# MAJOR PRESIDENTIAL DECISIONS

Richard Skolnik
**1803: Jefferson's Decision:**
The United States Purchases Louisiana

Robert Dallek
**1898: McKinley's Decision:**
The United States Declares War on Spain

Jordan Schwarz
**1933: Roosevelt's Decision:**
The United States Leaves the Gold Standard

Glenn Paige
**1950: Truman's Decision:**
The United States Enters the Korean War

# MAJOR PRESIDENTIAL DECISIONS

General Editor
**Fred L. Israel**
The City University of New York

CHELSEA HOUSE
New York, London
1980

*Cover designed by Techiya Rosenthal*

Copyright © 1980 by Chelsea House Publishers, a division of Chelsea House Educational Communications, Inc.

All rights reserved
Printed and bound in the United States of America

Library of Congress Cataloging in Publication Data
  Reprint of 4 works (1969-1970 editions) originally published by Chelsea House, New York, in series: The Decision making series.
  Includes bibliographies.
  CONTENTS: Skolnik, R. 1803: Jefferson's decision. — Dallek, R. 1898: McKinley's decision. — Schwarz, J. 1933: Roosevelt's decision. [etc.]
  1. Louisiana Purchase — Sources. 2. United States — History — War of 1898 — Sources. 3. Gold standard — History — 20th century — Sources. 4. Monetary policy — United States — History — 20th century — Sources. 5. Korean War, 1950-1953 — United States — Sources. I. Israel, Fred L. II. Series: Decision making series.
E333.M34    973         80-22040
ISBN 0-87754-218-X

Chelsea House Publishers
Harold Steinberg, Chairman & Publisher
Andrew E. Norman, President
Susan Lusk, Vice President

A Division of Chelsea House Educational Communications, Inc.
70 West 40 Street, New York 10018

**PART I**
**1803: Jefferson's Decision:**
The United States Purchases Louisiana

**PART II**
**1898: McKinley's Decision:**
The United States Declares War on Spain

**PART III**
**1933: Roosevelt's Decision:**
The United States Leaves the Gold Standard

**PART IV**
**1950: Truman's Decision:**
The United States Enters the Korean War

Note:
Each part contains its own Table of Contents and Bibliography.

# I

## 1803:
# JEFFERSON'S DECISION

## the UNITED STATES

## *PURCHASES*
## LOUISIANA

# Contents
## PART I
## 1803: Jefferson's Decision:
### The United States Purchases Louisiana
*Introduction*

Section One
The French Threat

| | |
|---|---:|
| *Commentary* | 1 |
| *1) Rufus King, Minister to England, to Secretary of State James Madison March 29, 1801* | 4 |
| *2) President Thomas Jefferson to Governor of the Mississippi Territory William C. C. Claiborne July 13, 1801* | 6 |
| *3) James Madison to Minister to Spain Charles Pinckney June 9, 1801* | 7 |
| *4) James Madison to Charles Pinckney May 11, 1802* | 10 |
| *5) James Madison to Minister to France Robert R. Livingston September 28, 1801* | 12 |
| *6) Rufus King to James Madison June 1, 1801* | 14 |
| *7) Rufus King to Robert R. Livingston January 16, 1802* | 16 |
| *8) Rufus King to James Madison February 5, 1802* | 18 |
| *9) Rufus King to James Madison February 27, 1802* | 19 |

## CONTENTS

10) Robert R. Livingston to French Foreign Minister Charles Talleyrand February 20, 1802 ... 20

11) Robert R. Livingston to James Madison February 26, 1802 ... 22

12) Robert R. Livingston to James Madison March 24, 1802 ... 23

13) Robert R. Livingston to James Madison April 24, 1802 ... 25

14) General Toussaint L'Ouverture to General Dessalines [n.d.] ... 27

15) General Charles Leclerc to the Minister of Marine, June 11, 1802 ... 28

16) General Charles Leclerc to First Consul Napoleon Bonaparte August 6, 1802 ... 29

17) General Charles Leclerc to the Minister of Marine September 13, 17, 1802 ... 31

## Section Two
## American Initiatives

*Commentary* ... 33

18) Lord Hawkesbury, British Foreign Secretary, to Rufus King May 7, 1802 ... 34

19) President Thomas Jefferson to Robert R. Livingston April 18, 1802 ... 36

20) President Thomas Jefferson to Pierre Samuel du Pont de Nemours April 25, 1802 ... 39

**CONTENTS**

21) *Pierre Samuel du Pont de Nemours to President Thomas Jefferson April 30, 1802*   42

22) *James Madison to Robert R Livingston May 1, 1802*   44

23) *Robert R. Livingston to James Madison September 1, 1802*   46

24) *Robert R. Livingston to James Madison November 11, 1802*   47

25) *Robert R. Livingston to James Madison January 24, 1803*   49

26) *President Thomas Jefferson to Robert R. Livingston, October 10, 1802*   50

Section Three
Crisis at New Orleans

*Commentary*   52

27) *Proclamation of Juan Ventura Morales, Intendant at New Orleans October 16, 1802*   54

28) *William E. Hulings, United States Vice Consul at New Orleans, to James Madison, October 18, 1802*   55

29) *James Madison to Charles Pinckney November 27, 1802*   56

30) *William C. C. Claiborne to James Madison January 3, 1803*   59

31) *William E. Hulings to James Madison January 20, 1803*   60

32) *Daniel Clark to James Madison March 8, 1803*   61

## CONTENTS

33) *James Garrard, Governor of Kentucky to President Thomas Jefferson November 30, 1802* — 62

34) *United States Senate February 16, 1803* — 63

35) *Report of the Special Committee January 12, 1803* — 70

36) *United States Senate February 27, 1803* — 73

37) *President Thomas Jefferson to the Governor of the Territory of Indiana, William H. Harrison, February 27, 1803* — 80

38) *James Madison to Charles Pinckney January 10, 1803* — 84

39) *Pierre Samuel du Pont de Nemours to President Thomas Jefferson October 4, 1802* — 85

40) *President Thomas Jefferson to Special Envoy to France James Monroe January 13, 1803* — 88

41) *President Thomas Jefferson to Robert R. Livingston, February 3, 1803* — 90

42) *President Thomas Jefferson to Pierre Samuel du Pont de Nemours February 1, 1803* — 91

43) *President Thomas Jefferson to James Garrard, January 18, 1803* — 95

44) *Editor's Comments,* The Frankfort (*Kentucky*) Palladium, *January 27, 1803* — 96

45) *William C. C. Claiborne to James Madison, March 27, 1803* — 97

46) *James Madison to James Monroe March 1, 1803* — 98

**CONTENTS**

| | |
|---|---|
| 47) *James Monroe to President Thomas Jefferson, March 7, 1803* | 100 |
| 48) *Robert R. Livingston to James Madison December 20, 1802* | 103 |
| 49) *Robert R. Livingston to James Madison January 24, 1803* | 104 |
| 50) *Robert R. Livingston to Napoleon Bonaparte, February 27, 1803* | 106 |

Section Four
Napoleon Decides to Sell

| | |
|---|---|
| *Commentary* | 111 |
| 51) *James Monroe to James Madison April 15, 1803* | 113 |
| 52) *Charles Talleyrand to Robert R. Livingston, February 19, 1803* | 114 |
| 53) *Charles Talleyrand to Robert R. Livingston, March 21, 1803* | 117 |
| 54) *Robert R. Livingston to James Madison March 3, 1803* | 118 |
| 55) *Robert R. Livingston to James Madison March 11, 1803* | 119 |
| 56) *James Madison to James Monroe April 20, 1803* | 121 |
| 57) *Robert R. Livingston to President Thomas Jefferson, March 12, 1803* | 122 |
| 58) *Rufus King to James Madison April 2, 1803* | 124 |
| 59) *James Madison to Robert R. Livingston and James Monroe, April 18, 1803* | 125 |
| 60) *Robert R. Livingston to James Madison April 11, 1803* | 130 |
| 61) *Robert R. Livingston to James Madison April 13, 1803* | 131 |

**CONTENTS**

62) *James Madison to Robert R. Livingston and James Monroe, March 2, 1803* — 138
63) *Robert R. Livingston and James Monroe to James Madison, May 13, 1803* — 144
64) *Lord Hawkesbury to Rufus King May 19, 1803* — 147

Section Five
Uncertainty Amidst Triumph

*Commentary* — 148

65) *President Thomas Jefferson to Dr. Hugh Williamson, April 30, 1803* — 152
66) *James Madison to Robert R. Livingston and James Monroe, July 29, 1803* — 153
67) *President Thomas Jefferson to General Horatio Gates, July 11, 1803* — 155
68) *James Madison to James Monroe July 30, 1803* — 157
69) *Albert Gallatin, Secretary of the Treasury, to President Thomas Jefferson August 18, 1803* — 159
70) *Albert Gallatin to President Thomas Jefferson, January 13, 1803* — 160
71) *President Thomas Jefferson to Albert Gallatin, January, 1803* — 163
72) *Robert R. Livingston to President Thomas Jefferson, June 2, 1803* — 164
73) *President Thomas Jefferson to Senator John Breckinridge of Kentucky August 12, 1803* — 165
74) *President Thomas Jefferson to Albert Gallatin, August 23, 1803* — 166
75) *President Thomas Jefferson to Attorney General Levi Lincoln August 30, 1803* — 167

## CONTENTS

76) *President Thomas Jefferson to Senator Wilson C. Nicholas of Virginia September 7, 1803* — 168

77) *Marquis d'Yrujo to James Madison September 27, 1803* — 171

78) *James Madison to Charles Pinckney October 12, 1803* — 172

79) *Message from the President of the United States, October 17, 1803* — 175

80) *Albert Gallatin to President Thomas Jefferson, October 28, 1803* — 178

81) *James Madison to Robert R. Livingston November 9, 1803* — 180

82) *Daniel Clark to James Madison October 20, 1803* — 182

83) *Proclamation of the United States Government to the People of New Orleans November 15, 1803* — 184

84) *Address of Governor William C. C. Claiborne to the Citizens of Louisiana, September 20, 1803* — 187

85) *A Contemporary Observation* — 189

86) *President Thomas Jefferson to Dr. Joseph Priestley, January 29, 1804* — 190

Bibliography — 192

*Introduction*

For most Americans at the time and for many since, the acquisition of the Louisiana Territory in 1803 appeared as an entirely natural and inevitable outgrowth of American expansion. The many apparently fortuitous circumstances associated with the transfer of this vast territory to the United States seemed sufficient proof that ineluctable, perhaps Divine, forces were at work. Few then considered the outcome as the result of a carefully conceived strategy which had been fraught with uncertainty. This unwillingness to recognize purposeful diplomatic efforts or to acknowledge the possibility of their failure can be explained by examining certain assumptions shared by most Americans of the early nineteenth century. They thought that America, situated on a virgin continent, would escape what they considered to be the degeneration of the Old World and would stand forth as a fresh land for a new race of men, a chosen people destined for greatness and world leadership. Such a destiny required that the United States be left to develop the Western Hemisphere freely, and to purge it, if necessary, of its differing or unprogressive elements. That foreign enclaves on the North American continent would dare to resist American expansion seemed both immoral and futile. Diplomatic posturing and political cross-pressures therefore could not divert the deeper, predetermined currents.

Recent historians, generally less beguiled by manifest destinies and territorial imperatives, have preferred to describe the Louisiana Purchase in terms more suitable to students of realpolitik and classic diplomacy. They have, however, too often dramatized the bizarre and fortuitous circumstances surrounding the episode, so that these elements of good fortune divert attention from the careful strategy pursued by the Jefferson administration. Attracted by the improbabilities and ironies of the situation, historians usually inject a note of cynicism as they compare the Federalists' original commitment to loose constitutional construction with their subsequent fears that the incorporation of Louisiana would distort the Constitution beyond recognition.

Napoleon's part in the affair generates interest; the wily Corsican allegedly bullied Spain into transferring Louisiana to France and then later turned a strategically untenable position into a windfall. His political virtuosity is further celebrated when it is recalled that he hoodwinked American innocents by selling them not only territory he could not defend but land that, having failed to honor certain stipulations of a treaty with Spain, he had never possessed. Finally, a somewhat patronizing attitude is assumed by historians as they reflect upon the supposed chagrin of America's two emissaries in France, Livingston and Monroe, when, lacking specific instructions, they were confronted with the dazzling opportunity of acquiring all of Louisiana. This conventional discussion invariably concludes with the rather obvious demonstration that America had, indeed, benefited handsomely from her somewhat reluctant purchase.

The Louisiana episode is a story of grand schemes and noble aspirations, the implications of which extended far beyond control of the unsettled land west of the Mississippi River. At stake on one hand was the possible restoration of a French Empire in the West. Napoleon, thwarted in his imperial plans in the East, notably in Egypt and India, saw the Caribbean and Louisiana as the bases for a renewed French Empire in the Western Hemisphere. Success in this enterprise would transform France into a power of unprecedented dimensions. His plans included the subjugation of the rich island of Santo Domingo, and it is here that a story of heroic proportions unfolds.

## Introduction

Aroused by the example of French revolutionaries, the Black slaves of the island had revolted, driven away their French masters, and achieved an effective level of freedom and independence—albeit not without the turmoil and dislocation of a civil war and a British invasion. Led by their military hero Toussaint L'Ouverture, these former slaves fought the reimposition of French hegemony. A French Empire in the West, therefore, could only begin with the destruction or re-enslavement of the people of Santo Domingo. Toussaint and Napoleon, remarkably kindred spirits, could not both prevail.

Other empires hung in the balance. Spanish riches from the New World had long been the lifeblood of the Spanish monarchy. For centuries the mineral wealth extracted from Central and South America had made Spain the envy as well as the target of other European powers, especially those affronted by her exclusivist colonial policies. At the close of the eighteenth century, however, the Spanish Empire appeared especially vulnerable. The French Revolution had aroused hopes of liberation among certain Spanish colonials at a time when the participation of Spain in the battle against revolutionary France had weakened the monarchy and loosened its hold over its colonies. Danger to Spanish possessions also arose from another quarter. Spanish officials along the Gulf of Mexico watched uneasily as waves of American frontiersmen encroached upon Spanish territory. What was to stop these thousands of Americans before they penetrated Spain's rich domains? Spanish officials were powerless as they wrestled with this problem. One solution they considered was to befriend the Americans, grant them what they demanded, and hope by so doing to postpone hostilities. Yet the American appetite, when whetted, was seemingly insatiable; such concessions might serve merely to fortify American aggressiveness. Because Spain was seeking a more effective policy, Spanish and French imperial requirements for a moment proceeded hand in hand. French possession of the Louisiana Territory would put one large building block of the new French Empire in place, while, for the Spaniards, French occupation of this region on the periphery of Spain's colonial heartland would serve as a formidable barrier against the turbulent Americans.

Europeans might bargain for American soil and plan empires there, but to Americans this was sheer delusion—or at least so they hoped. Not long after achieving independence Americans had begun to contemplate their future borders and power. Though some saw the expansion of the United States as potentially debilitating and welcomed the European settlement of the West as a restraining factor, a larger number preferred the vision of Americans bestriding the continent, working the soil, taming the forests, carrying forward the principles of democracy and liberty and, in short, performing God's work. To such people the existence of European holdings on America's borders was unnatural; they were malignant growths whose elimination was necessary to the future health of the American Republic.

Just at the time France and Spain were at work upon their grandiose schemes for the Western Hemisphere the Presidency passed to Thomas Jefferson, a man who was most expressive of America's continental ambitions. Jefferson maintained a heroic vision of America's destiny but avoided the strident, doctrinaire tones of the zealous imperialist. What concerned him most was not so much the extension of United States sovereignty across to the Pacific but the overspreading of that land by Americans who were committed to the practice and perpetuation of American ideals. Whether these people remained under the aegis of the government at Washington seemed to Jefferson, at this time at least, a matter of little significance. He was, however, disturbed by the haste with which Americans streamed westward, depopulating the East, depriving it of their talent and wealth, and often provoking the resent-

*Introduction*

ment of those remaining behind. To Jefferson's mind a controlled extension of American soil was much to be preferred. To his thinking the inevitability of such a movement precluded the need for haste. The Indians should be removed in an orderly and humane fashion, European territories should be purchased or obtained through the exertion of selective pressure, land should be laid out before settlement and then carefully given over to bonafide farmers, and eventually new states should be added to the Union following a period of political tutelage directed by the central government. Such a neat scheme would be seriously upset if Americans persisted in their headlong plunge toward the virgin lands of the West. The success of Jefferson's Louisiana policy would depend in fact upon his ability to control these restive spirits.

Such a regulated fulfillment of America's continental destiny could also be upset by the interposition of strong foreign influences along its borderlands. The French, English, and Spanish at one time or another had directed intrigues in the American West, hoping to carve out spheres of influence or to obtain territory with which to hedge in the Americans moving outward from the east coast. These efforts were aided by the vagueness of the boundary lines and the willingness of the Indians to ally themselves with whichever power maintained influence within the area. The inability of the American Government to establish an effective military presence on its borders, and the numerous American adventurers willing, for a price, to associate themselves with the schemes of foreign agents in the West, constituted grave security problems for the United States.

These problems, however, seemed trifling compared to the direct threat posed by Spain's secret transfer of Louisiana to France in 1800. As rumors of the retrocession reached America, anxious questions were raised. A relatively weak English Canada and a largely passive Spanish Empire could be tolerated for some time by Americans, but could an ambitious Napoleonic France peacefully coexist with the United States? Would the French again use their traditional talent for attracting Indian allies in order to erect a counterweight to American influence in the West? Would they use their control of the Mississippi River to lure western Americans from an attachment to the Union? Rather than permit the course of events to answer these questions, it would be far better to divert France at the start. Jefferson might have preferred a more leisurely contemplation of America's future, but the suspected intentions of the French left little time for such cerebrations. The administration was forced to devise a strategy to meet a crisis Jefferson called "the most important the United States have ever met since their independence."

It is clear that the events surrounding the transfer of Louisiana to France and its ultimate sale to the United States involved far-reaching imperial ambitions on the part of Spain, France, England, and the United States. The episode was a major event for the western powers; when it was over the patterns of hemispheric relationships had been permanently altered. France had staked its prestige and its resources on a renewed attempt for an empire in the New World. It had met with defeat in Santo Domingo and had hastily disposed of Louisiana. It would be some time before French imperial ambitions again would seek a major prize across the Atlantic. The devastation of Santo Domingo by the French and the elimination of Toussaint effectively destroyed whatever chances there had been for this Black republic to succeed in erecting a Caribbean Empire. The loss of the vast Louisiana Territory further demoralized a weakened Spain. Americans would now press even more insistently against Spain's exposed colonial frontiers in Florida, Texas, and Cuba. There could be little doubt that the once glorious Spanish Empire in the West had entered a period of rapid decay.

## Introduction

The extraordinary extension of American territory virtually assured the United States of ultimate domination of the continent. In control of so vast a territory the filling out of her "natural boundaries" could hardly be resisted. England, the rival of the Americans in the West, suddenly saw the balance swing strongly to the side of the United States. The struggle would continue, but an ultimate victory for the Americans seemed probable.

Administration leaders in Washington were not apt to dwell upon the Louisiana situation as an interesting conjunction of national destinies. They were confronted with what they chose to consider an immediate threat to the security, unity, and prosperity of the country. Ideologically committed to the search for a peaceful solution, and financially restricted to it, they planned their strategies as carefully and calmly as the highly volatile situation would allow. Popular histories of the incident neglect the deliberate preparations undertaken by Jefferson and his colleagues and emphasize instead the extraordinary good fortune of the Americans in having emissaries in Paris pressing for Louisiana just when the renewal of war in Europe made it expedient for Napoleon to sell it. While no interpretation of these events should omit these fortunate circumstances, it must also be recognized that Jefferson anticipated such a turn of events, and his plans were precisely to put the United States in a position to benefit from them when they occurred.

In a period when Americans considered themselves the darlings of providence there would seem to be little presumption in a plan which depended for its success upon the intervention of the kindly fates. It therefore remains to be related how the Jefferson administration drew together an extraordinary number of diverse strands, worked them into the design of its calculated decisions and succeeded in what Jefferson called a "noble acquisition."

# Section One

# The French Threat

*Commentary*

In the spring of 1801, shortly after Jefferson assumed the Presidency, rumors of a treaty transferring Spanish Louisiana to France spread through Washington causing deep concern to the new administration (Doc. 1). While Spanish possession of this territory was acceptable to the United States, a French Louisiana might threaten America's security. Would America's westward expansion be arrested? Would France continue to grant the same commercial rights on the Mississippi River and at New Orleans as Spain? Would the West be lured away from its attachment to the Union? These and other questions caused considerable anxiety within the administration. Jefferson described the situation as "very ominous" and admitted that "should France get possession of that country it will be more to be lamented than remedied by us." (Doc. 2) Lacking reliable information, Jefferson and Secretary of State James Madison counseled patience and expressed hope that circumstances overseas might change and that France might come to see the folly of its schemes for the Western Hemisphere. Charles Pinckney, the American Minister in Spain, was appraised of the situation and instructed to present the American point of view to the Spanish government (Docs. 3, 4). Madison then directed Robert Livingston, about to be sent to France as American Minister, to sound out the French and to attempt either to block their plans for Louisiana or to encourage them to grant commercial concessions (Doc. 5).

In Paris, Livingston confronted the august Charles Talleyrand, the French Foreign Minister, and from him received nothing but haughty evasions or bland assurances of friendship. Fortunately, the American Minister in England, Rufus King, was more successful in obtaining information (Docs. 6, 7). King reported that news reaching London indicated that France had already obtained Louisiana from Spain through a secret treaty and was indeed prepared to put into operation its imperial schemes for the Western Hemisphere (Docs. 8, 9). King, moreover, added that the British, although preoccupied by delicate peace negotiations underway with the French at Amiens, seemed to favor American efforts. British-American co-operation and the possibility of an alliance between the two nations would constitute a useful bargaining lever for the United States during the episode.

Livingston meanwhile continued to offer arguments to the French against any plan that involved their occupation of Louisiana (Docs. 10, 11, 12, 13). Talleyrand, however, professed no knowledge of any transfer of the territory to France. Leaving the diplomatic jousting to Talleyrand, Napoleon activated the first phase of his project to create a base for his empire in the New World. He planned to conquer Santo Domingo; only then would his forces occupy New Orleans. Napoleon entrusted to his brother-in-law, General Charles Leclerc, the task of subduing Santo Domingo and provided him with thousands of experienced troops. Before dispatching the invasion force though, Napoleon directed Louis Pichon, the French representative at Washington, to approach the American President and determine his reaction to such a move. Pichon found Jefferson prepared to accept the French expedition. In December 1801 Leclerc sailed for Santo Domingo, and it was there that the French army, the conqueror of Europe, found its match (Doc. 14). Even after Toussaint L'Ouverture, the island's Black leader, had been captured and deported, the savage struggle continued, a fact that gradually became known in the United States. Rufus King received news from an acquaintance in America that although "our intelligence has been generally that the Army of Leclerc made progress and was confident of success knowing as we do the policy of the French to put the best face on such affairs until they are obliged to abandon them, it is not impossible or improbable that the Blacks will maintain their liberty." In April 1802, Jefferson acknowledged that "the conquest of Santo Domingo will not be a short work. It will take considerable time to wear down a great number of souldiers [sic]." Fierce resistance by the natives and the devastations of yellow fever depleted General Leclerc's forces and caused him to despair of subjugating the island. Leclerc's letters to France vividly testify to his feelings of futility (Docs. 15, 16, 17). French energies had been diverted. The unsuccessful invasion of Santo Domingo provided Jefferson with additional time to counter the French threat in the West.

# 1

*Rufus King, Minister to England,
to Secretary of State James Madison
March 29, 1801*

[*State Papers, Correspondence Bearing upon the Purchase of the Territory of Louisiana* (Washington, D.C.: Government Printing Office, 1903), p. 3.]

*London*

Dear Sir:

In confirmation of the rumors of the day, Carnot's answer to Bailleul, published during the exile of the former, states the project which had been discussed in the Directory, to obtain from Spain a cession of Louisiana and the Floridas. A reference to that performance, copies of which I at the time sent to the Department of State, will show the manner in which it was expected to obtain the consent of Spain, as well as afford a clue to the views of France in seeking this establishment. What was then meditated, has, in all probability, since been executed. The cession of Tuscany to the Infant, Duke of Parma, by the treaty between France and Austria, forms a more compact and valuable compensation to this branch of the House of Spain than was formerly thought of; and adds very great credit to the opinion which, at this time, prevails, both at Paris and London, that Spain has in return actually ceded Louisiana and the Floridas to France. There is reason to know that it is the opinion of certain influential persons in France, that nature has marked a line of separation between the people of the United States living upon the two sides of the range of mountains which divides their territory. Without discussing the considerations which are suggested in support of this opinion, or the false consequences, as I wish to believe them, deduced from it, I am apprehensive that this cession is intended to have, and may actually produce, effects injurious to the union and consequent happiness of the people of the United States. Louisiana and the Floridas may be given to the French emigrants, as England once thought of giving them to the American tories; or, they may constitute the reward of some of the armies which can be spared at the end of the war.

I hear that General Collot, who was a few years ago in America, and a traveller in the Western country, and who for some time has been in disgrace and confinement in France, has been lately set at liberty; and that he, with a considerable number of disaffected and exiled Englishmen, Scotchmen, and Irishmen, is soon to proceed from France to the United States. Whether their voyage has any relation to the cession of Louisiana, is a matter of mere conjecture; but having heard of it in connexion with that project, I think proper to mention it to you.

What effect a plain and judicious representation upon this subject, made to the French Government by a minister of talents and entitled to confidence, would be likely to have, is quite beyond any means of judging which I possess; but on this account, as well as others of importance, it is a subject of regret that we have not such a character at this time at Paris.

> With perfect respect and esteem, I have the honor to be, dear sir, your obedient and faithful servant,
>
> RUFUS KING

*President Thomas Jefferson to
Governor of the Mississippi Territory
William C. C. Claiborne
July 13, 1801*

[Extract]

[*The Writings of Thomas Jefferson*, vol. 8, P. L. Ford, ed. (New York: G. P. Putnam's Sons, 1897), pp. 71-72.]

Washington

Dear Sir,

You will receive from the Secretary of State a commission as governor of the Mississippi territory, an office which I consider of primary importance, in as much as that country is the principal point of contact between Spain and us, & also as it is the embryo of a very great state. Independent of the official communications, which the Secretary of State will make to you from time to time, I cannot deny myself a few words, private & confidential, the object of which will be to contribute to the shaping your course to the greatest benefit, of the people you are to govern, and of the U. S. and to your own best satisfaction. With respect to Spain our dispositions are sincerely amiable and even affectionate. We consider her possession of the adjacent country as most favorable to our interests, & should see, with extreme pain any other nation substituted for them. In all communications therefore with their officers, conciliation and mutual accommodation are to be mainly attended to. Everything irritating to be avoided, everything friendly to be done for them. The most fruitful source of misunderstanding will be the conduct of their and our people at New Orleans. Temper and justice will be the best guides through those intricacies. Should France get possession of that country, it will be more to be lamented than remedied by us, as it will furnish ground for profound consideration on our part, how best to conduct ourselves in that case.

## 3

### *James Madison to Minister to Spain Charles Pinckney June 9, 1801*

[Extract]

[*State Papers, Correspondence Bearing upon the Purchase of the Territory of Louisiana* (Washington, D.C.: Government Printing Office, 1903), pp. 5–6.]

*Washington, Department of State*

On different occasions, since the commencement of the French Revolution, opinions and reports have prevailed that some part of the Spanish possessions, including New Orleans and the mouth of the Mississippi, had been or was to be transferred to France. Of late, information has been received through several channels, making it probable that some arrangement for that purpose has been concerted. Neither the extent of the cession, however, nor the consideration on which it is made, is yet reduced to certainty and precision. The whole subject will deserve and engage your early and vigilant inquiries, and may require a very delicate and circumspect management. What the motives of Spain in this transaction may be, is not so obvious. The policy of France in it, so far, at least, as relates to the United States, can not be mistaken. While she remained on the footing of confidence and affection with the United States, which originated during our Revolution and was strengthened during the early stages of her own, it may be presumed that she adhered to the policy which, in the treaty of 1778, renounced the acquisition of continental territory in North America, and was more disposed to shun the collisions threatened by possessions in that quarter, coterminous with ours, than to pursue objects to which the commanding position at the mouth of the Mississippi might be made subservient. Circumstances are not now the same. Although the two countries are again brought together by stipulations of amity and commerce, the confidence and cordiality which formerly subsisted have had a deep wound from the occurrences of late years.

Jealousies probably still remain, that the Atlantic States have a partiality for Great Britain, which may, in future, throw their weight into the scale of that rival. It is more than possible, also, that, under the influence of those jealousies, and of the alarms which have at times prevailed, of a projected operation for wrestling the mouth of the Mississippi into the hands of Great Britain, she may have concluded a preoccupancy of it by herself to be a necessary safeguard against an event from which that nation would derive the double advantage of strengthening her hold on the United States, and of adding to her commerce a monopoly of the immense and fertile region communicating with the sea through a single outlet. This view of the subject, which suggests the difficulty which may be found in diverting France from the object, points, at the same time, to the means that may most tend to induce a voluntary relinquishment of it. She must infer, from our conduct and our communications, that the Atlantic States are not disposed to enter, nor are in danger of being drawn, into partialities toward Great Britain unjust or injurious to France; that our political and commercial interests afford a sufficient guaranty against such a state of things; that without the cooperation of the United States, Great Britain is not likely to acquire any part of the Spanish possessions on the Mississippi; and that the United States never have favored nor, so long as they are guided by the clearest policy, ever can favor, such a project. She must be led to see again, and with a desire to shun, the danger of collisions between the two Republics from the contact of their territories; and from the conflicts in their regulations of a commerce involving the peculiarities which distinguish that of the Mississippi. Such are the general observations which the President has thought it proper should be communicated to you, that, knowing the light in which the subject is viewed by him, you may be less in danger of presenting it in any other. It is not expected that you will have occasion to make any positive use of them in relation to the councils of the French Republic, the Minister to which will be charged with that task. In relation to the Spanish Government, although the chief difficulty is not supposed to lie there, the President wishes you to cultivate a favorable disposition by every proper demonstration of the preference given by the United States to the neighborhood of that of every other nation. This may be the more important, as it is not improbable that her councils also may have been affected by rumors of proceedings in that country, connected with schemes of Great Britain for getting possession of New Orleans.

## James Madison to Charles Pinckney
## May 11, 1802

[*State Papers, Correspondence Bearing upon the Purchase of the Territory of Louisiana* (Washington, D.C.: Government Printing Office, 1903), pp. 27–28.]

*Washington, Department of State*

We are still without a line from you since your arrival at Madrid, and feel an increasing solicitude to hear from you on the subject of Louisiana. The latest information from Paris has confirmed the fact that it was ceded by a treaty prior to that of March, 1801; and, notwithstanding the virtual denial of the cession in the early conversations between Mr. Livingston and the Minister of Foreign Relations, a refusal of any explanations at present seems to admit that the cession has taken place. Still there are chances of obtaining a reversal of the transaction. The repugnance of the United States to it is, and will be, pressed in a manner that can not be without some effect: it is known that most of the French statesmen best informed on the subject, disapproved of it; the pecuniary difficulties of the French Government must, also, be felt as a check; whilst the prospect of a protracted and expensive war in St. Domingo; must form a very powerful obstacle to the execution of the project. The councils of England appear to have been torpid on this occasion. Whether it proceeded from an unwillingness to risk a fresh altercation with France, or from a hope that such a neighborhood between France and the United States would lead to collisions which might be turned to her advantage, is more than I can decide. The latter consideration might justly have great weight with her; but as her eyes may be more readily turned to the immediate and certain purposes to be answered to her rival, it is to be presumed that the policy of England will contribute to thwart the acquisition. What the intentions of Spain may be, we wait to learn from you. Verbal information from inofficial sources, has led us to infer that she disowns the instrument of cession, and will rigorously oppose it. Should the cession actually fail from this, or any other cause, and Spain retain New Orleans and the Floridas, I repeat to you the wish of the President, that every effort and address be employed to obtain the arrangement by which the territory on the east side of the Mississippi, including New Orleans, may be ceded to the United States, and the Mississippi made a common boundary, with a common use of its navigation for them and Spain. The inducements to be held out to Spain were intimated in your original instructions on this point. I am charged by the President now to add, that you may not only receive and transmit a proposition of guaranty of her territory beyond the Mississippi, as a condition of her ceding to the United States the territory, including New Orleans, on this side, but, in case it may be necessary may make the proposition yourself, in the forms required by our constitution. You will infer from this enlargement of your authority, how much importance is attached to the object in question, as securing a precious acquisition to the United States, as well as a natural and quiet boundary with Spain; and will derive from this consideration additional motives to discharge, with a prudent zeal, the task committed to you.

# 5

## James Madison to Minister to France Robert R. Livingston
### September 28, 1801

[Extract]

[*House Document 431*, 57th Cong., 2nd sess., pp. 6–8.]

*Washington, Department of State*

You have been already informed of the intention of the President that your departure to France should be hastened, and that you would be furnished with a passage in the Boston frigate, which, after landing you in Bordeaux, is to proceed to the Mediterranean.

From different sources information has been received that, by some transaction concluded or contemplated between France and Spain, the mouth of the Mississippi, with certain portions of adjacent territory, is to pass from the hands of the latter to the former nation. Such a change of our neighbors in that quarter is of too momentous concern not to have engaged the most serious attention of the Executive. . . . As soon as you shall have prepared the way by the necessary inquiries at Paris, it will be proper for you to break the subject to the French Government, and to make the use of these considerations most likely to give them their full weight. You will probably find it advantageous to press, in a particular manner, the anxiety of the United States to maintain harmony and confidence with the French Republic, the danger to which these will be exposed by collisions, more or less inseparable from a neighborhood under such circumstances, and the security which France ought to feel that it can not be the interest of this country to favor any voluntary or compulsive transfer of the possessions in question from Spain to France.

Among other topics to be employed on the occasion, you may, perhaps, find it eligible to remark on the frequent recurrence of war between France and Great Britain, the danger to which the Western settlements of the United States would be subject, of being embroiled by military expeditions between Canada and Louisiana, the inquietudes which would be excited in the Southern States, whose numerous slaves have been taught to regard the French as the patrons of their cause, and the tendency of a French neighborhood, on this and other accounts, to inspire jealousies and apprehensions which may turn the thoughts of our citizens toward a closer connection with her rival, and possibly produce a crisis in which a very valuable part of her dominions would be exposed to the joint operation of a naval and territorial power. Suggestions of these kinds must be managed with much delicacy, or rather the expediency of hazarding them at all, as well as the manner of doing it, must be left to your own information and discretion.

Should it be found that the cession from Spain to France has irrevocably taken place, or certainly will take place, sound policy will require in that state of things, that nothing be said or done which will unnecessarily irritate our future neighbors, or check the liberality which they may be disposed to exercise in relation to the trade and navigation through the mouth of the Mississippi; everything being equally avoided at the same time, which may compromise the rights of the United States beyond those stipulated in the treaty between them and Spain. It will be proper, on the contrary, to patronize the interests of our Western fellow-citizens by cherishing in France every just and liberal disposition toward their commerce. In the next place, it will deserve to be tried whether France can not be induced to make over to the United States the Floridas, if included in the cession to her from Spain, or at least West Florida, through which several of our rivers (particularly the important river Mobile) empty themselves into the sea. Such a proof on the part of France, of good will toward the United States, would contribute to reconcile the latter to an arrangement in itself much disrelished by them and to strengthen the returning friendship between the two countries; and by affording a fund for indemnifying and soothing our fellow-citizens who have suffered from her wrongs, would, in that view also, be a measure founded not less in an enlarged policy than in solid justice. The great importance of West Florida to the United States recommends to your patriotism the prudent use of every fair consideration which may favor the attainment of the object.

6

*Rufus King to James Madison*
*June 1, 1801*

[Extract]

[*State Papers, Correspondence Bearing upon the Purchase of the Territory of Louisiana* (Washington, D.C.: Government Printing Office, 1903), p. 4.]

*London*

On this occasion, among other topics of conversation, His Lordship (Hawkesbury) introduced the subject of

Louisiana. He had, from different quarters, received information of its cession to France, and very unreservedly expressed the reluctance with which they should be led to acquiesce in a measure that might be followed by the most important consequences. The acquisition might enable France to extend her influence and perhaps her dominion up the Mississippi; and through the Lakes even to Canada. This would be realizing the plan, to prevent the accomplishment of which, the seven years' war took place; besides, the vicinity of the Floridas to the West Indies, and the facility with which the trade of the latter might be interrupted, and the islands even invaded should the transfer be made, were strong reasons why England must be unwilling that the territory should pass under the dominion of France. As I could not mistake his Lordship's object in speaking to me on the subject, I had no difficulty or reserve in expressing my private sentiments respecting it; taking for my text the observations of Montesquieu, "That it is happy for trading Powers that God has permitted Turks and Spaniards to be in the world, since of all nations they are the most proper to possess a great empire with insignificance." The purport of what I said was, that we are contented that the Floridas remain in the hands of Spain, but should not be willing to see them transferred except to ourselves.

> With perfect respect and esteem, I have the honor to be, sir, your obedient and faithful servant,
>
> RUFUS KING

## 7

*Rufus King to Robert R. Livingston*
*January 16, 1802*

[*Life and Correspondence of Rufus King*, C. R. King, ed. (New York: G. P. Putnam's Sons, Inc., 1897), pp. 57–59.]

*London*

Dear Sir:

If you have received my letter of the 5th, the enclosure, the authenticity whereof I have no reason to doubt, will cast some light upon the subject of your last. During the negotiations of the Preliminaries, I conversed again and again *with the Prime Minister and Secretary of State for Foreign Affairs* concerning *the cession of Louisiana, who* assured me that the measure was *in their* view of much importance, and one which they could not see but with great concern; nevertheless that they were unable to interfere respecting it, for the same reason which compelled them to silence concerning other important objects, affecting the equilibrium of Europe, *and the* welfare *of Great Britain;* and I am disposed to credit the assurances made to me *that the cession* was neither a subject of enquiry nor discussion during the negotiation of the Preliminaries.

I have since more than once conversed with the same Persons, with the view of impressing upon them the great importance in a variety of respects *of this cession*, especially as it will affect the security *of their colonies,* and offers the means of rearing up and extending the commercial marine *of France*, the only sure foundation upon

16

## The French Threat 17

which she can raise a navy that will be able to cope *with that of England*. Reflection and views of this sort have produced a revision of the Question, but with no other effect than to confirm the decision before made; and you may infer with confidence that not a word has been *or will be said* upon the subject *at Amiens*.

In the explanations which took place concerning the Expedition that has lately sailed from *France*, it was *here* understood that it was to be wholly confined to the West Indies: the answer *to my* Enquiries was to this effect; lately however an opinion gains strength that a part of the force, *should the* situation of *St. Domingo* permit, *will be sent to New Orleans. I have* been explicitly told that no such authentic information has been *here* received, and that it is not likely to happen before the definitive Treaty is concluded. On the whole I am persuaded *that G. Britain will see with* much concern the accomplishment *of this cession;* that it is her interest, and that therefore she will be disposed, to throw impediments in the way of its being completed, but that she will *use no* open measure of opposition, nor such as would afford a Pretence to involve her in new difficulties.

## 8

*Rufus King to James Madison*
*February 5, 1802*

[*House Document* 431, 57th Cong., 2nd sess., p. 13.]

*London*

Sir:

I have seen a letter, dated Paris, February 26, which says, it is definitively settled to send a colony to Louisiana and Florida. General Bernadotte is to have the direction and command of it: preparations are making for the first expedition, whose departure will perhaps depend upon the accounts expected from St. Domingo. It is asserted that the Indian nations, adjoining to Florida, have agents, now here, for the purpose of making treaties with this country to unite themselves with the troops and settlers that may be sent hence. The establishment of this colony is a darling object, and will be pursued with ardor and upon a great scale, unless affairs of St. Domingo shall, for the moment, derange the plan. Louisiana, Guiana, and the desert islands of Tristan de Cunha, are each spoken of as places to which the rebellious and untractable negroes and people of color may be sent from St. Domingo and the other French colonies.

> With perfect respect and esteem, I have the honor to be, sir, your obedient and faithful servant,
>
> RUFUS KING

# 9

## *Rufus King to James Madison*
## *February 27, 1802*

[*House Document 431*, 57th Cong., 2nd sess., p. 15.]

*London*

Sir:

From all I can gather upon the subject we may consider the cession of Louisiana and the Floridas as an affair decided. Without doubt, you are fully aware of its various and extensive consequences. Has it occurred to you that the French Government will probably send thither a large body of people from France, and that it may add to them all the refractory and discontented blacks and persons of color of their West India colonies?

With perfect respect and esteem, etc.,

RUFUS KING

## *Robert R. Livingston to French Foreign Minister Charles Talleyrand February 20, 1802*

[*State Papers, Correspondence Bearing upon the Purchase of the Territory of Louisiana* (Washington, D.C.: Government Printing Office, 1903), p. 14.]

*Paris*

The undersigned, Minister Plenipotentiary of the United States, has seen, with some concern, the reserve of the French Government, with respect to the cession they have received from Spain of Louisiana.

He had hoped that they would have found a propriety in making such frank and open communications to him as would have enabled him to satisfy the Government of the United States that neither their boundary, nor the navigation of the Mississippi, secured by their treaties with Spain, would be, in any way, affected by the measure. It would also have been very satisfactory to him to have taken such arrangements with the Minister of Exterior Relations as would have had a tendency to dissipate the alarms the people of the Western territory of the United States will not fail to feel on the arrival of a large body of French troops in their vicinity; alarms which will probably be increased by the exertions of those Powers that are interested in keeping the two Republics from cementing their connection. The policy of the former Government of France led it to avoid all ground of controversy with the United States, not only by declining to possess any territory in their neighborhood, but by stipulating never to hold any. The undersigned does not, by this reference to the Treaty of 1778, mean to reclaim any rights under it, since, by the convention of Paris, 30th September, 1800, it is understood to be revoked; but merely to lead the French Government to reflect how far a regard to the same policy might render it conducive to the mutual interests of both nations to cover, by a natural barrier, their possessions in America, as France has invariably sought to do in Europe.

The undersigned prays the Minister of Exterior Relations (if the request is not inconsistent with the views of the Government) to inform him whether East and West Florida, or either of them, are included in the treaty made between France and Spain; and to afford him such assurances, with respect to the limits of their territory and the navigation of the Mississippi, heretofore agreed on between Spain and the United States, as may prove satisfactory to the latter.

If the territories of East and West Florida should be included within the limits of the cession obtained by France, the undersigned desires to be informed how far it would be practicable to make such arrangements between their respective Governments as would, at the same time, aid the financial operations of France, and remove, by a strong natural boundary, all future causes of discontent between her and the United States. The undersigned embraces this opportunity of renewing to the Minister of Exterior Relations his, etc.

# 11

## Robert R. Livingston to James Madison
## February 26, 1802

[Extract]

[*State Papers, Correspondence Bearing upon the Purchase of the Territory of Louisiana* (Washington, D.C.: Government Printing Office, 1903), p. 13.]

*Paris*

On the subject of Louisiana, I have nothing new. The establishment is disapproved by every statesman here as one that will occasion a great waste of men and money, excite enmities with us, and produce no possible advantage to the nation. But it is a scheme to which the First Consul is extremely attached; and it must, of course, be supported. You will find, by the enclosed note, that I have pressed an explanation on the subject, but I have received no answer. I have it, however, through a friend, from the First Consul, that it is by no means their intention to obstruct the navigation of the Mississippi, or violate our Treaty with Spain. General Bernadotte is understood to be designed for the command, and to have asked 10,000 troops.

## 12

## *Robert R. Livingston to James Madison*
## *March 24, 1802*

[Extract]

[*State Papers, Correspondence Bearing upon the Purchase of the Territory of Louisiana* (Washington, D.C.: Government Printing Office, 1903), pp. 20–21.]

*Paris*

On the business of Louisiana, they have, as yet, not thought it proper to give me any explanations, though I have omitted no opportunity to press the subject in conversation, and ultimately, by the note sent you on the 25th of February, (a duplicate of which was forwarded on the 28th), with a copy of another note enforcing the above, to which I have, as yet, received no answer.

The fact is, they believe us to be certainly hostile to this measure, and they mean to take possession of it as early as possible, and with as little notice to us as they can.

They are made to believe this is one of the most fertile and important countries in the world; that they have a much greater interest with the Indians than any other people; that New Orleans must command the trade of our whole Western country; and, of course, that they will have a leading interest in its politics. It is a darling object with the First Consul, who sees in it a means to gratify his friends, and to dispose of his armies. There is a man here, who calls himself a Frenchman, by the name of Francis Tatergem, who pretends to have great interest with the Creek nations. He has been advanced to the rank of General of Division. He persuades them that the Indians are extremely attached to France, and hate the Americans; that they can raise 20,000 warriors; that the country is a paradise, etc. I believe him to be a mere adventurer; but he is listened to, and was first taken up by the old Directors.

I can not help thinking that it would be advisable for the present Congress to take measures for establishing the Natchez, or some other port, and giving it such advantages as would bring our vessels to it without touching at Orleans. On this subject, however, you will form a better judgment than I can. I have but one hope left as to defeating this cession: it consists in alarming Spain and England. The Spanish Minister is now absent; but I have not failed to show, in the strongest light, to the Minister of Britain, the danger that will result to them from the extension of the French possessions into Mexico, and the probable loss of Canada, if they are suffered to possess it.

I have requested Mr. King to press this subject, also as opportunity offers. I enclose a copy of my last letter to him. If the treaty does not close soon, I think it would be advisable for us to meet at Amiens, and have accordingly proposed it to him.

I believe, such is the state of things here and such the desire for peace, that Britain may force them to relinquish Louisiana; particularly as the people here are far from desiring the establishment of any foreign colony which they consider as a weak point and drain for the population and wealth.

## 13

### *Robert R. Livingston to James Madison*
### *April 24, 1802*

[Extract]

[*State Papers, Correspondence Bearing upon the Purchase of the Territory of Louisiana* (Washington, D.C.: Government Printing Office, 1903), p. 23.]

*Paris*

The business most interesting to us, that of Louisiana, still remains in the state it was. The Minister will give no answer to any inquiries I make on that subject. He will not say what their boundaries are, what are their intentions, and when they are to take possession. And what appears very extraordinary to me, is, that by a letter I have just received from Mr. Pinckney, I find that he still supposes that the Floridas are not included in the cession: and he writes me that he has made a proposition to purchase them, which lies before the Minister, with whom he is to have a conference on the subject. You may, however, be fully assured that the Floridas are given to France; that they are at this moment fitting out an armament from here to take possession. This will be commanded by General Bernadotte. The number of troops designed for this object is between five and seven thousand. They will shortly sail for New Orleans, unless the state of affairs in St. Domingo should change their destination. You may act upon this information with absolute certainty, since I have no doubt of the channel through which I have received it. It would be wise immediately to take measures to enable the Natchez to rival Orleans. I have suggested the means: and I hope they will not be neglected by the Congress now sitting. That you may judge of the light in which this country is viewed by some here, I send you the extract of a paper that now lies before the Minister. If Congress makes the Natchez a free port, and if the state of affairs in St. Domingo should employ the troops designed for Louisiana, time will still be left for gold to operate here. But it must be plentifully and liberally bestowed, not barely in the assumption of debts, but in active capital, afforded in supplies, to aid their armaments in the islands. Give me your instructions as to the utmost amount, if, as you will be better able to judge than I can, the affairs of St. Domingo are likely to be protracted.

# 14

## *General Toussaint L'Ouverture to General Dessalines* [n.d.]

[Extract]

[As quoted in Ralph Korngold, *Citizen Toussaint* (Boston: Little, Brown, 1944), pp. 262–63.]

*Gonaïves, Santo Domingo*

There is no reason to despair, Citizen General, if you can succeed in depriving the troops that have landed of the resources of Port-Républicain. Endeavor by force or cunning to set fire to the city. It is entirely built of wood, so a few faithful emissaries should be able to do the work. . . .

Watch for the moment when the garrison will have been weakened by expeditions into the plains, and then try to take the city by surprise.

Do not forget that while we await the rainy season, which will deliver us of our enemies, fire and destruction remain our only resource. Bear in mind that soil bathed with our sweat must not be allowed to furnish the enemy with any means of subsistence. Render the roads impassable. Throw corpses of men and horses into all the wells. Order everything burned and destroyed, so that those who have come to enslave us may have constantly before their eyes an image of that hell they so richly deserve.

## 15

*General Charles Leclerc to the Minister of Marine, June 11, 1802*

[Extract]

[*Lettres du Général Leclerc* (Paris: Société de l'Histoire Des Colonies Française, 1937), p. 172.]

*Santo Domingo*

If the First Consul wishes to have an army in San Domingo in the month of October, he must have it sent from France, for the ravages of sickness here are too great for words. Not a day passes without my being told of the death of someone whom I have cause to regret bitterly. . . . Man cannot work here much without risking his life. Since my arrival in this country I have often been in very poor health from having worked too hard. The Government must seriously think of sending me a successor.

It is quite impossible for me to remain here more than six months. I reckon by that time to hand over the colony free from the state of war to the one who will be designated to replace me.

My health is so wretched that I would consider myself very fortunate if I can last that long.

## 16

*General Charles Leclerc to
First Consul Napoleon Bonaparte
August 6, 1802*

[Extract]

[*Lettres du Général Leclerc* (Paris: Société de l'Histoire Des Colonies Française, 1937), pp. 201–4.]

*Santo Domingo*

Death has wrought such frightful havoc among my troops that when I tried to disarm the North a general insurrection broke out.

❊   ❊   ❊

I entreated you, Citizen Consul, to do nothing which might make them anxious about their liberty until I was ready, and that moment was rapidly approaching. Suddenly the law arrived here which authorises the slave-trade in the colonies, with business letters from Nantes and Havre asking if blacks can be sold here. More than all that, General Richepanse has just taken a decision to re-establish slavery in Guadeloupe. In this state of affairs, Citizen Consul, the moral force I had obtained here is destroyed. I can do nothing by persuasion. I can depend only on force and I have no troops.

. . . Now, Citizen Consul, that your plans for the colonies are perfectly known, if you wish to preserve San Domingo, send a new army, send above all money, and I assure you that if you abandon us to ourselves, as you have hitherto done, this colony is lost, and once lost, you will never regain it.

My letter will surprise you, Citizen Consul, after those I have written to you. But what general could calculate on a mortality of four-fifths of his army and the uselessness of the remainder who has been left without funds as I have, in a country where purchases are made only for their weight in gold and where with money I might have got rid of much discontent? Could I have expected, in these circumstances, the law relating to the slavetrade and above all the decrees of General Richepanse re-establishing slavery and forbidding the men of colour from signing themselves as citizens?

I have shown you my real position with the frankness of a soldier. I am grieved to see all that I have done here on the point of being destroyed. If you had been a witness of the difficulties of all sorts which I have overcome, and the results I had obtained, you would grieve with me on seeing my position; but however disagreeable it may be, I still have hopes of succeeding. I make terrible examples, and since terror is the sole resource left me, I employ it. At Tortuga, of 450 rebels I had 60 hanged. To-day everything is in perfect order.

All the proprietors or merchants who come from France speak of slaves. It seems that there is a general conspiracy to prevent the restoration of San Domingo to the Republic. . . .

Send me immediately reinforcements, send me money, for I am in a really wretched position.

I have painted a pessimistic picture of my situation. Do not think that I am in any way cast down by what is happening. I shall be always equal to circumstances whatever they may be, and I shall serve you with the same zeal as long as my health permits me. It is now worse, and I am no longer able to ride. Bear in mind that you must send me a successor. I have no one here who can replace me in the critical situation in which the colony will be for some time. . . . Jérémie is in revolt. I have no other news from that quarter.

# 17

*General Charles Leclerc to the
Minister of Marine
September 13, 17, 1802*

[Extracts]

[*Lettres du Général Leclerc* (Paris: Société de l'Histoire Des Colonies Française, 1937), pp. 255ff.]

### Santo Domingo

If the French Government wishes to preserve San Domingo, it must, Citizen Minister, on the receipt of my letter give orders for *10,000* men to leave at once. They will arrive in Nivôse and order will be entirely established before the hot season. But if this malady is to last three months more, the Government must renounce the colony. . . .

Although I have painted such a horrible situation I ought to say that I am not without courage. . . . For four months now I exist merely by adroitness, without having any real force; judge if I can fulfil the intentions of the Government.

### Santo Domingo

The mountain chain from Vaillières up to and including Marmelade is in insurrection . . . I will be able to protect the plain only supposing that the malady stops in the first ten days of Vendémiaire. Since the 8 Fructidor it has assumed a new force, and I lose 100 to 120 men a day. To hold these mountains when I shall have taken them, I shall be *obliged to destroy all the provisions there and a great part of the labourers. I shall have to wage a war of extermination and it will cost me many men. A great part of my colonial troops have deserted and passed over to the rebels.* Let the Government send me 10,000 men independent of the reinforcements already promised to me. Let it send them at once by ships of the state and not by merchant vessels whose arrival is always slow. . . . Let it send me two million francs in coin and not in paper. . . . Or let it prepare for an interminable cruel war in San Domingo and perhaps the loss of the colony. It is my duty to tell you the whole truth. I tell it to you. . . . The news of the slavery re-established in Guadeloupe has made me lose a great part of my influence on the blacks. . . .

Bear in mind also the question of my successor for I am thinking seriously of quitting this country. . . .

. . . I leave this to go back to my bed, where I am hoping not to stay long. I wish you better health and more pleasant thoughts than mine. Since I am in this unfortunate country I have not had a moment's peace.

# Section Two

# American Initiatives

*Commentary*

Despite the diversion of French troops to Santo Domingo, Jefferson believed that the United States would eventually have to deal with a French occupation of Louisiana. Accordingly he advised his emissaries to approach the British on the possibility of a joint policy. The British government, judging from the May 7, 1802 letter of Foreign Secretary Lord Hawkesbury, favored some form of collaborative action (Doc. 18). Jefferson's increasing concern over Louisiana, his hostile though still temperate attitude toward France, and his receptivity to an Anglo-American *entente* were especially apparent in his lengthy dispatch to Livingston in the spring of 1802 as well as in a subsequent letter to Pierre Samuel du Pont de Nemours (Docs. 19, 20). Du Pont, a close friend of the President, cautioned against a British-American alliance and held out hope that a settlement with Napoleon, possibly involving a purchase of territory, could be reached (Doc. 21). Secretary of State James Madison instructed Livingston to explore the possibility of such a purchase, instructions which in fact conformed with Livingston's view that American money might well lead to concessions if it "be plentifully and liberally bestowed." (Doc. 22)

Although Livingston in Paris labored to present the American case to the French, an elusive Talleyrand and an enigmatic Napoleon kept him in a constant state of uncertainty (Doc. 23). Livingston was especially concerned that the French, when they arrived in Louisiana would ignore the right of deposit which Americans had enjoyed at New Orleans, a right indispensable to growing Western trade. Livingston pleaded for assurances on this matter but received little more than vague promises. His dispatches provide ample evidence of a man perplexed by countless evasions and ambiguous responses, oscillating between feelings of despair and bursts of hope for the final outcome (Docs. 24, 25). Jefferson, however, advised Livingston to remain calm and to avoid antagonizing the French (Doc. 26).

## 18

*Lord Hawkesbury, British Foreign Secretary, to Rufus King May 7, 1802*

[Extract]

[*House Document 431*, 57th Cong., 2nd sess., p. 27.]

*Downing Street*

Sir:

I have the honor to acknowledge receipt of your letter of the 21st ultimo.

*American Initiatives* 35

It is impossible that so important an event as the cession of Louisiana by Spain to France should be regarded by the King in any other light than as highly interesting to His Majesty, and to the United States; and should render it more necessary than ever that there should subsist between the two Governments that spirit of confidence which is become so essential to the security of their respective territories and possessions.

With regard to the free navigation of the Mississippi, I conceive that it is perfectly clear, according to the law of nations, that, in the event of the district of Louisiana being ceded to France, that country would come into possession of it subject to all the engagements which appertained to it at the time of cession; and that the French Government could, consequently, allege no colorable pretext for excluding His Majesty's subjects, or the citizens of the United States, from the navigation of the river Mississippi.

With regard to the second question in your letter, I can have no difficulty in informing you that no communication whatever has been received by His Majesty from the Government of France or Spain, relative to any convention or treaty for the cession of Louisiana or the Floridas; and I can, at the same time, most truly assure you that His Majesty has not in any manner, directly or indirectly, acquiesced in or sanctioned this cession.

In making this communication to you, for the information of the Government of the United States, I think it right to acquaint you that His Majesty will be anxious to learn their sentiments on every part of this subject, and the line of policy which they will be inclined to adopt in the event of this arrangement being carried into effect.

> I have the honor to be, with great respect,
> sir, your most obedient, humble servant,
>
> HAWKESBURY

# 19

*President Thomas Jefferson to
Robert R. Livingston
April 18, 1802*

[*The Writings of Thomas Jefferson*, vol. 8, P. L. Ford, ed. (New York: G. P. Putnam's Sons, 1897), pp. 143–47.]

*Washington*

Dear Sir:

A favorable and a confidential opportunity offering by Mr. Dupont de Nemours, who is revisiting his native country gives me an opportunity of sending you a cipher to be used between us, which will give you some trouble to understand, but, once understood, is the easiest to use, the most indecipherable, and varied by a new key with the greatest facility of any one I have ever known. . . .

The cession of Louisiana and the Floridas by Spain to France works most sorely on the U. S. On this subject the Secretary of State has written to you fully. Yet I cannot forbear recurring to it personally, so deep is the impression it makes in my mind. It compleatly reverses all the political relations of the U. S. and will form a new epoch in our political course. Of all nations of any consideration France is the one which hitherto has offered the fewest points on which we could have any conflict of right, and the most points of a communion of interests. From these causes we have ever looked to her as our *natural friend,* as one with which we never could have an occasion of difference. Her growth therefore we viewed as our own, her misfortunes ours. There is on the globe one single

## American Initiatives 37

spot, the possessor of which is our natural and habitual enemy. It is New Orleans, through which the produce of three-eighths of our territory must pass to market, and from its fertility it will ere long yield more than half of our whole produce and contain more than half our inhabitants. France placing herself in that door assumes to us the attitude of defiance. Spain might have retained it quietly for years. Her pacific dispositions, her feeble state, would induce her to increase our facilities there, so that her possession of the place would be hardly felt by us, and it would not perhaps be very long before some circumstance might arise which might make the cession of it to us the price of something of more worth to her. Not so can it ever be in the hands of France. The impetuosity of her temper, the energy and restlessness of her character, placed in a point of eternal friction with us, and our character, which though quiet, and loving peace and the pursuit of wealth, is high-minded, despising wealth in competition with insult or injury, enterprising and energetic as any nation on earth, these circumstances render it impossible that France and the U. S. can continue long friends when they meet in so irritable a position. They as well as we must be blind if they do not see this; and we must be very improvident if we do not begin to make arrangements on that hypothesis. The day that France takes possession of N. Orleans fixes the sentence which is to restrain her forever within her low water mark. It seals the union of two nations who in conjunction can maintain exclusive possession of the ocean. From that moment we must marry ourselves to the British fleet and nation. We must turn all our attentions to a maritime force, for which our resources place us on very high grounds: and having formed and cemented together a power which may render reinforcement of her settlements here impossible to France, make the first cannon, which shall be fired in Europe the signal for tearing up any settlement she may have made and for holding the two continents of America in sequestration for the common purposes of the united British and American nations. This is not a state of things we seek or desire. It is one which this measure, if adopted by France, forces on us, as necessarily as any other cause, by the laws of nature, brings on its necessary effect. It is not from a fear of France that we deprecate this measure proposed by her. For however greater her force is than ours compared in the abstract, it is nothing in comparison of ours when to be exerted on our soil. But it is from a sincere love of peace, and a firm persuasion that bound to France by the interests and the strong sympathies still existing in the minds of our citizens, and holding relative positions which ensure their continuance we are secure of a long course of peace. . . . I should suppose that all these considerations might in some proper form be brought into view of the government of France. Tho' stated by us, it ought not to give offence; because we do not bring them forward as a menace, but as consequences not controllable by us, but inevitable from the course of things. We mention them not as things which we desire by any means, but as things we deprecate; and we beseech a friend to look forward and to prevent them for our common interests.

If France considers Louisiana however as indispensable for her views she might perhaps be willing to look about for arrangements which might reconcile it to our interests. If anything could do this it would be the ceding to us the island of New Orleans and the Floridas. This would certainly in a great degree remove the causes of jarring and irritation between us, and perhaps for such a length of time as might produce other means of making the measure permanently conciliatory to our interests and friendships. It would at any rate relieve us from the necessity of taking immediate measures for countervailing such an operation by arrangements in another quarter. Still we should consider Orleans and the Floridas as equivalent for the risk of a quarrel with France produced by her vicinage. I have no doubt you have urged these considerations on every proper occasion with the government where you are. They are such as must have effect if you can find the means of producing thorough reflection on them by that government. . . . Every eye in the U. S. is now fixed on this affair of Louisiana. Perhaps nothing since the revolutionary war has produced more uneasy sensations through the body of the nation. Notwithstanding temporary bickerings have taken place with France, she has still a strong hold on the affections of our citizens generally. I have thought it not amiss, by way of supplement to the letters of the Secretary of State to write you this private one to impress you with the importance we affix to this transaction. I pray you to cherish Dupont. He has the best dispositions for the continuance of friendship between the two nations, and perhaps you may be able to make a good use of him. Accept assurances of my affectionate esteem and high consideration.

## 20

*President Thomas Jefferson to
Pierre Samuel du Pont de Nemours
April 25, 1802*

[Extract]

[Gilbert Chinard, *Correspondence of Dupont and Jefferson* (Baltimore: Johns Hopkins University Press, 1931), pp. 46–48.]

*Washington*

. . . I wish you to be possessed of the subject, because you may be able to impress on the government of

France the inevitable consequences of their taking possession of Louisiana; and though, as I here mention, the cession of New Orleans and the Floridas to us would be a palliation, yet I believe it would be no more, and that this measure will cost France, and perhaps not very long hence, a war which will annihilate her on the ocean, and place the element under the despotism of two nations which I am not reconciled to the more because my own would be one of them. Add to this exclusive appropriation of both continents of America as a consequence. I wish the present order of things to continue, and with a view to this I value highly a state of friendship between France and us. You know too well how sincere I have ever been in these dispositions to doubt them. You know too how much I value peace, and how unwillingly I should see any event take place which would render war a necessary resource; and that all our movements should change their character and object. I am thus open with you, because I trust that you will have it in your power to impress on that government considerations, in the scale against which the possession of Louisiana is nothing. In Europe, nothing but Europe, is seen, or supposed to have any right in the affairs of nations; but this little event, of France's possessing herself of Louisiana, which is thrown in as nothing, as a mere make-weight in the general settlement of accounts,—this speck which now appears as an almost invisible point in the horizon, is the embryo of a tornado which will burst on the countries on both sides of the Atlantic, and involve in its effects their highest destinies. That it may yet be avoided is my sincere prayer; and if you can be the means of informing the wisdom of Bonaparte of all its consequences, you have deserved well of both countries. Peace and abstinence from European interferences are our objects, and so will continue while the present order of things in America remain uninterrupted. There is another service you can render. I am told that

Talleyrand is personally hostile to us. This, I suppose, has been occasioned by the X Y Z history. But he should consider that that was the artifice of a party, willing to sacrifice him to the consolidation of their power. This nation has done him justice by dismissing them; that those in power are precisely those who disbelieved that story, and saw in it nothing but an attempt to deceive our country; that we entertain towards him personally the most friendly dispositions; that as to the government of France, we know too little of the state of things there to understand what it is, and have no inclination to meddle in their settlement. Whatever government they establish, we wish to be well with it. One more request,—that you deliver the letter to Chancellor Livingston with your own hands, and, moreover, that you charge Madam Dupont, if any accident happen to you, that she deliver the letter with her own hands. If it passes only through her's and your's, I shall have perfect confidence in its safety. Present her my most sincere respects, and accept yourself assurances of my constant affection, and my prayers, that a genial sky and propitious gales may place you, after a pleasant voyage, in the midst of your friends.

# 21

*Pierre Samuel du Pont de Nemours
to President Thomas Jefferson
April 30, 1802*

[Extract]

[Gilbert Chinard, *Correspondence of Dupont and Jefferson* (Baltimore: Johns Hopkins University Press, 1931), pp. 51–58.]

*New York*

One will say, and in this one certainly will be right, that if the British affect to let you become the second maritime power by offering the temptation of a passing alliance against Spain, they are laying a trap, and it is a mistake to trust them. The British detest and will always detest the second and even the third rate maritime powers. They would make you feel this in a harsh way were you to attain this honor which is more costly than useful. The persecutions that they would force on you would restore your alliance with France and all the blood shed in the interval would be lost.

Only France desires that you be a maritime power. Only England fears it.

These things being said, one will feel that you only need New Orleans and the delta of the Mississippi in order to insure a free and continuous outlet for the products of your western states and that a treaty of commerce in conjunction with your own ships will secure this outlet perfectly well. What answer can one give to that?

However, you prefer a treaty that cedes ownership to a treaty that cedes usage and I do not deny that this might be better for you, nor do I deny that this is not for France a matter of small importance.

But one must begin by agreeing on one point: namely, that the U. S. will never direct their desire toward the right bank of the river; that its usage will be equal and common to the two nations; and that the middle of the river's course will be a border between the two states. For it is really in the interest of three peoples and of the world that the powers of France and Spain should get together to repel the temptation that the U. S. might have one day to conquer Mexico.

This point being settled, one will wish to know what are your means of persuasion for obtaining the arrangement that you want? To say, "Give us this land or else we will take it" is not at all convincing. "We will defend it" is the first answer that enters the mind of every man. "We will prevent you" could tacitly be the second answer in the ordinary policy. And all the consequences that we want to avoid would then occur.

You want to obtain a territory that France possesses legitimately. If you were to say, "Give us that part of Louisiana that we want, give us the Floridas and we would make the English return Canada to you." If you were to say at least, "We pledge ourselves at the first war to assist you in obtaining possession of Canada." These would be mere proposals. They would also mean that talks are underway and I would go so far as to pledge that France would grant you through French Canada all the freedom of Commerce, all the outlets that the British are refusing you. But maybe the first point is higher than your credit with regard to England. Maybe you should not like to undertake the formal obligation of the second part, although you already seemed close to uniting with the English against us on account of Louisiana.

Where, then, lies your means of gaining and of convincing France to cede her property in a friendly way?

Alas, Mr. President, the freedom of conventions, the natural taste of all peoples and individuals for riches and the poverty that continuously assails great powers and from which only the second rate powers escape, leave you only one way when you do not have an exchange of the same nature to offer. It is acquisition; it is payment in money.

Calculate the cost of the very weak armament that you made three years ago. See what even the most successful war with France and Spain would cost and make a loan for part of it, say one-half of it. The two nations will have made a good bargain: you will have Louisiana and in all probability the Floridas for the least possible expense; and this conquest will be poisoned neither by hatred nor by human blood.

France will ask you the highest she can. You will offer the lowest you can. But offer enough in order to incite her to make up her mind before the taking of possession because the interest of the governors, of the prefects and of the commercial companies would become strong obstacles. These treaties must be concluded quickly: the more one bargains, the less one makes a good deal; the worst of all would be a break.

## 22

### *James Madison to Robert R. Livingston*
### *May 1, 1802*

[Extract]

[*House Document 431*, 57th Cong., 2nd sess., p. 24.]

*Washington, Department of State*

The cession of Louisiana to France becomes daily more and more a source of painful apprehensions. Notwithstanding the Treaty of March, 1801, and notwithstanding the general belief in France on the subject, and the accounts from St. Domingo that part of the armament sent to that island was eventually destined for Louisiana, a hope was still drawn, from your early conversations with M. Talleyrand, that the French Government did not mean to pursue the object. Since the receipt of your last communication, no hope remains, but, from the accumulating difficulties of going through with the undertaking, and from the conviction you may be able to impress, that it must have an instant and powerful effect in changing the relations between France and the United States. The change is obvious: and the more it can be developed in candid and friendly appeals to the reflections of the French Government, the more it will urge it to revise and abandon the project. A mere *neighborhood* could not be friendly to the harmony which both countries have so much an interest in cherishing; but if a possession of the mouth of the Mississippi is to be added to other causes of discord, the worst events are to be apprehended. You will consequently spare no efforts, that will consist with prudence and dignity, to lead the councils of France to proper views of this subject, and to an abandonment of her present purpose. You will also pursue, by prudent means, the inquiry into the extent of the cession—particularly whether it includes the Floridas as well as New Orleans—and endeavor to ascertain the price at which these, if included in the cession, would be yielded to the United States. I cannot, in the present state of things, be more particular on this head than to observe that, in every view, it would be a most precious acquisition, and that, as far as the terms could be satisfied by charging on the acquisition itself the restitution and other debts to American citizens, great liberality would doubtless be indulged by this Government. The President wishes you to devote every attention to this object, and to be frequent and particular in your communications relating to it.

## Robert R. Livingston to James Madison
## September 1, 1802

[Extract]

[*House Document 431*, 57th Cong., 2nd sess., p. 51.]

*Paris*

Sir:

I yesterday made several propositions to the Minister on the subject of Louisiana. He told me frankly, that every offer was premature; that the French Government had determined to take possession first; so that you must consider the business as absolutely determined on. The armament is what I have already mentioned, and will be ready in about six weeks. I have every reason to believe the Floridas are not included. They will, for the present, at least, remain in the hands of Spain. There never was a Government in which less could be done by negotiation than here. There is no people, no Legislature, no counsellors. One man is everything. He seldom asks advice, and never hears it unasked. His Ministers are mere clerks; and his Legislature and counsellors parade officers. Though the sense of every reflecting man about him is against this wild expedition, no one dares to tell him so. Were it not for the uneasiness it excites at home, it would give me none; for I am persuaded that the whole will end in a relinquishment of the country, and transfer of the capital to the United States. Their islands call for much more than France can ever furnish. The extreme hauteur of this Government to all around them will not suffer peace to be of long continuance. The French Minister at Lisbon, it is said, is coming home without taking leave. England is very sour; the debts due the Northern Powers unpaid, as well as ours, though their justice is admitted. Helvetia is still in arms; the little Cantons not acceding to the new form of Government.

## 24

### Robert R. Livingston to James Madison
### November 11, 1802

[Extract]

[*House Document 431*, 57th Cong., 2nd sess., pp. 61–64.]

*Paris*

France has cut the knot. The difficulty relative to Parma and Placentia, that stopped the expedition to Louisiana, has ended by their taking possession of the first, as you see by the enclosed paper. Orders are given for the immediate embarkation of troops (two demibrigades) for Louisiana; they will sail in about twenty days from Holland. The Government here will give no answer to my notes on the subject. They will say nothing on that of our limits, or of our right under the Spanish Treaty. Clarke has been presented to General Victor as a merchant from Louisiana. The General did not probably conceal his views, which are nothing short of taking exactly what they find convenient. When asked what they meant to do as to our right of *entrepôt*, he spoke of the treaty as waste paper; and the prefect did not know that we had such right, though it had been the subject of many conversations with the Minister, and of three different notes. The sum voted for this service is two millions and a half; as to the rest, they expect to compel the people to support the expenses of the Government, which will be very heavy, as the number of the officers, civil and military, with their suits, is great; and they are empowered to draw: so that the first act of the new Government will be the oppression of their people and our commerce. I believe you may add to this an early attempt to corrupt our people, and, if I may judge by the temper that the General will carry with him, an early attempt upon the Natchez, which they consider as the rival of New Orleans.

* * *

I am, dear sir, with the most respectful consideration, your most obedient servant,

R. R. LIVINGSTON

*Paris*

Sir:

After writing mine of this date, I called on the Minister and insisted on some positive answer to my notes. He told me that he was expressly instructed by the First Consul to give me the most positive assurances that the treaties we had entered into with Spain or them, relative to Louisiana, should be strictly observed. When I expressed my surprise that their officers should not be informed on that head, though on the eve of departing, he assured me that they would be furnished with copies of the treaties, and directed to conform strictly to them. I asked why these assurances were not given to me in the usual form, by replying to my notes? He said that he hoped that there would be no difficulty on that head, when the Consul should arrive (he is now absent). . . .

I shall endeavor to-day to see J. Bonaparte, though he has all along assured me that it was the Consul's intention to cultivate our friendship, and by no means to do anything that would endanger it. It will, however, be well to be on our guard, and, above all, to re-enforce the Natchez, and to give it every possible commercial advantage. If we can put ourselves in the situation to prevent the danger of hostility, I think we may hope that the dissatisfaction of inhabitants, the disappointment of officers, and the drain of money which the establishment will occasion, will facilitate our views after a very short time.

> I am, dear sir, with the most respectful consideration, your most obedient servant,
>
> ROBERT R. LIVINGSTON

## 25

*Robert R. Livingston to James Madison January 24, 1803*

[*House Document 431*, 57th Cong., 2nd sess., pp. 54–55.]

*Paris*

Sir:

I have just now heard of an opportunity from Havre. I am doubtful whether my letter will arrive in time for it. I therefore confine myself to inform you that General Bernadotte is named Minister to the United States, in the place of Otto, who will be employed here. General Bernadotte is brother-in-law to Joseph Bonaparte, is a very respectable man, and has the character of a decided republican. I have endeavored to impress upon him the necessity of making some arrangements relative to the debt previous to his departure, which he has much at heart. But neither he nor anybody else can influence the councils of the First Consul. You can hardly conceive anything more timid than all about him are; they dare not be known to have a sentiment of their own, or to have expressed one to anybody. . . . I confess to you I see very little use for a Minister here, where there is but one will; and that will governed by no object but personal security and personal ambition: were it left to my discretion, I should bring matters to some positive issue, or leave them, which would be the only means of bringing them to an issue.

    I am, &c.,

       Robert R. Livingston

# 26

*President Thomas Jefferson to*
*Robert R. Livingston*
*October 10, 1802*

[Extract]

[*State Papers, Correspondence Bearing upon the Purchase of the Territory of Louisiana* (Washington, D.C.: Government Printing Office, 1903), pp. 51–52.]

              *Washington*

Dear Sir,

  The departure of Madame Brugnard for France furnishes me a safe conveyance of a letter, which I cannot avoid embracing, although I have nothing particular for the subject of it. It is well, however, to be able to inform you, generally, through a safe channel, that we stand completely corrected of the error, that either the government or the nation of France has any remains of friendship for us. The portion of that country which forms an exception, though respectable in weight, is weak in numbers. On the contrary, it appears evident, that an unfriendly spirit prevails in the most important individuals of the government, towards us. In this state of things, we shall so take our distance between the two rival nations, as, remaining disengaged till necessity compels us, we may haul finally to the enemy of that which shall make it necessary. We see all the disadvantageous consequences of taking a side, and shall be forced into it only by a more disagreeable alternative; in which event, we must countervail the disadvantages by measures which will give us splendor and power, but not as much happiness as our present system. We wish, therefore, to remain well with France. But we see that no consequences, however ruinous to them, can secure us with certainty against the extravagance of her present rulers. I think, therefore, that while we do nothing which the first nation on earth would deem crouching, we had better give to all our communications with them a very mild, complaisant, and even friendly complexion, but always independent. Ask no favors, leave small and irritating things to be conducted by the individuals interested in them, interfere ourselves but in the greatest cases, and then not push them to irritation. No matter at present existing between them and us is important enough to risk a breach of peace; peace being indeed the most important of all things for us, except the preserving an erect and independent attitude. Although I know your own judgment leads you to pursue this line identically, yet I thought it just to strengthen it by the concurrence of my own. . . .

# Section Three

# Crisis at New Orleans

*Commentary*

Americans living in the eastern states remained calm as diplomats searched for a solution to the Louisiana question, but volatile Westerners needed but a spark to ignite their emotions especially since the conditions of the Mississippi River trade had never been entirely satisfactory to them. That spark soon came in the form of an October 1802 declaration by the Spanish Intendant at New Orleans revoking the right of deposit enjoyed by the Americans (Docs. 27, 28, 29, 30). Henceforth Westerners would be unable to store their goods at New Orleans before placing them aboard ocean-going vessels. Questions arose as to Spanish motives. Many saw the sinister hand of France behind the move, reasoning that the French preferred to receive Louisiana free of limitations to their authority and for this reason pressured Spain into withdrawing America's commercial privileges. Despite conflicting information from New Orleans, the administration, at least publicly, chose to view this declaration as simply the whim of the Intendant (Docs. 31, 32). If a subordinate had in fact touched off the situation, it might easily be remedied by application to the Spanish government. If Spain or France had ordered the suspension, then deeper problems were at hand.

Upon learning of the Intendant's declaration, the administration quickly announced that it would spare no effort to revoke it, but this statement did not dampen the public outcry. Phineas Bond, an English consul in the United States, observed that "Scarcely anything has happened since the Revolution . . . which has so much agitated the minds of all Descriptions of People in the U.S. as this Decree." Westerners feared economic ruination if shipments out of New Orleans ceased (Doc. 34). In addition, partisan Federalists in Congress, led by Senator James Ross of Pennsylvania, sought to embarrass the administration by urging aggressive measures, but Republican strength was sufficient to block specific measures, at least for the time being (Docs. 34, 35, 36). Thus Jefferson, who had hoped to avoid the pressures of public opinion and partisan recrimination, was forced to take immediate action at home and abroad (Docs. 37, 38).

Fortunately for Jefferson, as public pressure mounted, new information suggested a possible peaceful solution. In the fall of 1802 news arrived of General Leclerc's death in Santo Domingo. It now was evident that the French timetable for the conquest of that island had been seriously disrupted. Most important, Jefferson, on December 31, 1802, received word from Du Pont in France that a treaty with the French might be arranged wherein the United States could purchase New Orleans and the Floridas (Doc. 39). Encouraged by this news and obliged to allay the public clamor Jefferson decided to send James Monroe as a special envoy to France (Docs. 40, 41, 42). The President was not altogether optimistic about the outcome of Monroe's mission, although he realized that his decision had had a dramatic impact domestically. With one stroke, the administration had set back the Federalist War Hawks and soothed the inflamed tempers of the Westerners. Monroe departed and a tense country eagerly awaited the outcome of his mission (Docs. 43, 44, 45, 46, 47). Livingston meanwhile continued to write Washington asking for more explicit instructions, but was not overly confident of success (Docs. 48, 49, 50).

## 27

*Proclamation of Juan Ventura Morales, Intendant at New Orleans, October 16, 1802*

[*House Document 431*, 57th Cong., 2nd sess., pp. 54–55.]

As long as it was necessary to tolerate the commerce of neutrals which is now abolished, it would have been prejudicial to the province had the Intendant, in compliance with his duty, prevented the deposit in this city, of the property of the Americans, granted to them by the twenty-second article of the Treaty of Friendship, Limits, and Navigation, of the 27th of October, 1795, during the limited term of three years.

With the publication of the ratification of the Treaty of Amiens and the reestablishment of the communication between the English and Spanish subjects, that inconvenience has ceased. Considering that the twenty-second article of the said treaty takes from me the power of continuing the toleration which necessity required; since, after the fulfillment of the said term, this Ministry can no longer consent to it without an express order of the King; therefore, and without prejudice to the exportation of what has been admitted in proper time, I order, that from this date, the privilege which the Americans had of importing and depositing their merchandise and effects in this capital, shall be interdicted: and, that the foregoing may be publicly known, and that nobody may allege ignorance, I order it to be published in the usual places, copies to be posted up in the public *sitioes;* and that the necessary notice be given of it to the officers of finance, the administrator of rents, and otherwise, as may be necessary.

The present being given under my hand, and countersigned by the underwritten notary of finance *pro tempore,* in the office of Intendancy of New Orleans, October 16, 1802.

JUAN VENTURA MORALES

By order of the Intendant:
Pedro Pedesclaux.

28

*William E. Hulings, United States Vice Consul at New Orleans, to James Madison*
*October 18, 1802*

[*State Papers, Correspondence Bearing upon the Purchase of the Territory of Louisiana* (Washington, D.C.: Government Printing Office, 1903), p. 54.]

*New Orleans*

Sir:

I have the honor to enclose you an extract from a decree this day published by the Intendant of the Province of Louisiana, by which you will see that the Americans are no longer permitted to deposit their merchandise in this city. No information of any other place being appropriated for an American deposit is yet given; nor have we any reason to hope that the Government has such place in view. The season for the cotton from the Natchez, and other produce from the settlements higher up to come down, approaches. The difficulties and risks of property that will fall on the citizens of the United States, if deprived of their deposit, are incalculable; their boats being so frail, and so subject to be sunk by storms, that they can not be converted into floating stores, to wait the arrival of sea vessels to carry away their cargoes.

The port is also this day shut against foreign commerce, which can only be carried on by Spanish subjects, in Spanish bottoms.

I am, sir, with greatest respect,

WM. E. HULINGS

## 29

## *James Madison to Charles Pinckney*
## *November 27, 1802*

[*State Papers, Correspondence Bearing upon the Purchase of the Territory of Louisiana* (Washington, D.C.: Government Printing Office, 1903), pp. 63–65.]

*Washington, Department of State*

A letter from a confidential citizen at New Orleans, a copy of which is enclosed, has just informed us that the Intendant, at that place, by a proclamation, from which an extract is also enclosed, had prohibited the deposit of American effects stipulated by the Treaty of 1795; and, as the letter is interpreted, that the river was also shut against the external commerce of the United States from that port. Whether it be the fact or not that this latter prohibition has also taken place, it is evident that the useful navigation of the Mississippi so essentially depends on a suitable depository for the articles of commerce, that a privation of the latter is equivalent to a privation of both.

This proceeding is so direct and palpable a violation of the Treaty of 1795, that, in candor, it is to be imputed rather to the Intendant solely than to instructions of his Government. The Spanish Minister takes pains to impress this belief, and it is favored by private accounts from New Orleans, mentioning that the Governor did not concur with the Intendant. But, from whatever source the measure may have proceeded, the President expects that the Spanish Government will neither lose a moment in countermanding it, nor hesitate to repair every damage which may result from it. You are aware of the sensibility of our Western citizens to such an occurrence. This sensibility is justified by the interest they have at stake. The Mississippi is to them everything. It is the Hudson, the Delaware, the Potomac, and all the navigable rivers of the Atlantic States, formed into one stream. The produce exported through that channel last year amounted to one million six hundred and twenty-two thousand six hundred and seventy-two dollars from the districts of Kentucky and Mississippi only, and will probably be fifty per cent. more this year, (from the whole Western country. Kentucky alone has exported, for the first half of this year, five hundred and ninety-one thousand four hundred and thirty-two dollars in value,) a great part of which is now, or shortly will be, afloat for New Orleans, and consequently exposed to the effects of this extraordinary exercise of power. Whilst you presume, therefore, in your representations to the Spanish Government that the conduct of its officer is no less contrary to its intentions than it is to its good faith, you will take care to express the strongest confidence that the breach of the treaty will be repaired in every way which justice and a regard for a friendly neighborhood may require.

I have communicated the information received from New Orleans to the Chevalier d'Yrujo, with a view to obtain his immediate interposition, as you will find by the enclosed copy of a letter to him. He readily undertakes to use it with all the effect he can give it by writing immediately on the subject to the local authority at New Orleans. I shall write at the same time to Mr. Hulings, who will enforce, as far as he may have an opportunity, the motives for recalling the unwarrantable prohibitions. It is to be hoped that the Intendant will be led to see the error which he has committed, and to correct it before a very great share of its mischief will have happened. Should he prove as obstinate as he has been ignorant or wicked, nothing can temper the irritation and indignation of the Western country, but a persuasion that the energy of their own Government will obtain from the justice of that of Spain the most ample redress.

It has long been manifest that, whilst the injuries to the United States, so frequently occurring from the colonial officers scattered over our hemisphere, and in our neighborhood, can only be repaired by a resort to their respective Sovereigns in Europe, that it will be impossible to guard against most serious inconveniences. The instance before us strikes with peculiar force, and presents an occasion on which you may advantageously suggest to the Spanish Government the expediency of placing in their Minister on the spot, an authority to control or correct the mischievous proceedings of their colonial officers towards our citizens; without which any one of fifteen or twenty individuals, not always among either the wisest or best of men, may, at any time, threaten the good understanding of the two countries. The distance between the United States and the old continent, and the mortifying delays of explanations and negotiations across the Atlantic on emergencies in our neighborhood, render such a provision indispensable, and it can not be long before all the Governments of Europe, having American colonies, must see the policy of making it.

## William C. C. Claiborne to James Madison
## January 3, 1803

[*The Letter Books of W. C. C. Claiborne*, vol. 1, Dunbar Rowland, ed. (Jackson: Mississippi State Department of Archives and History, 1917), p. 253.]

*Natchez*

Sir,

The enclosed hand bill has this moment reached me; —it has every appearance of being an official publication—

The conduct of the Spanish Government in Louisiana, is indeed extraordinary; of late their acts manifest a determined hostility to the U. States.

The violation of the Treaty, so far as related to the deposit at Orleans, gave rise to much agitation in this Territory, and this recent attack upon every principle of friendly intercourse, and of those acts of civility which ought to take place, between two nations in a state of peace, has rendered the ferment still greater.

We have in this part of the Territory, about two thousand Militia, pretty well organized, and with a portion of this force (say six hundred men) my opinion is, that New Orleans might be taken possession of provided there should be only Spanish troops to defend the place.

I deem it my duty to inform you, that there are in Orleans and on the Coast, a number of Inhabitants devoted to the American interest, and in the event of hostilities, would most certainly join the American standard.

   I am &c

  (Signed) WILLIAM C. C. CLAIBORNE

## 31

*William E. Hulings to James Madison*
*January 20, 1803*

[Extract]

[Consular Despatches, New Orleans.]

*New Orleans*
Duplicate per Brig
*Mariner* via N York

About the 21st Octr. last I waited on the Govr. and had a conversation with him on the subject of the deposit; he assured me that he had opposed the Intendt. as far as he possibly coud, without taking the responsability on himself. That the Intendt. had done it on his own authority and responsability, as he knew of no orders from his C. Majesty for that purpose; all of which was confirmed to me by the Secrey. of Governt. [Don Andrés López y Armesto] the same day. Notwithstandg. the Govr. gave the matter up, and the Intendt's decree was, and continues to be strictly executed to the extreme prejudice of the Citizens of the United States; who are denied the rights of hospitality in distress, as exemplified in the Case of Col. John Ellis, and Majr. Wm. Gordon Forman, communicated to you in my letter of 25 Novr. ulto.—The Intendt. is very reserved even to his chief Officers, and choosing to consider me only as a private Stranger, avoids giving (as it appears to me) an Opportunity to say any thing about the business in question. Nor have I been able to learn from any of the heads of the Departmts. (with all of whom I am well acquainted) any thing that shou'd have come from the Intendt. relative to the authority on which he acted. The said Officers are generally of Opinion that no orders have been recd. by the Intendt.

## 32

*Daniel Clark to James Madison*
*March 8, 1803*

[Extract]

[Consular Despatches, New Orleans.]

*New Orleans*
*(Confidential)*

On the subject of the authority on which the Intendant has acted, there is among well informed People but one Opinion which is, that he merely executes the orders received from his Government. He is too rich, too sensible, and too cautious to take such a responsability on himself especially after meeting for such a length of time so decided an opposition from the Governor who in his official Correspondence on the subject which I have seen, says that the measures proposed were a direct and open violation* of the Treaty. It is much to be regretted that the Secretary of this Province Dn. Andres Lopez de Armesto and the Auditor or Judge, Dn. Nicolas Maria Vidal by whose opinion the Governor is guided are not men of firmness; as the old man tho almost incapable of an exertion from Age and infirmities would nevertheless have ordered the Intendant to be suspended from the exercise of his functions, had not his two Counsellors been wavering and indecisive and at last overawed by the tone and Spirit of the Intendant advised him to a compliance with the latters wishes. This determined Spirit of the Intendant is not natural to him, it is assumed because he feels himself supported, and you will recollect an expression of his which I formerly communicated that he was careless of the consequences of measures which he undertook in compliance with orders. In a conversation with the Auditor whom I reproached for submitting to the will of the Intendant he assured me that he had only done so on the perfect conviction that he had orders from the Minister to that effect, and desired me to recollect, that in the most trifling matters which involved any responsability, the assessor or himself were always consulted as his Guides on the occasion, for supported by the Opinion of one or the other he is discharged from all blame but if he acts without it he then takes the risk upon himself, and that he never would have dared to take so momentary an affair upon his own responsability without consulting any one, unless his orders had been express and so plain as to admit of no other interpretation whatever, and I could not avoid acknowledging the justness of his observation. . . .

## 33

### *James Garrard, Governor of Kentucky, to President Thomas Jefferson*
### *November 30, 1802*

[*State Papers, Correspondence Bearing upon the Purchase of the Territory of Louisiana* (Washington, D.C.: Government Printing Office, 1903), p. 57.]

*Frankfort, State of Kentucky*

Sir:

Two days ago, I received the enclosed letters from Dr. James Speed, and Mecker & Co., from New Orleans, together with a copy of a proclamation issued by Juan

Ventura Morales, Intendant of the Spanish Government of Louisiana, and which I do myself the honor to enclose for your information. The citizens of this State are very much alarmed and agitated, as this measure of the Spanish Government will, if not altered, at one blow, cut up the present and future prosperity of their best interests by the roots. To you, sir, they naturally turn their eyes, and on your attention to this important subject their best hopes are fixed. Permit me to request you will give me information on this business as soon as you can say, with certainty, what we may rely on; and let my solicitude on this occasion be my apology for this request.

With sentiments of respect, etc.,

JAMES GARRARD

## 34

*United States Senate
February 16, 1803*

[Extract]

[*Annals of Congress,* 7th Cong., 2nd sess. (Washington, 1851), pp. 94–96.]

MR. [JAMES] ROSS [Senator from Pennsylvania] rose and said, that two days ago he had the honor of stating some of his opinions to the Senate, respecting the alarming condition of our affairs upon the Mississippi; that in a very interesting part of his inquiry he had been called to order; that the Vice President had expressly determined him to have been in order, and also declared that there was no confidential information before the Senate relating to the late aggressions upon our rights in Mississippi: yet, not withstanding this declaration of the Vice President, as explicit as it was correct, Mr. R. said, the doors were actually closed and all further public discussions at that time prohibited. Yesterday the doors were again closed. He said it would be well recollected, that when this extraordinary measure was resorted to, he had given notice that he would not proceed further in the discussion, while the doors were shut, and that he would resume it whenever they should be opened. From that time to the present he had remained silent, but now, when a majority of the Senate had resolved that this discussion should be public, he would proceed to finish the remarks he had intended to make, and then offer his resolutions. He could not, however, avoid expressing his acknowledgments to the majority of that body, who had decided that this debate should be public, for although some gentlemen might be desirous to stifle, and smother in secrecy, an inquiry like the present, he firmly believed that there would always be firmness and independence enough in that House to meet in public the investigation of every subject proper for public deliberation.

MR. R. said he would not return to a repetition of what he had formerly stated, it would be sufficient to mention, that he had urged the importance of our rights in the navigation of the Mississippi, founded in nature, and acknowledged by compact. This was the great and only highway of commerce from the western country to the ocean. That the Spaniards after a long execution of this treaty, have now flagrantly violated it, and shut us out from all intercourse, and from the right of deposit: that they have plundered

## Crisis at New Orleans 65

our citizens upon the ocean; carried our vessels into their ports, and condemned them without the semblance of a trial. Our seamen have been cast into prison, and our merchants ruined. Thus assailed upon the ocean, and upon the land, by a long course of oppression and hostility, without provocation and without apology, he knew but one course we could take which promised complete redress of our wrongs. Experience had proved the compact was no security; the Spaniards either cannot or will not observe their treaty. If they are under the direction of a stronger Power, who will not permit them to adhere to their stipulations, or if they of their own accord inflict these indignities under a belief that we dare not resent them, it was equally incumbent upon us to act without further delay. The aggressors are heaping indignity upon you at your own door, at the very borders of your territory, and tell you, at the same time, they have no right to the country from whence they exclude you.

If they act thus without right, why not enforce yours by taking possession? Will you submit to be taken by the neck and kicked out without a struggle? Was there not spirit enough in the country to repel and punish such unheard-of insolence? Is not the magnitude of the interest at stake, such as to warrant the most vigorous and decisive course which can express public indignation? Go then, take the guardianship of your rights upon yourselves, trust it no longer to those who have so grossly abused the power they have had over it; reinstate yourselves in the possession of that which has been wrested from you and withheld by faithless men, who confess themselves no longer the owners of the country over which they are exercising these acts of injustice and outrage. Negotiation may, perhaps, be wise, but this is the effectual measure to support it; when it is seen that you have determined to support your just demands with force, that you have already taken into your hands an ample pledge for future security and good behaviour, your Ambassador will be respected and attended to. But what weight will his remonstrances have in any country of Europe, when they hear of no military preparation to vindicate your pretensions; when they learn that you have been chased out of a possession confessedly your right; that you have been insultingly told, Begone, you shall not buy, you shall not sell, you are such a nuisance we will have no intercourse with you!

Where is the nation, ancient or modern, that has borne such treatment without resentment or resistance? Where is the nation that will respect another that is passive under such humiliating degradation and disgrace? Your outlet to market closed, next they will trample you under foot upon your own territory which borders upon theirs! Yet you will not stir, you will not arm a single man; you will negotiate! Negotiation alone, under such circumstances, must be hopeless. No. Go forward, remove the aggressors, clear away the obstructions, restore your possession with your own hand, and use your sword if resistance be offered. Call upon those who are most injured, to redress themselves; you have only to give the call, you have men enough near to the scene, without sending a man from this side the mountains; force sufficient, and more than sufficient, for a prompt execution of your orders. If money be an object, one half of the money which would be consumed and lost by delay and negotiation, would put you in possession; then you may negotiate whether you shall abandon it and go out again.

* * *

MR. R. then read his resolutions, which are as follows:

"*Resolved,* That the United States have an indisputable right to the free navigation of the river Mississippi, and to a convenient place of deposit for their produce and merchandise in the island of New Orleans.

"That the late infraction of such, their unquestionable right, is an aggression hostile to their honor and interest.

"That it does not consist with the dignity or safety of this Union to hold a right so important by a tenure so uncertain.

"That it materially concerns such of the American citizens as dwell on the western waters, and is essential to the union, strength, and prosperity of these States, that they obtain complete security for the full and peaceable enjoyment of such their absolute right.

"That the President be authorized to take immediate possession of such place or places, in the said island, or the adjacent territories, as he may deem fit and convenient for the purposes aforesaid; and to adopt such other measures for obtaining that complete security as to him in his wisdom shall seem meet.

"That he be authorized to call into actual service any number of the militia of the States of South Carolina, Georgia, Ohio, Kentucky, Tennessee, or of the Mississippi Territory, which he may think proper, not exceeding fifty thousand, and to employ them, together with the military and naval forces of the Union, for effecting the objects above mentioned.

"That the sum of five millions of dollars be appropriated to the carrying into effect the foregoing resolutions, and that the whole or any part of that sum be paid or applied, on warrants drawn in pursuance of such directions as the President may, from time to time, think proper to give to the Secretary of the Treasury."

## February 23, 1803

[*Annals of Congress,* 7th Cong., 2nd sess., pp. 107–112.]

MR. [SAMUEL] WHITE, of Delaware, rose and addressed the Chair as follows: Mr. President, on this subject, which has on a former day been discussed with so much ability, and with so much eloquence, by my friend from Pennsylvania, the honorable mover of the resolutions, I shall submit the few observations that I may make, in as concise a manner as I am capable of, for it is very far from my wish to occupy the time or attention of the Senate unnecessarily.

\* \* \*

We can never have permanent peace on our Western waters, till we possess ourselves of New Orleans, and such other positions as may be necessary to give us the complete and absolute command of the navigation of the Mississippi. We have now such an opportunity of accomplishing this important object as may not be presented again in centuries, and every justification that could be wished for availing ourselves of the opportunity. Spain has dared us to the trial, and now bids us defiance; she is yet in possession of that country; it is at this moment within your reach and within your power; it offers a sure and easy conquest: we should have to encounter there now only a weak, inactive, and unenterprising people; but how may a few months vary this scene, and darken our prospects! Though not officially informed, we know that the Spanish provinces on the Mississippi have been ceded to the French, and that they will as soon as possible take possession of them. What may we then expect? When in the last extremity we shall be driven to arms in defence of our indisputable rights where now slumbers on his post with folded arms the sluggish Spaniard, we shall be hailed by the vigilant and alert French grenadier, and in the defenceless garrison that would now surrender at our approach, we shall see unfurled the standards that have waved triumphant in Italy, surrounded by impregnable ramparts, and defended by the disciplined veterans of Egypt.

I am willing, sir, to attribute to honorable gentlemen the best of motives; I am sure they do not wish to involve this country in a war, and God knows, I deprecate its horrors as much as any man; but this business can never be adjusted abroad; it will ultimately have to be settled upon the banks of the Mississippi: and the longer you delay, the more time you waste in tedious negotiations, the greater sacrifices you make to protract a temporary and hollow peace, the greater will be your embarrassments when the war comes on; and it is inevitable, unless honorable gentlemen, opposed to us, are prepared to yield up the best interest and honor of the nation. I believe the only question now in our power to decide, is whether it shall be the bloodless war of a few months, or the carnage of years.

## *February 24, 1803*

[*Annals of Congress,* 7th Cong., 2nd sess., (Washington, 1851), pp. 204–205.]

GOUVERNEUR MORRIS addressed the Chair. I have no hesitation in saying that you ought to have taken possession of New Orleans and the Floridas the instant your treaty was violated. You ought to do it now. Your rights are invaded—confidence in negotiation is vain; there is therefore no alternative but force. You are exposed to imminent present danger. You have the prospect of great future advantage. You are justified by the clearest principles of right. You are urged by the strongest motives of policy. You are commanded by every sentiment of national dignity. Look at the conduct of America in her infant years, when there was no actual invasion of right, but only a claim to invade. She resisted the claim; she spurned the insult. Did we then hesitate? Did we then wait for foreign alliance? No; animated with the spirit, warmed with the soul of freedom, we threw our oaths of allegiance in the face of our Sovereign, and committed our fortunes and our fate to the God of battles. We then were subjects. We had not then attained to the dignity of an independent Republic. We then had no rank among the nations of the earth. But we had the spirit which deserved that elevated station. And now that we have gained it, shall we fall from our honor?

35

## *Report of the Special Committee January 12, 1803*

[Extract]

[*State Papers, Correspondence Bearing upon the Purchase of the Territory of Louisiana* (Washington, D.C.: Government Printing Office, 1903), pp. 87–88.]

From the aforegoing view of facts, it must be seen that the possession of New Orleans and the Floridas will not only be required for the convenience of the United States, but will be demanded by their most imperious necessities. The Mississippi and its branches, with those other rivers above referred to, drain an extent of country, not less, perhaps, than one-half of our whole territory, containing at this time one-eighth of our population and progressing with a rapidity beyond the experience of any former time, or of any other nation. The Floridas and New Orleans command the only outlets to the sea, and our best interests require that we should get possession of them. This requisition, however, arises not from a disposition to increase our territory; for neither the Floridas nor New Orleans offer any other inducements than their mere geographical relation to the United States. But if we look forward to the free use of the Mississippi, the Mobile, the Apalachicola, and the other rivers of the West, by ourselves and our posterity, New Orleans and the Floridas must become a part of the United States, either by purchase or by conquest.

The great question, then, which presents itself is, shall we at this time lay the foundation for future peace by offering a fair and equivalent consideration; or shall we hereafter incur the hazards and the horrors of war? The Government of the United States is differently organized from any other in the world. Its object is the happiness of man; its policy and its interest, to pursue right by right means. War is the great scourge of the human race, and should never be resorted to but in cases of the most imperious necessity. A wise government will avoid it, when its views can be attained by peaceful measures. Princes fight for glory, and the blood and treasure of their subjects is the price they pay. In all nations the people bear the burden of war, and in the United States the people rule. Their Representatives are the guardians of their rights, and it is the duty of those Representatives to provide against any event which may, even at a distant day, involve the interest and the happiness of the nation.

We may, indeed, have our rights restored to us by treaty, but there is a want of fortitude in applying temporary remedies to permanent evils; thereby imposing on our posterity a burden which we ourselves ought to bear. If the purchase can be made, we ought not to hesitate. If the attempt shall fail, we shall have discharged an important duty.

War may be the result, but the American nation, satisfied with our conduct, will be animated by one soul, and will unite all its energies in the contest. Foreign powers will be convinced that it is not a war of aggrandizement on our part, and will feel no unreasonable jealousies toward us. We shall have proved that our object was justice; it will be seen that our propositions were fair; and it will be acknowledged that our cause is honorable. Should alliances be necessary they may be advantageously formed. We shall have merited, and shall therefore possess, general confidence. Our measures will stand justified not only to ourselves and our country, but to the world.

In another point of view, perhaps, it would be preferable to make the purchase, as it is believed that a smaller sum would be required for this subject, than would necessarily be expended, if we should attempt to take possession by force; the expenses of a war being, indeed, almost incalculable. The Committee have no information before them, to ascertain the amount for which the purchase can be made, but it is hoped that, with the assistance of two millions of dollars in hand, this will not be unreasonable. A similar course was pursued for the purpose of settling our differences with the Regency of Algiers, by an appropriation of one million of dollars, prior to the commencement of the negotiation, and we have since experienced its beneficial effects.

## United States Senate
## February 27, 1803

[Extract]

[*Annals of Congress*, 7th Cong., 2nd sess. (Washington, 1851), pp. 98–101.]

MR. [JAMES] BRECKINRIDGE observed, that he did not mean to wander in the field of declamation, nor, after the example of the honorable gentleman who had preceded him, endeavor to alarm or agitate the public mind; that he should endeavor to strip the subject of all improper coloring, and examine dispassionately the propriety of the measures which the Senate were called upon to sanction. He would be very brief.

What is the true and undisguised state of facts? Early in the session, the House of Representatives were informed, by a communication from the President, of the conduct of the Intendant at New Orleans. This communication stated, that he had taken measures to attempt a restoration of the right which had been violated; and that there were reasons to believe that the conduct of the Intendant was unauthorized by the Court of Spain. Accompanying this message were official papers, in which it appeared that the Governor of New Orleans had strongly opposed the conduct of the Intendant, declared that he was acting without authority in refusing the deposit, and indicated a disposition to oppose openly the proceeding. The Spanish Minister who resides here, also interposed on the occasion, and who stands deservedly high in the confidence of his Government, was clearly of opinion, that the Intendant was acting without authority, and that redress would be given so soon as the competent authority could interpose. From this state of things, and which is the actual state at this moment, what is the course any civilized nation who respects her character or rights, would pursue? There is but one course, which is admitted by writers on the laws of nations, as the proper one; and is thus described by *Vattel*, in his book, sec. 336, 338.

"A Sovereign ought to show, in all his quarrels, a sincere desire of rendering justice and preserving peace. He is obliged before he takes up arms, and after having taken them up also, to offer equitable conditions, and then alone his arms become just against an obstinate enemy, who refuses to listen to justice or to equity. His own advantage, and that of human society, oblige him to attempt, before he takes up arms, all the pacific methods of obtaining either the reparation of the injury, or a just satisfaction. This moderation, this circumspection, is so much the more proper, and commonly even indispensable, as the action we take for an injury does not always proceed from a design to offend us, and is sometimes a mistake rather than an act of malice: frequently it even happens, that the injury is done by inferior persons, without their sovereign having any share in it; and on these occasions, it is not natural to presume that he would refuse us a just satisfaction."

This is the course which the President has taken, and in which the House of Representatives have expressed, by their resolution, their confidence.

What are the reasons urged by the gentlemen to induce a different proceeding, an immediate appeal to arms? You prostrate, say the gentlemen, your national honor by negotiating, where there is a direct violation of a treaty! How happens it that our national honor has, at this particular crisis, become so delicate, and that the feelings of certain gentlemen are now so alive to it? Has it been the practice of this Government heretofore to break lances on the spot with any nation who injured or insulted her? Or has not the invariable course been to seek reparation in the first place by negotiation? I ask for an example to the contrary; even under the Administration of Washington, so much eulogized by the gentlemen last up? Were not the Detroit, and several other forts within our territory, held ten or a dozen years by Great Britain, in direct violation of a treaty? Were not wanton spoliations committed on your commerce by Great Britain, by France, and by Spain, to the amount of very many millions; and all adjusted through the medium of negotiations? Were not your merchants plundered, and your citizens doomed to slavery by Algiers, and still those in power, even Washington himself, submitted to negotiation, to ransom, and to tribute? Why then do gentlemen, who on those occasions approved of these measures, now despair of negotiation! America has been uniformly successful, at least in settling her differences by treaty.

But the gentleman is afraid that if we do not immediately seize the country, we shall lose the golden opportunity of doing it. Would your national honor be free from imputation by a conduct of such inconsistency and duplicity? A Minister is sent to the offending nation with an olive-branch, for the purpose of an amicable discussion and settlement of differences, and before he has scarcely turned his back, we invade the territories of that nation with an army of fifty thousand men! Would such conduct comport with the genius and principles of our Republic, whose true interest is peace, and who has hitherto professed to cultivate it with all nations? Would not such a procedure subject us to the just censure of the world, and to the strongest jealousy of those who have possessions near to us? Would such a procedure meet the approbation of even our own citizens, whose lives and fortunes would be risked in the conflict? And would it not be policy inexcusably rash, to plunge this country into war, to effect that which the President not only thinks can be effected, but is now actually in a train of negotiation? If, on the other hand, negotiation should fail, how different will be the ground on which we stand! We stand acquitted by the world, and what is of more consequence, by our own citizens, and our own consciences. But one sentiment will then animate and pervade the whole, and from thenceforth we will take counsel only from our courage.

But to induce us to depart from this proper, this safe, and honorable course of proceeding, which is pursuing by the President, the gentleman from Pennsylvania first, and the gentleman from Delaware again told you, that by such pacific measures you will irritate the western people against you; that they will not be restrained by you, but will either invade the country themselves, or withdraw from the Union and unite with those who will give them what they want. Sir, said Mr. B., I did not expect to hear such language held on this floor. Sir, the gentleman from Pennsylvania best knows the temper and views of the western people he represents, but if he meant to extend the imputation to the State I have the honor to represent, I utterly disclaim it. The citizens of Kentucky value too highly their rights and character to endanger the one, or dishonor the other. They deal not, sir, in insurrections. They hold in too sacred re-

## Crisis at New Orleans

gard their federal compact to sport with it. They were among the first to oppose violations of it, and will, I barter away this right for twenty-five years. The time indeed was, when not only irritation but disgust prevailed in that country; when, instead of sending fifty thousand men to seize on Orleans, an attempt was meditated, and a solemn vote taken in Congress to barter away this right for twenty-five years. The time indeed was, when great dissatisfaction prevailed in that country, as to the measures of the General Government; but it never furnished there, whatever it might have done elsewhere, even the germs for treasons or insurrections. The people I have the honor to represent are not accustomed to procure redress in this way. Instead of trampling on the Constitution of their country, they rally round it as the rock of their safety. But, unhappily, these times have passed away. Distrust and dissatisfaction have given place to confidence in, and attachment to those in whom the concerns of the nation are confided. I ask no reliance on my opinion for this fact, but appeal to the memorial of the Legislature of Kentucky to the present Congress, for the truth of this assertion. In this disposition of mind therefore, and from the sound sense and correct views and discernment of their true interest, which the people of Kentucky possess, I have no hesitation in pledging myself, that no such precipitate and unwarranted measures will be taken by them, as predicted by the gentlemen in the opposition.

*   *   *

Although he thought it incumbent on us, for the reasons he had stated, to try the effect of negotiation, yet, should that fail, he thought it incumbent on us also to be prepared for another resort. He considered this right, and upon a different footing from what we ever enjoyed it, so all-important, so indispensable to the very existence of the Western States, that it was a waste of words and time to attempt to portray the evils which a privation of it would produce; and he rejoiced to find that gentlemen with whom he had not been in the habit of voting on most political subjects so perfectly accord with him, that our precarious tenure of it must be changed. He hoped they were sincere in their declarations. If they were, the only difference between us now is, what are the proper means to obtain this great end? The course pursued by the President was, in his opinion, the only true and dignified course. It is that, and that only, which will certainly attain the object; and is the only one which will tend to unite cordially all parts of the Union. But we ought to be prepared, in case of a failure, instantly to redress ourselves. This, instead of having an evil, would, in his opinion, have a good effect on the negotiation. It would show, that although we are willing amicably to adjust our differences, yet that we are not only resolved on, but prepared for that resort which cannot fail to restore our violated rights. With that view, he would offer the following resolutions, as substitutes for those proposed by the gentleman from Pennsylvania.

He moved that the whole of the resolutions be struck out, expecting the word *"Resolved,"* and the following be substituted in their place—after the word *"Resolved,"*

> "That the President of the United States be, and he is hereby authorized, whenever he shall judge it expedient, to require of the Executives of the several States to take effectual measures to organize, arm, and equip, according to law, and

hold in readiness to march at a moment's warning, eighty thousand effective militia, officers included.

*Resolved,* "That the President may, if he judges it expedient, authorize the Executives of the several states to accept, as part of the detachment aforesaid, any corps of volunteers; who shall continue in service for such time, not exceeding —— months, and perform such services as shall be prescribed by law.

*Resolved,* "That —— dollars be appropriated for paying and subsisting such part of the troops aforesaid, whose actual service may be wanted, and for defraying such other expenses as, during the recess of Congress, the President may deem necessary for the security of the territory of the United States.

*Resolved,* "That —— dollars be appropriated for erecting, at such place or places on the western waters, as the President may judge most proper, one or more arsenals."

# 37

*President Thomas Jefferson to
Governor of the Territory of Indiana
William H. Harrison
February 27, 1803*

[Extract]

[*The Writings of Thomas Jefferson*, vol. 10, A. Lipscomb, ed. (Washington, D.C.: Thomas Jefferson Memorial Association, 1901), pp. 368–73.]

*Washington*

You will receive herewith an answer to your letter as President of the Convention; and from the Secretary of War you receive from time to time information and instructions as to our Indian affairs. These communications being for the public records, are restrained always to particular objects and occasions; but this letter being unofficial and private, I may with safety give you a more extensive view of our policy respecting the Indians, that you may the better comprehend the parts dealt out to you in detail through the official channel, and observing the system of which they make a part, conduct yourself in unison with it in cases where you are obliged to act without instruction. Our system is to live in perpetual peace with the Indians, to cultivate an affectionate attachment from them, by everything just and liberal which we can do for them within the bounds of reason, and by giving them effectual protection against wrongs from our own people. The decrease of game rendering their subsistence by hunting insufficient, we wish to draw them to agriculture, to spinning and weaving. The latter branches they take up with great readiness, because they fall to the women, who gain by quitting the labors of the field for those which are exercised within doors. When they withdraw themselves to the culture of a small piece of land, they will perceive how useless to them are their extensive forests, and will be willing to pare them off from time to time in exchange for necessaries for their farms and families. To promote this disposition to exchange lands, which they have to spare and we want, for necessaries, which we have to spare and they want, we shall push our trading uses, and be glad to see the good and influential individuals among them run in debt, because we observe that when these debts get beyond what the individuals can pay, they become willing to lop them off by a cession of lands. At our trading houses, too, we mean to sell so low as merely to repay us cost and charges, so as neither to lessen nor enlarge our capital. This is what private traders cannot do, for they must gain; they will consequently retire from the competition, and we shall thus get clear of this pest without giving offence or umbrage to the Indians. In this way our settlements will gradually circumscribe and approach the Indians, and they will in time either incorporate with us as citizens of the United States, or remove beyond the Mississippi. The former is certainly the termination of their history most happy for themselves; but, in the whole course of this, it is essential to cultivate their love. As to their fear, we presume that our strength and their weakness is now so visible that they must see we have only to shut our hand to crush them, and that all our liberalities to them proceed from motives of pure humanity only. Should any tribe be foolhardy enough to take up the hatchet at any time, the seizing the whole country of that tribe, and driving them across the Mississippi, as the only condition of peace, would be an example to others, and a furtherance of our final consolidation.

Combined with these views, and to be prepared

against the occupation of Louisiana, by a powerful and enterprising people, it is important that, setting less value on interior extension of purchases from the Indians, we bend our whole views to the purchase and settlement of the country on the Mississippi, from its mouth to its northern regions, that we may be able to present as strong a front on our western as on our eastern border, and plant on the Mississippi itself the means of its own defence. We now own from 31 to the Yazoo, and hope this summer to purchase what belongs to the Choctaws from the Yazoo up to their boundary, supposed to be about opposite the mouth of Acanza. We wish at the same time to begin in your quarter, for which there is at present a favorable opening. The Cahokias extinct, we are entitled to their country by our paramount sovereignty. The Piorias, we understand, have all been driven off from their country, and we might claim it in the same way; but as we understand there is one chief remaining, who would, as the survivor of the tribe, sell the right, it is better to give him such terms as will make him easy for life, and take a conveyance from him. The Kaskaskias being reduced to a few families, I presume we may purchase their whole country for what would place every individual of them at his ease, and be a small price to us,—say by laying off for each family, whenever they would choose it, as much rich land as they could cultivate, adjacent to each other, enclosing the whole in a single fence, and giving them such an annuity in money or goods forever as would place them in happiness; and we might take them also under the protection of the United States. Thus possessed of the rights of these tribes, we should proceed to the settling their boundaries with the Poutewatamies and Kickapoos; claiming all doubtful territory, but paying them a price for the relinquishment of their concurrent claim, and even prevailing on them, if possible, to *cede*, for a price, such of their own unquestioned territory as would give us a convenient northern boundary. Before broaching this, and while we are bargaining with the Kaskaskies, the minds of the Poutewatamies and Kickapoos should be soothed and conciliated by liberalities and sincere assurances of friendship. Perhaps by sending a well-qualified character to stay some time in Decoigne's village, as if on other business, and to sound him and introduce the subject by degrees to his mind and that of the other heads of families, inculcating in the way of conversation, all those considerations which prove the advantages they would receive by a cession on these terms, the object might be more easily and effectually obtained than by abruptly proposing it to them at a formal treaty. Of the means, however, of obtaining what we wish, you will be the best judge; and I have given you this view of the system which we suppose will best promote the interests of the Indians and ourselves, and finally consolidate our whole country to one nation only; that you may be enabled the better to adapt your means to the object, for this purpose we have given you a general commission for treating. The crisis is pressing; whatever can now be obtained must be obtained quickly. The occupation of New Orleans, hourly expected, by the French, is already felt like a light breeze by the Indians. You know the sentiments they entertain of that nation; under the hope of their protection they will immediately stiffen against cessions of lands to us. We had better, therefore, do at once what can now be done.

I must repeat that this letter is to be considered as private and friendly, and is not to control any particular instructions which you may receive through official channel. You will also perceive how sacredly it must be kept within your own breast, and especially how improper to be understood by the Indians. For their interests and their tranquility it is best they should see only the present age of their history. I pray you to accept assurances of my esteem and high consideration.

## 38

## *James Madison to Charles Pinckney*
## *January 10, 1803*

[*American State Papers,* vol. 2, *Foreign Relations,* Walter Lowrie and Matthew Clarke, eds. (Washington: Gales and Seaton, 1833), pp. 528–29.]

*Washington, Department of State*

Sir:

Since my letter of November 27th, on the subject of what had taken place at New Orleans, a letter has been received from the Governor of Louisiana to Gov. Claiborne, in which it is stated that the measure of the Intendant was without instructions from his Government, and admitted that his own judgment did not concur with that of the Intendant. You will find, by the printed documents herewith transmitted, that the subject engaged the early and earnest attention of the House of Representatives; and that all the information relating to it, possessed by the Executive prior to the receipt of that letter, was reported, in consequence of a call for it. The letter itself has been added to that report; but being confidentially communicated, it does not appear in print; a translation of it, however, is herewith enclosed. You will find, also, that the House has passed a resolution explicitly declaring that the stipulated rights of the United States on the Mississippi will be inviolably maintained. The disposition of many members was to give to the resolution a tone and complexion still stronger. To these proofs of the sensation which has been produced, it is to be added, that representations, expressing the peculiar sensibility of the Western country, are on the way from every quarter of it to the Government. There is, in fact, but one sentiment throughout the Union with respect to the duty of maintaining our rights of navigation and boundary. The only existing difference relates to the degree of patience which ought to be exercised during the appeal to friendly modes of redress. In this state of things, it is to be presumed, that the Spanish Government will accelerate, by every possible means, its interposition for that purpose; and the President charges you to urge the necessity of so doing with as much amicable decision as you can employ. We are not without hopes that the Intendent will yield to the demands which have been made on him: and to the advice which he will have received from the Spanish minister here. But it will be expected from the justice and good faith of the Spanish Government, that its precise orders to that effect will be forwarded by the quickest conveyance possible. The President wishes, also, that the expedient suggested in the letter above referred to, for preventing similar occurrences and delays, may also be duly pressed on that Government.

I have the honor to be, &c.

JAMES MADISON

# 39

## *Pierre Samuel du Pont de Nemours to President Thomas Jefferson*
## *October 4, 1802*

[*The Writings of Thomas Jefferson*, vol. 8, P. L. Ford, ed. (New York: G. P. Putnam's Sons, 1897), pp. 91–93.]

*Paris*

Mister President:

Our negotiation has not been as successful as I would have hoped. However, I'm far from considering it as being in such a bad way as Chancellor Livingston seems to believe. . . .

There can be no doubt that your treaties with Spain relating to borders of the two states and to commerce as well as to navigation on the Mississippi are to be respected, confirmed and renewed.

It is certain that it is the interest of France that the commerce of the U.S.A. should enjoy all of its rights even in New Orleans, and that the administrators sent there are convinced of this truth and seem disposed to regulate their behavior accordingly.

With regard to New Orleans and the Floridas: it seems to me that America wishes to take possession of them before entering into any negotiations. But after this preliminary will have been fulfilled, nothing heralds the refusal to negotiate.

If I were to give counsel to the two powers on this subject, I should propose the text included in the next page. I do this after having, I think, well calculated their respective interests.

## Article I

France will cede to the U.S. New Orleans and the two Floridas under the condition that France and its ships will have the right to exercise commerce as freely as the citizens and the ships of the U.S.A. and without paying any duty.

## Article II

The U. S. pledges themselves to induce no nation to participate in these advantages which are a special condition of the cession and to maintain with regard to commerce of other nations in this new territory which was not included in the stipulation of any previous treaty the principles and the levying of duties valid in American customs.

### Article III

France formally reserves for itself all the other territories dependent on Louisiana and which are situated on the right bank of the Mississippi.

Navigation on the River will be free and common to both nations.

### Article IV

The U. S. will pay France six million dollars as a price for the cession mentioned in Article I.

If you wish to go so far I do not lose hope of success whatever the current feelings may be and whatever the effect of the prejudice which in my view is unfounded, stemming from Santo Domingo where it was believed that your nation favors the black population rather than the white. And this is certainly better than to run the risk of submitting your people once again, justly proud of its independence, to the claws of the British leopard and of restoring the instruments of power or vengeance of your former oppressors who shall ever be to you false friends full of contempt and guile.

You see, Mr. President, that I speak to you with the freedom of a man honored by your friendship. Your friendship is very dear to me. I would like to deserve its continuation by rendering real services.

I have had the idea to make in Paris payments of dividends that the U.S.A. owe to French citizens. This would be a means toward further enhancing your credit and making known a spirit of goodwill, communication which I consider apt to promote your negotiations.

My son will explain to you all my ideas on this point. All of them are aimed at mutual advantage of the two nations.

## President Thomas Jefferson to Special Envoy to France James Monroe January 13, 1803

[Extract]

[*The Writings of Thomas Jefferson,* vol. 8, P. L. Ford, ed. (New York: G. P. Putnam's Sons, 1897), pp. 190–92.]

*Washington*

Dear Sir,

I dropped you a line on the 10th informing you of a nomination I had made of you to the Senate, and yesterday I enclosed you their approbation not then having time to write. The agitation of the public mind on occasion of the late suspension of our right of deposit at N. Orleans is extreme. In the western country it is natural and grounded on honest motives. In the seaports it proceeds from a desire for war which increases the mercantile lottery; in the federalists generally and especially those of Congress the object is to force us into war if possible, in order to derange our finances, or if this cannot be done, to attach the western country to them, as their best friends, and thus get again into power. Remonstrances, memorials &c. are now circulating through the whole of the western country and signing by the body of people. The measures we have been pursuing being invisible, do not satisfy their minds. Something sensible therefore was become necessary; and indeed our object of purchasing N. Orleans and the Floridas is a measure liable to assume so many shapes, that no instructions could be squared to fit them, it was essential then to send a minister extraordinary to be joined with the ordinary one, with discretionary powers, first however well impressed with all our views and therefore qualified to meet and modify to these every form of proposition which could come from the other party. This could be done only in full and frequent oral communications. Having determined on this, there could not be two opinions among the republicans as to the person. You possess the unlimited confidence of the administration and of the western people; and generally of the republicans everywhere; and were you to refuse to go, no other man can be found who does this. The measure has already silenced the Feds. here. Congress will no longer be agitated by them: and the country will become calm as fast as the information extends over it. All eyes, all hopes, are now fixed on you; and were you to decline, the chagrin would be universal, and would shake under your feet the high ground on which you stand with the public. Indeed I know nothing which would produce such a shock, for on the event of this mission depends the future destinies of this republic. If we cannot by a purchase of the country insure to ourselves a course of perpetual peace and friendship with all nations, then as war cannot be distant, it behooves us immediately to be preparing for that course, without, however, hastening it, and it may be necessary (on your failure on the continent) to cross the channel.

We shall get entangled in European politics, and figuring more, be much less happy and prosperous. This can only be prevented by a successful issue to your present mission. I am sensible after the measures you have taken for getting into a different line of business, that it will be a great sacrifice on your part, and presents from the season and other circumstances serious difficulties. But some men are born for the public. Nature by fitting them for the service of the human race on a broad scale, has stamped with the evidences of her destination and their duty.

## 41

*President Thomas Jefferson to
Robert R. Livingston
February 3, 1803*

[Extract]

[*The Writings of Thomas Jefferson*, vol. 8, P. L. Ford, ed. (New York: G. P. Putnam's Sons, 1897), pp. 209-10.]

*Washington*

A late suspension by the Intendant of N. Orleans of our right of deposit there, without which the right of navigation is impracticable, has thrown this country into such a flame of hostile disposition as can scarcely be described. The western country was peculiarly sensible to it as you may suppose. Our business was to take the most effectual pacific measures in our power to remove the suspension, and at the same time to persuade our countrymen that pacific measures would be the most effectual and the most speedily so. The opposition caught it as a plank in a shipwreck, hoping it would enable them to tack the Western people to them. They raised the cry of war, were intriguing in all the quarters to exasperate the Western inhabitants to arm & go down on their own authority & possess themselves of New Orleans, and in the meantime were daily reiterating, in new shapes, inflammatory resolutions for the adoption of the House. As a remedy to all this we determined to name a minister extraordinary to go immediately to Paris & Madrid to settle this matter. This measure being a visible one, and the person named peculiarly proper with the Western country, crushed at once & put an end to all further attempts on the Legislature. From that moment all has become quiet; and the more readily in the Western Country, as the sudden alliance of these new federal friends had of itself already begun to make them suspect the wisdom of their own course. The measure was moreover proposed from another cause. We must know at once whether we can acquire N. Orleans or not. We are satisfied nothing else will secure us against a war at no distant period; and we cannot press this reason without beginning those arrangements which will be necessary if war is hereafter to result. For this purpose it was necessary that the negotiators should be fully possessed of every idea we have on the subject, so as to meet the propositions of the opposite party, in whatever form they may be offered; and give them a shape admissible by us without being obliged to await new instructions hence. With this view, we have joined Mr. Monroe to yourself at Paris, & to Mr. Pinckney at Madrid, altho' we believe it will be hardly necessary for him to go to this last place. Should we fail in this object of the mission, a further one will be superadded for the other side of the channel. On this subject you will be informed by the Secretary of State, & Mr. Monroe will be able also to inform you of all our views and purposes.

## 42

*President Thomas Jefferson to Pierre Samuel du Pont de Nemours February 1, 1803*

[*State Papers, Correspondence Bearing upon the Purchase of the Territory of Louisiana* (Washington, D.C.: Government Printing Office, 1903), pp. 94–96.]

*Washington*

Dear Sir,

I have to acknowledge the receipt of your favors of August the 16th and October the 4th. The latter I received with peculiar satisfaction; because, while it holds up terms which cannot be entirely yielded, it proposes such as a mutual spirit of accommodation and sacrifice of opinion may bring to some point of union. While we were preparing on this subject such modifications of the propositions of your letter of October the 4th, as we could assent to, an event happened which obliged us to adopt measures of urgency. The suspension of the right of deposit at New Orleans, ceded to us by treaty with Spain, threw our whole country into such a ferment as imminently threatened its peace. This, however, was believed to be the act of the Intendant, unauthorized by his government. But it showed the necessity of making effectual arrangements to secure the peace of the two countries against the indiscreet acts of subordinate agents. The urgency of the case, as well as the public spirit, therefore induced us to make a more solemn appeal to the justice and judgment of our neighbors, by sending a minister extraordinary to impress them with the necessity of some arrangement. Mr. Monroe has been selected. His good dispositions cannot be doubted. Multiplied conversations with him, and views of the subject taken in all the shapes in which it can present itself, have possessed him with our estimates of everything relating to it, with a minuteness which no written communication to Mr. Livingston could ever have attained. These will prepare them to meet and decide on every form of proposition which can occur, without awaiting new instructions from hence, which might draw to an indefinite length a discussion where circumstances imperiously obliged us to a prompt decision. For the occlusion of the Mississippi is a state of things in which we cannot exist. He goes, therefore, joined with Chancellor Livingston, to aid in the issue of a crisis the most important the United States have ever met since their independence, and which is to decide their future character and career. The confidence which the government of France reposes in you, will undoubtedly give great weight to your information. An equal confidence on our part, founded on your knowledge of the subject, your just views of it, your good dispositions toward this country, and my long experience of your personal faith and friendship, assures me that you will render between us all the good offices in your power. The interests of the two countries being absolutely the same as to this matter, your aid may be conscientiously given. It will often perhaps, be possible for you, having a freedom of communication, *omnibus horis,* which diplomatic gentlemen will be excluded from by forms, to smooth difficulties by representations and reasonings, which would be received with more suspicion from them. You will thereby render great good to both countries. For our circumstances are so imperious as to admit of no delay as to our course; and the use of the Mississippi so indispensable, that we cannot hesitate one moment to hazard our existence for its maintenance. If we fail in this effort to put it beyond the reach of accident, we see the destinies we have to run, and prepare at once for them. Not but that we shall still endeavor to go on in peace and friendship with our neighbors as long as we can, *if our rights of navigation and deposit are respected,* but as we foresee that the caprices of the local officers, and the abuse of those rights by our boatmen and navigators, which neither government can prevent, will keep up a state of irritation which cannot long be kept inactive, we should be criminally improvident not to take at once eventual measures for strengthening ourselves for the contest. It may be said, if this object be so all-important to us, why do we not offer such a sum as to insure its purchase? The answer is simple. We are an agricultural people, poor in money, and owing great debts. These will be falling due by installments for fifteen years to come, and require from us the practice of rigorous economy to accomplish their payment; and it is our principle to pay to a moment whatever we have engaged, and never to engage what we cannot, and mean not faithfully to pay.

We have calculated our resources, and find the sum to be moderate which they would enable us to pay, and we know from late trials that little can be added to it by borrowing. The country, too, which we wish to purchase, except the portion already granted, and which must be confirmed to the private holders, is a barren sand, six hundred miles from east to west, and from thirty to forty and fifty miles from north to south, formed by deposition of the sands by the Gulf Stream in its circular course round the Mexican Gulf, and which being spent after performing a semicircle, has made from its last depositions the sand bank of East Florida. In West Florida, indeed, there are on the borders of the rivers some rich bottoms, formed by the mud brought from the upper country. These bottoms are all possessed by individuals. But the spaces between river and river are mere banks of sand; and in East Florida there are neither rivers, nor consequently any bottoms. We can not then make anything by a sale of the lands to individuals. So that it is peace alone which makes it an object with us, and which ought to make the cession of it desirable to France. Whatever power, other than ourselves, holds the country east of the Mississippi becomes our natural enemy. Will such a possession do France as much good, as such an enemy may do her harm? And how long would it be hers, were such an enemy, situated at its door, added to Great Britain? I confess, it appears to me as essential to France to keep at peace with us, as it is to us to keep at peace with her; and that, if this cannot be secured without some compromise as to the territory in question, it will be useful for both to make some sacrifices to effect the compromise.

You see, my good friend, with what frankness I communicate with you on this subject; that I hide nothing from you, and that I am endeavoring to turn our private friendship to the good of our respective countries. And can private friendship ever answer a nobler end than by keeping two nations at peace, who, if this new position which one of them is taking were rendered innocent, have more points of common interest, and fewer of collision, than any two on earth; who become natural friends, instead of natural enemies, which this change of position would make them. My letters of April the 25th, May the 5th, and this present one have been written, without any disguise, in this view; and while safe in your hands they can never do anything but good. But you and I are now at the time of life when our call to another state of being cannot be distant, and may be near. Besides, your government is in the habit of seizing papers without notice. These letters might thus get into hands, which, like the hornet which extracts poison from the same flower that yields honey to the bee, might make them the ground of blowing up a flame between our two countries, and make our friendship and confidence in each other effect exactly the reverse of what we are aiming at. Being yourself thoroughly possessed of every idea in them, let me ask from your friendship an immediate consignment of them to the flames. That alone can make all safe, and ourselves secure.

## 43

*President Thomas Jefferson to James Garrard
January 18, 1803*

[Extract]

[*The Writings of Thomas Jefferson,* vol. 8, P. L. Ford, ed. (New York: G. P. Putnam's Sons, 1897), pp. 202–03.]

I have determined with the approbation of the Senate, to send James Monroe, late governor of Virginia, with full powers to him and our ministers in France and Spain to enter with those governments into such arrangements as may effectually secure our rights & interests in the Mississippi, and in the country eastward of that. He is now here and will depart immediately. In the meantime knowing how important it is that the obstructions shall be removed in time for the produce which will begin to descend the river in February, the Spanish minister, has, at our request, reiterated his interposition with the Intendant of New Orleans.

I inclose you a resolution of the House of Representatives on this subject, which with the measures taken by the executive, will, I hope, furnish new grounds for the confidence which the legislature of Kentucky is pleased to express in the government of the U. S., and evince to them that that government is equally and impartially alive to the interests of every portion of the union.

## 44

*Editor's Comments*, The Frankfort (*Kentucky*) Palladium, *January 27, 1803*

[Extract]

[As quoted in A. P. Whitaker, *The Mississippi Question, 1795–1803* (Gloucester: Peter Smith, 1962), pp. 223–24.]

The attachment which the citizens of this State have long felt to the Union, has often been very undeservedly questioned by political writers in the papers of the Eastern States. When such writers as Coriolanus (who professes to be a republican) can prevail on themselves to give currency to the idea, we think it is high time, publicly to deny, in behalf of our fellow citizens, that any Power has, or, in all human probability, will have claims to their affection superior to the general government of the United States. Whatever may be the result of the present dispute with Spain—whatever may be the privations in consequence thereof—or however great the inducements to desert the Union,—the people of this state can never be brought "to enroll themselves as dependent provinces of Louisiana". . . . One sentiment only prevails on this subject, *a perfect reliance on the justice of the Federal Government and a determination to support its decision, let it cost what it will.*

## 45

## *William C. C. Claiborne to James Madison, March 27, 1803*

[Extract]

[*The Letter Books of W. C. C. Claiborne,* vol. 1, Dunbar Rowland, ed. (Jackson: Mississippi State Department of Archives and History, 1917), pp. 283–84.]

*Near Natchez*

Mr. Monroe's Mission is highly satisfactory to most of the reflecting Citizens of this territory; but there are some few Characters among us (from whose standing in society a contrary conduct was expected) who either from sinister views or sanguine temperaments reprobate the policy pursued, and have not been wanting in exertions to inflame the public and excite among them a spirit of discontent. But happily the reason and fears of these men having obtained the ascendancy of their passions, no difficulty has been experienced in suppressing in the bud such insurgent and disorderly efforts.

## 46

### James Madison to James Monroe
### March 1, 1803

[Extract]

[*State Papers, Correspondence Bearing upon the Purchase of the Territory of Louisiana* (Washington, D.C.: Government Printing Office, 1903), pp. 113–14.]

*Washington*

Dear Sir,

Since you left us we have no further intelligence from New Orleans, except a letter dated January 20th from the Vice Consular agent there, from which it appears that the letters to the Governor and Intendant from the Spanish Minister here had arrived about the 13th, and had not, on the 20th, produced the desired change in the state of things. The delay, however, does not seem to have been viewed by the Consul as any proof that the Intendant would not conform to the interposition. The idea continued that he had taken his measures without orders from his Government. There are letters (according to that from the Consul) for the Marquis Yrujo now on the way by land.

These will probably shew whether the Intendant will yield or not. The despatch vessel which carried the Marquis's letters is not yet returned. The detention of her beyond the allotted time is favorably interpreted by him, on the presumption that she waits for a satisfactory answer, which the pride of the Intendant postpones as long as possible.

The newspapers will have informed you of the turn given to the proceedings of Congress on the subject of New Orleans, &c. The propositions of Mr. Ross in the Senate, which drove at war thro' a delegation of unconstitutional power to the Executive, were discussed very elaborately, and *with open doors*. The adversaries of them triumphed in the debate, and threw them out by 15 votes against 11. On the motion of Mr. Breckenridge, measures of expenseless or cheap preparation, in the style of those which attended Mr. Jay's mission to G. Britain, have been agreed on in the Senate. It is uncertain whether even these will pass the House of Representatives. If they should, as is, perhaps, not improper, they will not be understood as indicating views that ought to excite suspicions or unfriendly sensations in either of the Governments to which your Mission is addressed. The truth is, that justice and peace prevail not only in the public councils, but in the body of the community; and will continue to do so as long as the conduct of other nations will permit. But France and Spain cannot be too deeply impressed with the necessity of revising their relations to us thro' the Mississippi, if they wish to enjoy our friendship, or preclude a state of things which will be more formidable than any that either of those powers has yet experienced. Some adjustments, such as those which you have to propose, have become indispensable. The whole of what we wish is not too much to secure permanent harmony between the parties. Something much better than has hitherto been enjoyed by the States is essential to any tolerable degree of it, even for the present. . . .

## James Monroe to President Thomas Jefferson
## March 7, 1803

[Extract]

[*State Papers, Correspondence Bearing upon the Purchase of the Territory of Louisiana* (Washington, D.C.: Government Printing Office, 1903), pp. 136–38.]

*New York*

Dear Sir,

I rec$^d$. yours of the 25. ulto. with one to M$^r$. Cepeda this morning, when I also rec$^d$. my instructions from the department of State, with all the other documents connected with my mission to France & Sp$^n$. The ship, Richmond, of ab$^t$. 400 tons burden, whose cabbin I have taken, cleared at the custom house on Saturday, my baggage was put on board, in expectation of sailing yesterday as M$^r$. Madison informed me my instructions ought to arrive by 8 in the morning; but it being Sunday, they were delayed till to-day. We are now detained by a snowstorm and contrary wind, but I shall sail as soon as it clears up, & the wind shifts.

The resolutions of M$^r$. Ross proved that the federal party will stick at nothing to embarrass the adm$^n$., and recover its lost power. They nevertheless produce a great effect on the publick mind and I presume more especially in the western country. The unanimity in the publick councils respecting our right to the free navigation of the river, and its importance to every part of the U States, the dissatisfaction at the interference of Sp$^n$. which will not be appeased while the power of a similar one exists, are calculated to inspire the hope of a result which may put us at ease forever on those points. If the negotiation secures all the objects sought, or a deposit with the sovereignty over it, the federalists will be overwhelmed completely: the union of the western with the Eastern people will be consolidated, republican principles confirmed, and a fair prospect of peace and happiness presented to our country. But if the negotiation compromises short of that, and leaves the management of our great concerns in that river, which comprise everything appertaining to the western parts of the U States, in the hands of a foreign power, may we not expect that the publick will be disappointed and disapprove of the result. So far as I can judge, I think much would be hazarded by any adjustment which did not put us in complete security for the future. It is doubtful whether an adjustment short of that would be approved in any part of the union; I am thoroughly persuaded it would not to the westward. If they were discontented, there would grow up an union of councils and measures between them and the Eastern people which might lead to other measures & be perverted to bad purposes. The Eastern towns, which govern the country wish war for the sake of privateering: the western would not dislike it especially if they were withheld from a just right, or the enjoyment of a privilege necessary to their welfare, the pursuit of which by force would create a vast expenditure of money among them. Their confidence is now reposed in the adm$^n$. from the best of motives,—a knowledge that it is sincerely friendly to their interests: it is strengthened by a distrust of these new *friends;* but an inquietude has been created by the late event, an inquiry has taken place which has shown that every part of the union especially the Eastern, is deeply interested in opening the river; that the attempt to occlude it on a former occasion was a base perhaps a corrupt intrigue of a few; their hopes and expectations have been raised, and it is probable they expect from the mission by a peaceful course everything which their enemies promised by war. The consequences of a disappointment are not easily calculated. If it restored the federal party to power and involved us in war, the result might be fatal. It therefore highly merits consideration whether we should not take that ground as the ultimatum in the negotiation which must in every possible event preserve the confidence & affection of the western people. While we stand well with them we shall prosper. We shall be most apt to avoid war, taking ten years ensuing together; and if we are driven by necessity into it, it is much better that it be under the auspices of a republican than a monarchial adm$^n$. These ideas are expressed in haste for y$^r$. consideration for I have not time to give them method or form. I shall most certainly labor to obtain the best terms possible, but it is for you to say, what are the least favorable we must accept. You will have time to weigh the subject & feel the publick pulse on it before anything conclusive may be done. I hope the French gov$^t$. will have wisdom enough to see that we will never suffer France or any other power to tamper with our interior; if that is not the object there can be no reason for declining an accommodation to the whole of our demands. . . .

## Robert R. Livingston to James Madison
## December 20, 1802

[Extract]

[*State Papers, Correspondence Bearing upon the Purchase of the Territory of Louisiana* (Washington, D.C.: Government Printing Office, 1903), p. 65.]

*Paris*

Sir:

I have received your favor by Mde. Broniau, and had, as you will find, anticipated your wishes in finding another manual to the First Consul. The consequence of which is, that I have, at this moment, a very strong memorial under his eye, and some projects which appear to be well received. But the subject is too delicate to treat here; when a safe conveyance offers I shall write to you more at large. The minister has changed his conduct much for the better, either because of our late difference, or because he suspects that I have another passage to the First Consul. France has not yet got Florida; but there is not much doubt that her negotiations on this subject will succeed, as Parma is a favorite object with Spain. Pray be explicit in the amount of what I may offer, and consider the value of the country—its importance to peace—the expensive establishment it will save, and its intrinsic worth, from the price of the land and actual revenue. I do not, however, mean that you should infer from this that my prospects of obtaining the object are great, because I find, as Mr. Talleyrand told me yesterday, the First Consul *entêté* with this project. But I have made so many converts, that I would wish, in case favorable circumstances should arise, to know how to act. If left to myself I may go beyond the mark. General politics you will collect from the papers I send. I have mentioned that the storm in England will blow over for the present; and the peace will not be lasting. The armament for Louisiana has not yet sailed; the civil officers are yet here, if I am rightly informed by the Minister from whom I had it yesterday.

## 49

### *Robert R. Livingston to James Madison January 24, 1803*

[*State Papers, Correspondence Bearing upon the Purchase of the Territory of Louisiana* (Washington, D.C.: Government Printing Office, 1903), pp. 81–82.]

*Paris*

Sir:

I have just now heard of an opportunity from Havre. I am doubtful whether my letter will arrive in time for it. I therefore confine myself to inform you that General Bernadotte is named Minister to the United States, in the place of Otto, who will be employed here. General Bernadotte is brother-in-law to Joseph Bonaparte, is a very respectable man, and has the character of a decided republican. I have endeavored to impress upon him the necessity of making some arrangements relative to the debt previous to his departure, which he has much at heart. But neither he nor anybody else can influence the councils of the First Consul. You can hardly conceive anything more timid than all about him are; they dare not be known to have a sentiment of their own, or to have expressed one to anybody. But I must defer writing to you more at large on this subject, as well as a full communication of a very delicate step that I have hazarded, which promised success for some time, but from which I, at present, hope for no important result. The Minister informs me that the expedition to Louisiana will sail shortly. General Bernadotte will go in about three weeks. He will have full powers to settle everything. I asked the Minister, what confidence you can have in any new offer to treat, when the last treaty is unexecuted; and if he had not better send out General Bernadotte with a treaty in his hand, than only with powers that will be suspected; and how he can make arrangements upon the debts, which must depend upon the Legislature? He answers this by saying, they want information as to right of deposit, &c. As to the debt, I have no hope that they have any intention to pay it, or even to fund it. From the disposition which I know to be entertained by some that go out with Victor, I have no doubt that they will provoke an Indian war, by paying them nothing; and that, in their solicitude to acquire wealth, they will act over again the tyranny of St. Domingo. It will be necessary, therefore, to take the position that will best guard you against the effects of these evils. As to myself, I am left wholly without any precise instruction how to act, or what to offer. Enclosed are two memoirs lately sent in, with as little effects as those that have gone before them; though I have reason to think that the Minister wishes well to my project for Louisiana, but the First Consul is immovable. I confess to you I see very little use for a Minister here, where there is but one will; and that will governed by no object but personal security and personal ambition: were it left to my discretion, I should bring matters to some positive issue, or leave them, which would be the only means of bringing them to an issue.

I am, &c.,

ROBERT R. LIVINGSTON

## 50

*Robert R. Livingston to
Napoleon Bonaparte
February 27, 1803*

[Extract]

[*State Papers, Correspondence Bearing upon the Purchase of the Territory of Louisiana* (Washington, D.C.: Government Printing Office, 1903), pp. 119-22.]

The . . . object that has awakened the sensibilities of the United States is, the change that is about to take place in the situation of Louisiana, heightened, as they are, by the silence which the Governments of France and Spain have observed, and still observe, with respect to their treaty, and the rights that the United States claim, and have long exercised, at New Orleans. I have pressed the Minister to some pointed declaration on the subject of our right of depot at New Orleans, on the limits as settled with Spain, and on the navigation of the Mississippi; for though it necessarily follows that those rights can not be injured by a change of jurisdiction, yet it would have been highly satisfactory to the United States to have received some such assurances upon these subjects as would have shown that the treaty between them and Spain was clearly understood, and served to overawe such of the officers of Government, as, emboldened by their distance from the Sovereign, might act from their own impressions. A recent event, citizen First Consul, has demonstrated the extreme sensibility of the United States on this subject. The Intendant of New Orleans having thought it proper to withdraw the right of depot, secured to the citizens of the United States by the Treaty of Madrid, a spirit of resentment has been manifested from one end of the Union to the other, and nothing but the interposition of the Spanish Minister, the disavowal of the act by the Governor of New Orleans, and the extreme solicitude of the American Government to avoid everything which might have a tendency to interrupt the harmony which at present so happily subsists between the United States and every power in Europe, could have prevented an immediate recurrence to arms; nor am I now without apprehension that, if nothing is done to calm their anxiety before the season for bringing down the produce of the country occurs, the Government will be compelled to follow the impulse of the people. Under these circumstances, citizen First Consul, it can not appear improper, prizing as I do, the connexion between our respective countries, to press for some such explicit and early declaration on the subject of our rights as will serve to calm the anxiety of the United States. Should the agents of France, who are to take possession of the Colony, continue the regulations in the face of the treaty which they may find established by the Spanish Intendant, a fatal blow will be struck at the future peace and harmony of both countries. That I may not intrude too far upon your patience, I will merely take the liberty to transport such loose hints as you may possibly think might be improved into some arrangements, alike useful to France and the United States, should you deem it proper to appoint some person to treat with me on this subject. But, in the meantime, as the moments are precious, and the United States will suffer extremely in their commerce, if the officers of France, who are directed to take possession, should not be explicitly instructed to respect the right of navigation and depot claimed by the United States, I must earnestly solicit some treaty; explanatory of the terms on which France has received the cession of Louisiana from Spain, and recognizing the rights of the United States. Should you, citizen First Consul, voluntarily add, as an expression of your good will, provisionally, in case the cession of the Floridas should be completed, a grant to the United States of the free passage through the rivers Mobile and Pensacola, together with a right of depot at their mouths, you would, while you were serving the commerce of France, confer an obligation on the United States that would greatly tend to strengthen the bands of friendship between the allied nations. For though the commerce of these rivers is, at present, very insignificant, yet, at some future period, when the country settles, it may become more important; and, in the meantime, the cession would derive considerable value from the evidence it would afford to the United States of your friendly disposition.

That France will never derive any advantage from the colonization of New Orleans and the Floridas, is fairly to be presumed, from their having been possessed, for more than a century past, by three different nations. While the other colonies of these nations were increasing rapidly, these have always remained weak and languid and an expensive burden to the possessor. Even at this moment, with all the advantages that New Orleans has derived from foreign capital, and an accession of inhabitants from the United States, which has brought its free population to about 7,000 souls, the whole of the inhabitants east of the Mississippi does not more than double that number; and those, too, are, for the most part, poor and miserable; and there are physical reasons that must forever render them inadequate to their own support, in the hands of any European nation. They are, however, important to the United States, because they contain the mouths of some of their rivers, which must make them the source of continual disputes. The interest that the

United States attach, citizen First Consul, to your friendship, and the alliance of France, is the principal cause of their anxiety to procure your consent to their accession of that country, and of the sacrifices that they are willing to make to attain it. They consider it as the only possible ground of collision between nations whom so many other interests unite. I can not, then, citizen First Consul, but express my doubt of any advantage to be derived to France from the retaining of that country in its whole extent; and I think I could show that her true interest would lead her to make such cessions out of them to the United States as would at once afford supplies to her islands, without draining the money of France, and rivet the friendship of the United States, by removing all ground of jealousy relative to a country of little value in itself, and which will be perpetually exposed to the attacks of her natural enemy, as well from Canada as by sea.

Should this idea not be so fortunate as to meet your approbation, there are still a variety of views in which, by a partial cession, permanent commercial advantages may be acquired; but it would be to intrude too much upon your time to detail them here, deeming them more proper subjects for discussion, if you should think it proper to render them the objects of a treaty.

Permit me, citizen First Consul, before I conclude, to mention a circumstance which embraces the interest both of France and the United States, and of humanity. The savages on the east side of the Mississippi are numerous and brave; considerable sums of money are annually expended by Spain in purchasing their friendship. Should these supplies be withheld, through neglect or misapplication, a universal massacre of the planters will ensue. Their detached situation renders it impossible to protect them. I am the more emboldened in making this observation, from the interest the United States have in turning your attention to this object, since, should this melancholy event take place, malignity, or those whose negligence or infidelity may have occasioned it, will not fail to impute it to the intrigues of the United States.

I pray you, citizen First Consul, to pardon the length of this letter, which you will have the goodness to attribute to my extreme anxiety to remove all causes of dispute between France and the country I represent, and to my conviction that some early and effectual arrangements are necessary to prevent those that already exist from growing to an alarming height. No evil can possibly arise from empowering the Minister, or such other person as you shall please, to treat with me on the subject of New Orleans; since even the appointment itself will have a conciliatory appearance, and you, citizen First Consul, will govern the negotiation, in which, I trust, nothing will be proposed on my part, that will not be equally beneficial to both France and the United States.

I have the honor, citizen First Consul, to remain, with the most profound respect and the highest consideration, your most obedient, humble servant,

Robert R. Livingston

# Section Four

# Napoleon Decides to Sell

*Commentary*

Meanwhile in Paris, Livingston, who resented Monroe's mission, accelerated his energetic but largely fruitless diplomatic efforts in the hope that negotiations might begin before Monroe arrived (Doc. 51). His dispatches, while occasionally brightened by hints of French concessions and good will, nevertheless indicated little progress on the question of a purchase or on any other matter of substance (Docs. 52, 53, 54, 55). Outwardly, the French appeared fully intent upon pursuing their plans for an empire in the Western Hemisphere. But Napoleon's expectation of a decisive victory in Santo Domingo had not materialized and Leclerc's death rendered the situation even more unpromising. In addition, the Spanish continued to resist the efforts of the French to obtain the Floridas as well as Louisiana, the former area being one the French deemed vital for the creation of a viable Louisiana. In response to American pressure, Spain also restored the right of deposit at New Orleans (Doc. 56), a move the French saw as distinctly inimical to their hopes of revoking American privileges in the area. Although French plans were in disarray, there was no visible weakening in the French bargaining position. As late as March 12, 1803, Livingston wrote "with respect to a negotiation for Louisiana I think nothing will be effected here." But curiously enough, Livingston recounted in the same letter the climactic confrontation between Napoleon and the British Ambassador, Lord Whitworth, a vivid incident that suggested that the resumption of European hostilities, an event Jefferson had long counted upon, would soon be forthcoming (Doc. 57). Subsequent British proposals, however, made it clear that though a general European war would aid America's efforts, England also had designs on Louisiana (Doc. 58). The administration, whose plans included the possibility of an alliance with Great Britain was fully alert to this matter (Doc. 59).

Livingston redoubled his efforts, apparently sensing that the fluid situation might favor the United States; he also hoped to obtain concessions before the arrival of Monroe. Disregarding diplomatic formalities, he pleaded with Talleyrand to "answer my last note with something positive." This message had requested that General Bernadotte, who was expected to leave for Washington, be given a note informing Jefferson that Livingston had begun fruitful discussions. Livingston wisely sent Talleyrand a copy of the militant Ross resolutions debated by Congress, resolutions which called for an immediate mobilization of troops.

Suddenly the impasse was broken. On April 11, 1803, Livingston reported to Madison that Talleyrand had casually inquired whether the United States would purchase all of Louisiana (Doc. 60). Shortly thereafter Napoleon directed his Finance Minister Barbé-Marbois to begin formal negotiations. The participation of Marbois, a close friend of Livingston, would surely indicate to the Americans that the French were earnest. At midnight on April 13, Livingston hurriedly wrote to Madison about matters which had transpired between Marbois and himself (Doc. 61). In a dramatic meeting beginning at 11 p.m., Marbois had announced that France would sell all of Louisiana to the United States if satisfactory terms could be obtained.

The next two weeks were anticlimactic. Monroe arrived and joined Livingston—neither welcomed the presence of the other at the negotiations—and they agreed despite instructions (Doc. 62) to bargain for the entire territory; both men soon realized that Napoleon would have it no other way (Doc. 63). The final agreement was signed on May 2, 1803. At the signing, Marbois, struck by the momentous nature of the event, assured the Americans that the treaty was "the noblest work of your lives." Livingston and Monroe were more restrained, no doubt uncertain of Jefferson's reaction when he learned that the two representatives had exceeded their instructions by purchasing not only New Orleans but the entire Louisiana territory. Some immediate comfort was derived, however, from the favorable manner in which England received news of the purchase (Doc. 64).

## 51

### *James Monroe to James Madison*
### *April 15, 1803*

[Extract]

[*State Papers, Correspondence Bearing upon the Purchase of the Territory of Louisiana* (Washington, D.C.: Government Printing Office, 1903), pp. 164–65.]

*Paris*

Dear Sir,

It is proper for me to mention to you in confidence some circumstances which I wish not to include in an official letter. I was informed on my arrival here by Mr. Skipwith that Mr. Livingston mortified at my appointment had done everything in his power to turn the occurrences in America, and even my mission to his account, by pressing the Government on every point with a view to show that he had accomplished what was wished without my aid: and perhaps also that my mission had put in hazard what might otherwise have been easily obtained. His official correspondence will show what occurred prior to my arrival & sufficiently proves that he did not abstain even on hearing that I was on my way, from the topics intrusted to us jointly.

* * *

## 52

*Charles Talleyrand to
Robert R. Livingston
February 19, 1803*

[Extract]

[*House Document 431*, 57th Cong., 2nd sess., pp. 142–43.]

*Paris*, Ventose, an 11

Sir:

The First Consul, in placing in my hands the memoir which you have presented to him, has ordered me to assure you that he has taken into serious consideration the objects you have had in view, and the various demands which you have presented.

## Napoleon Decides to Sell 115

He has, at the same time, caused a report to be made on all the subjects which may arise in consequence of these demands, and on the clauses of the convention between France and the United States, to which you refer. It is the intention of the First Consul (and he has charged me to make it known to you) that this convention shall be executed, in every particular, with scrupulous exactness.

The reflections contained in your memoir, in relation to the difficulties which, on the part of France, may attend its execution, do not apply, with the least foundation, either to the dispositions of the Government of the French Republic, or to the state of her finances. The First Consul is persuaded that the impressions by which you have on this point been misled, have been occasioned by your friendly solicitude; but these impressions are not supported by facts. No embarrassment exists in the finances of France. The French Government has the means, as well as the inclination, to be just; and if it should be placed in a position in which the discharge of its obligations would be attended with difficulties, it will know how to surmount those obstacles, and satisfy every claim that can be justly demanded.

* * *

As to the second question in your memoire, which relates to Louisiana, the First Consul would have preferred its having been the subject of a separate note. Affairs so different in their nature ought to be kept as much as possible apart, and should certainly not be united. It is entirely opposed to the maxims of Government, adopted by the Republic, to mingle important and delicate political relations with calculations of account and mere pecuniary interests.

The First Consul, always appreciating the motives which have induced you to insist on an explanation of the new relations which ought to exist between the two Republics, has charged me to inform you, that, aware of the solicitude, perhaps premature, but, in reality, natural and plausible, which the United States have manifested in this discussion, has come to the determination to send immediately to the United States a Minister Plenipotentiary, who will communicate on every point the information necessary to a final decision.

Under these circumstances, as well as in all others presenting topics for discussion between the two Governments, the First Consul desires that you shall give, on the subject of his dispositions towards the United States, the most positive and formal assurances, that attachment for your Republic, and esteem and personal consideration for its present Chief Magistrate, are national sentiments which, as a Frenchman, and as the chief of a people, the ancient and uniform friend of the American nation, he loves to profess, and of which he will always be under the pleasing obligation to furnish unequivocal proofs.

While I felicitate myself upon being, at this time, the medium by which these sentiments of the First Consul are expressed, allow me, sir, to renew the assurance of my high consideration.

CH. MAU. TALLEYRAND

## 53

*Charles Talleyrand to
Robert R. Livingston, March 21, 1803*

[Extract]

[*House Document 431*, 57th Cong., 2nd sess., pp. 153–63.]

*Paris*

Sir:

I see with pleasure, by the last letters from the French legation in the United States, that the excitement which had been raised on the subject of Louisiana has been allayed by the wisdom of your Government, and the just confidence which it inspires, to that state of tranquillity which is alone proper for discussion, and which, in the existing relations between the two nations, can not fail to lead to suitable explanations on difficulties arising from contingent circumstances, and draw still closer the bands by which they are mutually united. I ought to acknowledge, sir, that, in the publicity recently given to the proceedings respecting Louisiana, it is difficult to recognize the ancient sentiments of attachment and confidence with which France has always been desirous to inspire the people of the United States, and by which, from the first moment of their existence as an independent and sovereign nation, she has been induced to consider her relations with the United States as among the most important of her political relations.

On what account, then, either political or commercial, can the American nation view the proximity of France with so unfriendly an eye? Has the French Republic ever evinced a desire to arrest the prosperity of the United States, assume an influence to which she had no right, weaken her means of safety or annoyance, or place an obstacle in the way of their expanding commerce? Your Government, sir, ought to be persuaded that the First Consul entertains for the American nation the same affection with which France has been at all times animated; and that, among the advantages which he expects to derive from the possession of Louisiana, he estimates the additional means which will be at his command, to convince the Government and people of the United States of his uniformly liberal and friendly sentiments. . . .

## 54

### *Robert R. Livingston to James Madison March 3, 1803*

[Extract]

[*House Document* 431, 57th Cong., 2nd sess., pp. 114–15.]

*Paris*

Dear Sir:

This is merely to inform you that I have received your letter of the 18th of January, in which you notify me of Mr. Monroe's appointment. I shall do everything in my power to pave the way for him; and sincerely wish his mission may be attended with the desired effect. It will, however, cut off one resource on which I greatly relied; because I had established a confidence which it will take Mr. Monroe some time to inspire. Enclosed is a letter addressed to the First Consul himself, and sent him before I heard of Mr. Monroe's appointment. The Minister told me yesterday that I should have an answer to it in a few days. What that answer will be I know not: but

I have been indefatigable in my applications to everybody who will probably be consulted on this subject. When I arrived here I found Louisiana a very favorite object. Some books were published representing it as a paradise. I think I have greatly aided in dispelling this mania; and, had the Floridas been granted, and the necessary powers given me, I believe that something might have been effected; because at this moment there is not a man about the Court but inclines to our ideas upon the subject. The Floridas are still in the hands of Spain. I have explained the cause in my last: and not knowing how far we might succeed in our negotiations, or what sacrifices you would make, I have thought it best to use every exertion with the Spanish Ambassador and the British Minister to obstruct that negotiation.

## 55

### Robert R. Livingston to James Madison March 11, 1803

[Extract]

[*State Papers, Correspondence Bearing upon the Purchase of the Territory of Louisiana* (Washington, D.C.: Government Printing Office, 1903), pp. 140–41.]

*Paris*

I told you that M. Talleyrand had assured me that no sale would be heard of. You will find a passage in the note which was doubtless intended to convey that idea in very strong terms. As I know it to be the fixed determination of this Government to treat only in America, I have nothing more to do on this subject than to endeavor to get the right of depot left upon the footing it was till your negotiations are concluded. This I shall endeavor to effect. If, upon the arrival of Mr. Monroe, he can suggest anything better, I shall heartily concur with him. In treating with General Bernadotte, you will have every possible advantage. The nearer he views the object, the less he will value it. His dispositions are as friendly as possible to our Government and country; and his ideas relative to our connexion, and the little importance of Louisiana, exactly such as I would wish. My conversations with him on that subject were frequent and interesting; as well with Mr. Adet, who is much in his confidence, and who thinks exactly as I do. The great object that he will be instructed to keep in view will be, I think, from what I learn here, to keep the British out of the river, and to secure as much as possible of the carrying trade to France. Dupont de Nemours has shown me a plan that he gave to Consul Le Brun, of which I send you a copy. I have endeavored to convince those who may be consulted of its impracticability. The reasons are too obvious to make it necessary for me to state them to you. I have hinted at making the island of New Orleans an independent State, under the Government of Spain, France, and the United States, with a right of depot to each, subject to a duty on imports of one and a half per cent. in lieu of storage, wharfage, &c., suggesting the advantage that France would derive from being the only manufacturing nation of the three. The advantages of this to our carrying trade (while it left our revenue untouched) are obvious. And in such a treaty, arrangements might be made extremely advantageous to the Western people. The new nation must always feel its dependence upon us, and, of course, respect our rights. I should not have thought it worth while to mention this, had it not been that I gave an unsigned and informal sketch of it to Joseph Bonaparte: it may possibly be given to General Bernadotte. If, as I begin to believe, they do not get the Floridas, they will put the less value on New Orleans.

Things every day look more towards a rupture between this country and Britain; and though the politicians think otherwise, I believe a war not very distant.

# 56

## *James Madison to James Monroe*
## *April 20, 1803*

[Extract]

[*State Papers, Correspondence Bearing upon the Purchase of the Territory of Louisiana* (Washington, D.C.: Government Printing Office, 1903), p. 181.]

*Washington*

Dear Sir,

You will receive with this all the communications claimed by the actual and eventual posture of our affairs in the hands of yourself and Mr. Livingston. You will find, also, that the Spanish Government has pretty promptly corrected the wrong done by its officer at New Orleans. This event will be a heavy blow to the clamorous for war, and will be very soothing to those immediately interested in the trade of the Mississippi. The temper manifested by our Western Citizens has been throughout the best that can be conceived. The real injury from the suspension of the deposit was, however, much lessened by the previous destruction of the entire crop of wheat in Kentucky, by the number of sea vessels built on the Ohio, and by throngs of vessels from Atlantic ports to the Mississippi, some of which ascended to the Natchez. The permission, also, to supply the market at New Orleans, and to ship the surplus as Spanish property to Spanish ports, was turned to good account. The trial, therefore, has been much alleviated. Certain it is that the hearts and hopes of the Western people are strongly fixed on the Mississippi for the future boundary. Should no improvement of existing rights be gained, the disappointment will be great. Still, respect for principle and character, aversion to poor rates and taxes, the hope of a speedy conjuncture more favorable, and attachment to the present order of things, will be persuasive exhortations to patience.

## 57

### Robert R. Livingston to President Thomas Jefferson, March 12, 1803

[Extract]

[*House Document*, 431, 57th Cong., 2nd sess., pp. 144–46.]

*Paris*

With respect to a negotiation for Louisiana, I think nothing will be effected here. I have done everything I can, through the Spanish Ambassador, to obstruct the bargain for the Floridas, and I have great hope that it will not be soon concluded. The Ambassador tells me that the Consul often complains to him of the delay that business meets with: and, while Spain keeps the Floridas, Louisiana will be considered here as an object of little moment, as they are absolutely without ports in the Gulf, and so far facilitate your negotiations with General Bernadotte. I have had many interesting conversations with him, and have nothing to complain of. Remember, however, neither to wound his pride nor that of his nation; both being extremely irritable.

* * *

I broke off this part of my letter to attend Madame Bonaparte's drawing-room, where a circumstance happened of sufficient importance to merit your attention. After the First Consul had gone the circuit of one room, he turned to me, and made some of the common inquiries usual on those occasions. He afterwards returned, and entered into a further conversation. When he quitted me, he passed most of the other Ministers merely with a bow, went up to Lord Whitworth, and, after the first civilities, said: "I find, my Lord, your nation wants war again." L. W. "No, sir, we are very desirous of peace." First Consul. "You have just finished a war of fifteen years." L. W. "It is true, sir, and that was fifteen years too long." Consul. "But you want another war of fifteen years." L. W. "Pardon me, sir, we are very desirous of peace." Consul. "I must either have Malta or war." L. W. "I am not prepared, sir, to speak on that subject; and I can only assure you, citizen First Consul, that we wish for peace."

The prefect of the palace, at this time, came up to the Consul, and informed him that there were ladies in the next room, and asked him to go in. He made no reply, but, bowing hastily to the company, retired immediately to his cabinet, without entering the other room. . . . It is, then, highly probable that a new rupture will take place.

## 58

## *Rufus King to James Madison*
*April 2, 1803*

[*State Papers, Correspondence Bearing upon the Purchase of the Territory of Louisiana* (Washington, D.C.: Government Printing Office, 1903), pp. 156–57.]

*London*

In a late conversation with Mr. Addington, he observed to me, if the war happen, it would, perhaps, be one of the first steps to occupy New Orleans. I interrupted him by saying, I hoped the measure would be well weighed before it should be attempted; that, true it was, we could not see with indifference that country in the hands of France; but it was equally true, that it would be contrary to our views, and with much concern, that we should see it in the possession of England; we had no objection to Spain continuing to possess it; they were quiet neighbors, and we looked forward without impatience to events which, in the ordinary course of things, must, at no distant day, annex this country to the United States. Mr. Addington desired me to be assured that England would not accept the country, were all agreed to give it to her; that, were she to occupy it, it would not be to keep it, but to prevent another Power from obtaining it; and, in his opinion, this end would be best effected by its belonging to the United States. I expressed my acquiescence in the last part of his remark, but observed, that, if the country should be occupied by England it would be suspected to be in concert with the United States, and might involve us in misunderstandings with another Power, with which we desired to live in peace. He said, if you can obtain it, well, but if not, we ought to prevent its going into the hands of

France; though, you may rest assured, continued Mr. Addington, that nothing shall be done injurious to the interests of the United States. Here the conversation ended.

I have lately received your letter of January 29; and as soon as Lord Hawkesbury shall have named a time to receive me, which I have requested him to do, I will explain to him, in conversation, the President's views relative to the Mississippi.

## 59

## *James Madison to Robert R. Livingston and James Monroe, April 18, 1803*

[*State Papers, Correspondence Bearing upon the Purchase of the Territory of Louisiana* (Washington, D.C.: Government Printing Office, 1903), pp. 175–78.]

*Washington, Department of State*

Gentlemen:

A month having elapsed since the departure of Mr. Monroe, it may be presumed that, by the time this reaches you, communications will have passed with the French Government, sufficiently explaining its views towards the United States, and preparing the way for the ulterior instructions which the President thinks proper should now be given.

In case a convention and arrangement with France should have resulted from the negotiations with which you are charged; or, in case such should not have been the result—but no doubt should be left that the French Government means to respect duly our rights, and to cultivate sincerely peace and friendship with the United States—it will be expedient for you to make such communications to the British Government, as will assure it that nothing has been done inconsistent with our good faith, and as will prevent a diminution of the good understanding which subsists between the two countries.

If the French Government, instead of friendly arrangements or views, should be found to meditate hostilities, or to have formed projects which will constrain the United States to resort to hostilities, such communications are then to be held with the British Government, as will sound its dispositions, and invite its concurrence in the war. Your own prudence will suggest that the communications be so made as, on the one hand, not to precipitate France into hostile operations; and, on the other, not to lead Great Britain from the supposition that war depends on the choice of the United States, and that their choice of war will depend on her participation in it. If war is to be the result, it is manifestly desirable that it be delayed until the certainty of this result can be known, and the legislative and other provisions can be made here; and also of great importance, that the certainty should not be known to Great Britain, who might take advantage of the posture of things to press on the United States disagreeable conditions of her entering into the war.

It will probably be most convenient, in exchanging ideas with the British Government, to make use of its public Minister at Paris, as less likely to alarm and stimulate the French Government, and to raise the pretensions of the British Government, than the repairing of either of you to London, which might be viewed by both as a signal of rupture. The latter course, however, may possibly be rendered most eligible by the pressure of the crisis.

Notwithstanding the just repugnance of this country to a coalition of any sort with the belligerent politics of Europe, the advantages to be derived from the cooperation of Great Britain in a war of the United States, at this period, against France and her allies, are too obvious and too important to be renounced. And notwithstanding the apparent disinclination of the British councils to a renewal of hostilities with France, it will probably yield to the various motives which will be felt to have the United States in the scale of Britain against France, and particularly for the immediate purpose of defeating a project of the latter, which has evidently created much solicitude in the British Government.

The price which she may attach to her co-operation can not be foreseen, and, therefore, can not be the subject of full and precise instructions. It may be expected that she will insist at least on a stipulation that neither of the parties shall make peace or truce without the consent of the other; and as such an article can not be deemed unreasonable, and will secure us against the possibility of her being detached, in the course of the war, by seducing overtures from France, it will not be proper to raise difficulties on that account. It may be useful, however, to draw from her a definition, as far as the case will admit, of the objects contemplated by her, that whenever, with ours, they may be attainable by peace, she may be duly pressed to listen to it. Such an explanation will be the more reasonable, as the objects of the United States will be so fair and so well known.

It is equally probable, that a stipulation of commercial advantages in the Mississippi, beyond those secured by existing treaties, will be required. On this point, it may be answered at once, that Great Britain shall enjoy a free trade with all the ports to be acquired by the United States, on the terms allowed to the most favored nations in the ports, generally, of the United States. If made an essential condition, you may admit, that in the ports to be acquired within the Mississippi, the trade of her subjects shall be on the same footing for a term of about ten years with that of our own citizens. But the United States are not to be bound to the exclusion of the trade of any particular nation or nations.

Should a mutual guaranty of the existing possessions, or of the conquests to be made by the parties, be proposed, it must be explicitly rejected, as of no value to the United States, and as entangling them in the frequent wars of that nation with other Powers, and very possibly in disputes with that nation itself.

The anxiety which Great Britain has shown to extend her domain to the Mississippi, the uncertain extent of her claims from North to the South, beyond the Western limits of the United States, and the attention she has paid to the Northwest coast of America, make it probable that she will connect with a war on this occasion, a pretension to the acquisition of the country on the west side of the Mississippi, understood to be ceded by Spain to France, or at least of that portion of it lying between that river and the Missouri. The evils involved in such an extension of her possessions in our neighborhood, and in such a hold on the Mississippi, are obvious. The acquisition is the more objectionable, as it would be extremely displeasing to our Western citizens, and as its evident bearing on South America, might be expected to arouse all the jealousies of France and Spain, and to prolong the war, on which the event would depend. Should this pretension, therefore, be pressed, it must be resisted as altogether repugnant to the sentiments and to the sound policy of the United States. But it may be agreed, in alleviation of any disappointment of Great Britain, that France shall not be allowed to retain or acquire any part of the territory, from which she herself would be precluded.

The moment the prospect of war shall require the precaution, you will not omit to give confidential notice to our public Ministers and Consuls, and to our naval commanders in the Mediterranean, that our commerce and public ships may be as little exposed to danger as possible. It may, under certain circumstances, be proper to notify the danger immediately to the collectors in the principal ports of the United States.

## Napoleon Decides to Sell 129

A separate letter to you is enclosed, authorizing you to enter into such communications and conferences with British Ministers as may possibly be required by the conduct of France. The letter is made a separate one, that it may be used with effect, but without the formality, of a commission. It is hoped that sound calculations of interest, as well as a sense of right, in the French Government, will prevent the necessity of using the authority expressed in this letter. In a contrary state of things, the President relies on your own information, to be gained on the spot, and on your best discretion, to open with advantage the communications with the British Government, and to proportion the degree of an understanding with it to the indications of an approaching war with France. Of these indications, also, you will be best able to judge. It will only be observed to you that, if France should avow or evince a determination to deny to the United States the free navigation of the Mississippi, your consultations with Great Britain may be held on the ground that war is inevitable. Should the navigation not be disputed, and the deposit alone be denied, it will be prudent to adapt your consultations to the possibility that Congress may distinguish between the two cases, and make a question how far the latter right may call for an instant resort to arms, or how far a procrastination of that remedy may be suggested and justified by the prospect of a more favorable conjuncture.

These instructions have thus far supposed that Great Britain and France are at peace; and that neither of them intend at present to interrupt it. Should war have actually commenced, or its approach be certain, France will, no doubt, be the more apt to concur in friendly accommodations with us, and Great Britain the more desirous of engaging us on her side. You will, of course, avail yourselves of this posture of things, for avoiding the necessity of recurring to Great Britain, or, if the necessity can not be avoided, for fashioning her disposition to arrangements formed with Great Britain in reference to war, the policy of the United States requires that it be as little entangling as the case will permit.

# 60

## Robert R. Livingston to James Madison
## April 11, 1803

[Extract]

[*House Document 431*, 57th Cong., 2nd sess., pp. 157–58.]

*Paris*

These reasons, with the probability of war, have had, I trust, the desired effect. M. Talleyrand asked me this day, when pressing the subject, whether we wished to have the whole of Louisiana. I told him no; that our wishes extended only to New Orleans and the Floridas; that the policy of France should dictate (as I had shown in an official note) to give us the country above the river Arkansas, in order to place a barrier between them and Canada. He said, that if they gave New Orleans the rest would be of little value; and that he would wish to know "what we would give for the whole." I told him it was a subject I had not thought of; but that I supposed we should not object to twenty millions, provided our citizens were paid. He told me that this was too low an offer; and that he would be glad if I would reflect upon it, and tell him to-morrow. I told him that, as Mr. Monroe would be in town in two days, I would delay my further offer until I had the pleasure of introducing him. He added, that he did not speak from authority, but that the idea had struck him. I have reason, however, to think that this resolution was taken in Council on Saturday. On Friday, I received Mr. Ross's motion: I immediately sent it to M. Talleyrand, with an informal note expressive of my fears that it would be carried into effect; and requesting that General Bernadotte might not go till something effectual was done. I also translated it, and gave it to General Bernadotte, and pressed upon him the necessity of asking express instructions, in case he should find the island in possession of the Americans. He went immediately to Joseph Bonaparte. These, I believe, were exciting causes to the train we are now in, and which I flatter myself we shall be able, on the arrival of Mr. Monroe, to pursue to effect. I think, from every appearance, that war is very near at hand; and, under these circumstances, I have endeavored to impress the Government that not a moment should be lost, lest Britain should anticipate us.

* * *

P. S., 12th.—Orders are gone this day to stop the sailing of vessels from the French ports; war is inevitable; my conjecture as to their determination to sell is well founded; Mr. Monroe is just arrived here.

## 61

*Robert R. Livingston to James Madison*
*April 13, 1803*

[*House Document 431*, 57th Cong., 2nd sess., pp. 159–63.]

*Paris,* midnight

By my letter of yesterday, you learned that the Minister had asked me whether I would agree to purchase

Louisiana, &c. On the 12th, I called upon him to press this matter further. He then thought proper to declare that his proposition was only personal, but still requested me to make an offer; and, upon declining to do so, as I expected Mr. Monroe the next day, he shrugged up his shoulders, and changed the conversation. Not willing, however, to lose sight of it, I told him I had been long endeavoring to bring him to some point; but, unfortunately, without effect: that I wished merely to have the negotiation opened by any proposition on his part; and, with that view, had written him a note which contained that request, grounded upon my apprehension of the consequence of sending General Bernadotte without enabling him to say a treaty was begun. He told me he would answer my note, but that he must do it evasively, because Louisiana was not theirs. I smiled at this assertion, and told him I had seen the treaty recognizing it; that I knew the Consul had appointed officers to govern the country, and that he had himself told me that General Victor was to take possession; that, in a note written by the express order of the First Consul, he had told me that General Bernadotte was to treat relative to it in the United States, &c. He still persisted that they had it in contemplation to obtain it, but had it not. I told him that I was very well pleased to understand this from him, because, if so, we should not commit ourselves with them in taking it from Spain, to whom, by his account, it still belonged; and that, as we had just cause of complaint against her, if Mr. Monroe concurred in opinion with me, we should negotiate no further on the subject, but advise our Government to take possession. He seemed alarmed at the boldness of the measure, and told me he would answer my note, but that it would be evasively. I told him I should receive with pleasure any communication from him, but that we were not disposed to trifle; that the times were critical, and though I did not know what instructions Mr. Monroe might bring, I was perfectly satisfied that they would require a precise and prompt notice; that I was very fearful, from the little progress I had made, that my Government would consider me as a very indolent negotiator. He laughed, and told me that he would give me a certificate that I was the most importunate he had met with.

There was something so extraordinary in all this, that I did not detail it to you till I found some clue to the labyrinth, which I have done, as you will find before I finish this letter; and the rather, as I was almost certain that I could rely upon the intelligence I had received of the resolution to dispose of this country.

This day Mr. Monroe passed with me in examining my papers; and while he and several other gentlemen were at dinner with me, I observed the Minister of the Treasury walking in my garden. I sent out Colonel Livingston to him; he told him he would return when we had dined. While we were taking coffee he came in; and, after being some time in the room, we strolled into the next room, when he told me he heard I had been at his house two days before, when he was at St. Cloud; that he thought I might have something particular to say to him, and had taken the first opportunity to call on me. I saw that this was meant as an opening to one of those free conversations which I had frequently had with him. I accordingly began on the subject of the debt, and related to him the extraordinary conduct of the Minister, &c. He told me that this led to something important, that had been cursorily mentioned to him at St. Cloud; but as my house was full of company, he thought I had better call on him any time before 11 that night. He went away, and, a little after, when Mr. Monroe took leave, I followed him. He told me that he wished me to repeat what I had said relative to M. Talleyrand's requesting a proposition from me as to the purchase of Louisiana. I did so; and concluded with the extreme absurdity of his evasions of that day, and stated the consequence of any delay on this subject, as it would enable Britain to take possession, who would readily relinquish it to us. He said that this proceeded upon a supposition of her making so successful a war as to be enabled to retain her conquests. I told him that it was probable that the same idea might suggest itself to the United States; in which case, it would be their interest to contribute to render her successful, and I asked whether it was prudent to throw us into her scale? This led to long discussions of no moment to repeat. We returned to the point: he said, that what I had told him led him to think that what the Consul had said to him on Sunday, at St. Cloud, (the day on which, as I told you, the determination had been taken to sell,) had more of earnest than he thought at the time; that the Consul had asked him what news from England? As he knew he read the papers attentively, he told him that he had seen in the London papers the proposition for raising fifty thousand men to take New Orleans. The Consul said he had seen it too, and had also seen that something was said about two millions of dollars being disposed among the people about him, to bribe them, &c.; and then left him. That afterwards, when walking in the garden, the Consul came again to him, and spoke to him about the troubles that were excited in America, and inquired how far I was satisfied with his last note.

Here some civil things were introduced, for which I presume I am more indebted to the Minister's politeness than to his veracity; so let them sleep. He (Marbois) then took occasion to mention his sorrow that any cause of difference should exist between our countries. The Consul told him, in reply, "Well, you have the charge of the treasury; let them give you one hundred millions of francs, and pay their own claims, and take the whole country." Seeing, by my looks, that I was surprised at so extravagant a demand, he added that he considered the demand as exorbitant, and had told the First Consul that the thing was impossible; that we had not the means of raising that.

The Consul told him we might borrow it. I now plainly saw the whole business: first, the Consul was disposed to sell; next, he distrusted Talleyrand, on account of the business of the supposed intention to bribe, and meant to put the negotiation into the hands of Marbois, whose character for integrity is established. I told him that the United States were anxious to preserve peace with France; that, for that reason, they wished to remove them to the west side of the Mississippi; that we would be perfectly satisfied with New Orleans and the Floridas, and had no disposition to extend across the river; that, of course, we would not give any great sum for the purchase; that he was right in his idea of the extreme exorbitancy of the demand, which would not fall short of one hundred and twenty-five millions; that, however, we would be ready to purchase, provided the sum was reduced to reasonable limits. He then pressed me to name the sum. I told him that this was not worth while, because, as he only treated the inquiry as a matter of curiosity, any declaration of mine would have no effect. If a negotiation was to be opened, we should (Mr. Monroe and myself) make the offer after mature reflection. This compelled him to declare, that, though he was not authorized expressly to make the inquiry from me, yet, that, if I could mention any sum that came near the mark, that could be accepted, he would communicate it to the First Consul. I told him that we had no sort of authority to go to a sum that bore any proportion to what he mentioned; but that, as he himself considered the demand as too high, he would oblige me by telling me what he thought would be reasonable. He replied that, if we would name sixty millions, and take upon us the American claims, to the amount of twenty more, he would try how far this would be accepted. I told him that it was vain to ask anything that was so greatly beyond our means; that true policy would dictate to the First Consul not to press such a demand; that he must know that it would render the present Government unpopular, and have a tendency, at the next election, to throw the power into the hands of men who were most hostile to a connection with France; and that this would probably happen in the midst of a war. I asked him whether the few millions acquired at this expense would not be too dearly bought?

He frankly confessed that he was of my sentiments; but that he feared the Consul would not relax. I asked him to press this argument upon him, together with the danger of seeing the country pass into the hands of Britain. I told him that he had seen the ardor of the Americans to take it by force, and the difficulty with which they were restrained by the prudence of the President; that he must easily see how much the hands of the war party would be strengthened, when they learned that France was upon the eve of a rupture with England. He admitted the weight of all this: "But," says he, "you know the temper of a youthful conqueror; everything he does is rapid as lightning; we have only to speak to him as an opportunity presents itself, perhaps in a crowd, when he bears no contradiction. When I am alone with him, I can speak more freely, and he attends; but this opportunity seldom happens, and is always accidental. Try, then, if you can not come up to my mark. Consider the extent of the country, the exclusive navigation of the river, and the importance of having no neighbors to dispute you, no war to dread." I told him that I considered all these as important considerations, but there was a point beyond which we could not go, and that fell far short of the sum he mentioned.

I asked him, in case of a purchase, whether they would stipulate that France would never possess the Floridas, and that she would aid us to procure them, and relinquish all right that she might have to them. He told me that she would go thus far. I added, that I would now say nothing on the subject, but that I would converse with Mr. Monroe; and that I was sure to find him disposed to do everything that was reasonable, or could be expected to remove every cause of difference between the two countries. That, however, if any negotiation should go on, I would wish that the First Consul would depute somebody to treat with us, who had more leisure than the Minister for Foreign Affairs.

I said this to see whether my conjectures relative to him were well founded. He told me that as the First Consul knew our personal friendship, he having several times had occasion to speak of me and my family, and the principles that we held, he believed that there would be no difficulty, when this negotiation was somewhat advanced, to have the management of it put into his hands. He earnestly pressed me to make some proposition that was so near the First Consul's as to admit his mentioning it to him. I told him that I would consult Mr. Monroe, but that neither he nor I could accede to his ideas on the subject. Thus, sir, you see a negotiation is fairly opened, and upon grounds which I confess I prefer to all other commercial privileges; and always to some a simple money transaction is infinitely preferable. As to the quantum, I have yet made up no opinion. The field opened to us is infinitely larger than our instructions contemplated; the revenue increasing, and the land more than adequate to sink the capital, should we even go the sum proposed by Marbois; nay, I persuade myself, that the whole sum may be raised by the sale of the territory west of the Mississippi, with the right of sovereignty, to some Power in Europe, whose vicinity we should not fear. I speak now without reflection, and without having seen Mr. Monroe, as it was midnight when I left the Treasury Office, and is now near 3 o'clock. It is so very important that you should be apprized that a negotiation is actually opened, even before Mr. Monroe has been presented, in order to calm the tumult which the news of war will renew, that I have lost no time in communicating it. We shall do all we can to cheapen the purchase; but my present sentiment is that we shall buy. Mr. Monroe will be presented to the Minister to-morrow, when we shall press for as early an audience as possible from the First Consul. I think it will be necessary to put in some proposition to-morrow: the Consul goes in a few days to Brussels, and every moment is precious.

> I am, dear sir, with the most respectful consideration, your most obedient, humble servant,

ROBERT R. LIVINGSTON

# 62

## *James Madison to Robert R. Livingston and James Monroe, March 2, 1803*

[Extract]

[*State Papers, Correspondence Bearing upon the Purchase of the Territory of Louisiana* (Washington, D.C.: Government Printing Office, 1903), pp. 122-36.]

*Washington, Department of State*

Gentlemen:

You will herewith receive a commission and letters of credence, one of you as Minister Plenipotentiary, the other as Minister Extraordinary and Plenipotentiary, to treat with the Government of the French Republic on the subject of the Mississippi, and the territories eastward thereof, and without the limits of the United States. The object in view is to procure, by just and satisfactory arrangements, a cession to the United States of New Orleans, and of West and East Florida, or as much thereof as the actual proprietor can be prevailed on to part with.

* * *

The time chosen for the experiment is pointed out also by other important considerations. The instability of the peace of Europe, the attitude taken by Great Britain, the languishing state of the French finances, and the absolute necessity of either abandoning the West India islands, or of sending thither large armaments at great expense, all contribute at the present crisis to prepare in the French Government a disposition to listen to an arrangement which will at once dry up one source of foreign controversy, and furnish some aid in struggling with internal embarrassments. It is to be added, that the overtures committed to you coincide in great measure with the ideas of the person through whom the letter of the President of April 30, 1802, was conveyed to Mr. Livingston, and who is presumed to have gained some insight into the present sentiments of the French Cabinet.

* * *

There may be other objects with France in the projected acquisition; but they are probably such as would be either satisfied by a reservation to herself of the country on the right side of the Mississippi, or are of too subordinate a character to prevail against the plan of adjustment we have in view, in case other difficulties in the way of it can be overcome. The principles and outlines of this plan are as follows, viz:

ARTICLE 1. France cedes to the United States forever the territory east of the river Mississippi, comprehending the two Floridas, the island of New Orleans, and the islands lying to the north and east of that channel of the said river, which is commonly called the South

Pass, together with all such other islands as appertain to either West or East Florida; France reserving to herself all her territory on the west side of the Mississippi.

ART. 2. The boundary between the territory ceded and reserved by France, shall be a continuation of that already defined above the thirty-first degree of north latitude, viz: the middle of the channel or bed of the river through the said South Pass to the sea. The navigation of the river Mississippi in its whole breadth from its source to the ocean, and in all its passages to and from the same shall be equally free and common of the United States and of the French Republic.

ART. 3. The vessels and citizens of the French Republic may exercise commerce to and at such places on their respective shores below the said thirty-first degree of north latitude as may be allowed for that use by the parties to their respective citizens and vessels. And it is agreed that no other nation shall be allowed to exercise commerce to or at the same or any other place on either shore, below the said thirty-first degree of latitude. For the term of ten years, to be computed from the exchange of ratifications hereof, the citizens, vessels, and merchandises of the United States, and of France, shall be subject to no other duties on their respective shores, below the said thirty-first degree of latitude, than are imposed on their own citizens, vessels, and merchandises. No duty whatever shall, after the expiration of ten years, be laid on articles the growth or manufacture of the United States, or of the ceded territory, exported through the Mississippi in French vessels; so long as such articles so exported in vessels of the United States shall be exempt from duty: nor shall French vessels exporting such articles ever afterwards be subject to pay a higher duty than vessels of the United States.

ART. 4. The citizens of France may, for the term of ten years, deposit their effects at New Orleans, and at such other places on the ceded shore of the Mississippi, as are allowed for the commerce of the United States, without paying any other duty than a fair price for the hire of stores.

ART. 5. In ports of commerce of West and East Florida, France shall never be on a worse footing than the most favored nation; and for the term of ten years her vessels and merchandise shall be subject therein to no higher duties than are paid by those of the United States. Articles of the growth or manufacture of the United States, and of the ceded territory, exported in French vessels from any port in West or East Florida, shall be exempt from duty as long as vessels of the United States shall enjoy this exemption.

* * *

ART. 7. To incorporate the inhabitants of the hereby ceded territory with the citizens of the United States on an equal footing, being a provision which can not now be made, it is to be expected, from the character and policy of the United States, that such incorporation will take place without unnecessary delay. In the meantime they shall be secure in their persons and property, and in the free enjoyment of their religion.

* * *

The instructions, thus far given, suppose that France may be willing to cede to the United States the whole of the island of New Orleans, and both the Floridas. As she may be inclined to dispose of a part or parts, and of such only, it is proper for you to know that the Floridas, together, are estimated at one-fourth the value of the whole island of New Orleans, and East Florida at one-half that of West Florida. In case of a partial cession, it is expected that the regulations of every other kind, so far as they are onerous to the United States, will be more favorably modified.

Should France refuse to cede the whole of the island, as large a portion as she can be prevailed on to part with may be accepted; should no considerable portion of it be attainable, it will still be of vast importance to get a jurisdiction over space enough for a large commercial town, and its appurtenances, on the back of the river, and as little remote from the mouth of the river as may be. A right to choose the place would be better than a designation of it in the treaty. Should it be impossible to procure a complete jurisdiction over any convenient spot whatever, it will only remain to explain and improve the present right of deposit, by adding thereto the express privilege of holding real estate for commercial purposes, of providing hospitals, of having consuls residing there, and other agents who may be authorized to authenticate and deliver all documents requisite for vessels belonging to, and engaged in, the trade of the United States, to and from the place of deposit. The United States can not remain satisfied, nor the Western people be kept patient, under the restrictions which the existing treaty with Spain authorizes.

Should a cession of the Floridas not be attainable, your attention will also be due to the establishment of suitable deposits at the mouth of the rivers passing from the United States through the Floridas, as well as of the free navigation of those rivers by citizens of the United States. What has been above suggested in relation to the Mississippi, and the deposit on its banks, is applicable to the other rivers; and additional hints relative to them all may be derived from the letter, of which a copy is enclosed, from the Consul at New Orleans.

It has been long manifest that, whilst the injuries to the United States, so frequently occurring from the colonial officers scattered over our hemisphere and in our neighborhood, can only be repaired by a resort to their respective Governments in Europe, it will be impossible to guard against the most serious inconveniences. The late events at New Orleans strongly manifest the necessity of placing a power somewhere nearer to us capable of correcting and controlling the mischievous proceedings of such officers toward our citizens; without which, a few individuals, not always among the wisest or best of men, may at any time threaten the good understanding of the two nations. The distance between the United States and the old continent, and the mortifying delays of explanations and negotiations across the Atlantic on emergencies in our neighborhood, render such a provision indispensable; and it can not be long before all the Governments of Europe, having American Colonies, must see the necessity of making it. This object will likewise claim your special attention.

It only remains to suggest, that, considering the possibility of some intermediate violences between citizens of the United States and the French or Spaniards, in consequence of the interruption of our right of deposit, and the probability that considerable damages will have been occasioned by that measure to citizens of the United States, it will be proper that indemnification in the latter case be provided for, and that in the former it shall not be taken on either sides as a ground or pretext for hostilities.

These instructions, though as full as they could be conveniently made, will necessarily leave much to your discretion. For the proper exercise of it, the President relies on your information, your judgment, and your fidelity to the interests of your country.

JAMES MADISON

## Robert R. Livingston and James Monroe to James Madison, May 13, 1803

[Extract]

[*House Document 431,* 57th Cong., 2nd sess., pp. 191-94.]

*Paris*

Sir:

We have the pleasure to transmit to you by M. Dirieux a treaty which we have concluded with the French Republic for the purchase and cession of Louisiana. The negotiation of this important object was committed, on the part of France, to M. Marbois, Minister of the Treasury, whose conduct therein has already received the sanction of his Government, as appears by the ratification of the First Consul, which we have also the pleasure to forward to you.

An acquisition of so great an extent was, we well know, not contemplated by our appointment; but we are persuaded that the circumstances and considerations which induced us to make it will justify us in the measure to our Government and country.

Before the negotiation commenced we were apprized that the First Consul had decided to offer to the United States, by sale, the whole of Louisiana, and not a part of it. We found, in the outset, that this information was correct, so that we had to decide, as a previous question, whether we would treat for the whole, or jeopardize, if not abandon, the hope of acquiring any part. On that point we did not long hesitate, but proceeded to treat for the whole. We were persuaded that, by so doing, it might be possible, if more desirable, to conclude eventually a treaty for a part, since, being thus possessed of the subject, it might be easy, in discussion, at least, to lead from a view of the whole to that of a part, and with some advantages peculiar to a negotiation on so great a scale. By treating for the whole, whereby we should be enabled to ascertain the idea which was entertained by this Government of its value, we should also be able to form some estimate of that which was affixed to the value of its parts. It was, too, probable that a less sum would be asked for the whole, if sold entire to a single purchaser, a friendly Power, who was able to pay for it, and whom it might be disposed to accommodate at the present juncture, than if it should be sold in parcels either to several Powers or companies of individuals; it was equally so, if this Government should be finally prevailed to sell us a part, that some regard would be paid in the price asked for it to that which was demanded for the whole. Firstly, by treating for the whole, whereby the attention of this Government would be drawn to the United States, as the sole purchasers, we might prevent the interference of other Powers, as also that of individuals, who might prove equally injurious in regard to the price asked for it, whether we acquired the whole or any part of the territory. We found, however, as we advanced in the negotiation, that M. Marbois was absolutely restricted to the disposition of the whole; that he would treat for no less portion, and, of course, that it was useless to urge it. On mature consideration, therefore, we finally concluded a treaty on the best terms we could obtain for the whole.

By this measure, we have sought to carry into effect, to the utmost of our power, the wise and benevolent policy of our Government, on the principles laid down in our instructions. The possession of the left bank of the river, had it been attainable alone, would, it is true, have accomplished much in that respect; but it is equally true that it would have left much still to accomplish. By it our people would have had an outlet to the ocean in which no Power would have a right to disturb them; but while the other bank remained in the possession of a foreign Power, circumstances might occur to make the neighborhood of such Power highly injurious to us in many of our most important concerns. A divided jurisdiction over the river might beget jealousies, discontents, and dissensions, which the wisest policy on our part could not prevent or control. With a train of colonial governments established along the western bank, from the entrance of the river far into the interior, under the command of military men, it would be difficult to preserve that state of things which would be necessary to the peace and tranquillity of our country. A single act of a capricious, unfriendly, or unprincipled subaltern might wound our best interests, violate our most unquestionable rights, and involve us in war. But by this acquisition, which comprises within our limits this great river, and all the streams that enter into it, from their sources to the ocean, the apprehensions of these disasters is banished for ages from the United States. We adjust by it the only remaining known cause of variance with this very powerful nation; we anticipate the discontent of the great rival of France, who would probably have been wounded at any stipulation of a permanent nature which favored the latter, and which it would have been difficult to avoid, had she retained the right bank. We cease to have a motive of urgency, at least, for inclining to one Power, to avert the unjust pressure of another. We separate ourselves in a great measure from the European world and its concerns, especially its wars and intrigues. We make, in fine, a great stride to real and substantial independence, the good effect whereof will, we trust, be felt essentially and extensively in all our foreign and domestic relations. Without exciting the apprehension of any Power, we take a more imposing attitude with respect to all. The bond of our Union will be strengthened, and its movements become more harmonious by the increased parity of interests which it will communicate to the several parts which compose it.

* * *

## Lord Hawkesbury to Rufus King
## May 19, 1803

[*American State Papers*, vol. 2, *Foreign Relations*, Walter Lowrie and Matthew Clarke, eds. (Washington: Gales and Seaton, 1833), p. 560.]

*Downing Street*

Sir:

Having laid before the King your letter of the 15th of this month, in which you inform me that a treaty was signed at Paris on the 30th of last month, by the plenipotentiaries of America and France, by which the complete sovereignty of the town and territory of New Orleans, as well as of all Louisiana, has been acquired by the United States, I have received His Majesty's commands to express to you the pleasure with which His Majesty has received this intelligence, and to add that His Majesty regards the care which has been taken so to frame this treaty as not to infringe any right of Great Britain in the navigation of the Mississippi, as the most satisfactory evidence of a disposition on the part of the Government of the United States, correspondent to that which His Majesty entertains, to promote and improve that harmony and good understanding which so happily subsist between the two countries, and which are so conducive to their mutual benefit. I have it also in command to assure you, sir, that the sentiments which you have expressed in making this communication, are considered by His Majesty's Government as an additional proof of that cordiality and confidence which you have uniformly manifested in the whole course of your public mission, and which have so justly entitled you to the esteem and regard of His Majesty's Government.

# Section Five

# Uncertainty Amidst Triumph

*Commentary*

The spring and summer of 1803 brought splendid news for America. On April 19 Madison received word that the Spanish government had ordered the reopening of New Orleans to Americans and the restoration of the right of deposit. Jefferson, exalted at this triumph, noted that the United States had obtained "by a peaceable appeal to justice in four months, what we should not have obtained under seven years of war and the loss of 100,000 lives." (Doc. 65). In July American newspapers revealed that all of Louisiana was now American territory. The administration received the news warmly (Doc. 66). Jefferson saw the purchase as "replete with blessings to unborn millions of men. . . . The acquisition of New Orleans would of itself have been a great thing," he observed, "but that of Louisiana is inappreciable, because giving us the sole dominion of the Mississippi, it excludes those bickerings with foreign powers . . . and secures to us the course of a peaceable nation." (Doc. 67) Some reservations existed concerning both the provisions of the treaty and the consequences of the purchase. Although

## Uncertainty Amidst Triumph 149

Madison assured both Livingston and Monroe that they were justified in going beyond their instructions and negotiating for all of Louisiana, he was critical of Livingston's conduct (Doc. 68). The financial arrangements of the treaty were the primary source of displeasure. Rufus King and Secretary of the Treasury Albert Gallatin objected to the process whereby American securities issued to the French for payments were then sold by them to British and Dutch banks at a discount (Doc. 69). Arrangements for the repayment of American creditors also came under criticism, causing Jefferson to suggest a suspension of payments until a more suitable division of the funds could be arranged.

As Republicans prepared to celebrate their greatest triumph they were confronted by a grave dilemma. They had come to office firmly committed to the proposition that the acts of the national government were valid only when specifically authorized by the Constitution. They had long protested the Federalists' broad construction of the nation's fundamental law. Yet these same men were in the process of purchasing foreign territory from a foreign nation and ultimately incorporating it into the United States, although the Constitution provided no clear authority for such a procedure. To his credit, Jefferson seemed willing to confront this problem even before negotiations with the French showed any signs of success. In January 1803 Jefferson had asked Attorney General Levi Lincoln for a judgment on the legality of acquiring and incorporating Louisiana into the United States. Jefferson then forwarded Lincoln's opinion to Gallatin, who discovered little merit in the views of the Attorney General (Docs. 70, 71). The constitutional issue did not emerge again until the summer of 1803, when news of the purchase reached the United States. No longer was the question an academic one; a quick decision was necessary because the administration learned that France seemed to be dissatisfied with the treaty and would shortly move to annul it (Doc. 72). According to Livingston, "France is sick of the bargain . . . Spain is much dissatisfied and . . . the slightest pretense will lose you the treaty." Jefferson at this crucial juncture found himself increasingly uncertain as to the propriety of incorporating Louisiana. In fact, as soon as the treaty arrived in Washington, he drew up an amendment to the Constitution to allay his doubts. In later years Jefferson reflected upon this incident and upon his final decision to forego the amendment (Docs. 73, 74, 75, 76). In retrospect he acknowledged that the treaty had been extra-legal but offered the "superior ground" of "self-preservation of saving our society in danger" as constituting the "higher obligation" of his leadership.

Having resolved the constitutional issue, Jefferson faced two other major problems. One concerned the aforementioned rumors of French dissatisfaction with the treaty. In addition, news of the Louisiana Purchase brought angry protests from the Spanish government directed both at Paris and Washington (Docs. 77, 78). Spain declared the transaction illegal in view of France's earlier promise to not alienate Louisiana and to cede to Spain certain territories in Italy. To avert the French threat Jefferson decided upon a special session of Congress in October (Doc. 79) and suggested to Senator John Breckinridge of Kentucky that he prepare in advance the necessary legislation for ratifying the Louisiana treaty. Jefferson also cautioned Republicans to remain silent about the constitutional issue lest it become an excuse for France to retain Louisiana. Finally Jefferson urged that the government securities for payment be printed quickly and that a fast ship stand by to speed them overseas. Congress subsequently met in special session. The Republicans overrode Federalist opposition and passed the appropriate legislation. In short order the United States had met its part of the bargain.

## Uncertainty Amidst Triumph 151

Finally, Spanish notes of protest caused the administration to wonder whether that government would relinquish Louisiana. In the event that it did not, the United States seemed prepared to employ military pressure (Docs. 80, 81). Jefferson hinted that Spain's uncooperative attitude "may bring on acts of force," and his cabinet on October 4 unanimously agreed that, if necessary, force should be used to obtain New Orleans. General James Wilkinson received orders to ready his troops and the Governors of Kentucky and Tennessee were requested to raise volunteers. Indications were, however, that should Americans march on New Orleans they would encounter little resistance (Doc. 82).

The Louisiana affair ended without the flow of blood. As Americans in New Orleans were urging the populace to accept American rule, a rather unimposing force of American soldiers floated down the Mississippi and arrived at that port city. It met with no resistance, and on December 20, 1803, the United States assumed possession of Louisiana. American spokesmen assured the people of New Orleans that the transfer of ownership would result in great blessings and a bountiful future for them (Docs. 83, 84). However sincere, such assurances were not universally appreciated (Doc. 85). Nonetheless the vast expanse of Louisiana became a part of the American Republic (Doc. 86).

## 65

*President Thomas Jefferson to
Dr. Hugh Williamson, April 30, 1803*

[*State Papers, Correspondence Bearing upon the Purchase of the Territory of Louisiana.* (Washington, D.C.: Government Printing Office, 1903), p. 182.]

*Washington*

Dear Sir,

For the present we have a respite on that subject, Spain having without delay restored our infracted right, and assured us it is expressly saved by the instrument of her cession of Louisiana to France. Although I do not count with confidence on obtaining New Orleans from France for money, yet I am confident in the policy of putting off the day of contention for it till we have lessened the embarrassment of debt accumulated instead of being discharged by our predecessors, till we obtain more of that strength which is growing on us so rapidly, and especially till we have planted a population on the Mississippi itself sufficient to do its own work without marching men fifteen hundred miles from the Atlantic shores to perish by fatigue and unfriendly climate. This will soon take place. In the meantime we have obtained by a peaceable appeal to justice, in four months, what we should not have obtained under seven years of war, the loss of one hundred thousand lives, an hundred millions of additional debt, many hundred millions worth of produce and property lost for want of market, or in seeking it, and that demoralization which war superinduces on the human mind. To have seized New Orleans, as our federal maniacs wished, would only have changed the character and extent of the blockade of our western commerce. It would have produced a blockade, by superior naval force, of the navigation of the river as well as of the entrance into New Orleans, instead of a paper blockade from New Orleans alone while the river remained open, and I am persuaded that had not the deposit have been so quickly rendered we should have found soon that it would be better now to ascend the river to Natchez, in order to be clear of the embarrassments, plunderings, and irritations at New Orleans, and to fatten by the benefits of the depot a city and citizens of our own, rather than those of a foreign nation.

## 66

### *James Madison to Robert R. Livingston and James Monroe, July 29, 1803*

[Extract]

[*House Document 431*, 57th Cong., 2nd sess., pp. 222–24.]

*Washington, Department of State*

In concurring with the disposition of the French Government to treat for the whole of Louisiana, although the western part of it was not embraced by your powers, you were justified by the solid reasons which you give for it; and I am charged by the President to express to you his entire approbation for so doing.

This approbation is in no respect precluded by the silence of your commission and instructions. When these were made out, the object of the most sanguine was limited to the establishment of the Mississippi as our boundary. It was not presumed, that more could be sought by the United States, either with a chance of success, or perhaps without being suspected of greedy ambition, than the island of New Orleans and the two Floridas; it being little doubted that the latter was, or would be comprehended in the cession from Spain to France. To the acquisition of New Orleans and the Floridas, the provision was, therefore, accommodated. Nor was it to be supposed that in case the French Government should be willing to part with more than the territory on our side of the Mississippi, an arrangement with Spain for restoring to her the territory on the other side, would not be preferred to a sale of it to the United States. It might be added, that the ample views of the subject carried with him by Mr. Monroe, and the confidence felt that your judicious management would make the most favorable occurrences, lessened the necessity of multiplying provisions for every turn which your negotiations might possibly take.

\* \* \*

With respect to the terms on which the acquisition is made, there can be no doubt that the bargain will be regarded as on the whole highly advantageous. The pecuniary stipulations would have been more satisfactory if they had departed less from the plan prescribed; and particularly if the two millions of dollars in cash, intended to reduce the price to hasten the delivery of possession, had been so applied, and the assumed payments to American claimants placed on a footing specified in the instructions. The unexpected weight of the draft now to be made on the Treasury will be sensibly felt by it, and may possibly be inconvenient in relation to other important objects.

\* \* \*

I only add the wish of the President to know from you the understanding which prevailed in the negotiation with respect to the boundaries of Louisiana; and particularly the pretensions and proofs for carrying it to the river Perdido, or for including any lesser portion of West Florida.

> With high respect and consideration, &c.,
>
> JAMES MADISON.

## 67

### *President Thomas Jefferson to General Horatio Gates, July 11, 1803*

[*State Papers, Correspondence Bearing upon the Purchase of the Territory of Louisiana* (Washington, D.C.: Government Printing Office, 1903), pp. 220–21.]

*Washington*

Dear General,

I accept with pleasure, and with pleasure reciprocate your congratulations on the acquisition of Louisiana; for it is a subject of mutual congratulations, as it interests every man of the nation. The territory acquired, as it includes all the waters of the Missouri and Mississippi, has more than doubled the area of the United States, and the new parts is not inferior to the old in soil, climate, productions and important communications. If our Legislature dispose of it with the wisdom we have a right to expect, they may make it the means of tempting all our Indians on the east side of the Mississippi to remove to the west, and of condensing instead of scattering our population. I find our opposition is very willing to pluck feathers from Monroe, although not fond of sticking them into Livingston's coat. The truth is, both have a just portion of merit; and were it necessary or proper, it would be shown that each has rendered peculiar services, and of important value. These grumblers, too, are very uneasy lest the administration should share some little credit for the acquisition, the whole of which they ascribe to the accident of war. They would be cruelly mortified could they see our files from May, 1801, the first organization of the administration, but more especially from April, 1802. They would see, that though we could not say when war would arise, yet we said with energy what would take place when it should arise. We did not, by our intrigues, produce the war; but we availed ourselves of it when it happened. The other party saw the ease now existing, on which our representations were predicated, and the wisdom of timely sacrifice. But when these people make the war give us everything, they authorize us to ask what the war gave us in their day? They had a war; what did they make it bring us? Instead of making our neutrality the ground of gain to their country, they were for plunging into the war. And if they were now in place, they would now be at war against the atheists and disorganizers of France. They were for making their country an appendage to England. We are friendly, cordially and conscientiously friendly with England. We are not hostile to France. We will be rigorously just and sincerely friendly to both. I do not believe we shall have as much to swallow from them as our predecessors had.

## James Madison to James Monroe
## July 30, 1803

[Extract]

[*House Document 431,* 57th Cong., 2nd sess., pp. 225–26.]

*Washington*

Dear Sir,

I received your favor of ———— by Mr. Hughes, the bearer of the public despatches from you and Mr. Livingston. The purchase of Louisiana in its full extent, tho' not contemplated, is received with warm, and, in a manner, universal approbation. The uses to which it may be turned render it a truly noble acquisition. Under pendent management it may be made to do much good, as well as to prevent much evil. By lessening the military establishment otherwise requisite or countenanced, it will answer the double purpose of saving expence and favoring liberty. This is a point of view in which the Treaty will be particularly grateful to a most respectable descriptions of our Citizens. It will be of great importance, also, to take the regulation and settlement of that Territory out of other hands into those of the U.S., who will be able to manage both for the general interest and conveniency. By securing, also, the exclusive jurisdiction of the Mississippi to the mouth, a source of much perplexity and collision is effectually cut off. The communications of your colleague hither have fully betrayed the feelings excited by your message, and that he was precipitating the business soon after your arrival, without respect to the measure of the government, to yourself, or to the advantage to be expected from the presence and co-operation of the more immediate depository of the objects and sensibilities of his Country. It is highly probable that if the appeal to the French Government had been less hackneyed by the ordinary minister, and been made under the solemnity of a joint and extraordinary embassy, the impression would have been greater and the gain better.

*   *   *

My public letter will show the light in which the purchase of all Louisiana is viewed, and the manner in which it was thought proper to touch the policy of Mr. Livingston, in complaining that the communication did not authorize the measure, notwithstanding the information given that he was negociating for more than the East side of the Mississippi. The pecuniary arrangements are much disrelished, particularly by Mr. Gallatin. The irredeemability of the stock, which gives it value above par, the preference of the conditions to the true object in the cash payment, and the barring of a priority among them, are errors most regarded. The claims of the different creditors rest on principles as different.

## *Albert Gallatin, Secretary of the Treasury, to President Thomas Jefferson*
## *August 18, 1803*

[Extract]

[*The Writings of Albert Gallatin*, vol. 1, Henry Adams, ed. (New York: Antiquarian Press, Ltd., 1960), p. 142.]

*New York*

On the subject of Louisiana generally, Mr. King's opinions, both as relate to New Orleans and the upper country west of the Mississippi, seem to coincide with yours. He hinted, however, that more advantageous terms might have been obtained, and openly said that if our ministers did not think it safe to risk the object by insisting on a reduction of the price, they had it at least in their power to prescribe the mode of payment; that money might have been raised in England on much more advantageous terms if the mode had been left open to us; that [Cazenove], who was Talleyrand's privy counsel and financier, must have suggested the species of stock which was adopted, &c. He then asked me what could have been the reason which induced our ministers to agree to make an immediate cash payment for the American debts, instead of paying them in stock or more convenient instalments, as the creditors would have been perfectly satisfied to be paid that way, and *that* object at least did not seem to be one on which the French government would insist. I told him that I really could not tell, for I knew that mode or some similar one had been contemplated by the Administration, and I had not understood that any explanation on that subject had been received from our ministers. On my mentioning that the French Cabinet seemed to have believed that the question of peace or war was in their power, and that our ministers, being naturally under a similar impression, might have been induced to yield to more unfavorable terms than if they had contemplated war as certain, he observed that on the arrival of every messenger from France the correspondence of Lord Whitworth and Mr. Talleyrand had been communicated to him by the British Ministry, and that by the return of every messenger he had communicated its substance to Mr. Livingston, as well as his opinion of the certainty of war. We both concluded our conversation on that subject by agreeing that Mr. Livingston's precipitancy had been prejudicial to the United States. And he observed that Florida must necessarily fall in our hands, and that he hoped too much impatience would not be evinced on that subject.

70

## *Albert Gallatin to President Thomas Jefferson, January 13, 1803*

[Extract]

[*The Writings of Albert Gallatin,* vol. 1, Henry Adams, ed. (New York: Antiquarian Press, Ltd., 1960), pp. 111–14.]

*Washington, Department of the Treasury*

I have read Mr. Lincoln's observations, and cannot distinguish the difference between a power to acquire territory for the United States and the power to extend by treaty the territory of the United States; yet he contends that the first is unconstitutional, supposes that we may acquire East Louisiana and West Florida by annexing them to the Mississippi Territory. Nor do I think his other idea, that of annexation to a State, that, for instance, of East Florida to Georgia, as proposed by him, to stand on a better foundation. If the acquisition of territory is not warranted by the Constitution, it is not more legal to acquire for one State than for the United States; if the Legislature and Executive established by the Constitution are not the proper organs for the acquirement of new territory for the use of the Union, still less can they be so for the acquirement of new territory for the use of one State; if they have no power to acquire territory, it is because the Constitution has confined its views to the then existing territory of the Union, and *that* excludes a possibility of enlargement of one State as well as that of territory common to the United States. As to the danger resulting from the exercise of such power, it is as great on his plan as on the other. What could, on his construction, prevent the President and the Senate by treaty annexing Cuba to Massachusetts, or Bengal to Rhode Island, if ever the acquirement of colonies shall become a favorite object with governments, and colonies shall be acquired?

But does any constitutional objection really exist?

The 3d Section of the 4th Article of the Constitution provides:

1st. That new States may be admitted by Congress into this Union.

2d. That Congress shall have power to dispose of and make all needful rules and regulations respecting the territory or other property belonging to the United States.

Mr. Lincoln, in order to support his objections, is compelled to suppose, 1st, that the new States therein alluded to must be carved either out of other States, or out of the territory belonging to the United States; and, 2d, that the power given to Congress of making regulations respecting the territory belonging to the United States is expressly confined to the territory *then* belonging to the Union.

A general and perhaps sufficient answer is that the whole rests on a supposition, there being no words in the section which confine the authority given to Congress to those specific objects; whilst, on the contrary, the existence of the United States as a nation presupposes the power enjoyed by every nation of extending their territory by treaties, and the general power given to the President and Senate of making treaties designates the organs through which the acquisition may be made, whilst this section provides the proper authority (viz., Congress) for either admitting in the Union or governing as subjects the territory thus acquired. . . .

* * *

. . . To me it would appear:

1st. That the United States as a nation have an inherent right to acquire territory.

2d. That whenever that acquisition is by treaty, the same constituted authorities in whom the treaty-making power is vested have a constitutional right to sanction the acquisition.

3d. That whenever the territory has been acquired, Congress have the power either of admitting into the Union as a new State, or of annexing to a State with the consent of that State, or of making regulations for the government of such territory.

The only possible objection must be derived from the 12th Amendment, which declares that powers not delegated to the United States, nor prohibited by it to the States, are reserved to the States or to the people. As the States are expressly prohibited from making treaties, it is evident that, if the power of acquiring territory by treaty is not considered within the meaning of the Amendment as delegated to the United States, it must be reserved to the people. If that be the true construction of the Constitution, it substantially amounts to this: that the United States are precluded from, and renounce altogether, the enlargement of territory, a provision sufficiently important and singular to have deserved to be expressly enacted. Is it not a more natural construction to say that the power of acquiring territory is delegated to the United States by the several provisions which authorize the several branches of government to make war, to make treaties, and to govern the territory of the Union?

I must, however, confess that after all I do not feel myself perfectly satisfied; the subject must be thoroughly examined; and the above observations must be considered as hasty and incomplete.

> With respect, your affectionate servant.
>
> ALBERT GALLATIN

# 71

## *President Thomas Jefferson to Albert Gallatin, January, 1803*

[Extract]

[*The Writings of Albert Gallatin,* vol. 1, Henry Adams, ed. (New York: Antiquarian Press Ltd., 1960), p. 115.]

. . . You are right, in my opinion, as to Mr. L.'s proposition: there is no constitutional difficulty as to the acquisition of territory, and whether, when acquired, it may be taken into the Union by the Constitution as it now stands, will become a question of expediency. I think it will be safer not to permit the enlargement of the Union but by amendment of the Constitution. Accept affectionate salutations.

# 72

## Robert R. Livingston to President Thomas Jefferson, June 2, 1803

[Extract]

[As quoted in George Dangerfield, *Chancellor Robert R. Livingston of New York, 1746–1813*. (New York: Harcourt, Brace, & World, 1960), p. 372.]

They have been these two days past in Council & principally basting Mr. Marbois on the subject of the treaty for it seems that the consul is less pleased with it since the ratification than before—& I am persuaded that if he could conveniently get off he would. He says that the whole debt does not exceed four millions & that we have got 20. That delivering the ratifications to us was contrary to all form & that they must be recalled & given to Mr. Pichon to exchange & to this I believe we must consent as it is certainly regular tho' we shall first keep copies of the ratifications. He insists that if the stock is not delivered in the time prescribed the treaty is void. . . . In short he appears to wish the thing undone.

## President Thomas Jefferson to Senator John Breckinridge of Kentucky August 12, 1803

[Extract]

[*State Papers, Correspondence Bearing upon the Purchase of the Territory of Louisiana.* (Washington, D.C.: Government Printing Office, 1903), p. 235.]

*Monticello*

This treaty must of course be laid before both Houses, because both have important functions to exercise respecting it. They, I presume, will see their duty to their country in ratifying and paying for it, so as to secure a good which would otherwise probably be never again in their power. But I suppose they must then appeal to *the nation* for an additional article to the Constitution, approving and confirming an act which the nation had not previously authorized. The Constitution has made no provision for our holding foreign territory, still less for incorporating foreign nations into our Union. The executive in seizing the fugitive occurrence which so much advances the good of their country, have done an act beyond the Constitution. The Legislature in casting behind them metaphysical subtleties, and risking themselves like faithful servants, must ratify and pay for it, and throw themselves on their country for doing for them unauthorized, what we know they would have done for themselves had they been in a situation to do it. It is the case of a guardian investing the money of his ward in purchasing an important adjacent territory; and saying to him when of age, I did this for your good; I pretend to no right to bind you: you may disavow me, and I must get out of the scrape as I can: I thought it my duty to risk myself for you. But we shall not be disavowed by the nation, and their act of indemnity will confirm and not weaken the Constitution, by more strongly marking out its lines.

## President Thomas Jefferson to Albert Gallatin, August 23, 1803

[Extract]

[*The Writings of Albert Gallatin,* vol. 1, Henry Adams, ed. (New York: Antiquarian Press, Ltd., 1960), pp. 144–45.]

*Monticello*

. . . I enclose you the late letters of Livingston and Monroe for consideration, and to be returned to me when perused. You will find that the French government, dissatisfied perhaps with their late bargain with us, will be glad of a pretext to declare it void. It will be necessary, therefore, that we execute it with punctuality and without delay. I have desired the Secretary of the Navy so to make his arrangements as that an armed vessel shall be ready to sail on the 31st of October with the ratification, and, if possible, with the stock to France; if the latter can be got through both Houses in that time it will be desirable. Would it not be well that you should have a bill ready drawn to be offered on the first or second day of the session? It will be well to say as little as possible on the constitutional difficulty, and that Congress should act on it without talking. I subjoin what I think a better form of amendment than the one I communicated to you before. . . .

Louisiana as ceded by France to the United States is made a part of the United States. Its white inhabitants shall be citizens, and stand, as to their rights and obligations, on the same footing with other citizens of the United States in analogous situations. Save only that as to the portion thereof lying north of the latitude of the mouth of Arcansa River no new State shall be established, nor any grants of land made therein, other than to Indians in exchange for equivalent portions of lands occupied by them, until an amendment of the Constitution shall be made for these purposes.

Florida also, whensoever it may be rightfully obtained, shall become a part of the United States. Its white inhabitants shall thereupon be citizens, and shall stand, as to their rights and obligations, on the same footing with other citizens of the United States in analogous situations.

## 75

*President Thomas Jefferson to Attorney General Levi Lincoln August 30, 1803*

[Extract]

[*The Writings of Thomas Jefferson*, vol. 10, A. Lipscomb, ed. (Washington, D.C.: Thomas Jefferson Memorial Association, 1901), pp. 416–17.]

*Monticello*

. . . On further consideration as to the amendment to our Constitution respecting Louisiana, I have thought it better, instead of enumerating the powers which Congress may exercise, to give them the same powers they have as to other portions of the Union generally, and to enumerate the special exceptions, in some such form as the following:

"Louisiana, as ceded by France to the United States, is made a part of the United States, its white inhabitants shall be citizens, and stand, as to their rights and obligations, on the same footing with other citizens of the United States in analogous situations. Save only that as to the portion thereof lying north of an east and west line drawn through the mouth of Arkansas river, no new State shall be established, nor any grants of land made, other than to Indians, in exchange for equivalent portions of land occupied by them, until an amendment of the Constitution shall be made for these purposes.

"Florida also, whensoever it may be rightfully obtained, shall become a part of the United States, its white inhabitants shall thereupon be citizens, and shall stand, as to their rights and obligations, on the same footing with other citizens of the United States, in analogous situations."

I quote this for your consideration, observing that the less that is said about any constitutional difficulty, the better; and that it will be desirable for Congress to do what is necessary, *in silence*. I find but one opinion as to the necessity of shutting up the country for some time. We meet in Washington the 25th of September to prepare for Congress. Accept my affectionate salutations, and great esteem and respect.

76

*President Thomas Jefferson to*
*Senator Wilson C. Nicholas of Virginia*
*September 7, 1803*

[Extract]

[*House Document 431*, 57th Cong., 2nd sess., pp. 236–37.]

*Monticello*

Dear Sir,

Your favor of the 3d was delivered me at court; but we were much disappointed at not seeing you here, Mr.

## Uncertainty Amidst Triumph 169

Madison and the Governor being here at the time. I enclose you a letter from Mr. Monroe on the subject of the late treaty. You will observe a hint in it, to do without delay what we are bound to do. There is reason, in the opinion of our ministers, to believe, that if the thing were to do over again, it could not be obtained, and that if we give the least opening, they will declare the treaty void. A warning amounting to that has been given to them, and an unusual kind of letter written by their minister to our Secretary of State, direct. Whatever Congress shall think it necessary to do, should be done with as little debate as possible, and particularly so far as respects the constitutional difficulty. I am aware of the force of the observations you make on the power given by the Constitution to Congress, to admit new States into the Union, without restraining the subject to the territory then constituting the United States. But when I consider that the limits of the United States are precisely fixed by the treaty of 1783, that the Constitution expressly declares itself to be made for the United States, I cannot help believing the intention was not to permit Congress to admit into the Union new States, which should be formed out of the territory for which, and under whose authority alone, they were then acting. I do not believe it was meant that they might receive England, Ireland, Holland, &c., into it, which would be the case on your construction. When an instrument admits two constructions, the one safe, the other dangerous, the one precise, the other indefinite, I prefer that which is safe and precise. I had rather ask an enlargement of power from the nation, where it is found necessary, than to assume it by a construction which would make our powers boundless. Our peculiar security is in the possession of a written Constitution. Let us not make it a blank paper by construction. I say the same as to the opinion of those who consider the grant of the treaty-making power as boundless. If it is, then we have no Constitution. If it has bounds, they can be no others than the definitions of the powers which that instrument gives. It specifies and delineates the operations permitted to the federal government, and gives all the powers necessary to carry these into execution. Whatever of these enumerated objects is proper for a law, Congress may make the law; whatever is proper to be executed by way of a treaty, the President and Senate may enter into the treaty; whatever is to be done by a judicial sentence, the judges may pass the sentence. Nothing is more likely than that their enumeration of powers is defective. This is the ordinary case of all human works. Let us go on then perfecting it, by adding, by way of amendment to the Constitution, those powers which time and trial show are still wanting. But it has been taken too much for granted, that by this rigorous construction the treaty power would be reduced to nothing. I had occasion once to examine its effect on the French treaty, made by the old Congress, and found that out of thirty odd articles which that contained, there were one, two, or three only which could not now be stipulated under our present Constitution. I confess, then, I think it important, in the present case, to set an example against broad construction, by appealing for new power to the people. If, however, our friends shall think differently, certainly I shall acquiesce with satisfaction; confiding, that the good sense of our country will correct the evil of construction when it shall produce ill effects. . . .

## 77

### Marquis d'Yrujo to James Madison
### September 27, 1803

[*State Papers, Correspondence Bearing upon the Purchase of the Territory of Louisiana.* (Washington, D.C.: Government Printing Office, 1903), p. 243.]

*Vicinity of Philadelphia*

Sir:

On the 4th current I had the honor to intimate to you the extraordinary surprise with which the King my master had heard of the sale of Louisiana, made to the United States, in contravention of the most solemn assurances given in writing to His Majesty by the Ambassador of the French Republic near his person, and with the consent and approbation of the First Consul. The King my master charges me again to remind the American Government that the said French Ambassador entered, in the name of his Republic, into the positive engagement that France never would alienate Louisiana, and to observe to it that the sale of this province to the United States is founded in the violation of a promise so absolute that it ought to be respected; a promise, without which the King my master would, in no manner, have dispossessed himself of Louisiana. His Catholic Majesty entertains too good an opinion of the character of probity and good faith which the Government of the United States has known how to obtain so justly for itself, not to hope that it will suspend the ratification and effect of a treaty which rests on such a basis. There are other reasons no less powerful which come to the support of the decorum and respect which nations mutually owe each other. France acquired from the King my master the retrocession of Louisiana under obligations, whose entire fulfillment was absolutely necessary to give her the complete right over the said province; such was that of causing the King of Tuscany to be acknowledged by the Powers of Europe; but, until now, the French Government has not procured this acknowledgment promised and stipulated, either from the Court of London or from that of St. Petersburg. Under such circumstances it is evident that the treaty of sale entered into between France and the United States does not give to the latter any right to acquire and claim Louisiana, and that the principles of justice as well as sound policy ought to recommend it to their Government not to meddle with engagements as contrary in reality to her true interests as they would be to good faith, and to their good correspondence with Spain.

Such are the sentiments which the King my master has ordered me to communicate to the President of the United States; and, having done it through you, I conclude, assuring you of my respect and consideration towards your person, and of my wishes that our Lord may preserve your life, &c.

M. DE CASA YRUJO

## 78

### *James Madison to Charles Pinckney*
### *October 12, 1803*

[Extract]

[*House Document 431*, 57th Cong., 2nd sess., pp. 247–49.]

*Washington, Department of State*

Among the reasons which weighed with the President, as well as with Mr. Monroe, against attempting, at present, to procure from the Spanish Government the residuum of territory desired by the United States, is the ill-humor shown by that Government at the acquisition already made by them from France; and of which the language held to you by Mr. Cevallos, as communicated in your letter of ——, is a sufficient proof. A still fuller proof of the same fact is contained in three letters lately received from the Spanish Minister here; copies of which, with the answer to my two first, are herewith enclosed. I enclose also a copy of a letter written on the occasion to Mr. Livingston, which was rendered more proper by the probability, as well as by information from Paris, that efforts would be used by Spain to draw the French Government into her views of frustrating the cession of Louisiana to the United States.

In these documents you will find the remarks by which the objections made by the Spanish Government to the Treaty of Cession between the United States and France are to be combatted. The President thinks it proper, that they should, without delay, be conveyed to the Spanish Government, either by note from you or in conversation, as you may deem most expedient; and in a form and style best uniting the advantages of making that Government sensible of the absolute determination of the United States to maintain their right with the propriety of avoiding undignified menace and unnecessary irritation.

The conduct of Spain, on this occasion, is such as was, in several views, little to be expected, and as is not readily explained. If her object be to extort Louisiana from France, as well as to prevent its transfer to the United States, it would seem that she must be emboldened by an understanding with some other very powerful quarter of Europe. If she hopes to prevail on France to break her engagement with the United States, and voluntarily restore Louisiana to herself, why has she so absurdly blended with the project the offensive communication of the perfidy which she charges on the First Consul? If it be her aim to prevent the execution of the treaty between the United States and France, in order to have for her neighbor the latter instead of the United States, it is not difficult to show that she mistakes the lesser for the greater danger against which she wishes to provide. Admitting, as she may possibly suppose, that Louisiana, as a French Colony, would be less able, as well as less disposed, than the United States, to encroach on her southern possessions, and that it would be too much occupied with its own safety against the United States to turn its force on the other side against her possessions, still it is obvious, in the first place, that in proportion to the want of power in the French the colony would be safe for Spain; compared with the power of the United States, the colony would be insufficient as a barrier against the United States; and, in the next place, that the very security which she provides would itself be a source of the greatest of all the dangers she has to apprehend.

*  *  *

What is it that Spain dreads? She dreads, it is presumed, the growing power of this country, and the direction of it against her possessions within its reach. Can she annihilate this power? No. Can she sensibly retard its growth? No. Does not common prudence then, advise her to conciliate, by every proof of friendship and confidence, the good will of a nation whose power is formidable to her; instead of yielding to the impulses of jealousy and adopting obnoxious precautions which can have no other effect than to bring on, prematurely, the whole weight of the calamity which she fears? Reflections such as these may, perhaps, enter with some advantage into your communications with the Spanish Government; and, as far as they may be invited by favorable occasions, you will make that use of them.

Perhaps, after all this interposition of Spain, it may be intended merely to embarrass a measure which she does not hope to defeat, in order to obtain from France, or the United States, or both, concessions of some sort or other as the price of her acquiescence. As yet no indication is given that a resistance, by force, to the execution of the treaty is prepared or meditated. And if it should, the provisions depending on Congress, whose session will commence in two days, will, it may be presumed, be effectually adapted to such an event.

With sentiments, &c.,

JAMES MADISON

## 79

*Message from the President of the United States, October 17, 1803*

[Extract]

[*State Papers, Correspondence Bearing upon the Purchase of the Territory of Louisiana.* (Washington, D.C.: Government Printing Office, 1903), pp. 251–53.]

*To the Senate and House of Representatives of the United States:*

In calling you together, fellow-citizens, at an earlier day than was contemplated by the act of the last session of Congress, I have not been insensible to the personal inconveniences necessarily resulting from an unexpected change in your arrangements. But matters of great public concernment have rendered this call necessary, and the interest you feel in these will supersede in your minds all private considerations.

Congress witnessed, at their last session, the extraordinary agitation produced in the public mind by the suspension of our right of deposit at the port of New Orleans, no assignment of another place having been made according to treaty. They were sensible that the continuance of that privation would be more injurious to our nation than any consequences that could flow from any mode of redress; but, reposing just confidence in the good faith of the Government whose officer had committed the wrong, friendly and reasonable representations were resorted to, and the right of deposit was restored.

Previous, however, to this period we had not been unaware of the danger to which our peace would be perpetually exposed whilst so important a key to the commerce of the Western country remained under a foreign power. Difficulties too were presenting themselves as to the navigation of other streams, which arising in our territories, pass through those adjacent. Propositions had therefore been authorized for obtaining on fair conditions the sovereignty of New Orleans, and of other possessions in that quarter, interesting to our quiet, to such extent as was deemed practicable; and the provisional appropriation of two million dollars, to be applied and accounted for by the President of the United States, intended as part of the price, was considered as conveying the sanction of Congress to the acquisition proposed. The enlightened Government of France saw, with just discernment, the importance to both nations of such liberal arrangements as might best and permanently promote the peace, interests and friendship of both; and the property and sovereignty of all Louisiana, which had been restored to them, has, on certain conditions, been transferred to the United States, by instruments bearing date the 30th of April last. When these shall have received the constitutional sanction of the Senate, they will, without delay, be communicated to the Representatives for the exercise of their functions, as to those conditions which are within the powers vested by the Constitution in Congress. Whilst the property and sovereignty of the Mississippi and its waters secure an independent outlet for the produce of the Western States, and an uncontrolled navigation through their whole course, free from collision with other Powers, and the dangers to our peace from that source, the fertility of the country, its climate and extent, promise, in due season, important aids to our Treasury, an ample provision for our posterity, and a wide spread for the blessings of freedom and equal laws.

With the wisdom of Congress it will rest to take those ulterior measures which may be necessary for the immediate occupation and temporary government of the country; for its incorporation into our union; for rendering the change of government a blessing to our newly adopted brethren; for securing to them the rights of conscience and of property; for confirming to the Indian inhabitants their occupancy and self-government, establish friendly and commercial relations with them, and for ascertaining the geography of the country acquired. Such materials for your information relative to its affairs in general, as the short space of time has permitted me to collect, will be laid before you when the subject shall be in a state for your consideration.

*   *   *

TH. JEFFERSON

*Albert Gallatin to President
Thomas Jefferson, October 28, 1803*

[Extract]

[*The Writings of Albert Gallatin,* vol. 1, Henry Adams, ed. (New York: Antiquarian Press, Ltd., 1960), pp. 162-66.]

*Department of Treasury*

Dear Sir,

I have conversed with most of the Western members of Congress respecting the possibility of raising volunteers to assist the force already prepared for occupying New Orleans. I think that I have seen thirteen out of the seventeen who compose the delegation of the three Western States, and I believe that they have all conferred on the subject. Not only they appear to be strongly impressed with the importance of the subject, but some amongst them were more alarmed than I had expected, as it had been reported that the effective regular force at Fort Adams which may be spared did not exceed three hundred men. How that fact is I do not remember, but had believed that the regulars there would amount to double that number. The result of the conversation with those gentlemen, and which they requested might be communicated to you, is, that if the Executive shall think it necessary to call any militia or volunteers in that part of the country, it may be confidently relied on that within a fortnight after the reception of the orders by the Executives of Tennessee and Kentucky fifteen hundred horsemen, all of them volunteers and well selected, shall be at Nashville, and then proceed immediately to Natchez, which they may reach within twenty days afterwards at most. About one-third of that number might meet at Nashville a few days earlier, and march across the wilderness within a fortnight, the rest to follow in divisions of two or three hundreds as they met from the more distant parts; which will also be more convenient on account of forage for the horses. Every man shall carry his own provisions across, and will be completely accoutred and armed, unless, as there are muskets at Fort Adams, it should be thought more eligible to induce a number of the volunteers not to take their rifles, and to take muskets on their arrival. The idea of going by water must be abandoned so far as relates to an immediate expedition, because the water is too low, and then there are not on the spot any immediate means of transportation. All the gentlemen agree that as to the number of men, considering that all the crops are in, the season the most favorable in point of health of the whole year, and the general zeal of the country, five thousand men could be raised at once without any difficulty, and that the only struggle will be for having permission to go. The proportion agreed on is that Tennessee should send one-third, and Kentucky the other two-thirds.

❊ ❊ ❊

It is understood that if fifteen hundred effective volunteers are wanted to arrive at Natchez the requisition should be for two thousand two hundred and fifty, viz., seven hundred and fifty from Tennessee and fifteen hundred from Kentucky. As a measure which will cost nothing, will, in respect to Spain, add to their opinion of us, and may under certain circumstances be ultimately serviceable, to this force might be added ten thousand nominal men from the same States and Ohio, to be only enrolled or drafted and considered as ready to march whenever called upon. There has been something said of the want of galleys which would have been useful against those of Spain. Is not there one at Bayou Pierre?

Little reliance can be placed on the regular force at Massac, Kaskaskia, and Chickasaw Bluff, unless they have already received orders to proceed. Otherwise, on account of the low water, they will arrive too late. Yet there would be no harm in pressing by immediate orders their departure.

     Respectfully, your obedient servant

         ALBERT GALLATIN

## 81

### *James Madison to Robert R. Livingston, November 9, 1803*

[*State Papers, Correspondence Bearing upon the Purchase of the Territory of Louisiana.* (Washington, D.C.: Government Printing Office, 1903), pp. 264–65.]

       *Washington, Department of State*

Sir:

  In my letter of the 22d ultimo, I mentioned to you that the exchange of the ratifications of the treaty and conventions with France, had taken place here, unclogged with any conditions or reserve. Congress has since passed an act to enable the President to take possession of the ceded territory, and to establish a temporary Government therein. Other acts have been passed for complying with the pecuniary stipulations of those instruments. The newspapers enclosed will inform you of these proceedings.

  By the post which left this city for Natchez on Monday last, a joint and several commission was forwarded to Governor Claiborne and General Wilkinson, authorizing them to receive possession of and occupy those territories, and a separate commission to the former as temporary

Governor. The possibility suggested, by recent circumstances, that delivery may be refused at New Orleans on the part of Spain, required that provision should be made as well for taking as receiving possession. Should force be necessary, Governor Claiborne and General Wilkinson will have to decide on the practicability of a *coup de main* without waiting for the reinforcements, which will require time on our part, and admit of preparations on the other. The force provided for this object is to consist of the regular troops near at hand, as many of the militia as may be requisite, and can be drawn from the Mississippi Territory, and as many volunteers from any quarter as can be picked up. To them will be added 500 mounted militia from Tennessee, who, it is expected, will proceed to Natchez with the least possible delay.

M. Pichon has, in the strongest manner, pressed on M. Laussat, the French Commissary appointed to deliver possession, the necessity of co-operating in these measures of compulsion, should they prove necessary by the refusal of the Spanish officers to comply without them. On the 8th of October it was not known, and no indications have been exhibited at New Orleans, of a design, on the part of Spain, to refuse or oppose the surrender of the province to France, and thereby to us.

With high respect and consideration, &c.

JAMES MADISON

## 82

*Daniel Clark\* to James Madison*
*October 20, 1803*

[Extract]

[Consular Despatches, New Orleans.]

*New Orleans*

Whatever may have hitherto been the intentions of the Prefect, and these must have been regulated by the secret instructions received from his Court, the unexpected Cession of this Country to the U. S. and the political Situation of France have now rendered a change of measures necessary, and that decided enmity to the Individuals and Government of the U. S. which was so strongly marked in the Language and Actions of the Prefect has now given place to more pacific and friendly Views, and a more conciliatory Language and Conduct, and if I except a wish to gratify his Vanity by retaining possession of the Province a few days I believe he will place no obstacle whatever in the way of the delivery of it to the commissioners appointed by the U. S. for that purpose. Much trouble arising from etiquette may be expected, but as I flatter myself the Persons appointed for so important a Commission will be Men of talents and Experience and possess a knowledge of the World, this will be easily got over and it will require from such People but little exertions to make every thing easy and acceptable in the outset and reconcile all Parties to our Government from which the greatest Benefits are confidently expected.

\* Daniel Clark was a Delegate from the Territory of Orleans; elected to the Ninth and Tenth Congresses, he served from Dec. 1, 1806, to March 3, 1809.

## Uncertainty Amidst Triumph 183

In saying that I am confident we shall experience but little difficulty from the Prefect in taking possession I count fully on a sincere disposition at present on the part of France to fulfill its stipulations with us and the most positive orders given to the Prefect to comply with them—from the Man himself we have every thing to apprehend if left to the suggestions of his own violent temper and inclinations. He has however completely lost the confidence of the People of Louisiana, and would find no effectual support whatever at this Period, in an attempt to elude or delay the delivery of the Country.

* * *

With respect to the military force in this Province and its disposal I refer you to the inclosed Memorandum from which you will perceive that it is in itself trifling, is dispersed over a vast extent of Country, and cannot easily be concentrated. The Force of the Militia and the position of the different Settlements you are already in possession of, and it must be apparent that with a little exertion on the part of our Officers stationed in the Mississippi Territory, joined to the Militia of that Country and our numerous Partezans here, even before assistance could be sent from other Parts of the U. S., all Communication between the distant Settlements and the Capital could easily be cut off before they were aware of the Blow about to be struck and that our disposable Force in that Quarter, backed by threats of Vengeance on the part of the U. S. in case of opposition, would be sufficient even to put us in possession of New Orleans itself by a coup de main before effectual Measures could be taken for its defence.

* * *

Be pleased to assure the President that I shall carefully watch and advise you of every symptom indicative of a hostile or unfriendly disposition towards us from any

Quarter whatever and that I shall spare no pains or exertions to increase the attachment of the People of this Country to the Government of the U. S. . . .

> Your most obedient Servt.
>
> DANIEL CLARK

## 83

*Proclamation of the United States Government to the People of New Orleans November 15, 1803*

[Despatch no. 333 of Nov. 15, 1803, in James Robertson, *Louisiana under the Rule of Spain, France, and the United States, 1785–1807*, vol. 2. (Cleveland: Arthur A. Clark Co., 1911), p. 457.]

*The people of the United States to those of New Orleans.*

Brothers:

Spain has transferred the territory of Louisiana to France, and France to us. Spain has received for it the kingdom of Parma, and France fifteen millions of dollars [*duros*]. The transaction has been legitimate and attested by all solemnities that bind nations. But yet it is reported that Spain will try to destroy this contract and violate its honor.

The injustice and incivility of Spain will never inspire us with weakness or cowardice. We shall obtain our rights. But it belongs to you to decide whether you are disposed to share in them or to attack them for consideration of Spain. Equally in your hands too, is the acceptance of a part of our dominion or opposition to its course.

New Orleans, although old, is still very small, and the

states of our Union, although born but yesterday, have already made the progress of which humanity is susceptible. Your products, although planted in a paradise, appear to have been submerged or to have been destroyed by the cold, while those of our states up the river although with inferior advantages, flourish as if fed by the dew of heaven. That dew is the liberty and moderation of our government by which they are refreshed. Speedily will new blessings be seen to emanate from your weak energy; for instead of monopolies, you will have commerce, your towns will become cities, and from a province will be formed a nation.

Nature designed the inhabitants of Mississippi and those of New Orleans to be one single people. It is your peculiar happiness that nature's decrees are fulfilled under the auspices of a philosopher who prefers justice to conquest, whose glory it is to make man free and not a slave, and who delights in benevolence instead of splendor. Yet although he is careful of your happiness, he will not permit you to destroy it by obstructing our rights.

Your alternative is clear, for it consists only in making your small district, either a field of war or a garden of peace. Circumscribed as it now is, the most rigid discipline will not be able to free it from ruin. On your will only does it depend whether it is to be covered with ruins or with palaces.

Well may Spain counsel you to cry out that war may exist with all its horrors, but its intentions will not be to make you more happy. Spain purposes only to involve you in a war to further its own interests, and not to promote those of New Orleans. On our part, we recommend peace and all its blessings to you; and in this advice we find the interest of the benefits of free trade. Nature has united our interests into one whole. We are the children of the west, not of the east. Hence we shall not allow the old world to oblige us to forget that we both belong to the new.

You are interested parties in the cessions by which we reclaim you. The faith of governments is that of nations; and your loyalty was already bound up and united with us by a fitting chord.

The government of Spain, and later that of France, was able lawfully to dispose of your forces and wills so long as Louisiana belonged to them. But now no government may do so, since it has been ceded to us. Would you fail in the obligations which you contracted while you belonged to those governments, and in those which result from your union with us? United, then, by the bonds of alliance, can disloyalty, accompanied by war, monopoly, and provincial degradation appear more pleasing to you than good faith, accompanied by peace, commerce, and federal equality? It is, peradventure well, that Spain is trying to separate you from the brilliant destiny which is offered you, through the influence of jealousies or ministerial intrigues? Would you take their sword, and try vainly to prevent New Orleans from fulfilling its destiny? It is an obligation of friendship to hold back the arm of the maniac assassin from himself. We shall fulfil our duty.

We send you this address, because it is reported that Spain is trying to violate its faith, but we believe this to be calumny. From our cradle we have been accustomed to friendly intercourse with Spain; and that power has been just and honorable toward us, just as we have been toward it, and at the same time we have placed all our glory in rivaling its integrity. The good offices on one side and the other have engendered a friendship, which as long as it endures henceforth will be more intimate. But we look upon Spain as does a man his intimate friend, from whom he fears some injury. Doubt, affection, pain, and anger, alternately occupy his mind. The dispersion of this feeling by the continuation of integrity and good faith would be a new motive for reiterating his friendship and a new pledge of its continuation for the future.

When Spain sees that we are delivering to you and to

the descendants of its sons, formerly its subjects, all the advantages that we have been enabled to gain from the cession of Louisiana and all those which we may derive from our form of government, our policy and their gratitude will form a new link in the chain of national friendship. But if the corruption of Europe comes at the end to infest the honor and good faith of the Spaniards, fortune has placed you in the position that offers the greatest opportunity to practice honor and good faith in America as a right of your birth.

If a state in our Union fails in its faith by breaking our laws, or by a lack of the due loyalty, we would oppose it, as we shall oppose you; for we shall compel our laws to be respected and their obligations to be fulfilled by them. But first we would warn the public of such a state, just as now we are proceeding toward you, not as provincials or subjects, but as brothers and beloved fellow citizens.

## 84

### *Address of Governor William C. C. Claiborne\* to the Citizens of Louisiana, September 20, 1803*

[*House Document 431*, 57th Cong., 2nd sess., pp. 289–90.]

*New Orleans*

*Fellow-Citizens of Louisiana:*

On the great and interesting event now finally consummated—an event so advantageous to yourselves and

---

\* Governor Claiborne had assumed the powers formerly exercised by the Spanish Governor-general and Intendant of the Province of Louisiana.

so glorious to United America—I can not forbear offering you my warmest congratulations. The wise policy of the Consul of France has, by the cession of Louisiana to the United States, secured to you a connexion beyond the reach of change, and to your posterity the sure inheritance of freedom. The American people receive you as brothers, and will hasten to extend to you a participation in those inestimable rights which have formed the basis of their own unexampled prosperity. Under the auspices of the American Government, you may confidently rely upon the security of your liberty, your property, and the religion of your choice. You may with equal certainty rest assured that your commerce will be promoted and your agriculture cherished—in a word, that your true interests will be among the primary objects of our National Legislature. In return for these benefits, the United States will be amply remunerated if your growing attachment to the Constitution of our country, and your veneration for the principles on which it is founded, be duly proportioned to the blessings which they will confer. Among your first duties, therefore, you should cultivate with assiduity among yourselves the advancement of political information. You should guide the rising generation in the paths of republican economy and virtue. You should encourage literature; for without the advantages of education, your descendants will be unable to appreciate the intrinsic worth of the Government transmitted to them.

As for myself, fellow-citizens, accept a sincere assurance, that during my continuance in the situation in which the President of the United States has been pleased to place me, every exertion will be made on my part to foster your internal happiness, and forward your general welfare; for it is only by such means that I can secure to myself the approbation of those great and just men who preside in the councils of our nation.

WM. C. C. CLAIBORNE

# 85

## *A Contemporary Observation*

[Extract]

[C. C. Robin, *Voyages dans l'intérieur de la Louisiane . . . pendant les années 1802, 1803, 1804, 1805 et 1806*, 1 vol. (Paris: F. Brisson, 1807), p. 225.]

In the meantime, I saw the French flag slowly descending and that of the U.S. gradually rising at the same time. Soon a French officer took the first to wrap it up and bear it silently into the rear. The American flag remained stuck for a long time, in spite of the efforts to raise it as if it were confused at taking the place of that to which it owed its glorious independence. An anxious silence reigned at the moment among all the spectators who flooded the plaza, who crowded against the galleries, balconies and windows; and it was not until that flag had been quite boisted up that suddenly piercing cries of 'Huzza' burst from the midst of one particular group, who waved their hats at the same time. Those cries and that movement made more gloomy the silence and quietness of the rest of the crowd of spectators scattered far and wide—they were French and Spanish and were all moved and confounded their sighs and tears.

## 86

*President Thomas Jefferson to
Dr. Joseph Priestley, January 29, 1804*

[Extract]

[*State Papers, Correspondence Bearing upon the Purchase of the Territory of Louisiana* (Washington, D.C.: Government Printing Office, 1903), p. 274.]

*Washington*

I very early saw that Louisiana was indeed a speck in our horizon which was to burst in a tornado; and the public are apprized how near this catastrophe was. Nothing but a frank and friendly development of causes and effects on our part, and good sense enough in Bonaparte to see that the train was unavoidable, and would change the face of the world, saved us from the storm. I did not expect he would yield till a war took place between France and England, and my hope was to palliate and endure, if Messrs. Ross, Morris, &c. did not force a premature rupture, until that event. I believed the event not very distant, but acknowledge it came on sooner than I had expected. Whether, however, the good sense of Bonaparte might not see the course predicted to be necessary and unavoidable, even before a war should be imminent, was a chance which we thought it our duty to try: but the immediate prospect of rupture brought the case to immediate decision. The *denoument* has been happy; and I confess I look to this duplication of area for the extending a government so free and economical as ours, as a great achievement to the mass of happiness

## Uncertainty Amidst Triumph 191

which is to ensue. Whether we remain in one confederacy, or form into Atlantic and Mississippi confederacies, I believe not very important to the happiness of either part. Those of the western confederacy will be as much our children and descendants as those of the eastern, and I feel myself as much identified with that country, in future time, as with this; and did I now foresee a separation at some future day, yet I should feel the duty and the desire to promote the western interests as zealously as the eastern, doing all the good for both portions of our future family which should fall within my power.

# Bibliography

There is no full length scholarly study of the Louisiana Purchase. Numerous accounts exist, but these are within larger works dealing either with the major figures who participated in the event or with the general diplomacy of the American borderlands in the Napoleonic era. Source materials for the study of the Purchase are extensive and from them a generally complete view of the episode can be pieced together. Henry Adams (*History of the United States of America During the Administrations of Jefferson and Madison*, 9 vols. [New York, 1889–91]) emphasizes the President's hesitancy and finds little evidence that he acted with initiative, whereas Mary P. Adams ("Jefferson's Reaction to the Treaty of San Ildefonso," *Journal of Southern History*, vol. 21 [1955], pp. 173–88), for example, concludes that the military preparations ordered by Jefferson in 1802 and 1803 were notable and suggests that we have neglected this aspect of Jefferson's response. American Minister to France Robert Livingston receives mixed judgements for his part in the Purchase. George Dangerfield (*Chancellor Robert Livingston of New York, 1746–1813* [New York, 1960]) generally approves of Livingston's efforts to persuade a stubborn Talleyrand and a lofty Napoleon to abandon their plans for Louisiana while Gilbert Chinard (*Thomas Jefferson: The Apostles of Americanism* [Boston, 1939]) emphasizes Livingston's tendency to overplay his hand and rush toward a settlement before the arrival of Monroe. The negotiations between France and Spain over the Louisiana and Italian territories and, not unexpectedly, the actions and motives of Napoleon in this respect, continue to provoke scholarly speculation. And some historians, pondering the almost uncanny succession of favorable events which reinforced the American diplomatic position, have wondered whether Providence was indeed playing favorites.

The heart of the American diplomatic correspondence may be examined in W. Lowrie and M. Clark, *American State Papers, Foreign Relations*, 6 vols. (Washington,

D.C., 1832–59) or in the *State Papers and Correspondence Bearing upon the Purchase of the Territory of Louisiana* (Washington, D.C., 1903). Jefferson's correspondence, which is most revealing of the President's fears and anxieties, notwithstanding his hopes of final success, has been collected by Paul L. Ford, *The Works of Thomas Jefferson,* 12 vols. (New York, 1904) and *The Writings of Thomas Jefferson,* 10 vols. (New York, 1892–99). In addition, important letters bearing upon the episode are located in Andrew Lipscomb and Albert Bergh, eds., *The Writings of Thomas Jefferson,* 20 vols. (Washington, D.C., 1904). The importance of the Jefferson-Du Pont friendship to the successful outcome of the Louisiana affair can be seen in Gilbert Chinard, ed., *The Correspondence of Jefferson and DuPont de Nemours* (Baltimore, 1931).

Although Secretary of State Madison was active in the negotiations his collected correspondence (Gaillard Hunt, ed., *The Writings of James Madison,* 9 vols. [New York, 1908]) does not significantly add to the information we receive of him in the *State Papers.* Some useful letters of the Secretary of the Treasury, especially those relating to the constitutional aspects of the Louisiana acquisition, may be found in Henry Adams, ed., *The Writings of Albert Gallatin* (Philadelphia, 1879). The collected correspondence of Monroe (S. M. Hamilton, ed., *The Writings of James Monroe* [New York, 1903]) contain little that is pertinent. His *Autobiography* (Stuart Brown, ed., [Syracuse, 1959]) is also of marginal use. The role of Rufus King is amply revealed by the *State Papers,* but there is additional material in C. R. King, ed., *Life and Correspondence of Rufus King,* 5 vols. (New York, 1894–1900).

Away from Washington and in the Mississippi Territory, W. C. C. Claiborne kept a sharp eye on developments. His correspondence, found in Dunbar Rowland, ed., *Official Letter Books of W. C. C. Claiborne,* 6 vols. (Jackson, Mississippi, 1917), is therefore useful. Also of considerable value are the letters from New Orleans written by the unofficial American Consuls in residence there, especially those of Daniel Clark. An important portion of this material has been reprinted in the *American Historical Review,* vol. 32, pp. 801–24 and vol. 33, pp. 331–59 (1927–28). Documents from Spanish and French sources relating to the Purchase have been collected by James

Robertson, *Louisiana Under the Rule of Spain, France, and the United States, 1785-1807,* 2 vols. (Cleveland, 1911).

Two works related to the Louisiana Purchase are Arthur B. Darling, *Our Rising Empire, 1763-1803* (New Haven, 1940) and Arthur P. Whitaker, *The Mississippi Question, 1795-1803* (New York, 1934)—both excellent for their comprehensive view of the struggle of European powers for empire in the West. Bradford Perkins, *The First Rapprochement: England and the United States, 1795-1805* (Philadelphia, 1955) details the cooperative attitude that developed between those two nations in this period. Narrower in scope but of considerable interest to students of the Purchase are William Sloane, "Napoleon's Plan for a Colonial System," *American Historical Review,* vol. 4 (1899), pp. 439-55 and "World Aspects of the Louisiana Purchase," *American Historical Review,* vol. 9 (1904), pp. 507-21; Frederick Jackson Turner, "The Policy of France Toward the Mississippi Valley in the Period of Washington and Adams," *American Historical Review,* vol. 10 (1905), pp. 249-79; Mildred Fletcher, "Louisiana as a Factor in French Diplomacy from 1763-1800," *Mississippi Valley Historical Review,* vol. 17 (1930), pp. 367-77; C. L. Lokke, "Jefferson and the Leclerc Expedition," *American Historical Review,* vol. 33 (1928), pp. 322-28; Arthur P. Whitaker, "France and the American Deposit at New Orleans," *Hispanic American Historical Review,* vol. 7 (1931), pp. 485-502, and "New Light on the Treaty of San Lorenzo: An Essay in Historical Criticism," *Mississippi Valley Historical Review,* vol. 15 (1928-29), pp. 435-54.

Secondary accounts of some of the key American participants in the Louisiana diplomacy are in Irving Brant, *James Madison, Secretary of State, 1800-1809* (New York, 1953); George Dangerfield, *Chancellor Robert Livingston of New York, 1746-1813* (New York, 1960); Robert Ernst, *Rufus King* (Chapel Hill, 1968); and Lawrence Kaplan, *Jefferson and France* (New Haven, 1967). For appraisals of the domestic issues during this period see Morton Borden, *Parties and Politics in the Early Republic, 1789-1815* (New York, 1967); Noble Cunningham, *The Jeffersonian Republicans in Power* (Chapel Hill, 1963); and Norman K. Risjord, *The Old Republicans* (New York, 1965).

# II

## 1898: McKINLEY'S DECISION

## THE UNITED STATES

## Declares WAR on SPAIN

From IMPERIAL DEMOCRACY, © 1961, by Ernest R. May. Reprinted by permission of Harcourt, Brace & World, Inc.

Reprinted from Walter LaFeber: THE NEW EMPIRE: AN INTERPRETATION OF AMERICAN EXPANSION, 1860-1898. © 1963 by the American Historical Association. Used by permission of Cornell University Press.

# Contents
**PART II**
**1898: McKinley's Decision:**
The United States Declares War on Spain
*Introduction*

*Section One*
President Grover
Cleveland and the Cuban
Rebellion, 1895–1897

| | |
|---|---:|
| *Commentary* | 1 |
| *Secretary of State Richard Olney to Spanish Minister to the United States Dupuy De Lôme, April 4, 1896* | 2 |
| *De Lôme to Olney, June 4, 1896* | 8 |
| *President Grover Cleveland's Fourth State of the Union Message, December 7, 1896* | 13 |

*Section Two*
Congressional Pressure

| | |
|---|---:|
| *Commentary* | 18 |
| *United States Senate, April 6, 1897* | 18 |

*Section Three*
Report of McKinley's
Personal Envoy

| | |
|---|---:|
| *Commentary* | 32 |

*William J. Calhoun to President
William McKinley, June 22, 1897*     32

## Section Four
## McKinley's Predicament

   *Commentary*     44

   *Secretary of State John Sherman to
De Lôme, June 26, 1897*     44

   *Sherman to American Minister to Spain
Stewart L. Woodford, July 16, 1897*     47

   *Woodford to Sherman, Sept. 23, 1897*     52

## Section Five
## Rays of Hope

   *Commentary*     54

   *Reply of Foreign Minister Pio Gullón to
Minister Woodford's Note of
October 23, 1897*     54

   *Woodford to Sherman, November 13, 1897*     62

   *Woodford to Sherman, November 15, 1897*     65

   *Woodford to Sherman, November 26, 1897*     66

   *President William McKinley's First State of
the Union Message, December 6, 1897*     69

## Section Six
## Continuing Conflict

   *Commentary*     73

   *The American Consul-General in Havana
Fitzhugh Lee, to Assistant Secretary of
State, William Day, December 7, 1897*     73

   *Lee to Day, December 13, 1897*     75

   *Lee to Day, December 14, 1897*     76

| | |
|---|---|
| *Lee to Day, December 28, 1897* | **77** |
| *Diplomatic Note: United States of America to Spain, December 20, 1897 (Minister Woodford to Foreign Affairs Minister Pio Gullón)* | **78** |

## Section Seven
## The Anti-Autonomy Riots

| | |
|---|---|
| *Commentary* | 83 |
| *Lee to Day, January 15, 1898* | 83 |
| *Lee to Day, January 18, 1898* | 85 |
| *Lee to Day, January 21, 1898* | 86 |
| *United States House of Representatives January 20, 1898* | 90 |

## Section Eight
## The De Lôme Letter

| | |
|---|---|
| *Commentary* | 109 |
| *De Lôme's Letter December, 1897* | 109 |
| *Day to Woodford, February 9, 1898* | 112 |
| *Woodford to Sherman, February 11, 1898* | 112 |
| *United States House of Representatives February 14, 1898* | 113 |

## Section Nine
## Prelude to an Ultimatum

| | |
|---|---|
| *Commentary* | 117 |
| *Day to Woodford, March 3, 1898* | 117 |
| *Woodford to President McKinley, March 9, 1898* | 119 |
| *Woodford to the President, March 17, 1898* | 123 |

*United States Senate, March 17, 1898*     129

*Section Ten*
The Attitude of
the Powers

    *Commentary*     142

    *"The Powers and Spain"*     142

*Section Eleven*
The Decision for War

    *Commentary*     168

    *Woodford to the President, March 19, 1898*     168

    *Woodford to the President, March 19, 1898*     169

    *Day to Woodford, March 20, 1898*     170

    *Day to Woodford, March 26, 1898*     171

    *Day to Woodford, March 27, 1898*     173

    *Woodford to Day, March 27, 1898*     173

    *Day to Woodford, March 28, 1898*     175

    *Woodford to Day, March 31, 1898*     175

    *Woodford to the President, April 1, 1898*     179

    *Woodford to Day, April 2, 1898*     181

    *Spanish Minister to the United States Señor Polo de Bernabé to Sherman, April 3, 1898*     182

    *Woodford to the President, April 3, 1898*     184

    *Day to Woodford, April 4, 1898*     186

    *Sherman to Woodford, April 4, 1898*     187

    *Day to Woodford, April 4, 1898*     187

    *Joint Note of the Powers and President McKinley's Reply, April 6, 1898*     188

    *Woodford to Day, April 6, 1898*     189

| *Woodford to Day, April 6, 1898* | 191 |
| *Woodford to Day, April 7, 1898* | 192 |
| *Woodford to Sherman, April 8, 1898* | 194 |
| *Woodford to Day, April 9, 1898* | 196 |
| *Woodford to Day, April 9, 1898* | 197 |
| *Woodford to the President, April 10, 1898* | 198 |
| *Señor Polo de Barnabé to Sherman, April 10, 1898* | 199 |
| *Day to Woodford, April 10, 1898* | 202 |
| *Señor Polo de Bernabé to Day April 11, 1898* | 202 |
| *President McKinley to Congress April 11, 1898* | 203 |
| *Sherman to Woodford, April 14, 1898* | 212 |
| *Day to Woodford, April 17, 1898* | 213 |
| *Day to Woodford, April 19, 1898* | 214 |
| *Sherman to Woodford, April 20, 1898* | 215 |
| *"Ultimata"* | 216 |
| *Reaction: Approach to War* | 224 |
| Bibliographical Notes | 235 |

*Introduction*

On April 11, 1898, President William McKinley asked Congress "to authorize and empower" him "to take measures to secure a full and final termination of the hostilities between the Government of Spain and the people of Cuba, and to secure in the island the establishment of a stable government . . . , and to use the military and naval forces of the United States as may be necessary for these purposes."

During his thirteen months in office, McKinley had worked hard to avoid making such a request. Yet despite his devotion to a peaceful solution of Spanish-American differences over Cuba, the President finally found himself compelled to resort to force. Relying primarily upon the documentary record, or information which McKinley had before him at the time, this book attempts to give the student a picture of how the President arrived at his decision. That it could do this fully would be disputed by at least one historian, who recently wrote, "There are no historical sources that can reveal definitely why McKinley acted as he did in the spring of 1898."[*] This collection of materials, then, will give the student a general idea of the forces driving McKinley toward war and will acquaint him with some of the difficulties involved in explaining how a President or any leading political figure decides a major policy question.

❊    ❊    ❊

Long before McKinley took up his presidential duties on March 4, 1897, Spain's control of Cuba had aggravated relations with the United States. Though Spanish rule of

[*] J. Rogers Hollingsworth, ed., *American Expansion in the Late Nineteenth Century: Colonialist or Anticolonialist?* (New York, 1968), p. 5.

the island dated from 1511, nineteenth-century Americans assumed that the strategic location of Cuba, ninety miles from their shores, made it inevitable that the island would come under American influence or control. In response to this feeling, Presidents James K. Polk, Franklin Pierce and James Buchanan all had unsuccessfully sought to buy the island from Spain. Moreover, during the years 1868–1878, when the Cubans rebelled against Spain's archaic and exploitive rule, Presidents Ulysses S. Grant and Rutherford B. Hayes each seriously considered armed intervention to break Spanish power. Only the fact that Grant and Hayes were then occupied with other foreign issues saved the Spanish from a contest with American arms.

Much the same circumstances prevailed during President Grover Cleveland's second term. When a new Cuban revolution erupted at the beginning of 1895, a preoccupation with British-American differences over Venezuela allowed Cleveland and the American public to give only passing attention to the struggle. Once the Venezuela boundary dispute was settled, though, Cleveland could no longer afford to be passive. With the conflict in Cuba systematically destroying $40 million worth of American investments and $100 million in annual trade, with the American government bearing heavy naval appropriations to enforce neutrality, and with bipartisan pressure mounting in the Congress for recognition of Cuban belligerency, Cleveland felt compelled to do something to end the war. The President's first effort in April 1896, as the documents in Section One make clear, was a polite suggestion through his Secretary of State, Richard Olney, that Spain prevent American intervention through substantial concessions to the Cuban revolutionaries, including, if need be, a grant of autonomy. When this suggestion produced no change in Spanish policy and when the Republicans won the presidential election of 1896 on a platform including the demand that the United States "actively use its influences and good offices to restore peace

*Introduction*

and give independence to the Island," Cleveland warned Spain in his last State of the Union Message that "the United States is not a nation to which peace is a necessity. . . ." Cleveland, however, was unwilling to go beyond this. With but three months remaining to his term, he determined to leave the issue to his successor, William McKinley.

The new President found solving the Cuban crisis a demanding task. Initially eager to avoid public agitation of the issue and to give private diplomacy a chance to work, McKinley made no mention of Cuba in his Inaugural Address (March 4, 1897). Yet, as the excerpts in Section Two from the Senate debate of April 6, 1897, make clear, McKinley was under considerable pressure from Congress, and particularly from his fellow Republicans, to recognize Cuban belligerency. At the very least, it was clear to McKinley, an astute politician, that prolonged inactivity on his part and continued strife in the island threatened to disrupt the unity of his party.

Still, the President was unwilling to act in haste. Calling upon Republican friends in the House to block a joint congressional resolution recognizing Cuban belligerency, McKinley simultaneously appointed a skillful lawyer and former Union general, Stewart L. Woodford, to represent him in Madrid. Realizing that he faced a momentous problem, the President decided to educate himself fully about the state of Cuban affairs. With little more than consular dispatches and newspaper reports to rely on, both of which were highly critical of the Spanish and friendly to the Cuban cause, McKinley wished a first-hand estimate of military, political and economic conditions in the island from a trusted political friend. To this end, he dispatched William J. Calhoun of Ohio to Cuba in May 1897. Calhoun's report of June 22, 1897, which is printed in Section Three, undoubtedly made a strong impression on McKinley. It presented a grim picture of conditions: "The country outside of the military posts," Calhoun reported, "was practically depopulated. Every house had been burned, banana trees cut down, cane fields swept with fire, and everything in the shape of food destroyed. . . . I did not see a house, a man, woman or child; a horse, mule or cow, not even a dog; I did not see a sign of life, except an occasional vulture or buzzard sailing through the air. The country was wrapped in the stillness of death and the silence of desolation." Calhoun concluded, "The combined effect of the policy of waste and destruction, and that of the reconcentrado, will be the complete destruction of property, and the almost total elimination of the population." Though Calhoun did not see it as within the province of his mission to make recommendations or suggestions, he could not help but remark that "there will be no permanent peace in Cuba unless she is made free commercially, if not politically."

With this and other, similar reports before him, McKinley decided to launch a diplomatic campaign to persuade the Spanish to pacify Cuba, prevent American intervention, and head off a possible war. Between June and September, 1897, therefore, as the diplomatic documents in Section Four show, McKinley asked the Spanish to ponder "whether the time has not arrived when Spain, of her own volition, moved by her own interests and by every paramount sentiment of humanity, will put a stop to this destructive war and make proposals of settlement honorable to herself and just to her Cuban colony and to mankind." If Madrid could not initiate such a policy, it was well for her to understand, as McKinley explained, that American patience with continued Spanish efforts to suppress the Cuban rebels would soon run out. The importance of this warning, according to one historian, was that once made, McKinley "could not recede from this position, . . . a fact that did not escape his notice. It may well have determined all that followed, for he permitted himself the

## Introduction

right to judge Spain's conduct and to set the speed with which she made progress."*

With the assassination of Spain's conservative Premier, Antonio Cánovas, on August 8, 1897, and the elevation to power of a Liberal government under Mateo Sagasta, Madrid gave McKinley a conciliatory answer. As indicated in the diplomatic dispatches from Minister Woodford printed in Section Five, the new Spanish government announced the recall of the notorious Governor General of Cuba, Valeriano Weyler, and promised an end to the concentration camp policy as well as a grant of autonomy to the island, a grant to be proclaimed by the Queen Regent. While McKinley did not judge these promises as assuring an end to the rebellion and full settlement of Spanish-American differences, he nevertheless informed his countrymen in December 1897 of Spain's actions "in the direction of a better understanding" and of his decision to continue a policy of watchful waiting and restraint.

McKinley fully appreciated that his advice of patience might well suffer in the light of future events. For as the documents in Section Six show, at the same time that he urged Americans to give Madrid every possible chance to carry through on her pacification program, he heard from consuls in Cuba, that autonomy was unacceptable to both the insurgents and the loyal Spaniards in the island. Moreover, McKinley knew that the Spanish continued to blame the rebellion on America's failure to enforce her neutrality laws. Believing Madrid might yet use this as an excuse to abandon pacification plans, McKinley assiduously worked through diplomatic channels to refute this interpretation.

Yet whatever the President might try, events at the beginning of 1898, as the documents in Sections Seven and Eight show, were moving beyond his control. Riots in

*H. Wayne Morgan, *America's Road to Empire: The War with Spain and Overseas Expansion* (New York, 1965), p. 28.

Havana in January 1898, led by conservative Spanish officers against moderate newspapers which favored autonomy for Cuba, produced a feeling in the American Congress that only United States intervention would assure a satisfactory settlement of the rebellion and that only intense congressional pressure would compel the President to pursue such a course. Additional support for this view came on February 9 with the publication of a purloined letter written by the Spanish Minister to the United States, Enrique Dupuy de Lôme. Describing the President as "weak and a bidder for the admiration of the crowd" and indicating that Spain, or at least De Lôme, continued to hope for a military victory over the rebels which would make a grant of Cuban autonomy unnecessary, the letter gave newspapers around the country, and particularly those like the *World* and *Journal* in New York, the chance to renew their cry for action to free Cuba from Spain's immoral rule. The congressional response was equally strong, producing on February 14 a request to the President to publish Cuban consular reports. Since congressmen knew what these reports contained, the demand upon McKinley was tantamount to an invitation to present the Congress with a request for war.

But McKinley was still unwilling to accept the necessity of American intervention and war. The events of the following month, however, changed his mind. On February 15, the American battleship *Maine* blew up in Havana harbor with a loss of 260 men. Though an American naval court of inquiry found it impossible to assign specific blame beyond the explanation that an externally exploded submarine mine caused the disaster, American political leaders and journalists insisted on Spanish culpability and the urgent need for retaliatory measures. Further, however much McKinley may have wished to resist the pressure of these jingoes, he was mindful of the fact, as the documents in Section Nine reveal, that meaningful Spanish action to settle the Cuban conflict was unlikely.

## Introduction

Since autonomy was unacceptable to the insurgents and since a grant of independence was more than the Sagasta ministry could afford to concede, the Spanish appeared to be caught in an impasse. Finally, to add to the pressure on McKinley, Senator Redfield Proctor's first-hand report in the United States Senate on March 17 of unrelieved suffering in Cuba raised sentiment for intervention to a new high. Known as a conservative in general and a skeptic about atrocity reports from Cuba in particular, Proctor reinforced the already widespread feeling that humane considerations alone dictated American intervention to free the Cubans from Spanish rule. By the last week of March, McKinley stood convinced that he must put an ultimatum before Spain.

Before he committed himself to so conclusive a step, though, the President considered its effects upon the rest of Europe. Indeed, it is likely that McKinley first asked himself whether an ultimatum to Madrid would produce a coalition of European states ready to join or aid Spain in a war against the United States. As the narrative in Section Ten drawn from Ernest May's *Imperial Democracy* shows, the European governments were too divided among themselves to confront the Americans with such a united front. Though McKinley could not have known all the details May presents, he undoubtedly had a good general sense of the European mood.

Given this knowledge, the President, as the documents in Section Eleven illustrate, announced a series of conditions on March 27 which the Spanish had to meet to prevent American intervention. Madrid was to declare an armistice unilaterally until October 1, with the President to act as a mediator in all negotiations; secondly, there was to be an immediate end to the reconcentration policy and the introduction of a relief program with American aid; thirdly, if a settlement could not be reached by October 1, the President would become the final arbiter between the rebels and Spain. Although the Spanish knew McKinley's conditions by March 27 and although Madrid stated its unwillingness by March 31 either to declare an armistice without a rebel request for one or to accept the President as a final arbiter in the dispute, McKinley, for a variety of reasons also revealed in the last section of printed documents, did not put his war message before Congress until April 11.

By then, though, the Spanish had agreed to an immediate armistice, which meant that at the time of McKinley's war message, Madrid had complied with the two most important conditions in the American note of March 27. But this was not enough to head off a war. For, as revealed in another excerpt from Ernest May's *Imperial Democracy*, McKinley's demands upon the Spanish included an implicit condition that they make Cuba independent. Because "the State Department's security procedures," May writes, "were lax enough so that reporters often read and quoted from the most confidential dispatches, [Assitant Secretary William] Day and McKinley could not afford to be explicit in advising Woodford [on March 27] that their minimum terms included one which the conservative senators had not and would not have approved. In reality, their demands were that Spain end reconcentration, proclaim an armistice, *and* acknowledge that she would make Cuba independent if the President deemed it necessary." As May also shows, at other times and in other ways, McKinley let this last condition be known to Madrid. Hence, when he reluctantly addressed a war message to the Congress on April 11, it was with the feeling that Spain would not grant a condition which he believed essential to a settlement of the Cuban problem—a problem which to his thinking if not shortly settled would divide the country and bring on "a domestic crisis tantamount . . . to revolution."

If May sees domestic political considerations at the center of McKinley's decision for war, there are other historians who do not share this point of view. Walter

*Introduction*

LaFeber, for example, takes the position that business interests were more important in shaping McKinley's thinking in March and April than any other force in the United States.

As the student finishes these readings, he would do well to remember the question raised at the start of this introduction: do these documents and interpretations clearly establish what McKinley took into account before he asked Congress for a declaration of war? The answer has implications extending beyond an explanation of McKinley's decision to use force against Spain.

# Section One

# President Grover Cleveland and the Cuban Rebellion, 1895-1897

*Commentary*

When McKinley assumed the presidency in March 1897, the Cuban rebellion against Spanish rule had been in progress for almost two years, and the American government under the stewardship of President Grover Cleveland and Secretary of State Richard Olney had already established policy lines which McKinley could not ignore. As revealed in Olney's note of April 4, 1896, Washington had already placed itself on record as being vitally interested in Spain's Cuban policy, a policy which the Secretary of State attempted to liberalize. Spain politely but firmly refused to comply with American advice. Such a reply, however, as Cleveland made clear in his last State of the Union Message in December 1896, was unsatisfactory. Explaining that "it can not be reasonably assumed that the hitherto expectant attitude of the United States will be indefinitely maintained," Cleveland warned that "the United States is not a nation to which peace is a necessity." McKinley, though a member of the opposing political party beginning a fresh administration, could not abandon Cleveland's policies without seriously injuring American prestige; at the outset of his term circumstances and his predecessor had already carried McKinley part of the way toward war.

## Secretary of State Richard Olney to Spanish Minister to the United States Dupuy de Lôme, April 4, 1896

[Walter Lowrie and Matthew St. Clair Clark, eds., *American State Papers, Foreign Relations*, 1896–97, Washington, D.C., pp. 540–44.]

*Washington, Department of State*

Sir:

It might well be deemed a dereliction of duty to the Government of the United States, as well as a censurable want of candor to that of Spain, if I were longer to defer official expression as well of the anxiety with which the President regards the existing situation in Cuba as of his earnest desire for the prompt and permanent pacification of that island. Any plan giving reasonable assurance of that result and not inconsistent with the just rights and reasonable demands of all concerned would be earnestly promoted by him by all means which the Constitution and laws of this country place at his disposal.

It is now some nine or ten months since the nature and prospects of the insurrection were first discussed between us. In explanation of its rapid and, up to that time, quite unopposed growth and progress, you called attention to the rainy season which from May or June until November renders regular military operations impracticable. Spain was pouring such numbers of troops into Cuba that your theory and opinion that, when they could be used in an active campaign, the insurrection would be almost instantly suppressed, seemed reasonable and probable. In this particular you believed, and sincerely believed, that the present insurrection would offer a most marked contrast to that which began in 1868, and which, being feebly encountered with comparatively small forces, prolonged its life for upward of ten years.

It is impossible to deny that the expectations thus entertained by you in the summer and fall of 1895, and shared not merely by all Spaniards but by most disinterested observers as well, have been completely disappointed. The insurgents seem to-day to command a larger part of the island than ever before. Their men under arms, estimated a year ago at from ten to twenty thousand, are now conceded to be at least two or three times as many. Meanwhile, their discipline has been improved and their supply of modern weapons and equipment has been greatly enlarged, while the mere fact that they have held out to this time has given them confidence in their own eyes and prestige with the world at large. In short, it can hardly be questioned that the insurrection, instead of being quelled, is to-day more formidable than ever, and enters upon the second year of its existence with decidedly improved prospects of successful results.

Whether a condition of things entitling the insurgents to recognition as belligerents has yet been brought about may, for the purposes of the present communication, be regarded as immaterial. If it has not been, it is because they are still without an established and organized civil government, having an ascertained situs, presiding over a defined territory, controlling the armed forces in the field, and not only fulfilling the functions of a regular government within its own frontiers, but capable internationally of exercising those powers and discharging those obligations which necessarily devolve upon every member of the family of nations. It is immaterial for present purposes that such is the present political status of the insurgents, because their defiance of the authority of Spain remains none the less pronounced and successful, and their displacement of that authority throughout a very large portion of the island is nonetheless obvious and real.

\* \* \*

The consequences of this state of things can not be disguised. Outside of the towns still under Spanish rule, anarchy, lawlessness, and terrorism are rampant. The insurgents realize that the wholesale destruction of crops, factories, and machinery advances their cause in two ways. It cripples the resources of Spain on the one hand. On the other, it drives into their ranks the laborers who are thus thrown out of employment. The result is a systematic war upon the industries of the island and upon all the means by which they are carried on, and whereas the normal annual product of the island is valued at something like eighty or a hundred millions, its value for the present year is estimated by competent authority as not exceeding twenty millions.

Bad as is this showing for the present year, it must be even worse for the next year and for every succeeding year during which the rebellion continues to live. Some planters have made their crops this year who will not be allowed to make them again. Some have worked their fields and operated their mills this year in the face of a certain loss who have neither the heart nor the means to do so again under the present even more depressing conditions. Not only is it certain that no fresh money is being invested on the island, but it is no secret that capital is fast withdrawing from it, frightened away by the utter hopelessness of the outlook. Why should it not be? What can a prudent man foresee as the outcome of existing conditions except the complete destruction of the island, the entire annihilation of its industries, and the absolute impoverishment of such of its inhabitants as are unwise or unfortunate enough not to seasonably escape from it?

\* \* \*

Such a conclusion of the struggle can not be viewed

even by the most devoted friend of Cuba and the most enthusiastic advocate of popular government except with the gravest apprehension. There are only two strong reasons to fear that, once Spain were withdrawn from the island, the sole bond of union between the different factions of the insurgents would disappear; that a war of races would be precipitated, all the more sanguinary for the discipline and experience acquired during the insurrection, and that, even if there were to be temporary peace, it could only be through the establishment of a white and a black republic, which, even if agreeing at the outset upon a division of the island between them, would be enemies from the start, and would never rest until the one had been completely vanquished and subdued by the other.

The situation thus described is of great interest to the people of the United States. They are interested in any struggle for freer political institutions, but necessarily and in special measure in a struggle that is raging almost in sight of our shores. They are interested, as a civilized and Christian nation, in the speedy termination of a civil strife characterized by exceptional bitterness and exceptional excesses on the part of both combatants. They are interested in the noninterruption of extensive trade relations which have been and should continue to be of great advantage to both countries. They are interested in the prevention of that wholesale destruction of property on the island which, making no discrimination between enemies and neutrals, is utterly destroying American investments that should be of immense value, and is utterly impoverishing great numbers of American citizens.

On all these grounds and in all these ways the interest of the United States in the existing situation in Cuba yields in extent only to that of Spain herself, and has led many good and honest persons to insist that intervention to terminate the conflict is the immediate and imperative duty of the United States. It is not proposed now to consider whether existing conditions would justify such intervention at the present time, or how much longer those conditions should be endured before such intervention would be justified. That the United States can not contemplate with complacency another ten years of Cuban insurrection, with all its injurious and distressing incidents, may certainly be taken for granted.

The object of the present communication, however, is not to discuss intervention, nor to propose intervention, nor to pave the way for intervention. The purpose is exactly the reverse—to suggest whether a solution of present troubles can not be found which will prevent all thought of intervention by rendering it unnecessary. What the United States desires to do, if the way can be pointed out, is to cooperate with Spain in the immediate pacification of the island on such a plan as, leaving Spain her rights of sovereignty, shall yet secure to the people of the island all such rights and powers of local self-government as they can reasonably ask. To that end the United States offers and will use her good offices at such time and in such manner as may be deemed most advisable. Its mediation, it is believed, should not be rejected in any quarter, since none could misconceive or mistrust its purpose.

Spain could not, because our respect for her sovereignty and our determination to do nothing to impair it have been maintained for many years at great cost and in spite of many temptations. The insurgents could not, because anything assented to by this Government which did not satsify the reasonable demands and aspirations of Cuba would arouse the indignation of our whole people. It only remains to suggest that, if anything can be done in the direction indicated, it should be done at once and on the initiative of Spain.

The more the contest is prolonged, the more bitter and more irreconcilable is the antagonism created, while there is danger that concessions may be so delayed as to be chargeable to weakness and fear of the issue of the contest, and thus be infinitely less acceptable and persuasive than if made while the result still hangs in the balance, and they could be properly credited in some degree at least to a sense of right and justice. Thus far Spain has faced the insurrection sword in hand, and has made no sign to show that surrender and submission would be followed by anything but a return to the old order of things. Would it not be wise to modify that policy and to accompany the application of military force with an authentic declaration of the organic changes that are meditated in the administration of the island with a view to remove all just grounds of complaint?

It is for Spain to consider and determine what those changes would be. But should they be such that the United States could urge their adoption, as substantially removing well-founded grievances, its influence would be exerted for their acceptance, and it can hardly be doubted, would be most potential for the termination of hostilities and the restoration of peace and order to the island. One result of the course of proceeding outlined, if no other, would be sure to follow, namely, that the rebellion would lose largely, if not altogether, the moral countenance and support it now enjoys from the people of the United States.

In closing this communication it is hardly necessary to repeat that it is prompted by the friendliest feelings toward Spain and the Spanish people. To attribute to the United States any hostile or hidden purposes would be a grave and most lamentable error. The United States has no designs upon Cuba and no designs against the sovereignty of Spain. Neither is it actuated by any spirit of meddlesomeness nor by any desire to force its will upon another nation. Its geographical proximity and all the considerations above detailed compel it to be interested in the solution of the Cuban problem whether it will or no. Its only anxiety is that that solution should be speedy, and, by being founded on truth and justice, should also be permanent.

To aid in that solution it offers the suggestions herein

contained. They will be totally misapprehended unless the United States be credited with entertaining no other purpose toward Spain than that of lending its assistance to such termination of a fratricidal contest as will leave her honor and dignity unimpaired at the same time that it promotes and conserves the true interests of all parties concerned.

              I avail, etc.,

                          RICHARD OLNEY

## De Lôme to Olney
## June 4, 1896

[*Foreign Relations*, 1896–97, pp. 544–48.]

*Washington, Legation of Spain*

Mr. Secretary:

As I had the honor to inform your excellency some time ago, I lost no time in communicating to the minister of state of His Majesty the King of Spain the text of the note that your excellency was pleased to address to me, under date of the 4th of April last, in regard to the events that are taking place in the island of Cuba.

In his answer, dated May 22 last, the Duke of Tetuan [the Foreign Minister] tells me that the importance of the communication here referred to has led the Government of His Majesty to examine it with the greatest care and to postpone an answer until such time as its own views on the complicated and delicate Cuban question should be officially made public.

The minister of state adds that since the extensive and liberal purposes of Spain toward Cuba have been laid before the Cortes by the august lips of His Majesty in the speech from the throne, the previous voluntary decisions of the Spanish Government in the matter may serve, as

## President Cleveland and the Cuban Rebellion

they are now serving, as the basis of a reply to your excellency's note.

The Government of His Majesty appreciates to its full value the noble frankness with which that of the United States has informed it of the very definite opinion it has formed in regard to the legal impossibility of granting the recognition of belligerency to the Cuban insurgents.

\* \* \*

His Majesty's Government has read with no less gratification the explicit and spontaneous declarations to the effect that the Government of the United States seeks no advantage in connection with the Cuban question, its only wish being that the ineluctable and lawful sovereignty of Spain be maintained and even strengthened, through the submission of the rebels, which, as your excellency states in your note, is of paramount necessity to the Spanish Government for the maintenance of its authority and its honor.

\* \* \*

The Government of His Majesty and the people of Spain wish and even long for the speedy pacification of Cuba. In order to secure it, they are ready to exert their best efforts and at the same time to adopt such reforms as may be useful or necessary and compatible, of course, with their inalienable sovereignty, as soon as the submission of the insurgents be an accomplished fact.

The minister of state, while directing me to bring to the knowledge of your excellency the foregoing views, instructs me to remark how pleased he was to observe that his opinion on this point also agrees with yours.

No one is more fully aware of the serious evils suffered by Spaniards and aliens in consequence of the insurrection than the Government of His Majesty. It realizes the immense injury inflicted on Spain by the putting forth, with the unanimous cooperation and approbation of her people, of such efforts as were never before made in America by any European country. It knows at the same time that the interests of foreign industry and trade suffer, as well as the Spanish interests, from the insurgent system of devastation; but if the insurrection should triumph, the interests of all would not merely suffer, but would entirely and forever disappear amid the madness of perpetual anarchy.

It has already been said that, in order to prevent evils of such magnitude, the cabinet of Madrid does not and will not confine itself exclusively to the employment of armed force.

The speech from the throne, read before the national representatives, formally promised motu proprio, not only that all that was previously granted, voted by the Cortes, and sanctioned by His Majesty on the 15th of March, 1895, would be carried into effect as soon as the opportunity offered, but also by fresh authorization of the Cortes, all the new extensions and amendments of the original reforms, to the end that both islands may in the administrative department possess a personnel of a local character, that the intervention of the mother country in their domestic concerns may be dispensed with, with the single reservation that nothing will be done to impair the rights of sovereignty or the powers of the Government to preserve the same.

This solemn promise, guaranteed by the august word of His Majesty, will be fulfilled by the Spanish Government with a true liberality of views.

The foregoing facts, being better known every day, will make it patent to the fair people of other nations that Spain, far from proposing that her subjects in the West Indies should return to a régime unfit for the times when she enjoys such liberal laws, would never have withheld these same laws from the islands, had it not been for the increasing separatist conspiracies which compelled her to look above all to self-defense.

The Government of His Majesty most heartily thanks that of the United States for the kind advice it bestows on Spain; but it wishes to state, and entertains the con-

## President Cleveland and the Cuban Rebellion

fidence that your excellency will readily see, that it has been forestalling it for a long time past. It follows, therefore, as a matter of course, that it will comply with it in a practical manner as soon as circumstances make it possible.

Your excellency will have seen, nevertheless, how the announcement of this concurrence of views has been received.

The insurgents, elated by the strength which they have acquired through the aid of a certain number of citizens of the United States, have contemptuously repelled, by the medium of the Cubans residing in this Republic, any idea that the Government of Washington can intervene in the contest, either with its advice or in any other manner, on the supposition that the declarations of disinterestedness on the part of the Government of the United States are false and that it wishes to get possession of the island one of these days. Hence it is evident that no success would attend such possible mediation, which they repel, even admitting that the mother country would condescend to treat with its rebellious subject as one power with another, thus surely jeopardizing its future authority, detracting from its national dignity, and impairing its independence for which it has at all times shown such great earnestness, as history teaches. In brief, there is no effectual way to pacify Cuba unless it begins with the actual submission of the armed rebels to the mother country.

Notwithstanding this, the Government of the United States could, by the use of proper means, contribute greatly to the pacification of the Island of Cuba.

The Government of His Majesty is already very grateful to that of the United States for its intention to prosecute the unlawful expeditions to Cuba of some of its citizens with more vigor than in the past, after making a judicial investigation as to the adequacy of its laws when honestly enforced.

Still, the high moral sense of the Government of Washington will undoubtedly suggest to it other more effectual means of preventing henceforth what is now the case, a struggle which is going on so near its frontiers, and which is proving so injurious to its industry and commerce, a fact justly deplored by your excellency, being prolonged so exclusively by the powerful assistance which the rebellion finds in the territory of this great Republic, against the wishes of all those who love order and law.

The constant violation of international law in its territory is especially manifest on the part of Cuban emigrants, who care nothing for the losses suffered in the meanwhile by the citizens of the United States and of Spain through the prolongation of the war.

The Spanish Government, on its part, has done much and will do more every day in order to achieve such a desirable end, by endeavoring to correct the mistakes of public opinion in the United States and by exposing the plots and calumnies of its rebellious subjects.

It may well happen that the declarations recently made in the most solemn form by the Government of His Majesty concerning its intentions for the future will also contribute in a large measure to gratify the wish that your excellency clearly expressed in your note, namely—that all the people of the United States, convinced that we are in the right, will completely cease to extend unlawful aid to the insurgents.

* * *

When the Government of the United States shall once be convinced of our being in the right, and when that honest conviction shall in some manner be made public, but little more will be required in order that all those in Cuba who are not merely striving to accomplish the total ruin of the beautiful country in which they were born, being then hopeless of outside help and powerless by themselves, will lay down their arms.

Until that happy state of things has been attained Spain will, in the just defense not only of her rights but also of her duty and honor, continue the efforts for an early victory which she is now exerting regardless of the greatest sacrifices.

*   *   *

## President Grover Cleveland's Fourth State of the Union Message December 7, 1896

[F. Israel, ed., *The State of the Union Messages of the Presidents* (New York, 1967), vol. 2, pp. 1826–32.]

. . . The insurrection in Cuba still continues with all its perplexities. It is difficult to perceive that any progress has thus far been made toward the pacification of the island or that the situation of affairs as depicted in my last annual message has in the least improved. If Spain still holds Havana and the seaports and all the considerable towns, the insurgents still roam at will over at least two-thirds of the inland country. If the determination of Spain to put down the insurrection seems but to strengthen with the lapse of time and is evinced by her unhesitating devotion of largely increased military and naval forces to the task, there is much reason to believe that the insurgents have gained in point of numbers and character and resources and are nonetheless inflexible in their resolve not to succumb without practically securing the great objects for which they took up arms. If Spain has not yet reestablished her authority, neither have the insurgents yet made good their title to be regarded as an independent state. Indeed, as the contest has gone on, the pretense that civil government exists on the island, except so far as Spain is able to maintain it, has been practically abandoned.

Spain does keep on foot such a government, more or less imperfectly, in the large towns and their immediate suburbs; but that exception being made, the entire country is either given over to anarchy or is subject to the military occupation of one or the other party. It is reported, indeed, on reliable authority that at the demand of the commander in chief of the insurgent army the putative Cuban government has now given up all attempt to exercise its functions, leaving that government confessedly (what there is the best reason for supposing it always to have been in fact) a government merely on paper.

Were the Spanish armies able to meet their antagonists in the open or in pitched battle, prompt and decisive results might be looked for, and the immense superiority of the Spanish forces in numbers, discipline, and equipment could hardly fail to tell greatly to their advantage. But they are called upon to face a foe that shuns general engagements, that can choose and does choose its own ground, that from the nature of the country is visible or invisible at pleasure, and that fights only from ambuscade and when all the advantages of position and numbers are on its side. In a country where all that is indispensable to life in the way of food, clothing, and shelter is so easily obtainable, especially by those born and bred on the soil, it is obvious that there is hardly a limit to the time during which hostilities of this sort may be prolonged. Meanwhile, as in all cases of protracted civil strife, the passions of the combatants grow more and more inflamed and excesses on both sides become more frequent and more deplorable. They are also participated in by bands of marauders, who, now in the name of one party and now in the name of the other, as may best suit the occasion, harry the country at will and plunder its wretched inhabitants for their own advantage. Such a condition of things would inevitably entail immense destruction of property, even if it were the policy of both parties to prevent it as far as practicable; but while such seemed to be the original policy of the Spanish Government, it has now apparently abandoned it and is acting upon the same theory as the insurgents, namely, that the exigencies of the contest require the wholesale annihilation of property that it may not prove of use and advantage to the enemy.

It is to the same end that, in pursuance of general orders, Spanish garrisons are now being withdrawn from plantations and the rural population required to concentrate itself in the towns. The sure result would seem to be that the industrial value of the island is fast diminishing and that unless there is a speedy and radical change in existing conditions it will soon disappear altogether. That value consists very largely, of course, in its capacity to produce sugar—a capacity already much reduced by the interruptions to tillage which have taken place during the last two years. It is reliably asserted that should these interruptions continue during the current year, and practically extend, as is now threatened, to the entire sugar-producing territory of the island, so much time and so much money will be required to restore the land to its normal productiveness that it is extremely doubtful if capital can be induced to even make the attempt.

The spectacle of the utter ruin of an adjoining country, by nature one of the most fertile and charming on the globe, would engage the serious attention of the Government and people of the United States in any circumstances. In point of fact, they have a concern with it which is by no means of a wholly sentimental or philanthropic character. It lies so near to us as to be hardly separated from our territory. Our actual pecuniary interest in it is second only to that of the people and Government of Spain. It is reasonably estimated that at least from $30,000,000 to $50,000,000 of American capital are invested in plantations and in railroad, mining, and other business enterprises on the island. The volume of trade between the United States and Cuba, which in 1889 amounted to about $64,000,000, rose in 1893 to about

$103,000,000, and in 1894, the year before the present insurrection broke out, amounted to nearly $96,000,000. Besides this large pecuniary stake in the fortunes of Cuba, the United States finds itself inextricably involved in the present contest in other ways, both vexatious and costly.

Many Cubans reside in this country, and indirectly promote the insurrection through the press, by public meetings, by the purchase and shipment of arms, by the raising of funds, and by other means which the spirit of our institutions and the tenor of our laws do not permit to be made the subject of criminal prosecutions. Some of them, though Cubans at heart and in all their feelings and interests, have taken out papers as naturalized citizens of the United States—a proceeding resorted to with a view to possible protection by this Government, and not unnaturally regarded with much indignation by the country of their origin. The insurgents are undoubtedly encouraged and supported by the widespread sympathy the people of this country always and instinctively feel for every struggle for better and freer government, and which, in the case of the more adventurous and restless elements of our population, leads in only too many instances to active and personal participation in the contest. The result is that this Government is constantly called upon to protect American citizens, to claim damages for injuries to persons and property, now estimated at many millions of dollars, and to ask explanations and apologies for the acts of Spanish officials whose zeal for the repression of rebellion sometimes blinds them to the immunities belonging to the unoffending citizens of a friendly power. It follows from the same causes that the United States is compelled to actively police a long line of seacoast against unlawful expeditions, the escape of which the utmost vigilance will not always suffice to prevent.

These inevitable entanglements of the United States with the rebellion in Cuba, the large American property interests affected, and considerations of philanthropy and humanity in general have led to a vehement demand in various quarters for some sort of positive intervention on the part of the United States. It was at first proposed that belligerent rights should be accorded to the insurgents—a proposition no longer urged because untimely and in practical operation clearly perilous and injurious to our own interests. It has since been and is now sometimes contended that the independence of the insurgents should be recognized; but imperfect and restricted as the Spanish government of the island may be, no other exists there, unless the will of the military officer in temporary command of a particular district can be dignified as a species of government. It is now also suggested that the United States should buy the island—a suggestion possibly worthy of consideration if there were any evidence of a desire or willingness on the part of Spain to entertain such a proposal. It is urged finally that, all other methods failing, the existing internecine strife in Cuba should be terminated by our intervention, even at the cost of a war between the United States and Spain—a war which its advocates confidently prophesy could neither be large in its proportions nor doubtful in its issue.

❋   ❋   ❋

The correctness of this forecast need be neither affirmed nor denied. The United States has, nevertheless, a character to maintain as a nation, which plainly dictates that right and not might should be the rule of its conduct. Further, though the United States is not a nation to which peace is a necessity, it is in truth the most pacific of powers and desires nothing so much as to live in amity with all the world.

❋   ❋   ❋

# Section Two

# Congressional Pressure

*Commentary*

Like Cleveland, McKinley found moral, economic and political reasons to seek an end to the Cuban rebellion: stories of Spanish brutality and Cuban suffering aroused his moral indignation; American property losses had economic consequences which he could not long ignore; and political difficulties with congressional Democrats and Republicans made it imperative that he find some means of influencing Spanish conduct. As illustrated by the following excerpts from the discussion of April 6, 1897, in the United States Senate, it was the hope of jingoes like John T. Morgan of Alabama (Dem.) to force the President into official recognition of a Cuban rebellion and possibly even stronger action.

*United States Senate*
*April 6, 1897*

[*Congressional Record*, vol. 30, pt. 1, April 6, 1897, pp. 615–16, 618, 620–21.]

MR. MORGAN [DEM., ALA.]. I rise to a parliamentary inquiry.

THE VICE-PRESIDENT [GARRET HOBART]. The Senator from Alabama will state his parliamentary inquiry.

MR. MORGAN. Yesterday the Senate gave its unanimous consent that the joint resolution I introduced on the 1st instant should go over for consideration this morning. I desire to have it laid before the Senate.

THE VICE-PRESIDENT. The joint resolution is in order.

The Senate, as in Committee of the Whole, proceeded to consider the joint resolution (S.R. 26) declaring that a condition of public war exists in Cuba, and that strict neutrality shall be maintained.

MR. MORGAN. Let the joint resolution be read.

The joint resolution was read, as follows:

*Resolved by the Senate and House of Representatives, etc.,* That a condition of public war exists between the Government of Spain and the government proclaimed and for some time maintained by force of arms by the people of Cuba, and that the United States of America shall maintain a strict neutrality between the contending powers, according to each all the rights of belligerents in the ports and territory of the United States.

*   *   *

MR. MORGAN. A question of war or peace between this country and any foreign country, or a question of the existence of a war in any foreign country, is a matter of such grave importance to all the people of the United States that its consideration should always be entered upon with the utmost degree of deliberation and solemnity, and, as far as possible, it should be free from all the exasperations of feeling that we of course have when quarrels occur between us and other powers. It is in this view, and in this sense, and with this purpose, and only this, that I approach the subject this morning.

I do not wish to create a ferment in the United States about it. It is not necessary to do that, Mr.

President, if I were disposed to get up some public excitement, because the mind of the people of the United States is agitated and all their hearts are full of this subject. We are in the midst of a very trying situation that has never heretofore existed as it exists now. All the aggravations that surround us at this moment and the same sense of indignation have never heretofore existed, even in the various and frequent irritations that have occurred between Spain and the United States on the subject of her government in Cuba. We have tried so to feel, we have tried to so believe, and we have so conformed our conduct that it is a matter of indifference to us whether Spain shall persecute her own subjects in Cuba or not. I say we have tried to feel it and we have tried to believe it. At the same time the history of Spanish occupation in Cuba from the beginning of this century, and, indeed, far back of that period of time—but I will say from the beginning of this century, because our Government became concerned in it about that time—the history of Spanish occupation in Cuba has been so full of that absolute and heartless spirit of tyranny toward her own subjects as that it is not to be expected that a country organized as ours is, upon the basis of self-government and of the respect that is due from the Government to the citizen, should be free from very profound agitation, in view of the repeated and flagrant and very outrageous demonstrations of persecution that have been made by the Crown of Spain against her own subjects in the Island of Cuba.

*    *    *

Our people have suffered in one respect a degree of mortification and humiliation as well as a degree of personal distress that it has always been within the power of our Government to prevent. If the Government of the United States had taken care of its own people in the island of Cuba according to the full measure of its duty, many a life would have been saved in the former struggles and in the present one, much property would have been spared from destruction, great anguish of feeling would have been spared to our people, both native born and adopted. But the Government of the United States has not taken proper care of her own people in Cuba, and it is time that we begin to do so.

The object of the introduction of the joint resolution which is before the Senate to-day is to put the Government of the United States in a proper legal attitude toward the Government of Spain in Cuba, and to enable us simply to take care of our own citizens. I have always declared that this was my leading motive, and in fact my exclusive motive, as a Senator of the United States, in whatever support I have given to measures here in respect of our controversies and difficulties with Spain in the Island of Cuba. I have kept my mind fixed firmly and exclusively upon the duty of the Government of the United States to the citizens of the United States in the presence of this state of facts. I am trying to get from the Congress of the United States—and I hope the Executive will concur with us—a definition and statement of a legal status or situation which makes it possible for us, under the laws of nations, to protect the lives and property of our people in the Island of Cuba.

In accomplishing this result, Mr. President, it may turn out—and I would be very glad that it should —that assistance will be given to the people of the Island of Cuba in the establishment of their independence, in freeing themselves from an abominable yoke, which, so far as they are concerned, has never resulted in any benefit to the people there at all, but has been imposed upon them and maintained over them for the mere purpose of leeching out of them their substance and of keeping them as serfs and feudatories to the Crown of Spain and to the nobility and gentry of that country. I should be very glad that a result of that sort should follow; but whether that result shall follow, or one still more disastrous to the people of Cuba, nevertheless it is a duty that we can not abdicate to take care, so far as in us lies, of our people in that island.

In what way can we do that? That is the question which comes up here now. Can we do it by standing by and witnessing these wrongs inflicted upon them continually, aggressively, and redress them only by filing claims in the Department of State, to be urged against the Spanish Government after the war has ended and after Spain has become bankrupt? Can we accomplish this protection of our citizens by putting a price upon their blood and their sufferings, and by saying to Spain that "in the end of all of this, after the war is over, we shall charge up so many dollars and cents against you for these ruined and destroyed Americans, men, women, and children, and for their property"? In the former war we waited for ten years, and after the termination of that struggle we sent in our account, and we had a part of it allowed and a part of it disallowed, and the part that was allowed was only paid within the last two or three years. That has been nearly thirty years ago.

Now, can we afford to stand by here and see repeated, in a form that has become historic in Cuba, these wrongs and outrages against our own people, trusting to the settlement of an account for damages after the wrong has been done? . . . Shall we refuse to protect our people and deny to ourselves the right, the power, the opportunity, and the duty of providing for them as this struggle goes on?

Well, Mr. President, I hope that the Senate of

## Congressional Pressure 23

the United States at least will not agree that it is our duty to ignore these things, to pass them by silently and quietly. I hope that the expression on the part of the Senate will be now what it has been heretofore, a year ago, and still earlier than that—that we recognize the existence of public war in Cuba, attended with all the consequences under the laws of nations that belong to that legal situation; that we will stand neutral between these parties, and that we will execute the laws of neutrality, and especially those laws of neutrality which protect our own people.

* * *

Does war now exist in Cuba? Mr. President, that is a proposition that is absolutely so undebatable, so far beyond the domain of discussion, that I can not see how any sensible man can take it up for consideration when the answer lies immediately before him in every act that has occurred in the Island of Cuba within the past two years, and for a period much longer than that. With the vast army that Spain has sent there, with the drain upon her resources that is now threatening to bankrupt the kingdom, with a loss of thousands and tens of thousands of lives, with an opposing army which in the former revolution for the same causes never reached more than 10,000 men—volunteer soldiers—now reaching to the number of fifty or sixty thousand, with battle after battle fought in every part of that island, and with the occupation of that island from east to west, except in the larger, fortified towns, with the whole body of the country included within the lines of the Cuban army or within the power of their military influence—it is absolutely inadmissible, in view of those facts, to enter upon a discussion of that question. It is so palpable that no man in his senses, it seems to me, can possibly deny it.

* * *

... Here, then, is a war, flagrant and terrible, which has existed in the Island of Cuba for two years, and we want to know what are the rights of our people in that island, on the high seas, and in the United States, as they are affected by that war. We want to know what are their rights of property and their rights of commerce as they are affected by that war. We want to take some course in the Congress of the United States that will give to them every proper shelter and protection. That is what I understand we want to do, and if we do not accomplish that we ought at least to make the effort.

\* \* \*

The matter of the belligerency of a country foreign to us, recognized by the Government of the United States in whatever form the Government can make the recognition, seems to produce upon the minds of some people who try to comprehend it a sort of paralysis, and they imagine that there is something in it very profound and very obscure, hard to be understood, and still more difficult to be defined. Mr. President, it seems to me there is no difficulty in the matter. It is the simplest of all problems connected with our relations with foreign countries.

\* \* \*

... The declaration of belligerency on the part of the Government of the United States is not a hostile act. We did not complain of any hostility at the time Spain recognized the belligerency of the Confederate States, nor when Great Britain recognized their belligerency, although at that time there was very strong reason to believe, especially in the case of Great Britain, that their recognition of the belligerency of the Confederate States was in response to what they believed was the sentiment of the South that we would divide the Union and put ourselves under the

British flag. Yet the Government of the United States did not say to the Government of Great Britain, "That act on your part is a belligerent or an unfriendly act." By all means we did not say such a thing to Spain when she recognized the belligerency of the Confederate States. Then, if you recognize the belligerency of the Cubans, how can Spain say, in virtue of all the facts that have occurred there within the last two years and still exist, that a declaration of belligerency of the parties engaged in open war in Cuba is a hostile act toward Spain? It is impossible, Mr. President. A declaration of that sort on her part would be a mere pretext. She could not make the declaration in good faith.

\* \* \*

MR. HALE [REP., ME.]. Mr. President—

THE PRESIDING OFFICER. Does the Senator from Alabama yield to the Senator from Maine?

MR. MORGAN. Certainly.

MR. HALE. What evidence has the Senator to back up the statement he has made two or three times that prisons, places of incarceration, in Cuba are to-day filled with American citizens? I may say that I do not believe that to be the fact. I do not believe there is any evidence producible which establishes that fact, but of course I may be wrong; and I ask the Senator to state to the Senate what he has upon which to base his repeated statement that we ought to interfere now for the protection of the American citizens who lie in incarceration improperly on the Island of Cuba.

MR. MORGAN. In answer to the question of the honorable Senator from Maine, I must resort to a method of argumentation or statement which I understand is customary in the part of the country which he represents, and that is to answer one question by asking another. I should like to know of the Senator from Maine on what ground he predicates what he says is his belief that these statements are untrue? What information has he got and from whom? Who has denied it?

MR. HALE. I deny it.

MR. MORGAN. Who else?

MR. HALE. The Senator is an old—

MR. MORGAN. No; I'm not very old.

MR. HALE. And a very good lawyer. He is a young man in vigor—

MR. MORGAN. Oh, very.

MR. HALE. In power, and in earnestness; and he knows, as you know, Mr. President, and everybody knows, that it is the side which propounds the proposition that has got to report testimony and give evidence. I do not believe that the prisons of the Spanish authorities in Cuba are to-day filled with American citizens who are languishing in imprisonment, and making a reason why we should interpose down there. I have seen no testimony which shows that to be the case. I am willing that the State Department, which is the organ of the Government to consider these things, shall investigate that matter. I am willing that the Senator should go to the State Department and ask if that Department has evidence to this effect. I should like them to produce from the State Department papers, documents, and proofs, if he has them, of the proposition he maintains. But it is not for me, when I am doubtful and skeptical of these statements, to be asked to furnish my proofs. The Senator must furnish proofs.

MR. MORGAN. I accept very cheerfully indeed the onus probandi of any fact whatever that will relieve the honorable Senator from Maine from any unhappiness on account of his friends in Spain. I would hate to afflict him with any idea that a Spaniard is capable of any cruelty whatever. I would hate in his presence to refer to the transactions of the Duke of Alva, or to the Spanish Inquisition, or to the orders that are here which require the sacrifice by shooting and death and otherwise in any form—orders of General Weyler and formerly of Balmaceda—orders, Mr. President, that Secretary Fish, General Grant, and others said were a disgrace to humanity, a shock to the human sensibilities. I would dislike very much indeed to afflict the honorable Senator from Maine with any unhappiness at all in his supposition that there are perhaps no characters in the world so innocent as the Spaniards. I might prosecute that inquiry in the same direction and ask him why it is that he believes, as I know he does, that the Armenians have been sacrificed in Turkey. What evidence has the Senator that the Armenians have ever been butchered in Turkey?

MR. HALE. I do not want the Senator to escape from my question—

THE PRESIDING OFFICER. Does the Senator from Alabama yield to the Senator from Maine?

MR. MORGAN. Oh, yes.

MR. HALE. I do not want the Senator from Alabama to escape my question, which relates directly to the subject-matter of this debate, by references to the Duke of Alva, or to Spanish history in the past, or to the Armenians, or the Abyssinians, or what not. I want him to give the Senate some authority for his statement that one reason why we should intervene is because the Spanish prisons in Cuba to-day are stuffed with American citizens who languish in imprisonment there. My information is just the reverse. My information and my belief is that in the last six months, notably in the last six weeks, in every case where the proper authorities of the Government to whom are intrusted and who manage our diplomatic relations have intervened for the release of American citizens in Spanish prisons in Cuba the response has been at once made in a friendly tone, and that many, and nearly all, and for aught I know all, who have been arrested have been freed. I do not say that all have. But when the Senator says that those prisons are filled with American citizens I can only say that I do not believe it. I do not believe that the Senator is making a statement that he knows to be false. I do not think that he has complete information on the subject. And my attitude of doubtfulness in this matter is not in any way caused by friendship that I have for Spain. I care nothing about that. I am only seeking to adopt the course of proceedings in this case which is in accordance with the long record of diplomacy in this country for a hundred years, which has been not inflammatory, but conservative at every point where it can be reached.

MR. MORGAN. Now, if the honorable Senator has got done making his speech, which is all right, I will proceed and answer him as well as I can, and seriatum, too.

The Senator insists that he does not believe a word of this thing, that the Spanish prisons are stuffed with American prisoners. Perhaps the word "stuffed" grates upon the sensibilities of the Senator, and I will take that back and say "crowded," for I suppose that, according to the statements made by those who have come from there here, who are reputable people and who have made their statements to the State Department and also to the public press, as many as twenty prisoners confined in a room that is 19 feet long by 7 feet wide, without a place to lie down or a bench to sit upon, and with all of the inconveniences that it is possible to conceive of in such a situation, would be in rather a crowded state; and American citizens testify when they come out

## Congressional Pressure 29

that that is true. There is sworn testimony before this body now in the form of depositions that have been given before the Committee on Foreign Relations which proves these facts. That the Senator from Maine does not believe that is not shocking to me, for I do not think the Senator is capable of believing anything that casts the slightest impeachment in the world upon a Spaniard. I repeat, he seems to have some holy idea of the Spanish character which forbids him to acknowledge that under any circumstances one of these saintly murderers could have any harm or malice in his bosom.

MR. HALE. Now, let me say right there—

MR. MORGAN. No; I object. I am answering you now.

THE PRESIDING OFFICER. The Senator from Alabama declines to yield.

MR. HALE. I can not, of course, interrupt the Senator except by his consent.

MR. MORGAN. I am answering your argument now, and I object to any more interruptions on this subject.

Mr. President, we have a newspaper press in the United States, and I am very glad that we have, because through that agency we have acquired knowledge of what goes on in Cuba and elsewhere in the world, even in Armenia. In the main it turns out that the consensus of statement made by the American press in respect to a matter occurring in a foreign country is true. At all events, when they all concur in making a series of statements with one accord, it will put even the Senator from Maine upon the defensive to make some explanation or some statement on the subject. He says he has informed himself and does not believe what these papers state. When I ask him who his informant is, he declines to answer. I know who it is, and the world knows who it is. The Senator from Maine can not conceal the fact that he is in constant communication with the Spanish Government for the purpose of ascertaining the best way of defending them.

MR. HALE. Let me ask the Senator to repeat that statement.

THE PRESIDING OFFICER. Does the Senator from Alabama yield?

MR. HALE. I was talking with the Senator from Indiana and I did not hear what the Senator said.

MR. MORGAN. I stated that the Senator from Maine had said that he had sources of information which convinced him that these statements were untrue. Now, what are they?

MR. HALE. Not one single item of information that I have received as to the condition in Cuba comes from the Spanish authorities or any representative of them. I have talked with man after man who has visited Cuba within the last six months. I have letters, correspondence, and statements that, if this debate continues, I shall put before the Senate, showing my authority; and they come not from Spanish authorities, but from actual American citizens, with American names, American descent, American experience, and American residence.

MR. MORGAN. This statement that the Senator has made at last discloses where his sources of information come from. Do they contradict what the American papers say?

MR. HALE. They do not contradict what the American people say, but they contradict very squarely what the Senator from Alabama says; and I do not recognize that the Senator from Alabama, in seeking to inflame this condition and to bring about a condition of hostilities, represents the American people, Mr. President, by a great deal.

MR. MORGAN. It is a matter of indifference to me what the Senator thinks that I represent, Mr. President. I speak from what the American press has said here, and every man in this body knows what it is. The

American press has uniformly stated that not only were there many prisoners whose names were known in the prison houses of Habana, men and women, and even little children, but that there were very many whose names were entirely unknown to the world.

THE PRESIDING OFFICER. The hour of 2 o'clock having arrived, it is the duty of the Chair to lay before the Senate the unfinished business, which will be stated by the Secretary.

THE SECRETARY. A bill (S. 1035) to establish uniform laws on the subject of bankruptcies throughout the United States.

MR. HALE. If agreeable to the Senator from Massachusetts who has charge of the bankruptcy bill, I ask that the Senator from Alabama, if it is his preference to go on to-day, be allowed to proceed, laying aside the regular order temporarily and finishing his speech. I leave that to the Senator from Alabama.

MR. STEWART [REP., NEV.]. He can finish his speech to-morrow.

MR. HALE. That is as the Senator from Alabama prefers.

MR. MORGAN. I have no personal preference on the subject at all. At some time during this debate I intend to ask a vote of the Senate to proceed to the consideration of the joint resolution, whatever else may interfere, unless it is an appropriation bill, and I do not expect it to be very long before we reach that stage, because one thing or the other ought to be done—we ought either to make this declaration or we ought to drop the subject. We should let Mr. McKinley understand that he is to run this business without any advice or admonition on the part of the Congress of the United States, absolutely according to his own judgment, or else we should advise him that in our opinion a state of war exists in Cuba and that it is our duty to recognize it.

# Section Three

# Report of McKinley's Personal Envoy

*Commentary*

Since, as illustrated in the previous document, some uncertainty existed as to Spanish treatment of Americans in Cuba and conditions in general, McKinley sought the fullest possible information. As one means to this end, he sent a political friend, William J. Calhoun, to Cuba to assess the situation there. Calhoun presented McKinley with a comprehensive report on June 22, 1897, which drew a terribly bleak picture and added to the President's sense of urgency.

## William J. Calhoun to President William McKinley, June 22, 1897

[*Special Agents Reports*, vol. 48, Record Group 59, National Archives, Washington, D.C.]

I beg leave to submit the following report of the result of my observations while in Cuba on the special mission which you did me the great honor to trust to my care. I will preface what I have to say with the statement, that prior to going to Cuba I had read but little of the history of the island, or, of the war now going on there. The impressions I have formed, therefore, have been wholly derived from what I there saw and heard.

*Cause of the War*

The first question suggested to my mind was: What is the cause of this war? I knew the Cuban and the Spaniard were of the same race, that they had the same history and traditions, the same language and religion, and we would naturally expect them to live together in harmony, unless there was some serious reason for the intense hatred which now divides them. The first inquiry I made was along this line. I found the cause of the war could be assigned to conditions, partly economic, political and social. And there must be some material change in these conditions before any enduring peace or prosperity can come to, or remain with, the island. In my investigation I did not try to obtain statistical information. It would have been a laborious, if not a fruitless effort. There are no reliable statistics of trade or social conditions. In making my investigation I talked with all classes of men; with Spaniards both liberal and conservative; with Cubans and with the few foreigners whom I met. It was my desire to hear both sides, and to consider their conflicting statements in the most impartial spirit.

*Economic Cause*

It is my opinion that the principal cause of the war, and of all the discontent that has disturbed the social life of the island, can be found in the economic conditions that have prevailed there for many years past. Sugar is the principal product. It is the basis of Cuban commerce and

the main source of the island's wealth. The climate and soil are especially adapted to its production, and the labor employed is very cheap. The natural conditions surrounding the Cuban are such as to enable him to produce sugar in competition with any other part of the globe.
. . . The Cuban, for years past, has been limited for a market to the United States. Ninety-five per cent of Cuba's sugar is sold in our country. For the maintenance of the sugar industry, so important to its life and prosperity, Cuba is absolutely dependent on the United States. On the other hand, Cuba must import flour, lard, bacon, groceries, clothing, boots and shoes, furniture, and machinery of all kinds. For these necessaries of life it is wholly dependent on the outside world. They are not, and cannot be, produced on the island. The United States is the nearest and best market in which these supplies can be purchased. It is the only market in which the full measure of the exchange value of Cuba's sugar can be realized. Every law of trade or exchange prompts the Cuban to buy in this market. If left free to do so, he would be a liberal and willing purchaser.

In Spain there is no market for Cuban sugar, neither is that country a natural market wherein to buy Cuban supplies. In brief, there is no natural trade relations between Spain and Cuba.

It seems, however, to be the policy of Spain to force Cuba to buy the larger part of her supplies in the mother country. . . .

## Political Causes

Another complaint of the Cuban is that Cuba has been the football of Spanish politics. The government offices are uniformly filled by Spaniards, especially such offices as furnish opportunity for the exercise of power, or the accumulation of wealth. The favorites of the Spanish Ministry are given places in the Cuban Service. The Cuban feels he is debarred from public office; that the island is his home and country; that he ought to govern it; that whatever is honorable or profitable in its service ought to be open to his aspiration and ambition; and that the Spaniard is a foreigner and an intruder. In discussing this complaint with the Spaniards, they insisted it was not justified. They pointed to the local judiciary, most of the judges being native Cubans, to the many persons of like nativity holding positions under the municipal government of Havana, and to other notable instances where Cubans hold prominent places of power and trust. But the judge is appointed by, and holds his place and power subject to, the will and approval of Spain. The Cuban in the municipal government generally holds a minor position; he is a mere employee, such as book-keeper, clerk, copyist, etc. The rule is the offices of power and profit are held by the Spaniards, though there are some exceptions. The government in Cuba is more military than civil. Spain seems to trust more to the power of the soldier, than to the wisdom of the statesman.

But, the Cuban says, this monopoly of official place could be more easily endured, if the administration of public affairs was only patriotic and honest, instead of notoriously selfish and corrupt. There can be little doubt but that the government officials are, and for all time have been, grossly corrupt. . . .

The complaint of the Cuban is that the life of the island is being slowly but surely absorbed by Spain; that it is being despoiled by Spanish rapacity; that it is plundered by a corrupt officialism on the one hand and by the selfish demands of Spanish trade on the other; that Spain is like an octopus with Cuba in its grasp; in peace it slowly saps the life blood of its victim; when the latter struggles to be free, its enemy presses its tentacles deeper into the quivering flesh of the victim and will strangle it or stab it to death before it will let go.

## Social Conditions

I was informed there were no correct or reliable census reports of the population. The gross population is estimated to be about 1,500,000. A proper classification or division along lines of color or nativity is also hard to make. A prominent leader in Cuban politics estimated the peninsular Spaniards living on the Island, exclusive of the soldiers, at 130,000; the blacks and mulattoes at 700,000; and the white Cubans at 670,000. Other Cubans claim this estimate of the black population to be too high, that it does not exceed 400,000 or 500,000. . . .

The Spaniard has a contempt for the Cuban. He says the latter will not work; that he is envious and jealous of the former's success, achieved by industry and economy. The Cuban regards the Spaniard as selfish and rapacious, and hates him with an intensity that can neither be measured nor described. The division between them is as well marked and defined as though they were of separate and distinct races. As a rule, the Cuban, whether educated or not, is in sympathy with the insurgents. There are some notable exceptions, but they only serve to make the rule more prominent and pronounced. I went to Cuba with the impression that the insurgents were largely recruited from the lower classes; but, while it is true, as it is in all wars, that what are called the "common" people, bear the brunt of the battle, yet the insurgent army is representative of all classes and conditions of Cuban society.

## Military Situation

. . . As the war is now carried on, no one can foretell when or how it will end. It seems to be a question of endurance on both sides. The alleged pacification announced by General Weyler, as prevailing in the provinces of Pinar del Rio, Havana and Matanzas, is more theoretical than actual. . . . Pacification would imply that the people had resumed their usual avocations and society had been restored to its normal functions. But such is not the case in either of these three provinces. The tobacco and sugar plantations that are worked, are guarded by soldiers and the people are still away from their homes in the camps of the *reconcentrado*. The Spaniards insist that the rebellion is practically suppressed in Pinar del Rio, the extreme western province, I am inclined to the opinion this is largely true, that is, the tensity of the struggle is so far relaxed in that province that it no longer plays a part in the military problem. In Havana province the insurgents are active in skirmishes, raids and forays, but they hardly rise to the dignity of war. The main body of the insurgents is in the provinces of Santa Clara, Puerto Principe and Santiago. The war in the three western provinces which General Weyler calls pacified, may be likened unto a smouldering fire, the moment there is any relaxation of the attempt to suppress it, the flames will break out again with renewed fury. . . .

The insurgents have no hope of driving out the Spaniard by armed force; their only hope is to worry and harrass Spain to the point where she will sue for peace. Spain seems equally unable to make any prompt or decisive headway in crushing the rebellion. The rainy season has now set in, and it will be impracticable to make any effective or continued military movement until next fall. Thus, both parties face each other, both are weary and breathless, and the result is largely a question of endurance.

*      *      *

## The Reconcentrado

The principal feature of the war is what is called the *reconcentrado* movement. The country people, the laborers about sugar estates and the small farmers are called the "pacifico". The Spanish claim they were all openly or secretly in sympathy with the insurgents. They gave the latter information as to the movements of the troops, acted as spies and informers, killed the sick, wounded and struggling soldiers, and furnished the insurgents with supplies. As one means of weakening the insurgents it was determined to withdraw these people from their homes and concentrate them within the lines of the fortified posts. The order was issued directing them to leave their homes within a given limited period; any one failing to obey, or found outside the lines of the prescribed "zone" would be treated as active insurgents. In this way the people would be prevented from furnishing food or information to the insurgents, or recruits to their ranks. This order has been rigidly enforced. The troops drove the people away from their homes, tore down or burned their houses, laid waste their farms and compelled them to camp, as it were, within the military lines. They have built huts or "shacks" out of the bark and leaves of the palm trees, and many thousands of them are now living in this way. I travelled by rail from Havana to Matanzas. The country outside of the military posts was practically depopulated. Every house had been burned, banana trees cut down, cane fields swept with fire, and everything in the shape of food destroyed. It was as fair a landscape as mortal eye ever looked upon; but I did not see a house, a man, woman or child; a horse, mule or cow, not even a dog; I did not see a sign of life, except an occasional vulture or buzzard sailing through the air. The country was wrapped in the stillness of death and the silence of desolation. The blackened chimneys, dismantled houses and factories, and fire swept cane fields told the story of war's devastation. . . .

I was credibly informed that this waste and devastation prevails throughout the three western provinces. This policy of burning and destroying property was undoubtedly first inaugurated by the insurgents . . . but the Spaniards have adopted the same policy and have supplemented the

## Report of McKinley's Personal Envoy 39

destruction of the insurgents by making it thorough and complete. . . .

Around each post where the reconcentrado are located there is marked out what is called the "zone," or a limited territory within which the people are allowed to cultivate potatoes and other edibles. This is practically the only provision that is made for the support and maintenance of these people. I heard that the military forces distributed a few rations when the pacificos were first brought in, and in some instances the local civil authorities made a feeble effort to furnish them with food; but the latter can do but little for them. I also heard of details from the pacificos being taken into the country under the guard of the "guerrilleros" to hunt for food amid the desolate waste around them. There are many women, children and infirm men among these unfortunates who can do but little in their own behalf. The stronger and more aggressive ones manage to secure enough to support life; but for the weak and helpless there is little, if any, succor.

. . . The combined effect of the policy of waste and destruction, and that of the reconcentrado, whether so intended or not, will be the complete destruction of property, and the almost total elimination of the population.

### Political Possibilities

The war can only be settled in one of three ways:

> 1. The forcible suppression of the rebellion by the Spanish arms. To do this, means the almost total ruin and destruction of both life and property.
> 2. Reforms extended by Spain, which will give Cuba a liberal autonomy, with the privilege to levy her own taxes, and fix her own tariff duties.
> 3. The concession of Cuban Independence by Spain. Soon after I went to Havana, it was stated that the

reforms in administration proposed by the home government were on their way from Madrid, that they would be promulgated and an earnest effort made to put them in force. The proposed reforms are so limited in their scope, they leave so much power with Spain, and concede so little to Cuba, that in my opinion, nothing but force or necessity will cause the Cubans to accept them. They laugh at the reforms offered, and refuse to consider them. There will be no permanent peace in Cuba unless she is made free commercially, if not politically. Indeed the Spaniards did not seem to attach any particular significance to them. No promulgation or attempt to put them in force was made. It was apparently conceded that they were not radical enough to meet the situation.

I talked with a gentleman who was formerly the leader of the autonomist or liberal party. He is a man of great intellectual force and kindliness of heart. He is respected by every one, but has lost the confidence of the Cubans, by whom he was once adored, and is not wholly trusted by the Spaniards. He is, however, the most interesting character on the island. He is loyal to Spain, believes that autonomy is the solution of the problem. . . . He furthermore said he had studied the social and political conditions of Cuba for many years, he had led the sentiment that demanded a larger share of self-government and reform in administration, but, he was convinced that self-government was not practicable. The great mass of the people were ignorant, and untrained. Factional and turbulent conditions would arise that could only breed revolutions and disorder; the political disturbances of Santo Domingo would be re-enacted; and anarchy and chaos would result. The only hope for Cuba was in a continuance of the Spanish authority, with a gradual growth and enlargement of self-government. He also expressed the opinion

## Report of McKinley's Personal Envoy 41

that the proposed reforms ought to be accepted, and if put in practice in good faith peace would be restored and prosperity insured. I was convinced of the truth of a great deal that he said. I perhaps attached more importance to his opinion because of the fact he was the leader of the reform movement. But now, he has no influence with his people. He is a sad and silent spectator of a contest that is fought on lines he cannot approve, and whose miseries he cannot alleviate. The Cubans spoke kindly of him, acknowledged his great ability and conceded to him integrity of opinion and personal character.

I talked with many Spaniards, who were planters and business men. All their personal interests and fortunes are bound up in the fate of Cuba. They have a great fear of independence; they think it means revolutions and counter-revolutions; that there will be no peace, or stability to society or success to business. They pointed to every Latin-American country in the Western Hemisphere, and frankly admitted the failure of the race to successfully maintain a popular form of government. I found among these persons a decided willingness to accept annexation; in this desire they were prompted by commercial as well as political reasons.

Many of the Cubans, in fact nearly all of the business class, would be glad to have annexation. They did not seem to be sure of their ability to govern themselves, though they expressed a preference for the uncertainties and probable tumult incident to self-government, to a continuance of the Spanish rule with all its absolutism and rapacity. It is feared that the insurgents in the field will not listen to any proposition that will continue the sovereignty of Spain; and the Cubans in Havana seem disposed to consult the wishes of those who have sacrificed so much for liberty.

If it were not for the poor reconcentradoes, who are now bearing the brunt of the war, more of whom die with hunger and disease than do the soldiers on either side from casualties of battle, the problem would work itself out. It is largely a question of physical and financial endurance. If the former Spanish rule continues, and if the island is shut out from the American market, it will fall back in commercial importance, along side of Jamaica, Haiti and San Domingo. It will be worth nothing to Spain or any one else.

## Americans on the Island

I have no reliable data upon which to base an estimate of the number of native born Americans on the Island. I heard of but very few. It is safe, I think, to say that there are not a hundred on the whole island. Some of them were employed about the sugar factories and warehouses, as machinists, clerks, etc. They are out of employment and some of them are doubtless in need of assistance. But most of those who invoke assistance or protection on the ground of being Americans are naturalized citizens. Some of them are well to do planters and business men. They were educated in our colleges, and remained here long enough to become naturalized, then, they returned to Cuba where they have remained; they use their certificates of naturalization to protect their lives and their property. There is another class who have at some time worked in the cigar factories of Tampa or Key West, or have lived about New York and other cities; after a time they returned to the island and resumed their old relations to Cuban life. They seemed to have attached no importance to their naturalization until the war broke out, then, they hastened to the consulate offices and were registered. Many of them never pretended to be American citizens until they were arrested for political offenses, then they produce their certificates. This class have not always acted with that indifference to local political conditions that is supposed to be manifested by citizens of another country. The charge is made, that in many instances the certificates of naturalization are fraudulent, that they were purchased or obtained in violation of our laws of naturalization. I was credibly informed of one case where the party did not remain in the United States more than six months, when he was naturalized, then returned to Cuba and has remained there ever since.

The class of Americans who apply for relief are largely those who have been naturalized at some period of their lives; they were never registered at the consulate until the war broke out, and they are more largely identified with Cuba than with the United States.

It does not come within the province of any mission assigned me to make any suggestions or recommendations, I have tried to tell the story of Cuba and the conditions there prevailing as I saw and heard them. The island is one of the most unhappy and most distressed places on earth; it appeals to the sympathy of all, but the problem involved is so complicated and many-sided that it demands the best thought, the highest purpose of all who have to deal therewith.

I desire to say that in Cuba I was treated with great courtesy by every one, irrespective of political association.

I also beg to express to you my thanks for the confidence and trust you have reposed in me, and I indulge in the hope that our country may act wisely and well in the somewhat delicate relations we sustain to the wasted, desolated and blood-stained island.

Respectfully submitted

W. J. CALHOUN

# Section Four

# McKinley's Predicament

*Commentary*

The following documents indicate that in the summer of 1897 McKinley launched a diplomatic campaign to persuade Spain to place the Cuban conflict, in the words of his Minister to Madrid, Stewart L. Woodford, "in the sure way of being peacefully and finally ended." Judging from these documents, the President's motives for this campaign were those same moral, economic and political pressures which had made themselves felt from the start of his administration.

## Secretary of State John Sherman to De Lôme June 26, 1897

[*Foreign Relations*, 1896–97, pp. 507–08.]

*Washington, Department of State*

Sir:

Referring to the conversation which the Assistant Secretary, Mr. Day, had the honor to have with you on the 8th instant, it now becomes my duty, obeying the

## McKinley's Predicament 45

direction of the President, to invite through your representation the urgent attention of the Government of Spain to the manner of conducting operations in the neighboring Island of Cuba.

By successive orders and proclamations of the Captain-General of the Island of Cuba, some of which have been promulgated while others are known only by their effects, a policy of devastation and interference with the most elementary rights of human existence has been established in that territory tending to inflict suffering on innocent noncombatants, to destroy the value of legitimate investments, and to extinguish the natural resources of the country in the apparent hope of crippling the insurgents and restoring Spanish rule in the island.

No incident has so deeply affected the sensibilities of the American people or so painfully impressed their Government as the proclamations of General Weyler, ordering the burning or unroofing of dwellings, the destruction of growing crops, the suspension of tillage, the devastation of fields, and the removal of the rural population from their homes to suffer privation and disease in the overcrowded and ill-supplied garrison towns. The latter aspect of this campaign of devastation has especially attracted the attention of this Government, inasmuch as several hundreds of American citizens among the thousands of concentrados of the central and eastern provinces of Cuba were ascertained to be destitute of the necessaries of life to a degree demanding immediate relief through the agencies of the United States, to save them from death by sheer starvation and from the ravages of pestilence.

From all parts of the productive zones of the island, where the enterprise and capital of Americans have established mills and farms, worked in large part by citizens of the United States, comes the same story of interference with the operations of tillage and manufacture, due to the systematic enforcement of a policy aptly described in General Weyler's bando of May 27 last as "the concentration of the inhabitants of the rural country and the destruction of resources in all places where the instructions given are not carried into effect." Meanwhile the burden of contribution remains, arrears of taxation necessarily keep pace with the deprivation of the means of paying taxes, to say nothing of the destruction of the ordinary means of livelihood, and the relief held out by another bando of the same date is illusory, for the resumption of industrial pursuits in limited areas is made conditional upon the payment of all arrears of taxation and the maintenance of a protecting garrison. Such relief can not obviously reach the numerous class of concentrados, the women and children deported from their ruined homes and desolated farms to the garrison towns. For the larger industrial ventures, capital may find its remedy, sooner or later, at the bar of international justice, but for the labor dependent upon the slow rehabilitation of capital there appears to be intended only the doom of privation and distress.

\* \* \*

It is the President's hope that this earnest representation will be received in the same kindly spirit in which it is intended. The history of the recent thirteen years of warfare in Cuba, divided between two protracted periods of strife, has shown the desire of the United States that the contest be conducted and ended in ways alike honorable to both parties and promising a stable settlement. If the friendly attitude of this Government is to bear fruit it can only be when supplemented by Spain's own conduct of the war in a manner responsive to the precepts of ordinary humanity and calculated to invite as well the expectant forbearance of this Government as the confidence of the Cuban people in the beneficence of Spanish control.

Accept, etc.,

JOHN SHERMAN

## Sherman to American Minister to Spain Stewart L. Woodford, July 16, 1897

[*Foreign Relations*, 1897-98, pp. 558-61.]

Washington, Department of State

Sir:

Before you go to your post it is proper to state to you the President's views on the relation of your Government to the contest which is now being waged in Cuba. The same occasion requires that you should be made acquainted with the course which has been deemed best for the United States to follow under existing conditions.

During thirteen years of the past twenty-nine years the island of Cuba has been the scene of grave disorder and sanguinary conflict. On two distinct occasions the power and authority of the Spanish Crown have been arrayed against a serious and persistent effort of a large proportion of the population of the island to achieve independence. . . .

For more than two years a wholly unexampled struggle has raged in Cuba between the discontented native population and the mother power. Not only has its attendant ruin spread over a larger area than in any previous contest, but its effects have been more widely felt and the cost of life and treasure to Spain has been far greater. The strife continues on a footing of mutual destruction and devastation. Day by day the conviction gathers strength that it is visionary for Spain to hope that Cuba, even if eventually subjugated by sheer exhaustion, can ever bear to her anything like the relation of dependence and profit she once bore. The policy which obviously attempts to make Cuba worthless to the Cubans, should they prevail, must inevitably make the island equally worthless to Spain in the event of reconquest, whether it be regained as a subject possession or endowed with a reasonable measure of self-administration.

The recuperative processes, always painfully slow in an exhausted community, would necessarily be doubly remote in either of the latter contingencies, for in the light of events of the past twenty-nine years capital and industry would shrink from again engaging in costly enterprises in a field where neither proximate return nor permanent security is to be expected. To fix the truth of this assertion one need only regard the fate of the extraordinary efforts to rehabilitate the fortunes of Cuba that followed the truce of 1878. The capital and intelligence contributed by citizens of the United States and other countries, which at that time poured into Cuba seeking to endow the island with the marvelous resources of modern invention and advanced industrial processes, have now become submerged in the common ruin. The commerce of Cuba has dwindled to such unprofitable proportions that its ability for self-support is questionable even if peace was restored today. Its capacity to yield anything like adequate return toward the support of the mother country, even granting the disposition to do so, is a matter of the gravest doubt.

Weighing all these facts carefully and without prejudice, in the judgement of the President the time has come for this Government to soberly consider and clearly decide the nature and methods of its duty both to its neighbors and itself.

This Government has labored and is still laboring under signal difficulties in its administration of its neutrality laws. It is ceaselessly confronted with questions affecting the inherent and treaty rights of its citizens in Cuba. It beholds the island suffering an almost complete paralysis of many of its most necessary commercial functions by reason of the impediments imposed and the ruinous injuries wrought by this internecine warfare at its very doors; and above all, it is naturally and rightfully apprehensive lest some untoward incident may abruptly supervene to inflame mutual passions beyond control and thus raise issues which, however deplorable, can not be avoided.

In short, it may not be reasonably asked or expected that a policy of mere inaction can be safely prolonged. There is no longer question that the sentiment of the American people strongly demands that if the attitude of neutrality is to be maintained toward these combatants it must be a genuine neutrality as between combatants, fully recognized as such in fact as well as in name. The problem of recognition of belligerency has been often presented, but never perhaps more explicitly than now. Both Houses of Congress, nearly a year ago, adopted by an almost unanimous vote a concurrent resolution recognizing belligerency in Cuba, and latterly the Senate, by a large majority, has voted a joint resolution of like purport, which is now pending in the House of Representatives.

At this juncture our Government must seriously inquire whether the time has not arrived when Spain, of her own volition, moved by her own interests and by every paramount sentiment of humanity, will put a stop to this destructive war and make proposals of settlement honorable to herself and just to her Cuban colony and to mankind. The United States stands ready to assist her and tender good offices to that end.

It should by no means be forgotten that besides and beyond the question of recognition of belligerency, with its usual proclamation of neutrality and its concession of equal rights and impartial imposition of identical disabilities in respect to the contending parties within our municipal jurisdiction, there lies the larger ulterior problem of intervention, which the President does not now discuss. It is with no unfriendly intent that this subject has been mentioned, but simply to show that this Government does not and can not ignore the possibilities of duty hidden in the future, nor be unprepared to face an emergency which may at any time be born of the unhappy contest in Cuba. The extraordinary, because direct and not merely theoretical or sentimental, interest of the United States in the Cuban situation can not be ignored, and if forced the issue must be met honestly and fearlessly, in conformity with our national life and character. Not only are our citizens largely concerned in the ownership of property and in the industrial and commercial ventures which have been set on foot in Cuba through our enterprising initiative and sustained by their capital, but the chronic condition of trouble and violent derangement in that island constantly causes disturbance in the social and political condition of our people. It keeps up a continuous irritation within our own borders, injuriously affects the normal functions of business, and tends to delay the condition of prosperity to which this country is entitled.

No exception can be taken to the general proposition that a neighboring nation, however deeply disturbed and injured by the existence of a devastating internal conflict at its doors, may be constrained, on grounds of international comity, to disregard its endangered interests and remain a passive spectator of the contest for a reasonable time while the titular authority is repressing the disorder. The essence of this moral obligation lies in the reasonableness of the delay invited by circumstances and by the effort of the territorial authority to assert its claimed rights. The onlooking nation need only wait "a reasonable time" before alleging and acting upon the rights which it, too, possesses. This proposition is not a legal subtlety, but a broad principle of international comity and law.

The question arises, then, whether Spain has not already had a reasonable time to restore peace and been unable to do so, even by a concentration of her resources and measures of unparalleled severity which have received very general condemnation. The methods which Spain has adopted to wage the fight give no prospect of immediate peace or of a stable return to the conditions of prosperity which are essential to Cuba in its intercourse with its neighbors. Spain's inability entails upon the United States a degree of injury and suffering which can not longer be ignored. Assuredly Spain can not expect this Government to sit idle, letting vast interests suffer, our political elements disturbed, and the country perpetually embroiled, while no progress is being made in the settlement of the Cuban problem. Such a policy of inaction would in reality prove of no benefit to Spain, while certain to do the United States incalculable harm. This Government, strong in its sense of right and duty, yet keenly sympathetic with the aspirations of any neighboring community in close touch with our own civilization, is naturally desirous to avoid, in all rational ways, the precipitation of a result which would be painfully abhorrent to the American people.

For all of the reasons before stated the President feels it his duty to make the strongest possible effort to help bring about a result which shall be in conformity alike with the feelings of our people, the inherent rights of civilized man, and be of advantage both to Cuba and to Spain. Difficult as the task may seem now, it is believed that frankness, earnestness, perseverance, and a fair regard for the rights of others will eventually solve the problem.

It should be borne in mind from the start that it is far removed from the feelings of the American people and the mind of the President to propose any solution to which the slightest idea of humiliation to Spain could in any way be attached. But no possible intention or occasion to wound the just susceptibilities of the Castilian nation can be discerned in the altogether friendly suggestion that the good offices of the United States may now be lent to the advantage of Spain.

You are hereby instructed to bring these considerations as promptly as possible, but with due allowance for favorable conditions, to the attention of the Government of Her Majesty the Queen Regent, with all the impressiveness which their importance demands, and with all the earnestness which the constantly imperiled national interests of the United States justifies. You will emphasize the self-restraint which this Government has hitherto observed until endurance has ceased to be tolerable or even possible for any longer indefinite term. You will lay especial stress on the unselfish friendliness of our desires, and upon the high purpose and sincere wish of the United States to give its aid only in order that a peaceful and enduring result may be reached, just and honorable alike to Spain and to the Cuban people, and only so far as such aid may accomplish the wished-for ends. In so doing, you will not disguise the gravity of the situation, nor conceal the President's conviction that, should his present effort be fruitless, his duty to his countrymen will necessitate an early decision as to the course of action which the time and the transcendent emergency may demand.

As to the manner in which the assistance of the United States can be effectively rendered in the Cuban situation, the President has no desire to embarrass the Government of Spain by formulating precise proposals. All that is asked or expected is that some safe way may be provided for action which the United States may undertake with justice and self-respect, and that the settlement shall be a lasting one, honorable and advantageous to Spain and to Cuba and equitable to the United States.

For the accomplishment of this end, now and in the future, our Government offers its most kindly offices through yourself.

Respectfully yours,

JOHN SHERMAN

## Woodford to Sherman
## September 23, 1897

[*Foreign Relations*, 1897-98, p. 568.]

San Sebastian, Legation of the United States

Sir:

As arranged in my interview with the Spanish minister

of foreign affairs on Saturday last, September 18, I have to-day addressed him an official note setting forth the desires and wishes of the United States in regard to the Cuban question. . . .

I have the honor, etc.,

STEWART L. WOODFORD

# Section Five
# Rays of Hope

*Commentary*

Shortly after Woodford presented McKinley's demands on Madrid, the Conservative government fell from power and was replaced by a liberal regime which announced a comprehensive scheme for pacifying Cuba, including the recall of General Weyler, an end to the reconcentration policy and a grant of autonomy to the island. The following dispatches from Madrid to Washington put this information before McKinley and allowed him publicly to counsel continued restraint and watchful waiting in his first State of the Union Message, December 6, 1897.

## Reply of Foreign Minister Pio Gullón to Minister Woodford's Note of October 23, 1897

[*Foreign Relations*, 1897–98, pp. 582–89.]

*Palace, Ministry of State*
*October 23, 1897*

Excellency:

My worthy predecessor, the Duke of Tetuan, had the honor to receive, in regular course, the courteous and studied note which your excellency was pleased to address to him on the 23d of September last; but the Government, which has but now obtained the confidence of the Crown, being obliged to devote its initial labors to measures of internal concern which are demanded by every political change, took a genuine and thoughtful interest in having its first acts and its conduct clearly demonstrate that it was adopting with sincerity a new course, and a minute study of the matters in order to acquire an exact knowledge of them all being necessary, has perhaps delayed more than it would have wished the reply to the aforesaid note. Our desire to proceed with loyalty and frankness in our relations with the Government which your excellency so worthily represents at this court, and the obligation to the sentiments which your excellency is pleased to express, require that this preliminary explanation be made, to the end removing any imputation of doubts and vacillations on the part of one who, by reason of having attained to power with a defined programme, considers his honor engaged to its immediate realization without casuistic distinctions of unnecessary delays.

\* \* \*

The present Government of His Majesty is now most advantageously situated for investigating the points referred to and for securing the pacification of Cuba on the proper basis, since its own character, the antecedents of those who compose it, and the public and solemn promises which in the past and of its own sole initiative, it has made to the representatives of the country involved in the colonial policy of Spain and in the manner of conducting the war, a total change of immense scope, which must exercise considerable influence upon the moral and material situation of the Greater Antilla.

The Government of His Majesty, by reason of its firmly rooted convictions, in order to subserve the peninsular interests equally with those of the Antillas, and holding the resolute purpose to draw closer with ties of true affection the indissoluble bonds which unite the mother country with its cherished provinces beyond the seas, is determined to put into immediate practice the political system which the present president of the council of ministers announced to the nation in his manifesto of the 24th of June of this year. The acts accomplished by the present Government, notwithstanding the short time which has elapsed since its elevation to power, are a secure guaranty that not for anyone nor for anything will it halt in the path which it has traced, and which, in its best judgment, is that which will bring us to the longed-for peace.

To military operations, uninterrupted for a single day and as energetic and active as circumstances demand, but ever humanitarian and careful to respect all private rights as far as may be possible, must be joined political action honestly leading to the autonomy of the colony in such a manner that upon the full guaranty of the immutable Spanish sovereignty shall arise the new personality which is to govern itself in all affairs peculiar to itself by means of an executive organization and the insular council or chamber. This programme, which constitutes true self-government, will give to the Cubans their own local government, whereby they shall be at one and the same time the initiators and regulators of their own life, but always forming part of the integral nationality of Spain. In this way the Island of Cuba will form a personality with its own peculiar functions, and powers (atribuciones) and the mother country, moving in the sphere of action which is exclusively its own, will take charge of those matters—such as foreign relations, the army, the navy, and the administration of justice—which involve national requirements or needs.

In order to realize this plan, which it advocates as a solemn political engagement voluntarily assumed while its members were in opposition, the Government of His Majesty proposes to modify existing legislation so far as necessary, doing so in the form of decrees to admit of its more speedy application, and leaving for the Cortes of the Kingdom, with the cooperation of the senators and deputies of the Antillas, the solution of the economical problem and a patriotic and fair apportionment of the payment of the debt.

Thus broadly outlined, your Excellency, these are the measures, honorable to the Peninsula and just to Cuba, which the Government of Spain of its own volition and actuated only by patriotic aims and elevated humanitarian feelings proposes to make use of henceforth in order to put an end to the Cuban insurrection, assembling beneath the Spanish standard all the prominent men of the country, without distinction of origin or conduct, in order to oppose them to those professional agitators by nature and habit, who subsist only by strife and have no other object than rapine, destruction, and disorder. Military severity toward these destructive men will within a brief time prove the more advantageous and effective, since in the task to be performed by it will cooperate, of their own impulse, all those islanders who henceforth, feeling that they are the masters of their destinies, will find it to their own interest and advantage to put an end to ruinous and already unendurable excesses.

The formula for so auspicious a change will be henceforth peace, with liberty and local self-government, while the mother country will not fail to lend at the proper time the moral and material means in aid of the Antillean provinces, but will cooperate, on the contrary, toward the reestablishment of property, developing the inexhaustible sources of wealth in the island, and devoting itself especially to the promotion of public works and material interests, which, when peace shall have been assured, will rapidly increase, as was the case after the last war.

Having thus set forth the conciliatory, humane, and liberal purposes of the Government of His Majesty, in deference to the legitimate and justifiable interest which the

Cuban insurrection awakens on the part of the people and Government of the United States, I have now to consider certain of the statements contained in your note of the 23d September last.

Your Excellency is pleased to state therein that the President of the United States feels it his duty to make the strongest possible effort to contribute effectively toward peace, while giving friendly assurance that there is nothing further from his mind than the occasion or intention of wounding the just susceptibilities of Spain, but your excellency does not set forth the means of which the President might avail himself to attain those ends, neither do you recall the fact that on various occasions the Government of His Majesty has made special mention of several highly important means. It would be desirable to make clear a point of such elementary importance, and to state exactly, first of all, the nature of the proffered aid and the field wherein it would act, and then to decide as to its greater or less efficacy, since only by a previous and perfect knowledge thereof is it possible for both parties to reach a complete agreement.

The Spanish and American Governments agreeing in the same desire to secure immediate peace in Cuba, and both being interested therein, although in different degrees, the Government of His Majesty being interested as a sovereign and the United States in the character of a friend and neighbor, there will doubtless be found suitable bases for a friendly understanding, whereby Spain shall continue to put forth armed efforts, at the same time decreeing the political concessions which she may deem prudent and adequate, while the United States exert within their borders the energy and vigilance necessary to absolutely prevent the procurement of the resources of which from the beginning the Cuban insurrection has availed itself as from an inexhaustible arsenal.

On various occasions the Governments of His Majesty

have found themselves obliged to call the attention of the Government of the United States to the manner in which the so-called laws of neutrality are fulfilled in the territory of the Union. Despite the express provisions of those laws and the doctrines maintained by the American Government in the famous Alabama arbitration with regard to the diligence which should be used to avoid whatsoever aggressive act against a friendly nation, it is certain that filibustering expeditions have set forth and unfortunately continue to set forth from the United States, and that, in the sight of all men, there is operating in New York an insurrectionary junta which publicly boasts of organizing and maintaining armed hostility and constant provocation against the Spanish nation.

To effect the disappearance of such a state of things, as is demanded by general international friendship, would be, in the belief of the Government of His Majesty, the most effectual aid in the attainment of peace that the President of the United States could render. . . .

According to your Excellency's note, the President of the United States wishes His Majesty's Government either to formulate some proposition that will enable him to render his friendly offers effectual or to give assurance that pacification will speedily be secured by the efforts of Spain.

\* \* \*

His Majesty's Government . . . takes pleasure in notifying the United States Government that the pacification of the western provinces of the island has greatly progressed through the valiant efforts of the Spanish arms, and that it is confident of completing it in a short time, thanks to the energetic and unceasing efforts of its troops and the beneficial effect of the new and ample reforms, which are based upon principles of love, of forgiveness of the past, and of pardon to all who seek the protection of the historical banner of their country, and upon the assurance that the island shall henceforth govern itself, and that mutual affection shall draw closer the national tie which unites it to its former discoverer.

The problem being solved on these bases and in this manner, His Majesty's Government has no doubt of its ability to maintain a friendly understanding with the United States Government, and it does not hesitate to assert that when the internal system of the island of Cuba has been reorganized upon new principles the insurrectionary germs which have hitherto, unhappily, undermined it will disappear forever, thereby giving such security offered to domestic and foreign capital seeking advantageous investments in the island as will cause an abundant revival of the former wonderful prosperity to which the incomparable fertility of its soil entitles it.

It is not necessary to refer to the supposition of a continued prolongation of the struggle, nor to that of a change in the attitude of the United States toward the combatants. . . .

*   *   *

In this connection it is timely to remember that the American Government had to admit, in its note of April 4, 1896, that it was impossible to recognize the belligerency of the rebels at that time, although the insurrection was in a much more flourishing condition, and that, if Spain were withdrawn from the island of Cuba, the sole bond of union between the many heterogeneous elements in the island would disappear, which proves the necessity of her presence and the absurdity of the idea that there can be any other organization in the island possessing the attributes of lawful international personality. The insurgents, as has already been said on another occasion by His Majesty's Government, have always been and still are without any real civil government, fixed territory, courts of their own, a regular army, coasts, ports, navy, everything that the principal American writers on international law and statesmen require as preliminary to the discussion of a

## Rays of Hope

recognition of belligerency. . . . Under these circumstances it is impossible to admit that there can be a change in the attitude of the United States toward the combatants in Cuba.

As His Majesty's Government has decided, freely and deliberately, to establish autonomy in Cuba, there arises by the force of circumstances the case foreseen by the eminent Mr. Cleveland in his message of December 7, 1896; and, admitting the continuing international accountability (solidarity) of the governments which succeed each other in a country, it can not be doubted that the present most worthy President will agree with his predecessor that no just reason exists for conjecturing that the pacification of the island of Cuba will fail to be effected upon this basis. The Government of His Majesty the King of Spain expects with confidence from the rectitude, love of peace, and friendship of the President of the United States that he will aid it in this noble and humane undertaking, and that he will exert himself energetically to prevent the insurrection from receiving from the United States the moral and material aid which gives it its only strength and without which it would have already been subdued or would certainly be subdued very speedily.

It is, therefore, above all indispensably necessary that the President should decide upon his course toward Spain so far as regards the Cuban problem, and that he should state clearly whether he is ready to put a stop absolutely and forever to those filibustering expeditions which, by violating with the greatest freedom the laws of friendship, injure and degrade the respect which the American Government owes to itself in the discharge of its international engagements. . . .

* * *

## Woodford to Sherman
## November 13, 1897

[*Foreign Relations*, 1897–98, pp. 600–02.]

**Madrid, Legation of the United States**

Sir:

In my dispatch to you, No. 61, dated November 8 instant, I acknowledged receipt of your telegraphic dispatch dated November 6. I have since then indirectly caused the Spanish Government to know that our Government would regard an immediate change in the treatment of the noncombatant Cubans as the most effective guarantee of the change in the policy of Spain that can just now be given.

Yesterday afternoon I called by appointment on Señor Moret, minister for the colonies, to discuss the Solomon tobacco case. . . .

* * *

Señor Moret speaks excellent English, and when our interview about the tobacco case was ended I availed myself of the opportunity to have a full talk with him.

I told him that my Government discerned in the Spanish answer of October 23 hopeful indication of change in the policy of Spain, although the scope and effect of the Spanish programme remained still to be seen; that an immediate change in the treatment of the noncombatant Cubans would be an effective guarantee; that this is not a change dependent upon legislation or decree, and that the President accepted with the utmost gratification the pledge of the Spanish Government to conduct the war henceforth in humane and Christian methods.

Señor Moret at once replied that no one could be more anxious than himself to have the war conducted in humane and Christian methods; that the Spanish Government had instructed Marshal Blanco most fully in this regard, and that he was certain that Marshal Blanco would fully and loyally carry out the purpose and instructions of his Government. He added that before he had come into power he had publicly expressed his views about the conduct of the war in a speech at Zaragoza, and that he should not be as secretary in the room in which we then were unless his hands were free to see that his views about the humane conduct of the war could be carried out.

I then suggested that we should talk with each other plainly and fully, without diplomatic compliments and each man saying to the other just what two private citizens would say when discussing matters too serious to be veiled or concealed by courteous expressions. He assented, saying that he should be glad to have just such conversation with me.

I then remarked that should the Spanish Government feel it their duty to continue to insist upon their present view (as stated in their answer of October 23) that the Cuban insurrection is practically maintained by the sympathy and aid received from the people and territory of the United States, I hoped that he and his Government would clearly understand that the President believed that the United States Government had done more than its full duty, and must and would insist upon this attitude to the end or completion of any diplomatic correspondence that may take place, and that if thoroughly cordial relations are to be established and maintained between our two Governments it must be upon the basis of humane methods in the conduct of the Cuban war, on the just protection of American interests in Cuba, and on the practical establishment of such reforms in the administration of Cuba as would justify the expectation of permanent and prosperous peace.

He replied in substance that the Spanish Government must insist upon what they felt to be a just enforcement by the United States of our duties of neutrality, but that we could rely upon humane methods of warfare and the early and effective establishment of such an autonomy in Cuba as would enable the Cubans to govern themselves as wisely as they could in matters relating to their internal affairs.

Señor Moret told me that he would see that Marshal Blanco was instructed to keep Minister de Lôme informed by telegraph of the substance of each bando that he should issue with regard to the methods of conducting the war, and that Minister de Lôme would keep you constantly informed as to the same.

I then asked the Spanish minister when the decrees granting autonomy would probably be signed by the Queen and published. He replied that they were long and minute in their details; that they were being considered carefully, and would be ready for the signature of the Queen between November 23 and 25; that they would be published in the Official Gazette on the day after signature, and would then be furnished to me for transmission to my Government.

Upon my telling him that I should be glad to have a summary for transmission to the President in time to aid him in the preparation of his annual message to Congress, he told me that he would have a summary prepared, which I could translate and telegraph to the President on the day after the decrees were signed.

I then said to Señor Moret that if the changes promised in the conduct of the war were carried out promptly and thoroughly, and if the autonomy when decreed should be such as would give the Cubans actual and honest self-government in local affairs, I would earnestly advise my Government to refrain from interference in Cuba for a reasonable time so that the effect of what Spain is now trying to do might be clearly seen. Of course I added that this was only my individual assurance, but that I knew that the President is sincerely anxious to maintain true friendship with Spain, while he must do his duty in protecting just American interests.

Señor Moret then asked me if I thought it would be possible to negotiate a commercial treaty between Spain and the United States which should open the ports of Cuba and the United States to practically free reciprocal commerce. I replied that the "first corner to be turned is to secure peace, so that there shall be commerce worth having, and that then I believed that my Government would gladly do all that we could to promote large and profitable commercial relations between Cuba and the United States; but that this is a matter to be hereafter considered."

I have tried to give the substance of this most important conversation. It was so direct, so free from all diplomatic form and methods and so unreserved, that I venture to suggest that this letter be not placed upon the official files of your Department, until time and events shall demonstrate the result.

I have the honor, etc.,

STEWART L. WOODFORD

*Woodford to Sherman
November 15, 1897*

[*Foreign Relations,* 1897–98, p. 602.]

*Madrid, Legation of the United States*

Sir:

Yesterday, November 14, the Spanish minister of the colonies sent me copy of telegram received by him yesterday morning from Marshal Blanco, notifying the Spanish Government that he had signed a bando reestablishing the normal life of the country people, and had organized protective committees for the "reconcentrados" who could not at once obtain the general benefits secured to the country population.

I telegraphed you immediately in cipher as follows:

*November 14, 1897*

Secretary Sherman, Washington:

Spanish Government has just notified me that bando has been signed by General Blanco reestablishing normal life of country people, with necessary precautions and organizing protective committees for reconcentrados who can not at once obtain general benefits secured to country population. Daily food and medical assistance are also regulated at the charge of the State.

WOODFORD

I called promptly at the office of the Spanish minister to express the gratification of yourself and the President at the prompt action of the Spanish Government.

The Spanish ministry have confirmed their purpose of publishing decrees, signed by the Queen Regent, and granting autonomy to Cuba, not later than November 25th instant.

I have, etc.,

STEWART L. WOODFORD

*Woodford to Sherman*
*November 26, 1897*

[*Foreign Relations,* 1897–98, pp. 616–17.]

*Madrid, Legation of the United States*

Sir:

Yesterday afternoon, November 25th, the Queen Regent signed the three decrees extending the provisions of the Spanish constitution over Cuba, fixing the electoral laws of Cuba, and establishing the new system of autonomy therein. With great courtesy the Spanish ministry handed me a synopsis of the third decree establishing autonomy. What added to this courtesy was that a member of the cabinet brought it to me.

I have to-day telegraphed you in cipher as follows:

> Queen signed three decrees November 25. First two decrees confer on Spaniards resident in Antilles all rights enjoyed by peninsular Spaniards and extend electoral law of Spain to Cuba and Porto Rico. These two decrees are permitted by Spanish constitution and do not require to be ratified by Cortes. Third decree, granting autonomy, will be published November 27. This must be ratified by Cortes. Full synopsis of this decree was furnished me Thursday. Same will be cabled to Spanish minister at Washington with permission to show you. Synopsis of powers of Cuban parliament is as follows:
>
> The executive power, together with the chambers, can consider and vote on all subjects which may affect the domestic order of the island and its local interests without any limitation whatever. Matters of state (foreign relations), war, and marine only are excepted from their jurisdiction, in which the Governor-General acts by his own authority and as the delegate of the central Government. In addition to the legislative power of the insular chambers they will first receive the oath of the governor to preserve faithfully the liberties and privileges of the colony. Second, they will exact responsibility from the colonial secretaries. Third, they will have the right to apply to the central Government, through the governor, in order to propose to it the modification of the laws in force of a national character, in order to invite it to present new projects of law or

to take measures of an executive character which may be in the interest of the colony.

Besides its legislative powers over all local matters, the insular parliament has the power, first, to prescribe regulations upon the preparation of the electoral lists, upon the method of procedure for the election, upon the qualifications of the electors and the manner of exercising the suffrage, provided that its regulations do not affect the right of citizens to vote freely; second to dictate regulations relative to the compositions of the courts of justice, facilitating their organization with natives of the country or with lawyers who may have practiced in the courts of the colony; third, to make up the insular budget, as well for expenses as for revenue, without limitation of any kind, and to determine the revenues from which Cuba shall cover its proportionate part of the national budget. This national budget, or expenses of sovereignty, will be voted by the national parliament, with the assistance of the Cuban senators and deputies. Fourth, to initiate or take part in the negotiations of the National Government for making treaties of commerce which may affect Cuban interests; fifth, to accept or reject treaties of commerce which the National Government may have made when the Cuban government has not taken part in these negotiations; sixth, to form the colonial tariff, acting in the determination of the articles of mutual commerce between the Peninsula and the colonies in accord with the government of the metropolis. These articles will be determined in a list formed by and between both governments.

In all these subjects, which may be of common interest to Cuba and to the Peninsula, the Government before presenting a project of law, or the chambers before voting it, will hear the opinion of the central Government, to whom the proposed law will be communicated for this purpose, the correspondence which may for this purpose have taken place being published afterwards.

The conflicts of jurisdiction which may occur between the different municipal, provincial, and insular assemblies, or between the latter and the executive power, and which by reason of their character may not have been referred to the central Government, shall be submitted to the courts of justice.

*   *   *

## President William McKinley's First State of the Union Message, December 6, 1897

[*The State of the Union Messages of the Presidents,* vol. 2, pp. 1861–69.]

... The most important problem with which this Government is now called upon to deal ... concerns its duty toward Spain and the Cuban insurrection.

*   *   *

The instructions given to our new minister to Spain before his departure for his post directed him to impress upon that Government the sincere wish of the United States to lend its aid toward the ending of the war in Cuba by reaching a peaceful and lasting result, just and honorable alike to Spain and to the Cuban people. These instructions recited the character and duration of the contest, the widespread losses it entails, the burdens and restraints it imposes upon us, with constant disturbance of national interests, and the injury resulting from an indefinite continuance of this state of things. It was stated that at this juncture our Government was constrained to seriously inquire if the time was not ripe when Spain of her own volition, moved by her own interests and every sentiment of humanity, should put a stop to this destructive war and make proposals of settlement honorable to herself and just to her Cuban colony. It was urged that as a neighboring nation, with large interests in Cuba, we could be required to wait only a reasonable time for the mother country to establish its authority and restore peace and order within the borders of the island; that we could not contemplate an indefinite period for the accomplishment of this result.

No solution was proposed to which the slightest idea of humiliation to Spain could attach, and, indeed, precise proposals were withheld to avoid embarrassment to that Government. All that was asked or expected was that some safe way might be speedily provided and permanent peace restored. It so chanced that the consideration of this offer, addressed to the same Spanish administration which had declined the tenders of my predecessor, and which for more than two years had poured men and treasure into Cuba in the fruitless effort to suppress the revolt, fell to others. Between the departure of General Woodford, the new envoy, and his arrival in Spain the statesman who had shaped the policy of his country fell by the hand of an assassin, and although the cabinet of the late premier still held office and received from our envoy the proposals he bore, that cabinet gave place within a few days thereafter to a new administration, under the leadership of Sagasta.

The reply to our note was received on the 23rd day of October. It is in the direction of a better understanding. It appreciates the friendly purposes of this Government. It admits that our country is deeply affected by the war in Cuba and that its desires for peace are just. It declares that the present Spanish government is bound by every consideration to a change of policy that should satisfy the United States and pacify Cuba within a reason-

## Rays of Hope 71

able time. To this end Spain has decided to put into effect the political reforms heretofore advocated by the present premier, without halting for any consideration in the path which in its judgment leads to peace. The military operations, it is said, will continue, but will be humane and conducted with all regard for private rights, being accompanied by political action leading to the autonomy of Cuba while guarding Spanish sovereignty. This, it is claimed, will result in investing Cuba with a distinct personality, the island to be governed by an executive and by a local council or chamber, reserving to Spain the control of the foreign relations, the army and navy, and the judicial administration. To accomplish this the present government proposes to modify existing legislation by decree, leaving the Spanish Cortes, with the aid of Cuban senators and deputies, to solve the economic problem and properly distribute the existing debt.

In the absence of a declaration of the measures that this Government proposes to take in carrying out its proffer of good offices, it suggests that Spain be left free to conduct military operations and grant political reforms, while the United States for its part shall enforce its neutral obligations and cut off the assistance which it is asserted the insurgents receive from this country. The supposition of an indefinite prolongation of the war is denied. It is asserted that the western provinces are already well-nigh reclaimed, that the planting of cane and tobacco therein has been resumed, and that by force of arms and new and ample reforms very early and complete pacification is hoped for.

The immediate amelioration of existing conditions under the new administration of Cuban affairs is predicted, and therewithal the disturbance and all occasion for any change of attitude on the part of the United States. Discussion of the question of the international duties and responsibilities of the United States as Spain understands them is presented, with an apparent disposition to charge us with failure in this regard. This charge is without any basis in fact. It could not have been made if Spain had been cognizant of the constant efforts this Government has made, at the cost of millions and by the employment of the administrative machinery of the nation at command, to perform its full duty according to the law of nations. That it has successfully prevented the departure of a single military expedition or armed vessel from our shores in violation of our laws would seem to be a sufficient answer. But of this aspect of the Spanish note it is not necessary to speak further now. Firm in the conviction of a wholly performed obligation, due response to this charge has been made in diplomatic course.

Throughout all these horrors and dangers to our own peace this Government has never in any way abrogated its sovereign prerogative of reserving to itself the determination of its policy and course according to its own high sense of right and in consonance with the dearest interests and convictions of our own people should the prolongation of the strife so demand. . . . It is honestly due to Spain and to our friendly relations with Spain that she should be given a reasonable chance to realize her expectations and to prove the asserted efficacy of the new order of things to which she stands irrevocably committed. . . . Sure of the right, keeping free from all offense ourselves, actuated only by upright and patriotic considerations, moved neither by passion nor selfishness, the Government will continue its watchful care over the rights and property of American citizens and will abate none of its efforts to bring about by peaceful agencies a peace which shall be honorable and enduring.

# Section Six

# Continuing Conflict

*Commentary*

Though McKinley announced himself in favor of giving Spain's new Liberal government "a reasonable chance to realize her expectations," he also warned in his State of the Union Message that American patience was not infinite and that the United States might soon feel compelled to undertake "further and other action" in the form of "intervention to end the war." The following documents illustrate that McKinley had reason to believe that Spanish plans for reform might come to naught and that Spain might prove as obstinate as ever in her dealings with the United States.

## The American Consul-General in Havana, Fitzhugh Lee, to Assistant Secretary of State William Day, December 7, 1897

[*Senate Document No. 230*, 55th Cong., 2nd Sess., p. 13.]

*Havana, United States Consulate General*

Sir:

(The consul-general informs the Assistant Secretary

of State that measures for the relief of the reconcentrados are not sufficiently energetic to be effective, and that he is advised by the Governor-General that authority to admit articles of food and clothing from the United States to Cuban ports free of duty rested with the authorities at Madrid.)

I see no effects of the governmental distribution to the reconcentrados. I am informed that only $12,500, in Spanish silver, had been dedicated to the Havana province out of the $100,000 said to have been set aside for the purpose of relieving them on the island, and that reports from all parts of the province show that 50 per cent have already died and that many of those left will die. Most of these are women and children. I do not believe the Government here is really able to relieve the distress and sufferings of these people.

I am informed an order has been issued in some parts of the island suspending the distribution of rations to reconcentrados. The condition of these people is simply terrible.

I enclose herewith an official copy of the comparative mortality in Havana for the six months ending November 30. It will be perceived that there has been a great increase in the death rate, and without adequate means in the future to prevent it the mortality will increase. We hear of much suffering in the Spanish hospitals for want of food and among the Spanish soldiers. I hear, also that the Spanish merchants in some parts of the island are placing their establishments in the names of foreigners in order to avoid their provisions being purchased on credit by the military administration, and that the Spanish army is suffering much from sickness and famine, and that a great deal of money is needed at once to relieve their condition. In some parts of the island, I am told, there is scarcely any food for soldiers or citizens, and that even cats are used for food purposes, selling at 30 cents apiece.

It is a fair inference therefore to draw from the existing conditions, that it is not possible for the Governor-General of this island to relieve the present situation with the means at his disposal.

I am, etc.,

FITZHUGH LEE

*Lee to Day [Confidential],
December 13, 1897
(Received December 18)*

[Senate Document No. 230, 55th Cong., 2nd Sess., pp. 13–14.]

*Havana, United States Consulate General*

Sir:

I have the honor to make the following report:

The contest for and against autonomy is most unequal. For it, there are five or six of the head officers at the palace, and twenty or thirty other persons here in the city.

Against it, first, are the insurgents, with or without arms, and the Cuban noncombatants; second, the great mass of the Spaniards, bearing or nonbearing arms—the latter desiring, if there must be a change, annexation to the United States.

Indeed, there is the greatest apathy concerning autonomy in any form. No one asks what it will be, or when, or how it will come.

I do not see how it could be even put into operation by force, because as long as the insurgents decline to accept it, so long, the Spanish authorities say, the war must continue.

I am obliged to say, too, that the Government of this island has not been able to relieve from starvation the

Cuban population driven from their homes by the Weyler edict, and no longer attempts to do so.

I am, etc.,

FITZHUGH LEE

## Lee to Day
## December 14, 1897

[*Senate Document No. 230*, 55th Cong., 2nd Sess., p. 14.]

*Havana, United States Consulate General*

Sir:

I have the honor to report that I have received information that in the province of Havana reports show that there have been 101,000 "reconcentrados," and that out of that 52,000 have died. Of the said 101,000, 32,000 were children. This excludes the city of Havana and seven other towns from which reports have not yet been made up. It is thought that the total number of reconcentrados in Havana province will amount to 150,000, nearly all women and children, and that the death rate among their whole number from starvation alone will be over 50 per cent.

For the above number of reconcentrados $12,500, Spanish silver, was set aside out of the $100,000 appropriated for the purpose of relieving all the reconcentrados on the island. Seventy-five thousand of the 150,000 may be still living, so if every dollar appropriated of the $12,500 reaches them the distribution will average about 17 cents to a person, which, of course, will be rapidly exhausted, and as I can hear of no further succor being afforded, it is easy to perceive what little practical relief has taken place in the condition of those poor people.

I am, etc.,

FITZHUGH LEE

## Lee to Day
### December 28, 1897

[*Senate Document No. 230*, 55th Cong., 2nd Sess., pp. 14–15.]

*Havana, United States Consulate General*

Sir:

I have the honor to report that I have been informed by the authorities here that they are now engaged in forming an autonomistic cabinet and arranging for the members to take the required oath on the 1st January next, and also for an election to take place thirty days thereafter.

My present information is that most of the Spaniards will refrain from voting, and nearly all of the Cubans.

The feeling in Havana, and I hear in other parts of the island, is strong against it—the Cubans desiring an independent republic and the Spaniards preferring annexation to the United States rather than autonomy. On the night of the 24th instant there seems to have been a concerted plan over the island to testify the disapprobation of the people to the proposed autonomistic plans of the Spanish Government. It culminated in this city about 2 o'clock in the morning of the 25th, in the principal square of Havana, where a mob assembled with cries of "Death to autonomy!" and to General Blanco, and shouting "Viva Weyler!" These men came to the square with stones in their pockets, and some of them armed with weapons.

They made a demonstration, too, against the office of the Diario de la Marina, a paper published in this town favoring autonomy, but were dispersed by the military police and soldiers.

I am, etc.,

FITZHUGH LEE

*Diplomatic Note: United States of America to Spain, December 20, 1897*
*(Minister Woodford to Foreign Affairs Minister Pio Gullón)*

[*Foreign Relations*, 1897–98, pp. 646–47, 650–54.]

*Madrid, Legation of the United States of America*

Excellency:

In further reply to the note which your excellency addressed to me on the 23d of October last, I have now the honor to state that I communicated to my Government the full text thereof, together with copies of the manifesto issued by the Liberal party of Spain, through its honored chief, Señor Sagasta, on the 24th of June last, and to which manifesto your excellency referred in evidence of the consistent and sincere purposes of reform which animate the existing Government of His Majesty.

The President now instructs me to inform your excellency that the Government at Washington has given that extended consideration which their importance demands, not only to your note itself, but also to the remarkable and earnest declarations which such manifesto contains of the principles and purposes of the Liberal party, now intrusted with the Government of Spain. During the very time that these matters have been receiving the careful consideration of my Government the President has observed with peculiar satisfaction the encouraging signs which come to him alike from the Peninsula, from Cuba, and from the honored representative of Spain at Washington, of the singleness and earnestness of purpose wherewith His Majesty's Government and its responsible agents in Cuba are laboring to bring about an instant and permanent change in those conditions in that island which have so long distressed the Government and the people of the United States.

\* \* \*

## Continuing Conflict 79

After making these declarations touching the proclaimed policy of the Liberal Government of Spain toward Cuba and the measures already adopted and to be forthwith devised to render that policy effective, your excellency takes up that part of my note of September 23d last, which states that the President feels it his duty to make the strongest possible effort to contribute effectively toward peace, and your excellency remarks that my note makes no suggestion of the means of which the President might avail himself to attain that end. My omission of such suggestion is sufficiently explained in my concluding statements that the President had no desire to embarrass the Spanish Government by formulating precise proposals as to the manner in which the assistance of the United States could be effectively rendered, and that all that was asked or expected was that some safe way might be provided for action which the United States could undertake with justice and self-respect, so that the settlement should be a lasting one, honorable and advantageous to Cuba and equitable to the United States, to which ends my Government offered its most kindly offices. For the realization of this friendly offer I invited an early statement of some proposal under which that tender of good offices might become effective, or in lieu thereof satisfactory assurances that peace in Cuba would, by the efforts of Spain, be promptly secured.

The assurances tendered by your excellency on behalf of the Liberal Government of Spain lie in the line of this latter alternative.

Your excellency's note is silent as to the manner and form in which the Government of the United States might exert its good offices. Your excellency limits yourself to suggesting coincident but separate action by the two Governments, each in its domestic sphere, whereby, as your excellency says, "Spain shall continue to put forth armed efforts, at the same time decreeing the political concessions which she may deem prudent and adequate, while the United States exerts within its borders the energy and vigilance necessary to absolutely prevent the procurement of the resources of which from the beginning the Cuban insurrection has availed itself as from an inexhaustible arsenal." And thereupon your excellency proceeds to discuss at some length the supposed shortcomings of the United States as to the manner of fulfilling the neutrality laws in the territory of the Union, and as to the scope and sufficiency of those laws. This labored arraignment could scarcely fail to be received with mingled pain and sorrow by a Government which, like that of the United States, inspired by the highest sense of friendly duty, has for nearly three years endured almost insupportable domestic burdens, poured forth its treasure by millions, and employed its armed resources for the full enforcement of its laws and for the prevention and repression of attempted or actual violation thereof by persons within its jurisdiction.

\* \* \*

In the light of these indisputable facts, and with this honorable record spread before him, the President is constrained to the conviction that nothing can be more unwarrantable than the imputation by the Government of Spain that the Government of the United States has in any wise failed to faithfully observe and enforce its duties and obligations as a friendly nation.

In this relation it may be proper, if not indeed imperative, to inquire what those obligations are.

It is to be borne in mind that Spain has so far insisted that a state of war does not exist between the Government and the people of Cuba, and that Spain is engaged in suppressing domestic insurrection, which does not give her the right which she so strenuously denies to herself, to insist that a third nation shall award to either party to the struggle the rights of a belligerent or exact from either party the obligations attaching to a condition of belligerency.

## Continuing Conflict 81

It can not be denied that the United States Government, whenever there has been brought to our attention the fact or allegation that a suspected military expedition has been set on foot or is about to start from our territories in aid of the insurgents, has promptly used our civil, judicial, and naval forces in prevention and suppression thereof. So far has this extended and so efficient has my Government been in this regard that, acting upon information from the Spanish minister, or from the various agencies in the employ of the Spanish legation, vessels have been seized and detained in some instances when subsequent investigation showed that they were engaged in a wholly innocent and legitimate traffic. By using our naval and revenue marine in repeated instances to suppress such expeditions, the United States has fulfilled every obligation of a friendly nation. Inasmuch as Spain does not concede, and never has conceded, that a state of war exists in Cuba, the rights and duties of the United States are such, and only such, as devolve upon one friendly nation toward another in the case of an insurrection which does not arise to the dignity of recognized war.

*   *   *

A large part of your excellency's note is devoted to the discussion of a hypothetical change of attitude toward the combatants, involving the recognition of their belligerency. As my Government, with the largest attainable knowledge of all facts and circumstances pertinent to the case, has not yet determined upon that course, I do not see that any useful purpose can be subserved by present argument upon the stated premises.

Neither do I discern the utility of discussing the circumstances under which a case might arise for considering and acting upon the thesis advanced by your excellency on the authority of the argument before the tribunal of Geneva, that it is the duty of a nation to amend its laws if inadequate for the fulfillment of its international obligations of neutrality or to offer any comment thereon. The inadequacy of our neutrality laws is not admitted, nor is it proved by Spain in the light of the precedent to which appeal is had, inasmuch as the doctrine of Geneva was only applicable and applied to the case of a public war between recognized belligerents, a case which Spain does not concede to exist in the present instance.

Whatever just and humane measures may attain to a contented and recuperative peace in Cuba can not but win our admiration, and any progress toward its attainment can not but be benevolently viewed. In this path of kindly expectancy, and inspired now as always by the high purpose of fulfilling every rightful obligation of friendship, the United States proposes to persevere so long as the event shall invite and justify that course.

I can not better close this reply to your excellency's note than by repeating and affirming the words with which I concluded my note to the Spanish Government of September 23 last, "That peace in Cuba is necessary to the welfare of the people of the United States, and that the only desire of my Government is for peace and for that sure prosperity which can only come with peace."

* * *

# Section Seven

# The Anti-Autonomy Riots

*Commentary*

If McKinley had some hope of solving the Cuban crisis at the beginning of 1898, this hope was struck a sharp blow in the first month of the new year by events in Cuba and, in turn, by renewed pressure from the Congress. The following reports from Consul-General Fitzhugh Lee in Havana indicated that autonomy would not work, and excerpts from the *Congressional Record* illustrate the fact that the Democrats were using the Cuban issue to embarrass McKinley and the Republicans, probably forcing the President to consider more vigorous measures than he then cared to take.

## *Lee to Day*
## *January 15, 1898*

[*Senate Document No. 230,* 55th Cong., 2nd Sess., p. 19.]

*Havana, United States Consulate General*

Sir:

I have the honor to confirm the following cipher telegram to you:

Havana, January 12

Spanish officers with a mob at their heels make an attack upon four autonomist newspapers. The rioting continued until 1 p.m.

Havana, January 12

Apprehend serious disturbances as consequence of intense prevailing excitement. Antiautonomists began trouble, confining their attacks to autonomists. Rioting ceased, but many rumors. Consulate-general and palace heavily guarded.

Havana, January 13

Reports condition of affairs quiet. City under guard. Mobs yesterday cried, Death to autonomy and Blanco, and long live Weyler. The conflict is between Spanish factions. Some of the rioters proposed going to United States consulate. Ships not needed now, but may be later.

Havana, January 13

Spanish officers and mob attacked three newspaper offices, not four (as reported yesterday). Soldiers joined the mob when sent to defend the newspapers, and outside the palace shouted death to Blanco and autonomy. If Americans are in danger ships should be ready to move promptly for Havana. Uncertainty and excitement widespread.

Havana, January 14

A few casualties. Disorder last night and this morning and crowds shouting death to Blanco and autonomy. Fears nothing very grave at present.

(Noon. All quiet.)

Havana, January 15

Quiet prevails.

I have also the honor to acknowledge the receipt of the following cipher telegram, received yesterday from you:

Washington, January 14

Lee, Consul-General, Havana:

(Instructs him to maintain frequent communication with United States squadron in Key West as to state of affairs at Havana. He should also frequently advise the Department of the situation.)

I am, etc.,

FITZHUGH LEE

*Lee to Day [Confidential], January 18, 1898 (Received January 22)*

[*Senate Document No. 230*, 55th Cong., 2nd Sess., p. 20.]

*Havana, United States Consulate General*

Sir:

The recent disorders in this city are to be primarily attributed to a group of Spanish officers who were incensed at articles appearing in three of the newspapers of Havana, El Reconcentrado, La Discusion, and El Diario de la Marina. The first was very pronounced against General Weyler and his methods, the Discusion had been suppressed by Weyler, but its publication was permitted to be resumed by Blanco, and the last had been an ultra Spanish organ, but had been converted by the present authorities to autonomy.

It is probable that the Spanish officers were first provoked by the denunciations of Weyler in the columns of one of these papers and determined to stop it, and afterwards, being supported by the mob, turned the demonstration into an antiautonomistic affair.

I sent to-day an analysis of the autonomistic plan. The intense opposition to it on the part of the Spaniards arises from the fact that the first appointment of officers to put into form its provisions were made generally outside of their party in order to show the Cubans in arms that autonomy was instituted for their benefit and protection.

The intelligent Spaniards see no prosperity in the future, but rather other wars and more confusion in the same old attempts to make the waters of commerce flow in unnatural channels. The lower Spanish classes have nothing in mind when autonomy is mentioned except Cuban local rule; hence their opposition.

I am, etc.,

FITZHUGH LEE

P.S.—The paper referred to will go by the next steamer.

## Lee to Day, January 21, 1898
*(Received January 25)*

[*Senate Document No. 230*, 55th Cong., 2nd Sess., pp. 20–22.]

*Havana, United States Consulate General*

Sir:

I have the honor to transmit herewith a document containing "Observations regarding the decree which established on the Island of Cuba the autonomic regime," and two copies of the Havana Gazette containing the decree referred to.

I am, etc.,

FITZHUGH LEE

Observations Regarding the Decree which
Establishes on the Island of Cuba
the Autonomic Régime.

1. Article 3 grants to the insular chambers, together with the Governor-General, the power to legislate regarding colonial affairs "in the form and

terms designated by law." What law? Those decreed by the Cortes at Madrid? It appears so, because the provisions of a general character emanating from the said Cortes shall receive the name of laws, while the colonial legislative provisions shall be called statutes. And if the Cortes of the Kingdom is the one to fix the form and terms of the colonial resolutions, it has a powerful arm in its hands and can annul the action of the insular chambers.

2. The insular representation is composed of two bodies, with the same authority—the chamber of representatives and the council of administration. Article 4 provides that the chamber is formed by popular election; but that concessions, which at first seems extensive, when examined in its relations with the other powers given to the insular representation, is practically deficient. No colonial resolution can be in force unless it has been approved by the chamber and the council. The council, as we shall see later, from the nature of its composition, will be controlled by the Government in such a manner that the representatives of the people to the chamber will always find themselves in the power of the Government in some way. They will not be able to do anything, because if the council does not approve, or should modify the decision of the other house—the chamber—the latter's decisions will have no effect. The veto granted by article 43 will not be required.

3. The council of administration is composed of 25 members; 17 are appointed directly by the Government; the remaining 18 are elected by popular vote. To be elected a member of said council it is necessary to be a Spaniard (Spanish subject), 35 years of age, and possesing an income of $4,000 for two years previous to election. The formation of the council will be therefore controlled by the

Government, because the Government will appoint unconditionally the 17 members, and it will be very easy for the Government to find one or more votes among those owing their election to the people, the more so as the conditions required to be a counselor are favorable to those near the Government. In order to pass any measure the presence of a majority of those composing this legislative body is required. It will be very difficult to have all the 18 members elected by the people vote as a unit, and the absence of one or two will be sufficient to give the governmental members control of the body, or the vote be a tie.

If the members elected should stand together on any measure objectionable to the Government, they could be sent to their homes by the Governor-General, and he can instruct or direct the election of others more accommodating. On the other hand, the members by governmental appointment can be removed—their offices or positions cease with their lives. The Governor-General can not remove them. And to this end they will be carefully selected as faithful instruments of the Government, in whose hands the whole autonomistic machine will be placed. It is known that in Canada all senators are appointed by the Government; but it should be remembered that the Governor-General appoints them, with the advice and consent of its counselors or ministers, and that these counselors are elected by the parliament, and the parliament by the people, the result is, that in Canada the senators are representatives of the people, while here in Cuba the Government can control them.

4. As if the authority to veto was not sufficient (art. 43) and the power did not exist to suspend, close the sessions, and adjourn both bodies, or either of them, by the decree of the Governor-

## The Anti-Autonomy Riots 89

General, article 30 grants more authority or power to present [prevent?] or annul the freedom or liberty of the discussions of the colonial parliament, when, in the opinion of the Governor-General, the national interests will be affected by a colonial statute. The bill in question can not even be discussed unless previously authorized by the central government, and it is a limitation or restriction which has no precedent in any known autonomistic legislation. It is improper because the restriction arises before the debates show the character of the measure to be discussed. It reveals, besides, a mistrust or want of confidence of the mere discussion of the subject.

A Governor-General may decree that all bills or colonial statutes may be, in his opinion, contrary to the national interest and that nothing should be discussed in the local legislative bodies without the previous consent of the Madrid Government. All guarantees are for the Madrid power; there are none for the colony, except the one named in article 43, which fixes the limit within which the Madrid Government has to decide regarding the right of a veto which a colonial statute may have received from the Governor-General.

* * *

9. The Governor-General has the power to suspend the constitutional guarantees, apply legislation of public order (ley de órden público), and adopt any measures he may deem fit to maintain peace, etc. This power the Governor-General can exercise at will, without any limitation, because he is not obliged to hear the opinion of the council of secretaries (ministry), and thus the whole political system of the country lies with the Governor-General. The latter can therefore find any pretext for court-martial, the application of the code of military justice, and all that series of proclamations and orders

which have caused so much harm, and which rob the citizen of all guarantees and protection.

10. The distribution of the public debt of Cuba remains completely in the hands and subject to the decision of the Cortes of the Kingdom, which will try to assign to Cuba as much of it as it can, so that Spain will pay the smallest part.

Beyond all this, even, the fact remains and makes useless, while it exists, all orderly and pacific development of the autonomistic régime, and this fact is the existence of the volunteers in arms. The political party in power is unarmed, has no force of its own, while the Spanish radical (intransigente) party, which is in the opposition, is armed, having on its side the armed volunteers. Under such conditions there can be no genuine autonomistic government, because the opposition can ride over, whenever it pleases, the authority of the local government, and of which we had a very recent example, and it can have it repeated whenever the radical Spanish (intransigente) party so desire.

## *United States House of Representatives January 20, 1898*

[*Congressional Record*, vol. 31, pt. 1, pp. 797–802, 798–800, 801–02, 804–06.]

JOHN WILLIAMS [DEM., MISS.] Mr. Chairman, I feel a little embarrassed in discussing this question at this time. I heard a gentleman a moment ago say that he would "rather have a thousand dollars in his own pocket than to be talked about as the Republican party has been talked about here this morning and yesterday."

## The Anti-Autonomy Riots 91

I feel embarrassed in addressing myself to this question, and my embarrassment grows out of the fact that I doubt, after all that has happened, if it is right, if it is not absolutely cruel, to add the reenforcement of my strong right arm and "eagle brain and massive eye" and tongue tipped with eloquence to all of the other forces which have been hurling renunciations at the Republican party.

In fact, Mr. Chairman, I can conceive of but one excuse for what we are doing over on this side of the Chamber in connection with this matter of belaboring the Republican party about its foreign policy. That is the excuse that the Irishman gave when he was frailing the dead dog. Being asked why he was doing it, the dog was dead, he replied, "Yes; but, faith, I am trying to teach him that there is punishment after death." [Laughter.] I feel a little bit of hesitation about going on any further in this matter of belaboring the dead Republican carcass.

* * *

Now, I feel like giving a brief bit of history; and I want to mention a few of the rather inconsistent positions taken by the [Republican] chairman of our [foreign affairs] committee. The first was that there was no "public war" in the Island of Cuba, because all international law writers agree that wherever a state of public war exists it is a matter of right on our part and of justice to belligerents to recognize the fact, and that *the recognition of the fact of the existence of public war is a recognition of belligerency.* There is no mystery about it.

In the next breath he praised the McKinley Administration because it had stopped the "cruel warfare" that had been waged by one Weyler, and that this war was being now waged by Spain in a civilized manner. It must be, then, that this is not a public war, but just a private affair, between Cubans and

Spain, touching no one else, and with which the balance of the world has nothing to do! That is not exactly the definition of "private war" in the intendment of the books on international law, but it must be in the intendment of the gentleman!

Now, the next position taken by the gentleman from Illinois is that we can not now recognize that a state of public war exists in Cuba—in other words, recognize her belligerency—because rights of belligerency would not do the Cubans any good. Shades of history, of all people who have ever rebelled against their mother countries, what an important piece of information this is! What a great pity that George Washington, Nathanael Greene, and Thomas Jefferson, during the Revolution, when seeking recognition of belligerency at the hands of the powers of Europe, did not know that recognition of belligerency was of no advantage to America!

When the gentleman comes to his third position, he enters upon a very open field of diplomacy. He throws out one of those diplomatic "hints" practiced by Lord Beaconsfield, a hint thrown out into the atmosphere. He hints that the time may come—the time may be nearer than we think—when the McKinley Administration will brace itself up, not for the purpose of recognizing the belligerency, but for the purpose of recognizing and enforcing the independence of Cuba! What a great thing a hint is when thrown out by a diplomat! Ordinarily you would believe it better that men should make plain, explicit statements, leaving as little as can be to the imagination. That is true of ordinary mortals. But when it comes to diplomats like my colleague from Mississippi MR. [ALLEN], myself, and the gentleman from Illinois, we do things high-handedly by hints. If Cuba shall ever obtain freedom from the Republican Ad-

## The Anti-Autonomy Riots 93

ministration, I imagine she will be "hinted" into it!

Now, a little bit of history, gentlemen, for the record. A little over two years ago, in the last Congress, you told the people, and howled until you were hoarse, about the cowardice of Mr. Cleveland's Administration in not recognizing Cuban belligerency. With our aid you passed through this House a concurrent resolution favoring belligerency. In the last campaign you made the air resonant with a repetition of your war cries and appeals in behalf of "humanity and bleeding Cuba." When your convention met, you promised that you would try to give "peace and independence" to Cuba.

Now, I tell you, you are faced with a situation out of which you can not wriggle when we go before the people. Look at it! The Senate sent to the Committee on Foreign Affairs of this House a recognition of belligerency. It is sleeping there because you want it to sleep. When this bill now pending came into this House, we offered certain amendments, some recognizing belligerency and some independence. To them points of order were made by the Republican chairman of the Foreign Affairs Committee with the knowledge and approval of your Speaker and all your leaders. These amendments were perhaps obnoxious to the point of order. We will not rethrash that straw. But the point of order *need* not have been raised. It *would* not have been raised, if the Republican party had been willing to help Cuba. This evening we will move to recommit with instructions, against which motion the point of order can not justly lie. There is no doubt about that. Then we will have a yea-and-nay vote in this House, I trust, and put you upon record.

Then, if the point of order is made and it is held that it lies against the motion to recommit, we will appeal from the decision of the Speaker and get a yea-and-nay vote on that.

Then we have already sent to your Foreign Affairs Committee two bills recognizing the independence of Cuba. If you do not take up and pass them, if you do not bring them to the attention of this House, you can not go before the people afterwards and say, as so many of you have said, that while you have the warmest love for the struggling patriots and I wish to see liberty enthroned in Cuba, you have defeated our efforts in that direction because—and only because—we have not tried to consummate our aim in the right way.

Now, Mr. Chairman, I am no "jingo." I am the farthest from it. I am not arguing for Cuban annexation; this is not a question of annexation; it is a question at most of independence. It is totally unlike the Hawaiian question—the proposition to annex a country 2,000 miles from San Francisco and 4,000 miles from the mouth of the Nicaraguan Canal, for the purpose of enabling a sugar-planting plutocracy to rule through us ten or twenty times their number. Upon that question you would be deserting our traditional position as an American continental power, and trying to make of ourselves an intermeddling-maritime-world-power.

This is not a jingo question; it is a question of justice. All international law says that if there is a "state of public war" in the Island of Cuba to-day we have the right and we should, as a matter of justice to the Cubans, recognize the existence of the fact. The recognition of the existence of the fact is a recognition of belligerency. Nobody would have a right to complain, if in our discretion we exercised our right. It would be just *casus belli* to no power.

*  *  *

HENRY JOHNSON [REP., IND.] Mr. Chairman, I confess that I

have heard but very little of this debate, for I have been absent attending the hearings of the Banking and Currency Committee, of which I have the honor to be a member; but since coming into the Chamber a few moments ago I think I have gathered enough of the discussion to be able to understand its general drift, and I desire to submit a few observations upon the subject, which I trust will be found to be somewhat relevant.

So far as I am personally concerned, sir, I am perfectly willing to trust the Chief Executive of this nation in this troublesome Cuban matter. In my humble opinion his whole management of the affair since he came into office has been characterized by the utmost good sense, sound judgment, and exalted patriotism. He has conducted everything so adroitly as to steer clear of those things which menaced our peace and at the same time to obtain for us from Spain everything that we had a right to expect from her.

Under his administration of the problem American rights have been preserved, the prison doors in Cuba have been thrown open to our countrymen who were improperly restrained of their liberty, reparation has been made for injuries inflicted, and, largely in response to the sentiments which he has voiced, a complete change in the policy of Spain in its efforts to subjugate Cuba has been inaugurated. The old Spanish administration has fallen. That military chieftain who was waging war in Cuba contrary to the known usages of war has been recalled. For the old ministry there has been substituted a more liberal ministry—that of Sagasta.

In place of Weyler they have sent a general who is waging war according to the dictates of humanity and the code of civilized nations. Spain, too, is offering autonomy. Now, Mr. Chairman, that autonomy may not be according to our democratic ideas; but it is a great deal for a government constituted like the one which proffers it. It strikes me that under these circumstances there can be no wiser course for this Chamber, irrespective of party, than to uphold the sagacious, able, and patriotic hands of the President of the United States. His past conduct warrants us in the belief that our future will be secure with him. It is quite evident from all we hear that he is keeping a careful eye upon the condition of affairs in Cuba, and that in this matter he is being ably seconded by the distinguished gentleman of opposite politics who is now our consul in that island. He has promised us to see that American interests are jealously guarded, and that if the necessity arises he will act promptly to protect them.

Mr. Chairman, I read in the Washington Post this morning an editorial which, for good sense and conservative judgment, will compare favorably with any editorial that I have seen on this subject. I hope every gentleman of this House read it and pondered over it. It expresses the importance and gravity of the situation which now confronts us in this Cuban question so much better than I can possibly express it myself that if I had the article here I would be tempted to send it to the clerk's desk and have it read to the House. I commend it to the thoughtful perusal of gentlemen on the other side of this Chamber, and also to some on this side who seem disposed to rush with unbecoming haste toward that which may lead to great national embarrassment. If these gentlemen will read this editorial carefully and reflect over it, I trust that the hand of discretion will be laid on their fiery and impetuous natures and that the country may be saved from some menacing perils which their ill-advised conduct may possibly bring upon it.

It is all very proper, Mr. Chairman, for us to say that we sympathize with Cuba in this struggle for independence. It is all very commendable that as individuals we heartily desire to see the Cubans achieve their liberty. It may even be excusable for us to covet that island and desire that at some time it shall become a part of our own domain. But these are but one-sided, narrow, and superficial views of a great subject of national moment and importance. We must not forget that we are one of the family of nations; that there are certain rules of international law which are to be observed. We must not in our zeal to interfere in Cuban affairs set a precedent which may come home to plague us at some time in the future when we are least prepared to meet its force or avoid its effect.

There have been times in the past when, with very great propriety, we might have questioned the action of Spain—her conduct of the war against the insurgents. If so, I submit to this Chamber that the progress of events has removed very largely that ground of complaint. As I said a bit ago, the entire system of warfare there has been reversed. From being barbarous it has become civilized. I repeat it, the old administration in Spain that waged a different kind of warfare has been overthrown and a new and liberal administration has taken its place. A soldier is now in command of the Spanish forces on the Cuban Island who is doing all he can to pacify the insurgents and who is offering them a species of autonomy which, coming from Spain, is a marvel, though it may not be so liberal as to render it acceptable if tendered to people bred and constituted as our own.

Mr. Chairman, I sincerely lament the distress and suffering in Cuba.

It is well enough for us to contribute to the relief of the sufferings of the insurgents. We can do this consistently with our international obligations. Indeed, it is the exercise of the most commendable philanthropy to do so. But it is quite a different thing for us to exercise the high prerogatives which we possess as representatives of the American people and undertake, in violation of our international relations, to invade by force the internal affairs of that island and to give such a just provocation to Spain as may lead to consequences which we may subsequently very profoundly regret.

Mr. Chairman, our efforts along the line of pacification conducted through our President have been wonderfully successful. By what logic do gentlemen who did not intervene months ago under the barbarous and cruel policy of Spain then being pursued propose now to intervene when the very things which we insisted she should adopt as part of her policy toward that island have been adopted by her, and when she has, at our suggestion, renounced the methods of repression which we denounced with such emphasis?

MR. CLARK. Does not the gentleman know that in the last Congress the majority of Democrats in this House did vote to intervene? I may say all the Democrats, for it was only the personal adherents of Mr. Cleveland on this side, who never were Democrats, that voted against that step.

MR. JOHNSON. I wish it were possible that gentlemen could take a broader view on this subject than merely to consider it as something upon which they may hope to obtain a partisan advantage. We may be standing nearer the mouth of the crater than we realize. In our anxiety to avert Cuban bloodshed, let us be exceedingly cautious that we do not precipitate the flow of American blood. The hot-heads here, Mr. Chairman, ought to be restrained and obstructed.

The demand of the hour is for sensible and conservative men on this floor—men who are not influenced by considerations of party expediency or partisan advantage, but who are capable of taking a broad and patriotic view of the embarrassing and important subject. It is the ultimate and impartial verdict of the people as a whole that we should desire, and not the approval of a few incendiaries who would precipitate difficulties upon the country and involve us in complications which all would seriously regret.

❂  ❂  ❂

JEREMIAH BOTKIN [DEM., KAN.] I would like to ask the gentleman a question, with his consent.

MR. JOHNSON. I was going to say, Mr. Chairman—

MR. BOTKIN. Mr. Chairman, I would like to ask the gentleman from Indiana how he harmonizes his present position on the question of Cuban belligerency, or Cuban independence, with the Republican platform of 1896?

MR. JOHNSON. Oh, Mr. Chairman, there are two answers to the gentleman's question, either of which would be entirely satisfactory to a reasonable man. The first is that there is no man, no reasonable man, who reads the Republican platform to which the gentleman refers who can contend for a moment that it commits the Republican party to the policy that he insists upon.

Another answer is that I am going to act here on my individual judgment in matters of this character. I am going to act on circumstances as they develop themselves to me at the present time, and I am responsible to my conscience and to my constituents for the action which I shall take. [Applause.] I prefer to accept the wise and patriotic construction of the Republican platform which has been given to it by the President of the United States than the narrow construction which the gentleman would place upon it.

MR. BOTKIN. Does not the gentleman know that the people generally throughout the country and the masses of the Republican party have placed the same interpretation on the platform as that which I have suggested?

MR. JOHNSON. I do not know anything of the kind. I knew that the great fight in the last election was waged upon many questions, but that this one did not enter largely into the public estimation. It was dwarfed by others deemed to be more important. The Republicans of this country have placed no construction upon the Cuban plank of the party platform which would justify intemperate conduct upon our part as Representatives.

GALUSHA GROW [REP., PA.] Times have changed, anyhow.

MR. JOHNSON. I say, Mr. Chairman, that we may be standing nearer the verge of the crater than some gentlemen may imagine. I grant you that Spain is torn with internecine war. I grant you that her councils are divided. I grant you that she has not waged, so far, a successful war against Cuba, but at the same time the old Castilian spirit is not dead in her veins, and though she may be impotent to successfully resent our conduct, though she may be incapable of overcoming us in hostilities, yet we may, by our hotheaded conduct in this matter, force her to go to war in response to her pride and her courage.

We may involve ourselves in difficulties of the most extraordinary character. Can we defend ourselves in the forum of conscience before the cool, sober sentiment of this country if we do this? Can we defend ourselves under the law of nations in the eyes of the world if we do it? Everything we have demanded of Spain in the way of stopping her barbarities has been acceded to. Every indication of our desire she has studiously complied with with a view of avoiding difficulty with us.

## The Anti-Autonomy Riots 101

Shall we now, simply in pursuit of a sentiment, press her to that impassable point which will compel her to commence hostilities against us, and thus indirectly exercise the power to declare war which the Constitution imposes upon us, but which we have not the hardihood to exercise indirectly? Shall we provoke her into belligerency; shall we menace and shock the business interests of this country; shall we lay aside the matters of domestic legislation—those internal reforms so necessary for the benefit of the country and the prosperity of the people—to devise methods of prosecuting a great war?

\* \* \*

Who is there here who wants now, by the agitation of a war feeling, or by precipitating a war even with so impotent a power as Spain is claimed to be, to shake the business interests of this country to the foundation, to arrest all of our recuperation and development, to take our attention from these great measures of legislation which are absolutely indispensable to the prosperity of the people? Are you going to devote your time to voting men and munitions of war? Are you going to lay the groundwork for future pension rolls?

Are you going to distract the attention and legislation of the country from the bankruptcy act, which is demanded from many sections of the Republic and which is deemed to be necessary for the relief of the debtor? Are you going to lay aside the question of restricting immigration, that we may stop the coming to our shores from abroad of that element which is dangerous to our national existence and which we can no longer assimilate in the body politic? Are you going to abandon the great question of banking and currency reform which is being earnestly pressed upon your attention from all sections of the land and by men of all political parties, and in the proper solution of which is involved the happiness and prosperity of this great Republic?

* * *

MR. ALBERT BERRY [DEM., KY.] Will the gentleman permit me to ask him a question?

MR. JOHNSON. Yes, one more.

MR. BERRY. What does the gentleman from Indiana propose to do with the 200,000 people on that island who General Lee, our consul, tells us are there starving to death?

MR. JOHNSON. I propose, as the President of the United States has already done, that we shall call upon the warmhearted, generous, sympathetic American people to contribute out of their means for the purpose of alleviating this distress. I want to call the gentleman's attention to the fact that the man now in command of the Spanish army is not throwing any obstacles in the way of furnishing people with supplies, but is willing to do all he can to aid in the distribution.

I want to say another thing before I close. You demand forcible intervention, at least recognition, because of the suffering and bloodshed of this Cuban conflict. Tell me something. Can you dissociate war with this condition? Where did you ever know a war to be waged in the world's history that has not been accompanied with all the evils about which you are now so sympathetic?

It is not well enough for the Cubans to stop and calmly reflect when the olive branch is extended to them by Spain, to cease their hostilities at least long enough to hear what is being said to them in the way of pacification? Let us soberly ask ourselves whether or not the sentiment in this country which seeks to prolong these hostilities, which cares nothing for American interests and nothing for American lives in its anxiety to achieve its ends, had not better keep its mouth and its hand out of this controversy; whether

## The Anti-Autonomy Riots

it will not be better not only for Cuba but also for our own country, its progress and development, if we manifest a little common sense at this peculiarly troublesome juncture of our affairs.

* * *

JAMES ROBINSON [DEM., IND.] Mr. Chairman, the subject now under consideration is not new to the country or to the members of this House, very unfortunately to the people of Cuba, native and American, we have had this subject pressed upon us by red lines of blood, by loss of commerce, by wicked cruelty and devastation, till American patriotism rises and demands a recognition of Cuban rights.

For three long years, this time; and for ten years before the Cubans fought for freedom, and for three years now has this country gazed idly and stupidly on a scene of carnage, ruin, and death in our own immediate vicinity and presence, and denied a helping hand to these determined people. Why longer delay?

For many months this country has been ripe for action. Representatives in Congress, curbed by their patient wait for official information, have several times crystallized their judgment by unofficial and newspaper reports from the doomed and ravished districts, while the friends of Spain have each time doubted and discredited, till in the special session of Congress the Administration, longer unable to withstand the force of public opinion, revealed its secrets and confirmed the information long before secured.

In less than two days after the receipt of that official information, the Senate, with commendable patriotism, passed a joint resolution recognizing the Cubans as belligerents, and it has hung like Mohammed's coffin for months amid the entangling and mystifying rules of the House of Representatives. Not only was the action of the Senate in accord with party declarations in conventions, but it was in consonance with an enlightened sense of justice and humanity and perfectly consistent with the rules of international law.

With sentiment, justice, law, to guide us to action, should we yet longer delay? Should we not at once change the policy in Cuba from rude, barbaric, brute force and violence, without rules, to the rules of civilized warfare?

The Cubans are doing no more than we would do ourselves; no more than what our sires did do when they opposed the tyranny of England—threw off the yoke and made it possible in the Western World to have a continent of the free. They seek, as we did, to throw off the yoke of oppression and assume among the powers of the earth those rights to which the laws of nature and nature's God entitle them.

Does not the history of the ten years of disorders there before—does not this outbreak—establish that the spark of liberty there was not born to die?

Why, then, longer withhold our encouragement? The last Administration, too slow to act itself, "marshaled us the way that we were going," and outlined such a policy as we should pursue; but the Cleveland December message was seen to come and go; his Administration expired, and no time was fixed.

This Administration, declaring the facts which to my mind indicate a state of war in Cuba, on the 17th of last May sent to Congress a message to tell us that from 600 to 800 Americans were perishing on that fertile island that should flow with milk and honey; that Americans, driven from their homes in the country like sheep to the shambles, were immured in the cities without shelter, food, or raiment; Americans, who ought to have a guaranty of rights to breathe the air of that island, to live and move and have their being, are huddled together in pestilence-breed-

# The Anti-Autonomy Riots 105

ing towns and cities, and, escaping from the wrath of the sword and bullet, they are forced into the jaws of famine and disease.

For over two long years these scenes of carnage and destruction of life and property have been passing before us, two-thirds of the imports to this country from there gone and lost, three-fourths of our exports vanished, brutality, bloodshed, torture, and death "rushes red on our sight," no protection to Americans or their interests, no payment of losses from the bankrupt treasury of this effete and declining dynasty, and yet we are sometimes told that there is no God of Israel to guide us to the performance of our patriotic Christian duty. "O Judgment, thou hast fled to brutish beasts and men have lost their reason." No war in Cuba? Why, then, ask these extraordinary supplies? Why call upon this whole country for contributions for starving men? Representations of facts made, upon which it was urged that we vote this large sum of $50,000 in May to feed the hungry and clothe the naked and destitute Americans, only 90 miles across the water, so many of our people there without the guaranty of any protection to property, to honor, to life, and yet some say in their hearts there is no war.

By what standard are we to judge of war? By the number of soldiers engaged? If so, then 200,000 sent to Cuba or engaged there in three years should establish the fact. Is it to be determined by the fact of deaths, cruelties, starvation, and miseries? Under this standard the proof is made. Will you wait to say it till conflicting Governments are shown? Will you wait till loss of trade and danger to life and property and liberty of our own countrymen appear? If so, the time is ripe for action. Two hundred thousand humans already dead and in Cuban graves, 200,000 Spanish soldiers in Cuba to quell a disturbance that antijingoes say exists only in the imagination of a few weak and designing individuals of the press and in the Congress of the United States.

After three long years we find the promise of Spain to put down the rebellion unfulfilled. All students of history have lived long enough and know her history well enough to measure the distance between her promises and performance, words and acts. We have seen the agent of her tyrannical rule march across the island, leaving behind him, like the fiery meteor of night, a great red trail of blood. We have seen him gloat in satisfaction over an unvanquished foe. We have seen him return to safe retreats, immure the citizens, the objects of his vengeance, in towns and cities, and fleeing from fire, sword, and ravishment, we have seen them driven to starvation and death.

Is not this the retribution presaged by the Spanish Minister De Lôme's letter to Secretary of State Olney, between the diplomatic lines of which is written the exasperation of Spain at the action of some of our citizens and the slowness of our Government to aid her in this unholy struggle against a people on whose necks she wishes still to hold the tyrannical yoke? Read that letter, and, with the well-known Spanish character, do we not incur greater risks and complications by delay than would have come by a prompt recognition of the belligerency of the Cubans? Every day is fraught with greater danger. The interest of our trade, the safety of our people, warrant it; humanity demands it, not to speak of the eternal principles of patriotism and human liberty, which enforce our duties upon us.

Is it consistent with our interests that a revolution within 90 miles of our shores should continue for three long, bloody years, and can we be compelled to submit in patience to the disturbance and disorders which are the natural outgrowth of such conditions? Have we not rights as sacred as those of Spain, which, after three years of vain trial to regain a lost star in her wasting diadem, still shows with dogged persistency her inability?

* * *

A great duty devolves upon us, not only to the people so near us, but we owe a duty to ourselves, to our country, to our God. For these years patriotic hearts have fought for liberty, and tyranny 200,000 strong has sought to restrain and conquer, till to-day the eyes of nations are upon us, the eyes of trembling natives, 500,000 strong, with liberty kindled in their breasts, but hands not strong enough to strike—their eyes are upon us. All look this way to see if we will relapse into the pusillanimity of cowardice or assert our dignity and strength by a bold stroke of policy. Under the law of nations we only need the facts, first, of the existence of war; second, that our interests are affected.

Both are proven by the flood of light shed on these questions, by every source of legitimate news, and proven as conclusively as fact was ever proven in a court of law. Our efforts at mediation were met with a tone of complaint, that our Government had not done all it ought to smother the rebellion. The last Administration, full of tolerance, gave notice to the country and to Spain that a time would come when we would take action in Cuban affairs.

Sir, I would not stir the mind of any man to mutiny and rage, but if we fail to do our duty to suffering humanity, fighting for freedom, starving for freedom, murdered for freedom, sacrificing themselves in one of the most heroic battles ever fought by man for liberty, facing and meeting their fate, and shot like dogs for freedom—if, sir, under these conditions this free and liberty-loving people, through their Representatives assembled in this Capitol, does not stretch out its arm across the Gulf to rescue these patriots from the iron hand of that tottering monarchy, then I say, tear down your Capitol and let the plowshare run through the soil on which it rests, rather than let it stand as an emblem of a patriotic and enlightened people. [Applause on the Democratic side.]

The scheme of autonomy, conceived as it was in insincerity, unsanctioned by the organic law of Spain, with no safeguards of security for Cuba, will fail. The Cubans at the end of the ten years' war reluctantly entered into a treaty with Spain, nearly every provision of which was violated by the mother country, and the few that were observed were kept only upon the demand of the Government of the United States.

The loss of Cuba to Spain will be her gain. With the spirit of revolution permeating its people, Cuba will never be more profitable to Spain than were the American colonies in revolt to the British Crown. With all hope of profit swept away, nothing remains of Spain but the wasting of millions to preserve an empty honor, based upon an antiquated fiction of state pride, the breach of which would be far more profitable than the observance to this ancient, crumbling monarchy. Nor ought her pride be thus wounded, judging from the history of the past, by the loss of this fertile but incorrigible island.

\* \* \*

# Section Eight
# The De Lôme Letter

*Commentary*

Prospects for a settlement were further undermined with the publication on February 9, 1898, of a letter written by the Spanish Minister in Washington, Enrique Dupuy de Lôme. Insulting McKinley and indicating that Spain might be insincere in her autonomy policy, the letter touched off a new public and congressional outcry which culminated on February 14 in the passage of resolutions in both Houses of Congress calling upon the administration to publish American consular reports from Cuba. McKinley appreciated that the delivery of such reports to the Congress would be tantamount to a request for a declaration of war.

*De Lôme's Letter
December, 1897\**

[*Foreign Relations*, 1897–98, pp. 1007–08.]

*Washington, Legation of Spain*

His Excellency Don José Canalejas
My Distinguished and Dear Friend:

You have no reason to ask my excuses for not having

---

\*From internal evidence, this undated letter was probably written about the middle of December.

written to me. I ought also to have written to you, but I have put off doing so because overwhelmed with work and *nous sommes quittes.*

The situation here remains the same. Everything depends on the political and military outcome in Cuba. The prologue of all this, in this second stage (phase) of the war, will end the day when the colonial cabinet shall be appointed and we shall be relieved in the eyes of this country of a part of the responsibility for what is happening in Cuba, while the Cubans, whom these people think so immaculate, will have to assume it.

Until then, nothing can be clearly seen, and I regard it as a waste of time and progress, by a wrong road, to be sending emissaries to the rebel camp, or to negotiate with the autonomists who have as yet no legal standing, or to try to ascertain the intentions and plans of this Government. The [Cuban] refugees will keep on returning one by one, and as they do so will make their way into the sheepfold, while the leaders in the field will gradually come back. Neither the one nor the other class had the courage to leave in a body and they will not be brave enough to return in a body.

The [State of the Union] message has been a disillusionment to the insurgents, who expected something different; but I regard it as bad (for us).

Besides the ingrained and inevitable bluntness (groseria) with which is repeated all that the press and public opnion in Spain have said about Weyler, it once more shows that McKinley is, weak and a bidder for the admiration of the crowd, besides being a would-be politician (politicastro) who tries to leave a door open behind himself while keeping on good terms with the jingoes of his party.

Nevertheless, whether the practical results of it [the message] are to be injurious and adverse depends only upon ourselves.

## The De Lôme Letter

I am entirely of your opinions; without a military end of the matter nothing will be accomplished in Cuba, and without a military and political settlement there will always be the danger of encouragement being given to the insurgents by a part of the public opinion if not by the Government.

I do not think sufficient attention has been paid to the part England is playing.

Nearly all the newspaper rabble that swarms in your hotels are Englishmen, and while writing for the Journal they are also correspondents of the most influential journals and reviews of London. It has been so ever since this thing began. As I look at it, England's only object is that the Americans should amuse themselves with us and leave her alone, and if there should be a war, that would the better stave off the conflict which she dreads but which will never come about.

It would be very advantageous to take up, even if only for effect, the question of commercial relations, and to have a man of some prominence sent hither in order that I may make use of him here to carry on a propaganda among the Senators and others in opposition to the junta and to try to win over the refugees.

So, Amblard is coming. I think he devotes himself too much to petty politics, and we have got to do something very big or we shall fail.

Adela returns your greeting, and we all trust that next year you may be a messenger of peace and take it as a Christmas gift to poor Spain.

Ever your attached friend and servant,

ENRIQUE DUPUY DE LÔME

*Day to Woodford*
*February 9, 1898*

[*Foreign Relations*, 1897–98, p. 1008.]

*Department of State*
*Washington, D. C.*

There has appeared in the public prints a letter, addressed early in December last by the Spanish minister to Mr. Canalejas, and which the minister admits was written by him. It contains expressions concerning the President of the United States of such character as to end the minister's utility as a medium for frank and sincere intercourse between this country and Spain. You are, therefore, instructed to at once say to the minister of state that the immediate recall of the minister is expected by the President.

WILLIAM DAY
ACTING SECRETARY


*Woodford to Sherman*
*February 11, 1898*

[*Foreign Relations*, 1897–98, pp. 1008–09.]

*Madrid, Legation of the United States*

Dispatch concerning Spanish minister received. Have seen Spanish minister for foreign affairs. Resignation of Spanish minister had been asked and accepted by cable before our interview. The first secretary of legation at Washington will be placed at once in charge of the legation. New minister will be appointed at once, and will reach Washington in about 15 days. Full report by next mail.

STEWARD L. WOODFORD

## United States House of Representatives
## February 14, 1898

[*Congressional Record*, vol. 31, pt. 2, pp. 1681–82.]

LEMUEL QUIGG [DEM., N.Y.] Mr. Speaker, the Committee on Foreign Affairs have asked me to report another resolution with amendments.

THE SPEAKER. [THOMAS REED, REP., ME.] The Clerk will report the resolution.

The resolution was read, as follows:

> *Resolved by the House of Representatives,* That the Secretary of State be, and he hereby is, directed, if in his opinion not incompatible with the public interest, to inform the House what information, if any, has been received at the Department of State concerning the present condition of the reconcentrados in Cuba; whether or not they have been permitted to return to their estates; whether or not they, or any considerable number of them, are now on their estates; whether or not any zones, or considerable parts of zones, are now being cultivated by them, according to the reports received at the Department of State from American consuls or consular agents; what steps, if any, are shown by said consular reports to have been taken by the Spanish Government for feeding said reconcentrados, or for otherwise preventing them from starving and suffer-

ing; whether or not the Spanish Government has given the necessary military protection to enable the mills to grind cane, and what progress, if any, has been made in Spain's effort to induce the Cubans to accept autonomy.

SEC. 2. That the Secretary of State be directed, if in his opinion not incompatible with the public interest, to send to the House copies of all such reports from consuls, vice-consuls, and commercial agents of the United States in Cuba as may shed light upon the subjects above referred to, and as shall give information to the House and to the country concerning the condition of Cuba since the advent of the new régime under General Blanco.

With the following amendment:

In line 17, after the word "progress," strike out the words "if any has" and insert in lieu thereof "is shown by these reports to have."

So that it will read:

And what progress is shown by these reports to have been made in Spain's effort to induce the Cubans to accept autonomy.

MR. QUIGG. Mr. Speaker, when Congress assembled in December last, the President informed us in his annual message that the policy of concentration which had been adopted by the Spaniards in Cuba had, in deference to the repeated requests of our Government, been discontinued, and that a more humane method of dealing with the people of Cuba had been adopted in its stead. The object of this resolution is simply to ascertain what steps have been taken in Cuba, in pursuance to the announcement that was made by the Spanish Government to our Government, with regard to this matter.

I do not suppose that the House requires any

further information as to the character of the resolution, because it is apparent in its terms. Three months or thereabouts have elapsed since the new policy was undertaken in Cuba, and the purpose of the resolution is simply to ascertain what information the State Department has as to the steps that have been taken in Cuba to introduce the new and more humane policy.

I ask the previous question on the resolution.

*   *   *

HENRY COOPER [WISC.] Before the motion is put, I desire to ask the gentleman from New York a question. I understood the resolution as read to call for a report as to the present condition of the reconcentrados on the Island of Cuba. I was not present when the chairman of the Committee on Foreign Affairs made a speech on the 19th of January, but on looking up the RECORD I find that he stated in explicit terms that the Spanish Government had abandoned the policy of reconcentration and reversed the whole system. If that were true as to the reconcentrados on the island, did the committee know at the time the chairman of the committee made that statement whether or not that policy had been reversed? William D. Gibson, of the Philadelphia Press, said it had not been abandoned at all, but was in full force on the 20th of January, before Weyler was removed. What is the fact within the knowledge of the committee?

MR. QUIGG. If this resolution passes, the House will be put in possession of the precise facts. Instead of attempting to answer the gentleman on any information I may possess, which must have been had secondhand of course, I suggest that he vote for this resolution and then we will have all of the information directly from the State Department, and he will be fully informed and will not have to rely on the statements of the chairman of our committee or upon newspaper statements, but will have the full official information.

The previous question was ordered.

The amendment recommended by the committee was agreed to.

The resoution as amended was agreed to.

# Section Nine

## Prelude to an Ultimatum

*Commentary*

If events in the first six weeks of 1898 were not enough to force McKinley's hand, developments from the middle of February to the middle of March were: the destruction of the battleship *Maine* in Havana harbor on the night of February 15, growing evidence of Spanish inability to improve things in Cuba and Senator Redfield Proctor's speech on March 17 placed McKinley under intense pressure to make a bold move or lose control of his party and the country. The following diplomatic reports and the copy of Proctor's speech illustrate this point.

## *Day to Woodford* [*Personal and Confidential*] *March 3, 1898*

[*Foreign Relations*, 1897-98, pp. 680-81.]

Dear Mr. Woodford:

I have your favor of the 21st ultimo, as also your note of the 19th ultimo. I have, furthermore read your personal letters to the President, which have kept him so thoroughly advised of the situation. As to De Lôme, I agree with you that that incident is, fortunately, closed. The publication of the letter created a good deal of feeling among Americans, and but for the fact that it was a private letter, surreptitiously if not criminally obtained, it might have raised considerable difficulty in dealing with it diplomatically. As soon as we learned of its authenticity the first cable was sent to you suggesting the recall of the minister. De Lôme had been advised the day before, and cabled his resignation before the letter was brought to the Department. Your prompt and efficient method of dealing with the matter after its serious import was known, and your firm, dignified action in the interview with the minister, no doubt led to the satisfactory termination of the incident. Everybody that I see seems well pleased with it, and no one wished trouble about a matter of this kind. If a rupture between the countries must come, it should not be upon any such personal and comparatively unimportant matter. We sent you day before yesterday full instruction covering the Cuban situation, as you will see it is bad enough.

The De Lôme incident, the destruction of the *Maine*, have added much to the popular feeling upon this subject, although the better sentiment seems to be to await the report of the facts, and to follow the action of the President after the naval board has made its report. Whatever that report may be, it by no means relieves the situation of its difficulties. The policy of starvation, the failure of Spain to take effective measures to suppress the insurrection, the loss of our commerce, the great expense of patrolling our coast—these things, intensified by the insulting and insincere character of the De Lôme letter, all combine to create a condition that is very grave, and which will require the highest wisdom and greatest prudence on both sides to avoid a crisis. . . . The suggestion of the withdrawal of [consul] General Lee meets with no favor with the President. Like yourself, the General has been in the midst of surroundings often unfriendly, and has borne himself with dignity, patriotism, and courage, deserving the support, not the disapproval, of the Administration. As to the objectionable [American] newspapers, their sensational and unfounded reports are the cause of as much embarrassment at home as they can be abroad. The only remedy seems to be the sober sense and judgment of the people. There are many things, my dear General, which can not be written, but we all appreciate how difficult your position is and with what sagacity and fidelity you have discharged its manifold duties. I wish I could have a full talk with you. It may be that things will take such shape that the President will conclude to send a special messenger to you with full information, which no amount of writing could make available to you. The President highly appreciates your good work, and often speaks of it in the warmest terms.

I beg to add my personal assurances of confidence and esteem, and remain,

Very sincerely, yours

WILLIAM R. DAY


## Woodford to President McKinley
## March 9, 1898

[*Foreign Relations*, 1897–98, pp. 681–85.]

*Madrid, Legation of the United States*

Dear Mr. President:

Knowing how pressed you are for time, I fear you may find my letters somewhat prolix, but I know that you must wish all the light I can give you.

On Monday evening March 7, Señor ———, a well-known Spanish merchant, gave us a family dinner, at which were present his wife and daughter, my wife, daughter, a number of other Americans, and myself.

Before the dinner was over I came to the conclusion that Señor ——— was talking for a purpose. In the course of the conversation he began to speak, rather than talk, in a very logical and deliberate way, as if from a prepared brief. He said, in substance, that Spain had done all she could do or expected to do in recalling Weyler, in sending Blanco, in abandoning the policy of reconcentration, in establishing legitimate warfare, in rescinding the tobacco edicts, in encouraging planting and grinding, in establishing autonomy, in offering full pardon to all rebels, in permitting Cuba to make her own tariff regulations, and finally in entering deliberately and honestly on the negotiation of commercial treaties that should open the market of Cuba to reciprocal trade with the United States. That the great majority of the white people of Cuba had accepted autonomy; that planting was steadily increasing, and that the people were getting to work throughout the country wherever the rebels permitted. That the rebellion is now confined almost entirely to negroes; that there are few whites in the rebel forces, and these almost entirely officers. That the only hope of the rebellion is in the aid it gets from the United States and in the consequent expectation by the rebel chiefs that war will eventually come between the United States and Spain. That the rebellion can be kept alive in the swamps and in the hills indefinitely, because the negroes are perfectly acclimated, require little clothing and no regular rations, and can maintain guerrilla warfare and inflict great destruction of property. That the rebels can not achieve the independence of the island, while they can produce continuous disorder, suffering, and indefinite destruction of property. That there are but two possible solutions—either real autonomy under nominal Spanish sovereignty, or the actual occupation

## Prelude to an Ultimatum 121

and government of the island by the United States. That Cuban independence is absolutely impossible as a permanent solution of the difficulty, since independence can only result in a continuous war of races, and that this means that independent Cuba must be a second Santo Domingo. That autonomy, with real self-government of Cuba by Cubans, can and will succeed if the United States will openly advise it and place the moral power of the United States on the side of autonomy. That if the United States Government does nothing and will do nothing in aid of autonomy, then the rebellion must continue in keeping the island disturbed, although without any possibility of success in achieving independence, and that thus the rainy season will come and the present suffering, disorder, and disaster be continued throughout the approaching summer. That Spain is giving honest autonomy and will do anything and everything to make such autonomy successful except to abandon her sovereignty over the island. That the Spanish flag must remain the flag of Cuba until it is torn from the island by foreign force. That he had seen in the papers rumors of the willingness of the United States to buy Cuba, but that Spain will never sell Cuba to the United States. That no Spanish Government could do this and live. That if autonomy and military operations can not together succeed in putting an end to the rebellion and Spain should ever find herself compelled to abandon the island, she might be compelled to recognize its independence, but that she will never sell or cede the island to the United States. That the United States can never acquire Cuba with the consent of Spain, and that if the United States ever gets the island she must take it by conquest.

He said all this in a deliberate, thoughtful, and business-like way, without heat and without passion.

I believe that he expressed the average judgment of the Spanish and business classes.

He then asked me what more I thought Spain could

do to make autonomy stronger and give it sure hope of success. I simply replied that I had no advice to give or suggestion to make.

Upon his further pressing me, I asked if I might put a question and, on his assenting, I inquired whether it might not aid the insular government of Cuba in their efforts to break up the rebellion if they should propose to all the present officers of the insurgent army, below the rank of general, that such officers should be incorporated into the Spanish army, or if that be impracticable, into the local Cuban militia with the same rank and command that they now have in the insurgent army, and thus assure all the insurgents and their sympathizers that the local liberties of Cuba will be defended and secured by men who believe in the practical self-government of Cuba. He replied that such suggestion had been already made and possibly considered, but that he believed Spain would never consent to this.

I also understood him to say that he knew that Spain would be beaten in any struggle with the United States; that he feared such struggle to be inevitable, but notwithstanding this, that he and all good Spaniards would accept the issue of war without hesitation.

He then asked me why the people of the United States sympathized so strongly with the insurgents and are so strongly opposed to Spain now that Spain is doing so much and so sincerely for real autonomy and for the true self-government of Cuba by the white people of Cuba, adding that, although he had lived some years in New York, he had never thought that the serious business people of the United States wanted to annex Cuba.

* * *

Señor ———— came in this afternoon; said he had repeated [our] conversation of Monday evening (March 7) to Minister Moret, but had not yet seen Sagasta.

I took the opportunity to ask him why, in his judgment, if autonomy should succeed, Spain should not sell

Cuba, adding that I knew he believed Spain would either grant independence or fight before she would sell, but that I was curious to know why he, a cold clear-headed business man, should prefer independence (with race wars and destruction to all property interests) or war (with certain loss of Cuba as its result) to a peaceful transfer of the island to the United States with resulting cessation of expenditures and with present relief to Spanish finances. . . . Gathering himself together quickly, he said:

I fear war. My Government will not sell. You will not tell the rebels to lay down their arms and this means war.

I simply replied:

Perhaps your Government and your business associates may all be reflecting public opinion and perhaps down in your hearts, ministers and business men alike, each of you prefer to sell, but each is afraid to let the other know his thought.

He shrugged his shoulders, but made no reply.

* * *

## *Woodford to the President*
## *March 17, 1898*

[*Foreign Relations,* 1897-98, pp. 685-88.]

*Madrid, Legation of the United States*

Dear Mr. President:

In my No. 41, of March 9, I told you of Señor ——— call that afternoon and of Mr. ——— call that evening. On Saturday, March 12, Señor ——— came again; said that he had seen Minister Moret again on the 11th; that it was clear that autonomy would surely succeed if the

United States would openly advise the insurgents to lay down their arms; that if we would not do this the rebellion must continue; that Spain would never sell the island; that her honor is involved, and that autonomy having been granted, Spain would never surrender her sovereignty, except by force. All this was evidently inspired by Moret. I heard him with kindness, replied with courtesy, and kept my own counsel.

On March 15 I received Department instruction No. 147, dated March 1, and marked "confidential."

On March 16 I got Judge Day's letter of March 3, marked "Personal and confidential." These papers acquaint me with the situation in Cuba and at Washington on the dates when written.

The feeling here is despondent. Bread grows dearer; business more stagnant; public securities fall, and exchange on Paris and London rises.

As time has passed, my own impressions as to our possible duty and consequent action have changed. Permit me to tell you why and how.

In my first letter of August 10, from London, I wrote that "annexation by force might provoke protest, but should it come as the natural and logical result of successive conditions, I think it should be accepted as inevitable."

In my second of August 19 that "the current of events is setting toward the independence of Cuba or toward such autonomy as shall be practical independence," etc.

In my No. 11 of October 17 that restored peace may possibly bring a practical protectorate as a reasonable and desirable result. That I hoped not, for I feared that until the Cubans are taught by the hard lessons of experience they will prove very unsatisfactory wards in chancery and that to guarantee their acts will involve a serious and dangerous responsibility.

In my No. 19 of December 11 you will note that Min-

## Prelude to an Ultimatum 125

ister Moret told me on that day that he had very strong hopes that the practical pacification of the greater part of Cuba would be secured before the 1st of March, and that "I pressed upon him and Minister Gullón, whenever I met them, the necessity of very speedy and successful action."

The 1st of March has come and gone and peace is not yet secured. Department dispatch No. 147 bears that very date.

In my No. 31 of February 7 I wrote that it was then stated in Madrid "that the Spanish Government are disappointed in their efforts to break up the rebellion by autonomy or by influencing rebel chiefs, and doubt their ability to get the rebellion practically suppressed *before the rainy season begins.*"

What I then could only give as statement current in Madrid is now evident fact. With the exception of Minister Moret and those whom his splendid courage and personal magnetism inspire and control, I do not think that any thoughtful man in Madrid now believes that autonomy, and what is euphemistically called "influencing rebel chiefs," and military operations combined can practically suppress the rebellion *before the rainy season begins.*

Señor Sagasta, an experienced statesman, a loyal Spaniard, and a faithful friend of the Queen, waits hoping against hope. I think that he would do anything for peace that Spain would approve and accept. Señor Gullón evidently doubts whether peace can be maintained with the United States. I think that the Queen is disappointed and anxious. Well she may be, for she has struggled with admirable courage and wonderful faith for her son and her dynasty.

In that letter of February 7 I also reported that the present ministry had decided that they have made all the concessions to the United States that they can make, without endangering their own power and the continuance of the present dynasty; that they will do no more, and will fight, if what they have done does not secure our continued neutrality.

In my No. 33 of February 19 I confirmed my belief in the disposition and decision of the Spanish Government to make no further concessions.

My report No. 35 of February 26 gives résumé of situation after my personal interview with Ministers Gullón and Moret on February 25. You will remember that I had seen the Queen on the 22d.

In my No. 37 of March 2, I give Minister Moret's reasons for his faith in the success of autonomy as stated by himself. But even he practically admits that its success depends on the sympathy of our consul-general at Habana, and the friendship of the United States. His admission that the delay of one month in dissolving the old Cortes and convening the new one was due to the request of the insular government throws much light on the Cuban situation.

In that report of March 2 I called your attention to the evident fact that Spain will ask for more time within which to work out her policy. Autonomy is not yet successful. The new Cortes meets on April 25. The rainy season begins about May 1. Thereafter the Spanish army in Cuba can not fight in the open country, and can literally do nothing but sicken and die until the middle of September, or the first of October, while the acclimated insurgents can ravage the island at their will.

On the morning of March 9 the Madrid papers published the passage by our House of Representatives of the bill appropriating $50,000,000. As I wrote you that day, the Spanish Government and the Spanish people were simply stunned. When you advised and secured that action, you made settlement possible, although I hardly dare even yet to think it probable. While I have worked steadily and persistently for peace, I have never been optimistic. I have always realized the difficulties of the situation. I have sometimes feared that you might think me discouraged, but I am sure that you will not think that I have ever relaxed my efforts. To-day I have more faith in possible peace than I have had since I sailed from New York. The unanimous passage of the Cannon bill at Washington, and the reception of the news here in Madrid, give me this hope. The thought of sale is to-day in the air of Madrid. I think that the largest holders of the Spanish debt will soon advise the sale. But Señor Moret has now made a speech which I inclose, and in which he has taken very positive ground that autonomy will succeed. His speech is clever and strong. But even he may change. It is possible that you can buy Cuba and that such contingency may soon arise as may make it advisable for me to be authorized to at least discuss the matter with the Queen, or with Moret, if she or he should broach the subject. I believe that Spain, tired out and exhausted, threatened with practical famine, and confronted with the immediate necessity of tremendous outlay, would thank the Queen for her wisdom and courage should she dare to part with Cuba without war, and would sustain her even if she were compelled to change her ministry to secure this result.

I have advised, respectfully but earnestly, against annexation and against any protectorate, and have worked only for peace. This was the keynote of my interview with the British and other foreign ambassadors last September and October.

I have hoped that autonomy might be successful and might bring peace.

It now seems almost certain that autonomy can not succeed before the rainy season begins. This means that the present hell of famine and anarchy may continue in Cuba during all the coming summer. Should autonomy be supported by the great body of the educated and property-holding whites of Cuba, it will probably be strong enough next autumn to prevent effective good government by the insurgents. The insurgents, supported by the great majority of the blacks, and led by even a minority of enterprising and resolute whites, will probably be strong enough to prevent effective good government by the insular autonomic administration. This would mean and involve continuous disorder and practical anarchy.

The establishment of any form of protectorate still seems to me fraught with great and permanent danger. There is no general popular education in Cuba. The blacks and whites are quite even in numbers. The native Cubans and the Spanish residents are divided into hostile factions. Corruption in official rule has been for centuries the curse of Cuba. I do not believe that the population is to-day fit for self-government, and acceptance of a practical protectorate over Cuba seems to me very like the assumption of the responsible care of a madhouse. There are possible conditions under which a practical protectorate may be a reasonable and desirable result. But time and reflection have strengthened my first impression into deliberate judgment, and I pray that no conditions may arise under which we shall be responsible for the practical peace and good government of the island unless we have full power of ownership which shall enable us to compel good government.

Peace is still a necessity. Peace can hardly be assured by the insurgents through and under an independent government. Autonomy has not yet secured peace. I have at last come to believe that the only certainty of peace is under our flag and that with courage and faith we can minimize the dangers of American occupation and assure the blessings of American constitutional liberty.

I am thus, reluctantly, slowly, but entirely a convert to the American ownership and occupation of the island. If we recognize independence, we may turn the island over to a part of its inhabitants against the judgment of many of its most educated and wealthy residents. If we advise the insurgents to accept autonomy we may do injustice to men who have fought hard and well for liberty, and they may not get justice from the insular government should it once obtain control of the island. We may in either event only foster conditions that will lead to continuous disorder. If we have war we must finally occupy and ultimately own the island. If to-day we could purchase a reasonable price we should avoid the horrors and the expense of war, and you, as a soldier, know what war is, even when waged for holiest cause.

I therefore ask your permission to treat should the opportunity ever be presented. Whatever I might do in such contingency would be done tentatively and subject in all things to your constant knowledge and direction.

Should your judgment not approve my present request such knowledge will still be helpful, whatever may be the contingencies of the future.

Faithfully yours,

STEWART L. WOODFORD

## United States Senate
## March 17, 1898

[*Congressional Record*, vol. 31, pt. 3, pp. 2916–19.]

WILLIAM FRYE [REP., ME.] Mr. President, the Senator from Vermont Mr. Proctor, a Senator in whom the country has much confidence, and a conservative man, has just returned from a pretty careful investigation of affairs in Cuba, and has expressed a willingness to give to the Senate and the country his views; and some have desired that he may do so at the present moment.

        \*    \*    \*

REDFIELD PROCTOR [REP., VT.] Mr. President, more importance seems to be attached by others to my recent visit to Cuba than I have given it, and it has been suggested that I make a public statement of what I saw and how the situation impressed me. This I do on account of the public interest in all that concerns Cuba, and to correct some inaccuracies that have, not unnaturally, appeared in reported interviews with me.

My trip was entirely unofficial and of my own motion, not suggested by anyone. The only mention I made of it to the President was to say to him that I contemplated such a trip and to ask him if there was any objection to it; to which he replied that he could see none. No one but myself, therefore, is responsible for anything in this statement. Judge Day gave me a brief note of introduction to General Lee, and I had letters of introduction from business friends at the North to bankers and other business men at Habana, and they in turn gave me letters to their correspondents in other cities. These letters to business men were very useful, as one of the principal purposes of my visit was to ascertain the views of practical men of affairs upon the situation.

Of General Lee I need say little. His valuable services to his country in his trying position are too well known to all his countrymen to require mention. Besides his ability, high character, and courage, he possesses the important requisites of unfailing tact and courtesy, and withal, his military education and training and his soldierly qualities are invaluable adjuncts in the equipment of our representative in a country so completely under military rule as is Cuba. General Lee kindly invited us to sit at his table at the hotel during our stay in Habana, and this opportunity for frequent informal talks with him was of great help to me.

In addition to the information he voluntarily gave me, it furnished a convenient opportunity to ask him the many questions that suggested themselves in explanation of things seen and heard on our trips through the country. I also met and spent considerable time with Consul Brice at Matanzas, and with Captain Barker, a staunch ex-Confederate soldier, the consul at Sagua la Grande. None of our representatives whom I met in Cuba are of my political faith, but there is a broader faith, not bounded by party lines. They are all three true Americans, and have done excellent service.

*   *   *

## Sections Visited

There are six provinces in Cuba, each, with the exception of Matanzas, extending the whole width of the island, and having about an equal sea front on the north and south borders. Matanzas touches the Caribbean Sea only at its southwest corner, being separated from it elsewhere by a narrow peninsula of Santa Clara Province. The provinces are named, beginning at the west, Pinar del Rio, Habana, Matanzas, Santa Clara, Puerto Principe, and Santiago de Cuba. My observations were confined to the four western provinces, which constitute about one-half of the island. The two eastern ones are practically in the hands of the insurgents, except the few fortified towns. These two large provinces are spoken of to-day as "Cuba Libre."

Habana, the great city and capital of the island, is, in the eyes of the Spaniards and many Cubans, all Cuba, as much as Paris is France. But having visited it in more peaceful times and seen its sights, the tomb of Columbus, the forts—Cabana and Morro Castle, etc.—I did not care to repeat this, preferring trips in the country. Everything seems to go on much as usual in Habana. Quiet prevails, and except for the frequent squads of soldiers marching to guard and police duty and their abounding presence in all public places, one sees few signs of war.

Outside Habana all is changed. It is not peace nor is it war. It is desolation and distress, misery and starvation. Every town and village is surrounded by a "trocha" (trench), a sort of rifle pit, but constructed on a plan new to me, the dirt being thrown up on the inside and a barbed-wire fence on the outer side of the trench. These trochas have at every corner and at frequent intervals along the sides what are there called forts, but which are really small blockhouses, many of them more like large sentry boxes, loopholed for musketry, and with a guard of from two to ten soldiers in each.

The purpose of these trochas is to keep the reconcentrados in as well as to keep the insurgents out. From all the surrounding country the people have been driven in to these fortified towns and held there to subsist as they can. They are virtually prison yards, and not unlike one in general appearance, except that the walls are not so high and strong; but they suffice, where every point is in range of a soldier's rifle, to keep in the poor reconcentrado women and children.

* * *

There are no domestic animals or crops on the rich fields and pastures except such as are under guard in the immediate vicinity of the towns. In other words, the Spaniards hold in these four western provinces just what their army sits on. Every man, woman, and child, and every domestic animal, wherever their columns have reached, is under guard and within their so-called fortifications. To describe one place is to describe all. To repeat, it is neither peace nor war. It is concentration and desolation. This is the "pacified" condition of the four western provinces.

West of Habana is mainly the rich tobacco country; east, so far as I went, a sugar region. Nearly all the sugar mills are destroyed between Habana and Sagua. Two or three were standing in the vicinity of Sagua, and in part running, surrounded, as are the villages, by trochas and "forts" or palisades of the royal palm, and fully guarded.

## Prelude to an Ultimatum 133

Toward and near Cienfuegos there were more mills running, but all with the same protection. It is said that the owners of these mills near Cienfuegos have been able to obtain special favors of the Spanish Government in the way of a large force of soldiers, but that they also, as well as all the railroads, pay taxes to the Cubans for immunity. I had no means of verifying this. It is the common talk among those who have better means of knowledge.

### The Reconcentrados—The Country People

All the country people in the four western provinces, about 400,000 in number, remaining outside the fortified towns when Weyler's order was made were driven into these towns, and these are the reconcentrados. They were the peasantry, many of them farmers, some landowners, others renting lands and owning more or less stock, others working on estates and cultivating small patches; and even a small patch in that fruitful clime will support a family.

It is but fair to say that the normal condition of these people was very different from what prevails in this country. Their standard of comfort and prosperity was not high measured by ours. But according to their standards and requirements their conditions of life were satisfactory.

They lived mostly in cabins made of palms or in wooden houses. Some of them had houses of stone, the blackened walls of which are all that remain to show the country was ever inhabited.

The first clause of Weyler's order reads as follows:

I Order and Command:

>   First. All the inhabitants of the country or outside of the line of fortifications of the towns shall, within the period of eight days, concentrate themselves in the towns occupied by the troops. Any individual who, after the expiration of this period, is found in the uninhabited part will be considered a rebel and tried as such.

The other three sections forbid the transportation of provisions from one town to another without permission of the military authority, direct the owners of cattle to bring them into the towns, prescribe that the eight days shall be counted from the publication of the proclamation in the head town of the municipal district, and state that if news is furnished of the enemy which can be made use of, it will serve as a "recommendation."

Many, doubtless, did not learn of this order. Others failed to grasp its terrible meaning. Its execution was left largely to the guerrillas to drive in all that had not obeyed, and I was informed that in many cases the torch was applied to their homes with no notice, and the inmates fled with such clothing as they might have on, their stock and other belongings being appropriated by the guerrillas. When they reached the towns, they were allowed to build huts of palm leaves in the suburbs and vacant places within the trochas, and left to live, if they could.

Their huts are about 10 by 15 feet in size, and for want of space are usually crowded together very closely. They have no floor but the ground, no furniture, and, after a year's wear, but little clothing except such stray substitutes as they can extemporize; and with large families, or more than one, in this little space, the commonest sanitary provisions are impossible. Conditions are unmentionable in this respect. Torn from their homes, with foul earth, foul air, foul water, and foul food or none, what wonder that one-half have died and that one-quarter of the living are so diseased that they can not be saved? A form of dropsy is a common disorder resulting from these conditions. Little children are still walking about with arms and chest terribly emaciated, eyes swollen, and abdomen bloated to three times the natural size. The physicians say these cases are hopeless.

Deaths in the streets have not been uncommon. I was told by one of our consuls that they have been found dead about the markets in the morning, where they had crawled, hoping to get some stray bits of food from the early hucksters, and that there had been cases where they had dropped dead inside the market surrounded by food. Before Weyler's order, these people were independent and self-supporting. They are not beggars even now. . . .

## The Hospitals

Of these I need not speak. Others have described their condition far better than I can. It is not within the narrow limits of my vocabulary to portray it. I went to Cuba with a strong conviction that the picture had been overdrawn; that a few cases of starvation and suffering had inspired and stimulated the press correspondents, and that they had given free play to a strong, natural, and highly cultivated imagination.

Before starting I received through the mail a leaflet published by the Christian Herald, with cuts of some of the sick and starving reconcentrados, and took it with me, thinking these must be rare specimens, got up to make the worst possible showing. I saw plenty as bad and worse; many that should not be photographed and shown.

I could not believe that out of a population of 1,600,000, two hundred thousand had died within these Spanish forts, practically prison walls, within a few months past from actual starvation and diseases caused by insufficient and improper food. My inquiries were entirely outside of sensational sources. They were made of our medical officers, of our consuls, of city alcaldes (mayors), of relief communities, of leading merchants and bankers, physicians and lawyers. Several of my informants were Spanish born, but every time the answer was that the case had not been overstated. What I saw I can not tell so that others can see it. It must be seen with one's own eyes to be realized.

The Los Pasos Hospital, in Habana, has been recently described by one of my colleagues, Senator Gallinger, and I can not say that his picture was overdrawn, for even his fertile pen could not do that. But he visited it after Dr. Lesser, one of Miss [Clara] Barton's very able and efficient assistants, had renovated it and put in cots. I saw it when 400 women and children were lying on the floors in an indescribable state of emaciation and disease, many with the scantiest covering of rags—and such rags!—sick children, naked as they came into the world; and the conditions in the other cities are even worse.

* * *

### The Spaniard

I had little time to study the race question, and have read nothing on it, so can only give hasty impressions. It is said that there are nearly 200,000 Spaniards in Cuba out of a total population of 1,600,000. They live principally in the towns and cities. The small shopkeepers in the towns and their clerks are mostly Spaniards. Much of the larger business, too, and of the property in the cities, and in a less degree in the country, is in their hands. They have an eye to thrift, and as everything possible in the way of trade and legalized monopolies, in which the country abounds, is given to them by the Government, many of them acquire property. I did not learn that the Spanish residents of the island had contributed largely in blood or treasure to suppress the insurrection.

### The Cuban

There are, or were before the war, about 1,000,000 Cubans on the island, 200,000 Spaniards (which means those born in Spain), and less than half a million of negroes and mixed bloods. The Cuban whites are of pure Spanish blood and, like the Spaniards, dark in complexion, but oftener light or blond, so far as I noticed. The percentage of colored to white has been steadily diminishing for more than fifty years, and is not now over 25 per cent of the total. In fact, the number of colored people has been actually diminishing for nearly that time. The Cuban farmer and laborer is by nature peaceable, kindly, gay, hospitable, lighthearted, and improvident.

There is a proverb among the Cubans that "Spanish bulls can not be bred in Cuba"—that is, the Cubans, though they are of Spanish blood, are less excitable and of a quieter temperament. Many Cubans whom I met spoke in strong terms against the bull fights; that it was a brutal institution, introduced and mainly patronized by the Spaniards. One thing that was new to me was to learn the superiority of the well-to-do Cuban over the Spaniard in the matter of education. Among those in good circumstances there can be no doubt that the Cuban is far superior in this respect. And the reason of it is easy to see. They have been educated in England, France, or this country, while the Spaniard has such education as his own country furnishes.

### The Negro

The colored people seem to me by nature quite the equal mentally and physically of the race in this country. Certainly physically they are by far the larger and stronger race on the island. There is little or no race prejudice, and this has doubtless been greatly to their advantage. Eighty-five years ago there were one-half as many free negroes as slaves, and this proportion slowly increased until emancipation.

### The Military Situation

It is said that there are about 60,000 Spanish soldiers now in Cuba fit for duty out of the more than 200,000 that have been sent there. The rest have died, have been sent home sick, or are in hospitals, and some have been killed, notwithstanding the official reports. They are conscripts, many of them very young, and generally small men. One hundred and thirty pounds is a fair estimate of their average weight. They are quiet and obedient, and if well drilled and led, I believe would fight fairly well, but not at all equal to our men. Much more would depend on the leadership than with us. The officer must lead well and be one in whom they have confidence, and this applies to both sides alike. As I saw no drills or regular formation, I inquired about them of many persons, and was informed that they had never seen a drill. I saw perhaps 10,000 Spanish troops, but not a piece of artillery or a tent. They live in barracks in the towns, and are seldom out for more than the day, returning to town at night.

They have little or no equipment for supply trains or for a field campaign such as we have. Their cavalry horses are scrubby little native ponies, weighing not over 800 pounds, tough and hardy, but for the most part in wretched condition, reminding one of the mount of Don Quixote. Some of the officers, however, have good horses, mostly American, I think. On both sides cavalry is considered the favorite and the dangerous fighting arm. The tactics of the Spanish, as described to me by eyewitnesses and participants in some of their battles, is for the infantry, when threatened by insurgent cavalry, to form a hollow square and fire away ad libitum, and without ceasing until time to march back to town.

It does not seem to have entered the minds of either side that a good infantry force can take care of itself and repulse anywhere an equal or greater number of cavalry, and there are everywhere positions where cavalry would be at a disadvantage.

Having called on Governor and Captain-General Blanco and received his courteous call in return, I could not with propriety seek communication with insurgents.

I had plenty of offers of safe conduct to Gomez's camp, and was told that if I would write him, an answer would be returned safely within ten days at most.

I saw several who had visited the insurgent camps, and was sought out by an insurgent field officer, who gave me the best information received as to the insurgent force. His statements were moderate, and I was credibly informed that he was entirely reliable. He claimed that the Cubans had about 30,000 men now in the field, some in every province, but mostly in the two eastern provinces and eastern Santa Clara, and this statement was corroborated from other good sources. They have a force all the time in Habana Province itself, organized in four small brigades and operating in small bands. Ruiz was taken, tried, and shot within about a mile and a half of the railroad and about 15 miles out of Habana, on the road to Matanzas, a road more traveled than any other, and which I went over four times.

Arranguren was killed about 3 miles the other side of the road and about the same distance, 15 or 20 miles, from Habana. The Cubans are well armed, but very poorly supplied with ammunition. They are not allowed to carry many cartridges; sometimes not more than one or two. The infantry, especially, are poorly clad. Two small squads of prisoners which I saw, however, one of half a dozen in the streets of Habana, and one of three on the cars, wore better clothes than the average Spanish soldier.

Each of these prisoners, though surrounded by guards, was bound by the arm and wrists by cords, and they were all tied together by a cord running along the line, a specimen of the amenities of their warfare. About one-third of the Cuban army are colored, mostly in the infantry, as the cavalry furnished their own horses.

This field officer, an American from a Southern State, spoke in the highest terms of the conduct of these colored soldiers; that they were as good fighters and had more endurance than the whites; could keep up with the cavalry on a long march and come in fresh at night.

* * *

I have never had any communication, direct or indirect, with the Cuban Junta in this country or any of its members, nor did I have with any of the juntas which exist in every city and large town of Cuba. None of the calls I made were upon parties of whose sympathies I had the least knowledge, except that I knew some of them were classed as autonomists.

Most of my informants were business men, who had taken no sides and rarely expressed themselves. I had no means of guessing in advance what their answers would be, and was in most cases greatly surprised at their frankness.

I inquired in regard to autonomy of men of wealth and men as prominent in business as any in the cities of Habana, Matanzas, and Sagua, bankers, merchants, lawyers, and autonomist officials, some of them Spanish born but Cuban bred, one prominent Englishman, several of them known as autonomists, and several of them telling me they were still believers in autonomy if practicable, but without exception they replied that it was "too late" for that.

Some favored a United States protectorate, some annexation, some free Cuba; not one has been counted favoring the insurrection at first. They were business men and wanted peace, but said it was too late for peace under Spanish sovereignty. They characterized Weyler's order in far stronger terms than I can. I could not but conclude that you do not have to scratch an autonomist very deep to find a Cuban. There is soon to be an election, but every polling place must be inside a fortified town. Such elections ought to be safe for the "ins."

I have endeavored to state in not intemperate mood what I saw and heard, and to make no argument thereon, but leave everyone to draw his own conclusions. To me

## Prelude to an Ultimatum 141

the strongest appeal is not the barbarity practiced by Weyler nor the loss of the *Maine*, if our worst fears should prove true, terrible as are both of these incidents, but the spectacle of a million and a half of people, the entire native population of Cuba, struggling for freedom and deliverance from the worst misgovernment of which I ever had knowledge. But whether our action ought to be influenced by any one or all these things, and, if so, how far, is another question.

I am not in favor of annexation: not because I would apprehend any particular trouble from it, but because it is not wise policy to take in any people of foreign tongue and training, and without any strong guiding American element. The fear that if free the people of Cuba would be revolutionary is not so well founded as has been supposed, and the conditions for good self-government are far more favorable. The large number of educated and patriotic men, the great sacrifices they have endured, the peaceable temperament of the people, whites and blacks, the wonderful prosperity that would surely come with peace and good home rule, the large influx of American and English immigration and money, would all be strong factors for stable institutions.

But it is not my purpose at this time, nor do I consider it my province, to suggest any plan. I merely speak of the symptoms as I saw them, but do not undertake to prescribe. Such remedial steps as may be required may safely be left to an American President and the American people.

# Section Ten

# The Attitude of the Powers

*Commentary*

In considering whether he should take some bold step against Spain which might provoke a war, McKinley gave some thought to the response this might evoke from Europe's powers. As the following analysis of "The Powers and Spain" by Ernest May makes clear, there was no reason for McKinley to fear an anti-American coalition of European states.

## *"The Powers and Spain"*

[Ernest May, *Imperial Democracy* (New York, 1961), pp. 196–219.]

The German government had been the first seriously to consider aiding Spain in the crisis over its relationship with the United States. In the early autumn of 1897,

## The Attitude of the Powers 143

Kaiser Wilhelm II was at Rominten, one of his hunting lodges in the gloomy forests of East Prussia. Just back from a wearing but stimulating trip to Vienna, he found among correspondence forwarded from Berlin a dispatch from his ambassador in Madrid reporting the arrival of McKinley's new envoy, and predicting an American ultimatum with which the Spanish government would have to comply.

The fact that some such action by the United States had long been expected did not appear to modify the Kaiser's astonishment and outrage. He looked upon the regency in Madrid as a kindred monarchy. In his restless boyhood he had learned or half-learned many subjects, but one lesson that had fixed itself in his mind was the transcendent importance of the monarchical principle. He viewed officials of the French Republic as usurpers, and he could never understand how a legitimate ruler like Tsar Nicholas II trafficked with the heirs of those who murdered Louis XVI. He believed devoutly that those who wore crowns ruled by divine right. On the margin of his ambassador's letter now he scratched:

> The situation stands just thus: Cuba has belonged to Spain as a colony for hundreds of years. This is a European state. America wants "by fair means or foul"—apparently the latter—simply to relieve Spain of her colony. . . . Just to suffer this event, is Europe ready to do that . . . ? Shall we other monarchs look on placidly as a brave colleague of ours has her land and probably too—through Cuba's loss— her throne torn from her? Through the insolence of the Yankee, who will be secretly supported by John Bull? I believe it is now high time that we other monarchs . . . agree *jointly* to offer our help to the Queen in case the American-British Society for International Theft and Warmongering looks as if it seriously intends to snatch Cuba from Spain. A

common note which all of us Continentals sent to Uncle Sam and John Bull with the statement that we would mutually stand together and not allow Cuba to be stolen from H[er] M[ajesty] could not fail to have . . . effect. . . . Feeling in this connection among the great monarchs should be tested at once and reported upon to me.

In this fit of feeling, the Kaiser was troubled by no qualms about the prudence of helping Spain. America naturally repelled him. Surrounded by courtiers and military aides from the Junker class, he knew of the stress they felt from American competition. He had several times broached to Russian officials the notion of a European economic union against the United States. In his marginal note on the dispatch from Madrid, he commented that a move in behalf of Spain would serve two ends: "For one thing the rascals will see that Europe's kings really stand together and mutually share misfortune and joy and are not prepared to yield before republican money-madness; in the second place, it would be a very excellent device for furthering and establishing the continental union against America planned by myself and the Tsar."

The Kaiser's proposal was at once ill-considered, impulsive, rash, bold, and imaginative. In Berlin it was not given the studious inspection that it may have deserved. Emulating his industrious predecessor, Frederick the Great, Wilhelm wrote far too many marginal notes, and for all his earnestness, occasional brilliance, and famous memory, he failed to keep them all consistent. His officials had learned that he often contradicted himself, forgot, or flitted from one impulse to another. Some regarded the Emperor's marginalia as something like swearing, a means by which an excitable temperament relieved itself. Others frankly thought the monarch insane. The Imperial Chancellor, Prince Hohenlohe, worried about resemblances between Wilhelm and the mad King Ludwig II of Bavaria.

So startling a directive as one to plan a dé-*marche* in support of Spain caused bureaucrats in Berlin to tend to think less about its merits than about ways of circumventing it.

The new Foreign Minister, Bernhard von Bülow, was a master of this art. He could not afford to contradict or even argue with the Kaiser. For all his own self-confidence, he knew his dependence on imperial favor. Whether or not he thought of himself as a second and more polished Bismarck, he had to remember that Wilhelm had gotten rid of Bismarck, and Bülow was not even Chancellor yet. He may have felt at the time what he wrote later in his *Memoirs*—that the Kaiser's interest in the Spanish-American tangle was evanescent. Out of regard for his career, he had to seem to take the Kaiser seriously. The sort of words that he wrote for the Emperor's eyes were typified in a letter of February 1898, to Wilhelm's closest friend, Philip Eulenburg: "I hang my heart more and more every day on the Emperor. He is so remarkable . . . ! He combines in a manner that I have never before seen the soundest and most original intelligence with the shrewdest good sense. He possesses an imagination that can soar on eagle wings above all trivialities, and with it the soberest perception of what is possible and attainable. . . . What swiftness and sureness of apprehension!"

In his reply to the marginal note, Bülow suggested that, like a metaphysical poet, the Kaiser might have meant either more or less than he said. To the Emperor himself he offered congratulations on pointing out "the danger of American republican land-grabbing and arrogance for the future of monarchical Europe just as emphatically as he demonstrates the necessity for unity among the great powers in the face of this menace to their common interests." He promised "to initiate the necessary steps immediately."

At the same time, he wrote to Eulenburg, who was with the Kaiser at Rominten: "I trust it will comply with the All-Highest's intentions if, in carrying them out, I endeavor to prevent England and France from using a German action in behalf of Spain in order to embroil us in quarrels with America from which they themselves abstain or at our expense secure economic advantages." German trade with the United States, he observed, ran second only to that of England. Under the latest American tariff law, the United States could negotiate discriminatory treaties, and it would be imprudent to abandon this rich commerce to a rival. At the very least, Russia and France should be associated with any move in behalf of Spain. "If England and France abstain," he warned, "not only would the success of the action become doubtful, but this very fact could, from a political as well as an economic standpoint, bring us important disadvantages." Surely, the Foreign Minister implied, these considerations would present themselves to the Emperor's luminous intelligence.

A sounding from the court soon encouraged Bülow to go farther. A brief message came to him from Eulenburg. In the days before charges of homosexuality drove him to private life, Eulenburg enjoyed the reputation of having great influence with Wilhelm. He prided himself on serving as mediator between Kaiser and government, and he reported to Bülow that he too had taken exception to a German initiative in favor of Spain. He had suggested to the Emperor that Germany stay in the background, get Austria to sound out other courts, and let her take the credit or blame. The Kaiser had found this advice acceptable, saying: "The action is the thing. One must choose the most practical method."

With this report in hand, Bülow could presume to give advice. Since he had already talked with the most powerful member of the Foreign Ministry's permanent staff, Friedrich von Holstein, and found him averse to backing Spain, he could feel safe against rear attack from that sensitive, gifted, and industrious intriguer. In another telegram to Eulenburg, therefore, Bülow went on not only to approve the use of Austria as a front but to suggest that Austria try to use Spain, encouraging the Queen Regent to appeal to France, Russia, and Britain. Germany would thus take the last place in line instead of the leading role that the Kaiser had first proposed. Yet when Eulenburg showed this message to the Emperor, Wilhelm unhesitatingly scribbled some marginal notes adding up to complete concurrence.

Bülow gave the *coup de grâce* to the Kaiser's plan by forwarding an instruction to the German chargé d'affaires in Vienna. If the Cuban question should be brought up again, he directed, the German position should be made clear. Effective action would require unanimity among the powers, with the unqualified adherence of England and France. "Our most gracious master," he declared, "has . . . expressed his decision that Germany cannot for practical reasons anticipate the western powers in taking a positive stand on the Cuban question, though she will be ready to give the most earnest consideration to any appropriate proposals which come to us from London or Paris." The notion of German leadership for a combination against the United States had vanished like the memory of a dream.

*   *   *

The Austrian government, unlike the German, did undertake to marshal aid for Spain. Emperor Franz Josef had an affection for monarchy as deeply rooted if not as romantic as that of the German Kaiser. Moreover, he had a remote family tie to the Spanish Queen Regent. She was the niece of his favorite cousin, the Archduke Albert, and the daughter of the Archduke Charles Ferdinand. Franz Josef wished to see her at least keep her throne. But his impulses were totally unlike those of Wilhelm II. During fifty years of rule, he had kept to a fixed schedule and an almost monastic regimen, concentrating single-mindedly on the day-to-day administration of his motley and unstable empire. No such humor as the Kaiser's could even have entered his head. At most, he told his Foreign

Minister to do what could be done for Spain so long as it involved no risks or serious commitments for Austria.

The Foreign Minister acted, at any rate, as if these were his instructions. Count Agenor Goluchowski, who held the office, had, if anything, less verve and imagination than his imperial master. Casting up the account, Arthur J. May writes in *The Hapsburg Monarchy*, "Caution, passivity, conservation, safety first, last, and always were the guiding rules of the Ballplatz during the Goluchowski period." Like all Austro-Hungarian civil officials, Goluchowski was the Emperor's servant. A trim, impassive Galician Pole, he had been elevated suddenly from a provincial administrative post. He knew that he might be dismissed any morning and, like others before him, never see the Emperor again. He himself seemed indifferent to Spain's cause. In 1896, when Tetuán represented Spain as on the brink of collapse, Goluchowski shrugged his shoulders. There was no chance, he remarked to the Italian ambassador, of Europe's even giving platonic support. When the German chargé d'affaires talked with him in 1897, as a result of the instructions from Bülow, Goluchowski said he had no thought of taking an initiative in behalf of Spain.

His subsequent actions can only have resulted from hints or directives given by Franz Josef. In late November, 1897, he suddenly delivered an address to the Committee on Foreign Affairs of the Hungarian diet, warning Europe of the American economic peril. . . .

This address had its domestic uses. Hungarian liberals had launched an excited campaign for tariff autonomy; separatist feeling had received a boost from a recent speech by the German Kaiser extolling Hungary's accomplishments; these currents had become all the more dangerous because of violent disorders between Czechs and Germans in other parts of the empire. Goluchowski needed to show his concern with Hungary's agricultural interests. But it seems likely that he would not have given precisely

## The Attitude of the Powers 149

this address except at the direction of his Emperor, and it is plausible that Franz Josef suggested it partly as a test of European feeling toward the United States.

Soon afterward, Goluchowski did a virtual about-face on the question of joint European representations in Washington. Talking with diplomats in Vienna, he began to treat the notion seriously. By the end of 1897, the French ambassador was describing him as positively enthusiastic. The change of heart, as the Frenchman noted, came soon after the Emperor had accorded a long interview to the Spanish Minister for Foreign Affairs. Goluchowski claimed to be still unsure whether Austria should take an initiative, in view of the fact that France, Britain, Russia, and Germany were colonial powers while Austria was not, but he did endorse the principle, and it seems a safe guess that he did so because Franz Josef had been pressed into making some indefinite commitment to the Queen Regent.

As Spanish-American relations became more and more tense, the Austrian Minister tried as best he could to persuade some other government to lead a move in Spain's behalf. From diplomats in Vienna, he obtained an impression that France and Italy would join in a collective note to the United States, but only if all the powers co-operated. He already knew this to be the German attitude. In early March 1898, he told the French ambassador that Russia and Britain were the only two powers about which he had serious doubts. He thus hinted that France had only to beckon to her ally in order to become leader of a continental coalition.

\* \* \*

In the past, the French had shown no enthusiasm for action in behalf of Spain. When Tetuán asked European aid in 1896, France recoiled. Her policies were, in effect, those of her young Foreign Minister, Gabriel Hanotaux. Though Hanotaux endeavored to transact all official business before one o'clock so that he could return to his walk-up apartment and spend afternoons and evenings composing a biography of Richelieu, he had time to keep an autocratic hand over his subordinates and rarely, if ever, did he allow his decisions to be overridden in the cabinet. He recognized his country's economic stake in Spain and admitted to the Spanish ambassador that the French people sympathized with her. His own envoy in Madrid, the shrewd and worldly Marquis de Reverseaux, advised him not to dismiss Spain's appeal lightly. A war, he thought, would be "almost as prejudicial to the interests of Europe as to Spain." Hanotaux was not impressed.

※ ※ ※

During the course of the next year, it is true, the Foreign Minister came to feel less sure that support of Spain would be imprudent. He had long urged the Spanish government to institute reforms in Cuba and when Cánovas and then Sagasta finally did so, he offered congratulations, expressing regret only that Spain had not followed his advice earlier. The reforms seemed to him to put Spain in a stronger position as against the United States. Perhaps more important, they strengthened the case for Spain put forward with increasing fervor by right-wing Parisian newspapers. Hanotaux was not blind to feeling against America among French agrarians and against "Americanism" among orthodox Catholics. Coming himself from an agricultural community and revering the great French cardinals, Richelieu and Lavigerie, he sat in a right of center cabinet heavily dependent on rural electors and such clericalists as voted. With the Dreyfus case already bringing public opinion to a boil, Hanotaux may have begun to change his definition of prudence. Certainly, he was impressed by reactions elsewhere in Europe to the McKinley administration's new and higher tariff and by the disquiet which prospective American annexation of Hawaii was said to excite in Berlin and Tokyo. "The United States at this time are making many enemies," he mused on the margin of a dispatch, "—it is something to be watched. We could perhaps render a considerable service to Spain."

In this mood Hanotaux gave some thought to the possibility of leading a diplomatic offensive. Early in October 1897, soon after Woodford reached Spain, the Foreign Minister brought up the topic of Cuba in a cabinet meeting. There is no evidence of what he said. The archives show only that he carried with him detailed memoranda on French interests in the island and on past Spanish-American negotiations.

Not long after the cabinet session, however, he sent off an inquiry to St. Petersburg. Spain would appeal to France and Russia if the United States made fresh demands, he predicted. What would Russia's attitude be? At the same time, he telegraphed Reverseaux in Madrid, instructing him not to work too hard at discouraging the Spaniards. As a Foreign Ministry official noted in a memorandum, while "it is very important that we not become committed prematurely, we should also be alert to the danger of seeing Spain, convinced that she has nothing to expect from us, knock at other doors." Hanotaux had become more receptive to the notion of *démarche* by the powers.

He continued to flirt with this thought, even when no encouragement came except from Vienna and Madrid. The Russian government responded to his suggestion with little warmth, and Reverseaux reported the German ambassador in Madrid as definitely opposed. When Spain formally asked if she could count on French help in securing European support, Hanotaux could not answer one way or the other. Even after consulting the rest of the cabinet, he could only counsel the Spaniards to think again before appealing to the powers. In a talk with the Spanish ambassador, he asked rhetorically, "Is it not to be feared that a *démarche*, which, as Spain herself avows, could have only a purely platonic character, might wound the pride and arouse the sensibilities of a democracy so little accustomed to diplomatic forms and thus produce an effect contrary to the one hoped for?" He promised to inquire again about feeling in St. Petersburg. Not long after, he jotted on a memo slip, "I am very preoccupied with the increasing friction between Spain and the United States. Is there really nothing that can be done? The possibility of a war between the U.S. and Spain becomes probable and more and more dangerous."

Each day seemed, however, to make the problem more perplexing. The *Maine* issue brought fresh strain to Spanish-American relations. The conservative press in Paris devoted more and more space to attacks on the United States. In the Chamber of Deputies, the agrarian bloc aroused considerable response with a demand for further commercial reprisals against the United States. Since a general election was likely at any time, Hanotaux must have felt loath to invite criticism on the score of having failed to help Spain. As one of his ambassadors let slip later, he feared that war might bring revolution in Spain, that revolution might inflame feeling in France among monarchists on one side and radical republicans on the other, and that passions of either kind would hurt the middle-of-the-road Méline government in its appeal to the electorate. Powerful domestic considerations counseled action.

The general diplomatic situation, on the other hand, encouraged inaction. When the De Lôme letter made its sensation in the press, Hanotaux was struck by a sentence in it accusing England of encouraging war so that "Americans should amuse themselves with [Spain] . . . and leave her alone." Hanotaux called these words to the attention of his envoy in Washington. In early March, 1898, he learned of the visit paid to McKinley by Pauncefote, the English ambassador. He did not know, of course, that Pauncefote carried the secret proposal for Anglo-American co-operation in China, but he had reason to suspect something of the sort. France's Russian ally had just seized Port Arthur, and it seemed possible that the English government had asked American backing in China in return for a promise to discourage any European move in support of Spain. Hanotaux urgently asked France's ambassadors everywhere to report any information touching Anglo-American negotiations. There seemed risk that the French government might be damned at home if it failed to support Spain, endangered abroad if it did.

The situation in Asia remained clouded, and Hanotaux strongly advised the Spanish government against appealing to the powers. When Spain disregarded this counsel, the French government faced the necessity of answering. Hanotaux temporized. "France would willingly agree if all others did," he told the Austrian ambassador, "but . . . the *démarche* could work to the disadvantage of Spain if it were rejected and nothing ensued." He recorded his subsequent conversation with the Spanish ambassador, and noted, "I showed him that the abstention of England would lead to certain checkmate; I pointed out to him that Italy followed England, that Russia was very hesitant, and that we ourselves would be placed in the greatest embarrassment in the face of abstention by England." Hanotaux's position was almost as cautious and noncommittal as Bülow's.

Hanotaux soon found that many of his fears were baseless. The British government slowly made plain that it would not fight over Port Arthur. In addition, the chargé d'affaires in London, a young diplomat with excellent connections in English society, reported that Pauncefote had visited McKinley, not to make a pact with America, but to urge that the American government conciliate Spain. In England itself, he said, only "jingo journals" talked of Anglo-American friendship; "serious people" remembered past ill-will and thought that if Cuba fell, Britain's own possessions might become targets. He reported a conversation in which the permanent Under-Secretary of State for Foreign Affairs, Sir Thomas Sanderson, spoke of Britain's position as exactly parallel to that of France. During a space of two weeks, in the middle of March, 1898, the French Foreign Minister seemed to discover, in the first place, that there was no danger of an Anglo-American alliance in Asia and, in the second place, that Britain might actually join in some pan-European expression of sympathy for Spain.

On March 26 Hanotaux spoke publicly of possible intervention to preserve peace. During an interrogation in the Chamber of Deputies, he declared, "If the two parties, with common accord, seek sure and impartial friends to assist the friendly settlement of so serious a question, they will see every good intention to meet their desire, and ours will not be wanting." The Foreign Minister gave no ostentatious support to Spain. Indeed, he referred to the United States warmly as "a growing republic, sister to our own, full of ardor, confident of its worth, which urgently demands an end to evils which affect her interests and which have already endured for a long time." His speech nevertheless amounted to open encouragement of the *démarch* that Spain and Austria were proposing.

Through diplomatic channels, moreover, he suddenly took up the project with a will. Whereas he had once used Russia to protect France from a Spanish appeal, he now turned about. In his own hand he drew up a telegram to St. Petersburg, asking the Russian Foreign Minister "if he could not consent to join in a *démarche* altogether amicable and in no way wounding to the United States by some or all of the powers." He spoke to the German ambassador in Paris, saying confidently that common action by the powers might actually prevent war. When solicited by the Spanish government, he agreed to approach Britain. The French ambassador to England happened to be in Paris; Hanotaux promised to send him back with orders to press for a favorable British decision; he himself would talk with Salisbury when the Marquis passed through the French capital in the last days of

March. Overnight, the French government became sponsor for a European move in behalf of Spain.

But the French proposal had far less substance than the earlier project of the German Kaiser. In his speech, his messages to St. Petersburg, and even his conversations with the Spanish ambassador, Hanotaux made it perfectly clear that he had no thought of laying demands or threats in Washington. Diplomats and informed newspapermen both reported that McKinley desired to keep the peace. Hanotaux hoped to offer him Europe's moral aid. While sounding out Russia and England, he asked the French ambassador in Washington to speak with Secretary of State Sherman and say that France would not act without American consent. In seeking to maintain peace and to placate pro-Spanish opinion in France, Hanotaux did not intend to bruise American feelings. He had no thought whatever of building an anti-American alliance.

Even for a limited undertaking, however, the French government found it hard to secure Russian co-operation. The thirty-year-old Tsar yielded nothing to Wilhelm II or Franz Josef in his attachment to monarchism and exercised more autocratic power than either, but he had neither the disciplined will of the Austrian Emperor nor the impetuous intuition of the German Kaiser. The parts of Nicholas II's diary that have been published consist almost entirely of long passages on parties, family affairs, and religion, with hardly a word on matters of state. In records kept by men around him, he appears as a vague young man, saying little, endeavoring mainly to avoid offense, only rarely intervening capriciously in the business of his ministries. The result, to be sure, was not cabinet government as in a constitutional monarchy. Regardless of a Council of Ministers which convened from time to time, the Tsar's ministers reported individually to him and negotiated with one another like minor sovereigns. More often than not, the decisions which Nicholas made were those recommended by the last strong man to see him.

His policy with regard to the Spanish-American imbroglio was shaped by his Foreign Minister, Count Mikhail Nikolaevich Muraviev. Plucked from the legation in Copenhagen to succeed a Foreign Minister who died suddenly, Muraviev lacked both training and experience at court. It was even said of him that he could not compose a grammatical dispatch, and few observers failed to contrast his insularity with the cosmopolitanism of such of his colleagues as the Finance Minister, Count Sergei Witte. But Muraviev quickly worked his way into an influential clique. He seemed intuitively to grasp the whims that floated unspoken in the mind of the Tsar. When serious differences arose, he was often able to win a decision over more gifted rivals, and quickly won the power to deal at least with minor affairs much as he wished—and from the Russian standpoint the Spanish question clearly was a minor affair.

Muraviev wanted nothing to do with the Spanish-American quarrel. In 1896, when there had been risk of an appeal from Tetuán, his predecessor had been able to keep silence. Whether or not he was responsible for an editorial in a semiofficial journal warning Spain that no outside aid would come to her, he left the Spanish ambassador guessing that Russia would have answered favorably if all the other powers had. In 1897, however, Muraviev had to declare his views, for it was Russia's ally, France, that was putting the question. He spoke candidly to the French ambassador:

> In spite of our deep sympathies for Spain, the present state of our international relations requires the Imperial Government in this question to maintain the greatest reserve.
>
> The bonds of friendship which unite Russia to the United States prevent the Imperial Government from taking any action which could have an unfavorable effect on relations between the two countries

and be taken amiss by public opinion in the United States.

This attitude is dictated to the Imperial Government not only by its particular interests but also by considerations of a general order. . . . Intervention by one or two powers in the dispute would have no result except to complicate the situation and give the Cuban question an importance which it is, on the contrary, in the interests of the powers to minimize as much as possible.

It was conceivable, Muraviev remarked, that Russia might join in advising Spain to save face by accepting arbitration, but that was as far as she would go.

Since the French government still did not discourage the Spaniards, Muraviev spelled out for Hanotaux some of the considerations in his mind. On January 5, 1898, the French ambassador in St. Petersburg reported a conversation with the Foreign Minister: "Count Muraviev declared to me unhesitatingly that he would regard as inopportune any *démarche* in the United States by the powers. It seems to him dangerous to intervene in a question raised today by the United States. He would view as seriously disadvantageous the admission of the United States into any version of the concert of powers, for this could later be invoked as a precedent with regard to other questions, such as those in the Far East for example, where the European powers should all, in his opinion, remain united."

Muraviev's reluctance to become embroiled with the United States undoubtedly grew during the crisis that followed the seizure of Port Arthur. This risky venture had been undertaken at his insistence and against the advice of most other ministers. So long as there seemed danger of Britain's opposing this move with force, Muraviev dared not drive any other government into England's arms. He fought with Witte in order to make concessions to Japan in Korea and thus keep Japan neutral. He had been warned by his minister in Washington that the United States was likely to negotiate with Britain a new arbitration treaty which "might involve the United States in conflicts with other powers." It must have seemed obvious to Muraviev that Russia should not precipitate an Anglo-American *rapprochement* by gratuitously reproaching American conduct toward Spain.

He could not be sure, it is true, that this logic would seem so obvious to the Tsar. Newspapers which could be read by Nicholas said that American success against Spain would imperil monarchy and the established world order. Both *Novosti* and *Novoe Vremya* carried such declarations. In any case, Muraviev could not keep the moral issue from the Tsar's attention, for on March 25, 1898, the Spanish Queen appealed to Nicholas directly.

As it happened, this appeal coincided with an easing of tension in the Far East. Only a few days after the Queen Regent's message came, Muraviev received a note from the British government confirming what the press had predicted—that England would acquiesce in Russia's absorption of Port Arthur. This cheerful news did not change the Foreign Minister's mind about the Spanish issue. He remarked to the Austrian ambassador, one of his few foreign friends, "Any purely friendly action would be useless; any minatory action dangerous." The Russian ambassador in Madrid felt that Russia had no reason for interest in Spain's cause, and Muraviev evidently thought the same. On April 2, he told both the French and the Austrians that Russia would go along with a tender of good offices if all the other powers did so. His candid asides to ambassadors made it plain that he agreed without enthusiasm and that he might back out if complications threatened.

The Italian government, for whatever influence it may have had, adopted a position much like the Russian. Except for the British, it was the only one that wanted something from Spain. Anxious to block the expansion of

French influence in Africa, it wished to prevent the Spanish government from siding with France. At the time of Tetuán's first appeal to the powers, however, Foreign Minister Emilio Visconti Venosta had said frankly that Europe could not and would not assist Spain. When Spain renewed its appeal in 1898, his mind had not changed. He ultimately agreed to do whatever the others did, remarking to the Austrian ambassador in Rome that no power would challenge the United States if she refused to receive a collective note. The thought of anything beyond a mere gesture did not enter his mind.

Whether there could even be a gesture depended, of course, on the English government. Germany, Austria, France, and Italy had agreed to participate only if Britain did so. Russia expected a British refusal to release her from a similar pledge. And the British government was in the midst of that re-evaluation of her relations with the United States which followed the Venezuelan crisis. The world did not know of the proposed alliance in China, but it could read of speeches by Chamberlain and others on Anglo-American kinship. There seemed little reason to expect that Britain would participate in any action likely to offend the American government.

On the question of whether or not Britain should act at all, opinion among British officials divided. England had reason to desire Spanish good will, for if Spain should co-operate with a continental coalition, the straits of Gibraltar and British communications in the Mediterranean might be imperiled. Sir Henry Drummond Wolff, the ambassador in Madrid, wished his government to support Spain. He had encouraged Tetuán's project. Shortly before the memorandum was to go out, he wrote Salisbury enthusiastically of Spanish dependence on Britain and of Britain's great opportunity to make Spain her debtor by protecting Cuba from the United States. When the idea of a Spanish appeal to the powers was revived in the winter of 1897-1898, he went to the limit of discretion both in encouraging the Spaniards and in counseling his own government to agree.

*   *   *

In October 1897, when advised that Spain would soon solicit European support, Salisbury instructed Wolff to assure the Spanish government of Britain's sympathy but *not* of her willingness to give moral support. In 1898, when Spain became insistent, he tried to evade her pleas by speaking of American Anglophobia and saying that evidence of British backing would hurt rather than help the Spanish cause. Ill and absent from his desk during much of March and April, he did not have to make a final decision, and he evidently preferred not to do so. He left the question of Britain's participation in a European action up to the men who were acting for him.

In the Foreign Office, the permanent Under-Secretary, Sir Thomas Sanderson, took much the same view as Wolff. It was he who told the French chargé d'affaires that "serious people" distrusted the United States and that Britain's position was parallel to that of France. When the French government became sponsor for the proposed *démarche*, Sanderson privately advised the French chargé to persevere. The cabinet, he thought, could "associate itself" with such a move.

Arthur Balfour, who took Salisbury's place both in the Foreign Office and at the head of the cabinet, adopted the more cautious view. He first informed the Spanish ambassador that Britain could not give advice to the United States. He promised only to instruct the British ambassador in Washington to speak of Spain's desire for peace. When pressed by Austria and France as well as Spain, he then argued that any move would be premature so long as direct Spanish-American negotiations continued. He would promise nothing other than eventually to consult the cabinet.

The final decision resulted at least in part from intervention by Queen Victoria and, oddly enough, the Pope. On March 17 the Queen received María Cristina's personal appeal. "Poor thing," she sighed in her journal, and she wrote Lord Salisbury, "England should not refuse to join with the other Powers if asked." Her will was hardly law, of course, but it did command respect. Quite apart from her station and experience, she possessed a simple Tory conscience which sometimes shamed her clever and cynical ministers into unexpected acts of principle. Balfour received no direct word from Victoria, but he undoubtedly knew her wishes, and they probably had more influence with him than the counsel of Wolff or Sanderson.

During the two days between the summons to the cabinet and its actual sitting came the Pope's appeal to Spain which Spanish sources described as inspired by McKinley. In reality the inspiration came from Berlin. On March 8 a special courier left the German capital for the Vatican. On March 15 Bülow telegraphed Eulenburg that the Kaiser hoped for a papal tender of good offices. On March 27 he directed the German representative at the Vatican to tell the Pope that Spain was ready to give up Cuba and to propose that his Holiness employ some American clergyman to sound out feeling in Washington.

The Austrian ambassador in Berlin believed the whole idea to have been the Kaiser's. Remembering how the German-Spanish Carolines dispute had been settled by the Pope in the 1880's, Wilhelm hoped, he thought, to rescue Spain, improve his own standing with German Catholics, and at the same time undercut French influence at the Vatican. It seems at least equally probable that Bülow saw the likelihood of other powers agreeing to the joint *démarche* and sought, as a matter of pride, to frustrate a project which he had opposed from the outset. In any event, the German initiative brought the Pope's commission to [the American] Archbishop Ireland, Ireland's overoptimistic dispatch from Washington, Merry del Val's imprecise report to Madrid, and the ill-founded announcement by the Spanish government.

The British cabinet convened on April 4 under the impression that McKinley had actually sought papal intervention. McKinley had not yet contradicted the report, and the Foreign Office had received no communication from Pauncefote for several days. In discussion the English ministers evidently agreed that if the American President were so eager for peace, he would not resent a kindly move by the powers. After the meeting, Balfour called in the Austrian ambassador and told him Britain would join the others. His only condition was that the British ambassador in Washington should first talk with the President and make sure that McKinley was willing to receive a joint note.

The Austrian government had already drafted an instruction which all the powers were to send in identical form to their envoys in Washington. With little or no editing, its text received approval in the other capitals. All six Foreign Ministers thus directed their representatives to call on McKinley as soon as Pauncefote had given him advance warning and appeal "to the feelings of humanity and moderation of the President and of the American people in their existing differences with Spain." The result was the little ceremony that took place in the White House on April 6.

Despite all the precautions that preceded this joint *démarche*, it came close to involving the powers in some of the very complications they had foreseen and sought to avoid. McKinley not only omitted to mention the joint note in his message to Congress, but he actually spoke of intervening in Cuba in the name of humanity and civilization. Bellicose members of the House and Senate used similar language even more recklessly. European statesmen felt affronted that their representations had received so little regard. Their pride was engaged.

*    *    *

Once cautious decisions for joint action had been taken, moreover, governments in Europe were in danger of losing control over events. Their diplomatic representatives had more power to act on their own, and it was by no means certain that their deeds would conform with their governments' intentions. In Madrid the ambassadors met and agreed jointly to urge that Spain grant an armistice. The Austrian said that the Queen Regent had asked them to do so. The Frenchman contended that after the collective move in Washington, it was unnecessary for any of them to ask for further instructions. The Russian showed hesitation until the others persuaded him to join in. A step which did in fact irritate many Spanish politicians was taken without reference to ministers at home.

In Washington the same process started. The Austrian ambassador received a vague message from Vienna instructing him to consult his colleagues about the advisability of a second collective note. On April 11, just after the President's message to Congress, he met with the representatives of the other powers. The German, French, and Russian envoys felt that they should first obtain advice from home. After the meeting broke up, Pauncefote received a message from London which seemed to him adequate and appropriate. Signed by Sanderson, it informed him that Spain wanted the United States advised by the powers to accept the latest Spanish concessions. It ended, "We must leave any action on this request to your discretion."

Pauncefote asked the other ambassadors to come to his home on the afternoon of April 14. There he gave vent to feelings long suppressed. The French representative reported him as having said, "One cannot, without protesting in the name of conscience, allow to be committed the act of brigandage which the United States are preparing at this moment." Laying before his colleagues a draft of a new collective note, he proposed that they ask immediate authorization to present it to the Secretary of State.

The German ambassador had reservations about the wisdom of such a step. He raised the embarrassing question of what would ensue if the second note received no more attention than the first. He also suggested that a note to the Secretary of State was likely, in any case, to seem less important than the previous one, addressed to the President. At his instance, it was agreed that the ambassadors should recommend, instead of a new collective note, an identical note which each government could deliver to the American envoy accredited to it. They combined to frame a dispatch which each could send to his Foreign Minister. The text read:

> The time has come to dispel the erroneous impression which prevails, that armed intervention of the United States in Cuba . . . commands, in the words of the Message, the support and approval of the civilized world. Under these circumstances, Representatives of the Great Powers at Washington consider that their respective Governments might usefully . . . make it known that their approval cannot be given to an armed intervention which does not appear to them to be justified.

Like the original collective note, the proposed identical communications were to contain no threats. Unlike it, however, they were to be plainly critical of the United States. If they had been presented, other and more serious events might have followed.

Most of the ambassadors' governments seemed willing to run this risk. Goluchowski gave his instant approval. Hanotaux said France would go along with any move in which Britain participated, and he urged the English government to agree. Visconti Venosta remarked that he thought the note would serve no purpose but that Italy could not refuse. Muraviev told the Austrian ambassador that he thought it potentially dangerous, but only because it risked involving the United States in European questions in the future. He also made the interesting observation that McKinley had not spoken in the name of the great powers but in that of the civilized world. Nevertheless, he consulted the Tsar and announced that Russia would take part in any action agreed upon by the other powers.

Though the British ambassador in Washington had sponsored the project, the British government gave approval only conditionally. The Queen regarded America's behavior as "monstrous." She later wrote to Salisbury, If [the Americans] . . . declare Cuba independent really such a precedent *ought* to be *protested* against. They might just as soon declare Ireland independent!" Sanderson, who had been responsible for the instruction to Pauncefote, believed that outbreak of war would seriously threaten Britain's colonial holdings.

Balfour, who still held acting charge of the Foreign Office . . . doubted that the proposed note would be efficacious. On the other hand, he respected Pauncefote; "he is on the spot, and he is a man of solid judgment." He did not feel that there was time to obtain Chamberlain's opinion, though he probably could have guessed that the Colonial Minister would oppose any association with "the 'Concert of Europe' (*absit omen!*)." In any case, he temporized, writing that Britain would be ready to join in any representations in favor of peace and even "to make it quite clear that we have formed no judgment adverse to Spain," but, as he also wrote, "it seems very doubtful whether we ought to commit ourselves to a judgment adverse to the U.S., and whether in the interests of peace anything will be gained by doing so." Balfour thus suggested that the note should not be so harsh. . . .

It was the German Kaiser, curiously enough, who put a finish to the project. Bülow had agreed to the first collective note after all his subterfuges failed. Presented with the proposal for a second *démarche,* he took much the attitude of most other foreign ministers. He wrote the Kaiser, "I personally feel fairly indifferent . . . , although I think that a public branding of this wanton attack would be very appropriate."

The Kaiser did not agree. He wrote on the margin: "I think it perfectly mistaken, pointless, and therefore harmful. We should put ourselves in the wrong with the Americans." Wilhelm had become convinced that none of the powers would really act. His ambassador in Washington took the view that Goluchowski had voiced earlier —that only a show of naval force would make any impression on the Americans. And on the margin of another document the Kaiser wrote scornfully, "Ask Hanotaux how many cruisers he would send if the United States rejected a new appeal!"

Bülow consequently informed the Austrians that Germany could not participate. As soon as Hanotaux learned of this, he withdrew his own concurrence, and the entire project collapsed. The display of European unity had begun and ended with the ambassadors' visit to McKinley.

The Kaiser's original notion of a continental league against both Britain and the United States had vanished. His Foreign Minister was too adroit, too practical, too Europe-centered, too sensitive to ambivalence in public feeling. Spain's cause had been taken up ineffectually by the Austrian and French Foreign Ministers, who insisted from the outset on the principle of unanimity. Preoccupied with intra-European rivalries, Goluchowski, Hanotaux, and other diplomatists decided to postpone a confrontation with America until some later day. They were aware too of divisions in public opinion and of potential losses in trade and investment.

It is true that Spain did not offer Europe a perfect cause. Everyone knew that the Spanish government was corrupt and unstable; no one could doubt that the Cubans had legitimate grievances. The Spanish-American crisis did provide the powers with an opportunity to combine against the United States. Though their rulers were all emotionally on the side of Spain, yet they could not unite purposefully. And no such opportunity was to come again.

# Section Eleven
# The Decision for War

*Commentary*

The following documents offer a detailed picture of diplomatic and political developments immediately preceding America's declaration of war. Read by themselves, they might leave the student with the impression that McKinley's decision for war ignored the hopeful communications of his Minister in Madrid, Woodford, and of Spain's last-minute concessions. But these documents do not tell the whole story, for, as the concluding analyses by Ernest May and Walter LaFeber show, there were other, less obvious influences determining McKinley's actions.

*Woodford to the President*
*March 19, 1898*

[*Foreign Relations*, 1897–98, p. 692.]

*Madrid*

Unless report on the steamer *Maine* requires immediate action, I suggest that nothing be decided or done until after the receipt of my personal letters 43, 44, and 46, which my second secretary of legation will carry from Gibraltar Monday, March 21. I also suggest that you authorize me to tell the Queen informally, or any minister indicated by her, that you wish final agreement before April 15. If you will acquaint me fully with general settlement desired I believe Spanish Government will offer without compulsion and upon its own motion such terms of settlement as may be satisfactory to both nations. Large liberty as to details should be conceded to Spain, but your friendship is recognized and appreciated, and I now believe it will be a pleasure to Spanish Government to propose what will probably be satisfactory to you.

WOODFORD

## *Woodford to the President*
## *March 19, 1898*

[*Foreign Relations,* 1897–98, p. 693.]

*Madrid, Spain*

Dear Mr. President:

This morning I called at Señor Moret's house and showed him a telegram which I proposed to send you. He said that he could not approve it officially, as he had not yet the necessary authority, but that he would personally work with me to secure the results therein indicated. After leaving him I then telegraphed you in cipher as follows:

Señor Moret said to me this morning that justice to the Queen required him to assure me in the most positive manner that she had not been privy to or cognizant of any suggestion that she wished to talk with me about any possible cession of Cuba, either to the insurgents or to the

United States; that she wished to hand over his patrimony unimpaired to her son when he should reach his majority; and that she would prefer to abdicate her regency and return to her Austrian home rather than be the instrument of ceding or parting with any of Spain's colonies. I am sure that Mr. Moret to-day regards this [parting with Cuba] as inevitable, and is only seeking the way in which to do it and yet save Spanish honor. He will probably find the way to do it, even if he has to sacrifice himself. I hope this last may not be necessary. I do not believe it will be. Spain needs such men as he to-day, men of faith, courage, and sincerely patriotic purpose.

Please note what I say in my dispatch about April 15. I do not suggest a time limit officially stated. That might embarrass you as well as the Spanish Government. But I do regard it as very essential that they should see that the United States mean business, and mean it *now*.

Your resolute and wise action in getting authority from Congress to put the nation in condition both for defense and attack has made peace not only possible, but to-day I think it probable on such terms as you suggest. You see how my faith has strengthened.

Faithfully yours,

STEWART L. WOODFORD

## Day to Woodford
## March 20, 1898

[*Foreign Relations*, 1897–98, pp. 692–93.]

Department of State
Washington, D.C.

President is at loss to know just what your telegram 19th covers, whether loss of *Maine* or whole situation. Confidential report shows naval board will make unanimous report that *Maine* was blown up by submarine mine. This report must go to Congress soon. Feeling in the United States very acute. People have borne themselves with great forebearance and self-restraint last month. President has no doubt Congress will act wisely and immediate crisis may be avoided, particularly if there be certainty of prompt restoration of peace in Cuba.

*Maine* loss may be peacefully settled if full reparation is promptly made, such as the most civilized nation would offer. But there remains general conditions in Cuba which can not be longer endured, and which will demand action on our part, unless Spain restores honorable peace which will stop starvation of people and give them opportunity to take care of themselves, and restore commerce now wholly lost. April 15 is none too early date for accomplishment of these purposes. Relations will be much influenced by attitude of Spanish Government in *Maine* matter, but general conditions must not be lost sight of. It is proper that you should know that, unless events otherwise indicate, the President, having exhausted diplomatic agencies to secure peace in Cuba, will lay the whole question before Congress.

Keep President fully advised, as action of next few days may control situation.

DAY

*Day to Woodford*
*March 26, 1898 12:10 a.m.*
[*Foreign Relations*, 1897–98, p. 704.]

*Department of State*
*Washington*

The President's desire is for peace. He can not look upon the suffering and starvation in Cuba save with horror. The concentration of men, women, and children in the fortified towns and permitting them to starve is unbearable to a Christian nation geographically so close as ours to Cuba. All this has shocked and inflamed the American mind, as it has the civilized world, where its extent and character are known. It was represented to him in November that the Blanco government would at once release the suffering and so modify the Weyler order as to permit those who were able to return to their homes and till the fields from which they had been driven. There has been no relief to the starving except such as the American people have supplied. The reconcentration order has not been practically superseded. There is no hope of peace through Spanish arms. The Spanish Government seems unable to conquer the insurgents. More than half of the island is under control of the insurgents; for more than three years our people have been patient and forbearing; we have patrolled our coast with zeal and at great expense, and have successfully prevented the landing of any armed force on the island. The war has disturbed the peace and tranquility of our people. We do not want the island. The President has evidenced in every way his desire to preserve and continue friendly relations with Spain. He has kept every international obligation with fidelity. He wants an honorable peace. He has repeatedly urged the Government of Spain to secure such a peace. She still has the opportunity to do it, and the President appeals to her from every consideration of justice and humanity to do it. Will she? Peace is the desired end.

For your own guidance, the President suggests that if Spain will revoke the reconcentration order and maintain the people until they can support themselves and offer to the Cubans full self-government, with reasonable indemnity, the President will gladly assist in its consummation. If Spain should invite the United States to mediate for peace and the insurgents would make like request, the President might undertake such office of friendship.

DAY

## Day to Woodford
## March 27, 1898

[*Foreign Relations*, 1897–98, pp. 711–12.]

*Department of State*
*Washington*

Believed the *Maine* report will be held in Congress for a short time without action. A feeling of deliberation prevails in both houses of Congress. See if the following can be done:

First. Armistice until October 1. Negotiations meantime looking for peace between Spain and insurgents through friendly offices of President United States.

Second. Immediate revocation of reconcentrado order so as to permit people to return to their farms, and the needy to be relieved with provisions and supplies from United States cooperating with authorities so as to afford full relief.

Add, if possible:

Third. If terms of peace not satisfactorily settled by October 1, President of the United States to be final arbiter between Spain and insurgents.

If Spain agrees, President will use friendly offices to get insurgents to accept plan. Prompt action desirable.

DAY

## Woodford to Day
## March 27, 1898

[*Foreign Relations*, 1897–98, p. 713.]

I have today telegraphed you in cipher as follows:

Telegraphic instructions, signed "Day," dated

March 25, received Saturday evening, March 26. Do the words "full self-government" mean actual recognition of independence, or is nominal Spanish sovereignty over Cuba still permissible?

Instruct me fully as to what the words "with reasonable indemnity" mean and imply.

Under Spanish constitution, ministry can not recognize independence of Cuba or part with nominal sovereignty over Cuba. Cortes alone can do this and Cortes will not meet until April 25. If I can secure immediate and effective armistice or truce between Spanish troops and insurgents, to take effect on or before April 15, will this be satisfactory?

It is possible that I may induce Spanish ministry to submit the question of an early and honorable peace to the Cuban Congress, which will meet at Havana on May 4, and that Spanish Government will give such Cuban Congress all necessary authority to negotiate and conclude peace, provided such authority shall not diminish or interfere with the constitutional power vested by the Cuban constitution in the central government. If I can secure these two things with absolute and immediate revocation of concentration order may I negotiate? I believe that an immediate armistice means present and permanent peace. Also I believe that negotiations once open between insurgents and the Cuban government some arrangement will be reached during the summer which the Spanish home Government will approve, and that Cuba will become practically independent or pass from Spanish control. President of council of ministers wishes personal interview as to armistice, but I will not see him until . after I get your reply to this telegram.

WOODFORD

## Day to Woodford
### March 28, 1898

[*Foreign Relations*, 1897–98, p. 713.]

*Washington, Department of State*

Your cable 27th received. Full self-government with indemnity would mean Cuban independence. As to other matters see Sunday's telegram. Very important to have definite agreement for determining peace after armistice, if negotiations pending same fail to reach satisfactory conclusions.

DAY

## Day to Woodford
### March 28, 1898

[*Foreign Relations*, 1897–98, p. 713.]

*Washington, Department of State*

Important to have prompt answer on armistice matter.

DAY

## Woodford to Day
### March 31, 1898

[*Foreign Relations*, 1897–98, pp. 726–27.]

*Madrid, Legation of the United States*

Sir:

I have the honor to report that this (Thursday)

morning I received your cipher telegram, which I translate as follows:

*Washington, March 30, 1898*

Woodford, Minister, Madrid:

You should know and fully appreciate that there is profound feeling in Congress and the gravest apprehension on the part of most conservative members that a resolution for intervention may pass both branches in spite of any efforts which can be made. Only assurance from the President that if he fails in peaceful negotiations he will submit all the facts to Congress at a very early day will prevent immediate action on the part of Congress.

The President assumes that whatever may be reached in your negotiations to-morrow will be tentative only to be submitted as the proposal of Spain.

We hope your negotiation will lead to a peace acceptable to the country.

Wednesday, 4 p.m.

DAY

I at once telegraphed you in cipher as follows:

*Madrid March 31, 1898*

Assistant Secretary Day, Washington:

Received your dispatch dated Wednesday, 4 p.m., this morning. If Spanish Government accept our demands this afternoon without reservation or modification, I will receive Spanish suggestions tentatively and report by cable to-night for decision by the President. I will neither embarrass the President nor diminish the just demands of our Government.

WOODFORD

This afternoon at 4 o'clock I met the president of the

council, the minister for foreign affairs, and the minister for the colonies in our adjourned conference. The minister for the colonies acted as interpreter, as before.

I have to-night telegraphed you so fully, giving account of our conference, that I quote my telegram here.

*Madrid, March 31, 1898*

Assistant Secretary Day, Washington:

Adjourned conference held this afternoon, Thursday. All present. President of the council handed me Spanish propositions in writing, which I translated in their presence. The minister for the colonies examined and approved my translation, which begins here.

### *Catastrophe of the Maine*

Spain is ready to submit to an arbitration the differences which can arise in this matter.

### *Reconcentrados*

General Blanco, following the instructions of the Government, has revoked in the western provinces the bando relating to the reconcentrados, and, although this measure will not be able to reach its complete developments until the military operations terminate, the Government places at the disposal of the Governor-General of Cuba a credit of 3,000,000 of pesetas, to the end that the country people may return at once and with success to their labors.

The same Government will accept, nevertheless, whatever assistance to feed and succor the necessitous may be sent from the United States, in the form and conditions agreed upon between that sub-Secretary of State, Mr. Day, and the Spanish minister in Washington.

### Pacification of Cuba

The Spanish Government, more interested than that of the United States in giving to the Grand Antille an honorable and stable peace, proposes to confide its preparations to the insular parliament, without whose intervention it will not be able to arrive at the final result, it being understood that the powers reserved by the constitution to the Central Government are not lessened and diminished.

### Truce

As the Cuban Chambers will not meet until the 4th of May, the Spanish Government will not, on its part, find it inconvenient to accept at once a suspension of hostilities asked for by the insurgents from the general in chief, to whom it will belong in this case to determine the duration and the conditions of the suspension.

Spanish propositions end here. I told them I would telegraph their propositions to Washington verbatim, but that I did not believe the proposition relating to suspension of hostilities would be acceptable, and that the insurgents would not ask for it.

We parted without any appointment for further conference. I said that I would communicate the reply of my Government to the Spanish minister of foreign affairs.

Thursday night, 10 o'clock.

WOODFORD

I received all the propositions tentatively; did not commit my Government to any of them; promised to communicate all to Washington by telegraph, and expressly stated my belief that the one relating to suspension of hostilities would not be acceptable.

This proposition, taken in connection with the one relating to the "pacification of Cuba," does not mean immediate or assured peace. It means, when read with the other, continuation of this destructive, cruel, and now needless war.

I have written this in my own hand, as one of my two typewriters is sick, and the other is at work on the cipher dispatches I am sending to-night.

Very respectfully, yours,

STEWART L. WOODFORD

## *Woodford to the President*
## *April 1, 1898*

[*Foreign Relations*, 1897–98, pp. 727–28.]

Madrid, *Legation of the United States*

Dear Mr. President:

Yesterday's conference was a sorrow to me, for I have worked hard for peace. Last night I telegraph you as follows:

*Madrid, March 31, 1898*

President McKinley, Washington:

Have just telegraphed to the Department of State my official report of the adjourned conference held this afternoon, Thursday. It has turned, as I feared, on a question of punctilio. Spanish pride will not permit the ministry to propose and offer an armistice, which they really desire, because they know that armistice now means certain peace next autumn. I am told confidentially that the offer of armistice by the Spanish Government would cause revolution here. Leading generals have been sounded within the last week, and the ministry have gone as far as they dare go to-day. I believe the ministry are ready to go as far and as fast as they can and still save the dynasty here in Spain. They know that Cuba is lost. Public opinion in Spain has moved steadily toward peace. No Spanish ministry would have dared to do one month ago what this ministry has proposed to-day.

WOODFORD

The Spanish ministers said yesterday that their statement went as far as they could possibly go. Perhaps this is true, but they said the same some weeks ago and yesterday they yielded on two points. First, they are willing to arbitrate the *Maine* matter. Some days ago they talked fight if we should even suggest that they were responsible for the loss of the *Maine*. Secondly, they revoke the reconcentrado order, and place a large sum at General Blanco's disposal for the relief of the necessitous. It is not long since they denied the very existence of the horrible conditions they now admit.

There is no real war spirit here among the middle and lower classes. Last September most of the people were ready for war. The war spirit has been diminishing steadily and now prevails only among the aristocracy, the political classes, and the generals and officers of the army. The army is still the controlling factor in Spanish politics, and the attitude of the army constitutes the real danger to-day.

Faithfully, yours,

STEWART L. WOODFORD

## Woodford to Day
### April 2, 1898

[*Foreign Relations*, 1897–98, pp. 730–31.]

*Madrid, Legation of the United States*

Sir:

I have the honor to report that I have just telegraphed you, in cipher, as follows:

*Madrid, April 2, 1898*

Assistant Secretary Day, Washington:

Tuesday, March 29, I telegraphed to the President, being my personal No. 60. embodied, that telegram in my official dispatch to the Department of State, No. 195, dated March 30.

I telegraphed Spanish propositions in full on Thursday, March 31.

I telegraphed on Friday, April 1, my statement in full as made to Spanish ministers on March 29.

After most careful reflection I can not consider these Spanish propositions as satisfactory to the United States or just to Cuba. In view of my assurances, as given in my personal telegram No. 60 to the President, it becomes my duty to make this official statement.

Saturday, 5 p.m.

WOODFORD

I have worked hard for peace. I am hoping against hope, and still can not bring myself to the final belief that in these closing years of the nineteenth century Spain will finally refuse, on a mere question of punctilio, to offer immediate and effective armistice.

I still believe that immediate armistice will secure permanent and honorable peace with justice to Cuba and sure protection to our great American interests in that island. Men will not reason when their passions are inflamed. So long as they are fighting they will not negotiate. When they stop fighting they will begin to reach. Negotiations will follow and peace will come. If arms are now laid down on both sides they will not be taken up again.

Very respectfully, yours,

STEWART L. WOODFORD

*Spanish Minister to the United States
Señor Polo de Bernabé to Sherman
April 3, 1898*

[*Foreign Relations*, 1897-98, pp. 731-32.]

*Legation of Spain at Washington*

The envoy extraordinary and plenipotentiary of Spain has the honor to communicate to the honorable Secretary of State of the United States the following telegram which he has just received from his excellency the Governor-General of the island of Cuba:

> The insular government has resolved upon the publication in an extraordinary gazeta of a manifesto to the country setting forth the excellencies of autonomy, declaring that the colonial constitution is capable of reform in a full sense, and making a patriotic appeal to the insurrectionists to conclude a peace, after previous understanding and agreement. One of the paragraphs reads thus:
>
> "The provisional government ardently desires, and the facts bear testimony thereof, that all Cubans, without any exception whatever, shall join in the realization of the noble and fruitful work of rearing

peace and concord upon bases of unshakable firmness. The provisional government, following its own inspiration and being also the faithful interpreter of the earnest desires of the Government of the mother country, addresses itself to those Cubans who, in the arena of force, are striving to attain that which in its full reality and worth and without the perils or hazards of independence has already been attained—the triumph of right and justice with far-stretching horizons for the future and broad paths for the orderly and growing development of all the living forces of this community.

"Let the clash of arms cease; let us stretch forth our hands to each other; let us fraternally embrace within the beloved Cuban fatherland, regenerated by sacrifice and liberty; let us restore our hearthstones and gather around them with love; let us work in unity to the end that from the ruins of the past may arise great, strong, and prosperous the Cuban people; let us, the sons of Cuba, enter upon a frank and loyal understanding in order to deliberate with calmness and decide with skillful provision concerning the means which shall conduce by common accord to attain peace without shame for any and with honor for all; let hostilities be suspended, in order that the voice of patriotism may be heard among us, brothers, equally interested in the lot of Cuba. The provisional government hastens to take the initiative toward the attainment of the high ends which it thus sets forth, offering most solemnly all manner of guaranties, and relying ever upon the approbation of the Government of the mother country."

In transmitting to the Hon. John Sherman the foregoing telegram, which demonstrates the noble sentiments of concord and peace that animate alike the Government of His Majesty and the autonomous government of the island of Cuba, Don Luis de Bernabé avails himself of this opportunity to repeat to him the assurances of his highest consideration.

## *Woodford to the President*
## *April 3, 1898*

[*Foreign Relations*, 1897–98, p. 732.]

*Madrid, Legation of the United States*

Dear Mr. President:

I have been in communication with the Spanish minister all day, working hard for the last chance for peace. This evening, April 3, I telegraphed you in cipher as follows:

*Madrid, April 3, 1898*

President McKinley, Washington:

The minister for foreign affairs has just called and tells me confidentially that, according to news received by him, the Pope, at the suggestion of the President of the United States, proposes to offer to Spain his mediation in order that the Spanish Government grant an immediate armistice to Cuba, which will facilitate and prepare an early and honorable peace.

According to Señor Gullón's opinion, the Spanish Government will accede to the desires of the Holy Father, which are not political but humane. But he understands that the Spanish Government, going as far as it goes, asks that the United States will show their friendship for Spain by withdrawing our warships from the vicinity of Cuba and from Key West as soon as the armistice has been proclaimed. That the Spanish Government will continue this armistice so long as there are any reasonable hopes that permanent peace can be secured in Cuba. He asks your immediate answer as to withdrawal of warships at once after proclamation of armistice. I still believe that when armistice is once proclaimed hostilities will never be resumed and that permanent peace will be secured. If, under existing conditions at Washington, you can still do this, I hope that you will.

The Spanish minister for foreign affairs assures me that Spain will go as far and as fast as she can. The Austrian ambassador has heard me read this dispatch to this point and says that he will guarantee that Spain will do this.

If conditions at Washington still enable you to give me the necessary time I am sure that before next October I will get peace in Cuba with justice to Cuba and protection to our great American interests.

I know that the Queen and her present ministry sincerely desire peace and that the Spanish people desire peace, and if you can still give me time and reasonable liberty of action I will get for you the peace you desire so much and for which you have labored so hard.

I think there may be mistake in the telegram from Rome to the Queen, and that the words "at the suggestion of the President" may mean with the knowledge or with the approval of the President.

Sunday night, 10.

WOODFORD

Am too tired to-night to write further. Will report details of to-day's negotiations in my next.

Faithfully, yours,

STEWART L. WOODFORD

## Day to Woodford
## April 4, 1898

[*Foreign Relations*, 1897-98, pp. 732-33.]

*Washington, Department of State*

The President has made no suggestions to Spain except through you. He made no suggestions other than those which you were instructed to make for an armistice to be offered by Spain to negotiate a permanent peace between Spain and insurgents, and which Spain has already rejected. An armistice involves an agreement between Spain and insurgents which must be voluntary on the part of each, and if accepted by them would make for peace. The disposition of our fleet must be left to us. An armistice, to be effective, must be immediately proffered and accepted by insurgents. Would the peace you are so confident of securing mean the independence of Cuba? The President can not hold his message longer than Tuesday.

Two o'clock Monday morning.

DAY

## Sherman to Woodford
## April 4, 1898

[*Foreign Relations,* 1897–98, p. 733.]

*Washington, Department of State*

Congress may very possibly take decisive action middle or end of this week. You should notify the United States consul-general in Spain and cooperate with him in notifying the United States consular officers in Spain who are American citizens to arrange to leave their offices in charge of friendly power, and, if they desire, quietly prepare for departure from Spain upon notice, either special or public, of a rupture of relations.

If rupture comes you had better proceed to Paris and await further instructions.

SHERMAN


## Day to Woodford
## April 4, 1898

[*Foreign Relations,* 1897–98, p. 733.]

*Washington, Department of State*

We have received to-day from the Spanish minister a copy of the manifesto of the autonomy government. It is not armistice. It proves to be an appeal by the autonomy government of Cuba urging the insurgents to lay down their arms and to join with the autonomy party in building up the new scheme of home rule. It is simply an invitation to the insurgents to submit, in which event the autonomy government, likewise suspending hostilities, is prepared to consider what expansion if any of the decreed home-rule scheme is needed or practicable. It need scarcely be pointed out that this is a very different thing from an offered armistice. The President's message will go in Wednesday afternoon.

Monday night, 11 o'clock.

DAY

*Joint Note of the Powers and President McKinley's Reply, April 6, 1898*

[*Foreign Relations*, 1897–98, pp. 740–41.]

*Washington, D.C.*

The undersigned representatives of Germany, Austria-Hungary, France, Great Britain, Italy, and Russia, duly authorized in that behalf, address, in the name of their respective Governments, a pressing appeal to the feelings of humanity and moderation of the President and of the American people in their existing differences with Spain. They earnestly hope that further negotiations will lead to an agreement which, while securing the maintenance of peace, will afford all necessary guaranties for the reestablishment of order in Cuba.

The Powers do not doubt that the humanitarian and purely disinterested character of this representation will be fully recognized and appreciated by the American nation.

*Julian Pauncefote*, for Great Britain
*Holleben*, for Germany
*Jules Cambon*, for France
*Von Hengelmüller*, for Austria-Hungary
*De Wollant*, for Russia
*G. C. Vinci*, for Italy

## The President's Reply

The Government of the United States recognizes the good will which has prompted the friendly communication of the representatives of Germany, Austria-Hungary, France, Great Britain, Italy, and Russia, as set forth in the address of your excellencies, and shares the hope therein expressed that the outcome of the situation in Cuba may be the maintenance of peace between the United States and Spain by affording the necessary guaranties for the reestablishment of order in the island, so terminating the chronic condition of disturbance there, which so deeply injures the interests and menaces the tranquillity of the American nation by the character and consequences of the struggle thus kept up at our doors, besides shocking its sentiment of humanity.

The Government of the United States appreciates the humanitarian and disinterested character of the communication now made on behalf of the powers named, and for its part is confident that equal appreciation will be shown for its own earnest and unselfish endeavors to fulfill a duty to humanity by ending a situation the indefinite prolongation of which has become insufferable.

# Woodford to Day
# April 6, 1898

[*Foreign Relations*, 1897–98, p. 743.]

*Madrid, Legation of the United States*

Sir:

In continuation of my dispatch of this date, I have the honor to report that I have this afternoon at 6 o'clock sent to the Spanish ministers, who are now in conference, and by the hands of the secretary of this legation, an official note reading as follows:

*Madrid, April 6, 1898*

Excellency.
My Dear Sir:

I had hoped to be officially informed before 12 o'clock noon of this day that His Majesty's Government had proclaimed definite suspension of hostilities in the island of Cuba.

The President of the United States has this afternoon transmitted to the American Congress a message covering the entire Cuban question, with such recommendations as he has deemed necessary and expedient. The repose and welfare of the American people require the restoration of peace and stable government in Cuba. If armistice had been offered by the Government of Spain the President would have communicated that fact to Congress. He has recounted the conditions in Cuba, the injurious effect upon our people, the character and conditions of the conflict, and the hopelessness of the strife. He has not advised the recognition of the independence of the insurgents, but has recommended measures looking to the cessation of hostilities, restoration of the peace, and stability of government in the island. He has done this in the interests of humanity and for the safety and tranquillity of the United States.

Should His Majesty's Government arrive this day at final decision with regard to an armistice, I will telegraph the text of the same to my Government, should I receive it before 12 o'clock to-night. It will thus reach the President to-morrow (Thursday) morning in time to be communicated by him to Congress to-morrow (Thursday).

With sorrow deeper than I can express, I regret

that His Majesty's Government has not yet communicated to me its purpose to proclaim an immediate and effective armistice or suspension of hostilities in Cuba, lasting for a sufficient length of time to enable passions to cease and obtain permanent and honorable peace in Cuba, with the text of such proclamation.

I avail myself of this opportunity to renew to your excellency the assurances of my most distinguished consideration.

STEWART L. WOODFORD

To His Excellency Pio Gullón, Secretary of State.

Should I get any response to this note to the Spanish Government to-night, I will telegraph same to you.
Very respectfully, yours,

STEWART L. WOODFORD

## *Woodford to Day*
## *April 6, 1898*

[*Foreign Relations*, 1897-98, p. 743.]

*Madrid, Legation of the United States*

Sir:

I have the honor to acknowledge the receipt this evening of your cipher telegram of this date, which I translate as follows:

*Washington, April 6, 1898*

Woodford, Minister, Madrid:

The President's message will not be sent to

Congress until next Monday, to give consul-general at Havana the time he urgently asks to insure safe departure of Americans.

DAY

I hope that this will also give the Spanish Government the time in which to issue a frank and effective proclamation of such an armistice as may lead to early and honorable peace.

Very respectfully, yours,

STEWART L. WOODFORD

*Woodford to Day
April 7, 1898*

[*Foreign Relations*, 1897–98, p. 744.]

*Madrid, Legation of the United States*

Sir:

In view of the fact that the President's message covering the Cuban question was not sent to Congress on Wednesday, April 6 instant, as I had informed the Spanish Government, in my note to them dated April 6, would be done, it has seemed my duty, after most careful reflection, to withdraw the note in which I gave them this erroneous information. Accordingly I have this day addressed an official note to the Spanish minister for foreign affairs in the following terms:

*Madrid, April 7, 1898*

Excellency.
My Dear Sir:

Since sending to your excellency my note, No.

98, dated April 6 instant, I learn from my Government that the President of the United States has not sent to Congress his proposed message covering the entire Cuban question, with such recommendations as he might deem necessary and expedient. I am further officially informed that such message will not be sent to Congress until Monday next, April 11 instant. As the fact upon which the urgency of my note was based has thus been postponed, it becomes my pleasant duty to withdraw my said note, No. 98, dated April 6 instant. I do this gladly, as it is very far from the purpose of the United States even to seem to put any pressure upon the action of Spain.

I avail myself of this opportunity to renew to your excellency the assurances of my most distinguished consideration.

STEWART L. WOODFORD

To His Excellency Pio Gullón, Secretary of State.

Having in view the instructions of the Department to treat the Spanish Government with all possible courtesy and consideration, while maintaining firmly the interests and stating clearly the duties of the United States, I am sure that you will approve my action in thus withdrawing unreservedly my note of yesterday, which was reported in full to the Department in my dispatch, No. 211, dated April 6, 1898.

Very respectfully, yours,

STEWART L. WOODFORD

## Woodford to Sherman
## April 8, 1898

[*Foreign Relations*, 1897–98, pp. 744–45.]

*Madrid, Legation of the United States*

Sir:

I have the honor to report that on April 3d instant I gave out the following interview:

> In answer to the pressing request of the American and English newspaper correspondents in Madrid, General Woodford, the American minister, made to-day the following statement:
>
> The obligations of my diplomatic position absolutely forbid my granting any interview or giving the slightest intimation as to the present condition of the diplomatic negotiations intrusted to my care. I came to Spain under the instructions of the President to secure peace in Cuba, with permanent peace between the United States and Spain—a peace that should be built upon the bed-rock conditions of justice to Cuba, with assured protection to the great American interests in that island. I have labored steadily to obtain this result. I have never lost my faith, and, doubtful as conditions may seem to-day, I still believe that these great and good purposes of my President may yet be secured. I shall not desist in my labors for a just and honorable peace until the guns actually open fire, and my faith is still strong that war, with all its horrors, can be averted. Enough blood has been shed in Cuba already, and I can not believe that the closing hours of the nineteenth century will be reddened by conflict between Spain and the United States. My country asks for peace based upon conditions that

shall make peace permanent and beneficent, and I
have faith that Spain will yet do what is necessary
to assure justice for Cuba, and with justice peace is
certain.

This interview or statement was published in all the
leading English newspapers. I trust that its publication
has been useful.

Yesterday morning, April 7, the newspapers in Madrid were filled with erroneous statements, and efforts were made to incite mobs against the legation and against my residence. While I had no fears as to my personal safety, I thought it wise to allay the excitement and strengthen the conservative influences, which are growing stronger each hour in Madrid and which are working earnestly for peace. Accordingly I gave out the following statement, which was printed in all the Madrid papers last evening and in all the morning papers to-day, and which has been telegraphed to all the papers throughout Spain.

*United States Legation*
*Madrid, April 7, 1898*

* * *

The American minister has received nothing but courtesy from the people of Madrid during his residence here. He has never had the slightest apprehension for his own personal security or that of his family. He is working for peace, and, despite all rumors to the contrary, he still hopes that peace will be kept between Spain and the United States and that peace will very soon be again established in Cuba—a peace that shall be based upon absolute justice, with protection to the great American interests in that island and with the maintenance of the honor of Spain.

This publication has done good in Madrid and will

do good throughout Spain. The end is still very doubtful, and I am working from sense of duty rather than with strong faith in success. Still this is evident, and on this I base what hope is left to me: The sober sense of Spain is slowly but surely coming to the front, and a few days (if these few days can still be had) will see a crystallized, public sentiment that will sustain the present Spanish Government, if that Government has the immediate courage to do at once the things that are necessary for peace.

Very respectfully yours,

STEWART L. WOODFORD

*Woodford to Day*
*April 9, 1898*

[*Foreign Relations*, 1897-98, p. 746.]

*Madrid, Legation of the United States*

Sir:

I have the honor to report that I have just telegraphed you in cipher as follows:

*Madrid, April 9, 1898*

Assistant Secretary Day, Washington:

No change in situation. Spanish propositions of March 31 have not been modified. It is still possible that armistice may be declared. I will keep you fully advised.

WOODFORD

There are rumors this morning of a possible ministerial crisis, but I can not verify them at this moment.

Very respectfully yours,

STEWART L. WOODFORD

## Woodford to Day
## April 9, 1898

[*Foreign Relations*, 1897–98, p. 746.]

*Madrid, Legation of the United States*

Sir:

I have the honor to inform you that I have just telegraphed you in cipher as follows:

*Madrid, April 9, 1898*

Assistant Secretary Day, Washington:

Am just informed that armistice has been granted and that Spanish Government has communicated directly with the President. Please keep me fully advised.

WOODFORD

As I was dictating this dispatch I was sent for by the Spanish minister of foreign affairs. He told me that the Spanish Government had this day decided to grant an armistice in Cuba, at the request of the Pope and in deference to the wishes and advice of the representatives of the six great European powers; that the Spanish minister in Washington had been instructed to notify our Department of State, and that authority to proclaim the armistice had been cabled to the Captain-General in Cuba. He handed me written memorandum in Spanish stating officially the action of the Spanish Government.

I have at once telegraphed you in cipher as follows:

*Madrid, April 9, 1898*

Assistant Secretary Day, Washington:

Spanish minister for foreign affairs has just sent for me. The representatives of the European powers called upon him this morning and advised acquiescence in Pope's request for an armistice. Armistice has been granted. Spanish minister in Washington instructed to notify our Department of State and yourself. Authority has been cabled to General Blanco to proclaim armistice. I send verbatim memorandum just handed me by Spanish minister for foreign affairs, as follows:

"In view of the earnest and repeated request of His Holiness, supported resolutely by declarations and friendly counsels of the representatives of the six great European powers, who formulated them this morning in a collective visit to the minister of state, as corollary of the efforts of their Governments in Washington, the Spanish Government has resolved to inform the Holy Father that on this date it directs the general in-chief of the army in Cuba to grant immediately a suspension of hostilities for such length of time as he may think prudent to prepare and facilitate the peace earnestly desired by all."

I hope that this dispatch may reach you before the President's message goes to Congress.

WOODFORD

I will endeavor to acquaint myself fully with the inside condition of affairs here and will keep you advised.

Very respectfully,

WOODFORD

## *Woodford to the President*
## *April 10, 1898*

[*Foreign Relations*, 1897–98, p. 747.]

Madrid, Legation of the United States

President McKinley, Washington:

My personal No. 66. In view of action of Spanish

Government, as cabled Saturday, April 9, I hope that you can obtain full authority from Congress to do whatever you shall deem necessary to secure immediate and permanent peace in Cuba by negotiations, including the full power to employ the Army and Navy, according to your own judgment, to aid and enforce your action. If this be secured I believe you will get final settlement before August 1 on one of the following bases: Either such autonomy as the insurgents may agree to accept, or recognition by Spain of the independence of the island, or cession of the island to the United States.

I hope that nothing will now be done to humiliate Spain, as I am satisfied that the present Government is going, and is loyally ready to go, as fast and as far as it can. With your power of action sufficiently free you will win the fight on your own lines. I do not expect immediate reply, but will be glad to have an early acknowledgment of receipt.

WOODFORD

## Señor Polo de Bernabé to Sherman
## April 10, 1898

[*Foreign Relations*, 1897–98, pp. 747–49.]

*Legation of Spain at Washington*

The minister plenipotentiary of Spain has the honor to state to the honorable Secretary of State of the United States of America that Her Majesty the Queen Regent, acceding to the reiterated desires of His Holiness, and inspired by the sentiments of concord and peace which animate her, has given appropriate instructions to the general in chief of the army of Cuba, to the end that he shall concede an immediate suspension of hostilities for such time as he shall deem prudential, in order to prepare and facilitate people in that island.

* * *

The Government of Her Majesty, by this most important step, has set the crown to her extraordinary efforts to obtain the pacification of Cuba through the instrumentalities of reason and of right.

The autonomic constitution, which gives to the inhabitants of the island of Cuba a political system at least as liberal as that which exists in the Dominion of Canada, will within a short time enter upon the stage of complete development, when, after the elections have been held, the insular parliament will meet at Habana on the 4th of May next; and the franchise and liberties granted to the Cubans are such that no motive or pretext is left for claiming any fuller measure thereof.

Nevertheless as the island of Cuba is represented in the Cortes of the Kingdom, a privilege which is not enjoyed by any other foreign autonomic colony, the Cuban senators and deputies in the Cortes may there present their aspirations if they desire more.

* * *

The abrogation of the decree of reconcentration and the assistance of every kind which the Government of Her Majesty has granted and permitted to be extended to the reconcentrados have at last terminated a lamentable condition of things, which was the unavoidable consequence of the sanguinary strife provoked by a small minority of the sons of Cuba, and who have been mainly led and sustained by foreign influences.

No impartial mind, having full knowledge of the facts, which have never on any occasion been perverted, as those relating to the Cuban question have been and are now perverted, can justly impute to Spain remissness in endeavoring to reach the means of pacification of the island nor illiberality in granting privileges, liberties, and franchises for the welfare and happiness of its inhabitants. The Government of Her Majesty doubts not that this will be recognized by the United States Government, even as it must recognize the manifest injustice with which a portion of the public opinion of this country claims to discover responsibilities on the part of Spain for the horrible catastrophe which took place on the calamitous night of the 15th of February last. Her Majesty the Queen Regent, her responsible government, the Governor-General of Cuba, the insular government, and all the higher authorities of Habana displayed from the first moment the profound sorrow and the sentiments of horror which that measureless misfortune caused to them, as well as the sympathy which on that melancholy occasion linked them to the American Government and people.

\* \* \*

As for the question of fact which springs from the diversity of views between the reports of the Spanish and American boards, the Government of Her Majesty, although not yet possessed of the official text of the two reports, has hastened to declare itself ready to submit to the judgment of impartial and disinterested experts, accepting in advance the decision of the arbitrators named by the two parties, which is obvious proof of the frankness and good faith which marks the course of Spain on this as on all occasions.

The minister of Spain trusts that these statements, inspired by the earnest desire for peace and concord which animates the Government of Her Majesty, will be appreciated at their just worth by the Government of the United States.

*Day to Woodford*
*April 10, 1898*
*(about 6 p.m.)*

[*Foreign Relations*, 1897–98, p. 749.]

*Washington, Department of State*

The Spanish minister to-day informed me that authority had been given General Blanco to proclaim suspension of hostilities, and thereupon invited, on General's behalf, indication of nature and scope of such proclamation. Spanish minister had been answered that the President must decline to make further suggestions than those heretofore made known through you and through Spanish minister here, but that in sending in his message to-morrow the President will acquaint Congress with this latest communication of the Spanish Government and add any further information which Minister Polo may be in a position to furnish in regard to the nature and terms of General Blanco's action under the authorization so given him. The above is sent for your information. Your personal, No. 66, just received and fully noted.

DAY


*Señor Polo de Bernabé to Day*
*April 11, 1898*

[*Foreign Relations*, 1897–98, p. 750.]

*Washington, Royal Spanish Legation*

Dear Mr. Day:

I inclose herewith the official announcement of General Blanco's proclamation that I have received this morning and an English translation of said proclamation.

Believe me, etc.,

POLO DE BERNABE

## Suspension of Hostilities

Her majesty's Government, yielding to the reiterated wish expressed by His Holiness the Pope, has resolved, with the end to prepare and facilitate peace on this island, to decree a suspension of hostilities, and order me to publish it for said purposes.

In virtue thereof I have thought it expedient to order:

Article first. From the day following the receipt of this proclamation in each locality hostilities are declared to be suspended in the territory of the island of Cuba.

Article second. The details for the execution of the above article shall be the subject of special instructions that will be communicated to the different commanders in chief of the army corps for the most prompt and easy execution, according to the situation and circumstances of each.

Done at Habana the 7th day of April, 1898.

RAMON BLANCO

## President McKinley to the Congress
## April 11, 1898

[*Foreign Relations*, 1897–98, pp. 756–60.]

Obedient to that precept of the Constitution which commands the President to give from time to time to the

Congress information of the state of the Union and to recommend to their consideration such measures as he shall judge necessary and expedient, it becomes my duty now to address your body with regard to the grave crisis that has arisen in the relations of the United States to Spain by reason of the warfare that for more than three years has raged in the neighboring island of Cuba.

I do so because of the intimate connection of the Cuban question with the state of our own Union and the grave relation the course which it is now incumbent upon the nation to adopt must needs bear to the traditional policy of our Government if it is to accord with the precepts laid down by the founders of the Republic and religiously observed by succeeding Administrations to the present day.

* * *

Since the present revolution began, in February, 1895, this country has seen the fertile domain at our threshold ravaged by fire and sword in the course of a struggle unequaled in the history of the island and rarely paralleled as to the numbers of the combatants and the bitterness of the contest by any revolution of modern times where a dependent people striving to be free have been opposed by the power of the sovereign state.

Our people have beheld a once prosperous community reduced to comparative want, its lucrative commerce virtually paralyzed, its exceptional productiveness diminished, its fields laid waste, its mills in ruins, and its people perishing by tens of thousands from hunger and destitution. We have found ourselves constrained, in the observance of that strict neutrality which our laws enjoin, and which the law of nations commands, to police our own waters and watch our own seaports in prevention of any unlawful act in aid of the Cubans.

Our trade has suffered; the capital invested by our citizens in Cuba has been largely lost, and the temper and forbearance of our people have been so sorely tried as to beget a perilous unrest among our own citizens which has inevitably found its expression from time to time in the National Legislature, so that issues wholly external to our own body politic engross attention and stand in the way of that close devotion to domestic advancement that becomes a self-contained commonwealth whose primal maxim has been the avoidance of all foreign entanglements. All this must needs awaken, and has, indeed, aroused the utmost concern on the part of this Government, as well during my predecessor's term as in my own.

* * *

By the time the present administration took office a year ago, reconcentration—so called—had been made effective over the better part of the four central and western provinces, Santa Clara, Matanzas, Habana, and Pinar del Rio.

The agricultural population to the estimated number of 300,000 or more was herded within the towns and their immediate vicinage, deprived of the means of support, rendered destitute of shelter, left poorly clad, and exposed to the most unsanitary conditions. As the scarcity of food increased with the devastation of the depopulated areas of production, destitution and want became misery and starvation. Month by month the death rate increased in an alarming ratio. By March, 1897, according to conservative estimates from official Spanish sources, the mortality among the reconcentrados from starvation and diseases thereto incident exceeded 50 per centum of their total number.

... Reconcentration, adopted avowedly as a war measure in order to cut off the resources of the insurgents, worked its predestined result. As I said in my message of last December, it was not civilized warfare; it was extermination. The only peace it could beget was that of the wilderness and the grave.

Meanwhile the military situation in the island had

undergone a noticeable change. The extraordinary activity that characterized the second year of the war, when the insurgents invaded even the thitherto unharmed fields of Pinar del Rio and carried havoc and destruction up to the walls of the city of Havana itself, had relapsed into a dogged struggle in the central and eastern provinces. The Spanish arms regained a measure of control in Pinar del Rio and parts of Havana, but, under the existing conditions of the rural country, without immediate improvement of their productive situation. Even thus partially restricted, the revolutionists held their own, and their conquest and submission, put forward by Spain as the essential and sole basis of peace, seemed as far distant as at the outset.

*   *   *

The overtures of this Government, made through its new envoy, General Woodford, and looking to an immediate and effective amelioration of the condition of the island, although not accepted to the extent of admitted mediation in any shape, were met by assurances that home rule, in advanced phase, would be forthwith offered to Cuba, without waiting for the war to end, and that more humane methods should thenceforth prevail in the conduct of hostilities. Coincidentally with these declarations, the new Government of Spain continued and completed the policy already begun by its predecessor, of testifying friendly regard for this nation by releasing American citizens held under one charge or another connected with the insurrection, so that by the end of November not a single person entitled in any way to our national protection remained in a Spanish prison.

*   *   *

The war in Cuba is of such a nature that short of subjugation or extermination a final military victory for either side seems impracticable. The alternative lies in the physical exhaustion of the one or the other party, or perhaps of both—a condition which in effect ended the ten years' war by the truce of Zanjon. The prospect of such a protraction and conclusion of the present strife is a contingency hardly to be contemplated with equanimity by the civilized world, and least of all by the United States, affected and injured as we are, deeply and intimately, by its very existence.

Realizing this, it appeared to be my duty, in a spirit of true friendliness, no less to Spain than to the Cubans who have so much to lose by the prolongation of the struggle, to seek to bring about an immediate termination of the war. To this end I submitted, on the 27th ultimo, as a result of much representation and correspondence, through the United States minister at Madrid, propositions to the Spanish Government looking to an armistice until October 1 for the negotiation of peace with the good offices of the President.

In addition, I asked the immediate revocation of the order of reconcentration, so as to permit the people to return to their farms and the needy to be relieved with provisions and supplies from the United States, cooperating with the Spanish authorities, so as to afford full relief.

The reply of the Spanish cabinet was received on the night of the 31st ultimo. It offered, as the means to bring about peace in Cuba, to confide the preparation thereof to the insular parliament, inasmuch as the concurrence of that body would be necessary to reach a final result, it being, however, understood that the powers reserved by the constitution to the central Government are not lessened or diminished. As the Cuban parliament does not meet until the 4th of May next, the Spanish Government would not object, for its part, to accept at once a suspension of hostilities if asked for by the insurgents from the general in chief, to whom it would pertain, in such case, to determine the duration and conditions of the armistice.

The propositions submitted by General Woodford and the reply of the Spanish Government were both in the form of brief memoranda, the texts of which are before me, and are substantially in the language above given.

The function of the Cuban parliament in the matter of "preparing" peace and the manner of its doing so are not expressed in the Spanish memorandum; but from General Woodford's explanatory reports of preliminary discussions preceding the final conference it is understood that the Spanish Government stands ready to give the insular congress full powers to settle the terms of peace with the insurgents—whether by direct negotiation or indirectly by means of legislation does not appear.

With this last overture in the direction of immediate peace, and its disappointing reception by Spain, the Executive is brought to the end of his effort.

※ ※ ※

Nor from the standpoint of expediency do I think it would be wise or prudent for this Government to recognize at the present time the independence of the so-called Cuban Republic. Such recognition is not necessary in order to enable the United States to intervene and pacify the island. To commit this country now to the recognition of any particular government in Cuba might subject us to embarrassing conditions of international obligation toward the organization so recognized. In case of intervention our conduct would be subject to the approval or disapproval of such government. We would be required to submit to its direction and to assume to it the mere relation of a friendly ally.

When it shall appear hereafter that there is within the island a government capable of performing the duties and discharging the functions of a separate nation, and having, as a matter of fact, the proper forms and attributes of nationality, such government can be promptly and readily recognized and the relations and interest of the United States with such nation adjusted.

There remain the alternative forms of intervention to end the war, either as an impartial neutral by imposing a rational compromise between the contestants, or as the active ally of the one party or the other.

As to the first it is not to be forgotten that during the last few months the relation of the United States has virtually been one of friendly intervention in many ways, each not of itself conclusive, but all tending to the exertion of a potential influence toward an ultimate pacific result, just and honorable to all interests concerned. The spirit of all our acts hitherto has been an earnest, unselfish desire for peace and prosperity in Cuba, untarnished by differences between us and Spain, and unstained by the blood of American citizens.

The forcible intervention of the United States as a neutral to stop the war, according to the large dictates of humanity and following many historical precedents where neighboring States have interfered to check the hopeless sacrifices of life by internecine conflicts beyond their borders, is justifiable on rational grounds. It involves, however, hostile constraint upon both the parties to the contest as well to enforce a truce as to guide the eventual settlement.

The grounds for such intervention may be briefly summarized as follows:

First. In the cause of humanity and to put an end to the barbarities, bloodshed, starvation, and horrible miseries now existing there, and which the parties to the conflict are either unable or unwilling to stop or mitigate. It is no answer to say this is all in another country, belonging to another nation, and is therefore none of our business. It is specially our duty, for it is right at our door.

Second. We owe it to our citizens in Cuba to afford them that protection and indemnity for life and property which no government there can or will afford, and to that end to terminate the conditions that deprive them of legal protection.

Third. The right to intervene may be justified by the very serious injury to the commerce, trade, and business of our people, and by the wanton destruction of property and devastation of the island.

Fourth, and which is of the utmost importance. The present condition of affairs in Cuba is a constant menace to our peace, and entails upon this Government an enormous expense. With such a conflict waged for years in an island so near us and with which our people have such trade and business relations; when the lives and liberty of our citizens are in constant danger and their property destroyed and themselves ruined; where our trading vessels are liable to seizure and are seized at our very door by war ships of a foreign nation, the expeditions of filibustering that we are powerless to prevent altogether, and the irritating questions and entanglements thus arising —all these and others that I need not mention, with the resulting strained relations, are a constant menace to our peace, and compel us to keep on a semiwar footing with a nation with which we are at peace.

These elements of danger and disorder already pointed out have been strikingly illustrated by a tragic event which has deeply and justly moved the American people. I have already transmitted to Congress the report of the naval court of inquiry on the destruction of the battle ship *Maine* in the harbor of Havana during the night of the 15th of February. The destruction of that noble vessel has filled the national heart with inexpressible horror. Two hundred and fifty-eight brave sailors and marines and two officers of our Navy, reposing in the fancied security of a friendly harbor, have been hurled to death, grief and want brought to their homes, and sorrow to the nation.

The naval court of inquiry, which, it is needless to say, commands the unqualified confidence of the Government, was unanimous in its conclusion that the destruction of the *Maine* was caused by an exterior explosion, that of a submarine mine. It did not assume to place the responsibility. That remains to be fixed.

In any event the destruction of the *Maine,* by whatever exterior cause, is a patent and impressive proof of a

## The Decision for War

state of things in Cuba that is intolerable. That condition is thus shown to be such that the Spanish Government can not assure safety and security to a vessel of the American Navy in the harbor of Havana on a mission of peace, and rightfully there.

* * *

In view of these facts and of these considerations, I ask the Congress to authorize and empower the President to take measures to secure a full and final termination of hostilities between the Government of Spain and the people of Cuba, and to secure in the island the establishment of a stable government, capable of maintaining order and observing its international obligations, insuring peace and tranquillity and the security of its citizens as well as our own, and to use the military and naval forces of the United States as may be necessary for these purposes.

And in the interest of humanity and to aid in preserving the lives of the starving people of the island I recommend that the distribution of food and supplies be continued, and that an appropriation be made out of the public Treasury to supplement the charity of our citizens.

The issue is now with the Congress. It is a solemn responsibility. I have exhausted every effort to relieve the intolerable condition of affairs which is at our doors. Prepared to execute every obligation imposed upon me by the Constitution and the law, I await your action.

Yesterday, and since the preparation of the foregoing message, official information was received by me that the latest decree of the Queen Regent of Spain directs General Blanco, in order to prepare and facilitate peace, to proclaim a suspension of hostilities, the duration and details of which have not yet been communicated to me.

This fact with every other pertinent consideration will, I am sure, have your just and careful attention in the solemn deliberations upon which you are about to enter. If this measure attains a successful result, then our aspirations as a Christian, peace-loving people will be realized. If it fails, it will be only another justification for our contemplated action.

WILLIAM MCKINLEY

Executive Mansion, April 11, 1898

## *Sherman to Woodford*
## *April 14, 1898*

[*Foreign Relations*, 1897–98, p. 761.]

*Washington, Department of State*

House of Representatives, 324 to 19, passed yesterday afternoon resolution authorizing and directing the President to intervene at once to stop the war in Cuba, with the purpose of securing peace and order there and establishing, by the free action of the people thereof, a stable and independent government of their own, and empowering him to use the land and naval forces to execute that purpose.

Senate Committee on Foreign Affairs reported yesterday resolution declaring that the people of the Island of Cuba are and of right ought to be free and independent, demanding that Spain relinquish authority and government in Cuba and withdraw land and naval forces therefrom, and empowering the President to use Army and Navy and militia to carry resolution into effect. It will probably be decisively voted to-day.

Ultimate resolution in conference cannot now be forecast, but will doubtless direct intervention by force if need be to secure free Cuba. The situation is most critical.

JOHN SHERMAN

## Day to Woodford
## April 17, 1898

[*Foreign Relations,* 1897–98, pp. 761–62.]

*Washington, Department of State*

The Senate, Saturday evening, by 67 votes to 21, passed a resolution amending all of the House resolution after the enacting clause. It declares as follows:

"*Resolved,* By the Senate and House of Representatives of the United States of America in Congress assembled, First,

"That the people of the Island of Cuba are and of right ought to be free and independent, and that the Government of the United States hereby recognizes the Republic of Cuba as the true and lawful government of that island. Second,

"That it is the duty of the United States to demand, and the Government of the United States does hereby demand, that the Government of Spain at once relinquish its authority and government in the island of Cuba, and withdraw its land and naval force from Cuba and Cuban waters. Third,

"That the president of the United States be, and he hereby is, directed and empowered to use the entire land and naval forces of the United States and to call into the actual service of the United States the militia of the several States to such an extent as may be necessary to carry these resolutions into effect. Fourth,

"That the United States hereby disclaims any disposition or intention to exercise sovereignty, jurisdiction, or control over said island, except for the pacification thereof, and asserts its determination when that is accomplished to leave the government and control of the island to its people."

The House has taken a recess until 10 Monday morning, when vote will be taken on concurring in the Senate amendments. If the House nonconcurs conference follows. Ultimate form of resolution can not yet be foreseen.

Sunday morning, 1 o'clock.

DAY
ACTING SECRETARY

## Day to Woodford
## April 19, 1898

[*Foreign Relations*, 1897–98, p. 762.]

*Washington, Department of State*

At 3 this morning, after prolonged conference, the Senate and the House of Representatives adopted the joint resolution, the text of which was telegraphed to you Saturday night, omitting from the first section, the words, "And that the Government of the United States hereby recognizes the Republic of Cuba as the true and lawful government of that island." Vote in Senate, 42 to 35; in House, 310 against 6.

An instruction will be telegraphed you later, immediately on the President signing the joint resolution. In the meantime you will prepare for withdrawal from Spain and notify consuls to be ready for the signal to leave. If any consul is in danger he may quietly leave at his discretion.

DAY

## Sherman to Woodford
## April 20, 1898

[*Foreign Relations*, 1897–98, pp. 762–63.]

*Washington, Department of State*

You have been furnished with the text of a joint resolution voted by the Congress of the United States on the 19th instant (approved to-day) in relation to the pacification of the island of Cuba. In obedience to that act, the President directs you to immediately communicate to the Government of Spain said resolution, with the formal demand of the Government of the United States that the Government of Spain at once relinquish its authority and government in the island of Cuba and withdraw its land and naval forces from Cuba and Cuban waters. In taking this step the United States hereby disclaims any disposition or intention to exercise sovereignty, jurisdiction, or control over said island except for the pacification thereof, and asserts its determination when that is accomplished to leave the government and control of the island to its people under such free and independent government as they may establish.

If by the hour of noon on Saturday next, the 23rd day of April, instant, there be not communicated to this Government by that of Spain a full and satisfactory response to this demand and resolution whereby the ends of peace in Cuba shall be assured, the President shall proceed without further notice to use the power and authority enjoined and conferred upon him by the said joint resolution to such extent as may be necessary to carry the same into effect.

SHERMAN

## "*Ultimata*"

[Ernest May, *Imperial Democracy* (New York, 1961), pp. 152–159.]

From McKinley's standpoint there no longer seemed any alternative to an ultimatum. The antiwar front had practically disintegrated. After Proctor had declared himself for intervention, other previously conservative senators followed suit. The New York *Herald* changed its editorial policy just as the Chicago *Times-Herald* had. Its city editor wrote confidentially to McKinley, "Big corporations here now believe we will have war. Believe all would welcome it as relief to suspense." Whitelaw Reid advised the managing editor of his New York *Tribune* that war was inevitable and "it would be unwise for us to be the last persons to assent to it, or to seem to be dragged into the support of it." Elihu Root, then one of the leaders of the New York bar, wrote Theodore Roosevelt, "I sympathize with McKinley . . . ; but . . . if the administration does not turn its face towards the front and lead instead of being pushed, it seems to me it will be rolled over and crushed and the Republican party with it."

Even accepting the necessity for an ultimatum did not, however, relieve the President of his embarrassments. Jingoes were allies of the Junta; some held Cuban bonds; all had clamored for recognition of the existing insurgent government. Though erstwhile conservatives might have reconciled themselves to war, they were not ready to fight it solely in the interest of the Cubans. [Senator] Chandler wrote to [Charles A.] Dana, quoting Senator Elkins as saying it would be "folly . . . to spend 500 millions in a war for Cuba and then not get the property fought for. That he says is a plain business proposition." In drawing up his demands on Spain, the President felt he had to satisfy these divergent opinions, for he could still divorce himself neither from the jingoes nor their opponents.

## The Decision for War 217

He and Day solved this problem in characteristically subtle fashion—so subtle, indeed, that the surviving documents were later to mislead historians. At Senator Fairbanks' home, Day met with a group of conservatives from the upper house. Chandler, who heard about it later, listed Hanna, Allison, Aldrich, Hale, Spooner, and Platt of Connecticut as the others present. The last of these was Chandler's source, and Chandler quoted him as saying, "The understanding was that an armistice would be agreed to and negotiations opened with Spain for an autonomous government to the insurgents in Cuba, Spain not to relinquish her sovereignty. The final arbitration was to be left to the President of the United States if Spain and the Cubans couldn't agree." In accordance with this understanding, Day drew up a formal message for Woodford. Presumably he showed it to one or more of the senators. The concessions which it demanded from Spain were:

> First. Armistice until October 1. Negotiations meantime looking for peace between Spain and insurgents through friendly offices of President United States.
>
> Second. Immediate revocation of reconcentrado order so as to permit people to return to their farms, and the needy to be relieved with provisions and supplies from United States cooperating with authorities so as to afford full relief.
>
> Add, if possible:
>
> Third. If terms of peace not satisfactorily settled by October 1, President of the United States to be final arbiter between Spain and insurgents.

That was all. And since the Spanish government subsequently complied with the two essential conditions, granting an armistice and ending reconcentration, later readers of this document were to suspect that the American government wanted, not a negotiated settlement, but merely an excuse for war.

The fact was, however, that Day also sent Woodford other messages explaining that these itemized conditions did not limit and define all of America's demands. Indeed, on the very day before, Day had cabled the minister, suggesting in the name of the President that Spain offer the Cubans "full self-government, with reasonable indemnity."

After receiving the three-point message, Woodford asked what these earlier words meant, and Day replied: "Full self-government with indemnity would mean Cuban independence. . . . Very important to have definite agreement for determining peace after armistice." When Woodford reported later that he thought he could achieve an armistice and peace, Day asked him worriedly, "Would the peace you are so confident of securing mean the independence of Cuba?" Since the State Department's security procedures were lax enough so that reporters often read and quoted from the most confidential dispatches, Day and McKinley could not afford to be more explicit in advising Woodford that their minimum terms included one which the conservative senators had not and would not have approved. In reality, their demands were that Spain end reconcentration, proclaim an armistice, *and* acknowledge that she would make Cuba independent if the President deemed it necessary.

Believing that Woodford would make these requirements plain to the Spanish government, McKinley employed all his resource and guile to give Spain time to comply. Consul General Lee telegraphed that Americans still in Havana would be in danger if war came, and the President immediately called in members of Congress and sent copies of Lee's message to Capitol Hill. Even the most fevered of jingoes could see the force of Lee's advice. Chandler reported to Dana that no one resented an enforced wait, even though some radicals remained suspicious, "feeling that the delay will be utilized to get up some new scheme for holding on some terms the Spanish flag in Cuba." McKinley dealt with these suspicions by completing a message to Congress asking intervention to end the Cuban war. He exhibited it to a number of members of the Senate and House while declaring, "That message shall not go to Congress as long as there is a single American life in danger in Cuba."

With Congress temporarily appeased, the President employed every moment to persuade Spain that she should meet his conditions. Knowing Archbishop Ireland to be in direct communication with the Vatican, McKinley not only told him America's conditions but declared that he would be glad of any help the Holy See could give. He dared not entreat assistance too openly, and he was embarrassed when the Spanish government claimed that he had invited papal mediation. He had to deny having done so or having made any suggestions to Spain except through formal diplomatic channels.

Nevertheless, he continued these efforts furtively. He remained in contact with Archbishop Ireland; he invited the good offices of the House of Rothschild; he even went so far as to agree to combined diplomatic intervention by the great powers. Secretary of State Sherman, whose failing talents had been little used by the administration, was so thoroughly opposed to war that he spoke on his own initiative to the Austro-Hungarian minister, Baron von Hengelmüller, urging that the Austrian Emperor offer to mediate. Because he knew Sherman to be only nominally head of his department, Hengelmüller prudently consulted Day and was told that the President would reject any such European intervention out of hand. Others close to McKinley voiced the same opinion. Yet in the final period of grace, when Congress was only waiting for Americans to be evacuated from Cuba, both the President and Day relented.

The French ambassador suddenly heard what he regarded as inspired rumors that McKinley would welcome some European overture. Not long afterward Archbishop

Ireland came to the French embassy, directly from the President's study, to urge that the powers appeal to Spain to meet America's conditions and to the President, *"in the name of humanity,"* to accept. When the British ambassador called at the State Department to tell Day that the powers were discussing just such an appeal to the President and that his own instructions were to do whatever the United States requested, the Assistant Secretary did not reiterate what he had said earlier to Hengelmüller. On the contrary, he told the Englishman that while he doubted if any result could be achieved, he did not see how such action could do harm. When shown a collective note drawn up by the ambassadors, Day gave his full approval. Presumably he acted with the knowledge of the President.

The results of this truly extraordinary action by the administration were, in the first place, a little ceremony that took place in the White House on April 6. The envoys from Britain, France, Germany, Austria-Hungary, Italy, and Russia presented themselves. The Englishman, having served longest in Washington, read the note which they had all signed. It simply made "a pressing appeal to the feelings of humanity and moderation of the President and of the American people" and expressed the earnest hope "that further negotiations will lead to an agreement which, while securing the maintenance of peace, will afford all necessary guaranties for the reestablishment of order in Cuba." The President replied by reading a formal text expressing hope for peace but also speaking of America's "unselfish endeavors to fulfill a duty to humanity by ending a situation the indefinite prolongation of which has become insufferable." Owing to the caution which McKinley and Day had shown, this exchange produced no unfavorable publicity. Indeed, it created almost no stir in the press.

In the second place, and of far more importance to the President, there also resulted a *démarche* by the powers in Madrid. Though the Pope had already begged the Spanish government to grant an armistice, Woodford reported the cabinet as still divided. Then, on the morning of April 9, the six European ambassadors called on the Spanish Foreign Minister, just as they had earlier called upon McKinley. In the name of Europe, they asked that Spain accede to the request from the Vatican. And before the day was out, the government had agreed. Woodford, who had already declared that he would regard an armistice as equivalent to peace, cabled jubilantly to McKinley that victory could be and was being won.

The President felt no less elated. The first to bring him the news was Archbishop Ireland. Subsequently Ireland told the French ambassador that McKinley had been "delighted." Considering the assurances that Woodford had been sending him, the President must have believed that Spain had yielded to all his demands. After having wriggled and squirmed through so many tight places, McKinley could have a momentary feeling that it had all been worthwhile—that he had prevented a domestic rupture, brought peace and independence to Cuba, and spared his people a war.

But illusion was followed by disillusion. Even in his initial delight, McKinley may have been troubled by the fact that Ireland gave him no assurance of Spain's willingness to make Cuba free. He had made it quite clear to the Archbishop that this was an essential condition, and Ireland's silence hinted at a fact that McKinley did not know—that Spain had told the Vatican she "would accept no arbitration having as a condition the independence of Cuba." Unhappily for the President, the Spanish attitude soon stood revealed. When informing the State Department of the armistice decree, Depuy de Lôme's successor took pains to state in writing, "The autonomic constitution . . . gives to the inhabitants of the island of Cuba a political system at least as liberal as that which exists in the Dominion of Canada . . . ; and the franchise and liberties granted to the Cubans are such that no motive or pretext is left for claiming any fuller measure thereof." The Spanish minister had actually drawn up this memorandum on his own initiative, but the Americans could not know this fact. When Day asked him whether Spain would leave to the United States the final decision with regard to Cuba's sovereignty, the minister drew himself up and stiffly said, "No." The Assistant Secretary had to go sadly to the White House and inform the President that America's conditions had not been met.

McKinley may have made one last effort to bridle the Congress. There was a long cabinet meeting on the evening of April 10. According to a rumor picked up by the French ambassador, the President spoke at this meeting asking for delay in order to observe the effects of an armistice. Subsequently, however, he discussed this possibility with the Vice-President and various Republican senators and was warned in the strongest terms against changing the message he had already drafted and locked in the safe. Despite counterefforts by Democratic Senator Elkins and other conservatives, the President heeded this advice. At another cabinet session on the following morning, he announced that he would merely add to the original message a postscript mentioning the armistice decree and saying that Congress might take it into account. Though even the usually uncritical Secretary of the Navy regarded this postscript as a *non sequitur*, McKinley kept it as it was. Later on the morning of April 11, he sent it to Capitol Hill.

McKinley had drafted the message almost in the presence of jingo congressmen, yet had so written it as to ensure a little more delay. When perplexed by the necessity for navigating between radicals who wanted recognition of the insurgents and former conservatives who desired annexation, he had considered the possibility of just leaving the issue to Congress. In his papers there is a draft of a paragraph which would have done exactly that. But McKinley chose instead to take a stand characteristically somewhere vaguely between the two extremes. While advising Congress not to recognize the existing rebel regime, he proposed that an independent Cuban government eventually be given recognition. All he asked was power "to take measures to secure a full and final termination of hostilities between the Government of Spain and the people of Cuba," including authority to use the armed forces.

The vagueness of his words on the point of recognition guaranteed at least a delay of several days while Congress debated the more clear-cut alternatives. As a matter of fact, the Foreign Relations and Foreign Affairs Committees differed within themselves, and the two chambers differed with each other. The Senate committee reported out a resolution demanding Spanish withdrawal from the island and promising eventual independence. A minority of the committee urged an amendment recognizing the Republic of Cuba as then constituted, and this amendment carried. In the House, on the other hand, a resolution passed 324-19 which merely parroted the words of McKinley's message. As both Chandler and the French ambassador recognized, this uncertain language could conceivably allow the President to continue negotiations.

In all probability, McKinley had no thought of evading the manifest will of Congress and the people. During the time that was left to him, he did continue efforts to persuade Spain that she should declare her willingness to grant Cuba freedom. Woodford was informed in detail of the differences between the two chambers. The French ambassador, who was believed to have a direct channel to Madrid, was told that the President did not necessarily desire independence, that he might be able to preserve some semblance to Spanish sovereignty, but that he could do nothing unless assured by Spain that she would concede independence if necessary.

But Congress soon took away his initiative. Speaker Reed, who staunchly opposed war, had probably been responsible for the mild resolution enacted by the House. After the issue went to a conference committee, compromise was inevitable. The House conferees accepted the Senate's text. A vote in the lower chamber struck out the provision recognizing the insurgent government, and the upper body yielded to this verdict. Both agreed to demand that Spain relinquish sovereignty over the island, to authorize the use of armed forces by the President, and to pledge that the United States would not assume "sovereignty, jurisdiction, or control" over Cuba. On April 19, this resolution came to the President's desk.

He had no choice but to sign it, and once he had done so, he no longer possessed any power to prevent war. The only faint chance of peace that remained lay in a voluntary decision by Spain to abandon Cuba. McKinley had capitulated to the jingoes.

❦ ❦ ❦

## "Reaction: Approach to War"

[Walter LaFeber, *The New Empire: An Interpretation of American Expansion, 1860-1898* (Ithaca, 1963), pp. 397-406.]

McKinley had had the choice of three policies which would have terminated the Cuban revolution. First, he could have left the Spanish forces and the insurgents fight until one or the other fell exhausted from the bloodshed and financial strain. During the struggle the United States could have administered food and medicine to the civilian population, a privilege which the Spanish agreed to allow in March, 1898. Second, the President could have demanded an armistice and Spanish assurances that negotiations over the summer would result in some solution which would pacify American feelings. That is to say, he could have

*The Decision for War* 225

followed Woodford's ideas. Third, McKinley could have demanded both an armistice and Spanish assurances that Cuba would become independent immediately. If Spain would not grant both of these conditions, American military intervention would result. The last was the course the President followed.

Each of these policy alternatives deserves a short analysis. For American policy makers, the first choice was the least acceptable of the three, but the United States did have to deal, nevertheless, with certain aspects of this policy. If Spain hoped to win such a conflict, she had to use both the carrot of an improved and attractive autonomy scheme and the stick of an increased and effective military force. Spain could have granted no amount of autonomy, short of complete independence, which would have satisfied the rebels, and whether Americans cared to admit it or not, they were at least partially responsible for this obstinacy on the part of the insurgents. The United States did attempt to stop filibustering expeditions, but a large number nevertheless reached Cuban shores. More important, when the Spanish Minister asked Day to disband the New York Junta, the financial taproot of the insurgent organization, the Assistant Secretary replied that "this was not possible under American law and in the present state of public feeling." Woodford had given the Spanish Queen the same reply in mid-January. It was perhaps at this point that Spain saw the last hopes for a negotiated peace begin to flicker away.

Seemingly unrelated actions by the United States gave boosts to the rebel cause. The sending of the "Maine," for instance, considerably heartened the rebels; they believed that the warship diverted Spanish attention and military power from insurgent forces. When the vessel exploded, the New York Junta released a statement which did not mourn the dead sailors as much as it mourned the sudden disappearance of American power in Havana harbor. The Junta interpreted the passage of the $50,000,000 war appropriation measure during the first week of March as meaning either immediate war or the preparation for war. Under such conditions, it was not odd that the rebels were reluctant to compromise their objective of complete independence.

If the insurgents would not have accepted autonomy, no matter how liberal or attractive, then Spain might have hoped to suppress the rebels with outright force. To have done so, however, the Spanish government would have had to bring its army through the rainy season with few impairments, resume to a large extent the *reconcentrado* policies, and prevent all United States aid from reaching the rebels. The first objective would have been difficult, but the last two, if carried out, would have meant war with the United States. The State Department could not allow Spain to reimpose methods even faintly resembling Weyler's techniques, nor could the Department have allowed the searching of American vessels. McKinley and the American people hoped that Spain would stop the revolution, but they also insisted on taking from Spain the only tools with which that nation could deal with the Cubans.

Having found this first alternative impossible to accept, McKinley might have chosen a second approach: demand an armistice and ultimate pacification of the island, but attempt to achieve this peacefully over several months and with due respect for the sovereignty of Spain. This was the alternative Woodford hoped the administration would choose. He had reported during the two weeks before McKinley's message that the Spanish had given in time and time again on points which he had believed they could not afford to grant. In spite of the threat of revolution from the army, the Queen had granted a temporary truce. The American Minister continued to ask for more time to find a peaceful settlement. On April 11, the day the war message went to Congress, Woodford wrote the

## The Decision for War

President, "To-day it is just possible that Moret and I have been right [in our pursuit of peace], but it is too soon to be jubilant." The American Minister sincerely believed that the negotiations during the period of truce could, with good faith on both the American and Spanish sides, result in Spain evacuating the island. This would have to be done slowly, however. No sovereign nation could be threatened with a time limit and uncompromising demands without fighting back. The fact that Spain would not grant McKinley's demand for immediate Cuban independence makes the Spanish-American War which began in April, 1898, by no means an inevitable conflict. Any conflict is inevitable once one proud and sovereign power, dealing with a similar power, decides to abandon the conference table and issue an ultimatum. The historical problem remains: which power took the initiative in setting the conditions that resulted in armed conflict, and were those conditions justified?

By April 10 McKinley had assumed an inflexible position. The President abjured this second alternative and demanded not only a truce, but a truce which would lead to a guarantee of immediate Cuban independence obtained with the aid of American mediation. He moreover demanded such a guarantee of independence before the Cortes or the Cuban parliament, the two groups which had the constitutional power to grant such independence, were to gather for their formal sessions.

The central question is, of course, why McKinley found himself in such a position on April 10 that only the third alternative was open to him. The President did not want war; he had been sincere and tireless in his efforts to maintain the peace. By mid-March, however, he was beginning to discover that, although he did not want war, he did want what only a war could provide: the disappearance of the terrible uncertainty in American political and economic life, and a solid basis from which to resume the building of the new American commercial empire. When the President made his demands, therefore, he made the ultimate demands; as far as he was concerned, a six-month period of negotiations would not serve to temper the political and economic problems in the United States, but only exacerbate them.

To say this is to raise another question: why did McKinley arrive at this position during mid-March? What were the factors which limited the President's freedom of choice and policies at this particular time? The standard interpretations of the war's causes emphasize the yellow journals and a belligerent Congress. These were doubtlessly crucial factors in shaping the course of American entry into the conflict, but they must be used carefully. A first observation should be that Congress and the yellow press, which had been loudly urging intervention ever since 1895, did not make a maiden appearance in March, 1898; new elements had to enter the scene at that time to act as the catalysts for McKinley's policy. Other facts should be noted regarding the yellow press specifically. In areas where this press supposedly was most important, such as New York City, no more than one-third of the press could be considered sensational. The strongest and most widespread prowar journalism apparently occurred in the Midwest. But there were few yellow journals there. The papers that advocated war in this section did so for reasons other than sensationalism; among these reasons were the influence of the Cuban Junta and, perhaps most important, the belief that the United States possessed important interests in the Caribbean area which had to be protected. Finally, the yellow press obviously did not control the levers of American foreign policy. McKinley held these, and he bitterly attacked the owners of the sensational journals as "evil disposed . . . people." An interpretation stressing rabid journalism as a major cause of the war should draw some link to illustrate how these journals reached the White

House or the State Department. To say that this influence was exerted through public opinion proves nothing; the next problem is to demonstrate how much public opinion was governed by the yellow press, how much of this opinion was influenced by more sober factors, and which of these two branches of opinion most influenced McKinley.

Congress was a hotbed of interventionist sentiment, but then it had been so since 1895. The fact was that Congress had more trouble handling McKinley than the President had handling Congress. The President had no fear of that body. He told Charles Dawes during the critical days of February and March that if Congress tried to adjourn he would call it back into session. McKinley held Congress under control until the last two days of March, when the publication of the "Maine" investigation forced Thomas B. Reed, the passionately antiwar Speaker of the House, to surrender to the onslaughts of the rapidly increasing interventionist forces. As militants in Congress forced the moderates into full retreat, McKinley and Day were waiting in the White House for Spain's reply to the American ultimatum. And after the outbreak on March 31 McKinley reassumed control. On April 5 the Secretary of War, R. A. Alger, assured the President that several important senators had just informed him that "there will be no trouble about holding the Senate." When the President postponed his war message on April 5 in order to grant Fitzhugh Lee's request for more time, prowar congressmen went into a frenzy. During the weekend of April 8 and 9, they condemned the President, ridiculed Reed's impotence to hold back war, and threatened to declare war themselves. In fact, they did nearly everything except disobey McKinley's wishes that nothing be done until the following week. Nothing was done.

When the Senate threatened to overrule the President's orders that the war declaration exclude recognition of the Cuban insurgent government, McKinley whipped the doubters into line and forced the Senate to recede from its position. This was an all-out battle between the White House and a strong Senate faction. McKinley triumphed despite extremely strong pressure exerted by sincere American sentiment on behalf of immediate Cuban independence and despite the more crass material interests of the Junta's financial supporters and spokesmen. The President wanted to have a free hand in dealing with Cuba after the war, and Congress granted his wishes. Events on Capitol Hill may have been more colorful than those at the White House, but the latter, not the former, was the center of power in March and April, 1898.

Influences other than the yellow press or congressional belligerence were more important in shaping McKinley's position of April 11. Perhaps most important was the transformation of the opinion of many spokesmen for the business community who had formerly opposed war. If, as one journal declared, the McKinley administration, "more than any that have preceded it, sustains . . . close relations to the business interests of the country," then this change of business sentiment should not be discounted. This transformation brought important financial spokesmen, especially from the Northeast, into much the same position that had long been occupied by prointerventionist business groups and journals in the trans-Appalachian area. McKinley's decision to intervene placated many of the same business spokesmen whom he had satisfied throughout 1897 and January and February of 1898 by his refusal to declare war.

Five factors may be delineated which shaped this interventionist sentiment of the business community. First, some business journals emphasized the material advantages to be gained should Cuba become a part of the world in which the United States would enjoy, in the words of the New York *Commercial Advertiser*, "full freedom of development in the whole world's interest." The *Banker's*

*Magazine* noted that "so many of our citizens are so involved in the commerce and productions of the island, that to protect these interests ... the United States will have eventually to force the establishment of fair and reasonable government. The material damage suffered by investors in Cuba and by many merchants, manufacturers, exporters, and importers ... forced these interests to advocate a solution which could be obtained only through force."

A second reason was the uncertainty that plagued the business community in mid-March. This uncertainty was increased by Proctor's powerful and influential speech and by the news that a Spanish torpedo-boat flotilla was sailing from Cadiz to Cuba. The uncertainty was exemplified by the sudden stagnation of trade on the New York Stock Exchange after March 17. Such an unpredictable economic basis could not provide the springboard for the type of overseas commercial empire that McKinley and numerous business spokesmen envisioned.

Third, by March many businessmen who had deprecated war on the ground that the United States Treasury did not possess adequate gold reserves began to realize that they had been arguing from false assumptions. The heavy exports of 1897 and the discoveries of gold in Alaska and Australia brought the yellow metal into the country in an ever widening stream. Private bankers had been preparing for war since 1897. *Banker's Magazine* summarized these developments: "Therefore, while not desiring war, it is apparent that the country now has an ample coin basis for sustaining the credit operations which a conflict would probably make necessary. In such a crisis the gold standard will prove a bulwark of confidence."

Fourth, antiwar sentiment lost much strength when the nation realized that it had nothing to fear from European intervention on the side of Spain. France and Russia, who were most sympathetic to the Spanish monarchy, were forced to devote their attention to the Far East. Neither of these nations wished to alienate the United States on the Cuban issue. More important, Americans happily realized that they had the support of Great Britain. The *rapprochement* which had occurred since the Venezuelan incident now paid dividends. On an official level, the British Foreign Office assured the State Department that nothing would be accomplished in the way of European intervention unless the United States requested such intervention. The British attitude made it easy for McKinley to deal with a joint European note of April 6 which asked for American moderation toward Spain. The President brushed off the request firmly but politely. On an unofficial level, American periodicals expressed appreciation of the British policy on Cuba, and some of the journals noted that a common Anglo-American approach was also desirable in Asia. The European reaction is interesting insofar as it evinces the continental powers' growing realization that the United States was rapidly becoming a major force in the world. But the European governments set no limits on American dealings with Spain. McKinley could take the initiative and make his demands with little concern for European reactions.

Finally, opposition to war melted away in some degree when the administration began to emphasize that the United States enjoyed military power much superior to that of Spain. One possible reason for McKinley's policies during the first two months of 1898 might have been his fear that the nation was not adequately prepared. As late as the weekend of March 25 the President worried over this inadequacy. But in late February and early March, especially after the $50,000,000 appropriation by Congress, the country's military strength developed rapidly. On March 13 the Philadelphia *Press* proclaimed that American naval power greatly exceeded that of the Spanish forces. By early April those who feared a Spanish bombardment of New York City were in the small minority. More representative were the views of Winthrop Chandler who wrote Lodge that if Spanish troops invaded New York "they would all be absorbed in the population . . . and engaged in selling oranges before they got as far as 14th Street."

## Bibliographical Notes

Historical questions about late nineteenth-century imperialism in general and involvement in the Spanish-American War in particular have usually been dealt with in terms of why things happened rather than how they happened. A concise statement of the problem is given in the introduction to *American Expansion in the Late Nineteenth Century: Colonialist or Anticolonialist?*, edited by J. Rogers Hollingsworth (New York, 1968). A recent attempt to reduce this gap in our knowledge is Ernest R. May's stimulating discussion of how the United States rejected and then returned to its traditional anticolonialist attitude in the years between 1890 and 1903: *American Imperialism: A Speculative Essay* (New York, 1968).

In addition to May's *Imperial Democracy* and LaFeber's *The New Empire*, there are a number of books which deal either wholly or in part with McKinley and the onset of the Spanish-American War. The best biographical accounts of the President are Margaret Leech, *In the Days of McKinley* (New York, 1959), and H. Wayne Morgan, *William McKinley and His America* (Syracuse, 1963).

The best brief narrative of American entrance into the war is in H. Wayne Morgan, *America's Road to Empire: The War with Spain and Overseas Expansion* (New York, 1965). Julius Pratt, *Expansionists of 1898: The Acquisition of Hawaii and the Spanish Islands* (Baltimore, 1936), Frederick Merk, *Manifest Destiny and Mission in American History: A Reinterpretation* (New York, 1963), and Richard Hofstadter, "Cuba, the Philippines, and Manifest Destiny," in *The Paranoid Style in American Politics and Other Essays* (New York, 1965), all touch on the origins of the war in their discussions of the underlying causes of American imperialism at the close of the nineteenth century. The connection between the coming of the war and public opinion as expressed through newspapers is the subject of Joseph E. Wisan's *The Cuban Crisis as Reflected in the New York Press, 1895–1898* (New York, 1934), and George W. Auxier's "Middle Western Newspapers and the Spanish American War, 1895–1898," *Mississippi Valley Historical Review*, XXVI (March 1940), 523–34. John A. S. Grenville and George Berkeley Young focus more specifically on McKinley's role in "The Breakdown in Neutrality: McKinley Goes to War with Spain," which is chapter nine of their *Politics, Strategy and American Diplomacy: Studies in Foreign Policy, 1873–1917* (New Haven, 1966). They emphasize that international circumstances were at least as important as domestic ones in deciding McKinley on war.

# III

# 1933: ROOSEVELT'S DECISION

# the UNITED STATES

# Leaves the GOLD Standard

*The Hoover Administration*, Copyright © 1936, by William Starr Myers and Walter H. Newton. Renewal Copyright © 1964, by Margaret Barr Myers. Reprinted with the permission of Charles Scribner's Sons.

*John Maynard Keynes*, Copyright © 1955, by Seymour E. Harris. Reprinted with the permission of Charles Scribner's Sons.

*A Treatise on Money*, Volume II, Copyright © 1930, by John Maynard Keynes. Reprinted with the permission of Harcourt, Brace & World.

*Interpretations: 1933–1935*, Copyright © 1936, by Walter Lippmann. Renewal Copyright © 1964, by Allan Nevins. Reprinted with the permission of The Macmillan Company.

*The Economic Thought of Franklin D. Roosevelt and the Origins of the New Deal*, Copyright © 1956, by Daniel R. Fusfeld. Reprinted with the permission of Columbia University Press.

*Monetary Reform Movements: A Survey of Recent Plans and Panaceas*, Copyright © 1943, by Joseph Reeve. Reprinted with the permission of Public Affairs Press.

*On Our Way*, Copyright © 1934, by Franklin D. Roosevelt. Reprinted with the permission of The John Day Company, Inc.

*1933 Characters in Crisis*, Copyright © 1966, by Herbert Feis. Reprinted with the permission of Little, Brown and Co.

*The Secret Diary of Harold L. Ickes*, Copyright © 1953, by Harold Ickes. Reprinted with the permission of Simon & Schuster, Inc.

# Contents
## PART III
## 1933: Roosevelt's Decision:
### The United States Leaves the Gold Standard
*Introduction*

## Section One
## Public Pressures

| | |
|---|---:|
| *Commentary* | 1 |
| 1) *President Herbert Hoover's Monetary Orthodoxy* | 5 |
| 2) *The Assault on Gold: Seymour Harris on John Maynard Keynes* | 11 |
| 3) *Auri Sacra Fames: Keynes on Gold* | 20 |
| 4) *Handwriting on the Wall: An Editorial on Gold* | 24 |
| 5) *A Plan for Franklin D. Roosevelt: Irving Fisher on Reflation* | 27 |
| 6) *A Personal Triumph: The Elation of Irving Fisher* | 36 |
| 7) *The Great Decision: A Walter Lippmann Interpretation* | 40 |
| 8) *Conservatives for Inflation: The Committee for the Nation* | 44 |
| 9) *An Agrarian Perspective: The George Warren Thesis* | 47 |
| 10) *Would It Help Us to Go Off Gold?: A Qualified Affirmative* | 61 |

## Section Two
## Congressional Pressures

| | |
|---|---:|
| *Commentary* | 67 |

| | |
|---|---|
| 11) *The Debtor Needs a Devalued Dollar: A Southerner Speaks Out* | 70 |
| 12) *In the Greenbacker and Populist Spirit: A Voice from the Farm Belt* | 73 |
| 13) *Senator Elmer Thomas and His Amendment: A Critical Analysis* | 78 |
| 14) *The Fulfillment of Bryan's Dream: The Senate Silverites* | 89 |

## Section Three
## Roosevelt's Decision

| | |
|---|---|
| *Commentary* | 105 |
| 15) *The Quest for Balance: Roosevelt's Economic Philosophy* | 109 |
| 16) *Toward Inflation: Monetary Influences upon Roosevelt* | 116 |
| 17) *Roosevelt Meets the Press: The First Press Conference, March 8, 1933* | 121 |
| 18) *Roosevelt Reopens the Banks Without Gold: March 10, 1933* | 124 |
| 19) *Roosevelt Disdains Inflation: April 7, 1933* | 125 |
| 20) *The Quarterback Explains: April 19, 1933* | 127 |
| 21) *Politics and Monetary Policy: Raymond Moley's Perspective* | 131 |
| 22) *The Money Muddle: James Warburg Observes* | 138 |
| 23) *A Deliberate Course: Herbert Feis' Perspective* | 145 |
| 24) *The Roosevelt Style: Harold Ickes' Perspective* | 159 |
| 25) *The Last Word: Roosevelt Explains* | 162 |
| *Bibliography* | 166 |

## Introduction

The heated discussion, the story goes, occurred in Raymond Moley's Washington hotel suite during the early hours of Wednesday, April 19, 1933. The participants, Lewis Douglas, James P. Warburg, William Bullitt, and Moley had left the White House shortly before midnight after the President had informed his monetary advisers *fait accompli* that the nation had left the gold standard. The decision surprised them and while most of the capital slept, these men, four of Franklin Roosevelt's most conservative counselors, debated its consequences. Moley and Bullitt were uncertain of its meaning; Warburg and Douglas, on the other hand, believed it would precipitously upset international monetary cooperation. "Well," Douglas vehemently declared, "this is the end of Western civilization."

The question of monetary standards always has evoked tempestuous clashes throughout the normally irrational history of American capitalism. Whether it was the angry controversy which surrounded Andrew Jackson's Specie Circular of 1836, the demonetization "Crime of '73," or the Bryanite "Battle of the Standards" in 1896, Americans more often determined their allegiance to gold or silver currencies by emotional attachments than through any well-reasoned analysis of how these metals benefited either personal or societal needs. They frequently justified their preferences in metals by invoking standards of race, religion, and culture: Douglas was hardly the first to tie the fate of Western civilization to gold.

Douglas probably did not consider his pronouncement an exaggeration. Millions of Europeans and Americans for centuries had, like him, esteemed gold as the basis of the West's economy, believing that it distinguished a superior culture. Moreover, gold monometallists, asserted that politicians could not change the standard because they had no right to interfere with natural economic laws. It is perhaps difficult to understand how socially significant was one's advocacy of gold rather than silver. This economic issue divided the social classes in the last half of the nineteenth century and the "better elements" were devoted adherents to the standard; silver was distasteful to them as an aspect of egalitarianism. Bimetallism, they claimed, was an artificial compromise of the two standards.

During the nineteenth century gold became identified with world powers, silver with "inferior" nations. Only Asians, Slavs, Latins, and other "barbarians" had monetized silver. The empires traded with gold, the colonies with silver. In the United States, a parvenu nation ambitious to attain the stability of a world power, debtors tended to favor the white metal. The conventional wisdom held that a nation's status could be determined by the metal it esteemed. In the words of Senator John Sherman, perhaps the most influential American politician in financial matters during the Gilded Age, silver in the monetary standard would detach us "from the great commercial nations of the world and [force us to] join the inferior nations, where poverty or large populations compel them to the use of silver alone." The American destiny called for gold and greatness.

## II

For more than two decades following the Coinage Act of 1873, which excluded silver from coinage and made gold the sole monetary standard, rural Americans from the Cotton Belt to the Rockies cursed it as the "Crime of '73." After the Union had financed the Civil War by floating large blocs of government bonds, the Reconstruction Con-

*Introduction*

gresses had obliged bondholders by paying them in coin and then defined specie solely as gold, thereby demonetizing silver. Thus, while delighted investors redeemed securities purchased during the Civil War with gold, the poor and indebted found money harder to acquire as its value inflated. Debtors branded the 1873 deflationary law a class conspiracy and suspected links between Wall Street and the banks of Europe. Westerners were outraged by the coincidence of gold monetization and the development of profitable methods for mining the vast silver lodes recently discovered in the Rocky Mountain territories. Modern historians now conclude that there is no evidence that such a conspiracy existed, but history cannot always be derived from archives. Correctly or not, the sodbusters of the Great Plains and their western mining allies asserted that big bankers had combined with servile politicians to keep producers dependent upon capital.

All parties agreed that silver was the key to increasing the amount of money in circulation. This, in part, explains why silver created such an enduring strife in American society. Its growing abundance offered farmers, workers, and small businessmen an opportunity to demand more dollars for their labors. But in 1875 Congress passed the Resumption Act which provided for greenbacks supported only by gold. By the 1890's, Greenbackers, Populists, and monetary "reformers" made silver inflation their primary goal. The national depression which erupted in 1893 confirmed their belief that tight money accounted for their misery. The West had increased its political strength when Colorado joined the Union in 1876 followed by six more states—North and South Dakota, Montana, Washington, Idaho, and Wyoming—in 1889 and 1890. Democratic and Republican leaders could not ignore the congressional representatives and presidential electors from these states. Although Congress had passed compromise silver purchase laws in 1878 and 1890, the demands for inflation were not assuaged. Inflationists continued to blame the *de facto* gold standard for contractions in the economy.

President Grover Cleveland, however, blamed the Silverites for the depression of 1893. Arguing that they had taxed the confidence of investors and strained the revenue surplus of the Treasury, Cleveland, in June 1893, asked Congress to repeal the 1890 Sherman Silver Purchase Act. Congress reluctantly obliged the Chief Executive, but the issue split the nation and the Democratic party along sectional lines. Silver advocates from the rural South and West captured control of the Democratic National Convention in 1896, adopted a platform unacceptable to the northeastern gold faction, and nominated Nebraska's William Jennings Bryan for the Presidency. Thereafter the "Boy Orator of the Platte" challenged the "gold-bugs" and championed silver, making this issue into the most hotly debated one in the nation.

Free from the turbulence that marked the Democrats, the Republicans reaffirmed their faith in gold. In the 1896 "Battle of the Standards," William McKinley denied Bryan a single electoral vote north of the Mason-Dixon line and east of the Mississippi River. Few elections have revealed such intense sectional, class, and cultural bitterness as that of 1896, the last presidential contest of the nineteenth century. Moreover, Bryan's defeat foreshadowed another abortive attempt to pass a free silver law in 1898 and the exhausted silver movement subsided until another economic crisis was to revive it in the 1930's.

After McKinley's victory the gold forces, taking advantage of renewed prosperity and increasing world gold production, prevailed upon the GOP administration to formally adopt the gold standard. In March 1900 the President signed the Gold Standard Act which stipulated that one dollar would be worth 25.8 grains of gold with all forms of money in parity with this standard. During

*Introduction*

World War I the United States, like most nations, temporarily left the gold standard; gold stocks had diminished to such an extent that Congress empowered President Wilson to declare an embargo on gold exports. Nonetheless, the preference for gold persisted and in 1919 America became the first country to reinstate the standard. Throughout the 1920's American businessmen continued to honor the gold standard. The depression would test their faith.

### III

Depressions invariably weakened the psychological attachment to gold; the Great Depression almost destroyed it. In the wake of the downturn which followed the halcyon 1920's, dazed Americans wondered where all the money had gone. The depression presented a devastating collage of despair: breadlines, soup kitchens, and apple vendors were part of the urban landscape; factories with no orders to fill locked out their workers; farmers marched on state capitols to protest the burden of additional taxes, and threatened to lynch judges who carried out the law by foreclosing on property; Chicago teachers lived for months on credit and scrip because the city lacked funds for their salaries; and New York City, in supplication before the geniuses of Broad and Wall Streets to secure loans to sustain welfare recipients, was admonished that to qualify for the bankers' help it was necessary to cut its costly relief rolls.

These conditions are beyond the comprehension of most Americans entering the 1970's. A revolution in stability has occurred since World War II, and the depressions which plagued America in the nineteenth century now seem to be the result of relatively simple problems of economic management. In today's mixed economy, Washington juggles tax and credit rates and makes economic decisions to fund education, defense, public works, and relief; everyone in this country is at least indirectly affected by these decisions. We have flattened the business cycle's boom and bust; at this writing it is inflation, not deflation, that is our greatest trouble. It seems almost implausible that Americans in the 1930's did not conceive our mixed economy. Still, we owe those children of a darker age the courtesy of examining their precepts and policies before we condemn them for the sin of ignorance.

First, it is important to recall that depressions were endemic to the American economy. As President Hoover pointed out in 1931, the United States had experienced approximately fifteen such calamities of varying dimensions during the preceding century. The collapse of 1929 was hardly something unknown or unanticipated. Euphoric Americans hoped that the abundance of the 1920's heralded the end of these economic inversions. But the decline of 1929–30 was like the return of a familial black sheep whom everyone preferred to forget. Even so, the historic instability in the economy was reassuring, and it was believed that an upturn would follow the depression as a natural consequence. This depression was worse than most Americans could remember, but older persons compared it to the collapse of 1893, which ran its course in a few years. Thus, early in 1933, Charles Dawes, former Vice-President of the United States, banker, and former head of the Reconstruction Finance Corporation, confided to a friend that he was sure recovery would come within months; after all, he reasoned, the depression of the 1890's had lasted four years; 1933 was the fourth year of the current depression and he confidently expected that the economic cycle would by then have come full circle.

Such pointless analogies were commonplace in the 1930's. The Hoover years conventionally depicted the depression as a natural phenomenon requiring individual forbearance rather than collective government action. President Hoover set the tone by comparing proposed remedial legislation to laws exorcising a Caribbean hurri-

## Introduction

cane. (Within a year the President changed the analogy to medical science's conquest of disease.) He insisted that relief measures were futile and that recovery was imminent. Hoover's forecast early in 1930 of prosperity in 60 days was, at best, politically unfortunate. Nevertheless, it was his duty as President to reassure; he was no worse at this than his successors except in rhetoric and manner. The shibboleths of the times, now mercifully forgotten, required men to "sit tight," "pull in the belt," and "hold steady on the course."

Although most politicians regarded the depression with indifference during its first year, Hoover did not. Familiar with business psychology, he believed that in crises like this businessmen usually followed policies inimical to their own welfare. In severe economic dislocations industrialists played the percentages by liquidating capital, labor, wages, prices, and inventory. Such selfish tactics, Hoover reasoned, retarded recovery and further undermined confidence in the free market. Summoning manufacturers and bankers to the White House in 1930, he urged the industrialists not to lay off workers or slash wages. Their initial assent gratified the President. He supplemented this corporate cooperation with pleas to community relief agencies to coordinate their efforts with state and local governments. He converted the Presidency into a liaison for all agencies engaged in relief.

He refused, however, to make the Federal Government originate measures for relief. With an almost mystical faith in direct democracy, Hoover rejected the Federal Government as truly representative of a free people's will and insisted that the initiative for relief had to come from the people themselves. The only real democracy either lay outside of government or existed on local levels. If Washington functioned on behalf of the community, he believed that Americans would be relieved of initiative and responsibility and subjected to an enervating, paternalistic, collectivistic tyranny. Hoover's relief program entailed organizing the efforts of those who voluntarily cooperated with each other and with Washington to achieve an enlightened common purpose. And the American people generally concurred with this strategy; trust in it did not give way until the spring of 1932.

The federal role was administrative; Hoover excluded Congress from any major involvement in relief or recovery. He resisted all Democratic and Progressive proposals for direct federal relief or employment-producing public works. He accelerated public works projects already under way but declined to begin expensive new ones lest he expand budgetary deficits and weaken business confidence. While conditions deteriorated through most of 1931, Congress remained in adjournment from March to December awaiting a call from the President. Only as a last resort would Hoover request appropriations for relief.

Hoover's recommendation to Congress in December 1931 to create the Reconstruction Finance Corporation represented his first admission that the Federal Government had to provide something more than committees and conferences. The RFC had become a necessity because the bankers had failed him; he had asked them to pool their resources to save their weak brethren from bankruptcy and they had retorted that this responsibility belonged to the Federal Government. A precedent for the RFC had been set by the War Finance Corporation of the Wilson years. Hoover's agency, with a capitalization of $500,000,000 for loans to troubled credit institutions and railroads became the first peacetime federal effort to stabilize the economy by performing a capital function.

Yet this remained the outstanding inflationary deviation in an orthodox deflationary policy. Although criticized that his schemes were "trickle-down" solutions which aided only big businessmen, Hoover refused to extend federal loans to cities or small industries. With a self-deceiving

## Introduction

singlemindedness, the Administration sought a balanced budget, a feat which it had not accomplished since 1929. Declining revenues and increasing public needs rendered such household economics an impossibility. When Hoover and the Democratic leaders demanded a national manufacturers' sales tax to augment depleted revenues, House GOP Progressives and Democrats rebelled in March 1932. Throughout the spring of 1932 proposals for public works relief proliferated in Congress, and in May Hoover capitulated after stipulating that all projects be self-liquidating and reproductive. Only after vetoing the pork barrel Wagner-Garner bill did Hoover accept the Emergency Relief and Construction Act of 1932, which included RFC loans to the states for public works.

The President's monetary activities were likewise restrained. Britain left the gold standard in 1931 and fifteen nations followed suit. France, Italy, Belgium, Holland, and Switzerland held the line. Despite an acute drain on gold reserves throughout February 1932, Hoover steadfastly supported the United States standard. Aware that this policy was deflationary, Hoover tried to inflate credit in the Glass-Steagall Act of 1932 by permitting the Federal Reserve to lower the rediscount rate and release more gold to support currency. The President claimed that the origins of the depression were foreign and that to tamper further with gold would endanger all nations. The gold standard remained inviolate.

### IV

The Roosevelt Administration, by way of contrast, did not shrink from federal action, although this contrast did not in itself signify radicalism. During the 1932 campaign, Roosevelt had pledged himself to a balanced budget and his first inaugural address made a dutiful obeisance to the psychology of confidence. Of course there were crucial differences between the two Presidencies: a capacity to indulge in expedience freed the New Deal from the restraining business myths of the Hoover years. And, lest we give too much credit to Roosevelt, it should be remembered that every previous failure increased anxiety and opportunism in the public and Congress. After four winters of depression, the White House had a green light to try anything which might sustain hope in a despairing nation. Moreover, many of Roosevelt's staunchest congressional supporters were southern and western Democrats who, along with progressive Republicans, had vainly sought public works relief and direct federal aid programs for farmers. Roosevelt could not afford to disappoint these activists.

The day after his inauguration Roosevelt issued two significant proclamations: first he called the new Congress to Washington for a special session to begin in four days; then, employing his executive powers under the Trading with the Enemy Act of 1917, he stopped all gold transactions and proclaimed a national bank holiday. In one day's work, both Houses of Congress passed a banking law which few of the legislators had time to read. It gave the President broad discretionary powers over credit, currency, and gold and silver transactions. Gold hoarding and its export were forbidden, and sound banks in the Federal Reserve System were permitted to reopen only under licenses from the Treasury Department. The act temporarily succeeded in checking the money panic. Conservative enough to be endorsed by bankers and former Hoover administration officials, the banking law avoided radical nostrums while it aligned the government solidly behind the existing banking structure as a gesture of confidence. It seemed to be a natural extension of the Hoover policies. Hoover's Under Secretary of the Treasury Arthur L. Ballantine had played a prominent role in writing the measure. At a time when Bronson Cutting, progressive Republican Senator from New Mexico, believed that drastic re-

## Introduction

visions, even nationalization, of the banking system were in order, Roosevelt merely had shored up the existing structure. Referring to the radical rhetoric of the inaugural address, one representative gibed: "The President drove the money-changers out of the Capitol on March 4—and they were all back on the 9th."

Roosevelt proved to be just as conservative in fiscal matters. Hoover quixotically had attempted to balance the budget; Roosevelt vowed that he would not be as extravagant as his predecessor and would not incur a deficit. On March 10, he asked Congress for broad powers to cut $400 million in veterans' payments and $100 million in federal employees' salaries. Ninety House Democrats opposed this because it appeared that the income of veterans and government clerks paid for the RFC funds which aided the big bankers. Even so, in two days Congress complied. "Under the leadership of Franklin Roosevelt," William E. Leuchtenburg has written, "the budget balancers had won a victory for orthodox finance that had not been possible under Hoover."

But there were signs that Roosevelt would not continue to follow the dictates of conservative finance. When he began to form his cabinet in December, he deliberately ignored the pillars of the Democratic party, its hapless presidential candidates of the 1920's, James E. Cox, John W. Davis, and Alfred E. Smith. Instead he sought a progressive Republican to run his public works program from the Interior Department. Perhaps the most important post to be filled was Secretary of the Treasury; Carter Glass, "Father of the Federal Reserve," Wilson's head of the Treasury, and undisputed authority on the American financial system, received Roosevelt's first offer of his old portfolio. At 75, it was not difficult for the conservative Virginia Senator to decline on the grounds of ill health. It was, however, common knowledge that Glass expected Roosevelt to pursue an inflationary course and refused to associate himself with it. He believed that the President-elect sympathized with Senate inflationists like Cordell Hull, Burton K. Wheeler, George W. Norris, and Huey Long, all of whom advocated expanding the amount of currency in circulation in order to boost commodity prices. Roosevelt declined to commit himself to a firm sound-money position, and Glass stayed in the Senate where he could resist honorably all inflationary moves; neither of them ever regretted the Virginian's decision.

Inflationist panaceas had abounded in Congress throughout 1932, and the New Deal had to confront them. When the administration submitted its farm bill in mid-March, the inflationists seized the occasion to battle the gold standard, the source, they maintained, of many agrarian problems. They inserted a clause in the bill, the Thomas amendment, for inflating currency with a free coinage of silver. Roosevelt, conscious of his deflationary policies, agreed that the moment was politically propitious for an inflationary gesture. His compassion for the farmer was genuine, southern and western Democrats held powerful congressional positions, and he needed a harmonious party more than that yellow abstraction, gold. Fortunately for conservatives, Roosevelt insisted that authority to inflate currency properly belonged to the President, and Congress concurred with him.

The Thomas amendment, by requiring administration concessions, permitted Roosevelt to reappraise the official status of the gold standard. Since he had closed the banks and embargoed gold in March, the nation had been only technically on it. The review suited the purposes of many groups who for years had called for a flexible monetary system. Ever since its formation in 1921, the Stable Monetary Association had argued for a dollar based upon purchasing power instead of gold. An inspiration of "reflation" advocate Irving Fisher, the organization had links to Roosevelt; his uncle, Frederick A. Delano, had headed

## Introduction

it in the 1930's and his Secretary of Agriculture, Henry A. Wallace, had been a vice-president since its inception. Another anti-gold standard organization attempting to sway the New Deal was the Committee for the Nation. A heterogeneous group brought together in the waning days of the Hoover Administration by banker Frank A. Vanderlip, it included, among others, industrialist James H. Rand, Jr., of Remington Rand; retailer Lessing Rosenwald of Sears, Roebuck; Keynes-oriented publisher J. David Stern; its advisors were Fisher and "commodity dollar" theorist George Warren of Cornell University. The Committee united self-seekers, faddists, monetary cranks, and sophisticates with one common interest: an assault upon the gold standard.

Two external factors in their favor were the increasing isolation of the United States as a gold standard nation and the economic nationalism of Europe. Since most of the continent had forsaken gold, the dollar's convertibility in trade had been jeopardized. Great Britain's departure from the standard in 1931 represented a triumph for John Maynard Keynes, a British economist who had deplored its return to gold in 1925. Again and again Keynes had assailed the orthodox bankers of Britain, and the economic collapse seemed to support his arguments. Irving Fisher echoed Keynes' analysis but most Americans derided devaluation as "opportunism." Nevertheless, many businessmen and politicians clamored to follow the British lead and undoubtedly influenced Roosevelt.

No consensus of business attitudes existed in 1933. There were three schools of thought in America on inflation. First, reading right to left, orthodox conservatives bemoaned any suggestion of tampering with gold. "Let us make no mistake—controlled inflation is just sheer nonsense," Bernard Baruch warned. "It always starts out that way with good intentions, which have been used for the pavements of hell." Then came the objects of Baruch's despair, the "managed inflation" advocates, and, third, there were the silver monetizers whose influence was paramount in agriculture.

Many previously orthodox businessmen tended to be more expedient, a trend which favored conservative acceptance of Roosevelt's decision to leave the gold standard. Outside of Douglas, Baruch, and others who viewed a gold ban as the product of "mob rule," Roosevelt's decision terrorized very few people. Big Finance, never desiring that capital should go it alone, welcomed any federal help as enthusiastically as it had the Reconstruction Finance Corporation. Practical Wall Street men like J. P. Morgan cheered the White House for endeavoring to arrest the deflationary impetus. The Administration's move was, Morgan declared, "the best possible course under existing circumstances." In Chicago, Charles G. Dawes described the gold embargo as "the only thing that could be done," and Melvin A. Traylor, president of the First National Bank of Chicago, pronounced himself "entirely satisfied with it." Retailers forecast more sales as a result of it. A majority in Congress affirmed the wisdom of the decision. Even Republicans like Senators Arthur Vandenberg, David A. Reed, and the party's leader in the upper chamber, Charles L. McNary, approved. Because Americans now could compete for the export trade "for the first time in many, many months," Vandenberg believed that "Abandonment of the dollar externally may prove to be a complete answer to our problem, so far as the currency factor is concerned." It would be a long time before Americans had complete answers to the conundrum of recovery, but Roosevelt's decision certainly had given them further reason to hope.

## V

In the end, the gold standard decision gave prices a brief fillip and little more. Roosevelt's action demonstrated his uncertainty in monetary matters and his impatience

## Introduction

to resolve the nagging issues surrounding the exchange of gold. Counseled by monetary experts such as J. P. Warburg to devalue the dollar, Roosevelt went further than anticipated and yanked gold out from under the dollar. There is a lingering judgment held by many critics that Roosevelt went too far with the anti-gold group. According to that thinking, the Rasputin of the New Deal was George Warren, whom Eliot Janeway has described as "a famous quack . . . who practiced 'funny-money' alchemy. . . ." The President made the right decision at the right time. But, it is argued, by following other Warren notions, Roosevelt rubbed the luster from it.

Congress then passed a resolution abrogating the gold clause from all contracts, a move guaranteed to frighten most creditors as much as it relieved debtors. In October 1933, the Administration, acting on the price theories of George Warren, embarked upon a gold-buying program in an effort to remove it from circulation and boost commodity prices. Unfortunately, while Roosevelt halted the deflationary movement, gold buying only produced a stuttering of prices. Moreover, it disenchanted sound-money men who sought a flexible standard with controlled inflation. Because of this ill-advised scheme, capable men like Warburg and Dean Acheson abandoned the New Deal. Roosevelt finally put an end to the program in 1934 when Congress passed the Gold Reserve Act.

The New Deal has also been accused of ignoring the international consequences of its gold standard decision. Shunning an opportunity to forge multilateral agreements on the management of the world's money, Roosevelt opted for unilateral action. As *The Economist* of London later put it, "when a rich country, with a strong currency, voluntarily devalues by a very large percentage solely in order to facilitate its internal economic policy, it might be considered a very dangerous precedent and an incitement to the insanity of competitive depreciation." Of course, since the British were an early link in the chain of events, our cousins were bidding us to hearken unto their words rather than their deeds.

In addition to illustrating the New Deal's pragmatic activism, the gold standard decision demonstrated its economic nationalism. Roosevelt had hinted at this in his inaugural address by declaring that "the emergency at home cannot wait on . . . international readjustment." The Hoover Administration, however, operating on the assumption that reconstruction at home could not be achieved without stability abroad, had committed the New Deal to participation in an international economic conference in London that June. Although he might have disregarded it, Roosevelt cheerfully accepted Hoover's obligation. With Wilsonian idealism he sent a distinguished delegation headed by the Secretary of State to London. The conference had little chance for success; the French adamantly held firm to gold and the British, to achieve a favorable trade balance, had abandoned the standard but did not want other nations to follow their example. Stabilization of the international monetary system was a practical ideal but a remote possibility. During the meetings Roosevelt sent the delegates a candid, nationalistic message, giving many Europeans an opportunity to blame him for torpedoing a session which had no prospect of accord anyway. Except for the trade agreements which Cordell Hull bilaterally negotiated throughout the 1930's, the New Deal treated recovery as an exclusively domestic concern.

By the end of the decade the United States had learned that economic isolation was no more possible than political isolation. The international monetary chaos which grew out of World War I convinced Europe and America that cooperation after World War II was essential to all. Upon congressional approval of the Bretton Woods Agreements on July 31, 1945, the United States joined the International Monetary Fund, which had been organized

*Introduction*

to stabilize international currencies. Additional stabilization came with the Marshall Plan. Today, in an age when nations still fret about their balance of payments, gold outflows, and the devaluation of other currencies, these problems remind us of how little was resolved by the major decision Roosevelt made concerning the gold standard.

# Section One

# Public Pressures

*Commentary*

The issue of controlled monetary inflation among conservatives in 1933 divided the opportunistic from the orthodox. The Hoover Administration's economic policies had earned the approval of a conservative consensus but, after three depression winters with no recovery in sight, that accord had eroded. Business confidence weakened as the flight of gold overseas accelerated, endangering Hoover's defense of the American price in February 1932. Great Britain and several other nations had abandoned the gold standard the previous year; still, the White House made the gold value of the dollar as sacrosanct as a balanced budget. Hoover was not the usual orthodox economist, as his willingness to create the Reconstruction Finance Corporation attests. Inflating credit with public money, however, was acceptable; inflating the dollar by suspending gold payments was an anathema. Harris G. Warren, a historian sympathetic to the President, has written that Hoover "believed it was all right to play with credit, wrong to play with money." With an assist from the conservative Democratic leadership in passing the Glass-Steagall Bill of 1932, Hoover further expanded the quantity of available capital (Doc. 1). Later it became evident that this Hoover stratagem, like several others, had deferred rather than solved the crisis.

While a majority of the industrial and financial community probably endorsed Hoover's adherence to the price of gold, the number of supporters of controlled monetary inflation continued to enlarge. In the summer of 1932, a group of businessmen and farm leaders organized the Committee for the Nation dedicated candidly to the purpose of securing federal manipulation of the economy. Led by banker Frank A. Vanderlip, the committee abjured the gold standard in order to stem the deflationary trend (Doc. 8). Its members, hardly mavericks, included many respected bankers, manufacturers, retailers, and the most conservative farm group heads who lent a sort of pseudo-respectability to the inflation drive. One member, publisher J. David Stern, argued for an immediate gold embargo and the suspension of gold payments. In a May 1932 editorial, Stern drew an analogy between the depression crisis and the World War emergency, recommending that Hoover employ the powers given Wilson in 1917 to halt the gold flow, the very statutory precedent Roosevelt exercised when he closed the banks less than ten months later (Doc. 4).

But Stern, a progressive Democrat, was a renegade in business circles. He had been proposing public works and labor legislation which few businessmen would accept in the early 1930's. His economic philosophy presaged the federal economic policies of the sixties. In February 1933 Stern told an unsympathetic Senate Finance Committee that the nation should forget balanced budgets and spend millions to restore consumer purchasing power. Asked where he got such fanciful notions, Stern proclaimed himself a disciple of the British economist John Maynard Keynes, "the greatest economist living today." The senators evinced no knowledge of Stern's idol and scorned his proposals.

The movement to demonetize gold, however, owed a great deal to Keynes. For years he had derided the gold standard as an inhibiting anachronism to Britain's economic growth, and the British departure from it seemed to confirm his teachings. The British example impressed and influenced many Americans who incorporated Keynes' arguments into their own without acknowledging their debt to him (Doc. 2).

Indeed, in the history of the New Deal, Keynes is a spectre who never quite materializes as a decisive intellectual authority. Despite its later Keynesian penchant, there is no evidence that the Roosevelt Administration consciously heeded Keynes. Roosevelt conferred with him two years after the gold standard decision, but they were unimpressed with each other. That Stern remained one of the few Americans outside of academic circles familiar with Keynes' writings did not necessarily indicate a low intellectual level on this side of the Atlantic. Keynes' prose suffered in comparison to that of his later American adherents, although he managed to lighten his torpid essays on economics with a barbed wit. He displayed little patience for an orthodoxy which clutched the gold standard with irrational zeal (Doc. 3). Also, his advocacy of governmental manipulation of the economy led many Americans who neither knew nor read him to conclude that he was anti-capitalist. They were self-deceived; in fact, Keynes was an unconventional speculator whose investments bound him to an economic system he wanted to preserve in a flexible form.

Keynes' American counterpart was Yale economist Irving Fisher, a frequent consultant to Hoover, Roosevelt, and the Committee for the Nation. Keynes once hailed Fisher as "the economist who first influenced me strongly towards regarding money as a real factor in economic behavior." A monetary reformer since the 1890's, Fisher insisted that the dollar's value should be regulated and brought in line with the realities of purchasing power. As a bulwark against further deflation, he recommended a policy of "reflation," controlled inflation to be achieved by demonetizing gold. Prior to Roosevelt's inauguration, Fisher had warned the President-elect that "deflation has not reached its nadir and that to let it run its course without action is to invite disaster." He outlined a program of reflation which began with a suggestion to "abandon the gold standard entirely for a managed currency" (Doc. 5). Like many a trembling investor (he supposedly made a million dollars with shrewd speculation in the 1920's), Fisher yearned for a dose of inflation to bolster the sagging value of his securities and earnestly promoted his ideas with congressmen and New Dealers until the actual decision (Doc. 6).

Fisher notwithstanding, Roosevelt's gold policies owed most of their academic foundations to George F. Warren. The President had known Warren in New York and after he went to Washington he maintained contact with the Cornell professor of agricultural economics. Warren's book, *Prices,* co-authored by Frank A. Pearson, called for managed inflation by government manipulation of the price of gold primarily to benefit impoverished agrarians. This appealed greatly to the gentleman farmer in the White House. Because gold was plentiful, the Warren thesis went, the Administration should purchase it on the world market in order to deflate its price while concomitantly inflating commodity prices (Doc. 9). Secretary of Agriculture Henry A. Wallace and farm-minded senators endorsed the plan; Keynes, Walter Lippmann (Doc. 7), Dean Acheson of the Treasury Department, and Yale economist James Harvey Rogers, among others, disapproved of the plan except for its initial step of leaving the gold standard. The *New Republic* warned that juggling the price of gold should not be mistaken for a panacea since it disregarded the needs of workers, consumers, and other step-children of the economy (Doc. 10).

By April 1933, however, expediency among businessmen and economists had made the gold standard expendable in their struggle against economic depression.

# 1

## *President Herbert Hoover's Monetary Orthodoxy*

[William Starr Myers and Walter H. Newton, *The Hoover Administration: A Documented Narrative* (New York: Charles Scribner's Sons, 1936), pp. 169–72.]

*February 8, 1932:* The Reconstruction Finance Corporation now began to make loans.

*February 9, 1932:* The British again raised their tariffs.

Messrs. Meyer and Harrison of the Federal Reserve System, General Dawes from the Reconstruction Finance Corporation, and Secretary Mills called at the White House to report the peril into which the country's gold supply had fallen and also the imminent dangers to the gold standard. They reviewed the situation, saying that under the law the Federal Reserve banks must hold forty per cent of gold against currency issued and thirty-five per cent against their deposits, and in addition a minor gold fund must be held with the Treasury for redemption purposes. The coverage of the remaining sixty per cent of the Federal Reserve currency was by "eligible" securities (mostly commercial bills) held by the Federal Reserve banks. Various factors had come into play. Due to the foreign drain, over $1,000,000,000 of gold had been withdrawn from the monetary gold stock. Due to hoarding, the Reserve currency issued had swollen by $1,500,000,000 above normal, against which gold and eligible paper must be held. Due to slackness of business the Federal Reserve banks did not have the "eligible" paper to cover the sixty per cent with such paper and therefore had to increase the gold percentage of the Reserve by the amount of this deficiency. A memorandum was presented to the President which showed that through the interplay of these factors the "free" gold—that is to say the amount of gold which could be paid out to foreigners—had been reduced to $433,000,000.

The Board further furnished a list of foreign governments and citizens of other nations who held $1,393,500,000 on deposit or invested in short-term bills within the United States. They could take out about $900,000,000 of it on demand and the balance in less than ninety days. Of this, France alone held nearly $500,000,000. Under the prevailing conditions the free gold was being drawn down at the rate of $150,000,000 a week through hoarding and foreign demands, and a more rapid drain was threatened. On that basis we should be compelled to place an international embargo on gold or on the convertibility of the currency within two to three weeks. The memorandum, at the President's request given subsequently in more detail by the Reserve officials, showed that the amounts of deposits for account of the following countries or the holdings of short-term bills which were subject to demand or very short notice, were:

| | |
|---|---:|
| England | $142,533,000 |
| France | 491,740,000 |
| Germany | 38,158,000 |
| Italy | 30,616,000 |
| Netherlands | 41,042,000 |
| Canada | 136,712,000 |
| Latin America | 105,548,000 |
| Far East | 46,647,000 |
| All others | 195,545,000 |
| Total | $1,228,541,000 |

Reports of member banks of the Federal Reserve System showed that, on December 31, 1931, there was due from banks outside New York to banks in foreign countries, an additional $65,000,000. This probably was somewhat less on the current date.

The amount of monetary gold stock in the United States was shown to be as follows:

*Held by the U. S. Treasury*

| | |
|---|---|
| (a) Against gold certificates | $1,675,000,000 |
| (b) Reserve against U. S. Notes and Treasury Notes | 156,000,000 |
| (c) In general fund | 37,000,000 |
| (d) For Reserve Banks and agents | 1,628,000,000 |
| *Held in Reserve Banks* | 500,000,000 |
| Coin in circulation | 407,000,000 |
| Total | $4,403,000,000 |

If commercial bills were available to the Reserve banks or other coverage were made available, so that the gold reserve against Federal Reserve notes needed to be only the legal reserve of forty per cent, then the necessary gold to hold for this purpose would be $1,169,836,200, or would "free" from this source $902,144,000. It was stated by the Reserve officials that to attempt to call in gold or gold certificates and publicly to substitute Federal Reserve currency, would project a general panic. If this were done privately and when opportunity offered, it would be of no avail, as months would be required to get in even a few hundred million. In any event, the gold certificates now were being tightly hoarded.

The situation was rendered more imperative by the conviction in many circles both at home and abroad that, owing to the steady drain, we were on the same route to gold currency embarrassment that had been witnessed in Austria, Hungary, Germany, Great Britain, and other countries. In consequence, and aside from foreigners withdrawing their funds with increasing rapidity, a flight of capital from the United States had been started by some of our own citizens.

The President already had sought to fortify this situation by his proposal of October 6, 1931, at the joint conference of political leaders, to make other types of loans discountable by the Federal Reserve System. This was to enlarge the amount of "eligibles" available in the System, thus at the same time expanding the amount of credit available to business, and it had been agreed to at that time. He had recommended it in his message of December 6th. The Democratic members of the Senate committee would not act.

As a result of this conference (February 9th), it was decided that in order to relieve the situation, another effort must be made to enlarge temporarily the "eligibility" of commercial paper, and to make government bonds held by the Reserve banks temporarily legal as coverage of the currency above the forty per cent gold reserve. Such action would "free" over $1,000,000,000 of gold and thus allow full payment of foreign demands without endangering the gold standard. The President held that this must be for the emergency only. He at once requested Senators Watson and Robinson, the Republican and Democratic floor-leaders, together with Senators Glass, Bulkley, Walcott, and Townsend (the subcommittee of the Banking and Currency Committee), Secretary Mills, President Dawes of the Reconstruction Finance Corporation, and Governor Meyer of the Federal Reserve Board, to meet him at breakfast the following morning.

*February 10, 1932:* At this breakfast the President stated the danger to the gold standard, gave the figures and urged immediate action. He also took occasion to urge the immediate legislation he had asked for in respect to authorizing loans from the Reconstruction Finance Corporation or from Federal Reserve banks to closed banks upon their assets, in order that they might make earlier distribution to their depositors. General Dawes urged also a system of joint guarantees by banks eligible for loans from the Federal Reserve. A program was agreed upon after three hours of discussion. In the program, aside from extending "eligibility" and making "governments" a coverage to the currency, a provision was added for joint loans to not less than five banks. Senator Glass agreed to introduce a special bill covering these emergency points, but on condition that the provision for loans to closed banks should be omitted as he wanted to reserve this "attractive" feature to help carry along the general Banking Reform Bill.

The President agreed that if a good Banking Reform Bill could thus be quickly passed, it was worth yielding this point for the time being.

Having this agreement, the President at once called to the White House Speaker Garner, House Floor Leader Rainey, Minority Leader Snell, and Congressmen Steagall, Luce, Strong, and Beedy of the House Committee on Banking and Currency. The same ground was again gone over and an approval was given. The approval of the measure by Senator Glass very largely determined the action of the Democratic members, and they were frank to say so. In order to expedite passage through the House, inasmuch as the Democrats were in control and as he wanted to avoid any partisanship in its consideration, the President suggested that Mr. Steagall (Democrat), chairman of the committee, should introduce it there. It became known as the Glass-Steagall Bill. The market at once reacted to the removal of the fear. Wheat, cotton, and the securities markets commenced to move upward.

As it was impossible to disclose the actual situation in its entirety without creating senseless fears and a further rush for gold, the explanations given for the bills in Congress and elsewhere necessarily were rather inadequate. Due in part at least to this the legislation was denounced by certain bankers and other persons uninformed as to the underlying circumstances prompting the legislation.

It is important to note that on a later occasion, at Des Moines, Iowa, on October 4, 1932, when the danger was past, the President referred to the narrow margin by which we had escaped being forced off the gold standard and the provisions which had been devised to save us. . . .

# 2

*The Assault on Gold:
Seymour Harris on
John Maynard Keynes*

[Seymour E. Harris, *John Maynard Keynes: Economist and Policy Maker* (New York: Charles Scribner's Sons, 1955), pp. 164–73.]

Almost single-handedly, Keynes dealt the gold standard a blow or a series of blows from which it is not likely to recover. Its prestige is far below what it was in 1913, when Keynes began his onslaught.

It was natural for Keynes to raise questions about the gold standard. Under this standard, the price of gold is fixed by each country in terms of its domestic currency. Hence, exchange rates are fixed. Thus, if one ounce of gold equals twenty dollars in the United States and five pounds in Great Britain, then one pound equals four dollars. (The price of gold in the United States had not been changed from 1834 to 1933–1934.)

\* \* \*

Keynes admitted that the gold standard had functioned reasonably well in the nineteenth century. At least there had been a modicum of price stability. But he associated this stability with the increased recourse to gold use in the first half of the century, and the various measures for economizing gold in the second half. But looking forward in 1930, he anticipated an annual increment of gold of 2 per cent, against requirements of 3 per cent. Hence the danger of inadequate supplies of money. Moreover, the gold standard had worked tolerably well in the nineteenth century because with efficiency steadily rising there had been no serious problem of wage cutting as there was in the twentieth century as prices declined: in periods of falling prices wages simply would not have to rise to balance the gains of efficiency in the nineteenth century. The fall in prices reflected increased efficiency, and the gains were taken in stable wage rates as prices declined.

In a vigorous attack on an official committee's proposal to return to gold in 1925 (after the abandonment in 1914), Keynes wrote:

> I suspect that their criticisms may be based on theories, developed 50 years ago, which assumed a mobility of labor, a competitive wage level which no longer exists and that they have not thought the problem through over again in the light of the deplorably inelastic conditions of our industrial organism to-day.

But, despite Keynes' warnings, Great Britain returned to a gold standard, and with unfortunate results. In 1932, Keynes could write:

> The day must come, and not too far off, when our modern Midases will be filled to the teeth and choking. And that, perhaps, will be the moment which the ivory of heaven will choose for granting to our chemists the final solution of the problem of manufacturing gold and of reducing its value to that of a base metal.

As early as 1910, in one of his first written works, Keynes expressed approval of a widening of the gold points, which, since it involves an abandonment of fixed exchange rates, is a step away from gold. In his first book (1913), Keynes said that it was not likely that we would permanently leave our most critical economic adjustments "at the mercy of a lucky prospector, a new chemical process or a change of ideas in Asia." In an article in *The*

*Economic Journal* late in 1914, he looked forward to the end of gold's despotic control. But it was not until 1923, in his *Tract on Monetary Reform* that he mobilized his big artillery guns against the entrenched gold standard. Stability of prices was preferable to fixed exchanges, he now insisted. Thus if prices tend to fall (insufficient supplies of money), it would be possible under a managed currency to stop the fall by raising the price of gold in domestic currency. Then more gold would come in and hence more money created. Again, he pressed for a widening of the gold points. He would rely on managing the monetary standard, not only upon discount rate, the orthodox weapon, but also upon variations in gold points; and even offer to buy and sell forward exchange at fixed prices, the last a mechanism for influencing the rates on foreign loans relative to domestic loans. The objective of the last would be to influence gold supplies and exchanges through influencing capital movements. If more capital comes in (say), less gold goes out.

At this time, Keynes noted that the gold standard was no longer automatic; central banks had not reacted to gold flows in the orthodox manner even before the war, and they had learned to vary their reserves.

The gold standard is a barbarous relic, he now said.

> All of us, from the governors of the Bank of England downwards, are now primarily interested in preserving the stability of business, prices, and employment, and are not likely when the choice is forced on us, deliberately to sacrifice these to the outworn dogma, which had its value once, of £3:17:10½ per ounce.

> ... Whilst the economists dozed, the academic dream of a hundred years, doffing its cap and gown, clad in paper rags, has crept into the real world by means of the bad fairies—always so much more potent than the good—the wicked Ministers of Finance.

Since gold is a managed currency, Keynes contended the issue is not one of a managed versus automatic standard. Against a managed currency, "conservatism and skepticism join arms . . . Perhaps superstition comes in too; for gold still enjoys the prestige of its smell and colour."

Aware of the costs of both deflation and inflation, Keynes sought stability of prices. But this meant independence from gold. He reminded us that in A.D. 276, Aurelian fell by the hand of his assassin within a year of his deflation of the currency. He also suggested that Edward VII's debasement of the currency might be interpreted as a preference for stability of prices over stability of the exchanges; and Edward VII was in fact the forerunner of Irving Fisher, the father of the compensated dollar, though happier in being able to combine practice and theory.

Keynes' opposition to gold rested in part on foreign control of the gold standard. In the twenties, the United States and France called the tune, for they had most of the gold. The gold standard in Keynes' view had become a dollar standard. He was not very happy that the United States could, if it wished, deflate the British economy. In one sense, Keynes was pleased with American policy, for after all, the United States had a managed standard. The United States accepted gold in large quantities and would not put it to use. "It has been driven, therefore, to the costly policy of burying in the vaults of Washington what the miners of the Rand have laboriously brought to the surface." But unfortunately Keynes's satisfaction with Federal Reserve unorthodoxy clashed with his displeasure at a policy which made it more difficult for the British to create supplies of money required to keep employment high. Boom conditions in the United States would help Great Britain; but once the boom collapsed and the dollar then began to rise in value there would be danger for sterling if tied to the dollar. The United Kingdom would have to follow.

Moreover, the United States in its wisdom, may abandon the costly process of accumulating gold. The United States "can enjoy the latest scientific improvements, devised in the economic laboratory of Harvard, whilst leaving Congress to believe that no rash departure will be permitted from the hard money consecrated by the experience of Dungi, Darius, Constantine, Lord Liverpool and Senator Aldrich." Then the value of gold would fall greatly; and sterling tied to gold would fall and British prices rise. The United States can afford the luxury of a gold standard with its large fluctuations, but not the United Kingdom.

Keynes was not only against gold; he was at least equally critical of the policy of returning to the prewar parity of gold and sterling. Sterling had fallen to about $3.50 after World War I; and the authorities seemed determined to return to the prewar parity with gold and the dollar ( £1 = $4.86). In order to raise the value of the pound sterling to $4.86, it is obvious that either the supply of pounds sterling (that is, the supply of money) must decline or of dollars rise, or partly one and partly the other. Unfortunately, the United States economy went through a wringer in 1920–1921 which greatly reduced the number of dollars. Hence not only was it necessary to raise the value of sterling by about 40 per cent even if the dollar and gold had remained stable in value, but also to raise it further insofar as gold, and its equivalent the dollar, became more valuable. Hence the need for a great deflation of money and prices in Great Britain. The difficulties stemmed from the decision to return to prewar parity, as well as the functioning of gold (i.e., the rise in the value of the dollar).

Why did Keynes object to the return to a $4.86-pound sterling? Partly because this was an indication of renewed faith in gold. Partly because in his view the required deflation was to cause much trouble for the British economy. In 1924, he told the annual meeting of the Royal Economic Society "that we certainly live in a barbarous age, but our object should be to emerge from it, and if there is a new weapon forged for that purpose we have no right to overlook it." His plea was for an abandonment of gold.

His complaint against the official policy rested on

1. A fear that the result would be higher costs in Great Britain: wages and other costs would not decline in proportion to the increased dearness of sterling. Hence with the dollar and other currencies buying less British goods, the British would lose export markets. Here he distinguished between the markets sheltered from foreign competition where costs remained high and the non-sheltered markets subject to foreign competition. (High costs in non-sheltered domestic markets would, of course, keep costs and prices up.)

2. The fear that the pound sterling might be kept up temporarily through high money rates, which would attract foreign capital, with the result that the pound sterling would have an artificially high value —that is compared to British costs and prices, in relation to competitors' costs and prices. Moreover, the British high rates would work havoc with domestic employment.

3. The resultant attempt to bring wage rates down could not be justified on moral grounds and would have serious social and political effects. Those in the weakest position (e.g., school teachers and coal miners) would have to submit. As against Governor Norman of the Bank of England, who offered deflation applied with discrimination (a rise in the commodity value of the pound sterling) because he wanted varying adjustments in different indus-

tries, Keynes preferred a general attack, i.e., a devaluation.

As the time for the return to gold approached, Keynes became more embittered. In March 1925, he told a Parliamentary group that the correct approach was stable prices and unstable exchanges. Then Britain's competitive position could be maintained. Above all, he would not tie the hands of the Monetary Authority by a return to gold. "The worst of the controversy is that nine tenths of it is carried on by people who do not know the arguments on either side." Following the deflation after the Napoleonic Wars, he warned the members of Parliament, the country suffered twenty years of successive credit maladjustment and crisis unparalleled in British history, and revolution was barely averted. This was a warning of what to expect of deflation. The major objective should be to evolve a currency system fitted to domestic needs. A policy of monetary restriction at this time seemed insane. "To be sometimes in favor of cheaper money seems to them like being sometimes a Roman Catholic. . . ."

By April 18, 1925, he wrote prophetically: "It is in this chastened mood that the British public will submit their necks once more to the golden yoke—as a prelude, perhaps, to throwing it off forever at a not too distant date." But by May he admitted defeat: he acknowledged the gold standard could be maintained; but it was an unwise policy. Even as late as 1931, just before the abandonment of gold, Keynes still had to concede defeat—as he did in his *Treatise* in 1930. The world was against him. He would have to be satisfied with international cooperation to manage the gold standard.

Great Britain went through a bad period after the restoration of gold; and Keynes lost no opportunity in stressing the unfortunate results. In 1926, he pointed out that the coal industry was near ruin, textiles in despair at losses, iron and steel showed no profits, and wages were more out of line than in 1925. The only alternatives, Keynes reminded us in 1927, were a continuance of the current depression, or an assault on wages which the Cabinet had repudiated, or the transfer of resources that would have gone into foreign loans and exports to the task of improving the efficiency of domestic industries. In the course of the Macmillan Committee hearings, in the next few years, Keynes needled Pigou, Norman, and others unmercifully for their support of the return to gold. Thus, badgered in his attempt to save Great Britain from a contractionist policy resulting from the return to gold at the prewar parity, Keynes turned first to domestic investment and second to a protectionist policy. The former might provide the necessary increase of demand and employment, and the latter would protect against the resultant rise of imports, as, with a domestic investment policy, prices and income rose in Great Britain.

When Great Britain was finally driven off gold in September 1931, Keynes was exuberant. With sterling much cheaper and domestic costs unchanged, Great Britain once more was to be a low-cost country; real wages would fall to some extent but not unfairly; not only would imports fall but exports would rise; the rise in the cost of living should not be more than two fifths that of the rise in the price of gold and the dollar; foreign debtors would pay less in goods on past debts to Britain but this was an offset to previous increase in the real burden; half the world would have to follow Britain in its depreciation; those who would not would have themselves to blame for high costs. Keynes's forecasts were amply justified by the events.

Now Keynes could blast the officials of the United States and France who would hoard gold and not assume the responsibilities of a creditor nation. (Keynes had forgotten that in 1923 his position, and a dubious one, had been that foreign loans out of real savings would not help retrieve the gold held by the United States.) He reminded Americans of the Senator from the West who is supposed to have said: "We do not want your goods. We will not have your bonds. We have already got your gold. What we want is your money."

* * *

Keynes put across the message that the job of the monetary authority is to serve the economy, not the other way around. It is now considered proper and even orthodox policy to allow changes in exchange rates when supported by the underlying conditions. Not only is this basic policy of the International Monetary Fund, but many business men high in the administration of the Marshall Plan were in the forefront in urging Western Europe to adopt realistic exchange rates. No government in Great Britain could survive on a policy of adherence to gold. The gold standard is dead, if for no other reason, because the United States alone of the large countries is committed to a fixed price for gold. But this is no longer an international system. After forty years, Keynes's victory is almost complete.

# 3

## Auri Sacra Fames:
*Keynes on Gold*

[John Maynard Keynes, *A Treatise on Money*, vol. 2 (London: Macmillan and Co., Ltd., 1930), pp. 289-92.]

The choice of gold as a standard of value is chiefly based on tradition. In the days before the evolution of Representative Money, it was natural, for reasons which have been many times told, to choose one or more of the metals as the most suitable commodity for holding a store of value or a command of purchasing power.

Some four or five thousand years ago the civilised world settled down to the use of gold, silver and copper for pounds, shillings and pence, but with silver in the first place of importance and copper in the second. The Mycenaeans put gold in the first place. Next, under Celtic or Dorian influences, came a brief invasion of iron in place of copper over Europe and the northern shores of the Mediterranean. With the Achaemenid Persian Empire, which maintained a bimetallic standard of gold and silver at a fixed ratio (until Alexander overturned them), the world settled down again to gold, silver and copper, with silver once more of predominant importance; and there followed silver's long hegemony (except for a certain revival of the influence of gold in Roman Constantinople), chequered by imperfectly successful attempts at gold-and-silver bimetallism, especially in the eighteenth century and the first half of the nineteenth, and only concluded by the final victory of gold during the fifty years before the war.

Dr. Freud relates that there are peculiar reasons deep in our subconsciousness why gold in particular should satisfy strong instincts and serve as a symbol. The magical properties, with which Egyptian priestcraft anciently imbued the yellow metal, it has never altogether lost. Yet, whilst gold as a store of value has always had devoted patrons, it is, as the sole standard of purchasing power, almost a parvenu. In 1914 gold had held this position in Great Britain *de jure* over less than a hundred years (though *de facto* for more than two hundred), and in most other countries over less than sixty. For except during rather brief intervals gold has been too scarce to serve the needs of the world's principal medium of currency. Gold is, and always has been, an extraordinarily scarce commodity. A modern liner could convey across the Atlantic in a single voyage all the gold which has been dredged or mined in seven thousand years. At intervals of five hundred or a thousand years a new source of supply has been discovered—the latter half of the nineteenth century was one of these epochs—and a temporary abundance has ensued. But as a rule, generally speaking, there has been not enough.

Of late years the *auri sacra fames* has sought to envelop itself in a garment of respectability as densely respectable as was ever met with, even in the realms of sex or religion. Whether this was first put on as a necessary armour to win the hard-won fight against bimetallism and is still worn, as the gold-advocates allege, because gold is the sole prophylactic against the plague of fiat moneys, or whether it is a furtive Freudian cloak, we need not be curious to inquire. But before we proceed with a scientific and would-be unbiassed examination of its claims, we had better remind the reader of what he well knows—namely, that gold has become part of the apparatus of conservatism and is one of the matters which we cannot expect to see handled without prejudice.

One great change, nevertheless—probably, in the end, a fatal change—has been effected by our generation. During the war individuals threw their little stocks into the national melting-pots. Wars have sometimes served to disperse gold, as when Alexander scattered the temple hoards of Persia or Pizarro those of the Incas. But on this occasion war concentrated gold in the vaults of the Central Banks; and these Banks have not released it. Thus, almost through the world, gold has been withdrawn from circulation. It no longer passes from hand to hand, and the touch of the metal has been taken away from men's greedy palms. The little household gods, who dwelt in purses and stockings and tin boxes, have been swallowed by a single golden image in each country, which lives underground and is not seen. Gold is out of sight—gone back again into the soil. But when gods are no longer seen in a yellow panoply walking the earth, we begin to rationalise them; and it is not long before there is nothing left.

Thus the long age of Commodity Money has at last passed finally away before the age of Representative Money. Gold has ceased to be a coin, a hoard, a tangible claim to wealth, of which the value cannot slip away so long as the hand of the individual clutches the material stuff. It has become a much more abstract thing—just a standard of value; and it only keeps this nominal status by being handed round from time to time in quite small quantities amongst a group of Central Banks, on the occasions when one of them has been inflating or deflating its managed representative money in a different degree from what is appropriate to the behavior of its neighbours. Even the handing round is becoming a little old-fashioned, being the occasion of unnecessary travelling expenses, and the most modern way, called "ear-marking", is to change the ownership without shifting the location. It is not a far step from this to the beginning of arrangements between Central Banks by which, without ever formally renouncing the rule of gold, the quantity of metal actually buried in their vaults may come to stand, by a modern alchemy, for what they please, and its value for what they choose. Thus, gold, originally stationed in heaven with his consort silver, as Sun and Moon, having first doffed his sacred attributes and come to earth as an autocrat, may next descend to the sober status of a constitutional king with a cabinet of Banks; and it may never be necessary to proclaim a Republic. But this is not yet—the evolution may be quite otherwise. The friends of gold will have to be extremely wise and moderate if they are to avoid a Revolution.

## *Handwriting on the Wall:*
## *An Editorial on Gold*

[Editorial, *Philadelphia Record*, May 22, 1932, reprinted in *Congressional Record*, 72nd Cong., 1st sess., pp. 10935–36.]

The handwriting on the wall becomes clearer.

Within three months the United States must suspend gold payment.

If the Government waits until its hand is forced it courts disaster.

If the Government acts now it can arrest deflation, end depression, win back prosperity within 60 days.

Six months ago the *Record*, alone among all the newspapers in the United States, urged a gold embargo and suspension of gold payment. We said:

"If the Government fails to take the initiative now, its hand will be forced eventually, too late to do much good."

The *Record* repeats its warning. It is not now alone in its conviction. Trained economists, experienced bankers, clear-thinking business leaders, are agreed there is only one way to prevent chaos. The facts are obvious. The Government has allowed deflation to go so far that only most heroic measures will arrest and reverse the process.

Increased value of the dollar has literally bankrupted the Nation. In 1928 our national wealth was estimated at nearly $400,000,000,000 as against less than $200,000,000,000 of indebtedness. To-day national wealth is estimated at less than $200,000,000,000.

Wealth of the Nation is just as great as it was in 1928. The value of the dollar has changed.

But the total debts remain at $200,000,000,000 so that our debts are greater than our wealth—expressed in dollars—which spells National bankruptcy and ruin.

## Public Pressures 25

The only way out of this absurdity is to change the value of the dollar.

This can not be done by mild inflation or making additional credit available to our banks and large industrial organizations. It can only be done by deliberate cheapening of the dollar. We use the words "cheapening the dollar" rather than "stabilizing the dollar" because "cheapening" is unpleasant. Now is the time to force unpleasant verities upon a public that has been fed on the pap that prosperity is around the corner.

This nation is approaching a terrible crisis. Its fate depends on courage and intelligence in facing true facts and meeting them with its full strength.

We are in this terrible depression because the administration and Congress have failed to face facts. The administration has reluctantly and belatedly admitted the need of some inflation of our dwindling and sluggish currency. It has pretended that this mammoth task could be accomplished by "mild inflation," open market transactions of the Federal reserve banks.

It has thrown a sop to the inflationists by implying that the Federal reserve system is putting out new money through purchase of Government securities at the rate of $100,000,000 a week, and will continue this process until commodity prices are stabilized and deflation arrested.

Why not tell the truth?

At the rate gold is going out of the Federal reserve system, the Federal reserve banks will have to stop their open market transactions within six weeks. They will be pulled up short by dwindling gold reserve—the golden chain which has circumscribed any adequate action to cure the depression.

Hasn't the depression become big enough to be met in a big way? Can't the present situation be solved with the directness that Columbus showed when he smashed the end of an egg?

Why can't we fight this depression as we fought the war, when we declared an embargo on gold in 1917 and no one thought anything of it?

We should have put an embargo on gold to coincide in duration with the moratorium on allied debts.

It is obviously unfair to permit debtor nations to absorb our gold when they are not able to meet their national debt payments to us. President Hoover declared an embargo on allied debts but allows the subjects of these debtor nations to drain our gold and drive us toward destruction.

Is there anything sensible or ethical in such a course?

Are we in the grip of some strange obsession—the gold mentality, as Senator BORAH calls it—which makes us act irrationally whenever the precious metal is mentioned?

Since the depression became so intense that the administration could not pretend there was no depression, it has offered many remedies—all halfway measures.

Not one has succeeded in arresting depression and turning the tide.

The one possible exception is that the Reconstruction Finance Corporation did stop bank failures.

But unemployment is steadily increasing as volume of trade decreases. All statistical evidence of the economic position of this country grows more terrifying. Down come commodity price index, bank clearings, car loadings, stock and bond quotations.

This depression started in 1929. It has grown worse with increasing acceleration.

It is time that we acted with our full strength as we did in the war. Overnight Congress should give the President the right to declare a gold embargo, just as it gave that right to Woodrow Wilson in 1917. The President should act immediately on the power accorded him.

This should be followed by inflation on a war-time scale, so administered as to distribute purchasing power among the people.

# 5

## *A Plan for Franklin D. Roosevelt: Irving Fisher on Reflation*

[Irving Fisher to Franklin D. Roosevelt, February 25, 1933, *Roosevelt Papers,* Franklin D. Roosevelt Library, Hyde Park, New York.]

*February 25, 1933*
*President-Elect Franklin D. Roosevelt,*
*Hyde Park, N. Y.*

My dear President-Elect Roosevelt:

Thank you for your kind letter asking me to put in writing what I had hoped to tell you regarding my ideas on the depression and what needs to be done.

It is hard—impossible—to compress all I would say but I will try to save your precious seconds.

I feel that I must begin with a background of the present picture as I see it.

When your letter came, I was speaking with a friend who is a close observer of local working-class opinion. He was saying that he smelled "revolution". Professor [John R.] Commons has written you that there is already "revolution" among mid-west farmers, taking the law into their own hands. Probably no president since Lincoln inherited a more alarming situation because of the baffled rage of the unemployed and bankrupt, and those who fear becoming so without knowing what it is all about.

Last spring, before the House Ways and Means committee, I ventured to forecast that these things would happen unless Congress then did something to reflate the price level, that is deflate the dollar, and permit payment of commitments on something like the basis on which they were undertaken.

✻ ✻ ✻

Deflation inevitably and inexorably [sic] causes depression on all places and times. Mussolini through Signor Grandi in 1928 boasted that he could bring the lira up from 3 cents to 19.3 cents. He got as far as 5 cents and nearly bankrupted the country [Italy] in the process. Fortunately he then took advice from those (including myself who had an hour's interview with him in September, 1927) who had publicly predicted what would happen, and did happen, stopped the deflation at that point, with improvement at once. As you doubtless know, England got great improvement as soon as she went off the gold standard and secured reflation and lost much of it as soon as she failed to follow through. Japan and Brazil and, I have no doubt, other countries which I have not followed also gained from reflation. Sweden stopped deflation in 1931 and is the first country to openly and fully stabilize the purchasing power of any monetary unit. As the enclosed chart shows she has, every week since she began stabilizing the Krona, maintained a fixed price level within 1¾ per cent. This was done by the [Federal Reserve] Governor [Benjamin] Strong methods. The present situation in currency cries to heaven for reflation (up to a reasonable price level about half way back) and, after such reflation, for stabilization, like Sweden's.

Much of what President Hoover did and got done through the Glass Steagall act, the Federal Reserve bond buying and the Reconstruction Finance Corporation, though belated, has helped, and three times we seemed to be started on reflation. But many things conspired to set us back again: including the threat of higher taxes and the whole budget balancing ballyhoo, the terrible campaign of fear conducted by Hoover and Mills, the technocracy craze, the Wall Street revelations, the Michigan bank holiday.

The kernel of it all is that since the stock market crash we have had (1) over indebtedness, (2) consequent

## Public Pressures 29

distress selling to try to get out of debt, (3) consequent falling prices, deflation or a swelling dollar, (4) consequently *an increase in the real debt.*

Though the debts payable in America were (according to my "Booms and Depressions") reduced in number of dollars from 234 billions in 1929 to 197 billions in 1932, the dollar was so swollen that the latter 197 was the equivalent (in terms of the original dollars of 1929) of 302 billions! Now the dollar is still bigger. Each dollar of debts is 81% more burdensome than before we started down hill. In other words the liquidation *has not really liquidated* but, on the contrary *has actually aggravated,* the debts. That is the main secret of the depression, according to my studies. It means also that the real depression may only just be beginning! The idea of Senator Glass of "going through" to the bitter end is too horrible to contemplate. Few could pay debts with doubled dollars and on halved incomes.

The idea that we already are "nearly through" is wrong, we have not made any net progress whatever but our flounderings to get out of the debt bog has only sunk us deeper and deeper in terms of real things, cotton, wheat, lumber, etc. Those who do not see this are those who only count the dollars owed but do not *measure* each dollar. They have the "money illusion" that the dollar of 1933 is the same dollar as that of 1929. No accounting is correct which does not translate our varying dollar into a uniform measure. Such an accounting will give a jolt to anyone who has never tried it. It applies to our National Debt and to every fiscal problem, public or private. Yet 99% of our people, merchants, bankers, are fooling themselves just as in the opposite way the Germans did when the mark was falling. They refused to believe it until it had fallen 98%. I know: for I went to Germany in 1922 to test it and found practically everybody just as unconcious [sic] of the terrible shrinking of the mark as most of our people are today unconcious [sic] of the terrible swelling of the dollar. Though perhaps a few millions of our people have a glimmer of these facts and principles, the majority as yet do not.

You could make the majority see it. I can understand that in the campaign you felt it important not to give a handle to those who wanted to call you "another Bryan". And I am sure Hoover and [Ogden] Mills were "laying" for you. So the public are still mystified. Hoover and Mills find it hard to be consistent favoring "controlled credit expansion" but not "currency inflation". We need a rise in the price level by the only means it can be raised or ever has been raised—an increase in the quantity or velocity, or both, of the circulating medium whether credit, paper, or gold, or all three. Hoover and Mills are right in favoring "controlled credit expansion" but wrong in trying to put you in a hole by creating a legeng [sic] about some uncontrolled and incontrollable "inflation". Some day we may have to fight inflation again. I have all my life but Hoover and Mills have no real reason to fight it now unless it be "politics". What we are fighting now is deflation. It needs to be stopped and reversed just as in 1920 inflation needed to be stopped and reversed. The reversal in each case may well be called reflation. The reflation of 1929 was somewhat overdone and the reflation which you can and in my opinion should now bring about should not be overdone. There should be no trouble about that. The German example is clearly irrelevant. The English and Swedish examples are relevant. We are now headed for more deflation. It will be ruinous economically, politically, socially. It may mean the breaking of almost every bank and so the destruction of thirty or forty billions more of "deposit currency" the bankruptcy of half of our business, the unemployment of half of our workers. For falling prices turn profit to loss and compell [sic] shut downs as they have already.

## Public Pressures 31

Of course, someday the deflation process comes to an end, an end like the end of the Chicago conflagration when almost everything in its way has been burned up.

The budget could not than [sic] be balanced for even if half or three-quarters of our national income went to taxes that would not foot even the interest bill. In other words we are headed for the bankruptcy of the Federal Government as well as of the States and Cities. Probably we cannot really balance the budget even now and trying to do so has made more deflation and has made taxation more and more impossible. Secretary Mills has done grave harm by spreading the idea that balancing the budget is a magic formula for getting out of the depression. The effort to do [that] has and for the same reason defeated itself just as has the effort to liquidation, [sic] it swells the dollar i.e. reduces the price level.

These are the terrible and terrifying realities of the present situation.

Yet even balancing the budget can be readily done as soon as reflation comes. It will restore taxable income and reduce real debts. Without reflation *first* all efforts to balance the budget will increase real debts and reduce taxable resources.

The trouble is that since Governor Strong died and after the fight between the New York Federal Reserve Bank and the Federal Reserve Board we have had no great banker or great statesman who understood [sic] the situation. Mr. Hoover came nearest but he was late and half wrong while he only partly converted Mills. [Eugene] Meyer and [Carter] Glass have never seemed to understand at all. These men resent the criticism which we economists have leveled at them but deserve it. They are subject to the "Money Illusion" as set forth in my book of that name and seem to imagine that a price level is determined by supply and demand of commodities only. They are all able men in their specialties, but are as dangerous as a chauffeur who does not understand the car he runs. If you go by their advice, you may wreck the country and yourself. I say this with only the kindliest feelings for them and, of course, for you.

Senator Glass is a master of banking technique as Mills is of taxation technique and as Meyer is of accounting and investment. On these matters their advice would be worth ten times mine. But your problem now is none of these but one of the dollar's value concerning which there are only a few experts in the world. Among them are only a few bankers like Reginald McKenna and Lord D'Abernon and the Swedish Riksbank officials.

In 1932 McKenna said to me "You and I are the only people in the world who know about this subject". Of course he said this jokingly as there are scores of economists and bankers who do understand. But he had in mind an important but painful truth that the great majority do *not* understand and what is worse, do not understand that they do not understand. In my humble opinion these are the most dangerous men at this time, however they or others may fancy that they are "safe". I am, however, astonished to find the approaching unanimity among those who have really made an intensive study of the relations of money, credit, price levels. My book on Booms and Depressions reaches substantially the same conclusion as that of Sir Arthur Salter's on Recovery, the Second Effort. I enclose a copy of a letter from Sir Josiah Stamp and of extracts from letters received from Economists whose opinions are being collected for the "Committee for the Nation" representing leading industrialists and bankers.

McKenna has fought inflation and deflation alike, but at this time after drastic deflation he wants, as you may have seen, some corrective inflation. In his last report this president of the greatest bank in the world said: "I confess the thought of inflation, so long as it is controlled, does not alarm me. In these days the word no longer is a term of reproach, though some tender consciences find ease [sic] in using the innocent substitute, reflation."

Many today say they are opposed to inflation but want a rise in prices. Every great general rise in prices ever recorded has been due to inflation and every great general fall to deflation. (See my Money Illusion pp 41–4) There is no other way. The only choice is between a planned inflation and one coming from good luck, as possible in a few years from the new gold discoveries in South Africa.

If you will take your stand with such men as McKenna you have the opportunity of a generation to serve your fellow men and make a place in history beside Washington and Lincoln, having rescued your Country and the World from debt, Slavery and pauperism and safeguarded them against such disasters in the future.

Let me add that I believe that the right sort of announcement or proclamation on March 4 would reverse the present deflation overnight and would set us on the path toward new peaks of prosperity attainable in your administration and insure a re-election by a grateful people of whom I will be one.

This may seem tall talk but I am as optimistic of results if you take what it is my conviction is the only right road (reflation and stabilization) as I am pessimistic if you take the opposite road (deflation).

Reflation, speedy and effective, I believe, is easy if you know how. Many proposals for it are useless and may even produce deflation.

So, I urge you with more earnestness then I have ever urged anything in my life, to adopt, if you have not already, the money philosophy of Strong, McKenna the Riksbank, Salter, Stamp and others who know including the majority of economic experts in this field in which so few have specialized but in which so many uninstructed assume to know and simply mislead.

*   *   *

If I have been too longwinded or superfluous I hope you will forgive me; for I cannot repress my earnestness. Were it necessary I believe I would be willing to die to secure from you the boon I believe you can deliver to your waiting fellow countrymen. I still believe it might be worth your while to check up with me in a conference on the statements in this letter if you are skeptical.

Sincerely,
IRVING FISHER

### Sketch of possible program for reflation and stabilization

(1) Choose between present gold standard, cutting the gold content in two (this will not double the price level), abandon the gold standard entirely for a managed currency (and "pegged" foreign exchanges) and shifting to a commodity standard without any remaining fiction of a gold standard. This last is my preference, but the ultimate goal can be obtained by either of the other two courses, though *the first of the three will delay* and we need speed.

(2) If the second or third of the three devices is selected make a proclamation on March 4 the details of which will be based on the gold embargo act of 1917 still unrepealed. Nothing is to be gained by further proscription here. Mr. James H. Rand, Jr., President of Remington Rand, has worked out legal opinion in his possesion which you would surely ought to see. Premature publicity would hurt, to say the least.

(3) Reserve Finance Corporation to advance 50% to depositors their frozen deposits in failed banks.

(4) United States Insure bank deposits of all *existing* banks for one year.

(5) R. F. C. lend 25% of approved inventory values and of one year's payroll.

(6) Federal Reserve resume aggressive bond buying.

(7) Repeal the loan publicity clause as to R. F. C. loan.

(8) Stop the Wall Street investigation for the present.

(9) Issue stamp script (via Senator Bankhead & Congressman Pettingill).

\* \* \*

# 6

*A Personal Triumph:*
*The Elation of Irving Fisher*

[Irving Norton Fisher, *My Father Irving Fisher* (New York: Comet Press Books, 1958), pp. 273-76.]

A week before Roosevelt's inauguration he sent the President-elect a nine-page letter outlining his current suggestions for getting the country out of the depression. When the New Deal was scarcely a month old, he returned to Washington to help draft remedial legislation. His letters to Mother describe these hectic days, with particular reference to activities of The Committee for the Nation, consisting of such business leaders as James H. Rand:

Washington, April 8, 1933

I'm at a public stenographer's waiting for her to copy the manuscript of a bill for stabilizing the dollar after reflation of the price level. The President and most members of both houses of Congress now realize that we *must* do it. The only question is *how*.

I had had a long conference with Goldsborough, Senator Bulkley of Ohio and others. Prof. [George F.] Warren of Cornell came and Rand and several of the Committee for the Nation. The people working out the details now are ex-Senator Owen, Warren, myself and Goldsborough.

Washington, April 9, 1933

Owen, Warren, Rumely, Goldsborough and I have conferred all day and will meet tomorrow, which will be the third day. Rand, Vanderlip, etc. had one program and Goldsborough and Owen another. They are now combined and after the details are all worked out the result will be taken to the President, as the united suggestion of us all.

Washington, April 12, 1933

The Committee for the Nation have been having their sessions all day both before and after seeing the President. He did not commit himself, but I am confident that he is for reflation in some way and soon.

I had a talk with Att'y Gen'l Homer Cummings, who spoke quite frankly. I assume Sec'y Woodin is the stumbling block. It is interesting to see how people's moods here go up and down just as mine have done.

I think it is true that F. D. R. is ready to change his mind easily. I believe in this for myself, but it is very worrisome to have a President do it. He seems now to be wobbly about Bank Deposit Guarantee, because New York bankers via Woodin have questioned it again. But Senator Glass, now that he has been won over to it, is as determined for it as he was against it and resents Woodin's defection.

When the President's program was fully crystallized a week later and the gold standard definitely abandoned, Father expressed his elation in this letter to Mother:

Washington, April 19, 1933

Now I *am* sure—so far as we ever can be sure of anything—that we are going to snap out of this depression fast. I am now one of the happiest men in the world. Happy that we are to get back prosperity, happy to have had a share in the work which turned the scales and in the laying of the foundations years ago. I feel that this week marks the culmination of my life work. Even if I had no more of life, I would feel that what I have had has been as worth while as any man has a right to expect.

Even you haven't really known what I've been through this last month, between the mountain and the precipice. I felt that the only hope lay, not only for the country which is the important thing but for our own little selves, in Washington here; and the balance trembled back and forth. It is evident that F. D. R. has not until recently been sure which turn to take. Now that the right turn has been taken my work is over, except for details.

My next big job is to raise money for ourselves. Probably we'll have to go to Sister again, but I hope this can be avoided. I have defaulted payments the last few weeks, because I did not think it was fair to ask Sister for money when there was a real chance that I could never pay it back.

I mean that if F. D. R. had followed Glass we would have been pretty surely ruined. So would Allied Chemical, Sister, and the U. S. Gov't. The great prairie fire was ready to destroy everything before it. *Now* I can go to Sister with a clean conscience and a restored faith that she will not lose anything.

Today the peg which kept our dollar up in foreign exchange has been pulled out. And lo! The stocks and commodities soar at once! It seems miraculous to those not versed in these mysteries. And there will be grumbling and misunderstanding without end.

Washington, May 4, 1933

I'm just back from the U. S. Chamber of Commerce dinner at which President Roosevelt spoke. It is wonderful to have things coming my way so fast. He spoke of raising the price level and getting international cooperation.

The greatest news is that last night to a group of friends he definitely committed himself to reflation to the 1926 level and *stabilizing* at that level. We may thank God that we have a President who has the knowledge, understanding and courage to see and do what must be done.

# 7

## *The Great Decision:*
## *A Walter Lippmann Interpretation*

[Walter Lippmann, *Interpretations: 1933–1935* (New York: The Macmillan Co., 1936), pp. 50–53.]

In the series of financial crises which have followed one another since the summer of 1931 each nation has finally been forced to decide whether it would defend the gold parity of its currency or its own internal price level. No nation has been able to do both. No nation has been able to maintain the value of its currency in terms of gold and also to stabilize the domestic purchasing power of its currency. A choice has had to be made between keeping up prices at home and keeping up the gold value of the currency abroad.

The first great commercial power to be confronted with this choice was Germany, in the summer of 1931. The Germans elected to maintain the gold value of the reichsmark, and in order to do this they subjected themselves to the most drastic exchange control. They have succeeded in keeping their currency at its gold parity. But wholesale prices in Germany have fallen about fifteen per cent, and the German people have been subjected to a deflation which has been so terrific that it brought about a revolution.

The second great commercial power to face the issue was Great Britain in September, 1931. The British chose the opposite course. They elected to defend their price structure rather than the gold value of their currency. The pound sterling has therefore depreciated in the outer world. But the price level in Great Britain has been virtually stable, and though British industry remains depressed, there has been no acute crisis.

## Public Pressures 41

The third great commercial power to be confronted with the choice was the United States on March 4, 1933. The paramount question of the hour is whether we shall follow the German policy of defending the gold parity of the currency or the British policy of defending the internal price structure against continuing deflation. At the present moment the choice has not been made, for the Treasury, the Federal Reserve system, and the financial community are without a clear policy.

*   *   *

The decision which has now to be taken is the most important with which this Administration is likely to be confronted. For the evidence is now, I believe, conclusive that a decision to maintain the gold parity of currency condemns the nation which makes that decision to the intolerable strain of falling prices.

Now what has to be determined here is whether the efforts now being made to maintain the gold parity of the dollar shall be persisted in or whether the dollar shall be allowed without interference to find its exchange value with the other currencies of the world. If the decision is taken to keep the dollar as the dearest currency in the world, then, for as long as that experiment lasts, we must expect the American price level to be subjected to the forces of deflation. The prospect of an adequate expansion of credit to compensate for the furious liquidation which has been going on must be given up, and in all probability the whole program to expand purchasing power through expenditures on relief and public works. Where can such a policy end accept in such a revulsion of popular feeling as to make certain the acceptance by Congress of some scheme of really wild currency inflation?

*   *   *

If the Administration is wise, it will fix its attention first of all not upon the international value of the dollar but upon its domestic value. There are financial writers and some bankers who talk as if a great national interest were served by having a dollar which is from thirty to sixty per cent more valuable than the currencies which it once exchanged with on equal terms. In the name of common sense, what national interest is served by this tremendous and unprecedented overvaluation of the dollar? For eighteen months this overvalued dollar and the few currencies, like the franc, the reichsmark, and the guilder, which are at the gold parity with it, have been the conduits by which the impact of the world depression has been concentrated on the few countries which have remained fixed to the gold standard.

\* \* \*

Our conduit was broken on March 4th, and an honorable opportunity was then presented, through the forced suspension of the gold payments, to arrest the American deflation and to proceed to raise the American price level. All the commodity markets registered the conviction, in terms of enhanced prices, that the United States would, of course, seize the opportunity to relieve itself of the crushing burden of deflation. Thus far the opportunity has been fumbled. The Treasury, which is undermanned, overworked and so busy pruning the trees that it does not see the woods, has been too unsure of itself to adopt a policy which required courage and technical competence. The Federal Reserve system has been without leadership and has had no policy worthy of the name for the past eight weeks. As a result, without realizing the consequences or intending to suffer them, we have allowed a control of foreign exchange to be set up which, with the help of the British, maintains the dollar at an artificial overvaluation, and thus clamps down upon the American economy a deflationary policy.

\* \* \*

## Public Pressures 43

What are the consequences? On the one hand, the Administration is pushed further and further toward schemes like the farm bill, the thirty-hour bill, and these latest proposals for "mobilizing" industry, all of them hopelessly intricate devices to counteract the effect of a general fall in prices. On the other hand, Congress, which is hearing from home about the consequences of the deflation, is moving nearer and nearer to some form of inflation by fiat.

For those who wish to avoid both the kind of paternalism which is exemplified by the farm bill and the kind of inflation which is popular in Congress, there is a course of action open which has been tested by many countries and is almost certain to bring substantial relief. That course is to keep gold payments suspended, to let the dollar depreciate in terms of gold, and to support the government credit and the capital market by a policy of credit expansion which is regulated not by gold but by the price level. I do not say that this monetary policy will make us prosperous immediately. I do most thoroughly believe that it will stop the economic rot and permit us to recover. And I believe that if we fail to take this course the depression will become still deeper and still more acute.

*  *  *

That this policy will be regarded as gravely heretical by many experienced and accomplished men, I am fully aware. But these are times when men must be willing to accept the conclusions of the evidence as they see it, and be ready to take the risks of stating their conclusions. To my mind a study of the experience of the nations which have chosen one or the other of the two alternative courses provides overwhelming evidence that the safer and wiser course is to defend the internal price structure rather than the external value of the currency.

## 8

*Conservatives for Inflation:*
*The Committee for the Nation*

["Vanderlip Favors End of Gold Basis," *New York Times*, March 6, 1933, p. 6.]

A plan to deal with the financial situation by abandoning the gold standard and changing the country's banking and monetary systems was announced here yesterday by representatives of industry and farm organizations as the first move of a campaign to obtain Federal action on their suggestions. The plan was made public before the President's proclamation was issued.

Frank A. Vanderlip, chairman, said that the group was organized several weeks ago under the title of Committee for the Nation, to study various remedies for a bank crisis. The plan was embodied in an interim report, prepared on Feb. 26 for submission to business men and to members of Congress. It had been the intention of the backers of the plan to keep it secret temporarily and this was done until the nation-wide bank holidays made secrecy no longer necessary.

In its specific provisions, the interim report recommended a suspension of specie payments by the government; an embargo to halt gold exports; a restricted Federal guarantee of bank deposits; legislation for complete separation of investment and commercial banking, and an enforced increase of commodity prices.

### Devaluation of Dollar Suggested

To carry out this last aim the committee suggested "study" of a plan to "devaluate" the dollar by reduction of its gold content, in accordance with a fluctuating standard fixed by commodity price index numbers of the Department of Commerce. This proposal for a compensated dollar would have the same effect as inflation upon creditors, members of the committee admitted. They argued, however, that it would be a lesser evil than the outright issuance of flat money.

The details of the plan were submitted to the President's advisers, including Secretary of the Treasury Woodin, Mr. Vanderlip said, but as yet the administration has taken no stand on the proposals.

The plan was shown to Governor Lehman yesterday at his Park Avenue apartment. He inspected it but withheld comment.

## Signers of Report

Besides Mr. Vanderlip, persons who signed the interim report embodying the plan were:

J. H. RAND, JR., president Remington Rand, Inc., Buffalo.

FRED H. SEXAUER, president Dairyman's League Cooperative Association, Inc., New York.

FREDERIC H. FRAZIER, chairman of the board of the General Baking Company of New York.

JOHN HENRY HAMMOND, who is chairman of the board Bangor & Aroostook Railroad.

GENERAL R. R. WOOD, president Sears, Roebuck & Co., Chicago.

LESSING J. ROSENWALD, chairman Sears, Roebuck & Co., Philadelphia.

VINCENT BENDIX, president Bendix Aviation Corporation, Chicago.

SAMUEL S. FELS, president Fels & Co., Philadelphia.

E. L. NORTON, chairman Freeport Texas Corporation, New York.

PHILIP K. WRIGLEY, president William Wrigley Jr. Company of Chicago.

J. D. MILLER, president National Cooperative Council, Washington, D. C.

HARRY HARTKE, president National Cooperative Mill Producers Federation, Washington, D. C.

HOWARD E. COFFIN, chairman Southeastern Cotton, Inc.

R. J. ANDERSEN, assistant to the president Dairymen's League Cooperative Association.

EDWARD A. O'NEAL, president American Farm Bureau Federation.

L. J. TABER, Master National Grange.

GERARD S. NOLLEN, president Bankers Life Insurance Company.

FARNY R. WURLITZER, vice president Rudolph Wurlitzer Manufacturing Company.

E. I. MC CLINTOCH, Bayer Company.

WILLIAM J. MC AVEENY, president, Hudson Motor Car Company.

HENRY POPE SR., president, Bear Brand Hosiery Company, Chicago.

JOHN W. KISER, president, Phenix Manufacturing Co., Chicago.

WILLIAM A. WIRT, banker, Gary, Ind.

The survey on which the committee based its recommendations was prepared on the basis of reports by the National Industrial Conference Board and on interviews with bankers, industrialists and financial experts. Drawing an extremely pessimistic picture of the banking situation in the United States, the report called attention to the present situation regarding debt, bank failures, the general decline in purchasing power, the urban mortgage situation and the necessity for extensive financial operations by the government this year.

In its discussion of the gold standard the committee declared that the development of international securities markets had made it possible to transfer gold from one country to another "with telegraphic speed," since securities "can be turned into a bank deposit and thus into an effective demand for gold at short notice." This state of affairs, the report said, has resulted in an acute difficulty with respect to maintenance of the gold standard.

# 9

## *An Agrarian Perspective: The George Warren Thesis*

[George F. Warren, "Is Our Gold Standard Too Rigid?" *Forum*, vol. 89 (April, 1933), pp. 194–201.]

The economic catastrophe in which we find ourselves is due to a fall in commodity prices. What made prices fall? A correct diagnosis must precede a constructive policy. The reason why no progress has been made in curing the depression is that the cause of it is not generally known. One tabulation gives 118 assumed causes, about as many as the assumed causes of typhoid fever before the one cause was known.

* * *

So far as the writer has observed, no person who has studied the statistics of production has found any evidence to support the thesis that overproduction caused the depression, nor has he found any record of a person who now explains the depression on the basis of production who foresaw the depression. Correct forecasts were made on the basis of monetary factors.

There is a great difference between overproduction and underconsumption due to unemployment. If the trouble is overproduction, it can easily be cured by cutting production. If it is underconsumption, we must find a way to put the unemployed to work so that they can consume, rather than attempt to cut production to what an unemployed man can buy.

* * *

## Not a Business Cycle

The depression is not a business cycle. It has no more relationship to a business cycle than a tidal wave has to a tide. This is a collapse in the price structure from which there is no cyclical recovery. During such a collapse, several suppressed business cycles may occur. A favorable cycle in the textile and shoe industries occurred in 1932.

## Not Too Much Democracy

By specialization, each of us produces so much of something that each of us can have more of everything. The battery that keeps this modern machine running is the medium of exchange—money. When money is stable in value, the machine works well. When inflation occurs, it runs too fast. When deflation occurs, it stalls. Since the exchange of goods is stopped, unemployment occurs, and there is starvation in the midst of plenty.

The millions of unemployed in cities would like to produce goods that the farmers want in exchange for food. The farmers would like to exchange food for things that these unemployed persons would gladly produce. But the medium of exchange has broken down. It has also broken down as between workers within the cities. The unemployed carpenter would like to build a house for the unemployed textile worker, who, in turn, would like to make textiles in exchange for house rent. But since the exchange system has broken down, both are unemployed. In some cases, we have reversion to barter, but our civilization is too complex to allow this to go far.

Most of us believe in a society organized on the basis of individual initiative; that is, a capitalistic society. The operation of such a society depends on the medium of exchange. When the medium of exchange fails to function, the organization of society that depends on this medium is attacked. If we cannot invent a stable measure of value, there is danger of forcing some kind of a socialistic state that will attempt to regulate distribution and production by government action.

When the battery of an automobile fails to function, we should get a new battery rather than turn to a wheelbarrow. If we are to discard automobile transportation, it should be on the merits of the automobile and not on the accident of a defective battery. If we are to adopt state capitalism, socialism, or communism, it should be on the relative merits of these systems rather than because of a failure of the medium of exchange to function properly. The thing to correct is not the organization of society but the tool that is not working properly.

## *Not Tariffs*

The depression is not due to tariffs. We forget our time schedule. The depression of 1920 came at a time when we had a low Democratic tariff. Harding proposed to cure the depression by raising the tariff, and we have since cured it once more by the same method. The movement to raise tariffs all over the world has come as a result of falling prices. Tariffs are a futile attempt to prevent prices from falling when gold is rising in value. The way to get rid of tariffs is to restore prices, and tariffs will gradually be lowered. While excessive tariffs are a result of depression, they in turn cause further trouble.

## *Not Lack of Confidence*

Neither is the depression caused by lack of confidence. Here again, we must watch our time schedule. Certainly there was plenty of confidence in 1929; and ever since, there has been too much confidence. Many persons thought that the depression was over in the fall of 1929, in the fall of 1930, again in the fall of 1931, and again last fall. This over-confidence has continually led to further losses and has prevented the adoption of remedial measures. The Coué idea was given a good trial last year when the Federal Government helped credit agencies to expand credit, with the idea that confidence was the trouble. There is still misplaced confidence. Many persons think that we can start a building boom even though we have bankrupt supplies of buildings on the market.

\* \* \*

There are four factors in prices, not two, as is commonly supposed. This error has been the cause of innumerable business failures and of much foolish legislation. The price of wheat is the ratio of the supply of wheat and demand for it to the supply of gold and the demand for it.

Our present measure of value is a given weight of a single commodity, the value of which changes with the supply of this commodity, and the demand for it, in precisely the same way as the value of any other commodity changes.

The "money illusion" is as thoroughly dominant in this generation as was the illusion of a flat earth about which the sun revolved in the time of Galileo. It is almost as dangerous for an economist to challenge the money illusion as it was for Galileo to threaten the foundations of civilization by saying that the earth revolved.

## Relation of Gold to Prices

If the explanation of the depression is not to be found in the supply of commodities, we must turn to one of the other three factors for an explanation.

The demand for commodities was good at the time the collapse occurred. The severe unemployment has reduced demand, but this is primarily a result of, rather than the initial cause of the depression. The reduced demand resulting from depression is in turn a cause of further depression.

The supply of gold has not been keeping pace with the normal growth of business, but the supply of gold is sufficient to support prices at about the pre-war level with all the world back on a gold basis, and gold used with pre-war efficiency.

The depression was caused by the fourth factor in price—demand for gold. This was so low as to allow prices on a gold basis to double. This was followed by a demand so high as to cause the present depression.

## Why Did Prices Fall?

During the war, prices on a gold basis doubled. How did this occur? For the very simple reason that most of the world not only abandoned the gold standard—it stopped bidding for gold. Gold therefore moved to the few places where it was freely purchased. The low demand reduced its value. The value of gold is determined by world supply and world demand, not by location.

\* \*

## Deflation or Reflation?

The price level must be raised to the debt level, or the debt level must be lowered to the price level. This is a matter of grim reality that cannot be cured by psychology, confidence, or government lending.

We must choose between deflation and reflation. No country likes to change its monetary system, nor does any country like to go through wholesale bankruptcies and continue to have millions of unemployed. Our choice is not between two desirable things. It is between two undesirable things. Merely raising the well-known objections to either procedure does not commend the other. The question is: "Which is worse?"

If we wish to go through with deflation, we may as well proceed with the bankruptcies, foreclosures, and public defaults and get them over with. Merely postponing by lending some money or attempting to hold up the price of this thing or that thing, will accomplish very little.

At the new price levels, public and private debts are nearly equal to the national wealth. These debts will have to be reduced. The only plan thus far proposed for reducing them is bankruptcy and private adjustment. This will probably require three or four years for the major adjustment and a generation to complete the process. While the more serious part of this is taking place, bankrupt homes, farms, and other properties will always be for sale at less than new costs of construction, regardless of how long these costs may fall. Therefore little building of any kind is to be expected. Consequently most of the basic industries will operate at low capacity and severe unemployment will be continuous. Business cycles in such a period will be suppressed cycles.

The vigorous efforts to reduce taxes will do well if they succeed in making cuts equal to the new taxes necessary to feed the unemployed. Some shifting from real estate to other forms of taxation may occur.

Public debts will increase and some of the government units will find it impossible to meet their obligations. It will be years before taxpayers get these debts paid.

Adjusting a price level down requires much more time than adjusting it up. It is not difficult to adjust public and private debts to a higher price level, but it is very difficult to reduce them. To adjust debts up merely requires that the usual purchases be made at the new price level with the usual percentage of credit transactions. To adjust debts down means the slow process of bankruptcy. Bankruptcy acts like a house of cards—each bankruptcy starts another.

Large numbers of corporations will disappear by bankruptcy or by combination to avoid bankruptcy. Wholesale writing down of the capital of industrial plants, farms, and city real estate will be necessary. Costs of distribution will gradually decline so that prices paid to farmers will again come into adjustment with the prices which they pay. Much of this can be done in a half-dozen years. Probably it can be completed in a generation.

Some basic commodity prices have fallen too low even for the conditions, and will rise.

Innumerable measures will be tried in attempts to hold up prices of this or that thing. Tariffs, bounties, farm boards, domestic allotments, restrictions on trade between states under sanitary and other guises, pools, gentlemen's agreements, and many others will continue to be tried. Some of these may do a little good, but they will continue to result in disillusion and disappointment. Maintaining the present price of gold means bringing the whole debt and price structure down. To attempt to hold each individual thing up and yet bring down the whole is like sinking a ship but attempting to hold up each rivet and doorknob in it.

Nothing is gained by minimizing the gravity of the situation. Repeated confidence statements cannot change the fact. They discredit leadership and cause losses to innumerable individuals through false hopes. While the country has never before experienced as great deflation as we are now attempting, we have had experiences which indicate the probable length of the deflation disease. It usually takes six or seven years to go far enough with the bankruptcy process so that construction can begin, and it takes many more years fully to complete the process.

It is not improbable that the high value of gold will result in discoveries of it, so that a later generation will have inflation.

If the process is carried through, a new generation can be prosperous—except as foolish laws remain to plague it. Any price level is satisfactory after business is adjusted to it.

* * *

*Reflation*

The effect of any given rise in prices is the same regardless of the cause. If for any reason the price level is restored, it does not mean that all prices will rise equally. Many prices have not declined, or have declined little. Restoring the price level would relieve them of the necessity of declining. The major ones are debts and taxes. If commodity prices were raised, buying would begin because rising prices cause buying. Jobs would be available. Houses would be in demand. The debts and taxes on the houses and farms could be paid, and the debts would not have to be cut by bankruptcy.

Many charges, such as freight rates, doctors' fees, telephone rates, and the like, are already adjusted to the price level that would be established. They would not rise, but would be relieved from falling.

Costs of distribution would rise very little. Therefore, prices paid to farmers and other producers would rise much more than retail prices. This would bring farm prices into adjustment with other prices. It is sometimes said that two steps are necessary: first, restore the price level, and second, restore the relationships of farm prices to other prices. If the first step is taken, the second follows automatically.

As workers began to be employed, they would buy goods and clothing and start business. Later they would move back into their former homes which are now vacant. Real estate values would gradually be restored. To restore reasonably well balanced business relationships and get the population back to work will take time.

## *What Stabilization Means*

Stabilizing the commodity price level does not mean that any single commodity will be free from fluctuations in price due to the supply of it or the demand for it. It does mean that commodity prices as a whole may be freed from being swept up or down as a mass due either to world supply of gold or frantic changes in the demands for it. There are many proposals for limited or complete stabilization.

## *Credit Expansion*

Some persons believe that all that is necessary is to expand bank credit. The same persons by the same reasoning thought that prices would not fall. This was the reasoning back of the billions that were lent to other countries from 1922 to 1929.

Some say that "confidence" is all that is needed. To imagine that after the greatest period of monetary chaos in history we are suddenly to have such a phenomenal world-wide growth in confidence is certainly optimistic.

A gradual and slow increase in the amount of monetary circulation plus bank deposits per dollar of gold in the United States has been taking place for many years. There is no indication that the Federal Reserve System has speeded up this normal growth of circulation plus credit per dollar of gold. Whenever the normal is much exceeded, a reaction occurs.

By the management of credit, it is possible to throw commodity prices out of line with gold by a limited amount. There is no indication that any permanent change in this relationship can be accomplished in this way. Overexpansion of credit brings on a reaction, and so does overcontraction of credit. The policy of the Federal Government in 1932 was based on the theory that prices could be raised by credit. The Reconstruction Finance Corporation lent money to many agencies in the expectation that credit expansion by the Reconstruction Finance Corporation and the Federal Reserve Banks would raise prices and restore equities back of securities and start business activity. The policy did check contraction, temporarily; but only a rise in the price structure can stop bankruptcies and start employment. It is not possible to expand credit sufficiently to do this and still maintain the present price of gold.

## Currency Expansion

It is very easy to raise the price level by an expansion of the currency, but any expansion that is sufficient to restore prices of commodities to the debt level would make it impossible to continue to redeem each of the paper dollars with 23.22 grains of gold. There is no way of printing paper money that will make it possible materially to change the relative values of gold and commodities.

Any means of restoring prices will probably require suspension of gold payments while the plan is being discussed. This has now been done by all other important countries except those that have already cut the weight of gold in their money.

This does not mean wild inflation. The only cases of wild inflation have come after government bankruptcy. During the American and French Revolutions, both countries inflated until the money was "not worth a Continental." Similar inflation occurred during the German Revolution and attempts to pay reparations. Russia is in a revolutionary period and has had violent inflation.

England suspended gold payments for 24 years in the Napoleonic War period. She also suspended gold payments from 1914 to 1925 and now has suspended for more than a year. This makes a total of 36 out of 136 years off gold, but no case of wild inflation has occurred.

The United States has suspended gold payments four times, but even in the Civil War did not have wild inflation. Our average prices for the year 1864 were 193. Prices in England on a gold basis were 127. The worst inflation that has occurred since the Revolutionary War was on a gold basis in 1920, when prices averaged 226.

There is no danger of wild inflation except following revolution. If we should be forced to suspend gold payments, violent price fluctuations are to be expected for a time, but there is no cause for alarm about wild inflation.

## Re-valuation

Most of the continent of Europe has reduced the weight of gold in the monetary unit. It is probable that England and the 31 other countries that have suspended the gold standard will do the same. If so, this will leave the United States as one of the very few countries that attempt to maintain the pre-war price of gold regardless of the supply of it or demand for it.

By reducing the weight of gold in the dollar, any desired price level can be established. The future course of prices would depend on the future supply of gold and future demand for gold. Re-valuation is a simple emergency measure. It does not make provision for future stability. The question may well be raised as to whether the time has not come for the adoption of a more stable measure of value.

## Managed Currency

Two proposals have been advanced to provide for a permanently stable measure of value. One of these proposes a managed currency to be controlled in such a way as to keep the average of commodity prices stable. To operate such a system would require willingness and intelligence in the management, and freedom from influence by politics or desire for profit.

At innumerable times, after the failure of the gold standard, a managed currency has been operated with a considerable degree of success. England had such a currency from 1914 to 1925 and has had such a currency since September 1931. Prices in England since she left the gold standard have been more stable than prices here. Apparently, such a country as England could permanently operate such a currency successfully. The possibility of a managed currency should not be judged entirely by its success or failure when conditions are so bad that the gold standard has failed. Probably most countries will prefer a metal reserve.

## The Compensated Dollar

The compensated dollar is a proposal to establish by law a currency redeemable in gold, but the weight of gold for which the dollar would exchange would vary with the index number of wholesale prices of all commodities; that is, if prices rose 1 per cent, the weight of gold for which the dollar would exchange would rise 1 per cent. If prices fell 1 per cent, the dollar would exchange for 1 per cent less gold. The gold would be kept in bars in the Treasury and central banks. This would keep the dollar stable in buying power for the average of all commodities.

The dollar has to be rubber either as to weight or as to value. It cannot have a fixed weight and also have a fixed value. This proposal would give it a fixed value and a rubber weight. It raises the fundamental question as to whether a medium of exchange should be fixed in weight or fixed in value.

A scientific money is one with a constant buying power for all commodities rather than a fixed weight of one commodity. Our whole tax and debt structure rests on commodity prices. If this structure is to be kept sound either for the creditor or the debtor, it is commodity prices that need to be kept stable, not the weight of gold for which a dollar will exchange.

## Remonetization of Silver

By adopting bimetallism or symmetallism, it is possible to set any price level that is desired. If silver is remonetized, it should certainly be done by symmetallism, as proposed by the great English economist, Alfred Marshall. This proposal is now receiving considerable attention in England. It is very simple. Instead of having a dollar exchange for 23.22 grains of gold, it would exchange for some given weight of gold plus a given weight of silver. Since two commodities are more stable than one, and since silver production is less erratic than gold production, such a money would be more stable than gold. If once established, it would work in the same way in which the gold standard works, except for greater stability. It could be used as a basis for a compensated dollar.

## International Co-operation

Certainly international debts need reconsideration, but it is the debts owed by Americans to Americans in America that are the principal problem. Nothing that can be done about foreign debts will pay John Jones' mortgage on his house or farm. Bad as are the tariffs and trade restrictions set up by every country in the effort to hold up prices, the greatest problem of commerce is to re-establish the exchange system between Americans in America. To wait for endless conferences is futile. We should either deflate as quickly as possible, or reflate. No one but Congress has authority over our currency. If we adopt a wise monetary policy, it will have far-reaching international influence.

## *The Gold Clause*

A considerable number of bonds in the United States call for payment in a gold dollar of present weight and fineness. This does not apply to Federal Land Bank bonds or mortgages, nor to most of the mortgages of joint stock land banks and life insurance companies. These agencies agree to pay their creditors in lawful money and are therefore protected if they collect lawful money from their debtors.

The problem to-day is not whether creditors will be paid in any particular brand of a dollar, but whether they will get anything. Sometimes they get less than nothing, for they get a non-income-paying property with delinquent taxes. If the dollar is revalued Congress will probably invalidate such contracts.

# 10

## *Would It Help Us to Go Off Gold?:*
## *A Qualified Affirmative*

["Would It Help Us to Go Off Gold?" *The New Republic*, vol. 74 (March 1, 1933), pp. 59–61.]

Mr. H. N. Brailsford's article in this issue of *The New Republic* indicates why it will be difficult for Mr. Roosevelt to make a bargain by which the United States will concede something on war debts for a restoration of the gold standard by Great Britain. Even the more conservative forces in London, who look forward to a return to gold some time, though on a new parity, are not inclined to take that step before June 15.

In the meantime, the fact that the world has no stable medium of international exchange will obstruct revival of trade. And the agitation in the United States for inflation, already making rapid strides among the farmers, is likely to gain strength. In particular, the proposal to devaluate the dollar by a change in its gold content will be pushed. Mr. Brailsford's account of the British experience may be used to make out a good case for this course. It appears, according to his argument, that Britain has, by going off gold, at once relieved debtors and stabilized prices. Why, it will be said, should we not join the British, if not in going off gold entirely, at least in a depreciated currency which would relieve debtors at home and would repair the fault abroad between the gold dollar and the depreciated pound?

*The New Republic* has no superstitious reverence for the gold standard, and would welcome any good means for lessening the existing burden of debt. A relatively stable currency, capable of being held at a constant ratio to other currencies, is the ultimately desired objective, no matter whether it is based on gold or not. But we have grave doubts whether the proposal to change the gold content in the dollar—or even to abandon the gold standard entirely—would in itself accomplish the results which its proponents desire.

Let us be clear on one crucial point. If any change in the basis of currency is to relieve debtors at the expense of creditors, it must do so through a change in the prices of commodities and services. If, for instance, the farmer is to be rendered better able to pay the mortgage on his farm (without a reduction in the interest or principal of the mortgage), this result can be achieved only through an increase in the prices of wheat, hogs, cotton, etc. On this point Mr. Brailsford, usually an acute observer of economic affairs, seems to us to have made a slip. In what sense has going off gold reduced the British debt burden? British debts owed in countries still on gold have, of course, been rendered more onerous. British debts owed in countries which have gone off gold, and which use currencies linked to sterling, have not been affected at all. And British internal debts cannot have been lightened if British internal prices have not risen. If the manufacturer and the farmer receive no more for their products, and the wage earner's pay has not increased, it is now just as hard for them to pay their debts as it was before the gold standard crumbled. An inflation which does not increase prices, either relatively to other prices or absolutely, is not an inflation.

Could abandonment of the gold standard, or a reduction of the gold content in the dollar, affect prices in this country? Some advocates of such measures talk as if there were a magic process by which the passage of a law to this effect would overnight change the price of everything. They talk as if prices were directly related to gold. But of course that is not so. Gold operates in our system merely as a reserve back of currency and bank credit. It affects prices only in so far as it affects the value of the means of payment in use. If the available supply of currency and credit were insufficient because there was not enough gold in our reserves, an abandonment of the gold standard or a reduction of the gold content in the dollar would, by permitting expansion of currency and credit, tend to raise prices. But this is not the case. We have large excess reserves. The trouble is not that we have not a sufficient supply of currency and credit—in the banks. The trouble is that they are not being used in business and trade. We could change to a dirt standard without in the least affecting our internal price level. If business and trade actually were using all the credit now available without going off gold, we should probably have price increases which would more than satisfy the wildest inflationist.

It is only in foreign trade that a change in the gold standard might help. At present it costs a great deal for Great Britain and other countries which have gone off gold to buy in the United States. You have to pay a great many more pounds than before to buy a certain number of dollars. Therefore, it is argued, if we passed a law saying that a dollar were worth, say, only half as much gold as before, foreign nations could buy more of our wheat, cotton, automobiles, etc. This would tend to raise prices in the United States.

There is a possibility that this might happen, but in our opinion only a faint possibility. The exchange price of a currency on the gold standard appears to be held within narrow limits by the amount of gold which, by law, the unit of currency is worth. Let the price of the gold dollar rise too high in terms of gold pounds, and gold will flow from England to the United States until the old parity is resumed. Therefore it is easy to infer that if you change the gold content of either currency, you at once change their prices relative to each other. But, in a situation like the present, this is putting the cart before the horse. The pound did not depreciate in terms of the dollar because England went off the gold standard, but England went off the gold standard because the pound depreciated in terms of the dollar. The supply of pounds in the market seeking conversion to dollars was so much greater than the supply of dollars seeking pounds that there was a steady and enormous pressure on the price of the pound, too great for any possible flow of gold to remedy. Great Britain therefore had to stop the outflow of gold and let the price of the pound sink.

This means that the relative value of currencies is ultimately fixed, not by legislation or by gold standards, but by the relative demand for and supply of the currencies. This in turn depends on the balance of payments between the countries, arising from trade both visible and invisible, and from international financial transactions. Nothing at all would now happen to the exchange relationships between the pound and the dollar as a direct result of any legislation fixing another gold value of the dollar, or depriving it of gold value altogether. Pounds could buy more dollars only if Englishmen bought less than at present in the United States or invested and loaned less money here, or if Americans bought more in England than at present or loaned more money there.

Even assuming, however, that going off gold would in some way give rise to more European demand for American exports, there is still the probability that the potentially importing countries, all at present bent on national self-sufficiency, would increase tariffs and further restrict import quotas to neutralize American competition with their own producers. Unless something is done about these restrictions on trade, any other device aimed at world revival is certain to be futile.

The conclusion of the whole matter seems to be that in efforts to revive both domestic and foreign trade, tinkering with currencies is a blind alley. It is indeed desirable to promise stability in currencies and to facilitate stable exchanges. But any attempt to achieve this result by currency or banking policy alone is based on a misunderstanding of the way economic processes work, on a reversal of cause and effect. What we have to do is to control the relationships among prices and incomes, to regulate production, investment and the specific uses of credit. Only out of a successful and comprehensive effort to master our whole economic structure can a desirable effect on prices arise.

# Section Two

# Congressional Pressures

*Commentary*

Congressional agitation inspired much of the New Deal. The Black Thirty-Hour Bill provoked the National Industrial Recovery Act (NIRA). The abortive La Follette-Costigan bill of February 1932 prepared the way for the Public Works Administration and the Federal Emergency Relief Administration. The Wagner-Lewis and Dill-Connery bills, together with the Townsend Plan rumblings, moved a reluctant Roosevelt to support social security. Senator Robert F. Wagner of New York had written a version of the National Labor Relations Act a year before the demise of Section 7(a) of the NIRA obligated the President to protect the collective bargaining gains of organized labor. Congress "played a vital and consistently underestimated role in shaping the New Deal," Arthur M. Schlesinger, Jr., correctly observes. "In these early years, Congress was as often to the left of Roosevelt as to the right." Similarly, legislative initiative certainly played a large role in forcing Roosevelt's decision to jettison the gold standard.

Rural southern and western congressmen united in the early thirties in a campaign to boost commodity prices by devaluing gold. The Bryanite sentiment was surprisingly extensive. During the Hoover years, even a conservative Republican representative from Southampton County, Virginia, Menalcus Lankford, dared to question the worth of a gold standard the American people might "strangle" on (Doc. 11). Several agrarian legislators voiced economic biases that were distinctly reminiscent of the Greenbackers and Populists. Senator Smith W. Brookhart, a Republican Progressive from Iowa's corn country, charged that the gold standard protected the wealth of only a few while acting as a major cause of economic dislocation (Doc. 12). The leadership derided its Senate pariahs such as Brookhart, Huey Long, and Burton Wheeler, dubbing them "cranks" because of their peculiar monetary notions. But as it became more fashionable to fault the gold standard for low commodity prices, the agricultural bloc combined with inflationists from the silver states; the Thomas amendment to the agricultural bill of 1933 became the *sine qua non* for inflation.

As Joseph Reeve suggests, Senator Elmer Thomas of Oklahoma, author of the amendment, used his scant knowledge of economics to create an illusion of expertise (Doc. 13). Nevertheless, Thomas' amendment had wide appeal because of the relative ignorance of most lawmakers on monetary matters. Of course the Thomas solution seemed simplistic to conservatives, but many agrarians had come to believe that, in a nation of abundance, only a conspiracy by bankers could deny sustenance to the needy. The answer, therefore, lay in doing exactly what the moguls of Wall Street seemed to fear most, thereby breaking their stranglehold over money.

Inflation bills had proliferated in 1932, and in April 1933, the silver monetizers allied themselves with debtor farmers behind the Wheeler amendment to the farm bill (Doc. 14). On April 17, the Senate defeated Wheeler's Free Silver proposal but the Roosevelt Administration took note that the result would have been different if six senators had voted the other way. The stage had been set for passage of the more moderate Thomas amendment. Roosevelt had the option of controlling monetary inflation with Executive powers or antagonizing some of those Democrats who had been most loyal to him. The choice was never in doubt; the Thomas amendment, silver, and higher commodity prices won. The gold standard was doomed.

## 11

*The Debtor Needs a Devalued Dollar: A Southerner Speaks Out*

[*Congressional Record*, 72nd Cong., 1st sess. (Jan. 7, 1932), pp. 1460–61.]

Mr. [Menalcus] Lankford of Virginia. Mr. Speaker, this country, like a mighty giant arising groggy and unsteady from the knockout delivered it by the great depression, is becoming dimly and vaguely conscious of the fact that one of the main troubles it has had to contend with is the rising value of the dollar, and that probably the solution of its difficulties will be reducing the value of the dollar to somewhere near its commodity value.

Nations, States, cities, railroads, corporations of all kinds, and individuals are staggering beneath a load of debt that it is impossible to carry. With the rapid rise of the value of the dollar and the decline of commodity and all other values, it is impossible to meet these staggering obligations.

There is no possibility of bonds or obligations being reduced or canceled voluntarily, and unless the value of the dollar with which these obligations must be paid is decreased, no solution appears save universal bankruptcy, which will wipe them all out and allow us to start over again.

Certainly no one wants to contemplate such a dire remedy for existing conditions, but it seems to me that it is time for the country to give the most careful and painstaking attention to this question, and especially the holders of bonds, mortgages, and securities of all kinds, who would generally oppose any deflation in value of the dollar, for unless some relief is given they may wake up some fine morning to find their securities valueless.

## Congressional Pressures 71

The value of the dollar has risen so rapidly in the last two years that commodities which were worth $1 three years ago are now worth about 25 cents. In other words, commodity values have declined compared to the value of the gold dollar approximately 75 per cent, or the value of the dollar has risen 75 per cent. Either way it is an unhappy and unhealthy situation. This is true of real estate, cotton, wheat, tobacco, as well as of manufactured products.

Money—dollars—seems to be the only thing left that has value and in which the people have confidence. Farm products are worth next to nothing; farms and city real estate are invariably sold to the holder of the mortgage, for neither farms nor city real estate, nor commodities can compete with the dollar for the confidence of the man who has money to invest.

The result is the greatest era of hoarding in the history of the country—billions of idle capital hoarded, useless because the owners have more confidence and faith in dollars than anything they can buy with them; hence they save them and keep them out of the channels of trade where they would be beneficial to all.

The only way, therefore, it seems to me to bring them out of hiding and to put them into circulation is to decrease their value, so that they will seek investment in commodities, using this term in its broadest sense. As long as they have the high value placed on them to-day they will stay in hiding and not be exchanged for any commodity, real, personal, or mixed.

And yet it is with these same high-value dollars that the immense debts which burden States, cities, railroads, corporations, and individuals must be paid.

Business is gone, but the debts remain. All ambition, hope, enterprise is destroyed by the individual or group laboring under these impossible conditions.

Internationally what do we see? Practically every other large nation but the United States and France has abandoned the gold standard. It requires so much more of the goods, wares, and merchandise of these nations which have left the gold standard in exchange for our gold dollar that they are greatly hampered in selling to us, and our goods produced on a gold standard are so high in comparison with their commodity value that they can not buy from us.

The result may well be that our customers may soon seek other nations on a similar money standard with themselves with which to do business, and this trade, once established and connections once made, will be difficult, if not impossible, to recover.

I do not advocate abandoning the gold standard, neither do I believe in permitting the business and people of the United States to be strangled by the gold standard if such proves to be the case.

My suggestion is to reduce the value of the dollar as the only possible means by which the staggering load of debts can be paid, so that the vast amounts now in hiding will have to seek more profitable investment, and so that we in the United States can compete in foreign markets on a more equitable basis with the other nations who have abandoned the gold standard before it is too late and our foreign trade has sought other channels, and let the result be what it may to the gold standard. If it is sound and stands the strain in this time of great need, so well and good. If not, we had better seek another principle of exchange; and now that this question has reached a crisis, it is very well, it seems to me, for the leading economists of the country to study this question as never before to determine whether this is the best we can expect in our high state of enlightenment, or is there a better plan.

## 12

## *In the Greenbacker and Populist Spirit: A Voice from the Farm Belt*

[Smith W. Brookhart, "Let's Abandon the Gold Standard," *Forum*, vol. 88 (July 1932), pp. 10–12.]

According to the charts of Colonel Leonard P. Ayres, eminent statistician, we have had eight major depressions and eight cycles of inflation and depression in the past fifty years. Measurement of his graphs reveals scarcely thirty minutes of normal in the entire period, and now at the end of all our growth and development we find ourselves overwhelmed by the greatest bubble of inflation followed by the deepest and most persistent depression in all our history.

It is far from my purpose to charge all this calamity to the delinquency of the gold standard, but it has utterly failed to protect us, and I do think it is a substantial part among the causes of our troubles. Questions concerning it have been asked by the economists in scientific terms for a long time, and now they are being asked by the ordinary business man, the farmer, and the laborer. Is the gold standard a stable standard? Is it an honest standard? Did it give us prosperity? Did it drive us into our present and unyielding state of depression? Did it cause those former cycles of inflation and depression?

The bankers are still afraid to answer directly, although eight thousand banks have failed in spite of the protecting power of the gold standard and under the paternal care of the Federal Reserve System. And the statesmen talk in confidential terms only in the cloak rooms. The public is thus left to figure out its own conclusions. These conclusions are now coming with resounding force from every direction. They reached me a year ago with such emphasis that I decided to give them intensive study and answer them to my own satisfaction and, if possible, for the service of my constituency. . . .

## *Not World-Wide; Not Caused by War*

As I said, I do not claim the gold standard to be the only cause of our great depression, nor do I hold that its correction alone would restore prosperity. But neither do I believe that the depression is world-wide and that it was caused by the war. The Soviet Union is in the highest state of prosperity in all Russian history. Its 160 million people now have something to eat, and everyone has a job. There is no unemployment and no depression. Russia's prosperity is slackened by outside conditions, but it moves on irresistibly.

As for the war—when it began we were a debtor nation, owing other countries several billion dollars. In a little while we paid them all from war profits. After we entered the war the government levied taxes on other war profits and finally collected enough to lend more than 10 billion dollars to other countries; private industry and banking loaned even more—according to some estimates 15 or 16 billion dollars more. Meanwhile our national debt was paid down to 16 billion dollars. When all is totaled up we profited from the war. The foreign loans contributed to the causes of the depression, but they were not part of the war itself.

I find the causes of the depression at home—mainly in the laws of the Congress, assisted to some extent by state laws. Our annual national income in the prosperous years after the war was about 90 billion dollars. This was about $750 for each man, woman, and child, or $3750 for each family of five. In 1931 the national income was about 60 billion, or $500 for each individual and $2500 for each family of five. Now this is enough income, even in 1931,

## Congressional Pressures 75

to cure any depression and make everybody prosperous, *if it were properly distributed.* But most of it went to a few, less than 500,000, and as a result 7 million were turned out of work, and 12 million farmers were driven to the verge of bankruptcy with low prices for farm products. It was the unequal and unjust distribution that caused our trouble.

One of the causes of this maldistribution was the inflated gold standard which lowered commodity prices, raised interest rates, and oppressed all debtors.

Gold itself is a commodity. Like all commodities, it changes in value under the economic law of supply and demand or under the effect of civil laws that promote, restrict, modify, enlarge, or diminish its uses. When 25.8 grains of gold 90 per cent fine are arbitrarily selected by law as the gold standard dollar, that dollar can be stable only if its value does not change in relation to other commodities, and it can be honest only if governments or economic combinations are powerless to corrupt or manipulate its value.

The gold dollar does not meet either of these requirements. It always fluctuates in value with every change in production. If the production is low, the value is high; and that arbitrarily lowers the price level of all other commodities which must be measured in this inflated standard. At the same time the burden of all debts is increased in like proportion. We are under the weight of this burden at the present moment. In the general run of commodities, debts are double what they were a few years ago. This is directly due to what I call the dishonesty of the gold standard.

* * *

### 1/360 Billionth of the National Wealth

I do not claim that all economic evils can be corrected by a stabilization of the money standard. On the other hand, I do claim that there cannot be a complete recovery and permanent relief from the cycles of inflation and depression without a stabilization of the money standard.

*The national wealth itself should be the basis of the money standard.* It is unfair to select any one commodity, or two for that matter, and give them a monopoly of the business of being the money standard. The naming of gold or of gold and silver together as the exclusive standards for money at once surrounds them with artificial attributes and gives them a fiat value. Fiat value in any substantial proportion makes a money standard unsound. The only answer is to use the whole national wealth.

*   *   *

We all know that if 100 billion dollars of treasury notes were now issued as legal tender for debts, there would be great depreciation and an abnormal rise in all commodity prices. If a smaller amount were issued, the effect would be the same in a proportionate degree. In fact, we might issue enough to pay the whole national debt without undue inflation of prices. My bill therefore directs the Treasury to issue enough of this new money in payment of government obligations to restore the price ratio of 1926, and thereafter to keep this ratio constant as near as possible.

The 1926 ratio is regarded by many economists as near to normal, and that is probably true as to commodities in general, but it is still a discrimination as to agriculture. Therefore, the stabilization of the money standard alone will not restore business in general. If to this we could add a set-up that would give agriculture a cost of production price for its products, its restored buying power would start many wheels of industry, which, in turn, would restore the buying power of the unemployed, and that would start other wheels and put us on the road to a sound prosperity and not in a cycle of inflation and depression. This can never happen while any one commodity has a monopoly as the money standard.

Let me finally observe that if in addition we could abolish the competitive system of business, fix a coöperative wage for capital as we do for men, save the enormous waste of competition, and increase the forces of production, we could just as well have a 6% instead of a 4% increase in our wealth production, and a coöperative distribution which would make prosperity constant.

## *Senator Elmer Thomas and His Amendment: A Critical Analysis*

[Joseph Reeve, *Monetary Reform Movements: A Survey of Recent Plans and Panaceas* (Washington, D. C.: American Council on Public Affairs, 1943), pp. 148–61.]

The leading Congressional monetary reform strategist, Senator Elmer Thomas, received his political baptism in the campaigns of 1896 and 1900 as an ardent spokesman for the monetary doctrines of William Jennings Bryan. After making his fortune in legal work and land developments in Oklahoma, he came to Congress in 1923 for two terms in the lower house, and since then has served continuously in the Senate. During his very first session in Congress, he filed a bill for full payment of the bonus by the issuance of Federal Reserve bank notes, and later made occasional attacks upon the policies of the Federal Reserve System.

With the onset of the depression in 1929, Thomas was quick to urge monetary remedies. In December of that year he proposed an unsuccessful amendment to the Hoover tax reduction proposal providing additional public works appropriations of 160 million dollars, instead of surtax reductions. During the following two and a half years he fought for larger and larger provisions for public works and relief, as well as for more aggressive action by the Federal Reserve Board to check the deflation. His first real prominence as a monetary reform leader, however, came during the spring of 1932, when he led the fight in the Senate for immediate payment of the bonus by expansion of the currency. In his final appeal for passage of the Patman bill, he predicted that unless this or some other measure embodying monetary expansion was passed, "the great buildings on Wall Street will close and become the abode of bats and owls."

Re-elected by more than a two-to-one majority in the November 1932 elections, Thomas redoubled his monetary reform efforts in the lame-duck Congress. On January 13, 1933, he held the floor for six hours in a filibuster against the branch-banking provisions of the Glass banking bill and in support of the thesis that "the remedy is reflation, and if not reflation, then revolution." Unsuccessful in securing consideration for his own proposals to pay the deficits with currency, he turned to Wall Street itself, appealing to twelve outstanding bankers to halt their deflation and addressing stock and commodity brokers in behalf of "reasonable and controlled expansion of the currency." The advent of the Democratic administration in March, and the panic psychology of the bank holiday combined to give him the long-awaited opportunity for action. At the crucial moment in the debate upon the farm bill, he introduced an amendment, which, in its original version, gave the President virtually unlimited monetary powers of several varieties, and thus adroitly solidified the divergent monetary reform minorities into an unbeatable majority.

Catapulted into new prominence by the passage of the far-flung amendment bearing his name, Thomas became even more persistent in his pressure for monetary expansion, particularly after the sharp midsummer reaction. At first he concentrated upon convincing the President and the Reserve Board of the need for issuance of more currency. When Roosevelt chose the Warren gold purchase plan, however, the Oklahoman quickly came to his support, and soon thereafter began to decry "printing-press inflation," and to advocate "broadening the monetary base" by a full 50 per cent devaluation, or by the possible inclusion of silver.

*  *  *

Despite the vigor and persistence of his efforts Thomas's achievements were relatively meager. None of his own bills and resolutions ever came to a vote, and of four amendments approved by the Senate, three were quickly eliminated by conference committees, as opposition leaders had planned or anticipated. His sole victory, the inflationary amendment to the 1933 farm bill, represented a distinct compromise with his earlier aims, particularly in its permissive features. Moreover, the credit for its passage must be largely assigned to the effective propaganda of Coughlin, the Committee for the Nation, and the farm organizations, coupled with the unprecedented deluge of spontaneous demands for immediate action from a panic-stricken public. The Senator's efforts were perhaps indirectly responsible, in part, for the adoption of the gold-purchase and silver-purchase programs, but neither went far enough to satisfy his desires. Most disappointing of all to him, he was unable to secure the issuance of a single greenback.

## Basic Monetary Doctrines

The economic analysis with which the Congressional monetary reform leader supported his widely varying proposals was fairly consistent, since it was based upon his narrow definition of money as legal tender currency or "what one can spend with a stranger." He specifically excluded bank deposits as mere "credit-money," which was "imaginary" and based upon confidence, and hence could serve as a substitute for money in normal times only. The root-cause of all our economic troubles, Thomas held, was the scarcity of "real money" in actual circulation in comparison to the huge total of debts, interest, taxes, and other fixed obligations. To prove the shrinkage in the "actual circulation," he customarily cut official circulation figures for 1931 and later years approximately in half, by subtracting currency held in banks and arbitrary guesses of large amounts abroad and "hidden, buried, or hoarded." This doctored figure he compared with the peak circulation in 1920, noting the similar variations in farm and

## Congressional Pressures 81

general commodity prices between the two periods, and concluding that the large volume of "money in circulation" in 1920 was the cause of the high prices and prosperity then prevailing. The New Era prosperity, on the other hand, was based upon the dangerous inflation of "bankers' credit."

To explain the existing depression, the Senator used similar arguments. The shrinkage in the volume of the currency actually in circulation, coupled with the declining total of bank deposits after the inevitable crash of the 1926–29 credit inflation, had caused commodity prices to hit the toboggan. As they fell, debts and other fixed charges had become increasingly burdensome in terms of the products of farm, factory, and mine necessary to discharge them, causing impoverishment of the debtor class and cumulative economic distress. On April 1, 1932, he claimed that the debt burden had trebled because prices had fallen to one-third of the levels prevailing in 1920, and most of the debts had been incurred at these levels. In January 1933, he cited figures purporting to show that interest and tax payments alone would absorb more value than the total current national income. In such a situation, he declared, "it is a dishonest act to force the people to pay this increased value to satisfy the creditor and the tax gatherer."

While the Royal Oak priest blamed the "international bankers" for our troubles, Thomas placed full responsibility for the deflation and the depression on the Federal Reserve System. Controlling the financial policy of the United States, and thus largely dominating world economic conditions, "the Federal Reserve Board has its hands in the pockets of every man who lives on the face of the earth." The Board, he held, was vested with the duty and power to prevent economic catastrophe. Nevertheless, it allowed itself to be dominated by a few big New York banks, whose holdings of government bonds and other fixed investments increased in buying power in times of deflation; hence they vetoed all attempts to expand the currency.

In keeping with this picture of the Board's omnipotence and of the importance of the volume of "real money" in actual circulation, the Senator in several Januaries attacked the Federal Reserve System for "deliberately contracting the currency in circulation," though in each case the reduction represented merely normal or less than normal return of currency from the peak circulation during the Christmas season. Correspondingly, he criticized the open market purchase policy adopted in 1932, because it merely enabled the member banks to liquidate their indebtness, and actually reduced the volume of money in circulation. Most naïve of all were his remarks on February 22, 1933, applauding the increase in the circulation which had occurred during the preceding five weeks, and his condemnations after the bank moratorium because of the "deflation" represented by the return of hoarded cash to the banks.

On the basis of his own diagnosis, the Senator's remedial prescriptions were relatively plausible and simple. Such measures as the Reconstruction Finance Corporation, the Glass-Steagall Act, the Federal Reserve open market purchases, and the Glass-Borah amendment to the Home Loan Bank bill, he declared, had produced immediate, but purely temporary, stimuli to commodities and stocks merely on the false expectation that they would increase the amount of money in circulation. Hence, the sure cure was to force more actual money into circulation.

As long as we actually remained on the gold standard, Thomas insisted, our huge gold reserves were more than adequate legally to back all the necessary increases. After imposition of the gold-export embargo, he continued to dwell upon currency expansion as an essential goal, but began to place new emphasis upon gold-price adjustments, and later upon expansion of the monetary base by remonetization of silver. By August 1934, he was condemning the "fetish-worship of an unalterable gold dollar."

* * *

In the course of his numerous monetary reform crusades, the Senator repeatedly refused to express any preference for any specific type or method of currency expansion. On one occasion he declared that he was merely arguing for the principle "that we must have more money in circulation. I care not what kind—silver, copper, brass, gold or paper." At the Hippodrome rally in New York in November 1933, he agreed with Al Smith that gold dollars were better than "baloney dollars," but asserted that the trouble was that the people had neither. When the silver agitation resulted in legislation which merely gave a bonus to silver producers without substantial immediate monetary repercussions, he violently attacked the bill as a "3 per cent silver bill," pointing out that Oklahoma was not a silver-producing state, and asserting that "silver, as silver has no interest whatever for me. Unless we can use silver in some way to expand the currency and cheapen the dollar and raise commodity prices, I am not interested in any sense in silver."

Thomas likewise refused to specify how great an increase in the circulation would be necessary to restore prosperity, saying that it was a matter of trial and error. As his "yardstick of inflation," he advocated monetary expansion merely sufficient to raise commodity prices to a level that would permit producers to obtain their costs of production and sufficient profit for payment of taxes and interest, and gradual retirement of accumulated debts. In practice, he customarily translated this vague objective into the familiar 1926 wholesale commodity price level, and in several of his pronouncements he specifically condemned the prices prevailing in 1920 as excessively high. Later, he began to hint occasionally that the increased debt burdens accumulated since 1926 might eventually necessitate an even higher goal. In January 1932 he suggested that the expansion of the currency by as little as one billion dollars might suffice to achieve the 1926 price level and later he frequently cited figures in the neighborhood of two billion.

The Oklahoman's notion of the process by which monetary expansion would effect economic recovery adequately explains his uncertainty regarding the amount of new currency needed. Basing his analysis on the familiar quantity theory, he asserted:

> The value of money depends on the law of supply and demand; hence, the purchasing power of the dollar in the main depends upon the quantity of real dollars—gold, silver, and currency notes—in circulation. Under normal conditions and influences, any increase in the quantity of real dollars in circulation, lowers the value of purchasing power of such dollars. . . .

Moreover, he believed that "a declared policy of voluntary, premeditated and enforced inflation" of the currency, especially if directed to specific price level objectives, would cause dishoarding of currency and unthawing of frozen bank deposits, coupled with extension of new loans and creation of new bank deposits to take advantage of prospective price increases. Hence substantial increases in price levels might occur with very little actual "physical inflation." Thus, while apparently focusing his attention chiefly upon changes in the quantity of "real money" in circulation, he recognized in a crude manner the roles played by variations in the quantity of bank deposits and in the velocity of circulation of currency and deposits.

His emphasis upon the primary importance of currency expansion exposed him to heckling from senatorial opponents, who questioned the possibility of keeping any addition to the circulating currency from being immediately redeposited in the banking system. Such attacks the Oklahoman usually warded off with vague answers. On one occasion, however, he had to admit that the extra currency would eventually find its way to member banks and thence to the Reserve banks, first liquidating member bank indebtedness and then building up excess reserves. But this deposited currency, he insisted, would still be "in circulation," since "they could get it at any time they needed it." In another similar situation he dodged the question by declaring that the rise in prices produced by the increase in circulation (even though, by implication, temporary) would increase bank loans and business activity. Some of his later bills required the monetary authorities not only to issue adequate currency, but also to "keep [it] in circulation."

Thus, according to Thomas, currency expansion inevitably tended to raise commodity prices both directly and indirectly. Once prices began to climb, two powerful sets of forces would come into play which would immediately stimulate economic activity. First, as already suggested, the rise in prices, if generally expected to continue, would induce dishoarding and widespread anticipatory buying all along the line from consumer to manufacturer. Secondly, these developments would cause reopening of factories and expansion of employment, increased demand for farm products, and finally unthawing of frozen banks, as applicants for bank credit become more numerous and bankers more willing to accommodate them.

This emphasis upon the role of rising prices in stimulating anticipatory purchases was dominant in the picture drawn by the Senator on April 24, 1933 of the results to be expected from enactment of the Thomas amendment then pending, and it recurred less prominently on other occasions. As an argument for monetary expansion, it possesses considerable validity in times of extreme panic and widespread hoarding, when a drastic "shot in the arm" may prevent the economic pulse from coming to a complete standstill. An overdose of the remedy, however, is all too easy. Speculative price movements almost inevitably tend to overshoot the mark, or to create new maladjustments in place of the old. The monetary stimulant may well be too pleasant or too deceptively effective at the start, for the controlling authorities to act promptly enough to keep the rate of expansion within proper bounds. Application of the monetary brakes is a delicate maneuver, requiring much skill to prevent dangerous speculative reactions. Like most of his monetary reform colleagues, Senator Thomas was too prone to minimize the problems of control, both economic and political.

More frequently the Senator based his arguments for monetary expansion upon the relative inflexibility of debts, interest, and taxes. Higher prices, he reiterated, would enable farmers and other raw material producers to discharge these fixed obligations by selling a smaller proportion of their total production, thus restoring their "buying power" for the products of industry and inaugurating the usual upward spiral of expanding production, employment, and bank credit.

His emphasis upon the injustice done to the debtor class by the multiplied burden of debts and other fixed charges in times of deflation is part of this second approach. For example, his amendment to the 1933 farm bill, he claimed, potentially might transfer value of almost 200 billion dollars from the creditor, bondholding, and deposit-possessing class—"who did not buy it, did not earn it, do not deserve it, and must not retain it"—to the maltreated debtor and producer class. In this and similar statements, he not only tacitly assumed that all debts were contracted at much higher price levels, but also greatly exaggerated the cleavage between the so-called debtor and creditor classes by overlooking the large proportion of offsetting debts and credits. In later pronouncements, he apparently preferred to minimize the conflict of interest between debtors and creditors and to pose as a defender of both groups, holding that monetary expansion alone could "maintain the validity of contracts and the collectibility of legitimate debt claims." He also increasingly emphasized that the federal budget could be balanced only by greater tax revenues resulting from higher price levels.

The economic argument that rises in commodity prices, by outstripping fixed debt, interest, and tax charges, tend to stimulate business activity is legitimate as far as it goes. Thomas, however, was unaware of its full implications. In early statements he included salaries as a fixed charge, but later these were omitted, and in November 1933 he definitely declared that monetary expansion would raise wages and salaries, and thus increase buying power. Hence, purposely or otherwise, he failed to recognize the importance of the lag of money wages (the most important variable cost) behind commodity prices in stimulating recovery. Moreover, his assumption that existing debts had been incurred at the 1926 price level or thereabouts, led him to the fallacious belief that 1926 prosperity could be restored only by returning to 1926 "normal" prices. Instead of noting that gradual reductions in debts and their carrying charges, coupled with other hard-won cost-reduction, had made it possible for most producers to operate profitably at prices lower than the predepression levels, he claimed that debts had actually continued to increase and that, therefore, even higher prices might prove necessary to restore prosperity.

Finally, the Senator usually over-emphasized the importance of the farmer and the raw material producer in the national economy. In his Century of Progress address, he declared:

> Chicago lives and thrives on the prosperity of the farmer. When the farmer is prosperous, your implement manufacturers, your packers, your factories, your merchandise distributors and your great commercial

banks enjoy prosperity, and when the farmer is distressed, your factories are closed, your wage earners are unemployed, your banks are forced to ask Federal aid, your taxes go unpaid and your citizens, your corporations and your city face default, collapse and chaos. Every loss to agriculture is a direct loss to Chicago.

The possibility that boosts in food and raw material prices might decrease the real income of city consumers or raise industrial costs and thus retard recovery nowhere received mention. The sure remedy for all our troubles, both industrial and agricultural, was to raise the prices of "basic commodities."

*Summary*

Though Senator Thomas showed deeper insight into the role played by money in the economic system than did Father Coughlin, nevertheless important omissions and exaggerations distorted his analysis. His emphasis upon the predominant importance of the volume of currency in circulation was probably the most glaring deficiency, but his entire picture was grossly over-simplified, leading him to promulgate high-sounding half-truths, plausible only to the uninitiated. He deserves some credit for recognizing, in 1932, the futility of open market purchases and other indirect measures proposed to stimulate credit expansion; however, most of his own suggestions either involved inconsequential and temporary increases in the volume of the currency, or entailed eventual problems of control, of which he was scarcely aware. . . . In brief, though not completely blind to the larger problem, the Senator, like the radio priest, was much more interested in prescribing pills and poultices which would quickly restore vigorous activity to the ailing economic system, than in devising treatments to assure the continuance of economic health.

# 14

## *The Fulfillment of Bryan's Dream: The Senate Silverites*

[Jeanette Nichols, "Silver Inflation and the Senate in 1933," *Social Studies*, vol. 25 (January, 1934), pp. 12–18.]

The depression ills of 1933 caused a steady accumulation of inflation sentiment in the United States, with as many schemes for securing inflation as there were doctors who prescribed it. Monetary pills for the sick body politic appeal by their simplicity—it is so much easier to attribute distress simply to a lack of funds, than to ferret out the intricate, deep-seated, social causes of that lack. Hence the political usefulness of the inflation battle-cry, which has rung through every land periodically, ever since the dawn of history. Whether or not the currency would be expanded in the United States depended on many factors, one of which was the alignment of votes in the senate. There, during the first session of the seventy-third Congress, inflation steadily gained in strength and three dates stood out significantly in respect to silver.

Eastern press commentators were slow to realize the strengthening of the cheap money sentiment. The amassing of thirty-three votes on April 17 for the coinage of silver appeared to them surprising. Yet those thirty-three grew to forty-one by April 26, and they in turn by April 28 to fifty-three. Twelve hectic, astounding days, with ninety-one senators holding themselves within call most of the time. This movement progressed partly by the aid of those who wished to kill it. That is the irony of Fate, working through political instruments.

If Bryan's ghost stalked through the Senate chamber on the afternoon of Monday, April 17, it heard men speaking an ancient and familiar tongue. There were Senators Wheeler of Montana, King of Utah, and Pittman of

Nevada, all facing re-election in 1934, all talking about the remonetization of silver at 16 to 1. They said that they found the sentiment for it "overwhelming." Contributing somewhat to their argument was Mr. Norris (who, however, inclined more toward paper money and was not electioneering) of the ghost's old home bailiwick of Nebraska, an agricultural, rather than a silver-producing state. Most of the other principal speakers hailed from silver states; and they led a van of men from the West and South who voted that day for remonetization.

All fourteen senators from the seven silver states of Utah, Idaho, Montana, Arizona, Colorado, Nevada, and New Mexico (except Borah, Bratton, and Hayden) voted "aye." With them were Democrats and Republicans; but, with the exception of Couzens of Michigan, they were joined by no one from any state east of Wisconsin or north of North Carolina and Kentucky. An interesting picture in terms of economic geography—a picture adapted to enlargement.

The orators of the day, looking upon the countrywide misery, honestly desirous to alleviate it, although not always well grounded in monetary history, prescribed Bryan's own nostrum. Again, as in an earlier day, the demonetization of silver was limned forth as a most glaring evil. To that lonely cause a host of ill effects readily were attributed. It was no time to stress the contributions made to hard times by maldistribution, over-production, underconsumption, speculation, or distrust. It was a time to emphasize the need for trade with silver-absorbing countries, such as China and India, which import but do not export that metal.

But the wraith must have noticed that the orators of 1933 concerned themselves most repeatedly with the sad state of the export trade in agricultural products. From the hard-pressed farmer they expected a quick response. Men from silver-producing states scarce ventured openly to present their urgency as a naked demand for a special subsidy for mountain interests. They did not stress the fact that silver had been at an all-time New York low of 24¼¢ December 29, 1932, and had risen only to 28⅞¢ since. It was the farmer above ground, rather than the owner of mines in the bowels of the earth, for whom they pleaded.

In turn, senators from agricultural states broadened the base of their appeal, from farmers of the mid-continent to senators of the industrial states. They stressed the losses of the exporter of manufactured goods, since he also must be paid in dear American dollars rather than in cheap British pounds or Japanese yen; foreign purchasers were choosing to buy elsewhere—from firms operating in the lower priced industrial nations. Worse still, at home, the goods of countries whose currencies had fallen from the gold pedestal were surmounting the highest tariff wall which American ingenuity ever had erected. Of all this, much was said. It was music in the ears of the vindicated ghost, hearing again of the desperate plight of debtors, who again could not pay back in hard times money borrowed easily during a boom.

At the same time, the ghost of the Great Commoner noticed that the old gospel was vastly more "respectable" than it used to be. The Peerless Leader, in the days of his glory, had understood human emotions and their use so well that he had built up an inflation electorate of nearly six and one-half millions; they were taken chiefly from the ranks of silver producers, some unemployed workmen, debtors, and agriculturalists who were also debtors. As Bryan preached the doctrine, there was much of class warfare in it; and consequently there was one class (in addition to the well-to-do), which he scarcely succeeded in attracting; that was the naturally conservative, middle class of the industrial areas. But in 1933 many from it joined the cheap money group. They were confirmed in their inflation sentiments partly through a certain ineptitude among anti-inflationists, and greatly to the astonishment of the latter. The displacement of the gold standard god by inflation propaganda was extremely helpful to silver.

Among the people formerly supposed to desire what was termed "sound money" are the big bankers, the gentlemen who control the policies of the great radio networks, and the conservative press. Curiously enough, from each of these groups came a definite propulsion toward inflation, felt because of their influence upon the hundreds of thousands of Main Street conservatives who make up the "one-hundred-per-cent-Americans."

The contribution of Wall Street to inflation sentiment was partly one of disillusionment. The "average citizen" might not have been shaken from his acquiescence in the old shibboleth of the gold standard if the doors of the factories, retail businesses, and small banks had been the only ones to close. The terrific shock to him was the closing of the doors of *large* banks, the arrest of prominent bankers, and the hasty departure and continued absence from their country of outstanding business leaders.

In so far as Harriman, Insull, Mitchell, and Wiggin were discredited in the eyes of the nation, Wall Street lost sanctity. One of the wealthiest men in the United States found it in his heart to rise in the Senate and deride the "four M's," Morgan, Mellon, Mills, and Meyer, explaining that what the people want now is to choose their own autocrat, rather than starve under self-chosen autocrats. Apparently the fevered doctrine of American individualism, as applied to the worship of the clever man gifted in wealth-gathering, was a lost article of faith, although the United States Chamber of Commerce as late as November 18 doubted it. Citizens who never did it before, talked of wealth decentralization, of the transfer of this world's goods from the few who have to the many who have not. They joined the more radical classes in applause for the orator who talked of a sound, just, fair, and honest dollar which, through inflation, must displace the high, bloated, diseased, and dropsical dollar. They asked for cheap money but, fearful of a radical label, stipulated that it must be obtained through "controlled" inflation.

Possibly unaware of the inflamed state of much of the public mind toward financiers, banking experts during the excitement renewed attempts to obtain branch banking from Congress. But the man and woman of the rural and small town areas had little faith in banking leadership; they could not believe that the failure of small-town banks might be due somewhat to local limitations. Nor could they sense the desperate need for a better ordered system throughout the nation. They preferred, when they could, to trust their neighbor; they distrusted the motives of those who urged centralized control.

Powerful industrial interests, not particularly concerned in the silver futures market or in silver production, also helped silver by fostering inflation. The most notable of these groups was the famous "Committee for the Nation," composed of various manufacturing and dairy executives under the leadership of F. A. Vanderlip. They distinguished themselves by frankly admitting that vast sums had been irretrievably lost, and outlined a program for preventing inflation by restoring the price level. To read their recommendations, printed in the *New York Herald Tribune* of March 6, 1933, is to read a prospectus of many devices adopted by the President during the following six months. But those devices were necessarily so drastic as to radiate respectability to more historic inflation, such as greenbacks and bimetallism.

Further responsibility for the inflation demand could be laid at the doors of the radio. The inflationist of 1933, whatever his economic class, was more "informed" than in earlier depressions. He had been talked at over the radio, night and day, upon economic subjects, listening to what he would never bother to read about. In many cases the radio economics was of an elementary, if not a distorted, sort, administered in doses mixed according to the prejudices and objects of the speakers; but radio speeches strike listeners directly with the persuasive power of a living voice. They made many listeners feel that they were becoming "informed" on this abstruse and difficult subject.

The radio might even have elected Bryan. Did not a microphone orator in 1932 elect to the Senate a candidate admitted to have had, otherwise, not a ghost of a chance? Much more important, in 1933, was the influence of a certain popular, Sunday, radio hour. A powerful, convincing voice, bound up with a personality having by profession a vital appeal to a very large class of persons, spoke into a microphone at Detroit, hammering away upon the public mind in favor of inflation. November 5 Father Coughlin assured his listeners, "Sooner than you suspect, silver will be remonetized."

Next, we come to the inflation contribution of the conservative press, on which Fate played a scurvy trick. Literary critics scarcely classify the *Saturday Evening Post* as an inflammatory sheet; charges of radicalism preferably have been aimed at less successful and less popular weeklies. But times were hard for advertisers and their most popular medium shrank perforce from its pre-depression affluence of more than two hundred pages to less than one hundred.

In these restricted columns appeared, April 15, 1933, a detailed statement of disadvantages suffered by manufacturers in gold standard countries who must compete in world trade with those producing goods in countries having depreciated currencies. When the suffering nation is thoroughly demonstrated to be the United States, and the less unfortunate one to be England, the political usefulness of the article becomes such as would delight Senator Lodge himself!

It was forty years since Cameron, Chandler, Lodge, and Reed voiced the desire to marry silver to protection; but in the 1933 arguments many of theirs were repeated, and awakened response in the congressional breast, especially when they concerned such industries as steel and textiles, to mention but two badly hit by depreciation-competition.

The track to subsidy for industries has been well beaten through long years by efficient lobbyists. These know all the paths and by-ways laid out in the congressional mind by American political processes. It is natural to find excerpts from their press inserted in the *Congressional Record* during currency debate; and such excerpts show that even on the Atlantic seaboard "controlled" inflation had its advocates.

Oddly enough, in writing that cleverly illustrated article, "The Economic Drive Against America," Mr. Garet Garrett took pains to state that what he was advocating was most decidedly *not* an abandonment of the gold standard, but compensating surtaxes for exchange variations, which would debar imports under an unreasonably depreciated value. But there was nothing to prevent a silverite from making a present of a copy of the *Post* to each of his fellow senators, with useful deductions therefrom as to the respectability, the pure, unadulterated, one-hundred-per-cent-American quality of inflation through silver remonetization.

Since the currency issue is peculiarly adapted to political exigencies, any chance instrument like the Garrett article, has vastly more influence than a mountain of careful arguments deduced by specialists in economics. This must be so, because importunate constituents effectually deprive most Senators of opportunity and taste for study. Naturally, an anti-professorial set of mind is built up in those cases where the defense mechanism demands it. Incidentally it was displayed not less than four times upon the occasion of April 17's debate, when also Mr. Garrett was cited half a dozen times. Politically speaking, those economists who had been advocating inflation (whether by silver, paper, or other methods) owe Mr. Garrett and the *Post* a debt of gratitude.

Tricky Fate continued, after Wheeler's amendment was defeated, to make great sport of sober people's apparent intentions. Through the ensuing fortnight conservative political influence, opposing the steady progress of the inflationists, helped them considerably.

The same sentiment which pressed upon the legislative branch of the government, bore down upon the Executive, demanding inflation through silver remonetization, paper money, lessening the gold content of the dollar, and other means. The silver bills introduced into this Congress, cavorted all the way from brief bimetallic measures to intricate schemes of money based on gold, silver, copper, lead, zinc, and iron. Correspondents of the White House can have been no less fertile in suggestion. Inflation had a seat at the Cabinet table and its representatives among the "Little Cabinet." There was no small significance in the fact that the Secretary of Agriculture hailed from Iowa—the hotbed of agricultural unrest—and that Professor G. F. Warren was not against some use of silver in the monetary reserves. Watchers from the western end of Pennsylvania Avenue scarcely could have been surprised, therefore, when the silver vote on the Hill, where on January 24 it had stood at 18 to 56, by April 17 boasted totals of 33 to 43.

Hill and White House alike sensed in the inflation issue a challenge to leadership. Impatient voters, weary of timidity in the Hoover administration, wildly acclaimed leadership in that of Roosevelt. Of Congress they had not been saying the fairest things, and their idea of leadership seemed to be one man, rather than five hundred and thirty-one. This opinion senators and representatives had encouraged by admitting inability to agree, by delegating their powers and shifting their responsibilities. Conservative members, privately and publicly, were asserting that Congress was potentially more radical than the Executive. Further, there was a general demand on all sides for action —quick action—without too much regard for where it led.

Nevertheless, although repeated experience at the polls tends to foster certain types of caution, there were senators who remained unafraid. They knew that the Senate, like the House, was held in contempt among many people who do not stop to consider the basic principle of representative government. But they also knew that the fault in the last analysis lies close to the door of the electorate; and they made it clear that willingness to act and desire to lead were not all concentrated at the other end of the Avenue. At least six chose each his inflation star, to which he hitched his political wagon.

To the challenge of the thirty-three silver votes, the President responded quickly. He had made known his opposition to Wheeler's mandatory 16 to 1 proposition; but within about forty-eight hours after it mustered its increased following, he in effect declared the United States off the gold standard, announced that the dollar would be left to find its own level, and sponsored a compromise, permissive proposition (called the "Thomas" amendment), designed to ride through Congress on the skirts of the farm relief bill. That proposition carried something to mollify each one of the domestic inflation leaders, silver men, gold reduction men, paper men, all. It gave the President permission to act in each field if in his judgment advisable.

His action accomplished two objectives. It reasserted his leadership at home and strengthened his bargaining power abroad.

He reduced the ranks of the opposition in the Senate to the anti-inflationists, and even they must note that this compromise had more of "nay" than of "must." He left room for the widest possible divergence of opinion; conservatives could believe he really aimed to restore the gold standard among the chief nations as soon as political conditions permitted, and had endorsed the Thomas amendment only to prevent Congress from getting out of hand. Silver men could claim he aimed to remonetize silver throughout the world, or at least increase its use. Paper men could claim he planned an issue of greenbacks. Before night fell on this *coup d'état*, Mr. J. P. Morgan of New York City and Mr. Key Pittman of Tonopah, Neveda, were both praising the action of the Executive—for totally different reasons.

As for the international bearing of the President's action, he evidently knew something of how the United States position at the conference table in 1878, 1881, and 1892 was made ludicrous because she possessed no bargaining power. When the United States then begged an accord on silver, she faced an England bound tightly to the gold standard and there was no common ground on which to stand. Worse, there always loomed back of any action by American delegates, the question of a lack of support in Congress. But in April 1933, Robinson, Connally, and Pittman were urging the Senate, "We must not send our Government into any conference economically disarmed."

No sooner had the President sponsored the Thomas amendment than anti-inflationists inadvertently made sure of its adoption. The same presses which printed the full text of the amendment told the world that Senator Reed of Pennsylvania hoped to delay action until Congress had time to hear from the country. A sound legislative principle—which had worked to pass the economy bill. Obviously, the senator believed majority opinion repudiated inflation. But with each passing hour the opposite became more evident. From Middle West, South, West, and even East, the mails and wires disgorged a response which averaged contrary to Reed's expectations. His move fostered cheap money sentiment.

Fate jeered at the conservatives. Delay gave time for state legislatures to adopt inflation memorials, ironically based on the Garrett article. Delay gave new boldness to the advocates of a redistribution of wealth—some $200,000,000,000 were to change hands through this amendment. Delay gave time for arrival of slow letters, which were sent, the recipients said, because the poor could not afford telegrams for voicing their quick approval. More and more, personalities were indulged in; and the presence in Washington of ex-Secretary of the Treasury Mills, come to defeat the amendment, helped to increase its popularity.

The profiteers in this situation were the silver senators. Emboldened by the rage for cheap money, they worked openly to increase the market price of their home product. Many of their bills aimed to fix a silver price double that existing. They secured endorsement for an amendment empowering the President to provide for unlimited coinage, not at 16 to 1 but at a ratio between gold and silver to be determined by him. Thirteen Democrats who had voted against mandatory 16 to 1 supported this modified Wheeler proposal April 16, and it was adopted, 41–26. As four of the thirteen hailed from Illinois, Indiana, Connecticut, and New Hampshire, it was clear that silver inflation was moving eastward.

Two days later the silver senators secured an increase, from $100,000,000 to $200,000,000 in the amount of silver which the United States could take from debtor nations to relieve the silver market. This drew two Republicans not formerly voting with the silver men, from Michigan and Connecticut, and tallied at 53–32. In the silver votes of April 17 to April 28 was a lesson in political finesse:

|  |  |  |
| --- | --- | --- |
| April 17 | silver defeated | 33–43 |
| April 26 | silver victorious | 41–26 |
| April 28 | silver victorious | 53–32 |

However, while this was going on, an element of terror was creeping into the situation. Eastern as well as western senators queried, "Cannot unalleviated distress upset established government?" "Would Congress get out of hand?" conservatives asked. "Did the 'Thomas' amendment provide inflation enough?" westerners wondered. April 27 the radio news reporters had told a listening world that desperate farmers of Iowa were fighting the loss of their homes—armed with mud, sticks, ridicule, and a rope, used to frighten (but not to kill, be it noted) a judge in foreclosure proceedings. The shock was tremendous.

The next day martial law was declared in Iowa. In Washington the conservative Senator Dickinson from that state joined with seven more Republicans to help adopt the "Thomas" amendment. The vote this time was 64–21! On the same Friday they passed, 64–20, the farm relief bill with the "Thomas" amendment attached. About this vote there were two very striking things. Among the opposing twenty votes (not counting the pairs) were but three from west of the Mississippi, and two of these hailed from "Silver Dick" Bland's old state of Missouri. The only other states presenting a united front in opposition were one of the Middle West, Ohio, and the five eastern seaboard states of Delaware, Maine, New Jersey, Rhode Island, and Vermont.

Quickly Wheeler demonstrated that Ohio was not so conservative after all. The next Wednesday, May 3, he submitted a Senate resolution expressing it as the opinion of that body that the delegates to the International Economic Conference should "work unceasingly for an international agreement to remonetize silver" at 16 to 1 or better. The newly elected and enthusiastic inflationist senator from Idaho, Mr. Pope, had the pleasure of occupying the chair of the presiding officer when Wheeler introduced his resolution. It was laid on the table five days and then agreed to, without further discussion or objection.

With the resolution Wheeler submitted a statement favoring silver remonetization (ratio not ventured), signed by 96 Representatives; 19 of them came from districts east of the Mississippi, 8 from Ohio, 5 from Michigan, 3 from Illinois, 2 from Indiana, and 1 from Pennsylvania.

In this move Wheeler worked as a realist, within the bounds of the attainable. The House signatures were gathered without stipulating a ratio, which would have cut the list. Senate agreement was asked (without a record vote) to a Senate resolution, which operates merely as an expression of opinion, not to a joint resolution, which has the force of law.

Thenceforward the silver men were heartened by continual undermining of the position of gold. At the behest of Roosevelt, Congress passed a joint resolution with retroactive features for repeal of the gold payment clause in all obligations. Great Britain and lesser nations made war debt payments in silver. Preparatory to the Economic Conference, Senator Pittman grew increasingly optimistic, as it became clear that no general monetary agreement could precede the conference. He met gentlemen from Mexico when they came to see the President—most important because, while nearly 42% of the world's silver is produced in Mexico, United States interests control three-fourths of that production and practically all of the refining of it. He announced, May 19, a preliminary agreement on a 6-point silver program to be ratified at London.

In that city he had a busy and happy experience. The conference strengthened the silver cause in so far as it failed to agree on world gold stabilization. Pittman doubtless appreciated tremendously Roosevelt's refusal to peg the dollar; and while the conference dragged out its ineffectual existence he persuaded the delegates from countries holding large stocks of silver and from producing countries to sign an agreement associated with his name.

In it he posited an ultimate return to the gold standard, thereby furnishing Senator Wheeler an easy point of attack at home, while Pittman garnered his signatures abroad. Since the draft agenda had dismissed international bimetallism as impractical, he was in no position to urge it. India, China, and Spain, holding large silver stocks, agreed, July 22, not to sell more than 140,000,000 ounces through the next four years; Australia, Canada, the United States, Mexico, and Peru agreed to sell none and to withdraw from market 35,000,000 ounces yearly. This was in line with the draft agenda which suggested restriction of sales. Silver "withdrawn" was to be used for currency or otherwise retained from sale.

A supplementary agreement of July 26 apportioned the producers' withdrawals in such manner that the United States would withdraw about 70% of the yearly amount. How much of this might appear as currency was left for speculation. On this date the price of spot silver in New York was 36¾¢.

From August 10, when Pittman returned to the United States, until November 24, the date of this writing, the silver pot boiled merrily. Each of the many expressions of discontent over the working of the N.R.A., the A.A.A., the P.W.A. and all of the other heroic measures, added its quota to the general unsettlement. Since unsettlement is essential to their progress, the silver and greenback groups had reason to be grateful to Milo Reno and Albert H. Wiggin, to the coal strikes and the national Chamber of Commerce, to friends and enemies of the Administration, who so impatiently demanded an immediate cure for a long-standing disease. A loyal silverite must nightly pray that commodity prices shall not rise before they "do something for silver."

October was filled with the noise of fighting. Although the American Legion and A. F. of L. came out (October 4 and October 11) for "sound money" and against "unregulated inflation," inflation grew apace. October 21 Roosevelt announced that the government was about to buy domestic gold; October 29, that it would purchase foreign gold. The rumored order of November 17 for restricting the flight of capital seemed to exhaust the possibilities of exchange manipulation as a price-raising agent. Did this open the way for silver?

In the trans-Mississippi West meanwhile raged a battle royal. The Administration brought out the Commodity Credit Corporation and other plans for loans on cattle, wheat, and corn. If these succeeded, farm strikes would wane and inflation with them. If coördination of the N.R.A. and A.A.A. achieved its object, the commodity dollar, greenback, and silver men might fail in theirs. Senator Wheeler was determined not to fail. He spent those weeks addressing westerners over the radio and at many a Chamber of Commerce meeting. He must have been gratified at his reception out West but better was in store in the East. He found awaiting him a letter from an official of the Chamber of Commerce of Philadelphia, possibly the most conservative city in the United States, urging him to address its members; he could name his own date.

Meanwhile, inflation schemes hatched all over the country, and among the chicks was one lusty fellow of New York parentage but a hybrid strain, showing how, under the stress of trouble, financiers may stray. This bird was a dollar with a heart of gold, surrounded by silver. The metals were either to be actually minted in those relative positions or jointly used to back paper. This oddity proved again that money based on silver is less unpalatable to creditory tastes than unbacked paper. Senator Wheeler knew this.

Various senators tried to persuade Roosevelt to put into effect their pet plans. Upon India's ratification of the Pittman agreement (Nov. 21) Pittman announced the

United States was "obligated" to ratify, as the agreement was prepared with Roosevelt's approval. Outside of the silver group, inflation senators getting much publicity included Thomas of Oklahoma, Harrison of Mississippi, and Smith of South Carolina. As the President delayed specific endorsement, some senators uttered threats—that if he did not inflate before Congress met, Congress would repeal his powers and compel inflation. However, apportionment of the political spoils of an inflation victory might require time.

Out of the clash of conflict what will come? Silver men feel that somewhere in their territory lies the middle ground: the South with its paper and the East with its gold must lay down their arms before the West with its silver. They did it in 1878 and they may do it again. However, silver has very little political importance in any other nation today. Mr. Roosevelt is a realist, a man of much resource and great popularity. He may seek to divert inflation along new paths—away from Treasury vaults crammed with bullion. But of course he knows that a plan to succeed must appeal to national self interest and emotions. It must secure a majority vote in Congress.

# Section Three

# Roosevelt's Decision

*Commentary*

In the end, Roosevelt's decision to leave the gold standard was a personal one influenced by a great many factors: inflationist sentiment in Congress, the gold drain, foreign trade disadvantages for the nation, low commodity prices, Silverite agitation, the sophisticated arguments of businessmen and economists, and, perhaps most important of all, the social and economic precepts of the President himself. Roosevelt's public philosophy was, at best, ill-defined (Doc. 15). He deplored the instability and imbalance of our economic system. He believed that the Federal Government should be employed as an instrument of economic stabilization, and everything he read in the early years of the Depression confirmed his distaste for political inertia (Doc. 16). It seemed imperative that he devalue the dollar in order to increase consumption. How he could execute this remained unclear, but Franklin Roosevelt had a talent for converting uncertainty into the virtue of flexibility.

First he had to preserve confidence in the nation's banks and gold reserves. While preparations went apace for a special session of Congress to save the banks, Roosevelt used the Trading with the Enemy Act of 1917

*105*

to close them and cease gold transactions. No legislation, however, could inspire as much reassurance as the President's sanguine personality. On March 8 he sought the public's ears via the Washington press corps. Nevertheless, the crisis did not require complete candor. Asked whether the nation still respected the gold standard, Roosevelt was circumspect and disingenuous (Doc. 17). He obviously feared the consequences of the public's response more than those of his actions.

The following day both Houses of Congress approved the Administration's banking bill and Roosevelt extended the bank holiday. The law gave the President control over the exchange of gold, penalized hoarding of the metal, authorized the issuance of new Federal Reserve bank notes and the reopening of banks with liquid assets (Doc. 18). Exercising the powers of the law, Roosevelt forbade the exchange of gold in all transactions after March 6, thereby rendering the gold standard more a formality than a fact.

Roosevelt considered his action ephemeral but rumors spread that the nation had seen the last of the gold standard for a while. New Deal measures such as the closing of the banks and the Economy bill had been deflationary, Roosevelt admitted to a press conference on April 7 (Doc. 19). An infusion of more money would speed recovery, but, while saying nothing about remonetization, Roosevelt ruled out the radical step of printing additional dollars. The Thomas amendment forced a Presidential intercession in behalf of "managed inflation." On April 19 he announced the nation's departure from the gold standard (Doc. 20). Using the analogy of a football quarterback calling the next play on the basis of gained or lost yardage, the Chief Executive insisted that he had a "general plan" and a "perfectly definite objective" as he operated pragmatically from play to play. Still intent on avoiding a final commitment, Roosevelt hinted at a return to gold when the times were propitious.

## Roosevelt's Decision  107

Roosevelt had followed his own instincts on the gold standard despite some qualms and controversy within the Administration. Raymond Moley, leader of the Brain Trust during the campaign and later Assistant Secretary of State, remembers his great misgivings of the decision in his memoir of the New Deal. Recalling the debate among F. D. R.'s advisers, Moley suggests that the decision reflected no economic program, only an opportunistic surrender to the Senate inflationists in order to control their drive (Doc. 21). For Moley, the decision, although the right one in the context of 1933 need for managed inflation, had two unfortunate ramifications: it began a pattern of political opportunism which in turn precipitated expedient budgetary deficits leading to a ruinous inflationary trend.

James P. Warburg, a youthful Wall Street banker who had gone to Washington with Moley, also feared the prospect of unchecked inflation. An articulate conservative, Warburg urged the Administration to seek an international accord for a modified gold standard before embarking upon unilateral action. Warburg's diary describes how Roosevelt vacillated for a month before confronting his advisers with the gold standard decision *fait accompli* (Doc. 22). Yet Warburg did not seem sure that Roosevelt could have done anything else at that particular time.

Whereas Moley and Warburg tie the gold embargo directly to the Thomas amendment pressure, Herbert Feis, writing 30 years after the event, describes it as the capstone of a well-deliberated policy (Doc. 23). Feis, author of several studies in economic and diplomatic history, served both Hoover and Roosevelt as a State Department economic adviser. In his examination of the sequence of events beginning with the bank holiday, Feis depicts the gold embargo as inevitable under the circumstances. He does not completely discount the Thomas amendment's influence, but characterizes it as the concluding factor in a succession of considerations hastening the inevitable.

Roosevelt might have agreed with Feis. Judging from Secretary of the Interior Harold Ickes' description of Roosevelt's explanation to his Cabinet, the decision was calculated and not capricious (Doc. 24). Roosevelt, writing a year later, omitted any mention of inflationary pressure in Congress (Doc. 25). Two factors governed his decision: the flight of gold overseas and the need to curb deflation.

In sum, the writings of Warren and Fisher gave devaluation intellectual support, the acceptance of controlled inflation by the business community gave it moral support, and the Thomas amendment proponents gave it political support. The decision to take the United States off the gold standard was an idea that had come of age.

# 15

## *The Quest for Balance: Roosevelt's Economic Philosophy*

[Daniel R. Fusfeld, *The Economic Thought of Franklin D. Roosevelt and the Origins of the New Deal* (New York: Columbia University Press, 1955), pp. 251–57.]

The economic philosophy of Franklin D. Roosevelt, as it had developed by 1932, may be summarized briefly, and in general form. The private enterprise–private profit economy should not be abolished, but retained. However, its operations were not always benevolent and did not always promote the general welfare; hence those operations must be improved and supplemented by state and Federal government efforts whenever the need arose.

This economic philosophy was years in developing. Its beginnings lay in the *noblesse oblige* philosophy of the Hudson River gentry: less fortunate members of the community should be helped by the more fortunate. Roosevelt, however, was to go well beyond this philosophy. He became a spokesman for the idea that society owed a debt to those who suffered economic misfortunes: provision should be made for those persons as a duty of society and as a right of the individual, rather than as charity.

At Harvard Roosevelt had courses in economics that were centered on the economic problems of his time, courses that emphasized the growth of big business and economic concentration, the monetary problems of the period, and the growing maturity of America as the frontier disappeared. His professors were advocates of economic reform who took the attitude that the economic system was not to be judged on the basis of abstract principles alone, but on its performance as judged by its contribution to human welfare. Although it is difficult to estimate just what Roosevelt took from his Harvard courses, one thing is clear—the courses themselves were part of that intellectual-political ferment that was leading to Progressivism.

Roosevelt emerged from college when the Progressive movement was in its early stages. The theme of that movement was political and economic reform in the interest of the common man, and it emphasized that concentration of economic power was the major reason for the failure of American democracy to realize fully its potentialities. Roosevelt's schooling in progressivism made these two points major elements of his economic-political philosophy. In his early political career F.D.R. was in the progressive tradition, fighting bossism and big business, supporting welfare legislation, advocating conservation and other liberal causes. He was influenced by the example of his "Uncle Ted" Roosevelt; he supported the progressivism of Woodrow Wilson.

The ideas of progressivism were applied by Roosevelt in his career as Assistant Secretary of the Navy, where he had practical experience in dealing with monopoly in industry and in working with a pro-labor policy. His statements about economic problems were much more sophisticated after his Navy Department experience than they were before it. Of importance, too, in these years, was economic mobilization in World War I, which gave some idea of what the modern industrial economy can accomplish when directed by government leadership toward the achievement of a particular goal.

The tradition of progressivism was carried on by Governor Smith of New York in the twenties, taking the form of a program of welfare legislation. F.D.R. was one of Smith's strongest supporters. It was in these years that Roosevelt emerged as a party leader who emphasized the economic basis of political parties and sought to base the policies of the Democratic party on a truly "progressive" program that would promote the welfare of the common man.

Roosevelt was fundamentally a reformer who accepted the general framework of economic institutions of his time. He accepted the concept of private enterprise—but wanted to improve the performance of business. As early as 1914 he had differed with his superior, Secretary of the Navy Daniels, over the purposes of the government's armor plate plant: while Daniels wanted a plant large enough to produce all the government's requirements, if necessary, F.D.R. wanted only a pilot plant that would act as a "yardstick" to judge the performance of the navy's suppliers. In the twenties F.D.R.'s work with the American Construction Council indicated the type of reform he thought was necessary in business: businessmen themselves could improve the performance of industry by cooperation, and public service could become the goal of responsible business leaders. In this way business itself could set its own high standards, and reduce the influence of the speculator, the promoter, and monopolist. Roosevelt was not troubled by the possibility that the trade association might develop into an organ of monopoly. What Roosevelt condemned about modern American business enterprise was the development of monopoly and the concentration of economic power—as, for example, in his Tammany Hall speech of July 1929. He was not anti-business, but was opposed to monopoly and financial promotions.

One of the most interesting aspects of Roosevelt's economic thought was his advocacy of land-use planning. Beginning with a strong interest in farming that arose in the rural environment at Hyde Park, he was an early advocate of conservation and reforestation. His desire to preserve and strengthen rural life appeared at an early date, and was supplemented by acquaintance with the regional plan idea as it was applied to cities. Government development of water power resources, advocated by Governor Smith, was likewise promoted by Roosevelt. During the latter's terms as governor these threads emerged as a regional plan for New York, comprising a comprehensive land-use survey, reforestation, road construction and building of regional markets, electrification, and dispersal of industry into rural areas.

Supplementing F.D.R.'s reforming attitude toward business and agriculture was his advocacy of social welfare legislation: laws protecting the worker, unemployment insurance, and old age insurance.

Roosevelt's advocacy of reform was always tempered by political considerations as he sought the best methods of promoting his ideas in the particular circumstances of the moment. Although his individual utterances are not good guides to his thinking, there was, nevertheless, a considerable degree of consistency in his actions and statements. The road to reform, as Roosevelt trod it, was not always straight and narrow, but its windings were always in a consistent direction.

While Roosevelt's economic philosophy found its greatest strength in long-range reforms, particularly welfare legislation and land-use planning, it found its greatest weakness in finding policies to meet the depression emergency. There was little enough in progressivism or in the desire to help the underdog—or, indeed, in the orthodox economic thinking of the late twenties and early thirties—that would lead to effective anti-depression policies.

Roosevelt's economic thought did contain the germ of a comprehensive attack on the depression: his underconsumption theory of depression origins. His proposals to raise farm purchasing power and provide a better relief system for the unemployed were considered by Roosevelt to be means by which consumer spending could be increased. But if he had carried his underconsumption theory to its logical conclusion he would have advocated a large program of public works, and this he did not do.

By far the most important aspect of Roosevelt's program in 1932 was its acceptance of the principle of planning. F.D.R. did not advocate a system of comprehensive, central planning for the entire economy. But he did show a willingness to experiment with different kinds of planning to meet the needs of different areas of the economy.

The American people in 1932 had been prepared for such an approach by two developments. In the first place, government intervention in economic affairs had been growing for decades. Beginning with intervention in a few areas of the economy on a piecemeal basis—public utility regulation, acts regulating working conditions in factories, and the beginnings of conservation programs— the nation moved into the area of monetary controls with the Federal Reserve Act of 1914 and into the beginnings of farm relief in the twenties. With the onset of the depression Hoover went even further, attempting especially in the area of finance and credit to take effective action against the depression.

In the second place, the depression itself was so severe, and recovery from it seemed so far off, that many persons lost faith in the idea that a normal, natural recovery would quickly come. Maybe the freely operating market economy would ultimately bring about a recovery, but it would take so long and be so costly that the nation could not trust itself to the process. F.D.R. himself expressed this idea in his speech at Oglethorpe University on May 22, 1932, when he advocated planning to avoid depressions. Roosevelt recognized the mood of the nation, that it was willing to experiment with new and fairly drastic methods of ordering economic life, and developed several types of planning in the early New Deal.

The principle of land-use planning expressed by Roosevelt as Governor appeared in the early New Deal in the Tennessee Valley Authority and its program of cooperation between a government corporation, local government, and individuals for river valley development.

The Civilian Conservation Corps of the early New Deal was another form given to F.D.R.'s ideas of land-use planning.

In the 1932 campaign Roosevelt accepted the principle of planning as a means of raising farm prices; the result was the AAA legislation of 1933, encompassing benefit payments to farmers and restriction of output. Planning for agriculture was to be done by the Federal Department of Agriculture, with approval by the farmers.

In industry, trade associations were to "adjust production and consumption" through codes of fair practice supervised by government. Roosevelt's work with the American Construction Council in the twenties was a partial step in that direction, and his endorsement of the major principles of the Swope Plan at the Commonwealth Club in San Francisco on September 23, 1932, was the preamble to restriction of output and maintenance of prices by trade associations under the NRA codes.

All of these forms that were given to the principle of planning encompassed varying amounts of government direction, voluntary participation, and compulsory participation. They were experiments in new forms of social control, variations on the theme of planning in economic affairs. Aside from emergency banking legislation, the most striking aspects of the program of the "hundred days" of March-June, 1933, were NRA and AAA, and perhaps the most lasting monument of the early New Deal will be TVA.

The "positive state" as it was developing in the Roosevelt program encompassed more than planning in several forms, however. The framework within which private enterprise could operate was to be more closely defined and Federal regulations extended, i.e., railroad bankruptcy laws and securities regulation. Welfare legislation was to be extended through unemployment and old age insurance. The debtor was to be aided by government provision of farm credit and loans to home owners. An expanded program of unemployment relief was to be adopted. In many ways other than planning the Federal government was to take greater responsibility for the functioning of the economy.

Clearly, the Roosevelt program enunciated in 1932 and developed in the early New Deal represented a turning point in economic policy. Although it had its antecedents, including a number of measures adopted during the Hoover administration, it represented an important advance of government intervention into new fields, using a variety of new techniques. The "positive state" was advancing on all fronts: regulation of business activity, welfare legislation, planning.

Herbert Hoover, who discerned this aspect of Roosevelt's New Deal, did not clarify matters by his charge of socialism. Roosevelt's program was far from the fundamental beliefs of the socialists: he did not advocate Federal ownership of basic industries or comprehensive planning of economic life, nor did he reject the profit system as the motivating force for production and distribution. Hoover misstated the problem, and Roosevelt's answer that he was not a socialist disposed of the criticism as far as Roosevelt was concerned.

Nevertheless, a real problem remains: would Roosevelt's "positive state" preserve conditions in the economy within which private enterprise could operate with vigor and health? Roosevelt thought that it would, indeed, that such action as his program represented was essential to the preservation of private enterprise. Nevertheless, the problem remains more than twenty years later. Is the "positive state" a temporary stopping place on the road to socialism, or is it a true alternative?

# 16

## *Toward Inflation:*
## *Monetary Influences upon Roosevelt*

[Fusfeld, *The Economic Thought of Franklin D. Roosevelt,* pp. 190–94.]

As the bad times became worse, Governor Roosevelt sought to find policies that would meet the larger depression problem, not only at the state level, but in the area of national policy.

His mail was full of suggestions, many of them of the crackpot variety, for ways to end the depression. A recurring theme was the proposal to place the unemployed on farms where they would be able to raise their own food, and one correspondent wrote from a hobo jungle near Sacramento that a back-to-the-land movement was the only alternative to destruction of the "capitalistic" Federal government by a proletarian revolution. Other proposals were to limit wage earners to one per family, and to shorten the work day in order to spread work. One man sent F.D.R. a U. S. Department of Commerce pamphlet entitled "You Can Make It for a Profit," describing how to make furniture and other objects out of wood, with the suggestion that the unemployed could put themselves to work.

Roosevelt was actively looking for ways out of the depression. He had appointed his Committee on Stabilization of Industry in 1930, but, as we have seen, the Committee didn't think much could be done about cyclical swings in economic activity and as the depression worsened it was gradually transformed into a relief organization.

Nevertheless, Roosevelt's curiosity about depression remedies continued. In May 1931, he lunched with Sir George Paish, who had just completed his book, *The*

*Way to Recovery*, and who asked Roosevelt to write a foreword to it. He read Sir Arthur Salter's *Recovery: The Second Effort*, and thought it was "exceedingly interesting."

In 1931 Roosevelt invited Norman Lombard, then executive vice-president of the Stable Money Association, to attend the Governors' Conference on Unemployment at Albany and present his views on recovery. Lombard wrote a paper on "The Relationship Between Unemployment and Business Depressions and Monetary and Credit Policies," which he sent to Roosevelt in January 1931, and which formed the basis for his discussion at the conference.

Lombard began with the proposition that the supply of money and credit should be more effectively kept in line with the sound needs of business; if this were done the industrial machine would work more smoothly. Other remedies were necessary too, but monetary reform was essential. He phrased the argument in terms of the value of gold:

> If measures can be taken to stabilize the purchasing power of gold, to that extent will unemployment be reduced. Fluctuations in the purchasing power of gold, or of money, affect unemployment as follows: When gold increases in value that means that the general level of prices falls (because gold will buy more), and, when gold decreases in value, the general level of prices rises (because gold will buy less).

The evils of falling prices (depression) and rising prices (boom) were discussed, with Lombard maintaining that in order to prevent unemployment and unhealthy booms it was necessary "to stabilize the general level of prices, i.e., the purchasing power of money." Lombard recognized that while changing the monetary base had been proposed as a means of stabilizing the value of money, the supply of credit was more important. He concluded with the statement that "stabilization of the purchasing power of our unit of value should be the primary aim of monetary credit policy."

Lombard did not advocate the use of Fisher's "compensated dollar" as a means of stabilizing the price level. He proposed the use of credit controls that were already available, and suggested that F.D.R. take that position at the Governors' Conference.

In January 1931, Lombard wanted to control business fluctuations by stabilizing the level of prices. But during the depression prices had fallen to very low levels. Should they be stabilized there? It was becoming obvious to proponents of stable money that stabilization at prosperous levels was considerably different from stabilization at depression levels. Thus, interest shifted to efforts to raise the price level and then stabilize. This became the goal of the Committee for the Nation, formed by a number of businessmen in the summer of 1932. A major part of the Committee's proposal was the raising of the price of gold by 75 per cent in order "to bring the commodity price level to a 1926 base," and such action was urged on the New Deal early in 1933.

The transition from Lombard's view to that of the Committee for the Nation is a simple one. Lombard maintained at the 1931 Governors' Conference that price stability depended upon a stable value for gold. But if the problem were viewed as one of raising prices, then the price of gold should be raised. This is exactly the twist given to the idea by Professors Warren and Pearson and the Committee for the Nation. Indeed, the continuity of ideas is paralleled by a continuity of organization: when the Stable Money Association could no longer support itself it donated what assets it had to the Committee for the Nation "in the expectation that as soon as reflation was completed, the Committee would take up the project of stabilization as its major objective."

One connection between Roosevelt and these ideas was Irving Fisher himself. Although Fisher was never a close adviser of Roosevelt's at any time, in September 1932 he sent the Governor galley proofs of his book *Booms and Depressions* and later a specially prepared copy a month in advance of publication. The Governor, off on a campaign trip through the West, took the proofs along with him.

It was not Irving Fisher, but Professors George F. Warren and Frank A. Pearson of Cornell University who were most influential in bringing ideas of monetary manipulation to F.D.R.'s attention.

The theory of Warren and Pearson was expressed in a series of articles published in *Farm Economics* in the years 1931-33, and later in their book, *Prices*. According to their theory the general level of prices was determined by the ratio of monetary stocks of gold to the physical volume of production. Thus:

> For the thirty year period 1885 to 1914, monetary stocks of gold in the United States had to increase at the same rate as the physical volume of production in the United States in order to maintain stable commodity prices. If gold stocks increased more rapidly than the production of other things, prices rose; if gold increased less rapidly, prices fell.

Warren and Pearson felt that declining commodity prices were the result of a rising value of gold: gold had an excessive value in the postwar period because of increased demand for the metal as many nations returned to the gold standard. As long as the monetary unit was tied to gold it, too, would have an excessive value, and commodity prices would remain low.

What were the remedies? Warren and Pearson argued that "when a nation suspends gold payments, it can establish any internal price level that it desires." Three methods could be used: "forcibly maintaining the dollar at a low gold value," "reducing the amount of gold in the dollar," or "substituting another metal for all or a part of the gold in the dollar."

Once the price level had been raised by this method it was to be stabilized by the use of a "compensated dollar." Warren and Pearson in 1933 took over Fisher's idea:

> If prices rose 0.1 per cent in a week, the weight of gold purchasable by a dollar would be increased 0.1 per cent until any rise was corrected. If prices fell 0.1 per cent, the weight of the gold purchasable by the dollar would be decreased 0.1 per cent. . . . This would make the dollar have the same value at all times. It would be independent of the business cycle.

Henry Morgenthau, Jr., had studied under Warren at Cornell, and it was he who first brought the professor to the attention of Governor Roosevelt. As early as December 1930, Warren visited Roosevelt at Warm Springs, and he became an important adviser on agricultural matters. The Governor was familiar with the articles by Warren in *Farm Economics*, and in May 1932, he wrote that "I am doing a lot of studying down here on the fluctuating dollar. If we don't do something for stabilization, we will be headed for real trouble."

Ideas of raising prices by raising the price of gold—or what is the same thing, devaluing the dollar—were in the air during the early thirties, and Roosevelt was familiar with them. He had read Salter's book, he had heard Lombard's discussion of the relationship between gold and prices, Fisher's ideas had been put before him, and he was familiar with the arguments of Warren and Pearson. Roosevelt may not have been converted to the ideas of Warren and Pearson in 1932, but he certainly was familiar with them and with others of a similar nature.

* * *

## 17

*Roosevelt Meets the Press:
The First Press Conference, March 8, 1933*

[*The Public Papers and Addresses of Franklin D. Roosevelt*, vol. 2, Samuel I. Rosenmann, ed. (New York: Random House, 1938), pp. 33–37.]

❋   ❋   ❋

Q. What is going to happen after Thursday night, Mr. President, when the holiday ends? Are you going to call another one?

THE PRESIDENT: That depends on how fast things move.

Q. Depending on what Congress does too?

THE PRESIDENT: (*Nods*) Of course, in regard to certain phases of the financial situation, undoubtedly there will be necessary some additional proclamations. That includes, for example, the question of control of gold. That is obvious. As long as nobody asks me whether we are off the gold standard or gold basis, that is all right, because nobody knows what the gold basis or gold standard really is. . . .

❋   ❋   ❋

Well, we are still on the gold standard, and the more people who bring gold to have it made into money the better. . . .

❋   ❋   ❋

Well, of course on that question of the foreign trade in gold, for a good long time as a matter of actual fact the United States has been the only country on the gold standard. France has been theoretically on a gold standard, but nobody in France can take a bill to the bank and get gold for it; and, as far as imports and exports go in France, they have been Government-controlled. The same thing holds true in Switzerland and Holland. Only up to last Sunday night we have had free trade in gold; and now we haven't. . . .

* * *

Q. In your Inaugural Address, in which you only touched upon things, you said you are for sound and adequate . . .

THE PRESIDENT: I put it the other way around. I said "adequate but sound."

Q. Now that you have more time, can you define what that is?

THE PRESIDENT: No. (*Laughter.*) In other words—and I should call this "off the record" information—you cannot define the thing too closely one way or the other. On Friday afternoon last we undoubtedly did not have adequate currency. No question about that. There wasn't enough circulating money to go around.

Q. I believe that. (*Laughter.*)

THE PRESIDENT: We hope that when the banks reopen a great deal of the currency that was withdrawn for one purpose or another will find its way back. We have got to provide an adequate currency. Last Friday we would have had to provide it in the form of scrip, and probably some additional issues of Federal Bank notes. If things go along as we hope they will, the use of scrip can be very greatly curtailed, and the amounts of new Federal Bank issues, we hope, can be also limited to a very great extent. In other words, what you are coming to now really is a managed currency, the adequateness of which will depend on the conditions of the moment. It may expand one week and it may contract another week. That part is all off the record.

Q. Can we use that part—managed?

THE PRESIDENT: No, I think not. . . .
Q. Now you came down to adequacy; but you haven't defined what you think is sound. Don't you want to define that now?
THE PRESIDENT: I don't want to define "sound" now. In other words, in its essence—this is entirely off the record—in its essence we must not put the Government any further in debt because of failed banks. Now, the real mark of delineation between sound and unsound is when the Government starts to pay its bills by starting printing presses. That is about the size of it.
Q. Couldn't you take that out and give it to us? That's a very good thing at this time.
THE PRESIDENT: I don't think so. There may be some talk about it tomorrow.
Q. When you speak of a managed currency, do you speak of a temporary proposition or a permanent system?
THE PRESIDENT: It ought to be part of the permanent system—that is off the record—it ought to be part of the permanent system, so we don't run into this thing again. . . .

\* \* \*

## Roosevelt Reopens the Banks Without Gold: March 10, 1933

[Executive Order No. 6073, Rosenmann, ed., *Public Papers*, vol. 2, p. 55.]

Until further order, no individual, partnership, association, or corporation, including any banking institution, shall export or otherwise remove or permit to be withdrawn from the United States or any place subject to the jurisdiction thereof any gold coin, gold bullion, or gold certificates, except in accordance with regulations prescribed by or under license issued by the Secretary of the Treasury.

No permission to any banking institution to perform any banking functions shall authorize such institution to pay out any gold coin, gold bullion or gold certificates except as authorized by the Secretary of the Treasury nor to allow withdrawal of any currency for hoarding, nor to engage in any transaction in foreign exchange except such as may be undertaken for legitimate and normal business requirements, for reasonable traveling and other personal requirements, and for the fulfillment of contracts entered into prior to March 6, 1933.

## *Roosevelt Disdains Inflation:*
## *April 7, 1933*

[Rosenmann, ed., *Public Papers,* vol. 2, pp. 119–20.]

*   *   *

*Q.* There have been reports of the Administration coming around again to inflation and I wonder if you will say something about that—I mean actual inflation of the currency.

THE PRESIDENT: No, not putting it that way. I will tell you, off the record, about the problem. After all, you ought to know it. It is an old story.

So much of the legislation we have had this spring is of a deflationary character, in the sense that it locks up money or prevents the flow of money, that we are faced with the problem of offsetting that in some way. I would not say "inflation of the currency," because that is not the necessary meaning.

You see, upon the closing of the banks we put away somewhere around four billion dollars. It was probably locked up before, but people did not know it. Now it is locked up, and people do know it. That is deflationary.

The effect of cutting very nearly a billion dollars off the Government payroll, including the veterans' cuts, cutting down of departments and cutting off 15 percent of employees' pay—it would probably run to perhaps not quite a billion dollars but very nearly that—means that much loss in the flow of money. That is deflationary.

Now, on the other side of the picture, we have C.C.C. giving employment to about 250,000 people in the forests and on works of various kinds. That is

only $250,000,000 as an offset. Then there is $500,-
000,000 as an offset on direct relief to the States.
That means we have not yet caught up with the
deflation that we have already caused. Therefore, of
course, we are going to talk about methods to give
more people work or to raise commodity prices, which
would . . .

Q. The Farm Bill would do it.

THE PRESIDENT: The Farm Bill would do it, of course, because it will raise commodity prices. The Farm Mortgage Bill and the Home Credit Bill will help because they will cut down the debt obligations of the small, indivdual family man—the home man. That is all to the good.

Q. Lower rentals . . .

THE PRESIDENT: But the question is whether all those things are really inflationary. They are helpful.

Q. Might we have an expression from you that there is no disposition on the part of the Administration to inflate the currency itself? I mean to print currency in a manner other than has been done.

THE PRESIDENT: What do you mean, start the printing presses?

Q. Yes.

THE PRESIDENT: Off the record, we are not going to start the printing presses. That is silly.

\* \* \*

## The Quarterback Explains:
## April 19, 1933

[Rosenmann, ed., *Public Papers*, vol. 2, pp. 137–40.]

THE PRESIDENT: What is the news?

Q. There has been some talk again about inflation. I don't know . . .

THE PRESIDENT: How do you define inflation?

Q. I don't know what it is. (*Laughter.*)

THE PRESIDENT: Neither do I. I have gotten to the point where even a cigarette tastes bad.

Q. That is a sign of a cold?

THE PRESIDENT: Yes, it certainly is.

Has the State Department given you the social program yet?

Q. Yes, it has.

THE PRESIDENT: That is the only news of any real importance that I know of.

I will tell you another thing there is today. If I were writing a story, here is the way I would put it: I don't know whether you can hear me at the back of the room—my voice isn't particularly strong this morning, since I have a cold. If I were going to write a story, I would write it along the lines of the decision that was actually taken last Saturday, but which really goes into effect today, by which the Government will not allow the exporting of gold, except earmarked gold for foreign Governments of course, and balances in commercial exchange. That is for straight movement.

The whole problem before us is to raise commodity prices. For the last year, the dollar has been shooting up and we decided to quit competition. The general effect probably will be an increase in commodity prices. It might well be called the next step in the general program.

Q. In other words, let the dollar take care of itself?

THE PRESIDENT: Yes, let the dollar take care of itself by protecting it against foreign currencies, and letting it seek its own natural level instead of trying artificially to support it.

Q. This policy would raise prices here at home. On the agenda of the International Conference there is an item for raising prices all over the world.

THE PRESIDENT: Right.

Q. Can you give us any background on how that would be done internationally? By your policy it would be done nationally, but how would it be done internationally?

THE PRESIDENT: Of course, this really is a constructive move in the sense that it puts us in the same position with nearly all the other Nations of the world. We start on the same footing; and because we are such a large Nation, it ought to emphasize the necessity for all Nations getting together on a more stable basis.

Q. Yes?

THE PRESIDENT: It is a constructive move. It is a little bit like what happened nationally. What we had to do last March was to clear away the dead wood. We had been heading for a bank smash-up for a long time and what we did was a drastic thing, which was to clear away the dead wood and start afresh. Now, this is along the same general line. It puts us on a par with other Nations, and it is hoped eventually that it will aid somewhat to raise prices all over the world. However, as to what the actual details of that will be or the methods to be pursued, we don't know yet. There have been half a dozen different suggestions made. That is one of the things we are talking about.

*Q.* Can you explain the process by which this would tend to raise commodity prices here at home?

THE PRESIDENT: Here is a simple illustration: There are a good many commodities which are sold in terms of world trade. Well, for instance, cotton. Cotton is sold on a gold basis and, with the dollar where it has been, it works out to a certain number of cents. Therefore, if the dollar were to sell off 10 percent, the price of cotton in terms of dollars would go up 10 percent. . . .

*Q.* Have you any other ideas in mind on this so-called inflation or reflation as to the steps to be taken?

THE PRESIDENT: Nothing else. I think on the general subject, it is awfully difficult to particularize.

It is a little bit like a football team that has a general plan of game against the other side. Now, the captain and the quarterback of that team know pretty well what the next play is going to be and they know the general strategy of the team; but they cannot tell you what the play after the next play is going to be until the next play is run off. If the play makes ten yards, the succeeding play will be different from what it would have been if they had been thrown for a loss. I think that is the easiest way to explain it.

Here is a team that has a perfectly definite objective, which is to make a touchdown, so far as commodity prices go. The basis of the whole thing really comes down to commodity prices. And, this is entirely off the record, the general thought is that we have got to bring commodity prices back to a recent level, but not to the 1929 level except in certain instances. You take, for instance, city real estate in 1929. It was then altogether too high, and you ought not to bring city real estate back to the 1929 level. That is obvious. On the other hand, farm commodity prices were comparatively low in 1929 and have been going down since rather steadily for five or six years. So that it has got to be a definitely controlled inflation, because the man on the street does not understand it any more than the average banker understands it. It has got to be a controlled price level.

*Q.* Mr. President, is it still the desire of the United States to go back on the international gold standard?

THE PRESIDENT: Absolutely; one of the things we hope to do is to get the world as a whole back on some form of gold standard. . . .

*Q.* Is it all right for us to use that line about controlling the price level? You had been speaking off the record.

THE PRESIDENT: Yes, I think you can use that with the very definite thought in mind that we have to raise the price level but keep it from going too high.

*Q.* You spoke of some form of international gold standard. Does that imply the possibility of a lower gold content in the monetary units of the world?

THE PRESIDENT: Well, I would not put it that way. One of the things they are talking about—the economic end of the conference—is a different gold ratio, a different gold reserve to currency. You see, the old standard was 40 percent and there is talk of changing that ideal 40 percent standard, which was the old ideal, to something else.

*Q.* Would you describe this as another step toward a controlled or managed currency?

THE PRESIDENT: Currency? Yes, but I think you ought to couple with that the effort to get a more controlled credit, because the two go hand in hand.

\* \* \*

## Politics and Monetary Policy: Raymond Moley's Perspective

[Raymond Moley, *After Seven Years* (New York: Harper and Brothers, 1939), pp. 156–61.]

But to suppose for a moment that, once the bank crisis had passed, we thought we had achieved a permanent solution of the banking and financial problems is like imagining that Dr. James Alexander Miller, having pulled a tubercular patient through a critical case of pneumonia, would tell him that he was no longer in need of medical care. Yet that is just the kind of interpretation most of those who have written on the subject place upon the administration's course between March 13th, when the first of the banks were reopened, and April 19th, when the gold standard was suspended and Roosevelt publicly announced his acceptance of the power to inflate the currency under the Thomas amendment. The administration thought it had fixed everything, the story runs; it suddenly found it hadn't—either because it had opened too many unsound banks or because the millions of dollars of deposits frozen in banks still closed were discovered to be acting as a deflationary factor (this part of the story varies according to the conservatism of the writer); and so then it took the most attractive "out" by rushing into inflation.

Good stories—all of them—overlooking only the facts that Roosevelt recognized the need for pretty fundamental banking reform; that he was perfectly aware of the strength of inflationary sentiment in and out of Congress, and that his mind was open on the question whether the superdeflationary effects of the March crisis and the measures taken to deal with it would not require an antidote of drastic action.

This certainly isn't to imply that Roosevelt himself was "sold" on the idea of inflation before or immediately after his inauguration. I can testify that he wasn't. But he was very consciously waiting to see whether the effort to preserve the monetary standard after March 13th wouldn't entail greater sacrifices in terms of sinking money incomes than the American people would bear, or should be expected to bear, and wouldn't be overwhelmed by the political forces demanding what would amount to uncontrolled inflation.

I doubt that more than a handful of economists in the United States ever realized just how compelling the force of political circumstance was. Their idea seems to be that, from mid-February on, Roosevelt was beset by a few crackpot congressmen and senators (who could only "be counted upon to make a certain number of wild speeches"), a few businessmen and farm leaders organized under the title "The Committee for the Nation," and a couple of starry-eyed monetary experts; that Roosevelt mistook their voice for the voice of the people and therefore grossly overestimated the demand for inflation; and that if he had pulled a Grover Cleveland, "setting his face" against currency "tinkering," he could have exploded the myth of inflationary sentiment.

The cold fact is that the inflationary movement attained such formidable strength by April 18th that Roosevelt realized that he could not block it, that he could, at most, try to direct it.

Our realization of its growing momentum was, of course, a subjective process. For me, it was associated, curiously enough, with a little tune Will Woodin composed on the piano one night late in February after he and I had listened to Senator Burton K. Wheeler and ex-Senator Jonathan Bourne, Jr., expatiate for three hours on the advantages that would come from free coinage of silver. Will had called it "Lullaby in Silver" because he com-

## Roosevelt's Decision 133

posed it, he said, "to get this silver talk off my mind before I go to bed." After that night every time anyone talked to me of inflation, Will's "Lullaby in Silver" ran through my head until, by early April, the simple little tune had taken on the majestic proportions of a crashing symphonic theme in my consciousness.

But political judgments aren't made on the basis of such quirks of the imagination. The decisions of April 18th and 19th were the prosaic results of a counting of noses in the Senate.

No one doubted that inflation had a majority in the House. The only unknown was exactly how strong inflationary sentiment had grown in the Senate since January 24th, when eighteen votes were recorded in its favor. We found that out on Monday, April 17th, just before the Senate voted on Wheeler's amendment to the farm bill providing for the free coinage of silver at a ratio of sixteen to one.

Immediately after that measure was introduced, a Western senator put through a call to me. He was not, he explained, convinced that "sixteen to one" was sound. He wanted to support the administration if he could. But he had the "folks back home" to keep in mind and he simply couldn't afford, in any real test, to stand out against inflation. What could I suggest that he do?

I suggested that the senator watch the roll call, absent himself from the chamber until the end of the roll call, and then, if there were thirty votes for free silver, vote "No"; but if there were less than thirty votes for it, he might vote "Yes."

Several other senators called my office that day, put the same question, and got the same answer. Still others made inquiry through other channels. All told, we knew that well over ten senators either voted "No" on the Wheeler amendment or refrained from voting on it altogether, despite the fact that they were prepared to support inflation of some sort.

So, though the Wheeler amendment was defeated by a vote of 43 to 33, Roosevelt had conclusive evidence on April 17th that the Senate contained a majority in favor of inflation.

What alternative was there then? A clear one for the theorist working over his charts. But none for a President of the United States. As Walter Lippmann put it, the only questions left were "how inflation was to be produced and whether or not it would be managed and controlled."

Directly after the vote on the Wheeler amendment, Senator Elmer Thomas of Oklahoma introduced another authorizing the President to do any or all of the following things: (1) to issue greenbacks in meeting all forms of current and maturing federal obligations and in buying up United States bonds; (2) to fix the ratio of the value of silver to gold and provide for free coinage of silver by proclamation; and (3) to fix the weight of the gold dollar by proclamation.

Here were all three of the dreaded proposals for inflation bound up together in a way deliberately calculated to enlist all the inflationary support in Congress. And if there had been any doubt that it would succeed in so doing—which there wasn't—it would finally have been dispelled on the morning of Tuesday, April 18th.

Early that morning I was awakened by a telephone call from Senator Bulkley of Ohio. He gave me positive assurance that the Thomas amendment would go through as it stood unless the administration took a hand, and the most the administration could hope to achieve, he added, was congressional consent to vesting inflationary power in the President. Two minutes later Jimmy Byrnes telephoned the same message. I asked Jimmy to stop by, pick me up, and accompany me to the White House. (All through those weeks the nine-o'clock visit to the presidential bedside was routine.)

## Roosevelt's Decision 135

Before Jimmy left the White House that morning, it had been decided that Roosevelt would accept the Thomas amendment provided Thomas agreed to a thorough rewriting of it. Jimmy was entrusted with the responsibility of bringing Thomas around.

He succeeded. A few hours later Thomas handed F. D. R. a copy of his amendment, with the statement that he was agreeable to "minor changes" so long as the "big principle" of his measure wasn't destroyed.

That night there was scheduled a conference at the White House for discussion of the coming meetings with MacDonald and the other British representatives who were on the Atlantic en route to Washington. We joined the President promptly after dinner—Secretary Hull, Secretary Woodin, Senator Pittman, Herbert Feis, James Warburg, Budget Director Douglas, Bill Bullitt, and myself. But we never did get down to the business for which we'd gathered because, as we filed into the room, Roosevelt handed me the copy of the amendment Thomas had given him and said, "Here, Ray, you act as a clearing house to take care of this. Have it thoroughly amended and then give them the word to pass it." And then, turning to the others, "Congratulate me."

At that moment hell broke loose in the room. This was the first any of those present, except Woodin, Pittman, and I, knew of Roosevelt's decision that morning. Douglas, Warburg, and Feis were so horrified that they began to scold Mr. Roosevelt as though he were a perverse and particularly backward schoolboy. For two hours they argued the case, pacing up and down the room, interrupted more by each other than by the President's good-natured replies. Secretary Hull said nothing at all, but looked as though he had been stabbed in the back when, at one point in the rough and tumble, F. D. R. took out a ten-dollar bill, examined it, and said, "Ha! Issued by the First

National Bank of ——. That's in Tennessee—in *your* state, Cordell. How do *I* know it's any good? Only the fact that I think it is makes it so." And Will, who had protested a little when he heard the news earlier, did no more than whisper to me, "What's a Secretary of the Treasury to do when he's presented with a *fait accompli?*"

We left the White House close to midnight, and I rode with Key Pittman out to his house, making plans for the next day, before I returned to my hotel. When I reached my apartment, I found Douglas, Warburg, and Bullitt in my sitting room still violently discussing the "enormity" of the step Roosevelt was taking. The stream of talk went on for well over an hour then, and reached its crescendo with Lew Douglas', "Well, this is the end of Western civilization." Eventually the three men left, and I went to bed. Later, I heard the sequel. Neither Douglas nor Warburg slept that night. They wandered around the streets, bewailing the step that had been taken. At five in the morning they returned to the hotel and aroused Bullitt from sleep. Apparently they had to tell somebody the net result of all their travail; they had decided, at last, that they could not change the President's major decision and so they would concentrate on getting him to agree to one or two small limitations upon the powers conferred by the measure.

Early that Wednesday morning I went down to the Capitol, where, in the office of the foreign-relations committee, Pittman, Byrnes, a couple of draftsmen, and I began the two-day job of revision. That morning the President announced his decision to the press.

That night the announcement was made that henceforth, the export of gold would be prohibited. The United States had cut loose from the gold standard.

These are the facts, so far as I know them, about April 19th. Three-quarters of the explanation of what was behind them, Lindley has suggested, lay in the powerful sequence of events. But intimate observation of Roosevelt during those days has always made me believe that the element of circumstance played an even greater role. Rationalizations—the business of making a virtue of necessity—came after the decisions were made. It is true that those rationalizations, in turn, were to become the intellectual bridges to a silly and futile monetary policy— the brief adoption, in October, of Professor Warren's theory that changes in the gold price would cause commodity prices to vary proportionately. But if an active, choate desire to achieve a dollar whose gold content fluctuated with the price level played any appreciable part in determining Mr. Roosevelt's course in April, he certainly succeeded in concealing it from me.

Wool has been pulled over my eyes more than once. Perhaps it was then. Yet I believed and still believe that Roosevelt did not abandon the gold standard because of any positive theories about an "adjustable" dollar, but to prevent further deflation. I still believe that Roosevelt accepted the Thomas amendment only to circumvent uncontrolled inflation by Congress. I had the feeling that Roosevelt would baffle the "wild men" more effectively than a fundamentalist could, and that he could be trusted to resist the more dangerous forms of money magic. And all but the most/extreme gold-standard adherents seemed to share that feeling.

It's ironic that the one form of inflation that was at that time not feared at all—budgetary inflation—has, after six years, become the real menace to our financial solidarity, until for those who like to think of things in terms of ultimates, in terms of threats to Western civilization, it is, I suppose, as good a talking point as any.

## 22

*The Money Muddle:*
*James Warburg Observes*

[James P. Warburg Papers, Oral History Project, Columbia University, New York.]

### March 14 [1933, p. 147]

*10:45 A.M.* Talked to Perkins [the same James Perkins] after Union Pacific meeting and found that he and I are in full accord on foreign exchange policy. Talked also to Schubart here [Schubart was the foreign exchange manager of the Bank of Manhattan], who is likewise in accord. (In other words, both these people corroborated my feeling that we should not be supporting the dollar at all; that it was better for us to have the dollar go down.) Perkins told me that Altschul [that's Frank Altschul who was then the senior partner of Lazard Freres, a private banking house in New York] after flopping around a good deal, had also come to this conclusion.

### March 15 [1933, pp. 150–53]

*8:00 A.M.:* Woodin then left and Moley, Taussig and I got down to business on the main topic of the day, namely, the foreign exchange situation. I told Moley the conclusions I had reached and reported in detail my conversations with Perkins.

Concretely, I made the following recommendations:

1) That we do not attempt at this moment to decide whether we shall leave the gold embargo and return to a gold basis in the immediate future or at some later date.

2) That we do not put into force codified exchange restrictions on the German model, but back

up Kent's policy of stating broad intentions and relying on the cooperation and common sense of the banks on the Bank of England method.

3) That the widely held opinion, that a firm dollar in the exchange markets is a great sign of strength and a great thing for the country, was, in fact, erroneous; that it is in our interest at the present moment to have a cheap dollar in terms of the other exchanges,

a) because what England and France want us to do is to stay on the gold basis and continue in the same conditions that *has* gone on for the past months, in other words, be the playground for money that is afraid to stay at home;

b) because a firm dollar means for them deflation and falling commodity prices, whereas a weak dollar, or put the other way around, a strong pound means higher prices for commodities having an export market, such as cotton and wheat, with a tendency sympathetically to affect other commodity prices;

c) because there is tremendous and increasing pressure for inflationary relief from all possible sources and taking all possible forms. Unless some account is taken of this pressure and some concession made to it, Congress cannot be held in line. Cheapening of the dollar would make all these people happy at least for a certain length of time, and during this time it will be possible to develop a real program;

d) because even if devaluating the dollar to a certain extent may be something we shall regret having done, it is easier to remedy than to undo fifteen different relief measures taken heterogeneously and without proper correlation.

4) That the matter discussed in (3) should be made the object of very careful and intensive study immediately, but that irrespective of whether such

study would bear out my belief as stated in (3), we should at once arm ourselves with a stabilization fund.

The *reasons* for this last recommendation are:

a) that if we establish such a large fund, we serve notice that we are going to manage the dollar to what we consider our best advantage and that we are no longer going to be the football of European manipulation;

b) that the mere existence of such a fund will probably make it unnecessary to use it, but that we have in Fred Kent a man who is perfectly capable of matching brains with the management of the British stabilization fund (I pointed out this experience during the war);

c) that irrespective of whether we ever use the fund, it is a very much healthier way for us to sit down at the table with the British if we have a gun on our hip so long as we know that they are coming with a gun on their hip. It is very much easier to suggest that we both unbuckle our belts and lay the guns on the table than for us to make this suggestion to the British if they know and we know that we have no gun.

3:15 P.M.: Went over to the White House with Hull, Feis, and Taussig. We were shown into the Executive Office, but in order to get rid of interruption, moved over into the White House proper and were served tea during our discussion, which lasted over an hour and a half. I stated my suggestions to the President and he asked a considerable number of very searching questions. Feis took rather a bureaucratic, but not unhelpful position. Taussig was practically silent, and most of the discussion consisted of my answering questions asked by the President and the Secretary. The President finally said that he thought the suggestion had great merit and that he would like it pursued energetically at once. I said that I was not capable of working out the details of a stabilization fund but that Kent was, and suggested that I be permitted to ask him to come down at once; Feis suggested that George Harrison be asked to come too (*sic*). This latter was left rather vague. I went back to Moley's office and reported the conversation. Moley was delighted, but said very emphatically that Harrison should not be talked to.

### *April 11 [Entered in Diary for April 10]*

*12:30 A.M.*: After more rambling we [Taussig, Moley, Feis] finally got to usual point, that the tariff discussions are futile without exchange stabilization; that exchange stabilization is impossible without a definite gold policy here, and that too many people are playing with the idea of devaluing the dollar [including the President].

### *April 13 [1933, pp. 455–56]*

*9:00 P.M.*: Conference with FDR. [FDR and Warburg did not understand each other.] Should have mentioned that the President at the opening of our conversation, grinned at me and said, "Well, the Bank of Manhattan today asked for permission to ship $600,000 of gold and precipitated a tremendous argument in the Treasury. Some of them, including Ballantine, were for granting such license while others were opposed. I told them to grant this one license to your bank but not to grant any more." I told the President how it had come about and that I myself had told Kent to refuse the permission the bank had asked for and that it would be very foolish to issue such licenses.

### *April 18 [1933, pp. 492–93, 495–96, 498–99]*

*8:30 A.M.*: Breakfast with Moley, Bullitt and Woodin. We discussed gold shipments. Woodin is in favor of issuing licenses. I told him that I was entirely opposed to it, at least during the preliminary conversations with the British and French. Again, I am not sure that I convinced him.

Moley said that Senator Thomas was today going to introduce a resolution in the Senate, which would undoubtedly pass, authorizing the President to devalue the dollar or to turn loose the printing press, or I'd carry out any other form of inflation. Moley and Bullitt thought it would be harmless to have this happen and wanted me to work out a rider to this resolution, which would enable the President to carry out the Bunny [the debt plan]. I took just the opposite position and said that if such a resolution passed, it would make it very difficult for us to talk gold standard, etc. to the foreigners and that I thought by all means the resolution should be killed. Moley finally agreed and went off to the White House.

*8:45 to 11:30 P.M.*: With the President at the White House. For the first half hour Moley, Bullitt and I were alone with him; then Senator Pittman, Hull, Feis and Taussig appeared, followed shortly by Woodin and Lou Douglas.

The evening can, without exaggeration, be described as highly dramatic. The first thing the President did was to inform us, with a chuckle, that we had definitely abandoned the gold standard and that this would be announced tomorrow. He said that he had reached the definite decision to stop all export license on gold.

\* \* \*

As a *fait accompli*, there was no discussion. The President then said he did not want to discuss anything else for the time being except a very important matter which required immediate attention. He produced in printed form Senator Thomas' amendment to the farm bill (the thing we had killed yesterday morning), and said that he had told Senator Thomas in a conference a few hours before that he would accept this amendment, but that he would like it carefully rewritten. He made it very clear that the substance was not a matter for discussion, but that he wanted us to concentrate with great care on the form.

He said that the reason for the amendment was that unless something of this sort was done immediately Congress would take the matter in its own hands and legislate mandatory law instead of permissive. He then read us the bill which, in brief, authorizes the President to bring about inflation by any one of the four methods or any combination of the four methods. . . .

*　　*　　*

Before the arrival of the others I waged a lone battle and received very little support until Douglas and Woodin arrived. Thereafter Douglas and I carried the brunt of the attack with a certain amount of support from Hull, occasional wavering support from Pittman and Woodin, and a few timid observations by Feis. At the risk of being impudent I went so far as to say that I considered the passage of such a bill completely hare-brained and irresponsible, and that unless it were accompanied by a statement from the President that he had no intention of using the powers conferred, it would result in uncontrolled inflation and complete chaos; furthermore, that if it were accompanied by such a statement, it would put the President in a most unfair and impossible position. It was quite impossible to make the President see that converting our $21,000,000,000 of funded debt into currency, that is, into demand obligation, would bring about uncontrolled inflation. He and Moley took the position, more or less agreed to by Pittman, that at any time they could reverse the machinery and thus control the inflation—a view which I can only characterize as King Canute. Bullitt, much to my surprise, said very little after we had left the White House, but did not take the whole thing seriously.

We left the White House at 11:30. I came over to the hotel with Woodin and Douglas. Later on Moley, Taussig and Bullitt joined us and we debated until half past two, although Woodin went to bed very much earlier. Douglas and I took the position that if such legislation were allowed to pass it was perfectly futile to attempt to discuss anything with the foreigners and equally futile to discuss any other legislation of whatsoever nature because all programs would be completely knocked into a cocked hat.

### April 22 [1933, p. 535]

*2:15 to 5:00 P.M.:* At the British Embassy in conference with Sir Frederick Leith-Ross, Bewley and Oventon on the British side, and Hull, Pittman, Moley, Feis, Bullitt, Taussig and me. Leith-Ross began with a dissertation on how difficult everything had become because we had gone off the gold standard. His contention was that our action had been unnecessary and had made the entire problems of the Economic Conference exceedingly difficult, if not impossible. Hull made a brief statement of the conditions which precipitated our actions; Feis hemmed and hawed in elaborating the same, and from there on the conference developed into a debate between Leith-Ross and me. Leith-Ross said that he thought we should have taken measures to raise the domestic price level without going off gold. After considerable maneuvering, I jockeyed him into saying that he thought these measures should have consisted of doing just as we did do in the Thomas amendment. I said that if we had passed the Thomas amendment without first putting an embargo on gold, we would have driven American capital out of the country, and that this would have resulted in our taking a series of restrictive measures which were just the sort of nationalistic action that we had hoped international cooperation would avoid.

# 23

## *A Deliberate Course: Herbert Feis' Perspective*

[Herbert Feis, *1933: Characters in Crisis* (Boston: Little, Brown and Co., 1966), pp. 108–31.]

During the first hundred days, Roosevelt's handling of domestic economic affairs was dazzling; of foreign economic affairs, dizzying.

The measures which the new President employed for reopening the banks were in fact similar to those which Hoover's group had worked out, and he sailed along from day to day, enjoying the irony of his role as rescuer of our financial and banking system. When on the afternoon of March 8, as the main features of his emergency program were being settled, Felix Frankfurter entered his office, Roosevelt's first words of greeting were, "Well, Felix, they'll make a banker of me yet."

* * *

Before Roosevelt took office I received an inkling that he might decide that the United States had better leave the gold standard.

In February 1933 Tugwell was in Washington on other business. He came out to our house for luncheon and there he told me that the President-Elect had asked him about a week before to look up the legislation under which President Wilson had, during the First World War, embargoed gold shipments from the United States. He asked for my help in securing the information. I could foresee that if the word spread that the President-Elect was likely to order a cessation of gold shipments the outflow would turn into a flood. So fearful that if I talked to Secretary Mills himself my inquiry would travel to the White House at once and possibly excite some sort of public statement, I turned instead to my close working associate, Daniel Bell, the Assistant Secretary of the Treasury. I told him in the utmost confidence what information was wanted. Within a few minutes he called me back and gave me what he said were the pertinent legislative references. Tugwell having come to my office, I turned over the citations to him. I suggested that he ought to advise the President-Elect to have his own legal counsel study the subject thoroughly. He at once telephoned Hyde Park and gave Roosevelt the information in hand, with the suggestion that the lawyers be asked to review it. The President-Elect instructed Tugwell to ask Senator Thomas J. Walsh of Montana, who was to be designated Attorney General in the new cabinet (he died on March 2, on his way to the inauguration), to look into the matter. But that able Senator was away from Washington on a honeymoon with a young wife. Tugwell had to phone the President-Elect again. He was then told to turn for help either to Senator James Byrnes of South Carolina or to Senator Key Pittman, the silverite.

Tugwell hurried off to the Capitol to discuss the matter with one of them. Though uneasy, I felt obliged to refrain from telling even Secretary of State Stimson of Tugwell's request. I went about other business, but I was not allowed to let the matter slip out of my mind. Bell called on the telephone again to tell me he was sorry but the information he had given me was partly incorrect. I remarked at once that that was fine, just fine, and when he asked me why, I blurted out to him that it had already been sent "high, wide and far." When he asked me what that meant, I was called upon to tell him that it had been passed on to Hyde Park. Thereupon he exclaimed he thought it was necessary to tell Under-Secretary Ballantine what had happened, and ask him to come over to the State Department at once and bring along the Treasury lawyers. I asked him to wait before doing so.

Tugwell had told me he was taking the five o'clock train for New York. Looking at the clock I saw there was still a few moments before it would leave. I telephoned the stationmaster and asked him to inform Tugwell that it was imperative that he take a later train. A porter took off his bags while he telephoned me and we arranged to meet in Pittman's office. As he did not see any further need of consulting with Treasury officials, I phoned Bell and told him not to come to the State Department but rather to bury the subject in his mind. Then I phoned Ballantine and, though I could tell he was offended, pledged him to secrecy.

This was in a sense a silly injunction. For when I met Tugwell in Pittman's office they were already engaged in active pursuit of the information through lawyers in the Senate Legislative Bureau who might not feel obligated to maintain secrecy. After a brief talk I said I did not think that I could be of any further use at the moment. Pittman agreed and said he would complete the research and would phone Roosevelt. Before going out the door, however, I could not refrain from remarking again that if news of this action under consideration became public we might expect a great surge in the flow of gold out of the United States.

This inquiry and episode stimulated me to set down on March 3, the eve of the advent of the new group, my impressions of the international monetary situation. They were: (1) that only a handful of countries still maintained legal gold value for their currencies, but these included important countries such as France, Holland, Belgium and Germany, and they were fearful of being forced to abandon the gold standard; (2) that the recent fluctuation of currencies not on the gold standard had been large. For example, the value of the British pound in terms of the American dollar had recently swung all the way from

$3.20 to $3.70; (3) that stabilization need not mean the end of depreciation of currencies in terms of gold. One appealing possibility was the devaluation by agreement of the currencies of all countries that thought it advisable; and (4) that perhaps the British government could be induced *after* general devaluation to enter into a stabilization accord provided it was subject to review if Britain should again find it too hard to balance its foreign accounts without suppressing domestic economic activities. The most recent utterances of Prime Minister MacDonald and Chancellor of the Exchequer Chamberlain seemed to me more pliable than their earlier ones.

Should the American government at this time commit itself to maintaining the existing gold value of the dollar, even temporarily, I queried? Would it not rather be well advised to develop a program for general devaluation and provisional stabilization that might or might not be presented to the British and other governments depending on future circumstances?

I sent copies of this memo to Stimson, Mills, Hull and Moley. I do not remember whether any of them read it and spoke to me about it.

One of Roosevelt's first actions on taking office, as already told, was to close all banks, and in that connection to make exports of gold and silver and the transfer of capital out of the United States subject to license. But this could be and was construed by many as merely one feature of a temporary emergency program rather than a deliberate monetary policy. Secretary of the Treasury Woodin explicitly assured the country on March 5 that the United States had not gone off the gold standard.

* * *

On March 15 I was taken by Hull to tea with the President in the White House. James Warburg, consultant to Roosevelt about monetary policies, had been recommending that the American government maintain its virtual prohibition of gold exports and allow the value of the dollar to fall further in order to cause prices to rise and to avert other inflationary measures. He was of the opinion also that for the time being the question of whether or not to devalue the dollar ought to be left open; and that the government should set aside a large "stabilization fund" through which to manage and control movements in the value of the dollar. The President quizzed him about these views, with which I was in general accord. As recorded by Warburg in his journal, "The President finally said that he thought the suggestion had great merit and that he would like to see it pursued energetically at once." When Warburg told Moley of this conversation, Moley said he was delighted. But he was strongly opposed to consulting Harrison about the stabilization fund. Warburg proceeded to try to work out a plan whereby it would be operated by a foreign exchange division of the Treasury.

In anticipation of the scheduled talks with the foreign missions which were soon to flock to Washington, Warburg, with the President's knowledge and the approval of Woodin and Moley, had several talks about monetary matters with the British Treasury representative, Kenneth Bewley, the French financial attaché, Emmanuel Monick, and Paul Claudel, the French poet who was serving as ambassador. On March 30 Warburg reported to the President that they had agreed on many elements of a common monetary policy. Among these were: that the main countries should individually and collectively try to maintain stability of their currencies; that *ultimately* they should return to the gold standard; and that thereafter central banks should have a uniform rate of gold reserves against currencies and a supplementary one which could be in either gold or silver. Whether or not the dollar was to be devalued in terms of gold before this program was put into effect was left open.

A few days later, April 4, when the President had spent almost the whole morning reviewing with Hull, Moley, Warburg, Bullitt and myself the program to be discussed with the foreign missions, Warburg read his memorandum about monetary and fiscal actions. Roosevelt said he liked it. Warburg asked him whether, in the provision for ultimate return to the gold standard, he wished the question of devaluation of the dollar to remain undetermined. The President said that was exactly what he wanted.

\* \* \*

By the spring of 1933 diverse organizations and groups were crying aloud for some kind of monetary inflation or devaluation, or both. Most effective, probably, was the Committee of the Nation. Among its members were prominent merchants, such as the head of Sears Roebuck, some journalists, some Wall Street operators and some foreign exchange speculators. Their purpose was to get the United States off the gold standard and to bring about devaluation of the dollar from which they would profit either as speculators in foreign exchange or as business men. Another group, more conservative, who stood to gain by devaluation were those who had already exported gold or otherwise acquired liquid deposits in foreign banks. They conceived that they were merely protecting the value of their capital. More voluble and on the friendliest terms with the members of Congress were the advocates for the reincorporation of silver in the monetary system as an addition to monetary and banking reserves and the currency. These included such influential figures as Senator Key Pittman and Senator Elmer Thomas of Oklahoma. Their case for bringing back silver was spread among the populace by the broadcasts of the radio priest

## Roosevelt's Decision 151

of Detroit, Father Coughlin, who, it became known later, was speculating heavily in that metal either on his own account or on that of the Church. Then there were the exporters—especially of farm products—who had been at a disadvantage ever since Great Britain had gone off the gold standard and the value of sterling had fallen much below its previous parity with the dollar.

And lastly—and this is not authoritative classification —there were students of public affairs who thought that the time had come to break—or at least to brake—the control of the Federal Reserve System over the amount of paper money in circulation, and that the government should issue directly or indirectly other types of paper money to pay its bills and promote business activity.

Believers in the necessity of resorting to any or all such actions circulated in the corridors of the Senate and the House of Representatives and sought appointments with the President and the Secretary of the Treasury. They even infiltrated into my subordinate office in the State Department in order to present their arguments that the United States must cast off at least temporarily the restrictive bonds of the international gold standard. Some seemed self-interested, scheming and ignorant, but basically I was in accord with their intent and inclination.

The American government was now actually on the verge of going off the gold standard. During March and early April the government had issued a few licenses permitting the export of gold. The exchange value of the dollar had been declining slightly. The foreign exchanges were in confusion as a result of the uncertainty that still surrounded the intentions of the United States Treasury with respect to gold exports. These had been becoming increasingly profitable on paper; and it was becoming probable that the occasional issuance of licenses to export small amounts of gold would no longer be sufficient to support the dollar. The wish to exchange it for gold or other currencies was stimulated by the combined demand for some sort of swift and drastic inflation which was breaking loose in Congress. These impelled the President to end the pretense that we were adhering to the gold standard and assent to legislation which entrusted him with vast inflationary powers.

When the exchange markets opened on the morning of April 18, the dollar broke badly. The Treasury refused applications for licenses to export gold. The President had asked Secretary Hull to come to the White House that night to discuss the imminent conferences with the many foreign missions invited to Washington. The Secretary took Senator Pittman and me along. I went with the intention of using this fortuitous chance to plead with the President to postpone the Monetary and Economic Conference till midsummer, and preferably until the autumn. By that time, I thought, the American government would have more reliable knowledge of the extent and nature of actions required to stimulate recovery, and thus be able to determine with greater certainty what international engagements it might assume. But this intention was driven out of mind by what occurred.

When we entered the Red Room the President, seated, greeted us jovially. At his left, on a couch, Raymond Moley was bending forward, holding a small black notebook and a pencil (or pen). Warburg and Bullitt were there; our arrival evidently interrupted a lively conversation. Soon afterwards Secretary of the Treasury Woodin and Director of the Budget Douglas sauntered in.

The talk about the policies and proposals to be discussed with visiting foreign missions never got under way. For the President, with a chuckle, informed the assembled group that the American government was abandoning the gold standard. No more gold exports would be licensed; holders of paper currency would no longer be permitted to redeem it for gold. He averred that he had been impelled to take this action at this time because he had been informed—presumably by the Treasury and the Federal Reserve Bank of New York—that in order to maintain the existing value of the dollar in the face of withdrawals from the bank and a flight of capital, the American government might have to permit within a few days the export of one hundred million dollars or more of gold. The American gold-supply position was, the President knew, as strong as it had been in many years. Our stock of gold was adequate for a much larger volume of credit and Federal Reserve currency. Still he was afraid if the American government remained obligated to defend the dollar, the drain of these gold reserves might become unbearable, and the government and the banking system would have to clamp down hard on tendencies to expand. Moreover, he hated to think of the unearned gain which speculators would reap.

This wish—to prevent further loss of gold due to the defensive and speculative demands for it—was certainly one of the precipitating causes of his decision. But it was not the only one. Going off gold would, he thought, cause a rapid rise in dollar prices of goods and an increase in money incomes, so crucially needed by producers and debtors. It might enable him to avert introduction of those kinds of inflationary measures being demanded. It might aid American exports, especially of farm products. And lastly, it would put the American government in a better position to bargain with the British and other foreign governments about the relative gold values of their currencies.

I was not startled by our departure from the gold standard. Nor was I upset, since I had shared Keynes's opinion that it was absurd that the state of national and international affairs should be vitally affected by the supply, and ebb and flow, of that sterile metal, gold. Nor was anyone else present disturbed (except Douglas). The President's announcement, in short, did not make a sensation among the auditors; it evoked comments of approval and conjectures about its consequences, but no ejaculations of astonishment of protests.

* * *

The President, after the comments about leaving the gold standard trailed off, went on to say that he wished most of all to discuss with us another important matter which required immediate attention. Senator Thomas had informed him the previous day that because the Senate Agriculture Committee had come to the unanimous conclusion that the farmer could be saved only if the buying power of the dollar was greatly reduced, he had prepared an amendment to the Farm Bill. This, he had explained, would give the President discretionary authority to take any or all of four actions: (1) to issue paper currency in whatever quantities the President might direct; (2) to order the recoinage and free coinage of silver at such ratio to gold as he might wish; (3) to reduce the gold content of the dollar; and (4) to organize a dollar stabilization board to regulate the value of the dollar and thereafter to stabilize its value.

In the same letter in which he transmitted this information to the President, Thomas had pointed out that the commodity purchasing power of the dollar was about two and a half times what it had been not many years before. He had also stated that when the amendment was discussed in the Senate he was going to exhibit samples of corn, wheat, cotton and oats. "At the present prices," he had continued, "farmers must produce one quart of wheat and deliver same to market to secure one cent. He must produce three-quarters of a quart of shelled

*Roosevelt's Decision* 155

corn to receive half a cent, and must produce and deliver to market one quart of oats to secure half a cent, and must produce enough cotton, ginned, to fill an average-size pillow to equal the sum of five cents." The Senator indicated that he regarded this amendment as a statement of principles and that it was subject to revision in detail.

By the evening of April 18 this amendment had been set in print and was being studied by members of his committee and others. Moley had that morning discussed it with Bullitt, Woodin and Warburg, and had given Warburg to understand that the President was going to ask Thomas not to introduce this "resolution." But the President now told us that he had let Thomas know through Byrnes that he would not oppose it—provided it was amended in important particulars. Moley seems to have remembered his next words, although I do not. He said, "Here, Ray, you act as clearing house to take care of this. Have it thoroughly amended and give them the word to pass it." And turning to the rest of us he remarked, "Congratulate me."

When some of us began to expostulate, the President explained that he had decided to go along with the Thomas amendment because if he did not do so Congress was likely to pass a mandatory law instead of a permissive one even over his veto. The latest draft of the amendment was read aloud. Since Thomas had sent his letter to Roosevelt, the authority to issue notes had been stretched; in this printed text of the amendment the Treasury was to issue notes in currency denominations not only to pay at maturity any outstanding government obligations and to buy such obligations in the market *but also "to meet current expenses."* That additional clause, the President said, he was going to ask Thomas to strike out; and he was also going to suggest the addition of a provision for an amortization fund to retire these notes of an amount equal to the interest on the government obligations which they were used to purchase. Therefore, the President remarked, these Treasury notes would be quite different from the notorious "greenbacks," and the United States would not be entering into another greenback era.

This observation did not, however, convince us. Warburg, Douglas and I—interrupting each other—argued that granting to the President this wide-open power to issue Treasury notes would swiftly stimulate fears of inflation. If it were used it would cause speculative inflation not only of the currency but also of credit. It might bring into existence a great excess of liquid banking reserves, which could be the basis for speculative borrowing—by those who sought to gain by borrowing while prices were low and the value of the dollar high and then paying off their debts when prices soared and the value of the dollar fell.

Warburg also contended that resort to this authority would prevent the Federal Reserve System from regulating the value of currency. The President rejoined that it would be difficult to expand the currency through the Federal Reserve System because the government did not control it. Was not the influential Senator Carter Glass of Virginia —who had refused the offer to enter his cabinet as Secretary of the Treasury—even then trying to take away the small measure of control over the system that the government had? When the dissenters next warned that if, once this power were used and the price of commodities began to leap because of fear, he might find himself compelled to issue more and more in order to prevent a relapse, the President said that they were seeing spooks and exaggerating dangers. He did not directly answer the assertion that the mere possibility that this power might be used would stand in the way of a revival of a market for bonds.

The talk went on awhile longer and touched the other sections of the amendment, but not significantly. Warburg's reminiscent description in the account (which he later entered in the Oral History Project at Columbia University) of the way in which those present looked and acted corresponds roughly to my own memory of the scene. "Moley was in one of his satanic moods when he was delighted by this dramatic move of the President and rather amused by my discomfiture. Bullitt ditto. Bullitt thought this was a wonderful show—and great stuff. Hull never opened his trap. Pittman made sure we would buy silver and enable us to raise the price of silver. . . . Feis looked as though he was going to throw up. . . . Lew Douglas went to bat with me and Will Woodin, once he got through his head what it was all about, which took some time . . ."

The President, having listened with unruffled good nature, closed the argument. He reiterated his opinion that since the authority granted was optional people would not be alarmed, especially since he intended to make a statement that this power would only be used with great judiciousness. He was sure, he repeated, that it was better to arrange for Congress to pass a permissive inflationary act rather than one which would compel him to take inflationary measures.

At half past eleven when we straggled out of the White House, there seemed little reason to think that the objections cited had made much impression on the President. But Pittman, foreseeing that some of the arguments made against the currency provision would reappear in the Senate debate, remarked that it might be wise to consider a limitation of the power to issue these greenbacks in order to avoid a filibuster.

I walked home to Georgetown somewhat disturbed but with a sense that, in the end, the course actually followed would not be too impulsive or extreme. I learned later that Warburg and Douglas walked the streets for two hours, awakened Bullitt at five in the morning and continued to bewail the measures taken and to be taken.

The next evening Senators Pittman and Byrnes, Warburg, Douglas and Bullitt met with Moley in his room at the Carlton Hotel. They then redrafted the amendment in order to reduce the chance that it might incite an uncontrollable inflation. When Douglas reported to the President what they had done, he found him amenable and had no trouble getting him to agree to the more restricted range of delegated authority.

Thomas and his associates in the cause of inflation acquiesced to the limits imposed on the President's power to issue greenbacks. But they retained the provisions that looked toward devaluation of the dollar and upward valuation of silver.

## *The Roosevelt Style: Harold Ickes' Perspective*

[Harold L. Ickes, *The Secret Diary of Harold L. Ickes: The First Thousand Days, 1933–1936*, vol. 1 (New York: Simon and Schuster, 1953), pp. 23, 658–59.]

*Tuesday, April 18, 1933 . . .*

The Cabinet meeting this afternoon was given over entirely to a discussion of the economic situation. The President told of the drive that has been made on the dollar in Amsterdam, Paris, and London during the last few days. At first he decided to throw enough gold in to maintain the dollar but finally concluded not to do so. This is to be the national policy from this time on unless changed. This may mean that the dollar will go down to ninety cents or thereabouts. It may also mean a fluctuating dollar for some time, but in the end it is thought that we will be better off, and the world will be better off, if the dollar is not artificially maintained at a value disproportionate to the rest of the principal currencies of the world. It is likely also that the French franc will have to come down. The United States, in effect, went off the gold standard March 4, at the time of the banking crisis, except for the last two or three days when the dollar was being supported in the world market. We have been off the gold standard since then. There can be no doubt that with the Administration failing to support the dollar further, we are definitely off the gold standard and that it will be so recognized. I realize that I don't have an economic mind myself, so in matters of this sort I simply listen carefully and go along with what those who are better qualified than I decide should be our policy.

\* \* \*

*Monday, August 10, 1936 . . .*

He told me one interesting incident which I will set down. Shortly after the President took office in March and when he was being pressed to make important decisions in many matters, one night Bullitt was at the White House and found the President in the long corridor on the second floor. He was looking into the money question and certain new facts had just been brought to his attention. He asked Bullitt what he thought ought to be done and Bullitt said that we ought to go off gold. Then Senator Key Pittman came in and his opinion was asked. He said: "Go off gold." Raymond Moley was the third who came in and gave the same advice. There followed Secretary of the Treasury Woodin and the President waved cheerfully at him and said: "Hello Will, we have just gone off gold." Woodin, taken aback, said: "Have we?"

Bullitt thought this was a rare incident and so do I. Here was a momentous decision affecting the economic welfare of the country that was decided in such an offhand manner. Or appeared to be. The probabilities are that the President had been turning it over in his mind for some time and had already reached a conclusion for which he needed only certain supporting opinions. Admittedly it was a sound and wise decision from the point of view of the country and a timely one.

Then James P. Warburg and Lewis Douglas came in and the President told them what decision had just been arrived at. They fought and argued against it for a long time. When they left and stopped for a final word at the White House entrance, Douglas turned to Bullitt and said: "Bill, this means the end of Western civilization." Bullitt relates that he burst out laughing, and when Douglas asked him what he was laughing at, he said he had heard that statement made on many occasions and that it always made him laugh. At four o'clock that morning, Douglas and Warburg came to Bullitt's room in the Carlton. They told him that they had been walking the streets discussing the decision and that they had come to the conclusion that if Bullitt felt as he did about it, perhaps something might be said for it after all.

* * *

## 25

*The Last Word:*
*Roosevelt Explains*

[Franklin D. Roosevelt, *On Our Way* (New York: The John Day Co., 1934), pp. 58–63.]

The task of Secretary of the Treasury Woodin and of the Federal Reserve Board, the Reconstruction Finance Corporation, and the hard-working Treasury Department officials, was great. Every bank in the country, State and national, had been examined; the great majority had reopened. In the Treasury itself we had successfully surmounted the problem of borrowing enough money to meet necessary daily expenditures, although the Treasury was to all intents and purposes empty when we inherited it.

The earlier proclamations during the month of March had directed all persons in the possession of gold to surrender their gold to the banks. During this period we were of course still on the gold standard in the sense that gold could still be exported by our banks to meet foreign demands.

Early in April several symptoms began to give us grave worry concerning the gold reserve in banks in the United States. It was true that the total stock of gold here was adequate to meet all existing currency or credit needs. But, at the same time, recent history gave many examples of sudden and uncontrollable flights of gold caused by speculation or fear. Some Americans were, I regret to say, so alarmed about the future of their own country that they began to export their own capital. Others, I also regret to say, believed that if they could get their money into foreign currencies by exporting gold they would later be enabled to buy more dollars through an unpatriotic speculation. In Europe increasing pressure on our gold reserves was exerted by international speculators and by

162

banks and individuals, who sold American securities, bought American exchange and demanded payment in gold. The result was a great increase in the "earmarking" of gold in New York for foreign account, and probably, for actual export. A movement such as this could amount almost immediately, we believed, to at least half a billion dollars. Any acceleration of it might well cause us to lose a billion or even two billions of our gold reserve. The fact is that during the short suspension of the gold embargo in April we lost one hundred millions in gold.

It was at this point that Secretary Woodin and I decided that the time had come to prevent the export of any more gold.

This was accomplished on April twentieth through a very important Executive Order which stated:

> Until further order, the earmarking for foreign account and the export of gold coin, gold bullion or gold certificates from the United States . . . are hereby prohibited, except that the Secretary of the Treasury . . . may issue licenses authorizing the export of gold coin and bullion (a) earmarked or held in trust for a recognized foreign government or foreign central bank or the Bank for International Settlements, (b) imported for re-export or gold in reasonable amounts for usual trade requirements of refiners importing gold-bearing materials under agreement to export gold, (c) actually required for the fulfillment of any contract entered into prior to the date of this order, by an applicant who in obedience to the Executive Order of April 5, 1933, has delivered gold coin, gold bullion or gold certificates, and (d) with the approval of the President, for transactions which he may deem necessary to promote the public interest.
>
> Until further order, the Secretary of the Treasury is authorized . . . to investigate, regulate or prohibit

> . . . by means of licenses or otherwise, any transactions in foreign exchange, transfers of credit from any banking institution within the United States . . . to any foreign branch or office of such banking institution or to any foreign bank or banker, and the export or withdrawal of currency from the United States . . . by an individual, partnership, association or corporation within the United States . . .

Thus we served notice on the country and on the world that we proposed to maintain our gold reserves intact.

Many useless volumes could be written as to whether on April twentieth the United States actually abandoned the gold standard. In one sense, we did not because the legal gold content of the dollar was unchanged and because the Government and the banks retained all gold as the basis for currency. On the other hand, gold here in the United States ceased to be a medium of exchange.

The next morning the Secretary came in to see me. I think that he and I felt very happy because we had cut the Gordian knot. His face was wreathed in smiles, but I looked at him and said: "Mr. Secretary, I have some very bad news for you. I have to announce to you the serious fact that the United States has gone off the gold standard." Mr. Woodin is a good sport. He threw up both hands, opened his eyes wide and exclaimed: "My heavens! What, again?"

That order was the turning point. Its result was felt almost immediately. American exchange weakened in terms of foreign currencies; and the price level at home went up substantially. Everyone realized at last that we were serious in our purpose of conserving our own financial resources, that we proposed to maintain our currency, and that at the same time we had determined definitely to seek an increase in all values.

In talking with people about our basic economic troubles I have often drawn for them a picture showing two columns—one representing what the United States was worth in terms of dollars and the other representing what the United States owed in terms of dollars. The figures covered all property and all debts, public, corporate and individual. In 1929, the total of the assets in terms of dollars was much larger than the total of the debts. But, by the spring of 1933, while the total of the debts was still just as great, the total of the assets had shrunk to below that of the debts.

Two courses were open: to cut down the debts through bankruptcies and foreclosures to such a point that they would be below property values; or else, to increase property values until they were greater than the debts.

Obviously, the latter course was the only legitimate method of putting the country back on its feet without destroying human values. We recognized that the ultimate goal was far off and that many steps would have to be taken to arrive at that goal. We knew that we should have to face unreasonable speculation, as we actually did later on in June and July. We knew that there would be ups and downs, but that by keeping the objective constantly in mind and by using many methods and measures, we could at least make an honest effort to reach the goal. When the United States went off the gold basis in April, 1933, we did deliberately what many other nations, including Great Britain, had been compelled to do against their will. The country understood that the dollar was just as good a dollar as it had been before, and that, in fact, we proposed to make it a more honest dollar than it had been during the three and one-half years of constant and growing deflation.

## Bibliographical Notes

Students interested in the technical problems of monetary management in the New Deal are advised to consult the studies listed by William E. Leuchtenburg in *Franklin D. Roosevelt and the New Deal* (1963), p. 358. Often the best insights into the development of the New Deal's monetary policies are to be found in books written by administration participants, some of whom dissent from the policies, like James Warburg, *The Money Muddle* (1935); Raymond Moley, *After Seven Years* (1939) and *The First New Deal* (1966), Rexford Guy Tugwell, *The Brains Trust* (1968), and John Morton Blum, *From The Morgenthau Diaries: Years of Crisis, 1928–1938* (1959).

Biographies of the economists involved in the inflation movement, like Irving Fisher and George Warren, would be useful. We also need to know more about the Stable Monetary Association and the Committee for the Nation. There are several works on Keynes including those mentioned in the documents of this book, but for the story of the man and his American impact the student will find good-reading in the somewhat self-congratulatory book *The Age of Keynes* by Robert Lekachman (1966).

Despite the great impact of Congress upon the New Deal, historians have not dealt with the national legislature to any appreciable extent, one exception being James T. Patterson's outstanding monograph *Congressional Conservatism and the New Deal* (1967). The best study of the congressional silver inflationists can be found in Fred L. Israel's *Nevada's Key Pittman* (1963). Burton K. Wheeler has given us his autobiography *Yankee from the West* (1962). Unfortunately, there is no biography of Elmer Thomas. The South, its influence as prominent in Congress then as during any Democratic administration, is brilliantly characterized in George B. Tindall's *The Emergence of the New South, 1913–1945* (1967).

Students interested in federal recovery and depression relief policies before Roosevelt will find that Herbert Hoover's *Memoirs*, 3 volumes, (1951–52) and the William Starr Myers and Walter Newton history of *The Hoover Administration* (1936) are defensively pedantic and tediously written. Albert U. Romasco has done well in explaining Hoover's tactics in *The Poverty of Abundance: Hoover, the Nation, the Depression* (1965). Harris Gaylord Warren's admiration for Hoover does not prevent him from writing a critical narrative in *Herbert Hoover and the Great Depression* (1959). Irving Bernstein has an engrossing discussion of the relief issue during Hoover's term in *The Lean Years: A History of the American Worker, 1920–1933* (1960).

In dealing with almost any prominent public matter in this epoch, historians must confront the enigmatic personality of Franklin D. Roosevelt. Frank Freidel has the task of writing a definitive multi-volume biography of Roosevelt and has progressed through three *Franklin D. Roosevelt* volumes consecutively subtitled *The Apprenticeship, The Ordeal* and *The Triumph* (1952–56). Freidel has only elected Roosevelt to the Presidency and we await the inauguration of the New Deal. James MacGregor Burns has written an incisive and loving single volume biography, *Roosevelt: The Lion and the Fox* (1956). If the reader can tolerate the "Franklin and I" tone of it, Rexford Tugwell's *The Democratic Roosevelt* (1957) is most insightful and rewarding. A decade later the Tugwell industry produced *F.D.R.: Architect of an Era* (1967), a briefer exposition on the author's favorite person. Also, in the category of a reminiscent biography is Frances Perkins' *The Roosevelt I Knew* (1947), a pleasant and historically useful book.

New Deal historiography necessarily begins with Basil Rauch's *The History of the New Deal* (1944). Still, while there have been several overview treatments of the New Deal, the one which surpasses all others for scholarship, breadth, and understanding is William E. Leuchtenburg's *Franklin D. Roosevelt and the New Deal* (1963). Of course, the conscientious and curious student of the period must read Arthur M. Schlesinger, Jr.'s three volumes on *The Age of Roosevelt: The Crisis of the Old Order, The Coming of the New Deal* and *The Politics of Upheaval* (1957–60), which carry the reader from 1919 through the campaign of 1936. Even Schlesinger's detractors, who may be as legion as his admirers, must concede that his work compels the attention of everybody interested in the phenomenon called New Deal liberalism. Outside of books, there is one article which the reader should note because it is superbly suggestive: William E. Leuchtenburg, "The New Deal and the Analogue of War," in John Braeman *et al.*, editors, *Change and Continuity in Twentieth-Century America* (1964).

One thing which the Leuchtenburg article suggests is that we are, after nearly a quarter of a century since F.D.R., prepared to interpret the New Deal with a somewhat more dispassionate perspective. Just as Leuchtenburg employs Keynesian ideas to acquire a different appreciation of the New Deal, one of sorrow rather than adoration or anger, there are youthful historians who likewise are less concerned with disputation than comprehension. A model of modern evaluation is Ellis W. Hawley's *The New Deal and the Problem of Monopoly* (1966). Paul K. Conkin's *The New Deal* (1967) is a brief, fresh, provokingly interpretive analysis which unfailingly stimulates lively discussion. Both Hawley and Conkin should inspire the writing of many doctoral dissertations. There is some question as to whether Conkin is a "New Left" historian, but few would doubt Barton Bernstein's credentials for that appellation; his essay, "The New Deal: The Conservative Achievements of Liberal Reform," in Bernstein, editor, *Towards A New Past* (1967) is, at the least, challenging.

Finally, this reader has enjoyed the essays of popular economist Eliot Janeway in *The Economics of Crisis* (1968) and warmly recommends this witty, imaginative book on recent U.S. history that so adroitly defies all categorization.

# IV

## 1950: TRUMAN'S DECISION

### the UNITED STATES

### enters the KOREAN WAR

# Contents
## PART IV
## 1950: Truman's Decision:
### The United States Enters the Korean War
*Introduction*

Section One
Setting

    *Commentary*     1

1) *President Harry S Truman on
   United States Policy Toward Formosa
   January 5, 1950*     5

2) *Speech by Secretary of State
   Dean G. Acheson
   January 12, 1950*     7

3) *Speech by Dean G. Acheson
   March 7, 1950*     25

4) *Interview with Senator Tom Connally
   Democrat of Texas
   May 5, 1950*     30

5) *Associated Press Dispatch
   May 10, 1950*     31

6) *Ambassador to Korea John J. Muccio on
   Military Aid to Korean Security Forces
   June 9, 1950*     32

7) *Ambassador to the United States Chang Myun
   to President Syngman Rhee
   June 14, 1950*     35

8) *President Syngman Rhee to Chang Myun
   June 18, 1950*     39

9) *Speech by Special Ambassador
John Foster Dulles
June 19, 1950* — 42

## Section Two
## Occasion for Decision

*Commentary* — 46

10) *John E. James to
United Press International
June 25, 1950, 9:50 a.m.* — 47

11) *John J. Muccio to Dean G. Acheson
June 25, 1950* — 48

12) *John E. James to
United Press International
June 25, 1950, 10:30 a.m.* — 49

## Section Three
## The Decision to Engage
## the United Nations

*Commentary* — 51

13) *Deputy U.S. Representative
Ernest A. Gross
to Secretary-General Trygve Lie
June 25, 1950* — 55

14) *U.N. Commission on Korea
to Trygve Lie
June 25, 1950* — 56

15) *Statement of Ernest A. Gross
before the U.N. Security Council
June 25, 1950* — 58

16) *Resolution of the U.N. Security Council
June 25, 1950* — 64

17) *War in Korea
The New York Times
June 26, 1950* — 66

18) *George F. Kennan's Critique of the U.N. Policy* ... 69

## Section Four
## The Decision to Commit Air and Sea Forces

*Commentary* ... 71

19) *Radio Address by Marshal Kim Il Sung
June 26, 1950* ... 76

20) *U.N. Commission on Korea
to Trygve Lie
June 26, 1950* ... 85

21) *Statement by Harry S Truman
June 26, 1950* ... 90

22) *Speech by Senator Styles Bridges,
Republican of New Hampshire
June 26, 1950* ... 91

23) *Speech by Senator William F. Knowland,
Republican of California
June 26, 1950* ... 94

24) *Speech by Senator Tom Connally
June 26, 1950* ... 96

25) *Korean National Assembly to the
President and Congress of the United States
June 26, 1950* ... 100

26) *U.N. Commission on Korea
to Trygve Lie
June 26, 1950* ... 101

27) *General Douglas MacArthur's
Military Situation Report* ... 102

28) *Statement by President Harry S Truman
June 27, 1950* ... 103

29) *Speech by United States
Representative Warren R. Austin
June 27, 1950* ... 105

30) *Exchange of Telegrams between
Governor of New York Thomas E. Dewey
and Harry S Truman
June 27, 1950* — 108

31) *Speech by Representative Vito Marcantonio
American Laborite of New York
June 27, 1950* — 109

32) *Reply of Representative Abraham A. Ribicoff,
Democrat of Connecticut to Marcantonio
June 27, 1950* — 114

33) *Speech by Senator Robert A. Taft,
Republican of Ohio
June 28, 1950* — 116

34) *Reply of Senator Scott W. Lucas,
Democrat of Illinois, to Taft
June 28, 1950* — 125

35) *Joseph C. Harsch on
the Washington Response
to Truman's Decision
June 29, 1950* — 128

36) Pravda's *Comment on
President Truman's Statement
June 28, 1950* — 129

37) *Statement by Mao Tse-tung
June 28, 1950* — 131

38) *Ambassador to the Soviet Union
Alan G. Kirk to the Soviet
Minister of Foreign Affairs
June 27, 1950* — 132

39) *Deputy Minister of Foreign Affairs
Andrei Gromyko to Alan G. Kirk
June 29, 1950* — 133

40) *Statement by Dean G. Acheson
at a Press Conference
June 28, 1950* — 134

41) *Speech by Dean G. Acheson*
    *June 29, 1950* ........................................ 136

Section Five
The Decision to Commit
Ground Forces

   *Commentary* ........................................ 145

42) *Radio Order from Lieutenant*
    *General George E. Stratemeyer to*
    *Major General Earle E. Partridge*
    *June 29, 1950* ........................................ 149

43) *Joint Chiefs of Staff to*
    *General Douglas MacArthur*
    *June 29, 1950* ........................................ 150

44) *Recollections of Major General*
    *Edward M. Almond*
    *June 29, 1950* ........................................ 151

45) *Recollections of Marguerite Higgins*
    *June 29, 1950* ........................................ 158

46) *Recommendations of*
    *General Douglas MacArthur*
    *June 30, 1950* ........................................ 159

47) *Commander-in-Chief, Far East,*
    *to Joint Chiefs of Staff*
    *June 30, 1950* ........................................ 160

48) *White House Press Release*
    *June 30, 1950* ........................................ 161

49) *Speech by Senator Kenneth S. Wherry,*
    *Republican of Nebraska*
    *June 30, 1950* ........................................ 162

50) *Speech by Senator William F. Knowland*
    *June 30, 1950* ........................................ 165

51) *Ground Troops Move In*
    *The New York Times*
    *July 1, 1950* ........................................ 168

| | | |
|---|---|---|
| 52) | *Speech by Warren R. Austin*<br>*June 30, 1950* | 169 |
| 53) | *Verbal Orders of Major General*<br>*William Dean to Lieutenant*<br>*Colonel Charles Smith*<br>*June 30, 1950* | 173 |

*Bibliography* 174

*Introduction*

President Harry S Truman's dramatic decision to commit American combat forces to resist the North Korean Communist invasion of the Republic of Korea in June, 1950, constituted a multi-faceted turning point in the course of world politics after the Second World War. For America this decision involved the nation in its fourth largest war (now fifth after Vietnam), sacrificing 33,629 dead, and extending over more than three years to the uncertain July 27, 1953, armistice that still prevails in 1970. As initial military successes were disastrously reversed by Chinese Communist counter-intervention in October, 1950, dissatisfaction with the war became one of the main issues that brought down the Truman Administration and catapulted General Dwight D. Eisenhower into the Presidency in the election of 1952.

For Korea, the President's initial decision to fight and his later agreement to extend the United Nations' military objectives to include the occupation of North Korea had complex repercussions. The Republic of Korea was saved as a developing political, social, cultural, and economic collectivity, freed from North Korean Communist military subjugation. On the other hand, it was subjected to much deeper and more prolonged American influence than would have occurred if the Communist invasion had not taken place. Truman's decision also has had complex long range effects upon North Korea. American intervention meant the failure of a violent North

Korean Communist attempt to unify the country; it led to great damage from air and sea bombardment (spared South Korea); and it precipitated eight years of massive Chinese Communist military presence in the North. It is true that American intervention plus South Korean resistance prevented North Korean Communist reunification of the Korean nation. It is just as true that Chinese Communist intervention plus resistance by the remnants of the North Korean army prevented the reunification of the Korean nation under the auspices of the Republic of Korea and the United Nations. In the first case, Korea would have been united with very strong Soviet Russian influence (of Stalinist vintage) over the peninsula; in the second case, there would have been a very strong American influence (of a Truman-Dewey quality). Viewed from a hypothetically objective Korean standpoint in 1970, 20 years after Truman's decision, both parts of the nation have greater political and economic vitality than they had in 1950 and in international relations have achieved far greater degrees of autonomy from the powers that sponsored national division during the period from 1945 to 1948.

But the legacy of a bitter war remains. Two vast Korean armies totalling more than a million men face each other, fired by political hatred, across the Demilitarized Zone. There is fear in 1970 that, failing to incite armed guerrilla uprisings of the "people's war" variety, the North Korean Communists will again launch an armed invasion of the Republic of Korea, perhaps counting upon the growing opposition of the American public to military involvement in defense of the Republic of Vietnam to deter a repetition of Truman's 1950 decision. As long as Korea is not reunited and as long as two hostile armies remain poised in tense dialectical confrontation at mid-peninsula, the possibility that another American President will be faced with the occasion for another Korean decision is constantly present. If such a moment comes in the

*Introduction*

form of a powerful North Korean invasion of the South, then the precedent established by President Harry S Truman undoubtedly would have an exceedingly strong effect upon American decision making. But no one can reasonably be facile about multi-national decision making in the acute crisis situation that would be precipitated by the renewal of armed conflict on the Korean peninsula. All that one can say with confidence is that renewed killing in Korea would be a global as well as a Korean national disaster. It can only be hoped that Korean patriots and world political leaders will see this clearly.

The relationship between Truman's decision and the United Nations was noteworthy. In the aftermath of World War II, one of the favorite subjects for debate among American college students from 1945 to 1950 was the desirability of some form of "world government" in order to secure peace. Models discussed ranged from institutions that preserved national sovereignty to those that subordinated the nation state to higher authority. There was a good deal of discussion of the doctrine of "collective security" and it was argued that if the members of the League of Nations had been able to combine militarily against Italy when it invaded Ethiopia, then possibly the horrors of the Second World War could have been averted. It was thus significant that the first act of the United States Government upon being informed of the North Korean invasion of South Korea was to bring the event to the attention of the United Nations and to pursue further initial responses to this invasion under various Security Council resolutions. Cynical critics of Truman's decision have tried to portray this as merely the manipulation of an international symbol for purely selfish interests of national policy. In Communist terms, the "United Nations" became merely a "cloak to mask American aggression" against the Korean people. But a close study of the historical record and interviews with key participants in the decision, including President

Truman himself, discloses that there was a genuine commitment to the idea of strengthening the United Nations as an institution capable of securing world peace through collective resistance to armed aggression. The question of whether the conflict in Korea was an international or a civil war will perhaps continue to be debated, but in any case both Korean governments lay claim to national sovereignty and to specific territorial control. One of them, the Republic of Korea, addressed pleas to the United Nations and to the United States for assistance to repel the invasion. The unusually prompt and widespread support given to the United Nations effort in Korea by countries such as Ethiopia (a victim of Italian aggression), Britain, and France (prime objects of Nazi German assault) further evidenced concern for making the United Nations a more potent force for peace than the defunct League of Nations. Whether Truman's decision will be viewed by future historians as a true contribution toward establishing a principle of collective resistance to military aggression across national boundaries remains to be seen. At close range, that seems genuinely to have been President Truman's intent.

Truman's decision was of great importance for American relations with China. His decision to fight in Korea brought the United States closer to the Government of the Republic of China and further alienated it from the mainland Chinese People's Republic. If the North Korean People's Army had not invaded South Korea, then it seems highly probable that the Chinese Communists would have subjugated Taiwan without American opposition. In deciding to repulse the North Korean invasion, President Truman also decided in fact to guarantee the security of the Chinese Nationalist Government. This unexpected reversal of American policy further alienated Mao Tse-tung and the Chinese Communist leadership; embitterment deepened when Chinese and American infantrymen began to kill each other in the fall of 1950

*Introduction*

on the Korean peninsula. Thus American and Chinese involvement in the Korean War is one of the historical experiences that must be considered in thinking about American-Chinese relations.

Truman's decision is also of importance in assessing the past, present, and possible future of American relations with the Soviet Union. In the post-Stalin period Soviet scholars who specialize in Korean affairs have come to admit that the Korean War was not initiated by the United States, although they have continued to attribute it, publicly at least, to the initiative of President Syngman Rhee.

One must be frankly speculative in assessing the possibly changing impact of the Korean decision upon Soviet decision makers, but sometimes hypothetical analysis is inescapable. Although not discussed openly, is it not probable that the post-Stalinist leadership has tended to look upon the North Korean initiative as in part a Stalinist blunder? And until the Vietnamese conflict (as the Chinese revolution before it) called into question American capacity and will to save governments subjected to armed Communist assault, might not the probability of American intervention have been one of the expectations that dampened overt Soviet enthusiasm for "people's wars" and helped to widen the ideological rift between the Soviet Union and China? Might not also the "reasonableness" of the armistice settlement in 1953, preceded by the removal of General MacArthur from his command, have suggested to some Soviet leaders that peaceful negotiations with American leaders (when confronted with formidable force) was possible? That the Korean decision did not completely inhibit further movement of large Communist military units across formal political boundaries is illustrated by the experiences of Hungary and Czechoslovakia in Eastern Europe and of Vietnam and Laos in Asia. But not all Communist political decisions, of course, are attributable to Soviet direction. For

Soviet leaders Truman's decision in Korea probably continues to signify the dangerous possibility of a military response where vital American interests are threatened. A detailed case study of the Soviet withdrawal of offensive missiles from Cuba in 1962 might show that it was conditioned in part by recollections of Truman's 1950 decision in Korea.

In Truman's decision also lie elements relevant to the subsequent American military involvement in Vietnam. The alert reader will notice in the documents that follow references to strengthening American military support to the French in their colony of Indochina (now Vietnam). The invasion of South Korea was viewed by American policy makers in 1950 as possibly linked to expansionist drives by Communist forces in both East and Southeast Asia. Thus the North Korean decision to attack South Korea led to increased American military commitment in Vietnam and the Philippines as well as in China. It also led, of course, to a vast upswing in American military expenditures, thus increasing the capacity for further involvements in Asia and elsewhere. The Korean War, for example, had European repercussions in the strengthening of NATO. To understand subsequent American policy in Vietnam it is also undoubtedly important that Secretary of State Rusk, who served two Presidents as principal officer in charge of international relations from 1961 to 1969, contributed to Truman's 1950 Korean decision as the Assistant Secretary of State for Far Eastern Affairs. In this earlier assignment it must also be recalled that Secretary Rusk was one of the strong supporters of the United Nations as an instrument for achieving world peace. The personal experience of some American officials thus spanned the decisions in Korea and the subsequent decisions in Vietnam. As the generations involved in both sets of decisions fade from history all that will remain are impressions on the historical memory of their successors. In the 1960's Truman's Korean decision was a

## Introduction

living part of the experience of the American leaders who made policy toward Vietnam.

To call attention to these relevancies—for American politics, for unaccomplished Korean unification, for the United Nations, for American-Chinese and American-Soviet relations, and for American policy toward Vietnam—does not exhaust the potential implications of Truman's decision for American and international or world history. And no case study or set of documents can completely satisfy our search for understanding. History is lived as well as read and discussed. For we are close enough to the Korean decision to feel its repercussions; in a real sense it is still being made. Korea is still divided into Communist and non-Communist parts; and armies clash on a tense frontier. The immediate pre-1950 war issue is still very much the same: What will the American response be to a violent North Korean Communist attempt to overrun the Republic of Korea? Unlike President Truman, who in 1950 was caught very much "by surprise," readers of this book may have time to rehearse in advance what their likely response would be.

# Section One

# The Setting

*Commentary*

The North Korean attack upon the Republic of Korea came at a time when American foreign policy had created the impression that it was not prone to resist armed Communist expansion in Asia. This was greatly in contrast with American policy toward potential Soviet military expansion in Europe that had been accompanied by tough stands in Iran (1946), Greece (1947–48), and Berlin (1948), and the construction of a collective security military alliance in the North Atlantic Treaty Organization (1949). In Asia President Truman had decided and announced that the United States would not become militarily involved in the Chinese Civil War (Doc. 1). This had temporarily ended a dispute between the Departments of State and Defense. The Department of Defense had wanted the United States to take every possible diplomatic action to prevent the Chinese Communist invasion of the Chinese Nationalist government on the island province of Taiwan. The Department of

State had wanted the Defense Department to agree to make a military commitment that would back up diplomatic and political deterrence activities. Neither department was willing to do what the other wanted. The Defense Department argued that it did not have the capability to undertake the defense of Taiwan and the State Department argued that it did not want to risk American prestige in an empty propaganda campaign. Thus it was expected that the Chinese Communists would invade Taiwan in the summer of 1950 and it was American policy that the United States should do nothing about it.

In a speech before the National Press Club on January 12, 1950 (Doc. 2), Secretary of State Acheson omitted both Taiwan and Korea from a statement of the Pacific "defense perimeter" of the United States. In his view this was merely matching rhetoric with the realities of power that were as much the product of military as of diplomatic calculation. In his later opinion this speech was not as damaging an expression of a weak American commitment to Korea as was the House defeat of a supplemental Korean aid bill on January 19 by a vote of 192 to 191. Although he pleaded successfully in March for the subsequent continuance of aid to Korea, it will be noted that he felt it necessary to comment that the survival of the Republic of Korea "cannot, of course, be guaranteed" (Doc. 3). Remarks on May 4 by the Chairman of the Senate Foreign Relations Committee very explicitly revealed that Korea had a very low priority in American strategic thinking and that in the event of a major war with the Soviet Union (the main American concern of that period) Korea would not be defended (Doc. 4).

In Seoul, such statements of policy by high American officials were unsettling, especially in the face of renewed intelligence reports of a military buildup in North Korea and rumors of impending invasion (Doc. 5). These reports were generally discounted in American intelligence evaluations; internal subversion of the ROK was considered much more likely. There was a difference of opinion among American military and diplomatic officials in Korea about the relative capabilities of the North and South Korean armies. In general, the official reports of the Korean Military Advisory Group under Brigadier General William L. Roberts tended to underestimate North Korean capabilities and to overestimate those of South Korea. By contrast a June 9 statement by Ambassador Muccio in support of a request for Korean aid subsequently proved to be accurate and prophetic (Doc. 6). His estimate was discounted in Washington as an example of the special pleading normal when an ambassador identifies himself with the interests of a nation to which he is accredited.

The diplomatic efforts of President Syngman Rhee to secure an American guarantee of Korean security and increased armament were rather inept and ineffectual, relying mainly on a few obscure "influence peddlers" who attempted to approach American military leaders, pointedly avoiding the White House and the Secretaries of State and Defense. Correspondence between President Rhee and his ambassador to Washington, Chang Myun, that was subsequently captured and published by the North Korean Communist leadership was intended by them to show that Rhee and American leaders plotted to invade the North. In fact this correspondence shows that ROK diplomacy found little American receptiveness and had obtained substantially no new commitments prior to June, 1950. Great hopes were placed in a visit to Korea during June 18–20 by John Foster Dulles, State Department adviser, who was known to be sympathetic to the perilous predicament of the Republic of Korea (Docs. 7, 8). Ambassador Dulles, whose main responsibility was to work out a suitable peace treaty with Japan, took the trip to Korea on his own initiative and, although his encouraging remarks (Doc. 9) had been approved by the Assistant Secretary of State for Far Eastern Affairs, they represented no new commitment by either the Secretary of State or the President.

Communist propaganda during the Korean War and thereafter made much of a photograph showing Ambassador Dulles peering across the Thirty-eighth Parallel with binoculars, implying that he was a central figure in a master plot to conquer the Korean People's Democratic Republic. But surprise and confusion in both Seoul and Washington when the North Koreans finally attacked on June 25 (June 24, Washington time), compared with the well-ordered initiatives emanating from Pyongyang (Doc. 36), belied the Communist portrayal of Korean-American aggressive collusion.

On Sunday, June 25, 1950, Korean time (Saturday, June 24, in the United States), the President was spending a quiet weekend at home in Missouri; the Secretary of State was on his Maryland farm; the Chief American military adviser in Korea was in Yokohama, Japan, en route home; the acting chief of the military advisory group was also in Japan; the chief of the ROK Navy and the deputy chief of staff of the ROK Army were in Honolulu; many ROK officers were on weekend leave; General MacArthur's headquarters in Tokyo was on a normal weekend routine; and so forth.

When the North Korean attack came it was a great shock to the people of South Korea who had just been subjected to a vigorous campaign of North Korean peace propaganda contained in statements of June 7 and June 19, calling for amalgamation of the Seoul and Pyongyang representative assemblies and for a national election. The tragic gap between words and deeds that marked this event deeply undermined the confidence of the Korean people in the sincerity of the Korean Communist leadership and bequeathed a legacy of intense mistrust of Pyongyang statements concerning "peaceful unification."

## 1

*President Harry S Truman on
United States Policy Toward Formosa
January 5, 1950*

[*Department of State Bulletin,* Vol. XXII, No. 550, p. 79.]

The United States Government has always stood for good faith in international relations. Traditional United States policy toward China, as exemplified in the open-door policy, called for international respect for the territorial integrity of China. This principle was recently reaffirmed in the United Nations General Assembly resolution of December 8, 1949, which, in part, calls on all states—

> To refrain from (a) seeking to acquire spheres of influence or to create foreign controlled regimes within the territory of China; (b) seeking to obtain special rights or privileges within the territory of China.

A specific application of the foregoing principles is seen in the present situation with respect to Formosa. In the joint declaration at Cairo on December 1, 1943, the President of the United States, the British Prime Minister, and the President of China stated that it was their purpose that territories Japan had stolen from China, such as Formosa, should be restored to the Republic of China. The United States was a signatory to the Potsdam declaration of July 26, 1945, which declared that the terms of the Cairo declaration should be carried out.

The provisions of this declaration were accepted by Japan at the time of its surrender. In keeping with these declarations, Formosa was surrendered to Generalissimo Chiang Kai-shek, and for the past 4 years, the United States and the other Allied Powers have accepted the exercise of Chinese authority over the Island.

The United States has no predatory designs on Formosa or on any other Chinese territory. The United States has no desire to obtain special rights or privileges or to establish military bases on Formosa at this time. Nor does it have any intention of utilizing its armed forces to interfere in the present situation. The United States Government will not pursue a course which will lead to involvement in the civil conflict in China.

Similarly, the United States Government will not provide military aid or advice to Chinese forces on Formosa. In the view of the United States Government, the resources on Formosa are adequate to enable them to obtain the items which they might consider necessary for the defense of the Island. The United States Government proposes to continue under existing legislative authority the present ECA program of economic assistance.

## 2

*Speech by Secretary of State
Dean G. Acheson
January 12, 1950*

[*Department of State Bulletin,* Vol. XXII, No. 556, pp. 111–18.]

*Washington, D. C.*

This afternoon I should like to discuss with you the relations between the peoples of the United States and the peoples of Asia, and I used the words "relations of the peoples of the United States and the peoples of Asia" advisedly. I am not talking about governments or nations because it seems to me what I want to discuss with you is this feeling of mine that the relations depend upon the attitudes of the people; that there are fundamental attitudes, fundamental interests, fundamental purposes of the people of the United States, 150 million of them, and of the peoples of Asia, unnumbered millions, which determine and out of which grow the relations of our countries and the policies of our governments. Out of these attitudes and interests and purposes grow what we do from day to day.

Now, let's dispose of one idea right at the start and not bother with it any more. That is that the policies of the United States are determined out of abstract principles in the Department of State or in the White House or in the Congress. That is not the case. If these policies are going to be good, they must grow out of the fundamental attitudes of our people on both sides. If they are to be effective, they must become articulate through all the institutions of our national life, of which this is one of the greatest—through the press, through the radio, through the churches, through the labor unions, through the business organizations, through all the groupings of our national life, there must become articulate the attitudes of our people and the policies which we propose to follow. It seems to me that understanding is the beginning of wisdom and therefore, we shall begin by trying to understand before we announce what we are going to do, and that is a proposition so heretical in this town that I advance it with some hesitation.

Now, let's consider some of the basic factors which go into the making of the attitudes of the peoples on both sides. I am frequently asked: Has the State Department got an Asian policy? And it seems to me that that discloses such a depth of ignorance that it is very hard to begin to deal with it. The peoples of Asia are so incredibly diverse and their problems are so incredibly diverse that how could anyone, even the most utter charlatan believe that he had a uniform policy which would deal with all of them. On the other hand, there are very important similarities in ideas and in problems among the peoples of Asia and so what we come to, after we understand these diversities and these common attitudes of mind, is the fact that there must be certain similarities of approach, and there must be very great dissimilarities in action.

To illustrate this only a moment: If you will consider as an example of the differences in Asia the subcontinent of India and Pakistan, you will find there an area which is roughly comparable in size and population to Europe. You will find that the different states and provinces of that subcontinent are roughly comparable in size to the nations of Europe and yet you will find such differences in race, in ideas, in languages, and religion, and culture, that compared to that subcontinent, Europe is almost one homogeneous people.

## The Setting 9

Or take the difference, for instance, between the people and problems of Japan and Indonesia, both in the same Asian area. In Japan, you have a people far advanced in the complexities of industrial civilization, a people whose problems grow out of overpopulation on small islands and the necessity of finding raw materials to bring in and finding markets for the finished goods which they produce. In Indonesia, you find something wholly different—a people on the very threshold of their experience with these complexities and a people who live in an area which possesses vast resources which are awaiting development. Now, those are illustrations of complexities.

Let's come now to the matters which Asia has in common. There is in this vast area what we might call a developing Asian consciousness, and a developing pattern, and this, I think, is based upon two factors which are pretty nearly common to the entire experience of all these Asian people.

One of these factors is a revulsion against the acceptance of misery and poverty as the normal condition of life. Throughout all of this vast area, you have that fundamental revolutionary aspect in mind and belief. The other common aspect that they have is the revulsion against foreign domination. Whether that foreign domination takes the form of colonialism or whether it takes the form of imperialism, they are through with it. They have had enough of it, and they want no more.

These two basic ideas which are held so broadly and commonly in Asia tend to fuse in the minds of many Asian peoples and many of them tend to believe that if you could get rid of foreign domination, if you could gain independence, then the relief from poverty and misery would follow almost in course. It is easy to point out that that is not true, and of course, they are discovering that it is not true. But underneath that belief, there was a very profound understanding of a basic truth and it is the basic truth which underlies all our democratic belief and all our democratic concept. That truth is that just as no man and no government is wise enough or disinterested enough to direct the thinking and the action of another individual, so no nation and no people are wise enough and disinterested enough very long to assume the responsibility for another people or to control another people's opportunities.

That great truth they have sensed, and on that great truth they are acting. They say and they believe that from now on they are on their own. They will make their own decisions. They will attempt to better their own lot, and on occasion they will make their own mistakes. But it will be their mistakes, and they are not going to have their mistakes dictated to them by anybody else.

The symbol of these concepts has become nationalism. National independence has become the symbol both of freedom from foreign domination and freedom from the tyranny of poverty and misery.

Since the end of the war in Asia, we have seen over 500 million people gain their independence and over seven new nations come into existence in this area.

We have the Philippines with 20 million citizens. We have Pakistan, India, Ceylon, and Burma with 400 million citizens, southern Korea with 20 million, and within the last few weeks, the United States of Indonesia with 75 million.

This is the outward and visible sign of the internal ferment of Asia. But this ferment and change is not restricted to these countries which are just gaining their independence. It is the common idea and the common pattern of Asia, and as I tried to suggest a moment ago, it is not based on purely political conceptions. It is not based purely on ideological conceptions. It is based on a fundamental and an earthy and a deeply individual realization of the problems of their own daily lives. This new sense of nationalism means that they are going to deal with those daily problems—the problems of the relation of man to the soil, the problem of how much can be exacted from them by the tax collectors of the state. It is rooted in those ideas. With those ideas they are going forward. Resignation is no longer the typical emotion of Asia. It has given way to hope, to a sense of effort, and in many cases, to a real sense of anger.

Now, may I suggest to you that much of the bewilderment which has seized the minds of many of us about recent developments in China comes from a failure to understand this basic revolutionary force which is loose in Asia. The reasons for the fall of the Nationalist Government in China are preoccupying many people. All sorts of reasons have ben attributed to it. Most commonly, it is said in various speeches and publications that it is the result of American bungling, that we are incompetent, that we did not understand, that American aid was too little, that we did the wrong things at the wrong time. Other people go on and say: "No, it is not quite that, but that an American general did not like Chiang Kai-shek and out of all that relationship grows the real trouble." And they say: "Well, you have to add to that there are a lot of women fooling around in politics in China."

Nobody, I think, says that the Nationalist Government fell because it was confronted by overwhelming military force which it could not resist. Certainly no one in his right mind suggests that. Now, what I ask you to do is to stop looking for a moment under the bed and under the chair and under the rug to find out these reasons, but rather to look at the broad picture and see whether something doesn't suggest itself.

The broad picture is that after the war, Chiang Kai-shek emerged as the undisputed leader of the Chinese people. Only one faction, the Communists, up in the hills, ill-equipped, ragged, a very small military force, was determinedly opposed to his position. He had overwhelming military power, greater military power than any ruler had ever had in the entire history of China. He had tremendous economic and military support and backing from the United States. He had the acceptance of all other foreign countries, whether sincerely or insincerely in the case of the Soviet Union is not really material to this matter. Here he was in this position, and 4 years later what do we find? We find that his armies have melted away. His support in the country has melted away. His support largely outside the country has melted away, and he is a refugee on a small island off the coast of China with the remnants of his forces.

As I said, no one says that vast armies moved out of the hills and defeated him. To attribute this to the inadequacy of American aid is only to point out the depth and power of the forces which were miscalculated or ignored. What has happened in my judgment is that the almost inexhaustible patience of the Chinese people in their misery ended. They did not bother to overthrow this government. There was really nothing to overthrow. They simply ignored it throughout the country. They took the solution of their immediate village problems into their own hands. If there was any trouble or interference with the representatives of the government, they simply brushed them aside. They completely withdrew their support from this government, and when that support was withdrawn, the whole military establishment disintegrated. Added to the grossest incompetence ever experienced by any military command was this total lack of support both in the armies and in the country, and so the whole matter just simply disintegrated.

The Communists did not create this. The Communists did not create this condition. They did not create this revolutionary spirit. They did not create a great force which moved out from under Chiang Kai-shek. But they

## The Setting 13

were shrewd and cunning to mount it, to ride this thing into victory and into power.

That, I suggest to you, is an explanation which has certain roots in realism and which does not require all this examination of intricate and perhaps irrelevant details. So much for the attitudes of the peoples of Asia.

Let's consider for a moment another important factor in this relationship. That is the attitude of our own people to Asia. What is that fundamental attitude out of which our policy has grown? What is the history of it? Because history is very important, and history furnishes the belief on the one side in the reality and truth of the attitude.

What has our attitude been toward the peoples of Asia? It has been, I submit to you, that we are interested —that Americans as individuals are interested in the peoples of Asia. We are not interested in them as pawns or as subjects for exploitation but just as people.

For 100 years some Americans have gone to Asia to bring in what they thought was the most valuable thing they had—their faith. They wanted to tell them what they thought about the nature and relationship of man to God. Others went to them to bring to them what they knew of learning. Others went to them to bring them healing for their bodies. Others and perhaps fewer went to them to learn the depth and beauty of their own cultures, and some went to them to trade and they traded with them. But this trade was a very small part of American interest in the Far East, and it was a very small part of American interest in trade. It was a valid interest; it was a good interest. There was nothing wrong about it, but out of the total sum of the interests of the American people in Asia, it was a comparatively small part.

Through all this period of time also, we had, and still have great interests in Asia. But let me point out to you one very important factor about our interests in Asia. That is that our interests have been parallel to the interests of the people of Asia. For 50 years, it has been the fundamental belief of the American people—and I am not talking about announcements of government but I mean a belief of people in little towns and villages and churches and missionary forces and labor unions throughout the United States—it has been their profound belief that the control of China by a foreign power was contrary to American interests. The interesting part about that is it was not contrary to the interests of the people of China. There was not conflict but parallelism in that interest. And so from the time of the announcement of the open door policy through the 9-power treaty to the very latest resolution of the General Assembly of the United Nations, we have stated that principle and we believe it. And similarly in all the rest of Asia—in the Philippines, in India, in Pakistan and Indonesia, and in Korea—for years and years and years, the interests of Americans throughout this country have been in favor of their independence. This is where their independence societies, and their patriotic groups have come for funds and sympathy. The whole policy of our government insofar as we have responsibility in the Philippines was to bring about the accomplishment of this independence and our sympathy and help. The very real help which we have given other nations in Asia has been in that direction, and it is still in that direction.

Now, I stress this, which you may think is a platitude, because of a very important fact: I hear almost every day someone say that the real interest of the United States is to stop the spread of communism. Nothing seems to me to put the cart before the horse more completely than that. Of course we are interested in stopping the spread of communism. But we are interested for a far deeper reason than any conflict between the Soviet Union and the United States. We are interested in stopping the spread of communism because communism is a doctrine that we don't happen to like. Communism is the most subtle instrument of Soviet foreign policy that has ever been devised, and it is really the spearhead of Russian imperialism which would, if it could, take from these people what they have won, what we want them to keep and develop, which is their own national independence, their own individual independence, their own development of their own resources for their own good and not as mere tributary states to this great Soviet Union.

Now, it is fortunate that this point that I made does not represent any real conflict. It is an important point because people will do more damage and create more misrepresentation in the Far East by saying our interest is merely to stop the spread of communism than any other way. Our real interest is in those people as people. It is because communism is hostile to that interest that we want to stop it. But it happens that the best way of doing both things is to do just exactly what the peoples of Asia want to do and what we want to help them to do, which is to develop a soundness of administration of these new governments and to develop their resources and their technical skills so that they are not subject to penetration either through ignorance, or because they believe these false promises, or because there is real distress in their areas. If we can help that development, if we can go forward with it, then we have brought about the best way that anyone knows of stopping this spread of communism.

It is important to take this attitude not as a mere negative reaction to communism but as the most positive affirmation of the most affirmative truth that we hold, which is in the dignity and right of every nation, of every people, and of every individual to develop in their own way, making their own mistakes, reaching their own triumphs but acting under their own responsibility. That is what we are pressing for in the Far East, and that is what we must affirm and not get mixed up with purely negative and inconsequential statements.

Now, let me come to another underlying and important factor which determines our relations and, in turn, our policy with the peoples of Asia. That is the attitude of the Soviet Union toward Asia, and particularly towards those parts of Asia which are contiguous to the Soviet Union, and with great particularity this afternoon, to north China.

The attitude and interest of the Russians in north China, and in these other areas as well, long antedates communism. This is not something that has come out of communism at all. It long antedates it. But the Communist regime has added new methods, new skills, and new concepts to the thrust of Russian imperialism. This Communistic concept and techniques have armed Russian imperialism with a new and most insidious weapon of penetration. Armed with these new powers, what is happening in China is that the Soviet Union is detaching the northern provinces [areas] of China from China and is attaching them to the Soviet Union. This process is complete in outer Mongolia. It is nearly complete in Manchuria, and I am sure that in inner Mongolia and in Sinkiang there are very happy reports coming from Soviet agents to Moscow. This is what is going on. It is the detachment of these whole areas, vast areas—populated by Chinese—the detachment of these areas from China and their attachment to the Soviet Union.

I wish to state this and perhaps sin against my doctrine of nondogmatism, but I should like to suggest at any rate that this fact that the Soviet Union is taking the four northern provinces of China is the single most significant, most important fact, in the relation of any foreign power with Asia.

What does that mean for us? It means something very, very significant. It means that nothing that we do and nothing that we say must be allowed to obscure the reality of this fact. All the efforts of propaganda will not be able to obscure it. The only thing that can obscure it is the folly of ill-conceived adventures on our part which easily could do so, and I urge all who are thinking about these foolish adventures to remember that we must not seize the unenviable position which the Russians have carved out for themselves. We must not undertake to deflect from the Russians to ourselves the righteous anger, and the wrath, and the hatred of the Chinese people which must develop. It would be folly to deflect it to ourselves. We must take the position we have always taken—that anyone who violates the integrity of China is the enemy of China and is acting contrary to our own interest. That, I suggest to you this afternoon, is the first and the greatest rule in regard to the formulation of American policy toward Asia.

I suggest that the second rule is very like the first. That is to keep our own purposes perfectly straight, perfectly pure, and perfectly aboveboard and do not get them mixed-up with legal quibbles or the attempt to do one thing and really achieve another.

The consequences of this Russian attitude and this Russian action in China are perfectly enormous. They are saddling all those in China who are proclaiming their loyalty to Moscow, and who are allowing themselves to be used as puppets of Moscow, with the most awful responsibility which they must pay for. Furthermore, these actions of the Russians are making plainer than any speech, or any utterance, or any legislation can make throughout all of Asia, what the true purposes of the Soviet Union are and what the true function of communism as an agent of Russian imperialism is. These I suggest to you are the fundamental factors, fundamental realities of attitude out of which our relations and policies must grow.

Now, let's in the light of that consider some of these policies. First of all, let's deal with the question of military security. I deal with it first because it is important and because, having stated our policy in that regard, we must clearly understand that the military menace is not the most immediate.

## 18 TRUMAN'S DECISION

What is the situation in regard to the military security of the Pacific area, and what is our policy in regard to it?

In the first place, the defeat and the disarmament of Japan has placed upon the United States the necessity of assuming the military defense of Japan so long as that is required, both in the interest of our security and in the interests of the security of the entire Pacific area and, in all honor, in the interest of Japanese security. We have American—and there are Australian—troops in Japan. I am not in a position to speak for the Australians, but I can assure you that there is no intention of any sort of abandoning or weakening the defenses of Japan and that whatever arrangements are to be made either through permanent settlement or otherwise, that defense must and shall be maintained.

This defensive perimeter runs along the Aleutians to Japan and then goes to the Ryukyus. We hold important defense positions in the Ryukyu Islands, and those we will continue to hold. In the interest of the population of the Ryukyu Islands, we will at an appropriate time offer to hold these islands under trusteeship of the United Nations. But they are essential parts of the defensive perimeter of the Pacific, and they must and will be held.

The defensive perimeter runs from the Ryukyus to the Philippine Islands. Our relations, our defensive relations with the Philippines are contained in agreements between us. Those agreements are being loyally carried out and will be loyally carried out. Both peoples have learned by bitter experience the vital connections between our mutual defense requirements. We are in no doubt about that, and it is hardly necessary for me to say an attack on the Philippines could not and would not be tolerated by the United States. But I hasten to add that no one perceives the imminence of any such attack.

So far as the military security of other areas in the Pacific is concerned, it must be clear that no person can

## The Setting

guarantee these areas against military attack. But it must also be clear that such a guarantee is hardly sensible or necessary within the realm of practical relationship.

Should such an attack occur—one hesitates to say where such an armed attack could come from—the initial reliance must be on the people attacked to resist it and then upon the commitments of the entire civilized world under the Charter of the United Nations which so far has not proved a weak reed to lean on by any people who are determined to protect their independence against outside aggression. But it is a mistake, I think, in considering Pacific and Far Eastern problems to become obsessed with military considerations. Important as they are, there are other problems that press, and these other problems are not capable of solution through military means. These other problems arise out of the susceptibility of many areas, and many countries in the Pacific area, to subversion and penetration. That cannot be stopped by military means.

The susceptibility to penetration arises because in many areas there are new governments which have little experience in governmental administration and have not become firmly established or perhaps firmly accepted in their countries. They grow, in part, from very serious economic problems, some of them growing out directly from the last war, others growing indirectly out of the last war because of the disruptions of trade with other parts of the world, with the disruption of arrangements which furnished credit and management to these areas for many years. That has resulted in dislocation of economic effort and in a good deal of suffering among the peoples concerned. In part this susceptibility to penetration comes from the great social upheaval about which I have been speaking, an upheaval which was carried on and confused a great deal by the Japanese occupation and by the propaganda which has gone on from Soviet sources since the war.

Here, then, are the problems in these other areas which require some policy on our part, and I should like to point out two facts to you and then discuss in more detail some of these areas.

The first fact is the great difference between our responsibility and our opportunities in the northern part of the Pacific area and in the southern part of the Pacific area. In the north, we have direct responsibility in Japan and we have direct opportunity to act. The same thing to a lesser degree is true in Korea. There we had direct responsibility, and there we did act, and there we have a greater opportunity to be effective than we have in the more southerly part.

In the southerly part of the area, we are one of many nations who can do no more than help. The direct responsibility lies with the peoples concerned. They are proud of their new national responsibility. You can not sit around in Washington, or London, or Paris, or The Hague and determine what the policies are going to be in those areas. You can be willing to help, and you can help only when the conditions are right for help to be effective.

That leads me to the other thing that I wanted to point out, and that is the limitation of effective American assistance. American assistance can be effective when it is the missing component in a situation which might otherwise be solved. The United States cannot furnish all these components to solve the question. It can not furnish determination, it can not furnish the will, and it can not furnish the loyalty of a people to its government. But if the will and if the determination exists and if the people are behind their government, then, and not always then, is there a very good chance. In that situation, American help can be effective and it can lead to an accomplishment which could not otherwise be achieved.

*Japan.*—Now, with that statement, let's deal very briefly—because the time is going on and I am almost equaling my performance in the Senate and House—let's deal very briefly with some of the problems. Let's take the situation in Japan for a moment. There are three great factors to be faced. The security matter I have dealt with. Aside from that, there are the economic questions and the political questions. In the political field, General MacArthur has been very successful and the Japanese are hammering out with some effort, and with some backsliding, and regaining and backsliding again of progress, a political system which is based on nonmilitaristic institutions.

In the economic field, we have not been so successful. That is in very large part due to the inherent difficulty of the problem. The problem arises with the necessity of Japan being able to buy raw materials and sell goods. The former connections of Japan with the mainland and with some of the islands have been disrupted. That has produced difficulties. The willingness of other countries to receive Japanese goods has very much contracted since the war.

Difficulties of currency have added to those problems. But those matters have got to be faced and have got to be solved. Whether they are solved under a treaty or if the procedural difficulties of that are too great under some other mechanism, they must be solved along lines which permit the Japanese greater freedom—complete freedom if possible—to buy what they need in the world and to sell what they have to offer on the mainland of Asia, in southeast Asia, and in other parts of the world. That is the nature of the problem and it is a very tough one. It is one on which the occupation authorities, the Japanese government, ourselves, and others are working. There can be no magic solution to it.

*Korea.*—In Korea, we have taken great steps which have ended our military occupation, and in cooperation with the United Nations, have established an independent and sovereign country recognized by nearly all the rest of the world. We have given that nation great help in getting itself established. We are asking the Congress to continue that help until it is firmly established, and that legislation is now pending before the Congress. The idea that we should scrap all of that, that we should stop half way through the achievement of the establishment of this country, seems to me to be the most utter defeatism and utter madness in our interests in Asia. But there our responsibilities are more direct and our opportunities more clear. When you move to the south, you find that our opportunity is much slighter and that our responsibilities, except in the Philippines and there indirectly, are very small. Those problems are very confusing.

*Philippines.*—In the Philippines, we acted with vigor and speed to set up an independent sovereign nation which we have done. We have given the Philippines a billion dollars of direct economic aid since the war. We have spent another billion dollars in such matters as veterans' benefits and other payments in the Philippines. Much of that money has not been used as wisely as we wish it had been used, but here again, we come up against the matter of responsibility. It is the Philippine Government which is responsible. It is the Philippine Government which must make its own mistakes. What we can do is advise and urge, and if help continues to be misused, to stop giving the help. We cannot direct, we should not direct, we have not the slightest desire to direct. I believe that there are indications that the Philippines may be facing serious economic difficulties. With energetic, determined action, they can perhaps be avoided or certainly minimized. Whether that will be true or not, I can not say, but it does not rest within the power of the American Government to determine that. We are always ready to help and to advise. That is all we can and all we should do.

*Asia.*—Elsewhere in southeast Asia, the limits of what we can do are to help where we are wanted. We are organizing the machinery through which we can make effective help possible. The western powers are all interested. We all know the techniques. We have all had experiences which can be useful to those governments which are newly starting out if they want it. It cannot be useful if they don't want it. We know techniques of administration. We know techniques of organizing school districts, and road districts, and taxation districts. We know agricultural and industrial techniques, all of which can be helpful, and those we are preparing to make available if they are wanted, where they are wanted, and under circumstances where they have a fighting chance to be successful. We will not do these things for the mere purpose of being active. They will not be done for the mere purpose of running around and doing good, but for the purpose of moving in where we are wanted to a situation where we have the missing component which, if put into the rest of the picture, will spell success.

The situation in the different countries of southeast Asia is difficult. It is highly confused in Burma where five different factions have utterly disrupted the immediate government of the country. Progress is being made in Indochina where the French, although moving slowly, are moving. There are noticeable signs of progress in transferring responsibility to a local administration and getting the adherence of the population to this local administration. We hope that the situation will be such that the French can make further progress and make it quickly, but I know full well the difficulties which are faced by the Foreign Minister of France and my admiration and respect for him are so great that I would not want one word I say to add a feather to the burden that he carries.

In Malaya, the British have and are discharging their responsibility harmoniously with the people of Malaya and are making progress.

*Indonesia.*—In Indonesia, a great success has been

achieved within the last few weeks and over a period of months. The round table conferences at The Hague in which great statesmanship and restraint were displayed, both on the Dutch and the Indonesian side, have resulted in this new government being formed. Relations of this government with the Dutch will be very good, and the Dutch can furnish them great help and advice, and we will be willing to stand by to give whatever help we can rightly and profitably give. That situation is one which is full of encouragement although it is full of difficulty also.

*India and Pakistan.*—As one goes to the end of this semicircle and comes to India and Pakistan, we find really grave troubles facing the world and facing these two countries there, both with respect to Kashmir, and to the utter difficulties—economic difficulties growing out of the differences in devaluation, settlement of monetary plans back and forth, et cetera. We know that they have assured one another, and they have assured the world, that as stubborn as these difficulties may be and difficult as they may be of solution, they are not going to resort to war to solve them. We are glad to hear those assurances and the whole world is glad to hear it, but we know also that the problems are in such a situation and in such an area that they are most inflammable, and we believe that in addition to these most desirable assurances there should be some accommodation of wills to bring about a result as soon as possible.

In India and in Pakistan we are willing to be of such help as we can be. Again, the responsibility is not ours. Again we can only be helpful friends. Again the responsibility lies with people who have won their freedom and who are very proud of it.

So after this survey, what we conclude, I believe, is that there is a new day which has dawned in Asia. It is a day in which the Asian peoples are on their own, and know it, and intend to continue on their own. It is a day in which the old relationships between east and west are gone, relationships which at their worst were exploitation, and which at their best were paternalism. That relationship is over, and the relationship of east and west must now be in the Far East one of mutual respect and mutual helpfulness. We are their friends. Others are their friends. We and those others are willing to help, but we can help only where we are wanted and only where the conditions of help are really sensible and possible. So what we can see is that this new day in Asia, this new day which is dawning, may go on to a glorious noon or it may darken and it may drizzle out. But that decision lies within the countries of Asia and within the power of the Asian people. It is not a decision which a friend or even an enemy from the outside can decide for them.

3

## *Speech by Dean G. Acheson*
## *March 7, 1950*

[*Department of State Bulletin,* Vol. XXII, No. 559, pp. 454–55.]

*Washington, D.C.*

I appreciate the invitation to appear before your Committee with Mr. Hoffman to explain to you briefly why I feel the continuation of the Korean economic recovery program for a second year is of real importance to the success of American foreign policy. I shall indeed be brief because I know that, although I myself was not present, this matter was fully discussed with you by

26 TRUMAN'S DECISION

Mr. Webb and Mr. Hoffman* only a few months ago. In addition, I have referred to the importance of our Korean program in discussions we have had during the present session.

I believe the main questions we have to consider are: (1) the importance of the proposed continuation of the economic recovery program to the success of our over-all policy toward Korea and (2) the part which our Korean policy plays in United States policy for the Far East.

First as to Korea: You will recall that the United States has taken the leadership among the nations to attain the realization of our fundamental declaration made at Cairo in 1943 with the United Kingdom and China (and later joined by the U.S.S.R.) "that in due course Korea should become free and independent." When our own efforts to persuade the U.S.S.R. to join in holding free elections to establish a united country were unsuccessful, we referred the matter to the United Nations. The General Assembly has used and is using its best efforts to bring about the accomplishment of this end, desired by all the Korean people. The success of its efforts has, thus far, been limited to assisting in the establishment of a free government, the Republic of Korea, in what was formerly the area of United States occupation.

Upon the establishment of the Republic, the United States undertook to assist it to survive and develop as a democratic, representative government. To do this, the United States is providing the Republic with political support. Through our information and educational programs, we are seeking to help the Republic develop a sound educational system founded on principles of representative democracy. At the request of the Republic, we are maintaining there a Military Advisory Group to assist in training Korean security forces and to insure the effi-

* Mr. Webb and Mr. Hoffman are the Under Secretary of State and Administrator of the Economic Cooperation Administration, respectively.

cient employment of United States military assistance by those forces. Supplementing the prior transfer of military equipment under the Surplus Property Act, the Congress has authorized under the Mutual Defense Assistance Act the extension of military aid to Korea. And the Congress has recently authorized the Economic Cooperation Administration to undertake a program intended to bring the economy of the Republic as nearly as possible to a self-supporting basis. In doing so the Congress authorized the expenditure in the fiscal year 1950 of the total sum of 120 million dollars.

By means of these and related measures, the United States hopes to achieve the objective of strengthening the Republic of Korea to the point where it can (1) successfully withstand the threat of expanding Communist influence and control arising out of the existence in north Korea of an aggressive Soviet-dominated Communist regime and (2) serve as a nucleus for the eventual peaceful unification of the entire country on a democratic basis.

The testimony presented to your Committee by Mr. Hoffman, Mr. Webb, and other witnesses at the time of hearings on the bill authorizing the program for fiscal year 1950 indicated very plainly that the authority requested was to carry out the first year of a planned 3-year program intended to help Korea make substantial progress toward a self-supporting economy. The program for which authority is now requested for fiscal year 1951 is the second year of this 3-year program. Since Mr. Hoffman will go into the economics of the program with you, I will not attempt to do so beyond saying that the Department of State has participated in the preparation of the program which he will outline and supports it fully.

Second, as to the place of this proposal in our overall Far Eastern policy, I have said that the United States is taking the leadership among the nations in helping the people of Korea attain the goal of a united independent nation, free from foreign domination. As a result of this initiative, the United States today is looked to not only by the people of Korea but by the peoples of the Far East and, in fact, by the people of democratic nations everywhere as the leader in the struggle for the survival of a Korean Republic, both for itself and as a possible nucleus for the eventual peaceful unification of that country.

Broadly speaking, the United States foreign policy in the Far East is directed toward encouraging and assisting the efforts of the peoples of that area to improve their welfare and security, to stabilize and develop their economies, to strengthen free institutions, and to advance the cause of self-government free from outside domination. Korea is one place in which the United States can continue to take well-defined positive steps to help a free democratic country to survive in the face of efforts of communism to engulf it. Hundreds of millions of people of Southern and Southeastern Asia and the islands of the Pacific are now in a period where they must choose between the roads toward democracy or totalitarianism. As the President said in his message to the Congress on Korean aid in June of last year:

> Korea has become a testing ground in which the validity and practical value of the ideals and principles of democracy which the Republic is putting into practice are being matched against the practices of communism which have been imposed upon the people of north Korea. The survival and progress of the Republic toward a self-supporting, stable economy will have an immense and far-reaching influence on the people of Asia. Such progress by the young Republic will encourage the people of southern and southeastern Asia and the islands of the Pacific to resist and reject the Communist propaganda with which they are besieged. Moreover, the Korean Republic, by demonstrating the success and

tenacity of democracy in resisting communism, will stand as a beacon to the people of northern Asia in resisting the control of the Communist forces which have overrun them.

The people of Asia, as well as the people of Korea, have been able to see the way in which economic assistance from the United States has contributed already to the ability of the Korean people to move toward economic independence. The Economic Assistance Program has increased agricultural production and the well-being of the large farming population of Korea. It has given food to the families of the industrial workers and, by increasing production, has brought about mounting employment. It has made possible a small surplus for export as a source of foreign exchange with which necessities may be imported. This progress, together with the rehabilitation of factories, mines, and fishing facilities important to the Korean economy, has helped to give them faith in their form of government, strength to resist the constant pressures of communism, and confidence in their future.

There is one further and fundamental question which must be considered: That is the probability of ultimate success of the effort of the Korean Republic to survive. In recent debates, a number of Members of the Congress have indicated their feeling that the possibility of failure makes them doubt the wisdom of the United States giving a helping hand in this effort. It is my belief that American policy should be based on determination to succeed rather than on fear of the possibility of failure. Despite the problems with which the Republic of Korea is beset, both internally and externally, and despite its necessarily limited experience in self-government and paucity of technical and administrative know-how, conditions of stability and public order have continued to improve and the threat of Communist overthrow appears at least temporarily to have been contained.

There is good reason to hope from progress made thus far that with our assistance, the Republic of Korea can survive and thrive. This cannot, of course, be guaranteed. However, it continues to be true that without our assistance there can be no such hope.

# 4

*Interview with Senator Tom Connally, Democrat of Texas*
*May 5, 1950*

[Extracts]

[*U.S. News and World Report*, Vol. XXVIII, No. 18 (May 5, 1950), pp. 29–30.]

A. After all, the people make the issues. If you're out campaigning and some fellow gets up and says, "What about Korea?" what are you going to do? You can't duck under the table. You've got to talk.

* * *

Q. *Do you think the suggestion that we abandon South Korea is going to be seriously considered?*
A. I am afraid it is going to be seriously considered because I'm afraid it's going to happen, whether we want it to or not. I'm for Korea. We're trying to help her—we're appropriating money now to help her. But South Korea is cut right across by this line—north of it are the Communists, with access to the mainland—and Russia is over there on the mainland. So that whenever she takes a notion she can just

overrun Korea just like she probably will overrun Formosa when she gets ready to do it. I hope not, of course.

Q. *But isn't Korea an essential part of the defense strategy?*
A. No. Of course, any position like that is of some strategic importance. But I don't think it is very greatly important. It has been testified before us that Japan, Okinawa and the Philippines make the chain of defense which is absolutely necessary. And, of course, any additional territory along in that area would be that much more, but it's not absolutely essential.

5

*Associated Press Dispatch
May 10, 1950*

[*New York Times*, May 11, 1950, p. 14.]

*Seoul*

Defense Minister Sihn Sung Mo warned South Korea today that invasion by Communist North Korea was imminent. Mr. Sihn said intelligence reports indicated the North Koreans were moving in force toward the south.

## 6

*Ambassador to Korea John J. Muccio on Military Aid to Korean Security Forces June 9, 1950*

[*Department of State Bulletin*, Vol. XXII, No. 573, pp. 1048-49.]

In order to implement United States policy objectives and assist the Korean people in the achievement of their aspirations toward a united and independent democratic statehood, this Government has adopted a policy which includes (1) political support of the Government of the Republic of Korea within and outside the United Nations; (2) economic assistance designed to achieve a stable economy and a greater measure of self-sufficiency; (3) vigorous information and education programs; and (4) as a final step, and one without which both United States assistance and the efforts of the Korean people would be unavailing, military aid to the Korean security forces.

The uniquely compelling urgency which attaches to the military assistance requirements of the Republic has been brought about by virtue of the presence on its very frontiers (and not more than 30 miles from the capital city of Seoul) of an aggressive Soviet-dominated Communist regime which is publicly committed to the destruction of the Republic, by force of arms if necessary. The resultant serious problems of internal and external security threaten the continued survival of the Republic as an independent democratic nation.

There can be little doubt that the policies and intentions of the north Korean regime, which are but manifestations of the expansionist policies of the Soviet Union, are aimed at achieving eventual Communist domination of the entire peninsula. In order to prevent this threat from becoming an actuality, the United States has assisted the Korean security forces through (1) the transfer, prior to, and during United States troop withdrawal, of military equipment and supplies with a replacement value of more than 56 million dollars; (2) the establishment of a Military Advisory Group to assist in the training and development of those security forces; and (3) the passage by the United States Congress of the Mutual Defense Assistance Act which provides for continued support of those forces during fiscal year 1950.

The Korean Government has exhibited a willingness and ability to utilize this aid effectively. Internally, the Government is achieving increasingly favorable results in the vigorous campaign now being waged against Communist guerrillas. The fact that armed guerrilla strength has been reduced from an estimated peak of 2,000 to 577 men from September 1949 to April 1950 and that more than 5,000 guerrillas have been killed during that same period may be taken as a measure of the success of army and police operations.

Although the threat of north Korean aggression seems, temporarily at least, to have been successfully contained, the undeniable matériel superiority of the north Korean forces would provide north Korea with the margin of victory in the event of a full-scale invasion of the Republic. Such superiority is particularly evident in the matter of heavy infantry support weapons, tanks, and combat aircraft with which the U.S.S.R. has supplied and continues to supply its Korean puppet. It has been aggravated also by the recent Communist successes in China which have increased considerably the military potential of the north, particularly by releasing undetermined numbers of Korean troops from the Chinese Communist armies for service in Korea. The threat to the Republic will continue as long as there exists in the north an aggressive Communist regime desiring the conquest and domination of the south. It is, therefore, vital that the Republic's security forces, which are almost entirely dependent upon the United States for logistical support, be maintained on an effective defensive level of equality, in manpower, equipment, and training, in relation to those which immediately threaten it.

I am convinced that termination of United States military assistance after 1950 would mean both a nullification of the success which the security forces have thus far achieved in maintaining internal and external security and the substantial loss of the investments which we have made in the form of both military and economic assistance. Furthermore, the political support which this Government and the majority of the United Nations has extended the Republic in its struggle to survive would be rendered meaningless, and millions of people in the Far East who are now faced with the choice between communism and democracy would lose faith in the United States and would rapidly succumb to the aggressive tactics of Communist expansion.

On the other hand, it is my confirmed opinion that continued military assistance to the Republic of Korea is the best assurance not only for the protection of our investment but also for the successful implementation of our policy with respect to both that country and the entire Far East.

## 7

*Ambassador to the United States
Chang Myun to President Syngman Rhee
June 14, 1950*

[*Facts Tell* (Pyongyang: Foreign Languages Publishing House, 1960), pp. 187–91.]

*Washington, D.C.*

Your Excellency,

I arrived in Washington June 10 (Saturday) with my family, and I am happy to report that my wife's condition is good. She stood the strain of the trip better than I expected, and is now under the care of a heart specialist here. We are both most grateful to Your Excellency for the many kindnesses extended to us and for your graciousness in arranging our trip.

On the day of my arrival, I arranged a small dinner party in honor of Mr. Dulles. It was necessary that we have the party that day, because Mr. Dulles is leaving Washington today, and Saturday (June 10) was the only possible opportunity he had to meet with us. We had Mr. and Mrs. Dulles, Mr. Dean Rusk (Mr. Rusk has succeeded Mr. Walton Butterworth as Director of the Office of Far Eastern Affairs), Mr. and Mrs. Niles Bond, and Mr. and Mrs. Allison. Mr. Allison is in the Office of Northeast Asian Affairs, and will go with Mr. Dulles on his tour of the Far East. I had ample opportunity for a full discussion with Mr. Dulles, and was asked many questions. This visit Mr. Dulles is about to make is most important in view of the fact that he has a strong voice in preparing decisions of the State Department concerning the Far East. I am confident that his visit may bring about a change in the Department's policy with regard to the Far East. I impressed upon him how much our people are looking forward to his visit, in the hope that it will bring about a firmer stand in the State Department on the anti-Communism issue. I summed up the hopes of our people and our Government as to Mr. Dulles' part as follows:

> 1. He should make a strong statement, assuring Koreans that the United States will stand behind Korea both in peace and in trouble, both economically and militarily. His statement should declare that Korea should be placed within the United States' line of defense in the Pacific. (Mr. Dulles said at this point that the United States had never made an official commitment with respect to military support with any country, except under the Atlantic Pact, and there were qualifications even in that agreement. He said that not even the Philippines had any such agreement with the United States. But, he added, he was certain that the United States would not abandon Korea, and that he is even now preparing a statement to the effect that Korea would be backed by the United States. He said he would assure the Korean people that the United States would assist them).
>
> 2. We want more planes and long range guns in order to render our defenses more effective.
>
> 3. Korea should participate in peace treaty negotiations with Japan, because we have fought the Japanese longer and more than any other country.
>
> 4. Korea should take an active part in the formation of a Pacific Pact, if such a Pact ever comes

into being, and we would like to see the United States take an active part in the formation of the pact. (I regret, I told Mr. Dulles, that Korea was left out of the Baguio meeting, despite the specific promise of an invitation from the President of the Philippines himself. Dulles comment was "You didn't miss much.")

5. We want to see that Formosa will be protected by the United States because of its invaluable strategic location.

In conclusion, I told Mr. Dulles that his visit would, we believed, mean a general revision of the Far Eastern policy of the United States, and that we look forward to his precise and accurate powers of observation to effect a drastic change in the American Far Eastern policy. I told him that his coming to Korea would be regarded as the visit of an angel of peace, trying to impress upon him the importance of his presence in the eyes of our people, and also the responsibility that our hopes place upon him. I urged him to visit the 38th parallel and see for himself the situation. He is leaving today at 6 p.m. to go directly to Korea. I will see him off at the airport. He is accompanied by Mrs. Dulles. I hope Your Excellency will give him a big reception, and I am confident that you will do all you can to make his short stay pleasant. I would recommend that he be invited to a military review.

In this connection, I might add that yesterday (June 13) I had a long talk with Mr. Carl McCardle, who is going to the Far East with Mr. Dulles. We sent you a factsheet on Mr. McCardle's background last week. Mr. McCardle put many questions to me regarding Your Excellency, and I answered him specifically and with the purpose of clearing up the rumors and reports regarding you which have not been favorable. At the end of our conversation, which lasted more than an hour, he seemed to understand much more clearly. I gave him a copy of "Japan Inside Out" which he said he would read on the plane, together with some material we furnished him. He told me that he was most anxious to see you, and that he wants to go to the 38th parallel. He also would like to attend the opening session of the Assembly. He promised me that he would do his utmost to bring an accurate picture of conditions in Korea to the people of the United States, and told me that he shares most of Mr. Dulles' political views. I hope Your Excellency will show him such courtesies as you deem proper. As for an exclusive interview, there are some disadvantage [sic] inherent in granting it, because, as has been pointed out to us, if one newspaperman is permitted to interview Your Excellency exclusively and to quote you directly, the other correspondents in Seoul will have immediate queries from their superiors as to why they have not succeeded in securing such interviews. As a result, some ill feeling might develop. I am confident, however, that Your Excellency's judgement in this matter will be considered and correct. Together with Mr. McCardle, Mr. William Matthews, who is editor-publisher of the Arizona Daily Star, at Tucson, Arizona, will accompany Mr. Dulles' party. We were informed here that Mr. Matthews passport could not be sent to us in time for a visa and returned to the West Coast (he is joining the Dulles party in Seattle tomorrow) and upon this advice from Mr. Dulles office, we cabled His Excellency the Foreign Minister requesting a waiver of visa in Mr. Matthews' case. He is recommended by Mr. Dulles.

With sentiments of loyalty and esteem, I am

Respectfully yours,

JOHN M. CHANG

# 8

## *President Syngman Rhee to Chang Myun June 18, 1950*

[*Facts Tell*, pp. 197–99.]

*Seoul*

Thank you for your letters of June 14.

Mrs. Rhee and I are very glad to learn that Mrs. Chang is feeling well and is under the care of a good specialist there.

I am very glad that you had a chance to entertain Mr. Dulles and his party before he left. By now you have no doubt a copy of his speech at the Assembly. He went to the SD and told them that [sic] he wanted to say and they fully approved.

What you wrote in your letter that Mr. Dulles said that the United States has never made any official commitment not even the Philippines etc. I wish to point out to you that all those who are in the perimeter are automatically included in the defense line. Even if there is no pact signed it is the policy of the United States to supply these countries. Besides, the psychological effect of being in the defense line is already a moral commitment.

I had several conversations and an hour's talk today and he fully agreed that the Southeast Asia pact does not mean anything. He also agreed that Communist China should not be admitted to the UN. It would be an act of appeasement toward the Soviet Union. He agreed with all my policy and no doubt will do his best after his return.

There is one thing I want to tell you. When a party like this comes the next time you have to try to find out why some of the people are attached to it. Mr. McCardle went along to other conferences and he is filing his report in an official way in the White House to give his impression about the things he observes as an unofficial guest. Mrs. [sic] Matthews was sent by the White House in particular to report to the President and it is said that his report will count just as much as the report of Mr. Dulles if not more. These are valuable information I should get through your office. Fortunately we were tipped of the purpose of his presence in the party.

Miss Louise Yim is leaving for the States tomorrow and I asked her to take this letter along. She is trying to get a final settlement of the Pfeiffer Foundation which will amount to $140,000 for the construction of her school buildings. It might be that you get inquiries from different sources and I know you will do all you can to help her in getting this endowment. This endowment granted to her will do a great deal for Korean education. As you know there is no other school in that part of our city and it would be of great advantage if this school could be developed in such a manner as to enable all the students in that area to be taken care of. As you know the school facilities are inefficient and the great need for new buildings is the most essential one particularly since the compulsory school system has been adopted by the Legislature. We are in a great dilemna [sic] as there are not enough schools to accept students. Everything could be done so that the construction work of new buildings can begin. Therefore, do all you can and also ask Mr. Namkoong to help her in every way possible.

In regard to the Los Angeles question. I have received several letters from both parties and it still seems the best to let the resignation of Mr. Min stand with the understanding that he returns to Korea. If there is any possibility for Mr. Min to obtain a position with the U.S.

## The Setting 41

Army in Monterey the Government will consider an extension. By now you will be already in the clear if that can materialize otherwise, tell him the Foreign Office is unable to retract the former request for Mr. Min to return at the end of the month.

I cannot understand what is meant by saying that Chang and his family have no funds for returning. As I explained to you in Seoul our Government has already deposited his and his family's passage to the American Steamship Co. I cannot understand why he has not conted [sic] them as requested before he complains about his inability to pay his passage. We have wired KORIC* several times that his passage was deposited for May and then transferred for the June sailing. I also understood that you were authorized to inform the new clerk to pay his railroad fare from Los Angeles to Seattle.

It is up to you to settle the affairs of the office of the consulate. It is certain that you will have to give the secretary at least a month's notice. Miss Park has to be clearly instructed as to her office hours and her duties. She must keep the books and other things. We should be very sure that she is doing her best in the office.

I intended to give these instructions through the Foreign Office but as Miss Yin is leaving I may not have time to get the orders out on time.

* Cable address of the South Korean Embassy in Washington.

## 9

*Speech by Special Ambassador
John Foster Dulles
June 19, 1950*

[*Department of State Bulletin*, Vol. XXIII, No. 574, pp. 12–13.]

*Seoul*

The American people salute the Korean nation. We honor the valiant struggle you are making for liberty—human liberty and national liberty.

The American people enlisted in that struggle 175 years ago. We were, then, few, poor, divided, and menaced. There were only about 3 million of us. We were living precariously off the soil and the seas. We had been divided by loyalties to 13 rival sovereign states. We were closely pressed by the great military powers of that time —Spain to the south, England and France to the north, and Russia, which had moved into our continent, in the west. Nevertheless, our founders saw that Providence had given our people a unique opportunity to show that a free society could develop a spiritual, intellectual, and material richness which could not be matched by a society of dictatorship and that, if we took advantage of that opportunity, our example would stimulate men elsewhere to cast off the shackles of despotism. From its beginning, our effort was consciously related to the general welfare of mankind.

We went through many dark days and long nights. But our experiment succeeded. Our conduct and example, despite many faults, did help to show the infinite possibilities of free men, and it encouraged men everywhere to pry loose the grip of despotism and to take command of their own destiny. The nineteenth century was, in most of the world, an era of human liberation.

But the battle between liberty and despotism is never-ending. It has no limits either in space or in time. It is part of the constant struggle between good and evil, a struggle that seems to have been ordained for the testing of man.

Despotism, thrown onto the defensive in the nineteenth century, has resumed the offensive in the twentieth century. Already, the United States has twice intervened with armed might in defense of freedom when it was hard-pressed by unprovoked military aggression. We were not bound by any treaty to do this. We did so because the American people are faithful to the cause of human freedom and loyal to those everywhere who honorably support it.

Today, the Korean people are in the front line of freedom, under conditions that are both dangerous and exciting. You emerged from over 40 years spent under Japanese militarism. But you have not emerged into conditions of placid ease. Instead, you encounter a new menace, that of Soviet communism. It denies the spiritual worth and dignity of the individual human being. It insists that all men should be regimented into a pattern of conduct made for them in Moscow. It seeks to impose that degrading concept upon all men everywhere.

Taking advantage of Japanese surrender terms, Soviet communism has seized in its cruel embrace the Korean people to the north of the 38th Parallel; and, from that nearby base, it seeks, by terrorism, fraudulent propaganda, infiltration, and incitement to civil unrest, to enfeeble and discredit your new Republic, hoping, no doubt, that the people might, in despair, accept the iron discipline of the Soviet Communist Party.

That is a hard test for those who are only newly training in the practice of representative government.

Some observers felt that your task was a hopeless one. You have proved them to be wrong. Your faith and your works have confounded the skeptics. You have already held two general elections in an atmosphere free of terrorism, and a very high percentage of all eligible voters have participated. Out of your electoral processes, has come a stable and representative government. You have developed a strong, disciplined, and loyal defense establishment. Through hard work, you are steadily improving your country's economic condition.

There is solid ground for encouragement. No doubt, there are difficult days ahead and many problems yet unsolved, some internal, some external. But what has already happened shows that it lies within your power to achieve the goal of a Korea that is strong and free. Nothing can prevent that if you persist in your resolute will to be free, and if each of you individually exercises the self-controls that are required for the general good. A free society is always a society of diversity. That is the secret of its richness. But also it is a society in which men must voluntarily curb their individualism to the extent needed to enable the nation as a whole to avoid frustration and to achieve creation.

As you establish here in South Korea a wholesome society of steadily expanding well-being, you will set up peaceful influences which will disintegrate the hold of Soviet communism on your fellows to the north and irresistibly draw them into unity with you. Never, for a minute, do we concede that Soviet Communists will hold permanently their unwilling captives. No iron curtain can indefinitely block off the attracting force of what you do if you persist in the way you have been going.

You are conducting what may go down in history as the Great Korean Experiment, an experiment which, in its way, can exert a moral influence in the twentieth century as profound as that which, in the nineteenth century, was exerted by what was then called the Great American Experiment. That is why the eyes of the free world are fixed upon you. You carry the hopes and aspirations of multitudes.

The American people give you their support, both moral and material, consistent with your own self-respect and your primary dependence on your own efforts.

We look on you as, spiritually, a part of the United Nations which has acted with near unanimity to advance your political freedom, which seeks your unity with the north and which, even though you are technically deprived of formal membership, nevertheless requires all nations to refrain from any threat or use of force against your territorial integrity or political independence.

The American people welcome you as an equal partner in the great company of those who comprise the free world, a world which commands vast moral and material power and resolution that is unswerving. Those conditions assure that any depotism [sic] which wages aggressive war dooms itself to unutterable disaster.

The free world has no written charter, but it is no less real for that. Membership depends on the conduct of a nation itself; there is no veto. Its compulsions to common action are powerful, because they flow from a profound sense of common destiny.

You are not alone. You will never be alone so long as you continue to play worthily your part in the great design of human freedom.

# Section Two

# Occasion for Decision

*Commentary*

John E. James, a United Press International correspondent in Seoul, gave the world its first news of the outbreak of fighting in Korea (Doc. 10). This earned him a coveted "world beat" in journalism's hall of fame, which he later attributed to his midwestern father's advice to "get up early and go to work." Early on Sunday morning of June 25, Jack James was on the way to his downtown Seoul office when he accidentally met a military intelligence officer and bumped into one of the biggest stories of any journalist's lifetime. James' first cable reached Washington on Saturday evening June 24, and formed the basis of a UPI request to the State Department for confirmation at 9:04 p.m. (Korean time was 13 hours in advance of Washington time; thus this was 10:04 a.m. Sunday, June 25, in Korea.) The first official report of the United States Ambassador to Korea, John J. Muccio, arrived in Washington at 9:26 p.m. (Doc. 11). Ambassador Muccio's reputation as a cautious and careful observer was an important factor in assessing his report on the situation.

The Ambassador's cable was soon followed by a second dispatch from Jack James (Doc. 12).

These three reports formed the informational basis for the first American reaction to the fighting in Korea. A small group of officials hurriedly gathered at the State Department, including Dean Rusk, Assistant Secretary of State for Far Eastern Affairs (who had been the first Assistant Secretary for United Nations Affairs during 1949–50), John D. Hickerson, Assistant Secretary of State for United Nations Affairs, and Frank Pace, Jr., Secretary of the Army. They conferred by telephone with Secretary of State Acheson who was then at his Sandy Spring, Maryland, farm. In turn Secretary Acheson conferred with President Truman in Independence, Missouri. Based on these three cables American leaders had to decide what was happening in Korea and what, if anything, to do about it.

## 10

*John E. James to*
*United Press International*
*June 25, 1950,  9:50* A.M.

[Glenn D. Paige, *The Korean Decision* (New York: The Free Press, 1968), p. 88.]

New York

25095 JAMES FRAGMENTARY REPORTS EXTHIRTY EIGHTH PARALLEL INDICATED NORTH KOREANS LAUNCHED SUNDAY MORNING ATTACKS GENERALLY ALONG ENTIRE BORDER PARA REPORTS AT ZERO NINETHIRTY LOCAL TIME INDICATED KAESONG

FORTY MILES NORTHWEST SEOUL AND HEADQUARTERS OF KOREAN ARMYS FIRST DIVISION FELL NINE AYEM STOP ENEMY FORCES REPORTED THREE TO FOUR KILOMETERS SOUTH OF BORDER ON ONGJIN PENINSULA STOP TANKS SUPPOSED BROUGHT INTO USE CHUNCHON FIFTY MILES NORTHEAST SEOUL STOP LANDING EXSEA ALSO REPORTED FROM TWENTY SMALL BOATS BELOW KANGNUNG ON EASTERN COAST WHERE REPORTEDLY OFFCUT HIGHWAY ENDITEM NOTE SHOULD STRESSED THIS STILL FRAGMENTARY AND PICTURE VAGUE SYET JAMES

## 11

*John J. Muccio to Dean G. Acheson*
*June 25, 1950*

[*United States Policy in the Korean Crisis*, Department of State Publication 3922, Released July, 1950, p. 11.]

*Seoul*

According to Korean Army reports which are partly confirmed by Korean Military Advisory Group field adviser reports, North Korean forces invaded Republic of Korea territory at several points this morning. Action was initiated about 4 a.m. Ongjin was blasted by North Korean artillery fire. About 6 a.m. North Korean infantry commenced crossing the [38th] parallel in the Ongjin area, Kaesong area, and Chunchon area, and an amphibious landing was reportedly made south of Kangnung on the east coast. Kaesong was reportedly captured at 9 a.m., with some ten North Korean tanks participating in the operation. North Korean forces, spearheaded by tanks, are reportedly closing in on Chunchon. Details of the fighting in the Kangnung area are unclear, although it seems that North Korean forces have cut the highway. I am conferring with Korean Military Advisory Group advisers and Korean officials this morning concerning the situation.

It would appear from the nature of the attack and the manner in which it was launched that it constitutes an all-out offensive against the Republic of Korea.

MUCCIO

## 12

*John E. James to
United Press International
June 25, 1950, 10:30 A.M.*

[Glenn D. Paige, *The Korean Decision*, pp. 96–97.]

New York

25103 JAMES ADD 25095 REPORTS SAID ATTACKS LAUNCHED IN HEAVY RAIN AFTER MORTAR ARTILLERY BARRAGES WHICH BEGAN FOUR AYEM SUNDAY MORNING STOP KAESONG WHICH LIES PRACTICALLY ON PARALLEL ONLY MAJOR CITY REPORTED TAKEN STOP TANKS SUPPOSEDLY BROUGHT INTO PLAY THERE PARA KAESONG ABOUT FIFTY MILES ALONG ONE KOREAS BEST ROADS FROM SEOUL STOP MILITARYERS HERE HOWEVER SAID NORTHERN FORCES COULD PROBABLY STOPPED AT IMJIN RIVER WHICH CAN CROSSED BY VEHICLES EITHER ALONG SINGLE RAILWAY BRIDGE OR BY HANDPOWER FERRY PARA

THERE APPARENTLY NONO ACTION DIRECTLY NORTH SEOUL AT CHOSONGNI WHICH PROVIDES SHORTEST ROUTE FOR INVASION SUDKOREAN CAPITAL AND IS ONE OF TRADITIONAL ROUTES THROUGHOUT KOREAN HISTORY STOP THERE SOME OPINION HERE THAT ATTACKS WHICH BEEN HEAVIEST IN EAST AND WESTERN PORTIONS OF PENINSULA MIGHT BE FEINTS DESIGNED DRAW SUDKOREAN STRENGTH AWAY FROM THIS ROUTE PARA NORTH KOREANS SUPERIOR AIRFORCE NOTNOT USED STOP WEATHER TOO BAD IF USE INTENDED PARA OBSERVERS SEOUL SAY MAJOR ATTACK THIS TIME NOTNOT IN NORTHS FAVOR STOP RAINY SEASONS JUST BEGINNING RICE PADDYS ARE FULL OF WATER ROADS CAN BECOME MORASS MAKING TRANSPORT SUPPLY AND OPERATIONS OF TANKS AND AIRFORCE DIFFICULT TO IMPOSSIBLE PARA STILL NOTNOT CERTAIN WHAT SCOPE OR STRENGTH OF ATTACKS ARE BUT ONE OFFICER SAID QUOTE THIS LOOKS LIKE REAL THING UNQUOTE PARA THERE BEEN NONO UNUSUAL ACTIVITY REPORTED RECENTLY FROM NORTH OF PARALLEL REGARDING TROOP MOVEMENTS OR CONCENTRATIONS SUPPLYS WHICH WOULD INDICATE MAJOR ATTACK STARTING HOWEVER ENDS JAMES

# Section Three

# The Decision to Engage the United Nations

*Commentary*

Secretaries Hickerson and Rusk were unanimous in recommending to Secretary Acheson that the North Korean attack should be brought to the attention of the United Nations Security Council. Secretary Acheson agreed; so did President Truman. Since there was so little information to go on, Secretary Acheson advised the President that he saw no reason for him to return to Washington from the weekend vacation he had planned in Missouri.

Because Warren Austin, the Representative of the United States to the United Nations, was at home in Vermont, the burden of alerting the Security Council fell upon his deputy, Ambassador Ernest A. Gross, and Assistant Secretary Hickerson. At first they conferred by telephone with U.N. Secretary-General Trygve Lie. Later Ambassador Gross confirmed these conversations in an official note (Doc. 13). Throughout the night of Saturday, June 24, officials at the Department of State and in New York worked to prepare a draft resolution that would be presented to the Security Council. In the meantime, sometime before 10:30 a.m., Sunday morning, a report was received directly from the United Nations Commission on Korea (UNCOK) in Seoul (Doc. 14). This was considered exceptionally important by American officials since it meant that the United Nations would not be asked to act upon information limited to American sources.

Ambassador Gross presented the draft resolution during a Security Council meeting that began at 2:00 p.m., Sunday, June 25 (Doc. 15). The Soviet representative was absent from this meeting since for six months the Soviet Union had boycotted all U.N. meetings where the Republic of China was represented. The Soviet position was that only the Chinese People's Republic merited the position assigned to "China" in the U.N. Charter, although speculation at the time held that the Soviet Union did not expect the United Nations to take any effective action related to Korea. As a result of debate and discussion several changes were made in the American resolution (compare Doc. 15 with Doc. 16) before it was passed at 5:45 p.m. on June 25 by a vote of 9 to 0 with one abstention (Yugoslavia). China, Cuba, Ecuador, Egypt, France, India, Norway, and the United Kingdom joined the United States in supporting the resolution that labeled the North Korean invasion as "armed attack" and called upon both parties to the conflict to cease hostilities. Moreover the U.N. Commission on Korea was asked to report further on the situation.

Immediate enthusiasm for the United Nations action was widespread. Some delegates had taken the unusual action of voting for the resolution without waiting for instructions from their home governments. The North Korean invasion seemed to pose a challenge to the very existence and usefulness of the United Nations as an international institution whose purpose was to seek world peace. An editorial in *The New York Times*, published on June 26 (Doc. 17) summarized the American reaction to the Korean fighting and the U.N. resolution up to that point. Among top American officials State Department counselor George F. Kennan was virtually alone in considering the decision to lay the Korean conflict before the Security Council to have been a mistake (Doc. 18). Partly because he was out of communication in a farm outside Washington with no telephone, he did not take part in the decision to engage the United Nations. Later he was confident that had he been present at the State Department on Saturday night he could have convinced Secretary Acheson, and through him the President, to repel the North Korean invasion without United Nations involvement.

By 2:45 p.m., Washington time, on June 25, the military situation in Korea seemed so serious that Secretary Acheson advised the President to return to Washington. In response the President asked that a group of advisers meet with him that evening at Blair House. Just before entering a dinner meeting that began at 8:00 p.m. President Truman was heard to declare softly "We can't let the U.N. down." Thirteen officials joined the President for discussion: five from the State Department and eight from the Department of Defense. They included Secretary Acheson and Under Secretary of State James E. Webb, Assistant Secretaries Hickerson and Rusk, and Ambassador-at-Large Philip C. Jessup. Defense officials included Secretary Louis A. Johnson, Secretary Frank Pace, Jr. (Army), Secretary Francis P. Matthews and Admiral Forrest P. Sherman (Navy), and Secretary Thomas K. Finletter and General Hoyt S. Vandenberg (Air Force). The chairman of the Joint Chiefs of Staff, General Omar N. Bradley, also attended.

The President opened the meeting by saying that he had an "open mind" and requested individual opinions. Preceding the evening's discussion the participants heard a report of General MacArthur's views on the strategic importance of Formosa brought back by Secretary Johnson and General Bradley on June 24 after a visit to Tokyo. Secretary Acheson presented the following suggestions for consideration: (1) That General MacArthur be authorized to furnish the Republic of Korea with military equipment in excess of that already authorized under the Mutual Defense Assistance Program, (2) that American airplanes be employed to cover the evacuation of American women and children from the port of Inchon near Seoul, (3) that the Air Force be authorized to destroy North Korean tanks and airplanes that attempted to interfere with the evacuation, (4) that consideration be given to further assistance that might be rendered in support of the Security Council resolution just passed or to any subsequent resolution, and (5) that the Seventh Fleet be ordered to prevent a Chinese Communist invasion of Taiwan as well as a Nationalist assault on the Chinese mainland.

At the end of the discussion the President approved substantially all of Secretary Acheson's recommendations, except that he wanted to "sleep on" the final one. At this time the military situation in Korea did not appear to be so crucial that the Blair House conferees were confronted by a decision "to intervene or not to intervene." In order to obtain more information it was agreed that General MacArthur should be directed to send a reconnaissance party to Korea for a direct report from the combat area. The President set a tone of firm resolve and the participants shared his apparent determination to take positive action. The strength of the Republic of Korea Army was still overestimated and it was thought that the South Koreans might contain the attack. There was little clarity about Soviet intentions but it seemed that Soviet leaders, intimately involved in North Korea, had exhibited some degree of willingness to risk war. With atomic superiority, the United States was thought to be more powerful than the U.S.S.R., although to an indeterminate degree. The President and his advisers were pleased by the strong determination to resist North Korean "aggression" that had characterized the deliberations of the U.N. Security Council.

During the discussion of air support for the evacuation of American civilians it was expected that American fighter pilots should have a rather wide leeway in attacking the armor spearheading the North Korean drive toward Seoul. But General Bradley resisted making these expectations explicit in orders sent to General MacArthur. In his opinion, the pilots would be combative enough without being encouraged. This turned out to be incorrect. No written orders immediately came out of the first Blair House conference and General MacArthur was informed of the President's decisions only in an improvised telecommunications exchange. Nearly 24 hours later the President's advisers learned that American aircraft were *not* attacking the North Korean tanks.

13

*Deputy U.S. Representative to the U.N.
Ernest A. Gross to
Secretary-General Trygve Lie
June 25, 1950*

[*United States Policy in the Korean Crisis,* pp. 11–12.]

Dear Mr. Secretary-General:

I have the honour to transmit herewith the text of the message which I read to you on the telephone at three o'clock this morning, June 25, 1950.

Will you be good enough to bring the message to the

immediate attention of the President of the United Nations Security Council.

> Faithfully yours,
>
> ERNEST A. GROSS

[Enclosure]

The American Ambassador to the Republic of Korea has informed the Department of State that North Korean forces invaded the territory of the Republic of Korea at several points in the early morning hours of June 25 (Korean time).

Pyongyang Radio under the control of the North Korean regime, it is reported, has broadcast a declaration of war against the Republic of Korea effective 9 p.m. e.d.t. June 24.

An attack of the forces of the North Korean regime under the circumstances referred to above constitutes a breach of the peace and an act of aggression.

Upon the urgent request of my Government, I ask you to call an immediate meeting of the Security Council of the United Nations.

## 14

*U.N. Commission on Korea to Trygve Lie*
*June 25, 1950*

[United Nations, Security Council. U.N. doc. S/1496.]

GOVERNMENT OF REPUBLIC OF KOREA STATES THAT ABOUT 04:00 hrs 25 JUNE ATTACKS WERE LAUNCHED

## The Decision to Engage the United Nations 57

IN STRENGTH BY NORTH KOREAN FORCES ALL ALONG THE THIRTY EIGHTH PARALLEL. MAJOR POINTS OF ATTACK HAVE INCLUDED ONGIN PENINSULA, KAESONG AREA AND CHUNCHON AND EAST COAST WHERE SEABORNE LANDINGS HAVE BEEN REPORTED NORTH AND SOUTH OF KANGNUNG. ANOTHER SEABORNE LANDING REPORTED IMMINENT UNDER AIR COVER IN POHANG AREA ON SOUTHEAST COAST. THE LATEST ATTACKS HAVE OCCURRED ALONG THE PARALLEL DIRECTLY NORTH OF SEOUL ALONG SHORTEST AVENUE OF APPROACH. PYONGYANG RADIO ALLEGATION AT 13:35 hrs. OF SOUTH KOREAN INVASION ACROSS PARALLEL DURING NIGHT DECLARED ENTIRELY FALSE BY PRESIDENT AND FOREIGN MINISTER IN COURSE OF CONFERENCE WITH COMMISSION MEMBERS AND PRINCIPAL SECRETARY. ALLEGATIONS ALSO STATED PEOPLES ARMY INSTRUCTED REPULSE INVADING FORCES BY DECISIVE COUNTER ATTACK AND PLACED RESPONSIBILITY FOR CONSEQUENCES ON SOUTH KOREA. BRIEFING ON SITUATION BY PRESIDENT INCLUDED STATEMENT THIRTY SIX TANKS AND ARMOURED CARS USED IN NORTHERN ATTACKS AT FOUR POINTS. FOLLOWING EMERGENCY CABINET MEETING FOREIGN MINISTER ISSUING BROADCAST TO PEOPLE OF SOUTH KOREA ENCOURAGING RESISTANCE AGAINST DASTARDLY ATTACK. PRESIDENT EXPRESSED COMPLETE WILLINGNESS FOR COMMISSION BROADCAST URGING CEASE FIRE AND FOR COMMUNICATION TO UNITED NATIONS TO INFORM OF GRAVITY OF SITUATION. ALTHOUGH NORTH KOREAN DECLARATION OF WAR RUMOURED AT 11:00 hrs. OVER PYONGYANG RADIO, NO CONFIRMATION AVAILABLE FROM ANY SOURCE. PRESIDENT NOT TREATING BROADCAST AS OFFICIAL NOTICE. UNITED STATES AMBASSADOR, APPEARING BEFORE COMMISSION, STATED HIS EXPECTATION REPUBLI-

## 58 TRUMAN'S DECISION

CAN ARMY WOULD GIVE GOOD ACCOUNT OF ITSELF.

AT 17:15 hrs. FOUR YAK-TYPE AIRCRAFT STRAFED CIVILIAN AND MILITARY AIR FIELDS OUTSIDE SEOUL DESTROYING PLANES, FIRING GAS TANKS AND ATTACKING JEEPS. YONGDUNGPO RAILROAD STATION ON OUTSKIRTS ALSO STRAFED.

COMMISSION WISHES TO DRAW ATENTION OF SECRETARY-GENERAL TO SERIOUS SITUATION DEVELOPING WHICH IS ASSUMING CHARACTER OF FULL SCALE WAR AND MAY ENDANGER THE MAINTENANCE OF INTERNATIONAL PEACE AND SECURITY. IT SUGGESTS THAT HE CONSIDERS [SIC] POSSIBILITY OF BRINGING MATTER TO NOTICE OF SECURITY COUNCIL. COMMISSION WILL COMMUNICATE MORE FULLY CONSIDERED RECOMMENDATION LATER.

## 15

*Statement of Ernest A. Gross before the U.N. Security Council June 25, 1950*

[United Nations Security Council, Fifth Year, *Official Records*, No. 15, 473rd Meeting, pp. 4–8.]

Mr. Gross (United States of America): At 4 o'clock in the morning of Sunday, 25 June, Korean time, armed forces from North Korea commenced an unprovoked assault against the territory of the Republic of Korea. This assault was launched by ground forces along the 38th parallel and the Ongjin, Kaesong, and Chunchon sectors, and by amphibious landings in the east coast in the

## The Decision to Engage the United Nations 59

vicinity of Kangnung. In addition, North Korean aircraft have attacked and strafed Kimpo airport in the outskirts of the capital city of Seoul.

The facts and a general outline of the situation have now been reported by the United Nations Commission on Korea, and are reflected in document S/1496, to which the President has referred. Under these circumstances, this wholly illegal and unprovoked attack by North Korean forces, in the view of my Government, constitutes a breach of the peace and an act of aggression. This is clearly a threat to international peace and security. As such, it is of grave concern to my Government.

It is a threat which must inevitably be of grave concern to the Governments of all peace-loving and freedom-loving nations. A full-scale attack is now going forward in Korea. It is an invasion upon a State which the United Nations itself, by action of its General Assembly, has brought into being. It is armed aggression against the Government elected under United Nations supervision. Such an attack strikes at the fundamental purposes of the United Nations Charter. Such an attack openly defies the interest and authority of the United Nations. Such an attack, therefore, concerns the vital interest which all the Member nations have in the Organization. The history of the Korean problem is well known to the members of the Council. At this critical hour I shall not review that history in detail.

May I be permitted to recall just a few of the milestones in the development of the Korean situation? A Joint Commission of the United States of America and the Union of Soviet Socialist Republics sought unsuccessfully, for two years, to agree at ways and means of bringing to Korea the independence which we assumed would automatically come when Japan was defeated. This two-year deadlock prevented 38 million people in Korea from getting the independence which it was agreed was their right. My Government, thereupon, sought to hold a Four Power Conference, at which China and the United Kingdom would join the United States and the Soviet Union in seeking agreement on the independence of Korea. The Soviet Union rejected that proposal.

The United States then asked the General Assembly to consider the problem. The Soviet Union opposed that suggestion. The General Assembly, in resolution 112 (II) of 14 November 1947, created the United Nations Temporary Commission on Korea. By that resolution, the General Assembly recommended the holding of elections not later than 31 March 1948 to choose representatives with whom the Commission might consult regarding the prompt attainment of freedom and independence for the Korean people. These elected representatives would constitute a national assembly and establish a national government of Korea. The General Assembly further recommended that, upon the establishment of a national government, that government should, in consultation with the Commission, constitute its own national security forces and dissolve all military or semi-military formations not included therein. The General Assembly recommended that the national government should take over the functions of government from the Military Command and from the civilian authorities of the North and South, and arrange with the occupying Powers for the complete withdrawal from Korea of their armed forces, as early as practicable and, if possible, within ninety days.

Elections were held in South Korea and the Commission observed them. A Government in South Korea was set up as a result of the elections observed by the Commission. The Commission was unable to enter North Korea because of the attitude of the Soviet Union.

The United Nations Temporary Commission on Korea, in its report to the third session of the General Assembly[*], stated that not all the objectives set forth for it had been

[*] See *Official Records of the third session of the General Assembly, Supplement No. 9.*

## The Decision to Engage the United Nations 61

fully accomplished and that, in particular, unification of Korea had not yet been achieved. Notwithstanding the frustrations and the difficulties which the Temporary Commission had experienced in Korea, the General Assembly, at its third session, in resolution 195 (III) continued the Commission's existence and requested it to go on with its efforts to bring North and South Korea together.

One aspect of resolution 195 (III) adopted by the third session of the General Assembly should, I feel, be particularly emphasized. The General Assembly declared that a lawful government had been established in Korea as a result of the elections observed by the Commission, and declared further that this was the only lawful government in Korea. This is a most significant fact. The General Assembly declared further that the Government of Korea was based on elections which were a valid expression of the free will of the electorate of that part of Korea, and which were observed by the United Nations Commission. In the light of this declaration, my Government, on 1 January 1949, extended recognition to the Government of the Republic of Korea, and more than thirty States have, since that time, also accorded recognition to that Government.

The United Nations Commission worked toward the United Nations objectives of the withdrawal of occupying forces from Korea, the removal of the barriers between the regions of the North and the South and the unification of that country under a representative government freely determined by its people.

In 1949, as in 1948, the Commission's efforts to attain access to North Korea, which included direct intercourse with the Northern authorities and endeavours to negotiate through the Government of the USSR, were fruitless. The Commission was unable to make progress either towards the unification of Korea or toward the reduction of barriers between the Republic of Korea and the Northern author-

ities. The Commission reported to the General Assembly\*
that the border of the 38th parallel was becoming a scene
of increasingly frequent exchanges of fire and armed
raids, and that this constituted a serious barrier to friendly
intercourse among the people of Korea.

The Commission observed the withdrawal of United
States forces, which was completed on 19 June 1949.
Although it signified its readiness to verify the fact of
the withdrawal of the occupation forces of the Soviet
Union from North Korea, the Commission received no
response to its message to the USSR, and, therefore, could
take no action.

At its fourth session, the General Assembly, in
resolution 293 (IV) adopted on 21 October 1949, again
directed the Commission to "seek to facilitate the removal of barriers to economic, social and other friendly
intercourse caused by the division of Korea." The General
Assembly also authorized the Commission "in its discretion to appoint observers, and to utilize the services and
good offices of one or more persons, whether or not
representatives on the Commission."

The United Nations Commission on Korea is presently
in Seoul, and we have now received its latest report.

I have submitted a draft resolution [S/1497] which
notes the Security Council's grave concern at the invasion
of the Republic of Korea by the armed forces of North
Korea. This draft resolution calls upon the authorities
in the north to cease hostilities and to withdraw their
armed forces to the border along the 38th parallel. It
requests that the United Nations Commission on Korea
observe the withdrawal of the North Korean forces to
the 38th parallel and keep the Security Council informed
on the implementation and execution of the resolution.
The draft resolution also calls upon all Members of the
United Nations to render every assistance to the United

\* See *Official Records of the fourth session of the General Assembly, Supplement No. 9, volume I.*

*The Decision to Engage the United Nations* 63

Nations in the carrying out of this resolution, and to refrain from giving assistance to the North Korean authorities. With the President's permission, I should like to read the draft resolution in full.

*"The Security Council*

*"Recalling* the finding of the General Assembly in its resolution of 21 October 1949 that the Government of the Republic of Korea is a lawfully established government having effective control and jurisdiction over that part of Korea where the United Nations Temporary Commission on Korea was able to observe and consult and in which the great majority of the people of Korea reside; and that this Government is based on elections which were a valid expression of the free will of the electorate of that part of Korea and which were observed by the Temporary Commission; and that this is the only such government in Korea;

*"Mindful* of the concern expressed by the General Assembly in its resolutions of 12 December 1948 and 21 October 1949 of the consequences which might follow unless Member States refrained from acts derogatory to the results sought to be achieved by the United Nations in bringing about the complete independence and unity of Korea; and the concern expressed that the situation described by the United Nations Commission on Korea in its report menaces the safety and well being of the Republic of Korea and of the people of Korea and might lead to open military conflict there;

*"Noting* with grave concern the armed invasion of the Republic of Korea by armed forces from North Korea,

*"Determines* that this action constitutes a breach of the peace,

"I. *Calls upon* the authorities in North Korea
"(a) To cease hostilities forthwith; and
"(b) To withdraw their armed forces to the 38th parallel;
"II. *Requests* the United Nations Commission on Korea
"(a) To observe the withdrawal of the North Korean forces to the 38th parallel; and
"(b) To keep the Security Council informed on the execution of this resolution.
"III. *Calls upon* all Members to render every assistance to the United Nations in the execution of this resolution and to refrain from giving assistance to the North Korean authorities."

16

*Resolution of the U.N. Security Council
June 25, 1950*

[United Nations, Security Council. U.N. doc. S/1501.]

*The Security Council*

*Recalling* the finding of the General Assembly in its resolution of 21 October 1949 that the Government of the Republic of Korea is a lawfully established government "having effective control and jurisdiction over that part of Korea where the United Nations Temporary Commission on Korea was able to observe and consult and in which the great majority of the people of Korea reside; and that this Government is based on elections which were a valid expression of the free will of the electorate of that part of Korea and which were observed by the Temporary Commission; and that this is the only such Government in Korea";

*Mindful* of the concern expressed by the General Assembly in its resolutions of 12 December 1948 and 21 October 1949 of the consequences which might follow unless Member States refrained from acts derogatory to the results sought to be achieved by the United Nations in bringing about the complete independence and unity of Korea; and the concern expressed that the situation described by the United Nations Commission on Korea in its report menaces the safety and well being of the Republic of Korea and of the people of Korea and might lead to open military conflict there;

*Noting* with grave concern the armed attack upon the Republic of Korea by forces from North Korea,

*Determines* that this action constitutes a breach of the peace,

I. *Calls for* the immediate cessation of hostilities; and

*Calls upon* the authorities of North Korea to withdraw forthwith their armed forces to the thirty-eighth parallel;

II. *Requests* the United Nations Commission on Korea

(a) To communicate its fully considered recommendations on the situation with the least possible delay;

(b) To observe the withdrawal of the North Korean forces to the thirty-eighth parallel; and

(c) To keep the Security Council informed on the execution of this resolution;

III. *Calls upon* all Members to render every assistance to the United Nations in the execution of this resolution and to refrain from giving assistance to the North Korean authorities.

## 17

*War in Korea*
The New York Times
*June 26, 1950*

[*The New York Times*, June 26, 1950, p. 26.]

The Soviets' puppets in North Korea have set the match to the powder train. The world's major concern now is whether the universal conflagration can be avoided. The United States has acted promptly and the United Nations has done likewise. Whether their action, as at present projected, will be sufficient to restore the peace is problematical.

The powder train was laid in a long series of clashes with the Soviet Union. The 38th Parallel, established initially merely as a military marker to facilitate the acceptance of Japanese surrender, was quickly turned by the Soviet Union into an impassable political barrier. Behind this barrier was established the now familiar puppet regime, and this regime was supplied with a Soviet-trained and Soviet-equipped army. The Russians, having blocked every attempt at agreement or unification, then ostentatiously withdrew their own army—or said they did—and called upon the United States to do likewise. The United States ended its occupation but had meanwhile given substantial help in the formation of a free and democratic government—installed and recognized under the express guidance and approval of the United Nations. In the United Nations the Soviet Union under-

## The Decision to Engage the United Nations

took to prevent these steps but did not succeed. Nevertheless, it prevented the entry of the lawful government of Korea into the United Nations and has attempted at every turn to impede and discredit the young republic. These moves have also failed.

Meanwhile, for two years, a Soviet-inspired conspiracy of sabotage, infiltration, terrorism and treason has sought to destroy the Korean government from within. This campaign also has failed, as American officials have recently testified. The next move, therefore, is frontal attack. It is obviously Soviet-authorized, but we may be sure that there will be loud disclaimers from Moscow. It will be represented as a "natural" and "spontaneous" uprising of patriotic Koreans against "imperialism." The North Koreans have already added the familiar dodge of representing their assault as a retaliation. This is Hitler's famous "counteract with pursuit."

Neither the United States nor the United Nations, however, will be taken in by such transparent fiction. They recognize that this is not a "local" dispute and that the peace of the world hangs on what can be done about it.

The United States, thus far, has done two things. It has dispatched some military materials to South Korea and it has taken the diplomatic initiative in getting the matter before an immediate and emergency session of the United Nations Security Council. What the materials are has not been disclosed. Whether they can be sufficient to offset the complete air superiority of the Russian-supplied North Korean forces is not yet known.

Meanwhile, the United Nations has given overwhelming support to the United States resolution branding the North Korean invasion as an act of aggression, calling for a cease-fire and a withdrawal, and asking for support for South Korea and abstention of any aid to North. This is moral support for South Korea, but something more than moral support may be required.

Behind the prompt United Nations action must be, of course, the realization of the vital stake that the organization has in this issue. The lawful Korean Government is uniquely a United Nations creation. The invasion of its territory and an act of aggression against it is, in effect, an aggression against the United Nations and a direct defiance of its will and of its processes. If it cannot cope with this situation it may not survive in its present form.

Nevertheless, that coping presents some grave problems and difficulties. The Soviet Union, one of the five permanent members of the Security Council, chose to ignore the summons to the emergency session. It will obviously be the Soviet position, therefore, that any action of the body is illegal and will be disregarded by the Russians. This is another attempt at veto by walkout.

The question, however, may well be more academic than real. The Soviet Union would disregard any action of the United Nations that it did not like in any case. What is real, here, is how firmly the will of the peace-loving world can be expressed and how closely it can be united in expressing that will.

The effects of this situation on the United States will be no less far-reaching. What happens in Korea will affect every political and military position of the United States in the Pacific. If South Korea is lost to the Communists there must be an immediate revision of our defenses in respect to Japan and Alaska. The whole charter of the peace-treaty discussions will have changed abruptly. The position of Okinawa will have been modified and its needs changed. The Philippines will appear in a different military aspect. There will have to be a decision about Formosa.

What this adds up to is that war in Korea will, in the immediate future, force upon the United States the necessity for a decisive and unequivocal policy and program in respect to Asia. Thus far we have temporized and improvised. Our time for that ran out when the

North Korean tanks crossed the border. We can lose half a world, at this point, if we lose heart.

# 18

## George F. Kennan's Critique of U.N. Policy
[n. d.]

[George F. Kennan, *Memoirs 1925–1950* (Boston: Little, Brown and Co., 1967), p. 490.]

I never approved of the involvement of the United Nations in the Korean affair, or understood the rationale for it. This was, after all, an area in which we had taken the Japanese surrender and accepted the responsibilities of occupation. There was as yet no peace treaty with Japan to define its future status. We had accepted the responsibilities of military occupation in South Korea, and the fact that we had withdrawn our own combat forces did not mean, in the continued absence of a Japanese peace treaty, that these responsibilities were terminated. We had a perfect right to intervene, on the basis of our position as occupying power, to assure the preservation of order in this territory. We needed no international mandate to make this action proper. Nor did the Charter of the United Nations require us to involve the organization in such a conflict. Article 107, while somewhat ambiguous, conveyed the general impression that problems arising immediately from the recent war were not to be considered proper subjects for the attention of the UN. This was, finally, a civil conflict, not an international one; and the term "aggression" in the usual international sense was as misplaced here as it was to be later in the case of Vietnam. The involvement of the United Nations, hastily brought about by my colleagues in the State Department before I returned from my farm on that fateful Sunday, was thus in no way necessary or called for; and the later invocation of a UN resolution to justify military operations extending beyond the parallel seemed to me to represent an abuse, rather than a proper utilization, of the exceptional confidence accorded to us at that time by the international community.

# Section Four

# The Decision to Commit Air and Sea Forces

*Commentary*

The Security Council resolution of June 25 had no observable effect upon North Korean decisions. They continued what appeared to be a well-planned and well-executed invasion. At 9:30 a.m., Monday, June 26, (8:30 p.m., Sunday, in Washington) the supreme North Korean leader Marshal Kim Il Sung made a radio broadcast in which he clearly announced his goal of unifying the Korean peninsula by military means (Doc. 19). As seen from this statement North Korean objectives were certainly not to restore the *status quo ante* at the Thirty-eighth Parallel. The North Korean invasion of the South also was not justified as a preemptive attack forced by fear of a joint ROK-American invasion of the North. North Korean military action was justified solely on the grounds that the ROK Army had attacked the North. But no evidence has ever been produced to that effect, even during the exhilarating, free atmosphere of the overthrow of the Rhee Administration in 1960. Then and for nearly 10 months thereafter Koreans were at liberty to expose past evils and did so with a vengeance. Not a word was said, in the revolutionary atmosphere, to link President Rhee with precipitating the Korean War. If the Rhee Administration had initiated the attack this was a time in history when the voice of Korean truth would have been heard. Nothing on this subject was heard except continued distrust of Korean Communist treachery in substituting violence for proclaimed peaceful intent to achieve national reunification. The June 26 report of the United Nations Commission on Korea (Doc. 20) is a more accurate portrayal of the conditions surrounding the outbreak of fighting.

At about 10:00 a.m. on the morning of June 26, President Truman issued a statement that summarized the measures that had been taken up to that time (Doc. 21). A decision to commit combat forces still had not been made. In the Congress, Senators Bridges (Doc. 22) and Knowland (Doc. 23) were militant in urging the President to take positive action. At the same time the Republican Party policy group held a caucus and passed a resolution that the Korean fighting should not be allowed to drag the United States into war. Neither the President nor Secretary Acheson seemed specially cognizant of what Senators Bridges, Knowland, or other critics were saying at this particular time. Nor did they seem to be especially aware or sensitive to the charges that they had been "soft on Communism" that were parts of the political campaign of Wisconsin Senator Joseph R. McCarthy. An attempt was made to answer Senators Bridges and Knowland by Senator Tom Connally, Chairman of the Foreign Relations Committee, but since he did not know at this time what the President was ultimately going to do (as the President himself did not) he could only answer in "vague, hypothetical terms" (Doc. 24).

By late afternoon on Monday the military reports

being received from Korea had become increasingly grim. The Korean Ambassador, Chang Myun, visited President Truman and presented to him an appeal for assistance from the Korean National Assembly (Doc. 25). A similar request for support was addressed to the U.N. Secretary-General. A contemporary report from UNCOK further reflected the gravity of the situation (Doc. 26).

At 6:30 p.m. Secretary Acheson, who had been working alone in his office since late afternoon, called in his advisers and announced that he had drafted a course of action for coping with the crisis. The group worked on the recommendations he had drafted until a little after 7:00 p.m. when they went to dinner. At 7:29 p.m. Secretary Acheson telephoned the President and advised him that in his opinion it was time to call another meeting of his advisers.

They met at 9:00 p.m. at Blair House. Substantially all who had attended the first meeting were present except Under Secretary Webb, on duty at the State Department. He was said to have been "put in the dog house" by the President because on Sunday he had attempted to precipitate discussion of American domestic political implications of the events in Korea.

The President asked for General MacArthur's report on the latest military situation; this was presented by General Bradley (Doc. 27). Then the President again asked for the individual opinions of his advisers, beginning with Secretary Acheson. The Secretary of State presented a five-point proposal that he and his aides had just drafted: (1) that the Navy and Air Force be instructed to give the fullest possible support to the South Korean Forces and that such support be limited to the area south of the Thirty-eighth Parallel, (2) that orders be issued to the Seventh Fleet to prevent an attack upon Formosa, that the Chinese Nationalist Government be told to desist from operations against the mainland, and that the Fleet be ordered to secure the compliance of the latter, (3) that American forces in the Philippines be strengthened and that increased military assistance be rendered to the Philippine Government, that military assistance to Indochina (Vietnam) be accelerated and that a military mission be sent there, and (5) that Ambassador Austin be instructed to report any action taken under the above recommendations to the United Nations.

After discussion these suggestions were approved without substantial modification. A group went to the Pentagon to convey the decisions to General MacArthur. President Truman later called this "the toughest decision I had to make as President."

General MacArthur wanted to announce the impending American military support at once in order to bolster South Korean morale, but permission was refused him since the President had informed neither the Congress nor the American people. The General circumvented this injunction by allowing the news to be broadcast only in the Korean language and denying all inquiries about it in Tokyo. The President officially announced his decisions at noon on Tuesday, June 27 (Doc. 28) after meeting with congressional leaders. Upon Secretary Acheson's recommendation the President decided not to ask the Congress for a joint resolution in support of American military involvement in the fighting. The Secretary of State feared impairment of American morale and unity by partisan attacks upon present and past policy that would probably accompany such a debate.

At 3:00 p.m. on Tuesday the U.N. Security Council met again. At 11:45 p.m., after requested delays by delegates who attempted to secure instructions from their home governments, a resolution proposed by Ambassador Austin was approved without modification (Doc. 29) by a vote of 7 to 1 with 2 abstentions. The United Kingdom, France, China, Cuba, Ecuador, Norway, and the United States supported the resolution; Yugoslavia opposed it; India and Egypt abstained. There was thus an interval of

## The Decision to Commit Air and Sea Forces 75

slightly more than 24 hours between the time President Truman decided to fight in Korea and the time when the U.N. Security Council formally called for "urgent military measures . . . as may be necessary to repel the armed attack and to restore international peace and security in the area." According to Secretary-General Lie this discrepancy was "more apparent than real" because diplomatic consultations in the U.N. previously had shown that there were enough votes to support military countermeasures against the North Korean invasion.

Governor Thomas E. Dewey of New York, who had opposed Truman in the 1948 election, set the tone of an overwhelmingly favorable domestic and international response to the President's decisions (Doc. 30). But there was dissent, too, such as that of Representative Vito Marcantonio (Doc. 31), who was answered by Representative Abraham Ribicoff (Doc. 32), and that of influential Republican Senator Robert A. Taft (Doc. 33), who was answered by Senate majority leader Scott W. Lucas (Doc. 34). The sense of overall unity within Washington, however, was vividly described by Joseph C. Harsch of the *Christian Science Monitor* (Doc. 35). Compared with the acrimony surrounding the Vietnam War, in the 1960's, the sense of national unity initially surrounding the American military commitment in Korea is noteworthy.

The Soviet response to Truman's decision as expressed in a front-page *Pravda* commentary (Doc. 36) was expectedly critical but relatively temperate compared with the strident reaction of Mao Tse-tung as reported in the Peking *Jen-min Jih-pao* (Doc. 37). The impression that the Soviet Union would respond moderately to Truman's decisions was reinforced by an exchange of diplomatic notes. This was initiated on June 27 by an American request that the Soviet Union disavow responsibility for the attack and use its "good offices" with the North Koreans to get them to withdraw (Doc. 38). The Soviet

76 TRUMAN'S DECISION

response on June 29 indicated that the conflict in Korea was an internal affair in which outside interference was impermissible (Doc. 39).

A timely review of the President's decisions up to this point was given by Secretary Acheson in a press conference on the afternoon of Wednesday, June 28 (Doc. 40) and in an address before the American Newspaper Guild on June 29 (Doc. 41).

Ground combat troops still had not been ordered into Korea. It was still hoped that air and sea power in support of the ROK Army could turn the tide of battle.

19

*Radio Address by
Marshal Kim Il Sung
June 26, 1950*

[*Kim Ilsŏng sŏnjip* (Selected Works of Kim Il Sung) (Pyongyang: Korean Workers Party Press, 1954), Vol. III, pp. 1–12. Translated by Glenn D. Paige.]

Dear countrymen!
Beloved brothers and sisters!
Officers and men of our People's Army!
Guerrillas active in the southern part of the Republic!
On behalf of the Government of the Korean Democratic People's Republic I make the following appeal to all:

The army of the traitorous rebel Syngman Rhee's puppet government on June 25 began a general attack all along the Thirty-eighth Parallel against territory north of the Parallel. Brave constabulary units of the Republic resisted the attack of the enemy and engaged in a merciless battle that brought about the demoralization of the Syngman Rhee puppet government's army.

The Government of the Korean Democratic People's Republic discussed the situation that had arisen and ordered the People's Army to begin a counterattack and to destroy the armed forces of the enemy. In accordance with the instructions of the Government, the People's Army repulsed the enemy from the territory north of the Thirty-eighth Parallel and advanced 10 to 15 kilometers into the territory south of the Thirty-eighth Parallel. The People's Army liberated several cities such as Onjin, Yŏnan, Kaesŏng, Paekch'ŏn, and many villages.

Despite the struggle of all patriotic and democratic forces of our Fatherland to achieve unification of the Fatherland by peaceful means, the traitorous rebel Syngman Rhee-ites opposed the people and launched a civil war of fratricidal extermination.

As all the world knows, for a long time the Syngman Rhee traitors, opposing peaceful unification, have prepared for a civil war of fratricidal extermination. Even though the people of South Korea are struggling to keep from starvation, the Syngman Rhee puppet government wasted the greater part of its budget, which was forcibly collected through excessive taxes, on increased military armament and preparations for a fratricidal civil war of extermination.

For this fratricidal civil war of extermination the Syngman Rhee reactionaries moreover made furious rear area preparations.

They established a reactionary police system in South Korea; drove all democratic political parties and social organizations underground; arrested, imprisoned, and murdered patriotic, progressive persons; and repressed anyone who expressed even the slightest dissatisfaction with the Rhee reactionary system and its war preparations.

The traitorous rebel Syngman Rhee-ites, who are the unspeakable enemy of the Korean people, in the process of carrying out their anti-people, reactionary policies, imprisoned and murdered tens of thousands of our Fatherland's best sons and daughters.

The Syngman Rhee traitorous rebels in order to mask their preparations for civil war incessantly created conflict incidents along the Thirty-eighth Parallel, caused the Fatherland and the people to fall into a state of uneasiness, and planned to place responsibility for these provocative conflict incidents upon the authorities of our People's Republic.

It must be pointed out that in the process of preparing a "northern expedition," the Syngman Rhee traitorous rebels at the direction of the American imperialists even set out on the path of conspiring with Japanese militarists, the most thoroughgoing enemies of the Korean people.

The Syngman Rhee rebels, seeking to preserve their selfish greed and control, made our Fatherland into a military strategic base for American imperialism in Asia. Furthermore, as a source of natural resources to feed the profits of American monopoly capitalism, they placed the economy of the southern part of the Fatherland under the control of the American monopoly capitalists.

Seeking to enslave our Fatherland by economic means, the American imperialists finally ruined the national economy of the southern part of the Republic.

The American imperialists took away many essential natural resources of our Fatherland such as rice, tungsten, and graphite at low prices.

Dominated by American capitalism, medium and small entrepreneurs and shopkeepers could not escape bankruptcy.

Production has stopped in the southern part of the Fatherland; the majority of factories and manufacturing plants have been closed, producing several million unemployed; and farmers, who even today have not yet received land, and the people are wandering about in hunger.

Dear countrymen!

## *The Decision to Commit Air and Sea Forces* 79

The Government of the Korean Democratic People's Republic, seeking to avoid the bloodshed of a fratricidal civil war of extermination, together with all patriotic, democratic political parties and social organizations and all the people of our Fatherland, has made every effort to achieve unification of our Fatherland by peaceful means. Already, in April 1948, at the joint North-South meeting of the representatives of the various political parties and social organizations, the first step was taken to unify our country by peaceful means.

However, the Syngman Rhee traitorous rebels caused this first step to fail and, with the support of the American imperialists and their running dogs the so-called U.N. Commission on Korea, fabricated separate "elections" in South Korea on May 10, 1948, and strengthened preparations for an armed attack upon the northern part of our Fatherland.

A step toward peaceful unification of our country was made in June of last year in the proposal for general elections made by seventy-two patriotic political parties and social organizations, meeting under the auspices of the Fatherland Front; this aimed at achieving the peaceful unification and complete independence of the Fatherland.

Although all the Korean people warmly supported and approved this proposal, the Syngman Rhee rebels also, of course, caused it to fail.

Reflecting the desires of all the people yearning for the peaceful unification of Korea, the Fatherland Unification Democratic Front on June 7, 1950 again made a proposal directed toward peaceful unification of the Fatherland.

However the Syngman Rhee rebels, branding as traitors those who had supported the proposals of the Fatherland Front concerning peaceful unification of the Fatherland, again caused failure of this proposal to be realized.

On June 16, 1950, the Standing Committee of the

Supreme People's Assembly, Korean Democratic People's Republic, proposed that the Supreme People's Assembly of the Korean Democratic People's Republic and the South Korean "National Assembly" be united into a single all-Korean legislative body as a means of achieving peaceful unification of the Fatherland. This proposal expressed indomitable and tenacious trust in the unification, independence, and democratic development of the Fatherland and was based upon the hopes of the various political parties and social organizations.

And how did the Syngman Rhee rebels reply to this just proposal that expressed the ardent desires of the entire Korean people?

The Syngman Rhee rebels, betraying the interests of the Korean people replied to the earnest desires of all the Korean people for peaceful unification of the Fatherland with a fratricidal civil war of extermination.

However, what kind of objectives do these reactionary traitors hope to gain out of this fratricidal civil war of extermination?

Through this fratricidal war of slaughter, the Syngman Rhee rebels hope to set up in the northern part of the Republic the unprecedented, anti-people, reactionary system of rule that remains in the South as a remnant of Japanese imperialism and to rob our people of the democratic reforms and successes that have been achieved.

The Syngman Rhee reactionary traitors want to rob the farmers in the northern part of the Republic of the land that they received from the landlords through land reforms based on the principle of confiscation without compensation and distribution without payment—and give them back again to the landlords; furthermore they want to steal all the democratic freedoms and rights that have been won by the Korean people in the northern part of the Republic.

The Syngman Rhee rebels want to turn our Fatherland into an American imperialist colony and to make the Korean people into slaves of American imperialism.

Dear brothers and sisters!

A great crisis has been inflicted upon our Fatherland and people. In order to cope with this crisis, what must be done?

The Korean people in this war against the Syngman Rhee traitorous rebels must defend to the death the Korean Democratic People's Republic and its Constitution; must destroy the anti-people, fascist Syngman Rhee puppet government in the South, liberating the southern part of the Republic from the rule of the Syngman Rhee rebels; furthermore, the Korean people must set up true organs of people's power—people's committees—in the South and must complete the unification of the Fatherland under the flag of the Korean Democratic People's Republic to form a strong, democratic, independent state.

The war waged by us for unification of the Fatherland, independence, freedom and democracy against the fratricidal civil war of extermination begun by the Syngman Rhee traitorous rebels is a just war.

Dear countrymen!

The entire Korean people once again have risen in opposition to enslavement by foreign imperialists and stand as one in a struggle of national salvation to overthrow and destroy the Syngman Rhee traitorous rebels. Everywhere they stand ready to sacrifice themselves and certainly they will win victory.

All the Korean people must always clearly watch out for and become increasingly vigilant against every action and movement of the American imperialists who stand behind the Syngman Rhee rebels.

Our People's Army must show courage, boldness, and initiative in defending to the death the various democratic reforms and achievements in the northern part of the Republic, in saving our countrymen in the southern part of the Republic from reactionary rule, and in bringing about the unification of the Fatherland.

The officers and men of our People's Army arise from the people and are the best sons and daughters of the Fatherland and the people. They are the Korean People's Army, educated and trained in love of the Fatherland and the people, armed with the most recent, modern, and best weapons, and possessed of the noble consciousness that they must always fight for the interests of the Fatherland and people.

The people in the northern part of the Republic must change over all their activities to a wartime basis and must mobilize all their forces to smash the enemy mercilessly in short order.

Every enterprise must be subordinated to the tasks of achieving war objectives and mopping up the enemy; we must organize all-people's aid to the People's Army; the front must be continually augmented and reinforced; all necessities must be swiftly supplied; emergency transportation of military goods must be secured; and the most all-embracing warm-hearted assistance should be given to wounded soldiers.

We must organize all activities in the People's Army rear areas solidly so as to respond completely to the demands of the fighting front.

In the rear areas, there must be merciless struggle against deserters and those who spread false propaganda; the tasks of exposing and purging spies and saboteurs must be organized at once.

Our enemies are cunning and treacherous; everywhere they will spread lies and deception.

We must not be duped by evil propaganda; the authorized agencies of the Republic must punish those persons who injure the all-people's war for unification, freedom, and independence.

The workers, technicians, and office workers of the northern part of the Republic must exercise high vigilance in all the factories, manufacturing plants, rail transport facilities, and transportation and communications agencies

## The Decision to Commit Air and Sea Forces 83

in order to guard against enemy infiltration. They must exert every effort to fulfill the duties entrusted to them faithfully, making wise efforts to ensure prompt and effective responses to the demands from the front.

The farmers of the northern part of the Republic must exert every effort to ensure the food supplies of the People's Army and to produce more agricultural products. They must also give every possible assistance to ensure the victory of the People's Army.

The men and women guerrillas in the southern part of the Republic must develop the guerrilla movement more ferociously and bravely; the broad masses of the people must be brought more into the guerrilla units; and liberated areas must be expanded or created. In the enemy rear areas the enemy must be attacked and mopped up. To disrupt the enemy's battle plan, staff headquarters should be attacked. Such things as railroads, roads, bridges, telegraph lines, and telephone lines must be cut and destroyed, using every means, so as to disrupt . . . communications between the fighting front and the enemy rear area. Everywhere traitors must be punished. People's committees, the organs of people's power, must be revived, and positive support must be given to the People's Army.

Countrymen in the southern part of the Republic must not obey the orders of the Syngman Rhee puppet government, must oppose their decrees and directions, and must carry out their destructive activities so as to make the enemy's rear area organization a confused missing link.

The workers of the South must resist everywhere, organize a general strike, cause an uprising, and must save all the factories, manufacturing plants, mills, mines, railroads, and other places of work from destruction by the fleeing enemy. They must welcome the People's Army and assist them in all possible ways to be victorious.

Farmers in the South must not give food to the

enemy, must protect this year's harvest, must participate fully in the guerrilla movement, and must give the utmost support and assistance to the People's Army.

Individual entrepreneurs, medium and small businessmen, and tradesmen must help the People's Army, and must cooperate in the struggle to liberate our national economy from the American monopoly capitalists.

The literati and intelligentsia of the South must assist the war against the Syngman Rhee rebels in order to secure the unification and freedom of the Fatherland and to achieve conditions for the development of national culture. They must participate positively in the ranks of the political propagandists, exposing mercilessly the crimes of the Syngman Rhee rebels and performing the function of agitators in organizing a mass uprising.

Officers and men of the South Korean puppet government's "National Defense Army"!

Your real enemies are the Syngman Rhee rebels. Not missing this opportunity for the Fatherland and the people, you must thoroughly root out the Syngman Rhee rebels. You must come over to the side of the People's Army and the partisans and must cooperate in the all-people's struggle for the unification and freedom of the Fatherland.

You must win an honorable place in the ranks of fighters for the freedom and independence of the Fatherland by stepping forth against the enemies of our people.

Dear countrymen, brothers and sisters! I call upon all the Korean people to gather more solidly under the authority of the Korean Democratic People's Republic in order to destroy and sweep away quickly the armed power and police system of the Syngman Rhee rebels.

Let us gain the heroic victory of securing the unification and independence of the Fatherland—something for which all our people yearn.

The history of mankind shows that when a people have risen prepared to face death in the struggle to achieve their freedom and independence they have always been victorious.

Our cause is a just cause.

Victory will certainly be on the side of our people.

I am confident that our righteous struggle for the Fatherland and the people will definitely be victorious.

The time has come to bring about the unification of our country. Let us go forward bravely with self-confidence and conviction in victory.

Devote all our strength to support the front and the People's Army!

Devote all the strength of our people to mopping up and annihilating the enemy!

Long live the Korean people who have risen in a righteous all-people's war!

Long live the Korean Democratic People's Republic!

Forward to victory!

## 20

*U.N. Commission on Korea to Trygve Lie June 26, 1950*

[United Nations, Security Council. U.N. doc. S/1505.]\*

The Commission submits following Summary Report on background events preceding twenty-fifth June outbreak of hostilities.

\* Due to transmission difficulties, this cable has been received in a garbled form and is subject to correction. [A revision of this original document can be found in U.N. doc. S/1505/Rev. 1, August 21, 1950.]

1. For the past two years the North Korean regime has by violently abusive propaganda, by threatening gestures along the 38th parallel and by encouraging and supporting subversive activities in the territory of the Republic of Korea pursued tactics designed to weaken and destroy the Government of the Republic of Korea established under the auspices of the United Nations Temporary Commission on Korea and recognized by the General Assembly during the same period the United Nations Commission on Korea has been the target for repeated propaganda broadcasts which denied its legality, dubbed it futile, and subjected its individual members to abuse. This campaign has been relentlessly pursued during the past eight months while the economy of the young Republic remains shaky and the deliberations of the First National Assembly have been frequently stormy and critical of the Administration. There have been distinct signs of improvement in recent months in both economic and political stability of the country. In early April the Korean Army and police climaxed a winter offensive against northern supported guerrillas operating in South Korea by smashing two guerrilla battalions totalling some 600 men soon after their crossing of the parallel. At the same time internal security and domestic morale have been strengthened by suppression of subversive elements.

2. Although the North Korean regime by its radio, propaganda and support of subversive elements endeavoured to prevent the holding of effective general elections on 30 May, these elections which were observed by the Commission were on the whole successfully conducted and in an atmosphere of law and order.

3. This new Assembly succeeded the Republic's First National Assembly, which was elected in May 1948, under the supervision of UNTCOK [sic] unlike the 1948 elections which middle of the road parties boycotted for fear that elections in only half Korea would make permanent the artificial barrier at the 38th parallel. All parties ex-

cept the underground Communist participated in 1950 elections although the two largest parties in the previous Assembly, the Pro-Government and the Opposition both suffered heavy losses and the most significant gains were made by those moderate elements which had boycotted the 1948 elections. The New Assembly with some 130 Independents out of a total 210 Members convened on 19 June 1950 in a hopeful atmosphere conducive to continued progress in the building of an effective representative Government in an economically healthy State. The initial sessions have indicated determination to tackle the Administration in a critical spirit for its numerous shortcomings.

4. At the beginning of June the North Korean regimes Pyongyang radio gave the widest publicity to an article calling for intensification of measures aimed at unifying Korea and on 3 June a communique stated that the signing by 5,300,000 Northerners of an appeal for peace and unification meant that a renewed struggle for national unification was beginning.

5. On 7 June radio Pyongyang began to broadcast at repeated intervals a letter of Appeal from the Democratic Front for attainment of unification of Fatherland to all Democratic political parties and social organizations in Korea proposing elections throughout Korea following the meeting of a proposed consultative council.

6. The tone of the appeal indicated an ostensible change in the North's previous attitude in spite of such conditions as the exclusion from the Council, as traitors, of nine TMP leaders in the South Korean Government, and the statement that UNCOK would not be permitted to interfere in the task of unification. Included among the addresses UNCOK sent a representative across the parallel to receive the text on 10 June and convey personally to three northern representatives the Commission's desire for peaceful unification.

7. The three northern representatives came South

## 88 TRUMAN'S DECISION

next day carrying copies for all but a few of the leading parties and political personalities of the Republic. They were immediately placed under detention by the South Korean authorities who have since tried to induce them to switch sides by showing the facts in the South. The Southern action of detaining "envoys of peace" has been denounced violently by the Northern radio. At a hearing the Commission was assured by all three of their good treatment by Southern authorities, of their sincere belief in the good intentions of the Northern regime though admitting their eyes had been opened through direct observation to numerous Northern misconceptions of facts on political personalities of the Republic.

8. They were immediately placed under detention by the South Korean authorities who have since tried to induce them to switch sides by showing the facts in the South. The Southern action of detaining "envoys of peace" has been denounced violently by the [word not clear]. Received all traitors including Premier Ki Il Sung [sic] if elected with open arms and give the due positions if they repented and resolved to devote themselves to establishing a sound basis for the Republic of Korea.

9. Subsequently the [word not clear] letter was replaced by another plan for peaceful unification prepared by the Praesidium of the Peoples' Supreme Assembly of the Northern Regime. This contemplated a procedure which involved the convening of the North and South Assemblies into a single legislative assembly but was accompanied by objectionable conditions similar to those of earlier appeal.

10. Both appeals have been denounced by the South Korean press, political parties, and leaders as sheer propaganda. An apparent intention of these appeals was to split the unity prevailing in the South Korean National Assembly by encouraging those who had opposed the 1948 elections to think there was a real possibility of peaceful unification by negotiation.

## The Decision to Commit Air and Sea Forces 89

11. Meanwhile the Commission had agreed to mediate if its good offices were acceptable to both parties in an exchange of important political prisoners originally suggested by the North. On 10 June Commission made clear its unwillingness to jeopardize exchange in any way although North Korea rejected on 20 June proposed Commission role arrangements for exchange were still pending at time of invasion.

12. In the light of the evidently increasing strength of the Republic of Korea in recent months and the utterly unexpected invasion on 25 June the radio propaganda offensive calling for early unification by peaceful means seems to have been intended solely for its screening effect.

13. General Kim Il Sung in radio broadcast this morning at 0930 hours reiterated the North Korean claim first made at 1335 hours that South Korea having rejected every Northern proposal for peaceful unification had crowned its iniquity by launching an invasion force across the parallel in the sector of Haeju CMA thus precipating [sic] North Korean counter attacks for which it would have to assume the consequences.

14. In the same broadcast the Premier called for a struggle to the [word not clear] in order to secure unification and punish "traitors," calling for mass risings and sabotage in South Korea. The Commission has no evidence to justify in any respect the Northern allegations. All the evidence continues to point to a calculated co-ordinated attack prepared and launched with secrecy.

## 21

### Statement by President Harry S Truman
### June 26, 1950

[*United States Policy in the Korean Crisis*, pp. 16–17.]

I conferred Sunday evening with the Secretaries of State and Defense, their senior advisers, and the Joint Chiefs of Staff about the situation in the Far East created by unprovoked aggression against the Republic of Korea.

The Government of the United States is pleased with the speed and determination with which the United Nations Security Council acted to order a withdrawal of the invading forces to positions north of the 38th parallel. In accordance with the resolution of the Security Council, the United States will vigorously support the effort of the Council to terminate this serious breach of the peace.

Our concern over the lawless action taken by the forces from North Korea, and our sympathy and support for the people of Korea in this situation, are being demonstrated by the cooperative action of American personnel in Korea, as well as by steps taken to expedite and augment assistance of the type being furnished under the Mutual Defense Assistance Program.

Those responsible for this act of aggression must realize how seriously the Government of the United States views such threats to the peace of the world. Willful disregard of the obligation to keep the peace cannot be tolerated by nations that support the United Nations Charter.

## 22

*Speech by Senator Styles Bridges,
Republican of New Hampshire
June 26, 1950*
[Extracts]

[*Congressional Record*, 81st Cong., 2nd sess. (June 26, 1950), pp. 9154–55.]

MR. BRIDGES. Mr. President, this is a solemn hour in the history of the world. The free people of all nations are looking to the United States for leadership. The leaders of the slave nations also are looking to the United States. On our immediate actions will hinge the plans of the Kremlin for other conquests.

Mr. President, will we continue appeasement? Will we wait for the dust to settle? Will we discover 6 months, or 6 years from today what we should have done today?

I say that now is the time for decisive action. Now is the time to draw the line. Now is the time to tell all the world, unmistakably, that America will not surrender, equivocate, appease, or hesitate.

Yesterday, on Sunday, June 25, 1950, we learned of the dastardly, unprovoked attack on the Republic of Korea. From all the information at my command, I am amazed to learn that apparently the American Government was not apprised through our intelligence services of the proposed attack.

I supported unification of the armed services. I

supported the creation of the Central Intelligence Agency, which was supposed to prevent another surprise such as the Pearl Harbor attack. Yet from all the information I can obtain neither the State Department nor the Department of Defense was informed by the Central Intelligency Agency of the impending attack. Both claim that neither had any warning of it. It was such a surprise that the head of our military mission was far away, in Tokyo. It came as a complete surprise, even though the North Korean Communist armies were at the borders of South Korea, and had been for some time.

* * *

In my judgment, the time is here for us to draw a line.

What is running through the minds of the peoples of the free world? They are wondering when their turn will come. They are looking to the United States. They know we gave away Manchuria and found excuses not to intervene in China. They know we allowed Poland to fall. They know what has happened in Czechoslovakia, Rumania, and Bulgaria. They know the Russian military might. The free peoples know that Stalin's armies are poised on many frontiers. They weigh Stalin's success against our success. Forty-one times the Soviet veto has prevailed in the United Nations in effect to block peace. To the one-sixth of the world which Stalin ruled in 1945 he has added another one-sixth, until now he has one-third of the world in slavery.

It is not enough to fight communism with ideas and economic assistance as we have done in Korea. It is not enough to bring moral pressure to bear. The Soviets have no idea which can stand before our ideal of human freedom. The Cominform has no economic weapon to counter free enterprise. Com-

## The Decision to Commit Air and Sea Forces 93

munism offers no moral resistance to the concepts of Christianity. But these weapons are not enough. Communism is everywhere equipped with tanks, artillery, and war planes.

I realize that it is considered politically unwise to advocate a strong policy, because some people say that a strong policy might lead us to war. But the Cominform has thrown down the gauntlet. If we pick it up, there may be a risk of war. I realize it is politically smart to back away from international incidents, from situations which may lead to the loss of American lives. But let us be completely honest. Is there any way to avoid war with Soviet Russia? Is there any way to prevent armed conflict? Yes; I believe there are two ways:

First. We can continue our present course. It is the way of appeasement. It is surrender on the installment plan. We postpone war, and we finally became the largest slave state.

Second. We can call communism's bluff. I think it would work. I believe the Cominform is too crafty to risk a full scale armed conflict with the free world. But it is a calculated risk. Let us be frank. It might lead to war.

But the only course open to America is to preserve its freedom.

We should take a stand today firmly and forthrightly.

It is my wish today to invite attention to the desirability of taking a calculated risk, the desirability of establishing a line in the world. Beyond this line we should announce we shall not permit Russia nor the Communist satellites to penetrate.

Mr. President, we have the Korea war on our hands today, and some of our leaders appear not to be interested. Some shrug their shoulders. I know the attitude of some persons on the subject. It was the same before World War II. Hitler was a serious menace to world peace, but Hitler was never the menace in his day that Russia is today——

## 23

*Speech by Senator William F. Knowland,
Republican of California
June 26, 1950*

[*Congressional Record*, 81st Cong., 2nd sess. (June 26, 1950), pp. 9157–58.]

MR. KNOWLAND.

* * *

The Republic of Korea is not likely to be saved by a United Nations resolution alone.

No competent observer of the world scene can believe that the satellite north Korean regime took this major step of a full-scale overt aggressive action without prior consultation and approval of the Soviet Government. It is not likely that they will be too impressed with resolutions alone.

Time is of the essence. We must constantly keep in mind that Holland was overrun by Nazi Germany in 5 days and Denmark in 2. The Security Council meets again Tuesday afternoon at 5 o'clock.

If there is any prolonged debate or if obstructionism is practiced by the Soviet Union and its satellites the free people of Korea may lose their liberty while diplomats are talking.

Mr. President, at this point in my remarks I

## The Decision to Commit Air and Sea Forces

wish to insert the latest Associated Press dispatch from Seoul dealing with the Korean situation. It reads in part as follows:

> A Communist northern spearhead swept within 9 miles of Seoul tonight and fears were expressed it may reach the city before dawn.
>
> Southern resistance at Uijongbu, only 12 miles away, collapsed before the Russian-backed forces hammering at them with tanks and artillery.
>
> The American Embassy burned its important secret papers in a huge bonfire. The air raid sirens screeched. The city was buzzing after four northern planes strafed downtown streets.

* * *

If international communism can destroy this free people, what hope is there that the chaotic condition in Viet Nam can be stabilized, or that world opinion can be mobilized to support the colonial areas of Hong Kong or Malaya, the chaotic internal conditions of a disunited Burma, or the Kingdom of Siam, which would be almost completely surrounded, or even India and Pakistan, with international communism already pressing in along a wide and difficult front.

The destruction of the Republic of Korea would be catastrophic. It is my belief that Korea and the other nations I have just mentioned must be looked upon as a unit. If this nation is allowed to succumb to an overt invasion of this kind, there is little chance of stopping communism anywhere on the continent of Asia.

Time is rapidly running out. Difficult decisions cannot be permanently pushed aside. In these closing days of June 1950, the Congress, the American people, and the free world, must be prepared to make a prompt decision.

The peace of the world will not be saved by abject surrender to the pressures of international communism any more than it was at Munich 12 years ago. Appeasement then, as now, is but surrender on the installment plan.

# 24

## Speech by Senator Tom Connally
## June 26, 1950

[*Congressional Record*, 81st Cong., 2nd sess. (June 26, 1950), pp. 9158–60.]

MR. CONNALLY. Mr. President, I have listened to the addresses of the Senator from New Hampshire [Mr. Bridges] and the Senator from California [Mr. Knowland]. The subject they have discussed is, of course, of transcendent importance to the United States, and, for that matter, to the peace of the world. It involves questions which we cannot solve at the moment. We cannot settle here and now exactly what we should do, but I wish to say that the United Nations Security Council has acted with promptness, and I hope with decision. We should wait until all the facts have been disclosed, and we should take counsel with the United Nations without unduly seeming to arrogate unto ourselves authority to settle the problem here at home.

MR. KNOWLAND. Mr. President, will the Senator yield?

## The Decision to Commit Air and Sea Forces 97

MR. CONNALLY. Yes; I yield.

MR. KNOWLAND. The able chairman of the Foreign Relations Committee does not believe, does he, that the North Korean troops are going to be stopped merely by a resolution of the United Nations?

MR. CONNALLY. No. I have not said that. That question certainly implies that the Senator from Texas at least thinks that it might be done by a resolution. But we have set up the United Nations, and when it decides upon the course that ought to be pursued, we will then be in a better position to judge our responsibility, and what we should do, than we are today. If it takes more than resolutions, the United Nations can take action beyond resolutions.

MR. KNOWLAND. Mr. President, will the Senator yield?

MR. CONNALLY. I should prefer to wait a minute. I should like to answer one question before I get shot in the ribs with another question. [Laughter]. I know the astuteness of the Senator from California. I know how many questions he has concealed about his person, and how prolific he is in expressing his own views upon every question that attracts any attention whatever.

Mr. President, some will say that the advice from Northern Korea cannot be stopped by resolution of the United Nations. That is very true. Others will say the United Nations has no armed forces which it could call into action. That is true. But the United Nations in its over-all power and in its over-all authority would have authority and would have power to call upon any nation or any group of nations that are members of the United Nations to supply troops if the United Nations determines that the use of troops is justified and is necessary.

I now yield to the Senator from California.

MR. KNOWLAND. Has the Senator explored the fact that when the United Nations Security Council meets tomorrow afternoon, if any action is proposed forthwith, the Soviet Government might return just long enough to exercise its veto against any action, and then does the Senator from Texas believe that we should sit back and twiddle our thumbs and do nothing?

MR. CONNALLY. I will say to the Senator that I do not undertake to anticipate all the possibilities. Of course, the veto is involved somewhat, but some of the nations other than Russia might do a little vetoing themselves. If the United Nations cannot act, they might together pursue a course over and above the powers of the United Nations. The freedom-loving people of the world might agree among themselves that we shall not permit this palpable breach of the peace; that this overt attack, without provocation and without justification, upon a free people and a free republic will not be tolerated by other free governments in the world. That is a possibility. I ask the Senator from California if he does not agree that that is a possibility. Does the Senator answer the question or not?

* * *

Mr. President, some Senators speak as if they wanted to declare war tomorrow. The Senator from New Hampshire said we could not depend on other courses, and that there was only one course left to us. He did not say "declare war," but the clear implication of his remarks was that we could not go any further, that we had to make a stand and, if necessary, we had to make an armed stand.

Mr. President, those questions are being considered. The Secretary of State and the Secretary of Defense this morning were before the Appropriations Committee. I was there as an observer. They were not permitted, because of instructions by higher authority, to discuss such questions before that committee at this particular time, because, after all, the responsibility does not rest upon the Chiefs of Staff, the responsibility does not rest on the Secretary of Defense, but the responsibility rests upon the President of the United States; and the President of the United States does not want to take a course which might involve the people of the United States in war until all aspects of the matter have been considered.

The responsibilities of the United States shall be considered. The safety of free peoples shall be considered, and the national security and the national interest of the United States must be considered.

I feel sure that Senators need not become unduly alarmed. The President of the United States is not going to neglect the interests of the United States or its people. He is not going to tremble like a sycophant before the Russian power. He is not going to surrender our rights or the rights of free peoples.

This is a plain and an aggravated case. The United Nations was created to prevent just such occurrences as this one, to prevent armed aggression by one nation upon the territory or the sanctity of another nation. Of course, we have seen in the press statements to the effect that North Korea claims that South Korea provoked this incident. However, that claim will not stand the light of examination, it will not stand any investigation or examination, because it is not true.

## 25

*Korean National Assembly to the President and Congress of the United States June 26, 1950*

[*United States Policy in the Korean Crisis*, p. 17.]

Beginning in the early morning of 25 June, the North Korean Communist Army began armed aggression against the South. Your Excellency and the Congress of the United States are already aware of the fact that our people, anticipating an incident such as today's, established a strong national defense force in order to secure a bulwark of democracy in the east and to render service to world peace. We again thank you for your indispensable aid in liberating us and in establishing our Republic. As we face this national crisis, putting up a brave fight, we appeal for your increasing support and ask that you at the same time extend effective and timely aid in order to prevent this act of destruction of world peace.

## 26

*U.N. Commission on Korea
to Trygve Lie
June 26, 1950*

[United Nations, Security Council. U.N. doc. S/1503.]

NORTH KOREAN ADVANCES HAVE CREATED DANGEROUS SITUATION WITH POSSIBILITIES OF RAPID DETERIORATION. IMPOSSIBLE ESTIMATE SITUATION WHICH WILL EXIST TOMORROW IN SEOUL. IN VIEW COMMISSION'S PAST EXPERIENCE AND EXISTING SITUATION COMMISSION CONVINCED NORTH KOREA WILL NOT HEED COUNCIL RESOLUTION NOR ACCEPT UNCOK GOOD OFFICES. SUGGEST HAVE COUNCIL GIVE CONSIDERATION EITHER INVITATION BOTH PARTIES AGREE ON NEUTRAL MEDIATOR EITHER TO NEGOTIATE PEACE OR REQUESTING MEMBER GOVERNMENTS UNDERTAKE IMMEDIATE MEDIATION. COMMISSION DECIDED STAND BY IN SEOUL. DANGER IS THAT CRITICAL OPERATIONS NOW IN PROGRESS MAY END IN MATTER OF DAYS AND QUESTION OF CEASE FIRE AND WITHDRAWAL NORTH KOREAN FORCES SUGGESTED COUNCIL RESOLUTION PROVE ACADEMIC.

## 27

*General Douglas MacArthur's Military Situation Report June 26, 1950*

[Harry S Truman, *Memoirs: Years of Trial and Hope*, Vol. II (Garden City: Doubleday & Company, 1956), p. 337.]

Piecemeal entry into action vicinity Seoul by South Korean Third and Fifth Divisions has not succeeded in stopping the penetration recognized as the enemy main effort for the past 2 days with intent to seize the capital city of Seoul. Tanks entering suburbs of Seoul. Govt transferred to south and communications with part KMAG opened at Taegu. Ambassador and Chief KMAG remaining in the city. FEC mil survey group has been recalled, under this rapidly deteriorating situation.

South Korean units unable to resist determined Northern offensive. Contributory factor exclusive enemy possession of tanks and fighter planes. South Korean casualties as an index to fighting have not shown adequate resistance capabilities or the will to fight and our estimate is that a complete collapse is imminent.

## 28

*Statement by President Harry S Truman
June 27, 1950*

[*United States Policy in the Korean Crisis*, p. 18.]

In Korea the Government forces, which were armed to prevent border raids and to preserve internal security, were attacked by invading forces from North Korea. The Security Council of the United Nations called upon the invading troops to cease hostilities and to withdraw to the 38th parallel. This they have not done but on the contrary have pressed the attack. The Security Council called upon all members of the United Nations to render every assistance to the United Nations in the execution of this resolution. In these circumstances I have ordered United States air and sea forces to give the Korean Government troops cover and support.

The attack upon Korea makes it plain beyond all doubt that Communism has passed beyond the use of subversion to conquer independent nations and will now use armed invasion and war. It has defied the orders of the Security Council of the United Nations issued to preserve international peace and security. In these circumstances the occupation of Formosa by Communist forces would be a direct threat to the security of the Pacific area and to United States forces performing their lawful and necessary functions in that area.

Accordingly I have ordered the Seventh Fleet to prevent any attack on Formosa. As a corollary of this action I am calling upon the Chinese Government on

Formosa to cease all air and sea operations against the mainland. The Seventh Fleet will see that this is done. The determination of the future status of Formosa must await the restoration of security in the Pacific, a peace settlement with Japan, or consideration by the United Nations.

I have also directed that United States Forces in the Philippines be strengthened and that military assistance to the Philippine Government be accelerated.

I have similarly directed acceleration in the furnishing of military assistance to the forces of France and the Associated States in Indochina and the dispatch of a military mission to provide close working relations with those forces.

I know that all members of the United Nations will consider carefully the consequences of this latest aggression in Korea in defiance of the Charter of the United Nations. A return to the rule of force in international affairs would have far-reaching effects. The United States will continue to uphold the rule of law.

I have instructed Ambassador Austin, as the Representative of the United States to the Security Council, to report these steps to the Council.

## 29

*Speech by United States
Representative to the U.N.
Warren R. Austin
June 27, 1950*

[U.N. Security Council, Fifth Year, *Official Records*, No. 16, 474th Meeting (June 27, 1950), pp. 3-4.]

*U.N. Security Council*

MR. AUSTIN (United States of America): The United Nations finds itself confronted today with the gravest crisis in its existence. Forty-eight hours ago the Security Council, in an emergency meeting, determined that the armed invasion of the Republic of Korea by armed forces from North Korea constituted a breach of the peace. Accordingly, the Security Council called for a cessation of hostilities forthwith and the withdrawal by the North Korean authorities of their armed forces to the 38th parallel. The Security Council also requested the United Nations Commission on Korea to observe the withdrawal and to report. Finally, the Security Council called upon all Members to render every assistance to the United Nations in the execution of the resolution, and to refrain from giving assistance to the North Korean authorities.

The decision of the Security Council has been broadcast to the Korean authorities and is known to them. We now have before us the report of the United Nations Commission for Korea, which confirms our fears. It is clear that the authorities in North Korea have completely disregarded and flouted the decision of the Security Council. The armed invasion of the Republic of Korea continues. This is, in fact, an attack on the United Nations itself. The North Korean authorities have called upon the established Government of the Republic to surrender.

It is difficult to imagine a more glaring example of disregard for the United Nations and for all the principles which it represents. The most important provisions of the Charter are those outlawing aggressive war. It is precisely these provisions which the North Korean authorities have violated.

It is the plain duty of the Security Council to invoke stringent sanctions to restore international peace. The Republic of Korea has appealed to the United Nations for protection. I am happy and proud to report that the United States is prepared as a loyal Member of the United Nations to furnish assistance to the Republic of Korea.

I have submitted a draft resolution [*S/1508/ Rev. 1*] which I ask the Council to consider favourably as the next step to restore world peace. Its text is as follows:

"*The Security Council,*

"*Having determined* that the armed attack upon the Republic of Korea by forces from North Korea constitutes a breach of the peace;

"*Having called* for an immediate cessation of hostilities; and

"*Having called* upon the authorities of North Korea to withdraw forthwith their armed forces to the 38th parallel; and

"*Having noted* from the report of the United Nations Commission for Korea that the authorities in North Korea have neither ceased hostilities nor withdrawn their armed forces to the 38th parallel, and that urgent military measures are required to restore international peace and security; and

"*Having noted* the appeal from the Republic of Korea to the United Nations for immediate and effective steps to secure peace and security,

"*Recommends* that the Members of the United Nations furnish such assistance to the Republic of Korea as may be necessary to repel the armed attack and to restore international peace and security in the area."

This is the logical consequence of the resolution concerning the complaint of aggression upon the Republic of Korea adopted at the 473rd meeting of the Security Council on 25 June 1950 and the subsequent events recited in the preamble of this resolution. That resolution of 25 June called upon all Members "to render every assistance to the United Nations" in the execution of this resolution, and "to refrain from giving assistance to the North Korean authorities". This new draft resolution is the logical next step. Its significance is affected by the violation of the former resolution, the continuation of aggression, and the urgent military measures required.

## 30

*Exchange of Telegrams between
Governor of New York Thomas E. Dewey
and President Harry S Truman
June 27, 1950*

[*The New York Times*, June 28, 1950, p. 4.]

### Dewey to Truman

I whole-heartedly agree with and support the difficult decision you have made today to extend American assistance to the Republic of Korea in combatting armed Communist aggression. Your action there, in Formosa, the Philippines and Indo-China was necessary to the security of our country and the free world. It should be supported by a united America.

### Truman to Dewey

I am grateful for your message and hasten to assure you that I shall find strength and courage in your brave words. The wholehearted pledge of support which you give will be a source of inspiration and fortitude as we gird ourselves for the difficult tasks ahead. We have taken our stand on the side of Korea and our pledge of faith to that nation is a witness to all the world that we champion liberty wherever the tyranny of Communism is the aggressor.

## 31

*Speech by Representative Vito Marcantonio,
American Laborite of New York
June 27, 1950*

[Extract]

[*Congressional Record*, 81st Cong., 2nd sess. (June 27, 1950), pp. 9268–69.]

* * *

MR. MARCANTONIO. Mr. Chairman, we have heard words read here by our distinguished majority leader which I think will mark a disastrous course, and the words I am using do not adequately describe the disastrous consequences this course will have on the people of the United States unless checked by the people themselves.

I refer specifically to these words the majority leader read from the President's statement:

> In these circumstances I have ordered United States air and sea forces to give the Korean Government troops cover and support.

Then again the president is quoted:

> Accordingly I have ordered the Seventh Fleet to prevent any attack on Formosa.

This means the utilization of Americans in our Armed Forces in two civil wars, one that is taking place in Korea and one that is well nigh completed in China. For all purposes, we were at war with the government and people of Korea, and we might as well face it, the moment these words were enunciated.

I would be remiss to the things in which I believe if I did not stand up here and state my opinion on this matter. After all, Mr. Chairman, you live only once, and it is best to live one's life with one's conscience than to temporize or accept with silence those things which one believes to be against the interests of one's people and one's nation.

The argument is advanced here that this action can be justified as a result of the United Nations Charter. That has been the tenor of the argument. I disagree with any such contention. However, I say that when we agreed to the United Nations Charter we never agreed to supplant our Constitution with the United Nations Charter. The power to declare and make war is vested in the representatives of the people, in the Congress of the United States. That power has today been usurped from us with the reading of this short statement by the President to the people of the world. We here in Congress are asked to supinely accept this usurpation of our right as representatives of the American people. We have abdicated it for I have heard no protest, I have heard not a single word against it. I have no other recourse but to stand up and point out exactly what this action is, how it violates our Constitution, our democratic traditions, and how it deprives the American people of the right to express themselves on the vital question of war and peace, a power and a right properly vested in the representatives of the American people, the Congress, by those who wisely wrote our Constitution.

I know we are going to have and we have been having a lot of war drum beating. The beating of the war drums has been such that they may drown

## The Decision to Commit Air and Sea Forces 111

out reason. But I think it is time, before it is too late, that we pause and take inventory of what has happened in Asia.

We have been warned time and time again and all signs in Asia have been pointing to what? That the people of Asia, the people of China, have been seeking national liberation, and that aspiration for national liberation has been and is supreme in the very existence of the people of Asia. In China we spent $3,000,000,000 on Chiang Kai-shek. He controlled the mainland, he controlled the Government, he controlled the army, he controlled everything. Our 3,000,000,000 did not save him, because I tell you neither $3,000,000,000, nor any amount of billions, would ever defeat the desire of 400,000,000 Chinese to establish for themselves their own form of government, no more than billions of dollars could have stopped us to establish [sic] for ourselves our own form of government in 1776.

THE CHAIRMAN. The time of the gentleman from New York [Mr. Marcantonio] has expired.

MR. MARCANTONIO. Mr Chairman, I ask unanimous consent and the indulgence of this Committee to proceed for five additional minutes.

THE CHAIRMAN. Is there objection to the request of the gentleman from New York?

There was no objection.

MR. MARCANTONIO. I thank the Committee for giving me this extra time.

So the people of China asserted themselves. Formosa is just as much a part of China as Staten Island is a part of New York. Here we are told that the United States Fleet is to intercede and to interfere and attempt to stop the people of China from carrying out their own will in their own country.

I remember the words I said here on February

7 about Korea. I stated in the well of this house that the defense of tyranny was never in the best interests of the people of the United States. I pointed out the similarity between the rottenness that existed in the Chiang Kai-shek government and that existing in the South Korean Government—the imprisonment of 40,000 people; the harsh exploitation of the people, the feeling of unrest, and the contempt for the rulers of South Korea on the part of the general masses of the people. It was a government imposed on the people of Korea by force of arms, a police state; and I stated at that time that that Government could not long endure, that it would be wiped out by the will of the people of Korea.

I also said at that time that you cannot take a nation and draw a line through it and divide it and split into two countries a nation which is an ethnic unity, a people united culturally and racially over the centuries. But we tried to do it. The United Nations itself recognized that that could not be done, and set up a United Nations commission to bring about a united country in Korea, and to carry out the will of the people for a united and independent country. The tyrannical rulers of South Korea continued to deny this legitimate aspiration of the people, ruthlessly suppressed every endeavor on the part of the people to achieve this objective and thus created an irrepressible conflict.

Here now we are sending American aviators to lay down their lives, sending American sailors to lay down their lives, and who knows how soon it will be before our infantry will be sent to lay down their lives to defend, aid and abet tyranny and perpetrate aggression against the Korean people who strive for a united and independent nation.

Now, you may want this action. I do not. I know that the American people will not want this

## The Decision to Commit Air and Sea Forces 113

action when they think it over, and I know that they will thrust through this terrible dark cloud of war that has been descending on them. Oh, yes, you can indulge in attacks on communism. You can keep on making impassioned pleas for the destruction of communism, but I tell you that the issue in China, in Asia, in Korea and in Viet Nam is the right of these peoples to self-determination, to a government of their own, to independence and national unity.

Remember one thing: A bomb was dropped on Hiroshima. It had terrible consequences, but it did not frighten the people of China and it did not frighten the people of Korea. For again, these people despite the terror of the atom bomb have refused to abandon their efforts for national liberation. They will no more abandon this objective than the American people did during our Revolution.

I also say, Mr. Chairman, that in the light of this background that before this action can be taken this question should be debated here and decided here. The vote must be taken here by us as representatives of the American people whether or not American aviators and American seamen shall be shot down, their blood spilled in defense of tyranny in a conflict similar to our own Civil War. That is a power which is vested in us by the Constitution. I shall do all that I can—alone perhaps, but living with my conscience—to oppose this course which is not in the defense of the best interests of the American people.

War is not inevitable; there are alternatives, but this declaration on the part of President Truman is an acceptance of the doctrine of the inevitability of war. I stand here and challenge that doctrine. I say that the ingenuity of Americans and people all over the world challenge this doctrine.

## 32

*Reply of Representative Abraham
A. Ribicoff, Democrat of
Connecticut, to Marcantonio
June 27, 1950*

[Extract]

[*Congressional Record*, 81st Cong., 2nd sess. (June 27, 1950), pp. 9269–70.]

MR. RIBICOFF. Mr. Chairman, I agree with the gentleman from New York that war is not inevitable; but certainly if we were to follow his advice this Nation would gradually surrender nation after nation to Soviet imperialism. I think war under those circumstances would be inevitable.

The gentleman from New York says that the action of the President will lead to disaster. I contend that any other action by the President of the United States would lead to disaster.

I think there are striking parallels between what has happened in Korea and what happened in the recent past. We must stop, look, listen, and counsel with one another. The gentleman from New York talks as if this were an action by Korean patriots; this is an action by pawns of Soviet imperialism. What difference is there in the action of northern Koreans today and the actions which led to the Second World War? Talk about parallels. This is similar to Mussolini's invasion of Ethiopia, this is

## The Decision to Commit Air and Sea Forces 115

similar to Hitler's reoccupying the Rhineland, this is an exactly similar parallel to Japan's moving into Manchuria. Time after time it has been proven that inaction, that willingness to shut one's eyes to injustice eventually leads to war. Appeasement and indifference will not stop wars. We know that Russian imperialism seeks the domination of all the world. Let us not think that should the United States sit idly by and do nothing as one nation after another is conquered by Russia and Russian satellites that the United States itself would remain free. Under those circumstances there would be no alternative, the United States of America would stand by itself in a world completely dominated by Soviet Russia, a world where the entire balance of power, and economic, and material, and military resources would be in the hands of the Soviet Union.

Certainly the President of the United States cannot sit idly by, nor this Congress, and condone such circumstances or permit them to continue throughout the world. I feel that the next 50 years will determine the course of western civilization for the next 2,000 years. People of power, courage, and purpose will make that decision. Let us hope they will be people endowed with decency and a sense of freedom; and certainly, if we are to be successful and the civilization that we know is to remain, it is most important that the United States recognize the freedom of people all over the world and not stand idly by and allow Russia to take one nation after another as she has done in the past. That, itself, will lead to war and the action of the President in putting a stop to what is happening in Korea I cannot help but feel will restrict the further spreading of any general war because Russia when she realizes the determination of the United States will stop at that point. She stopped in Berlin, she stopped in Greece, she stopped in Iran. If we want peace we will get it if we are strong. "Peace through strength" should be the slogan of the United States. We should not continue to back away time and time again because Russia seeks to make a move unilaterally and we allow her to make the move. If successful, from that time on she probes further and further and further.

I am sure that the people of the United States of America will back up the conduct of the President of the United States because the conduct of the President of the United States today will lead to peace, not to war. If the President of the United States followed the advocacy of the gentleman from New York it would lead to a general world war and if it continues much longer we of the United States of America will ourselves have our back to the wall. I am sure that the Congress and people of this country will back the President of the United States in this important issue and not the gentleman from New York [Mr. Marcantonio].

## 33

*Speech by Senator Robert A. Taft, Republican of Ohio June 28, 1950*
[Extracts]

[*Congressional Record*, 81st Cong., 2nd sess. (June 28, 1950), pp. 9319–23.]

MR. TAFT. Mr. President, I desire to speak with reference to the Korean crisis, and at a later time to ask permission to put into the RECORD a number of documents which deal with the basic consideration of that crisis.

Early on Sunday morning, June 25, the Communist-dominated Republic of North Korea launched an unprovoked aggressive military attack on the Republic of Korea, recognized as an independent nation by the United Nations. On the same day the Security Council of the United Nations adopted a resolution noting with grave concern the armed attack upon the Republic of Korea from forces from North Korea, and determining that this action constituted a breach of the peace. The resolution called for the immediate cessation of hostilities, for the withdrawal of the armed forces of North Korea to the thirty-eighth parallel, and for the United Nations Commission on Korea to make informational reports; and called "upon all members to render every assistance to the United Nations in the execution of this resolution and to refrain from giving assistance to the North Korean authorities." This resolution was adopted by a vote of nine members, Russia being absent, and Yugoslavia abstaining.

The attack did not cease, and on Tuesday, June 27, the President issued a statement announcing that he had "ordered United States air and sea forces to give the Korean Government troops cover and support." He also announced that he had ordered the Seventh Fleet to prevent any attack on Formosa, and that he had directed that United States forces in the Philippines be strengthened, and that military assistance to the Philippine Government and the forces of France and the associated states in Indochina be accelerated.

On the same day, last night, the United Nations adopted another resolution definitely recommending "that the members of the United Nations furnish such assistance to the Republic of Korea as may be necessary to repel the armed attack and restore international peace and security in the area." This vote was adopted by seven members of the Security Council; I am informed, I am not absolutely certain, Yugoslavia voting "no," and India and Egypt refraining from voting, Russia still being absent. American air and sea forces have moved into Korea and are partaking in the war against the northern Korea Communists.

No one can deny that a serious crisis exists. The attack was as much a surprise to the public as the attack at Pearl Harbor, although, apparently, the possibility was foreseen by all our intelligence forces, and should have been foreseen by the administration. We are now actually engaged in a de facto war with the northern Korean Communists. That in itself is serious, but nothing compared to the possibility that it might lead to war with Soviet Russia. It is entirely possible that Soviet Russia might move in to help the North Koreans and that the present limited field of conflict might cover the entire civilized world. Without question, the attack of the North Koreans is an outrageous act of aggression against a friendly independent nation, recognized by the United Nations, and which we were instrumental in setting up. The attack in all probability was instigated by Soviet Russia. We can only hope that the leaders of that country have sufficient judgment to know that a world war will result in their own destruction, and will therefore refrain from such acts as might bring about such a tragic conflict.

Mr. President, Korea itself is not vitally important to the United States. It is hard to defend. We have another instance of communism picking out a soft spot where the Communists feel that they can make a substantial advance and can obtain a moral

## The Decision to Commit Air and Sea Forces 119

victory without risking war. From the past philosophy and declarations of our leaders, it was not unreasonable for the North Koreans to suppose that they could get away with it and that we would do nothing about it.

The President's statement of policy represents a complete change in the programs and policies heretofore proclaimed by the administration. I have heretofore urged a much more determined attitude against communism in the Far East, and the President's new policy moves in that direction. It seems to me that the time had to come, sooner or later, when we would give definite notice to the Communists that a move beyond a declared line would result in war. That has been the policy which we have adopted in Europe. Whether the President has chosen the right time or the right place to declare this policy may be open to question. He has information which I do not have.

It seems to me that the new policy is adopted at an unfortunate time, and involves the attempt to defend Korea, which is a very difficult military operation indeed. I sincerely hope that our Armed Forces may be successful in Korea. I sincerely hope that the policy thus adopted will not lead to war with Russia. In any event, I believe the general principle of the policy is right, and I see no choice except to back up wholeheartedly and with every available resource the men in our Armed Forces who have been moved into Korea.

*   *   *

Furthermore, it should be noted that there has been no pretense of consulting the Congress. No resolution has ever been introduced asking for the approval of Congress for the use of American forces in Korea. I shall discuss later the question of whether the President is usurping his powers as Commander in Chief. My own opinion is that he is doing so; that there is no legal authority for what he has done. But I may say that if a joint resolution were introduced asking for approval of the use of our Armed Forces already sent to Korea and full support of them in their present venture, I would vote in favor of it.

I have said that the present crisis is produced by the bungling and inconsistent policies of the administration.

First, at Yalta and at Potsdam we agreed to the division of Korea along the thirty-eighth parallel, giving the Russians the northern half of the country, with most of the power and a good deal of the industry, and leaving a southern half which could not support itself, except on an agricultural basis. This was in line with a very foolish policy which paid for Russian assistance against Japan, which we did not need, by presenting Russia with the Kurile Islands, half of Sakhalin Island, the control of Manchuria, and the control of northern Korea. Apparently someone at Yalta saw the thirty-eighth parallel drawn on the map and did not take the trouble to suggest a more sensible line, if Korea had to be divided at all. The agreement was a part of the sympathetic acceptance of communism as a peace-loving philosophy, which has made Russia a threat to the very existence of the world.

Second, the Chinese policy of the administration gives basic encouragement to the North Korean aggression. If the United States was not prepared to use its troops and give military assistance to Nationalist China against Chinese Communists, why should it use its troops to defend Nationalist Korea against Korean Communists? That certainly must have seemed a fairly logical conclusion to those who have

## The Decision to Commit Air and Sea Forces 121

inaugurated this aggression. The Communists undoubtedly considered that Korea was very much less important than China to the United States, and that they could get away with their grab of Korea, as the Chinese Communists got away with theirs in China. The general policy of doing nothing in China was reaffirmed by Secretary Acheson in a speech before the National Press Club as recently as January 12 of this year.

* * *

In the President's statement there is a direct repudiation of the policies of Secretary Acheson declared in January of this year. The use of United States air and sea forces in Korea overrules the policy of American withdrawal and the defense of the Okinawa-Japanese line. The statement that "the occupation of Formosa by Communist forces would be a direct threat to the security of the Pacific area and the United States forces performing their lawful and necessary functions in that area," is directly contrary to the statement of Secretary Acheson that Formosa has no military value and that "we are not going to get involved militarily in any way on the Island of Formosa."

The President now says that the determination of the future status of Formosa must await the restoration of security in the Pacific, a peace settlement with Japan, or consideration by the United Nations. This is a direct overruling of Secretary Acheson's position on January 5 to the effect that it was wholly unnecessary to wait for a treaty with Japan because Formosa's position had been definitely settled by the Cairo and Potsdam agreements.

The furnishing of military assistance to Indochina contradicts Secretary Acheson's statement that all the United States could do in Southeast Asia was to provide advice and assistance when asked, and that the responsibility was not ours.

Mr. President, since I approve of the changes now made in our foreign policy, I approve of the general policies outlined in the President's statement. I feel that we must back up our troops, where they have been sent by the President, with unstinted support. Whether the President chose the right time for his new policy, or the right place, can be discussed in the future. I suggest, however, that any Secretary of State who has been so reversed by his superiors and whose policies have precipitated the danger of war, had better resign and let someone else administer the program to which he was, and perhaps still is, so violently opposed.

[Applause on the floor and in the galleries.]

THE PRESIDING OFFICER (Mr. Gillette in the chair). The rules of the Senate forbid any demonstration of approval or of disapproval.

MR. LUCAS. Mr. President, a point of order.

THE PRESIDING OFFICER. The Senator will state it.

MR. LUCAS. Mr. President, the sad part of it is the fact that it was Senators who were violating the rule.

MR. TAFT. Mr. President, I have only a few words to say on the legal right of the President's act.

Although I should be willing to vote to approve the President's new policy as a policy, and give support to our forces in Korea, I think it is proper and essential that we discuss at this time the right and power of the President to do what he has done. I hope others will discuss it, because I have not thoroughly investigated the question of the right and the power of the President to do what he has done.

His action unquestionably has brought about a de facto war with the Government of northern Korea. He has brought that war about without consulting Congress and without congressional approval. We

## The Decision to Commit Air and Sea Forces 123

have a situation in which in a far distant part of the world one nation has attacked another, and if the President can intervene in Korea without congressional approval, he can go to war in Malaya or Indonesia or Iran or South America. Presidents have at times intervened with American forces to protect American lives or interests, but I do not think it has been claimed that, apart from the United Nations Charter or other treaty obligations, the President has any right to precipitate any open warfare.

It is claimed that the Korean situation is changed by the obligations into which we have entered under the Charter of the United Nations. I think this is true, but I do not think it justifies the President's present action without approval by Congress. I stated when we were discussing the bill to implement the United Nations Charter that I felt that once the American representative on the Security Council voted in favor of using armed forces then the President was entitled to go ahead and use those forces without further action by Congress. I objected to the bill because it gave the President unlimited power to tell our representative on the Security Council how he must vote so that he could commit the country to the use of armed forces without congressional authority. I felt that giving the President the right to tell our representative on the Security Council how he should or should not vote, in effect gave him the right to put the United States into war, provided the other sections of the bill were complied with.

*　*　*

Other questions arise out of the United Nations Charter which I think should be explored. At least, they should be debated by this body.

Article 27 provides that decisions of the Security

Council on all matters shall be made by an affirmative vote of seven members, including the concurring votes of the permanent members. The word "veto" was never used in the United Nations Charter. It simply provides that there must be the concurring votes of the five permanent members. In this case Soviet Russia has not voted. They never even appeared at the meeting. It is suggested, I understand, that gradually, under the practice adopted, a veto must be expressed by a negative vote; even though that seems directly contrary to the language of article 27. I am not a student of that subject. I merely suggest that the question, and the fact that Korea is not a member of the United Nations, ought to be explored and debated very fully by the Senate. I do not think there is any immediate rush about it. I merely do not like to have this action go by with the approval of the Senate, if it is what it seems to me, namely, a complete usurpation by the President of authority to use the Armed Forces of this country. If the incident is permitted to go by without protest, at least from this body, we would have finally terminated for all time the right of Congress to declare war, which is granted to Congress alone by the Constitution of the United States.

## 34

*Reply of Senator Scott W. Lucas,
Democrat of Illinois, to Taft
June 28, 1950*
[Extracts]

[*Congressional Record,* 81st Cong., 2nd sess. (June 28, 1950), pp. 9327-29.]

MR. LUCAS. Mr. President, I had not expected to speak on this matter today. However, in view of the remarks made by the able Senator from Ohio, I am constrained to speak briefly in reply to some of the points made by the Senator.

\* \* \*

Mr. President, under the resolution and under the statement made by the members of the Security Council, in my humble opinion the President had the right to do what he has done. Such a resolution cannot be enforced unless some military action is taken.

Not only that, but even assuming that the President does not have any jurisdiction under the United Nations Charter to do what he did, as is contended by the Senator from Ohio, I should like to call the attention of the Senate and of the country to what our Nation has done in the past. Able and sincere Senators have argued, over the course of history, about how far the President of the United States can go as Commander in Chief of the military forces of this country. I call attention to the fact that those who discuss that matter, and those who follow the argument made by the Senator from Ohio today, apparently have forgotten the course this country pursued.

I read now from remarks I made in the Senate on November 4, 1941:

> Those who make that argument apparently have forgotten the course this country has pursued when international pirates have destroyed American lives and property in the past. The Barbary wars yield an interesting instance in this respect. The ruler of Tripoli, having declared war against the United States on March 14, 1801, started attacking American vessels. A naval force dispatched to the Mediterranean in anticipation of the event had received orders to blockade Tripoli and destroy her shipping. There was no declaration of war on our part when that was done. This the Navy proceeded to do. The interesting feature in that case is that the nature of the fleet's task was limited by the belief of President Jefferson that in the absence of congressional authorization "measures of defense" only were in order. These measures of defense, to be undertaken without congressional authority and laid down by Jefferson at that time, went rather far. The instructions regarding them included the following—

This is what Thomas Jefferson as Commander in Chief of the Army and Navy, advised the Navy to do at that time—

> You will then distribute your forces in such a manner as your judgment shall direct,

## The Decision to Commit Air and Sea Forces

so as to best protect our commerce and chastise their insolence by sinking, burning, or destroying their ships and vessels wherever you shall find them.

* * *

Every Senator who knows anything about history, every Senator who knows anything about the past, must realize, if he is honest with himself, that the act performed by the President of the United States was within his right, and within the traditions and precedents which have been established more than a hundred times in the history of this Republic.

* * *

Mr. President, notwithstanding the seriousness of the hour, irrespective of the crisis before us, we hear the Senator from Ohio tell the country and the world that the President of the United States is responsible for the start of this de facto war. What a travesty upon justice. Mr. President, the Senator from Ohio grudgingly goes along with the general policy at the present time, but proceeds to charge bungling and inconsistency in the foreign policy, as though he had the remedy and panacea for everything. I am certain the country is sorely grieved because the Senator from Ohio has not been the chief architect of our foreign policy.

* * *

Mr. President, this is a fateful hour in the history of the American Republic. Men may dig up all the presumed and supposed mistakes they want to dig up if they so desire. They can continue to do so at a time when there should be unity in this country, instead of attempts being made to divide the people of America. At this very moment, Mr. President, when our fleet is on its way to Formosa, when our troops are at this very time in Korea—at least the air and some of the ships near by are there—it seems to me that we ought to close ranks, and forget what happened at Potsdam and Yalta, because digging up those old sores will get nowhere so far as giving the American people the kind of unity they ought to have. The only thing such action does is to help Mr. Stalin. Obviously, it will lift the morale of troops in Northern Korea. Every time a speech of this kind is made under such extraordinary circumstances, Mr. President, I undertake to say that we are playing directly into the hands of the Communists, the very people we ought to be fighting tooth and nail, instead of fighting among ourselves.

## 35

*Joseph C. Harsch on the Washington Response to Truman's Decision June 29, 1950*

[*Christian Science Monitor*, June 29, 1950, p. 1.]

I have lived and worked in and out of this city for 20 years. Never before in that time have I felt such a sense of relief and unity pass through this city.

The most curious thing about the affair was the June 27 gloom from a belief that the administration would miss the boat and do something idle or specious. The decision to act already had been taken, yet almost everyone was assuming there would be no action. When it came there was a sense first of astonishment and then of relief. Mr. Truman obviously did much more than he was expected to do, and almost exactly what most individuals seemed to wish he would do. I have never seen such a large part of Washington so nearly satisfied with a decision of the government.

36

Pravda's *Comment on President Truman's Statement June 28, 1950*

[*Pravda*, June 28, 1950, p. 1. Translated by Glenn D. Paige.]

On June 27 the President of the United States of America made a special statement about the events in Korea.

The events in Korea, now the focus of world attention, show with full clarity that the imperialist instigators of war, having attained their objective, are not going to stop in mid-course. As is known, on June 25 a provocative attack by the troops of the puppet government of South Korea unleashed military actions on Korean territory. In response, the constabulary units and troops of the Korean Democratic People's Republic took active measures and, obeying the orders of their government, went over to a counterattack, carrying the military action south of the 38th Parallel.

The Government of the Korean Democratic People's Republic had an opportunity several times to show its consistency in defending the interests of the Korean people, its democratic development, its independence, and its patriotic desires for unification. Already at the beginning of June of this year the United Democratic Unification Front and the Presidium of the Supreme People's Assembly of Korea in Pyongyang, expressing the will of the Korean people, set forth a proposal to achieve the peaceful unification of the country. The Syngman Rhee clique answered this proposal on June 25 by beginning an internecine fratricidal war.

The Syngman Rhee clique has set off on the path of military adventure. They counted in advance upon the military assistance of their overseas patrons. Now the aggressive plans of their protectors are beginning to be revealed.

As is shown by the statement of Truman, he has ordered the air and sea forces of the United States to give armed "support" to the army of that traitor to the Korean people Syngman Rhee. At the same time the American president has ordered the 7th American Fleet "to prevent an attack upon Formosa"; this constitutes an order concerning the de facto occupation of a part of Chinese territory by American armed forces.

This statement means that the Government of the United States of America has undertaken a direct act of aggression against the Korean Democratic People's Republic and against the Chinese People's Republic.

Truman's statement and actions, unprecedented in the international relations of the post-war period, are just one more indication that the American ruling circles no longer limit themselves to preparation for aggression, but have gone over to direct acts of aggression.

But haven't they gone too far?

The American government with characteristic disregard for international law has rudely trampled upon the United Nations Charter, acting as if the United Nations did not even exist.

The question arises: Who authorized the American

*The Decision to Commit Air and Sea Forces* 131

government to take such a step? In sending their forces into action did the government of the U.S.A. obtain the agreement of the Security Council to which Truman and Acheson declare their faithfulness? Where and when did the Security Council decide to free the hands of the government of the U.S.A. to undertake this act of direct aggression?

As is known, neither the United Nations nor any other international organ empowered the government of the U.S.A. to take those actions related to Korea and China that Truman announced yesterday.

Undertaking their open aggressive act, the American government apparently intended to present the United Nations with a fait accompli.

37

*Statement by Mao Tse-tung*
*June 28, 1950*

[*Jen-min Jih-pao* (People's Daily), June 29, 1950, p. 1. Translated by Glenn D. Paige.]

The Chinese people long ago made it clear that the affairs of all nations should be handled by the peoples concerned. The affairs of Asia should be handled by Asians, and not by Americans. American aggression cannot but evoke widespread determined resistance on the part of Asian peoples. Although Truman announced last January 5 that the United States would not intervene on Taiwan, he himself has just proven the hypocrisy of that statement and at the same time has broken every international agreement by the United States that it would not interfere in the internal political affairs of China. The fact that America has thus revealed its imperialist character is of great benefit for China and the peoples of Asia. American interference in the domestic political affairs of Korea, the Philippines, Taiwan, and other areas is completely unjustified. The sympathy of the Chinese people and of the great masses of people throughout the world is going to be on the side of the victims of aggression and not on the side of the American imperialists. They will neither be taken by imperialist bribes nor be intimidated by imperialist threats. Imperialism has a bold front but is empty within because it does not have the support of the people. People of China and peoples of the world arise! Prepare thoroughly! Defeat every provocation of American imperialism!

## 38

*Ambassador to the Soviet Union Alan G. Kirk to the Soviet Minister of Foreign Affairs June 27, 1950*

[*United States Policy in the Korean Crisis*, pp. 63–64.]

My Government has instructed me to call to your attention the fact that North Korean forces have crossed the 38th parallel and invaded the territory of the Republic of Korea in force at several points. The refusal of the Soviet Representative to attend the United Nations Security Council meeting on June 25, despite the clear threat to peace and the obligations of a Security Council member under the Charter, requires the Government of the United States to bring this matter directly to the attention of the Government of the Union of Soviet Socialist Republics. In view of the universally known fact of the close relations between the Union of Soviet Socialist Republics and the North Korean regime, the United States Government asks assurance that the Union of Soviet Socialist Republics disavows responsibility for this unprovoked and unwarranted attack, and that it will use its influence with the North Korean authorities to withdraw their invading forces immediately.

## 39

*Deputy Minister of Foreign Affairs Andrei Gromyko to Alan G. Kirk June 29, 1950*

[*United States Policy in the Korean Crisis,* p. 64.]

1. In accordance with facts verified by the Soviet Government, the events taking place in Korea were provoked by an attack by forces of the South Korean authorities on border regions of North Korea. Therefore the responsibility for these events rests upon the South Korean authorities and upon those who stand behind their back.

2. As is known, the Soviet Government withdrew its troops from Korea earlier than the Government of the United States and thereby confirmed its traditional principle of noninterference in the internal affairs of other states. And now as well the Soviet Government adheres to the principle of the impermissibility of interference by foreign powers in the internal affairs of Korea.

3. It is not true that the Soviet Government refused

to participate in meetings of the Security Council. In spite of its full willingness, the Soviet Government has not been able to take part in the meetings of the Security Council inasmuch as, because of the position of the Government of the United States, China, a permanent member of the Security Council, has not been admitted to the Council, which has made it impossible for the Security Council to take decisions having legal force.

## 40

*Statement by Dean G. Acheson
at a Press Conference
June 28, 1950*

[*The New York Times*, June 29, 1950, p. 10.]

There are a few points which I should like to make before we go into the questions about the matter which I am sure is uppermost in all of your minds. This is the announcement by the President yesterday of decisions which he had taken. I will not go into those decisions in detail, but make some points about them.

The first point I want to make is our feeling of deep gratitude here in the Department, and responsibility also, for the almost unanimous world reaction which has come from the action taken by the United Nations, and from the announcement by the President of his ac-[sic]\* been taken in support of the United Nations.

In all parts of the world where free opinion exists there has been an immediate response—a response to the realization that this was, if there ever was in the world,

\* Line omitted in the original text.

## The Decision to Commit Air and Sea Forces 135

a test of whether the United Nations was going to survive.

The attack was the most cynical, brutal, naked attack by armed forces upon an undefended country that could occur. The world has understood that, and it was understood that the actions taken by the United States have been in support of the United Nations.

The second point I want to make is that as soon as we knew that this attack had taken place, and had immediately conveyed that information to the President and gotten his instructions, it was the view of the President, and of the entire Government of the United States, that our first responsibility was to report this to the United Nations. This was done in the middle of the night on Saturday, June 24, and a meeting of the Security Council was called on Sunday, June 25. From then on, all action in Korea has been under the aegis of the United Nations. That is a very important point.

The next point that I want to make is one that I am sure you understand. It is that the entire action of the Government of the United States, since a late hour on Saturday when this information came to us, has been taken under Presidential leadership and direction. Here, as in many other situations in the years which I have been Under Secretary and Secretary, the President has been faced with the most difficult decisions which had to be made quickly, and after taking full advice he has assumed the responsibility and he has made the decision.

The fourth point I would like to make is that there has been complete unity among the President's advisers, civil and military. The Departments of State and Defense have worked practically as one department ever since this matter arose, and in anticipation of possible difficulties of this sort, so that we were able on the shortest possible notice to present completed staff work to the President. He had the view of his advisers without having differences among his advisers.

The fifth point I should like to stress is the unity

which existed at the President's meeting yesterday, at which the Secretary of Defense and I, and our advisers, were present with the Congressional leaders. Here, again, the understanding of the problem, the understanding of the actions taken showed complete unity.

The sixth point I should like to make is that with very few expections [sic] the press and the radio of the United States has been unified in its comments upon what was done, and the necessity for doing it. I assume, and I think I assume justly, that that attitude on the part of the press and the radio indicates that there is similar unity among the people of the United States.

Finally I should like to leave with you the thought that the complexities and difficulties of the international situation are great. This is a time for very steady and sober talk and actions. It is not a time for general speculation, for trying to stir up difficulties which do not exist, for imagining possibilities which are remote.

It is a time for the very greatest steadiness and it is a time, as I have often said in the past, where, more than ever, you gentlemen share with the officials of the Government a very deep responsibility, which I feel sure you are quite aware of.


41

*Speech by Dean G. Acheson
June 29, 1950*

[*Department of State Bulletin*, XXIII, No. 575, pp. 43–46.]

*Washington, D.C.*

I would like to review with you the facts of the situation which I am sure is uppermost in your minds—

## The Decision to Commit Air and Sea Forces 137

the events which have been taking place and are now going on in Korea.

I think you will agree that this has been what newspaper men call a fast-breaking story.

The immediate events of the story go back less than 5 days. On Saturday afternoon—it was just before daybreak of Sunday morning in Korea—without warning and without provocation, Communist forces of the north launched a coordinated full-scale assault on the Republic of Korea. After heavy artillery fire, Communist infantry began crossing the 38th parallel at three points, while amphibious forces were landing at several points on the east coast, some 20 miles to the south.

First reports to reach the capital at Seoul, 30 miles below the 38th parallel, were fragmentary and confused. There had been small border forays on many previous occasions, and the magnitude of this attack was not immediately clear.

Our Ambassador at Seoul, John Muccio, immediately got in touch with Korean Army headquarters, through our Military Advisory Group, and, as soon as it became evident that this was more than another border incident, he cabled the State Department.

Ambassador Muccio's cable reached the State Department code room at 9:26 Saturday night, having crossed an inquiry the Department had sent to him a few minutes before, based on the first press flash on the action.

Within a matter of minutes, the message was decoded and the Department was alerted for action.

By 10:30 p.m., our Assistant Secretary for Far Eastern Affairs, Dean Rusk, and the Secretary of the Army, Frank Pace, were conferring at the Department.

By 11:00, Secretary Pace had alerted the Department of Defense, a full operating staff was on duty at our Bureau of Far Eastern Affairs, and I had discussed the situation by phone with the President.

Action developed along two fronts in the State Department during the night.

One group of Department officers worked through the night preparing for a meeting of the Security Council which we had immediately requested. The United Nations had established the Republic of Korea and had, since early 1948, maintained a Commission in Korea. We, therefore, felt a primary responsibility to bring this matter to the immediate attention of the United Nations.

By Sunday afternoon, within 20 hours of the time the first official word of this invasion was received here, the Security Council had taken its first action. Representatives of 10 member nations of the Security Council had been assembled from their Sunday places of rest— the eleventh was the representative of the Soviet Union, who stayed away. After hearing the report of the United Nations Commission concerning the unprovoked act of aggression, the Security Council passed a resolution which called for an immediate end to the fighting and for the assistance of all members in restoring the peace. All actions taken by the United States to restore the peace in Korea have been under the aegis of the United Nations.

Another group of Department officers, meanwhile, were working with their colleagues in the Defense Department, consulting on measures to be taken within the framework of existing policy and plans and the emergency orders of the President.

The President flew to Washington. By the time he had arrived, at 7:20 Sunday evening, completed staff work and recommendations had been prepared and were laid before him. The Departments of State and Defense had worked as one department, with complete agreement and coordination of effort.

During Sunday night and early Monday morning, actions flowing from the conference with the President were set in motion. General MacArthur was authorized to respond at once to urgent appeals from the Government of Korea for additional supplies of ammunition and in a matter of hours was flying into Korea loaded transport planes with fighter protection to assure their safe arrival. At about the same time, the Seventh Fleet with all men aboard was steaming north out of Subic Bay, to be on hand in case of need.

It became possible on Monday to get a clearer picture of the military situation, by sifting the fragmentary and sometimes conflicting reports we had been receiving from many different sources.

From the size and speed of the Communist attack, it was evident that it was a premeditated action; that it had been carefully plotted for many weeks before. The initial thrust, supported by planes and tanks, had clearly caught the Korean Government troops by surprise. Although the defending forces rallied and launched several small counteractions, it did not appear that they were in a position to bar the tank-and-plane-supported Communist thrust down the corridor to the capital city.

By Monday night, in the light of this situation, recommendations were prepared by the President's civil and military advisers on the course of action to be taken. In preparing these recommendations, it was clear to all concerned that this act of aggression had brought in issue the authority and, indeed, the continued existence of the United Nations and the security of the nations of the free world, including the United States and its forces in the Pacific. These recommendations were prepared with the sober realization of the issues involved and with the full agreement of all the President's advisers.

As in many other situations which have arisen in the years in which I have served as Under Secretary and Secretary, the President was faced with difficult decisions which had to be made quickly. And as in the previous cases, the President assumed the responsibility, made the decisions, and has given leadership and direction to the entire action of the Government of the United States.

Consultations with Congressional leaders on Tuesday morning demonstrated a complete unity in understanding the problem and the course of action which needed to be taken.

At Tuesday noon, the President announced the actions which this Government would take to support the United Nations and uphold a rule of law in the Pacific area.

In the interval between the meetings of the Security Council on Sunday and again on Tuesday, the United Nations Commission on Korea had confirmed the fact that the Communist authorities in North Korea had ignored the cease-fire order and defied the authority of the United Nations. Therefore, the Security Council recommended at a meeting Tuesday night that member nations give aid to the Republic of Korea and help to restore peace and security to the area.

Yesterday—4 days after the fighting began—the fall of Seoul was confirmed, but American air and sea support for Korean Government troops was beginning to make itself felt, and peace-loving nations the world over were able to hope that this act of brutal, unprovoked, and naked aggression would not be allowed to succeed.

It may be useful at this point to review briefly the background of recent history against which the present act of aggression against Korea is to be considered.

Since the nineteenth century, American missionaries, doctors, and educators have been especially active in Korea, so that through the years of Japanese occupation, which began in the first decade of this century, the Korean people came to regard the United States as a symbol of the freedom and independence to which they aspired.

In the Cairo Declaration of December 1943, the United States, the United Kingdom, and China pledged their determination that Korea would become free and independent. This pledge was reaffirmed in the Potsdam Declaration of July 26, 1945, and was subscribed to by the Soviet Union when it entered the war against Japan 13 days later.

The defeat of Japan made it possible for Korea to look forward to the realization of its desire for independence.

## The Decision to Commit Air and Sea Forces

On the day following the first Japanese offer of surrender, which was made on August 10, 1945, the Secretary of War submitted to the Secretary of State a plan for the arrangements to be followed in accepting the surrender of Japanese troops in various places. To meet the immediate problem, it was proposed that the nearby Soviet troops accept the surrender of Japanese armed forces in Korea down to the 38th parallel and that American troops be brought up from Okinawa and the Philippines to accept the surrender of Japanese troops in the southern part of Korea. This arrangement was approved by the Joint Chiefs of Staff, the State-War-Navy Coordinating Committee, and the President and, after it had been accepted by Generalissimo Stalin, was incorporated in the first general order to be issued by General MacArthur as Supreme Commander for the Allied Powers on September 2, 1945.

Soviet troops had occupied the northern part of Korea on August 12. The Soviet desire and intention to put troops into Korea had been made evident at the Potsdam discussions, 1 month before. On September 8, American troops had been landed to accept the surrender of the Japanese in the southern part of Korea, and we began efforts to negotiate with the Soviet Union for the unification and independence of the country.

We soon found that the Soviet Union considered the 38th parallel not as a line drawn on a map for the sake of administrative convenience but as a wall around their preserve.

At the Moscow meeting of Foreign Ministers in December 1945, a joint commission for the unity and independence of Korea was agreed to between the Soviet Union and ourselves, but we found that every effort to give effect to this agreement and previous agreements was blocked by Soviet intransigence.

The United States was unwilling to permit this situation to delay further the realization of Korean independence.

This Government therefore laid the question of Korean independence before the United Nations. The General Assembly of the United Nations, in November 1947, called for an election in Korea under the observation of a United Nations Commission, to choose a representative national assembly for the purpose of drafting a democratic constitution and establishing a national government.

The Soviet Union refused to allow the United Nations Commission to enter its zone. Consequently, the right of the Korean people to participate in a free election to establish a free government was confined to southern Korea. The election was held there, and the Government of the Republic of Korea was established on August 15, 1948.

It has been the aim of the United States to provide the people of the Republic of Korea with sufficient assistance and support to enable them to progress through their own efforts toward freedom and independence. The transfer of functions from the United States Army Military Government to Korean agencies was carried out progressively from the moment of the establishment of the Republic.

The United States has continued to give assistance and support to the Republic, both within the framework of the United Nations and directly. We have trained and equipped Korean defense forces, we have extended economic aid and technical advice, fostered exchange of students and professors, and, in general, done everything possible to help the people of Korea in establishing a democratic political and economic structure responsive to their needs.

The Government of the Republic of Korea was accepted by the United Nations, in December 1948, as the validly elected, lawful Government of the area in which elections were permitted—and the only such Government in Korea. The General Assembly established a reconstituted Commission to continue to work for unification

## The Decision to Commit Air and Sea Forces

and a representative government for the entire country.

The United States recognized the new government on January 1, 1949. Many other members of the United Nations have since done the same. Membership of the Republic of Korea in the United Nations has been blocked by the Soviet veto.

Meanwhile, the 38th parallel had become a part of the Iron Curtain. Behind that curtain, the Soviet Union established a Communist regime. The formal creation of this regime was proclaimed on September 9, 1948, as the so-called "Democratic People's Republic of Korea," claiming jurisdiction over the entire country. This regime has lived, as it was created, in complete defiance of the United Nations.

The great single fact which stands out from this summary history is that a peaceful people ruled by a sovereign independent government of their own choosing, brought into being by the United Nations and recognized by the great majority of the free nations of the world, was attacked in a cynical and brutal act of aggression.

We are confronted with a direct challenge to the United Nations. Whether this organization, which embodies our hopes for an international order based on peace with justice and freedom, can survive this test will depend upon the vigor with which it answers the challenge and the support which it receives from free nations.

The President has enunciated the policy of this Government to do its utmost to uphold the sanctity of the Charter of the United Nations and the rule of law among nations. We are, therefore, in conformity with the resolutions of the Security Council of June 25 and June 27, giving air and sea support to the troops of the Korean Government. This action, pursuant to the Security Council resolutions, is solely for the purpose of restoring the Republic of Korea to its status prior to the invasion from the north and of reestablishing the peace broken by that aggression.

In order that the Communist movement may not further threaten the security of the Pacific area by force of arms, we shall increase military assistance to the Philippines and to the forces of France and the Associated States in Indochina.

The President has also ordered the Seventh Fleet to prevent any attack on Formosa, and we have called upon the Chinese Government on Formosa to cease all air and sea operations against the mainland. This action is not intended to determine the future status of Formosa, which can be settled only upon the restoration of peace and security in the Pacific, a peace settlement with Japan, or consideration by the United Nations.

As a further measure toward the restoration of peace, we have, through our Embassy in Moscow, asked the Soviet Government to exercise its influence with the North Korean authorities for the withdrawal of the invading forces and the cessation of hostilities in Korea.

In conclusion, the action of the United States Government in Korea is taken in support of the authority of the United Nations. It is taken to restore peace and security to the Pacific area.

It is taken in the conviction that peace and security cannot be obtained by sacrificing the independence of nations to aggression.

Free men the world over have spoken out with one voice since this dawn attack was launched days ago. They endorse our resolve and stand with us in support of the United Nations. Those Governments in a position to provide armed forces to assist in the support of the Republic of Korea are already taking steps to provide that support.

It is now clear to all—if indeed, it was not clear before—that free nations must be united, they must be determined, and they must be strong, if they are to preserve their freedom and maintain a righteous peace. There is no other way.

# Section Five

# The Decision to Commit Ground Troops

*Commentary*

The President's decision to commit Air Force and Navy units in battle support of the ROK forces explicitly had limited their scope of action to the area south of the Thirty-eighth Parallel. The initial American decision to fight in Korea was strictly intended *to restore the status quo ante,* that is, to drive the North Korean invasion force back across the parallel. In the period after June 26 several of the President's diplomatic and military advisers became concerned that the order for military engagement might somehow be interpreted as an indication of readiness to engage the Soviet Union in war, or at least to fight Soviet forces if they appeared in the Korean combat zone. Thus these advisers wanted to keep the conflict "limited" and to make very explicit the fact that if Soviet forces were encountered the American units

145

should defend themselves but not engage in offensive operations unless ordered by Washington.

The restriction of military action to South Korea, the territory of the victim of aggression, was questioned in congressional debate and was found to hamper the operations of field commanders. This was especially true of the Air Force which could not attack the North Korean base from which Soviet-made fighters and bombers were attacking the South. In the early morning of Thursday, June 29, Korean time (Wednesday evening in Washington), General MacArthur flew to Korea for a one-day reconnaissance of the battle area. En route, aboard his special aircraft, the "Bataan," he listened to his air commander Lieutenant General George E. Stratemeyer explain the problems that his pilots were encountering. General MacArthur, without hesitation and without waiting for authorization from Washington, gave Stratemeyer permission to attack the principal North Korean airfield near Pyongyang (Doc. 42). This second breach of the strict letter of his instructions in the first week of the war was later defended by the General as falling within the discretion normal to a field commander.

In any case, at 5:00 p.m. on June 29, Washington time, a meeting of the National Security Council was held, presided over by the President and attended by the Joint Chiefs of Staff, in which General MacArthur was authorized to extend his air and sea operations against "military targets" in North Korea (Doc. 43). The same meeting authorized the use of a limited number of ground troops for the purpose of securing a port-airfield beachhead in the Pusan-Chinhae area about two hundred miles south of the fighting front. Members of the Joint Chiefs of Staff later recalled that they approved the limited commitment of ground troops at this time to ensure the safe evacuation of American civilians from Korea, an operation which had not yet been completed. They still had not decided to order American infantrymen into direct combat with the North Korean People's Army. The further recommendations of General MacArthur were awaited.

In Korea, General MacArthur found confusion; only about 24,000 ROK soldiers could be accounted for (Doc. 44). Flying back to Japan shortly after 6:15 p.m., June 29 (5:15 a.m., Thursday, Washington time) the General told correspondent Marguerite Higgins who was with a group of journalists aboard the "Bataan" that he would recommend the commitment of American ground troops as soon as he returned to Tokyo (Doc. 45). In flight, the General drafted his recommendations in pencil on a pad of paper held in his lap (Doc. 46).

There is an inexplicable gap between the time when the General returned to Tokyo (9:15 a.m. Thursday, June 29, Washington time) and the time when his first official recommendation to deploy ground troops in combat reached Washington (sometime before 4:57 a.m., Friday, June 30, Washington time) (Doc. 47). After preliminary discussions between General MacArthur and General Collins, Secretary of the Army Frank Pace, Jr., telephoned the President at 4:57 a.m. and told him that General MacArthur had recommended sending one regimental combat team to Korea at once to be followed by augmentation of the American ground combat forces to two division strength. This time the ground force authorization was for direct combat action. General MacArthur had insisted: "Time is of the essence and a clear-cut decision without delay is essential." The President agreed immediately to send the regimental combat team to Korea but delayed decision on the two-division augmentation until he had time to confer with his advisers.

At 9:30 a.m. the President met with the Secretaries of State and Defense, the Service Secretaries, the Joint Chiefs of Staff and other advisers; the meeting lasted only 30 minutes. The President explained the decisions he had made and asked for further recommendations. The conferees agreed with General MacArthur's recommendations and he was given "full authority to use the troops under his command." A White House press release issued at about noon explained the ground troop decision in restrained language: "General MacArthur has been authorized to use certain supporting ground units" (Doc. 48). Later it was explained that the full force and intent of the contemplated infantry engagement could not be communicated to the American public at this time because it would have given advance information to the enemy which would have imperilled the lives of the soldiers.

Just prior to the White House press statement, the President met with congressional leaders to explain his most recent decisions. Senator Kenneth S. Wherry, Republican of Nebraska, was openly critical of the President during this meeting and later that afternoon carried his dissatisfaction to the floor of the Senate (Doc. 49). Republican Senator William F. Knowland responded in defense of the President's constitutional authority to engage in this "police action" (Doc. 50). But despite criticisms the commitment of ground forces seemed to be accepted by domestic public opinion as virtually "inevitable" (Doc. 51).

There was strong support for American actions within the United Nations and a statement by Ambassador Austin before the Security Council on Friday, June 30, expressed the prevailing atmosphere there (Doc. 52).

The phrase "police action" originated when a journalist questioned the President during a news conference on June 29. He asked, "Would it be possible to call this a police action under the United Nations?" Quoted indirectly, as was the journalistic custom in 1950, the President was said to have agreed that that was exactly what it amounted to. As American ground soldiers engaged North Korean and Chinese infantry in three years of bitter fighting, the phrase "police action" became a term of scorn among the troops. For them it was unmistakably war. The tragedy of their initial ill-preparedness for Korean combat is poignantly conveyed by the verbal orders that sent the first ground soldiers to battle in Korea (Doc. 53).

## 42

*Radio Order from Lieutenant General George E. Stratemeyer to Major General Earle E. Partridge*
*June 29, 1950*

[Roy E. Appleman, *South to the Naktong, North to the Yalu* (Washington: Government Printing Office, 1960), p. 44.].

Take out North Korean Airfield immediately. No publicity. MacArthur approves.

## 43

*Joint Chiefs of Staff to
General Douglas MacArthur
June 29, 1950*

[Extracts]

[*Military Situation in the Far East,* Hearings before the Committee on Armed Services and the Committee on Foreign Relations, U.S. Senate, 82nd Cong., 1st sess. (Washington: Government Printing Office, 1951), Part I, p. 536.]

In support of resolutions of the United Nations approved on the 25th of June and transmitted on the 28th, and the 27th of June transmitted—as a certain reference—you will employ naval and air forces available to the Far East Command to provide fullest possible support for South Korean forces by attack on military targets so as to permit these forces to clear South Korea of North Korean forces.

Employment of Army forces will be limited to essential communications and other essential service units except that you are authorized to employ such Army combat and service forces as to insure the retention of a port and air base in the general area of Pusan-Chinhae.

By naval and air action you will defend Formosa against invasion or attack.

* * *

You are authorized to extend your operations in Northern Korea against air bases, depots, tanks, farms, troop columns, and other purely military targets, if and when this becomes essential for the performance of your mission, as given in a preceding paragraph, or to avoid unnecessary casualties to our forces. Special care will be taken to insure that operations in North Korea stay well clear of the frontiers of Manchuria or the Soviet Union.

The decision to commit United States air and naval forces and limited Army forces to provide cover and support for South Korean troops does not constitute a decision to engage in war with the Soviet Union if Soviet forces intervene in Korea. Decision regarding Korea, however, is taken in full realization of the risk involved. If Soviet forces actively oppose our operations in Korea, your forces should defend themselves but should take no action to aggravate the situation, and you should report the situation to Washington.

## 44

*Recollections of Major General Edward M. Almond*
*June 29, 1950*

[*Interlocking Subversion in Government Departments,* Hearings before the Subcommittee to Investigate the Administration of the Internal Security Act and Other Internal Security Laws of the Committee on the Judiciary, U.S. Senate, 83rd Cong., 2nd sess., Testimony of Lt. General Edward M. Almond (Retired) (Washington: Government Printing Office, 1954), Part XXV, pp. 2059–62.]

SENATOR WELKER. General, will you describe to the committee, sir, the opening days of the Korean war as viewed from your position as the Chief of Staff, including the first inspection trip, and the telecon?

GENERAL ALMOND. Well, I recall right off the bat that

those were very hectic days. They were particularly a jolt to me because, on Sunday morning, which was the 25th of June, having had a week of General Bradley and Mr. Johnson visiting to our area, we were concerned with almost a 20-hour schedule to see that they got to the right places, that they had the right conferences, to do the preparing for these conferences where it was our function.

In general, we had been pretty busy. So on that particular morning, I went down to my office with the idea of shuffling a few papers on Sunday and going home at least by 2 o'clock in the afternoon. I had been in my office only some 20 minutes when the first telegram came from Korea, from our little communication detachment we had over there with Ambassador Muccio's diplomatic group. That said that a border incident happened on the Ongjin Peninsula, which is at the mouth of the Han River, in western Korea. In about 30 minutes we got another such message. In the next 2 hours or two hours and a half we had 5 messages that stretched all the way across the 38th parallel, roughly. From the first one we were concerned, but we thought perhaps it had been a border raid. But when we got them scattered all across the front, we knew that something unusual was bound to happen and was happening. We transmitted each one of those, as I recall it, as rapidly as possible to the Pentagon to show that something was brewing. That has all been established, I am sure.

The next day—after the 25th of June—or the next 2 days, here in America, realization having taken place also of something unusual, we were directed to send a group to Korea as General MacArthur's reconnaissance party to determine just what was going on. We sent Major General Church of our staff and 14 officers from our headquarters by plane, destination Seoul. They landed at Suwon, Korea. The

## The Decision to Commit Ground Troops 153

condition of the Korean Army had deteriorated so in that period of 2 days that Major General Church never got to Seoul. On June 29, General MacArthur and a small staff flew to Korea. We found Major General Church on the 29th, 2 days later, there at Suwon.

We had continued to observe the deteriorating situation on June 25, 26, 27, and 28. General MacArthur got query after query, wanting to know just what was happening. So, again, as he went to Formosa later on, he decided to go to Korea. He took the key members of his staff. I, as chief of staff, was a member of it. We flew to Suwon airport and landed at almost the instant that two YAK North Korean planes dropped a bomb on the end of the runway. We sent our plane back to Pusan after we landed. It was to come back and pick up the group at 4 o'clock that afternoon, which it did.

At 20 minutes to 4, as we were coming down the road from the direction of Seoul, where we had been the latter part of the day, two YAK's came over again and dropped two more bombs on the end of the runway, which delayed General MacArthur's plane coming in to pick him up to take him back to Tokyo. His purpose in going to Korea was to have first-hand information, not only of what the Korean Army was doing, but what the President of the Nation thought about it, what our own United States Ambassador thought, what the Chief of Staff of the Korean Army was thinking about doing in the face of all this debacle that was happening.

We arrived, I would say, at 10:30 in the morning. We went to a little schoolhouse where General MacArthur found General Church and his 14 officers from Tokyo, our officers. They had had 2 days to sense throughout the southern part of Korea what was going on.

There we met with Mr. Rhee, the President of

the Republic; Mr. Muccio, our Ambassador in Korea; the Chief of Staff of the South Korean Army, and a lot of lesser lights.

General MacArthur began his query by asking General Church to have his officers, or himself, give the situation as he understood it. To make a long story as short as possible, General Church gave us the current situation on June 29 with the assistance of some of his officers who had been out and who had more intimate information than he had received in the last few hours. General Church said, "This morning we knew of 8,000 men in hand in the Korean Army, 8,000 out of 100,000." He said, "As far as we can tell, they are straggling all over South Korea, coming down all the roads, and even across the mountains. They all have their rifles and ammunition, but apparently nobody is fighting." He said, "I have just received a report that we now have in groups standing along the road 8,000 more, and I hope to have 8,000 more tonight, all stragglers."

That made 24,000, if he got them, out of 100,000 supposedly combat forces. That just gives you an example of how deteriorated that situation had gotten. That had a considerable bearing on our deployment into Korea within the course of the next week.

General MacArthur then asked Mr. Rhee what his concept of the condition was, and Mr. Rhee gave a very brief statement. To be a little facetious, it amounted to about the statement that "We are in a hell of a fix."

SENATOR WELKER. And he was in a hell of a fix.

GENERAL ALMOND. Undoubtedly. And we recognized it and so did he. General MacArthur then asked the chief of staff of the Korean Army what his plan was in the emergency. His reply was that he was going to mobilize 2 million youths in South Korea and repel the invasion, which had already happened. That was a little impractical. Mr. Muccio then gave his impression and he gave a very sound one. I have the highest respect for Mr. Muccio. I never saw him before, and I haven't seen him since, except during the Korean war, but he had real courage in the interpretations that he gave us and his attitude toward repelling the invasion. General MacArthur then said, "Well, I have heard a good deal theoretically, and now I want to go and see these troops that are straggling down the road."

We got three old, broken down cars and got them there at Suwon, 30 miles out of Seoul, the capital. We drove to the south bank of the Han River, where we could see the enemy firing from Seoul to targets on the south bank. We were within probably a hundred yards of where some of these mortar shells were falling. It was safe enough, so we had no worry. Going up that road from Suwon for a distance of 30 miles, we passed many trucks, many stragglers, many men in groups, all smiling, all with rifles, all with bandoliers of ammunition around them, all saluting, showing that they were disciplined—they recognized that some dignitary was coming along. We had some MP's with us, some Korean MP's, and some policemen clearing the road. They all smiled. General MacArthur made the remark. He said, "It is a strange thing to me that all these men have their rifles and ammunition, they all know how to salute, they all seem to be more or less happy, but I haven't seen a wounded man yet." That indicated that nobody was fighting, that they had lost their leadership and that is what happened. The best men in the world can't fight without coordination and determination.

Some fight better than others individually as guerrillas. But anyhow, that gave him the idea of just how bad the situation was. We then returned to Suwon and took off, as I told you, between YAK bombings, and went back to Tokyo. I think that night we began a series of telecon conferences with our Government here, in the Pentagon, which enabled General MacArthur to personally, from personal observation, interpret how bad the situation was.

It was during that period just before and during this trip to Korea that it became known to us, much to our surprise, I will say, and much to General MacArthur's surprise, that this country was going to participate in armed action in Korea. None of our plans had involved this, had included this. Our plan and our mission was to evacuate our diplomatic and military training personnel (KMAG) from Seoul in case of adversity. We had done that by June 28. But in these telecons, it developed that it had been decided by the United Nations to intervene in Korea in some way. The first manner was by the way of supply. When we learned that we were to supply the Korean armed forces, the question went back "Where do we land these supplies and how?"

As I recall it, it was stated that we would put these in at Pusan, the southern port. The reply that went back from our headquarters was to the effect that Pusan might not exist in our hands any too long, and perhaps not more than a day or two longer. "How would we land the supplies then?" The directive then came back. It must be remembered that in the meantime we had received the instructions that the United States Air Force and the United States Navy would assist the South Koreans in opposing the NK forces and in restoring order.

We knew from our trip to Korea on June 29 that the South Koreans had lost their capacity to restore order anywhere for the reasons that I have

## The Decision to Commit Ground Troops

just recounted. Our rejoinder to that concept of "restoring order" was that this could be looked upon with little confidence. Whereupon, we were directed to place defense forces to protect the port of Pusan in Korea to the extent of one regiment of infantry so that supplies to the ROK government could be sent by us from Japan.

The rejoinder that the Pentagon received from that statement was that "that is totally inadequate." That reply by General MacArthur caused a suspension of conversation over the telecon, to be resumed 30 minutes later.

In 30 minutes the telecon was resumed, whereupon General MacArthur was authorized to use the forces necessary in his opinion to protect the port of Pusan. The question then came, "Do you require any further instructions?" The answer was "No." That terminated the telecon and General MacArthur immediately ordered three divisions under General Walker, the bulk of the Eighth Army, to Korea because he knew the situation was so bad that nothing short of a fundamentally sound military movement would salvage it. I don't think you have to have me to testify that even that wasn't enough for the next 3 months. The immediate action that was taken was barely enough to drag along so that General Walker could maintain the semblance of a continuous line in the defense of Pusan, called the Pusan perimeter.

## 45

*Recollections of Marguerite Higgins*
*June 29, 1950*
[Extracts]

[Marguerite Higgins, *War In Korea* (Garden City: Doubleday, 1951), pp. 33–34.]

General MacArthur had come away from his frontline view of the South Korean retreat with the conviction that if America wanted to save Korea, ground troops would have to be committed. "It is certain that the South Koreans badly need an injection of ordered American strength," he told me. "The South Korean soldiers are in good physical condition and could be rallied with example and leadership. Give me two American divisions and I can hold Korea."

* * *

Now we had a job to do. On the plane that night General MacArthur said, "The moment I reach Tokyo, I shall send President Truman my recommendation for the immediate dispatch of American divisions to Korea. But I have no idea whether he will accept my recommendation."

## 46

*Recommendations of
General Douglas MacArthur
June 30, 1950*

[Douglas MacArthur, *Reminiscences* (New York: McGraw-Hill Book Company), p. 334.]

The South Korean forces are in confusion. Organized and equipped as a light force for maintenance of interior order, they were unprepared for attack by armor and air. Conversely they are incapable of gaining the initiative over such a force as that embodied in the North Korean Army. The South Koreans had made no preparations for defense in depth, for echelons of supply or for a supply system. No plans had been made, or if made were not executed, for the destruction of supplies or materials in the event of a retrograde movement. As a result they have either lost or abandoned their supplies and heavier equipment and have absolutely no system of intercommunication. In most cases the individual soldier in his flight to the south has retained his rifle or carbine. They are gradually being gathered up by an advanced group of my officers I sent over for the purpose. Without artillery, mortars and anti-tank guns, they can only hope to retard the enemy through the fullest utilization of natural obstacles and under the guidance of leadership of high quality. The civilian populace is tranquil, orderly and prosperous according to their scale of living. They have retained a high degree of national spirit and firm belief in the Americans. The roads leading south from Seoul are crowded with refugees refusing to accept the Communist rule.

It is essential that the enemy advance be held or its impetus will threaten the over-running of all of Korea. The South Korean Army is incapable of counteraction and there is a grave danger of a further breakthrough. If the enemy advances continue much further, it will threaten the Republic.

The only assurance for holding the present line and the ability to regain later the lost ground is through the introduction of United States ground combat forces into the Korean battle area. To continue to utilize the forces of our air and navy without an effective ground element can not be decisive. Unless provision is made for the full utilization of the Army-Navy-Air team in this shattered area, our mission will at best be needlessly costly in life, money and prestige. At worst, it might be doomed.

## 47

*Commander-in-Chief, Far East, to Joint Chiefs of Staff*
*June 30, 1950*

[*Military Situation in the Far East,* Hearings before the Committee on Armed Services and the Committee on Foreign Relations, U.S. Senate, 82nd Cong., 1st sess. (Washington: Government Printing Office, 1951), Part II, p. 1012.]

On 30 June 1950, CINCFE informed the Joint Chiefs of Staff, after a reconnaissance of the Korean battle are [sic], that the South Korean Army was in confusion. Supplies and equipment had been abandoned or lost. Without artillery, mortars, and antitank guns, the most the South Koreans could hope to accomplish would be to retard the advance of the enemy. The South Korean Army was incapable of united action, and there was grave danger of a further breakthrough. CINCFE further stated that the only assurance of holding the Han River line and to regain lost ground would be through the commitment of United States ground combat forces into the Korean battle area. Accordingly, he stated, if authorized, it was his intention to move immediately a United States regimental combat team to the combat area in Korea as the nucleus of a possible buildup of two divisions from Japan for early offensive action in accordance with his mission of clearing South Korea of North Korean forces.

## 48

## *White House Press Release*
## *June 30, 1950*

[*United States Policy in the Korean Crisis,* pp. 24–25.]

At a meeting with Congressional leaders at the White House this morning, the President, together with the Secretary of Defense, the Secretary of State, and the Joint Chiefs of Staff, reviewed with them the latest developments of the situation in Korea.

The Congressional leaders were given a full review of the intensified military activities.

In keeping with the United Nations Security Council's request for support to the Republic of Korea in repelling the North Korean invaders and restoring peace in Korea, the President announced that he had authorized the

United States Air Force to conduct missions on specific military targets in Northern Korea wherever militarily necessary and had ordered a Naval blockade of the entire Korean coast.

General MacArthur has been authorized to use certain supporting ground units.

## 49

*Speech by Senator Kenneth S. Wherry,*
*Republican of Nebraska*
*June 30, 1950*

[Extracts]

[*Congressional Record*, 81st Cong., 2nd sess. (June 30, 1950), pp. 9537–38.]

MR. WHERRY. Mr. President, a sigh of relief has swept across the country that, at last, at long last, the President has accepted the suggestion of some of us that he draw a line, that he stop his vacillation in the Pacific.

The President's action is belated, and therefore it will be more difficult to protect countries threatened by the tide of communism.

The administration let China slip into the hands of Moscow-directed Communists, with one excuse or another. How many hundreds of thousands of lives were lost, as a result of this appeasement of Soviet Russia is anyone's guess.

These terrible, ghastly failures by the administration cannot now be swallowed up with a show of flag-waving and cries of emergency, hurry up, and do not question this or that.

It was high time that the President acted, because the breath of the Communist dragon has begun to breathe upon the Philippines, and the entire Pacific was and still is in jeopardy.

President Truman has acted to draw a line. At last, at long last, he says to the Communist hordes, "thus far and no further." But there is a long row to hoe, and much more to be done, very much more. This action by the President is only a beginning.

The American people long ago had lost confidence in Secretary Acheson. His resignation is now definitely in order. His appeasement policies now stand repudiated by the President.

* * *

The next step is for the President to call the Congress into a joint session, give the facts and a complete review of what has taken place, and give Congress his recommendations.

The junior Senator from Nebraska voted for the United Nations Charter when it was before the Senate for ratification. The junior Senator from Nebraska was assured on the Senate floor that the constitutional power of Congress to declare war was in no way modified by the Charter. Others have contended on the floor of the Senate that regardless of the provisions of the United Nations Charter the President had full authority to act in the emergency in Korea, and order our troops into action.

This point was argued by the majority leader, who gave precedents for the President's action. But I want to point out that in these precedents all the actions taken were for the protection of American lives and property. This was a very different situation than was brought about by the President's ordering air power and warships to southern Korea.

It seems to the junior Senator from Nebraska in

all fairness the President should not have acted under the resolution passed by the United Nations without congressional authorization. Perhaps there was an immediate emergency. Perhaps time did not permit. I am not questioning the President's sincerity at all. However, Congress was in session, and this was a possibility. I refer to it only as a way in which I think it should have been done if it could possibly have been done that way.

But the practical side of this is whether the President acted within the constitutional processes, or whether he acted under the resolution adopted by the United Nations.

One thing he did not do, and that was to call the Congress of the United States, which is now in session, into a joint session, and there reveal to us the facts that he knew and make his recommendations at that time, so that the Congress, the legislative branch, could determine and assume the responsibilities, which the Congress should assume and thereby bring about the unity which must be had all along the line among not only Members of Congress but the American people. No doubt full authority and funds would have been voted by the Congress to prepare for the protection of American interests. At least I would have been one who would have given the President that assurance.

While it is too late now, and nothing would be accomplished by trying to amend what has been done, the junior Senator from Nebraska calls attention to this as a notice for future conduct, in the event that this present situation develops into something much more serious than it is now.

## 50

*Speech by Senator William F. Knowland
June 30, 1950*
[Extract]

[*Congressional Record*, 81st Cong., 2nd sess. (June 30, 1950), pp. 9539–40.]

MR. KNOWLAND. It seems to me that at this critical hour in our Nation's history we need, more than at almost any other time, a united American public opinion and a united Congress upholding the hands of the President of the United States. By that I do not mean that at the proper time and place there will not be room for constructive analysis of some of the measures which have been taken or have not been taken, but, as one Member of the Senate on this side of the aisle, and as a member of the Committee on Armed Services, it seems to me that during the next 10-day period 13 men in the Kremlin are going to be making a decision fateful for themselves and for the world. I cannot help believing that in part their decision may be based on whether or not they believe the President of the United States has overwhelming support in the Congress and in the country for the necessary action he has taken.

Mr. President, certainly there are few who disagree that at some time a line had to be drawn in Asia, as one has been drawn in Europe. Certainly there are few who will disagree that had Korea been permitted to go down the drain, as Ethiopia was in an earlier year, as Manchuria was when the Japanese war lords invaded her, as Austria and Czechoslovakia were allowed to go, that would not have been the road of peace. As has been pointed out on the floor of the Senate many times before, the world should have learned then, as it should now, that appeasement is but surrender on the installment plan.

Mr. President, I am not one of those who dispute the powers of the President of the United States to take the necessary police action. I believe that he has been authorized to do it under the terms of our obligations to the United Nations Charter. I believe he has the authority to do it under his constitutional power as Commander in Chief of the Armed Forces of the United States.

Certainly the action which has been taken to date is not one which would have required, or one in which I believe it was desirable to have, a declaration of war, as such, by the Congress of the United States. What is being done is more in the nature of police action.

It is a well-known fact that when there are widespread disorders it is of great importance to bring them under control immediately, and to use sufficient force to bring them under control at the earliest possible moment. It is a fact well known by fire departments in this land that if a fire department can get to a fire in the first 5 or 10 minutes of a blaze it has a much better chance of saving the neighborhood than it has if it gets there half an hour late.

I wish to say that I was a little concerned by one statement of my distinguished friend, the junior Senator from Nebraska. I perhaps may have misunderstood him—I wrote it down—when he said, "Perhaps there was an immediate emergency." I do not think that there is any "perhaps" to the situation. The invasion of South Korea was a well-organized move. The invaders moved in a surprise Pearl Harbor type of attack. They were making rapid progress with armored forces down through the broad valley that leads to the city of Seoul, the capital of the Republic of Korea.

We must always keep in mind that in this age of the atom and the airplane minutes and hours count in a situation of this kind. I believe, Mr. President, that had not the President of the United States acted forthwith as he did after bringing the matter quite properly to the attention of the United Nations, which adopted its first resolution, the entire resistance in South Korea might have collapsed, and then, if we were to save the United Nations, we would still ultimately have had to take the action which the President of the United States took, but it might have meant an amphibious landing on a hostile shore. Any American who had any experience or who observed the difficulties of an amphibious operation either in the Pacific or on the Normandy shores, should know that that would have been very costly in American lives and in the lives of the men of other member states of the United Nations. So I think the President of the United States quite properly moved in to preserve so much of South Korea, to whom we had great obligations, that when the announcement was made today that additional American forces would go there, they would be able to land on friendly shores and not on hostile shores.

## 51

*Ground Troops Move in*
The New York Times
*July 1, 1950*

[*The New York Times*, July 1, 1950, p. 14.]

Events in Korea are still running a logical and inevitable course. One must take the order to use United States ground troops in support of the South Koreans in that light. We are basically committed, along with other United Nations members, to the defense of Southern Korea. That means the U.N. must provide whatever is necessary to save the country from occupation. The South Koreans were not equipped to withstand this attack. When the American forces withdrew last year, the South Korean Army was left with the means of guaranteeing internal security, not fighting off aggression by tank columns and airplanes. The Russians, in arming, training and directing the North Korean forces for this attack, based their calculations on the weakness of the southern forces.

Once the decision to back the South was taken, there could be no strict limitation on the means to do so. There is something dramatic and decisive about the use of ground troops, partly because throughout history they have been the symbol as well as primary instrument of war, and partly because ground troops mean the physical occupation of terrain. Yet, looked at logically, there is not much difference between using American airmen or American sailors, and using American soldiers on land.

It is clear now that this could not have been avoided, any more than the order to bomb north of the thirty-eighth parallel and to blockade the whole peninsula. To stop short of the necessary measures now would be folly. The United Nations cannot lose this first great battle in defense of peace and freedom, nor can the United States, which is now so deeply committed, contemplate a failure. South Korea must and will be saved.

## 52

### Speech by Warren R. Austin
### June 27, 1950
[Extract]

[United Nations Security Council, Fifth Year, *Official Records*, No. 17, 475th Meeting, June 30, 1950, pp. 9–12.]

*U.N. Security Council*

I appreciate the perception of Mr. Chauvel in saying that we, at this table, have a dual mission and represent, on the one hand, our Governments and, on the other, the collective entity called the United Nations. I wish to say a few words about our collective duty. I know it is impossible physically to divide myself in two, but it is morally possible to emphasize the second aspect of our functions, namely, our collective duty. Speaking as the representative of a Member of the United Nations and of the Security Council, and as an officer of the United Nations, and having our collective duty primarily at heart, I want to express gratitude to the Government of India for its magnificent response to the questions which could not be communicated to it the other night but which finally reached it. The cause of justice and peace is strengthened by this positive help from a great nation such as India.

I wish to call the Council's attention to the fact that, at a meeting with Congressional leaders at the White House this morning, the President of the United States, together with the Secretary of Defense, the Secretary of State and the Joint Chiefs of Staff, reviewed the latest developments of the situation in Korea. The Congressional leaders were given a full review of the intensified military activities. In keeping with the request of the United Nations Security Council for support to the Republic of Korea in repelling the North Korean invaders and restoring peace in Korea, the President announced that he had authorized the United States Air Force to conduct missions on specific military targets in North Korea wherever militarily necessary and had ordered a naval blockade of the entire Korean coast. Furthermore, General MacArthur had been authorized to use certain supporting ground units. This statement has also been released at the White House.

In addition to this, I desire to inform the Council of the following statement made yesterday by the Secretary of State:

> The President has enunciated the policy of this Government to do its utmost to uphold the sanctity of the Charter of the United Nations and the rule of law among nations. We are therefore, in conformity with the resolutions of the Security Council of 25 June and 27 June, giving air and sea support to the troops of the Korean Government. This action, pursuant to the Security Council resolutions, is solely for the purpose of restoring the Republic of Korea to its status prior to the invasion from the North and of re-establishing the peace broken by that aggression. The action of this Government in Korea is taken in support of the authority of the

## The Decision to Commit Ground Troops 171

United Nations. It is taken to restore peace and security in the Pacific area.

I should also like to inform the Security Council that the United States authorities in the Korean area are giving the United Nations Commission on Korea every possible assistance in order that it may perform its mission. The Commission is returning to Korea; I am informed that an advance group of the Commission has already arrived in Pusan. The United States authorities have been requested to make every effort to procure the necessary facilities so that the entire Commission may function in Korea with the least possible delay.

In my capacity as an officer of the United Nations, and in order to assist the United Nations as best I can in its most crucial test since I have been in this position, I think it necesary that certain outstanding facts should be placed on record. They are historical, and probably would not fade from the scene, but it is well for us to charactize these attitudes and these acts in the light of our own vision of the scene and the atmosphere in which we live. To me the outstanding elements in this crucial situation are the brave attitudes and deeds not merely of the members of the Security Council but of all those Members of the United Nations who have responded so quickly to the inquiry of the Secretary-General. The reason why these attitudes are important is, I think, that they spring from the positive will of those Members. They glorify the interest, the initiative, the devotion and the consecration of those Members to the great principles for which we are united. Their action is spontaneous to be sure; it appears before us in the brilliant record just read to us today by the Assistant Secretary-General, succeeding the resolutions which we passed. This devotion to peace, determination to make the sacrifice, positive will to face those who would employ devices of all kinds to prevent collective action by the peace-loving nations of the world, mark this period of our history, and those nations will be surrounded with glory for the action they have taken unhesitatingly, voluntarily and spontaneously.

This proves another significant thing, which is that the present situation is one between an aggressor and the United Nations; it is the violation of order, it is the trampling upon morality, it is the attempt to destroy small countries that has aroused the world—that is, the peace-loving, freedom-desiring world.

By the communications which we have listened to and by the collective acts in various regions of the globe, the people, through their Governments, have responded to the bugle call of the great principles of non-aggression, political independence, personal freedom and security from violence and lawlessness. It is the reaction against those deadly foes of freedom, honour and security which has made them come together in this great response, which is a laudable chapter in the history of collective international efforts for peace.

Another thing which ought to be marked, I think, although it should not be emphasized over the fundamental principles that are vindicated in this action, is significant because it differs somewhat from our past history. It is that the freedom-loving people of the world have overcome every obstacle that has been erected in their minds or in their politics in order to take this strong, clear and definite position. By these acts they have overcome timidity, they have overcome the fear that they might perhaps violate some technicality or some strict construction raised solely for the purpose of paralysing or even killing collective action by the United Nations to attain its noble purposes. For this reason the record made here today is luminous and will throw light into the dark places of the world.

## 53

*Verbal Orders of Major General
William Dean to Lieutenant
Colonel Charles Smith
June 30, 1950*

[Appleman, *South to the Naktong, North to the Yalu*, p. 60.]

When you get to Pusan, head for Taejon. We want to stop the North Koreans as far from Pusan as we can. Block the main road as far north as possible. Contact General Church. If you can't locate him, go to Taejon and beyond if you can. Sorry I can't give you more information. That's all I've got. Good luck to you, and God bless you and your men.

## Bibliography

The most detailed case study of the United States decision to defend the Republic of Korea against armed invasion is Glenn D. Paige, *The Korean Decision: June 24–30, 1950* (New York: The Free Press, 1968), which is based in part on interviews with former President Truman, Secretary of State Acheson, Secretary of Defense Johnson, and other officials. The best contemporary journalistic narrative of the decision may be found in Beverly Smith, "The White House Story: Why We Went to War in Korea," *Saturday Evening Post* (November 10, 1951), pp. 22 ff. One of the reasons for the detailed accuracy of the Smith article is that it was based in part upon the notes of a young White House staff member, George M. Elsey, who was a former history major at Princeton and wished to record the chronological sequence of a major historical event as it unfolded.

Among accounts by direct participants in the decision, those by President Harry S Truman, *Memoirs: Years of Trial and Hope*, Vol. II (Garden City: Doubleday & Co., Inc., 1956) and Dean G. Acheson, *Present at the Creation* (New York: Norton, 1969) are most important. Recollections of other participants in the two Blair House conferences that led to intervention in the Korean fighting may be found in *Military Situation in the Far East*, Hearings before the Committee on Armed Services and the Committee on Foreign Relations, U.S. Senate, 82nd Cong., 1st sess., to Conduct an Inquiry into the Military Situation in the Far East and the Facts Surrounding the Relief of General of the Army, Douglas MacArthur from His Assignment in That Area (Washington: Government Printing Office, 1951.)

Since Truman's decision caught the main military executor of it by surprise, the accounts by General Mac-

Arthur and his former aides are of interest more for their criticism of pre-decisional events and for evidences of improvisation rather than as insights into the initial decision to fight itself. Although a baffling 17-hour "delay" remains to be explained (see Paige, *op. cit.*, pp. 239–40), various aspects of the MacArthur record are important in explaining his recommendation to send ground troops to Korea. Consult, for example, General of the Army Douglas MacArthur, *Reminiscences* (New York: McGraw-Hill, 1964) and Major General Courtney Whitney, *MacArthur: His Rendezvous with History* (New York: Alfred A. Knopf, 1956.) A future historian with access to the message files between the Defense Department and General MacArthur's headquarters in Tokyo especially for the period June 28–30 will be able to prepare an exact chronology of events. Two official Army publications, not at all uncritical, that give useful military information on pre-June 25 Korea are Roy E. Appleman, *South to the Naktong, North to the Yalu* (Washington: Government Printing Office, 1960) and Robert K. Sawyer, *Military Advisers in Korea: KMAG in Peace and War* (Washington: Government Printing Office, 1962).

The views of the then Secretary-General of the United Nations on the Korean decision may be found in Trygve Lie, *In the Cause of Peace* (New York: The Macmillan Co., 1954).

The most "sensational" book published in the United States about the Korean decision is I. F. Stone, *Hidden History of the Korean War* (New York: Monthly Review Press, 1952). This book was translated into many languages and is well-known in intellectual circles throughout the world. Recently it has been republished. Stone's major thesis is that there was some kind of collusion between Syngman Rhee, Chiang Kai-shek, John Foster Dulles, and the American Right Wing, to instigate a North Korean attack and thus trick the United States into firm military support of both the Republic of China and the Republic of Korea. Stone's hypothetical case had so little basis in fact and appeared so ridiculous at the time of publication that it largely escaped critical comment. Only one book, written in Japanese, effectively disposes of the main empirical bases of Stone's hypotheses: Naoi Takeo, *Chōsen senran no shinjitsu* (The Truth About the Korean War) [Tokyo: Democratic Japan Society, 1953.] For example, Stone makes much of a Pentagon spokesman's statement that the United States knew about the impending outbreak of war because it had evacuation ships standing by at Inchon Harbor. Naoi points out that there was only one small Chinese freighter (passenger capacity—12) and a loaded Norwegian fertilizer ship in the harbor at that time. This was hardly adequate for several hundred women and children and certainly represented no anticipatory planning. Stone accepts statements of military officers in an unusually uncritical manner.

Any reader of the Paige book cited above can critically evaluate the Stone book as it pertains to the period June 24–30, 1950 for himself. Readers who wish to go directly to the most forceful argument that the Pyongyang leaders have presented for the thesis that they were attacked by the United States and the Republic of Korea should consult a Communist collection of apparently captured documents *Facts Tell* (Pyongyang: Foreign Languages Publishing House, 1960). These documents portray a situation exactly contrary to the North Korean thesis of South Korean aggression. The documents reveal that Rhee was ill-armed and that the United States was reluctant to provide a heavy weapons buildup.

In comparing and critically evaluating the Paige and Stone books the reader will find it useful to keep two additional things in mind. First, Korean Communist leaders have never claimed that their invasion of the Republic of Korea was pre-emptive, initiated in self-defense against imminent attack from the South. Their official claim is that on June 25 the South Koreans attacked them and that subsequently they called a meeting of the political committee of the Party Central Committee and an emergency Cabinet meeting which (a) called for a withdrawal of the invasion and (b) then ordered a counterattack aimed at Korean unification. This is how they portray the beginning of what they call the "Fatherland Liberation War." This is clarified on the basis of the study of North Korean sources by a leading Japanese scholarly expert on the Korean War, Shinobu Seizaburō, *Chōsen sensō no boppatsu* (The Outbreak of the Korean War) (Tokyo: Fukumura, 1969). Readers may also wish to recall that when the Rhee Administration was overturned in Seoul in April, 1960, after police killed demonstrating students—a period followed by a year of remarkably free conditions of civil liberties—not a single word was said to link the origins of the war, a Korean national tragedy, with discredited President Rhee's leadership.

Thus, as far as who attacked whom first is concerned, there is no "hidden history" of the Korean War. What *is* something of a mystery is the set of relationships among Kim Il Sung, Stalin, and Mao Tse-tung in the pre-invasion period. Students of history curious about this will have to wait until decision making case studies and documentary collections are compiled and made available in Pyongyang, Moscow, and Peking.